Social Change, Charisma and International Behaviour: Toward a Theory of Foreign Policy-making in the Third World

Institut Universitaire de Hautes Etudes Internationales
Collection de Relations Internationales

4

Social Change, Charisma and International Behaviour: Toward a Theory of Foreign Policy-making in the Third World

BAHGAT KORANY

1976
A. W. SIJTHOFF - LEIDEN
Institut Universitaire de Hautes Etudes Internationales
GENÈVE

To my family and Margaret

Acknowledgements

For the help and encouragement received during this research work I feel indebted to a long list of institutions and persons that cannot all be enumerated here.

But my first thanks must go to the Graduate Institute of International Studies (Geneva) and its director Professor Jacques Freymond, for all the help given in my research programme. Professors Harish Kapur and Jean Siotis of the Graduate Institute never hesitated to offer advice and encouragement. A long-term gratitude goes to my friend, Bruce Graham, Professor of Government at University of Sussex, England. I extend my gratitude too to many of my compatriots, both inside and outside Egypt, and to Nagy Tawfik of the F.A.O. go special thanks. I am also grateful to the many analysts of both International and Comparative Politics whose scholarship proved very valuable to me as can be seen in the numerous footnotes acknowledging my debts.

I would not have been able to procure all the data included in this work if it were not for the efforts and kind help of the personnel of the libraries of the Graduate Institute, the U.N. Library, the I.L.O. Library (Geneva), the British Museum, Chatham House, School of African and Oriental Studies (London), American University (Beirut) and Arab University (Beirut).

Very special thanks go to Laurence Bordier who has deciphered my Egyptian hieroglyphics.

Last but not least, my deep gratitude goes to Margaret, my wife. Without her varied and sustained help and encouragement, this work might have taken much longer to complete.

Brief table of contents

Table of contents

Pages

CHAPTER II

Pages

CHAPTER III

Pages

PART TWO

NON-ALIGNMENT AS A FOREIGN POLICY ORIENTATION

CHAPTER IV

CHAPTER VII

Pages

PART FOUR

THE IMPACT OF NON-ALIGNMENT ON THE CONTEMPORARY INTERNATIONAL SYSTEM

CHAPTER IX

List of tables and figures

Introduction

Social scientists agree that social change is a constant process, whether it is reflected in such characteristics of the contemporary international system as nuclear deterrence or the rise of "third world" actors. But when a discipline like political science is confronted with new phenomena that have to be described and explained, its existing paradigm and tools of analysis often prove inadequate. This *malfunction* necessitates the sharpening and adaptation of existing concepts and methodologies, which in its turn creates a *sense of crisis* in the discipline. This sense of crisis pushes some of the discipline members to a *search for a new paradigm* "appropriate" for the new context. This soul-searching continues until a *methodological and conceptual reorientation* enjoys a certain consensus. If, after the Second World War, the study of International Relations moved from "Utopianism" to "Realism", and in the 1960's from this latter to "Behaviouralism", and seems to be moving in the 1970's even further toward " Post-Behaviouralism" (to quote the 1969 Presidential address of the American Political Science Association), the methodological-conceptual reorientation, however, does not yet seem to have materialised.

The sense of crisis is even more characteristic of such subfields as the "Politics of Developing Areas", or—if we prefer—"the underdeveloped study of underdeveloped countries". [1]

---

[1] For a sociologist's point of view, see Frank, André : *Sociology of Development and Underdevelopment of Sociology,* London, Pluto Press, 1971. For the point of view of Political Science, see : Halpern, Manfred : "Toward Further Modernization of the Study of New Nations" : *World Politics,* XVII (1964), pp. 157-181, and Wilner, Ann R. : "The Underdeveloped Study of Political Development", *World Politics,* XVI (1964), pp. 468-482. For a more general, as well as an anthropologist's point of view, see Stavenhagen, Rodolfo : "Decolonising Applied Social Sciences", a talk at the Graduate Institute in April 1971, but was to be published in *Human Organization.* Similarly in International Law, some scholars question "the traditional legal view of wars of national liberation" which considers them "a category of internal wars and as such are not subject to internal legal regulation". They advocate "development

Let us consider our substantive issue : the third world foreign policy of non-alignment. Contrary to the "theory of alliances", [2] no comprehensive analysis of the bases of non-alignment, or even an operational definition of the concept, [3] has been established. Indeed, non-aligned countries themselves may share part of the responsibility. As recently as their 4th Summit (Algiers, September 1973), they were still debating the definition of their foreign policy orientation in order to achieve consensus. Even the date of the first use of the term "non-alignment" is still in doubt. Krishna Menon said he used it for the first time in the U.N. in 1953-1954 and Nehru did not like it. [4] But Nehru himself had already used the term during a debate on foreign affairs on March 28, 1951 (a speech entitled : "We Will not Compromise", *Nehru's Speeches,* pp. 191-203).

But even if we all agree on the partial responsibility of third world actors themselves, is it not the task of scholarship to attempt systematisation, creating order out of the apparent unconnectedness of social phenomena ? Let us consider the conceptual issue that figures in almost all International Relations textbooks—"system"—and specifically the concept of "subsystem" that is applied to non-alignment as a foreign policy orientation. The survey of published definitions of the subsystem concept, offered by 22 subsystem analysts between 1958 and 1971, results in an inventory of 21 attributes to identify the subsystem. These attributes range from "proximity or primary stress on a geographic region" to "a regional equilibrium of local forces". But the average agreement among analysts is .21, and the agreement between Kaiser and Zartmann, for instance, is .14, between Brecher and Michael Haas .13, between Hoffmann and Modelski .00, between Michael Haas and Hoffmann .00 ; even Shepherd and Zartmann (as we shall see in Chapter V), who were both applying "subsystem theory" to "Black Africa", also scored .00 agreement. [5]

---

or adjustment" or even the adoption of "new instruments ... [which] would be drafted from the beginning with the *specific conditions* of wars of national liberation in view". See Abi-Saab, Georges : "Wars of National Liberation and the Laws of War", *Annals of International Studies* (Geneva), III (1972), pp. 93-119 (emphasis added).

[2] Holsti, Ole R., Hopmann, P. Terence, and Sullivan, John : *Unity and Disintegration in International Alliances : Comparative Studies,* New York and London, Wiley-Interscience Publications, 1973.

[3] Two criteria are adopted here to identify a non-aligned actor : (*a*) non-participation in East-West military blocs, as the 1961 Cairo Preparatory Conference required ; and (*b*) invitation to full membership in the non-aligned subsystem.

[4] Brecher, Michael : *India and World Politics : Krishna Menon's View of the World,* London, O.U.P., 1968, p. 3.

[5] Thompson, William : "The Regional Subsystem : a Conceptual Explication and a Propositional Inventory", *International Studies Quarterly,* XVII (1973), pp. 89-119.

These present difficulties of political analysis (both substantive and conceptual) necessitate and justify risks of attempting a conceptual mapping of foreign policy-making in the third world. [6] The objective is to disentangle relevant foreign policy variables or determinants and establish linkages that might not appear at first glance. This conceptual mapping would be even more useful when the variables are drawn from different conceptual islands (*e.g.* modern systems theory, theories of conflict, decision-making . . .) and from the home territories of other academic disciplines (*e.g.* sociology, social psychology, anthropology) ; for in this case efforts at interdisciplinary integration can be consolidated and bridges can be extended toward the work of theory-oriented researchers in other areas. How did I attempt to cope with such a taxing task for the single researcher ? This can best be grasped by organising this introduction around five main issues :

I. The Diagnosis of the Research Problem ;
II. The Remedy I am Suggesting to Deal with the Problem ;
III. Methodological Principles Followed ;
IV. Potential Payoffs of this Study ; and
V. Research Problems Encountered and the Solutions Adopted.

I. **How Did I Diagnose the Problem to be Researched ?**

A cursory survey of different paradigms of International Relations—whether classical or behavioural—would reveal that there are two widespread assumptions : (*a*) the interchangeability assumption : elaboration of universal "models" where all actors are considered interchangeable "eggs in the same basket", and/or (*b*) the "small-state-as-pawn" assumption : when a distinction is made between "small underdeveloped powers" and "big developed powers", but the former are generally assumed to be objects of the latter's competition, "pawns" in the East-West conflict rather than entities in their own right.

This study is based on two alternative assumptions : (*a*) rather than continuing a tradition of an International Relations verging on becoming

[6] Conceptual mapping is a necessary step in a systematisation of our knowledge about third world foreign policy-making and a means of singling out limitations and loopholes as the first step to coping with them. See Rosenau, James : "Pre-Theories and Theories of Foreign Policy" in Barry Farrel (ed.) : *Comparative and International Politics,* Evanston, Northwestern U.P., 1966, pp. 27-93 ; and Smith, Brewster : "A Map for the Analysis of Personality and Politics", *Journal of Social Issues,* XXIV (1968), pp. 15-29.

a literature of (big) power politics, a contrary assumption is that considerable enrichment and relevance in current International Relations is to be achieved by means of explorations into the typical perceptual orientations and foreign policy patterns of third world states [7] ; and (*b*) contrary to the interchangeability assumption, the emphasis here is on the socio-psychological attributes that characterise these actors and underscore their designation by such suggestive (if somewhat oversimplified) labellations as "developing countries", "modernising states", or "Third World" members.

To sum up then : the underlying premise adopted here is that non-alignment at the global level is only the visible tip of the iceberg, for there is much to be discovered within these countries themselves to account for the choice and mode of practice [8] of this foreign policy.

After this diagnosis, how did I proceed ? This brings me to the second main issue : the organisation of this research work.

II. The Remedy or the Treatment

The nine chapters of the study follow three basic steps :

1. In the first place, since conceptualisation about third world foreign policy is to be situated within current attempts at theory-building in International Relations, there must be an analysis of the relevant literature to determine what the leading scholars have to say on the "basic questions", and to examine critically their conceptual bases as far as they are related to our topic. In this way the conceptual-methodological contributions and limitations of other approaches are brought to our attention. Moreover, this first step provides some justification for the alternative methodological assumptions and/or conceptual decisions that will have to be made. Consequently, chapters I and II analyse critically samples of the dominant schools in International Relations and emphasise their methodological and/or conceptual limitations. Chapter I shows why the "power school" suffers from both conceptual crudeness and empirical failure in its attempt to explain third world foreign policy. In chapter II the payoffs of both modern systems theory and the decision-making model are exploited. The

---

[7] For relevant attempts in this same direction, see, for instance : Huopaniemi, Jukka : *The Roles of Non-Alliance,* Research Reports No. 23/1971, Institute of Political Science, University of Helsinki ; and Rothstein, Robert : *Alliances and Small Powers,* New York, Colombia U.P., 1968.

[8] Incidentally, this constitutes a bridge between International Relations and Comparative Politics in Political Science in general and in third world political analysis in particular.

first (modern systems theory) is used to account for the systemic setting, the operational environment within which third world states act *(i.e.* the contemporary international system), which constitute conceptually the external variable in any balanced account of their foreign policy-making process. The second (the decision-making model) permits the shift from the global level to the actor-oriented level and emphasises the psychological environment, [9] the perception of third world policy-makers. This critical evaluation of the different schools in International Relations reveals not only their payoffs but also their limitations and hence permits us to explicit our two basic assumptions that underly the second necessary step.

2. The development of a conceptual framework attuned to our research objectives. This conceptual framework presents the basic concepts used to indicate eventual hypotheses and to contain supporting data. Consequently, chapter III is an elaboration of the "situation-role model". Though the model's bases in other social sciences are explicited and the advantages of interdisciplinarity are emphasised, the political scientist must be more than a mere borrower. Therefore, three-quarters of this chapter III are devoted to how the situation-role model is to be applied in foreign policy analysis, and the chapter ends by showing in matrix form how the proposed model can account for the phenomenon of non-alignment as well as the model's place in current International Relations theorisation.

3. The third necessary step is the application of the researcher's model through the use of empirical data, a process which will indicate patterns of similarity and difference among third world actors that concern us here. This is the objective of the rest of the study from chapter IV through to the beginning of chapter IX. Chapter IV treats the common attributes that characterise third world actors and that made the majority choose non-alignment as a foreign policy. Though third world actors' position in, and perception of, a stratified international system is dealt with, the chapter's main focus is on how the prismatic or malintegrated political system (a summary variable of third world societies) is linked to the choice of non-alignment. Problems of social change and "identity crisis", social disorganisation and ethnic fractionalisation, systemic strain and political conflict, "charismatic leadership" and "nationalised" socialism are treated both conceptually and empirically. These are the major societal-psychological features correlated with the adoption of non-alignment, and hence

[9] For a discussion of the environment in foreign policy analysis, see: Brecher, Michael, Steinberg, Blema, and Stein, Janice: "A Framework for Research on Foreign Policy Behaviour", *Journal of Conflict Resolution,* XIII (1969), pp. 75-102; and Brecher, Michael: *The Foreign Policy System of Israel,* London, O.U.P., 1972.

constitute the hidden part of the iceberg. The linkage is emphasised by formulating the integrative function of non-alignment in the prismatic political system as an explicit hypothesis.

Inter-actor variations notwithstanding, the attributes of their "common situation" justify the treatment of non-aligned actors as an international subsystem in Chapter V. Problems like subsystem boundary and regulatory mechanism, interaction among members of the non-aligned subsystem, behavioural heterogeneity among non-aligned actors, are conceptualised and operationalisation is suggested. Official declarations and reports of non-aligned actors have been scrutinised and at least 22 newspapers and other news sources (ranging from *Beirut Express* to Malaysia's *Straits Times* and passing by China's *Hsinhua* and India's *Hindu*) have been employed to make up for the lack of data on this important aspect of non-alignment.

But non-alignment is not only a foreign policy orientation or a subsystem, but also the behaviour of an individual actor. It was, then, found that analysts' use of "foreign policy" as their dependent variable is too general to be operationally useful, and consequently an analytical distinction was made between foreign policy *orientation* and foreign policy *behaviour*. Chapters VI-VIII are devoted to this latter . A pioneer third world actor—Nasser's Egypt—was chosen as a "crucial experiment". Egypt is a founder-member of the non-aligned subsystem, and Nasser's country was the early advocate of this policy among both Arab and African actors. But strangely enough, no book-length systematic study has been published about Egypt's non-alignment either in English, French or Arabic. Consequently, in addition to its conceptual function as a 'crucial experiment', the choice of Egypt allowed us to make up for the lack of data on this actor's pattern of non-aligned behaviour—especially since indigenous sources in Arabic were scrutinised. [10]

Chapter VI, then, uses events data to apply the general analysis of the third world 'common situation' to Egypt's third world 'specific situation'. The 3-year period following the advent of the military regime, a period which manifested a search for a foreign policy until non-alignment was adopted, was analysed in detail, not only to provide systematic data on this period, but more importantly to attest to the plausibility of our hypothesis about the integrative function of non-alignment in the prismatic political system. Chapter VII attempts the linkage between non-alignment and the other variables characterising the 'national component' of third world actors' 'situation' (recent colonisation, state of economic underdevelop-

[10] For the advantages and disadvantages of doing research on one's own country, see the discussion by the Indian social anthropologist Srinivas, M. N.: "Some Thoughts on the Study of One's Own Society", in his *Social Change in India*, University of California Press, 1969, pp. 147-165.

ment, and perceived geo-cultural distinctiveness). This is followed by a treatment of Egypt's pattern of non-aligned behaviour (1952-1970) to show the influence of these domestic variables on the country's international behaviour as well as inter-variable association. The tracing of the pattern of Egypt's non-alignment shows—in conformity with the proposed 'situation-role' model—how 'personalised' the policy-making process in non-aligned actors is, and since inter-actor variations characterise non-aligned behaviour, these two aspects (leader personality variable/inter-actor variations) are linked together in chapter VIII to pave the way for an eventual typology of non-aligned behavioural patterns. Two charismatic and key leaders (Nehru and Nasser) of two pioneering, but different, non-aligned actors are chosen to show how and why two close third world pioneers can differ in their foreign policy behaviour. Their divergent patterns of political socialisation are traced and compared as a means to account for the behavioural specificities of non-aligned India and non-aligned Egypt.

Chapter IX brings us back to the macro-systemic level where we pick up the hypothetical "peace function" of non-alignment, first stated in chapter II. Conflicting "theories" concerning the "most appropriate" systemic structure for systemic stability (bipolarity versus multipolarity) are confronted and critically evaluated. Then the impact of non-alignment on systemic structure and systemic conflict is conceptualised, before it is put to the test in four different empirical cases of conflict in the contemporary international system. The empirical analysis points out the crucial importance of some intervening variables (*e.g.* conflict issue, conflict sequence, communication patterns among conflict protagonists) that govern both the effectiveness and/or limitations of non-aligned actors' impact on the conflict-management process.

Thus while focussing its analysis on the linkage between the socio-psychological attributes of third world societies and their foreign policy making process, this organisation of the study nevertheless guaranteed an integrated, holistic approach that could test hypotheses on three levels of analysis : that of the global system, that of the third world society itself and, thirdly, that of the charismatic leader. This brings me to the third main issue in this introduction.

III. Methodological Principles Adopted

(*a*) Though the work is interdisciplinary, it is not limited to the mere borrowing of "foreign" concepts from other social sciences but, more importantly, it is concerned with how to transform rather than transfer, and adapt rather than adopt, these imported concepts to the concerns of International Relations analysts.

(*b*) I also chose to adopt a multimethodological approach for it was felt that in the present "transitional stage" of our discipline we need to invest in all available resources, concerned mainly with how useful they are for the purpose at hand rather than with considering them for their own sake as "traditional" or "behavioural", qualitative or quantitative. Consequently, the techniques of analysis used ranged from quantitative indicators, scales, tables, and events data, to the analysis of novels and other literary material. Thus heterogeneity of foreign policy behaviour among non-aligned actors, for instance, is traced in the public declarations and views of third world statesmen before it is measured and tabulated. Similarly, political conflict in Egypt's prismatic political system is measured by the level-of-conflict indicators, but also problems of social change and societal-psychological conflict, as analysed by Egyptian novels and other indigenous literary sources, were amply discussed.

(*c*) A third methodological principle concerns the "relevance versus precision" controversy in International Relations. I tried to keep a balance between the richness of relevance and the precision of observable measurement. Moreover, I have tried to attenuate the risk of specialised jargon acting as a barrier to communication for the non-specialised but interested reader. I followed the advice of the sociologist C. Wright Mills : "To have mastered the research language, method and theory is to have become a conscious thinker, a man at work trying to be continuously aware of the assumptions and implications of whatever he is about. (But) to be mastered by 'method', 'theory' and 'language' is simply to be kept from working."

What, then, is the result of all this effort ? This brings me to the fourth main issue in this introduction.

IV. Potential Payoffs of this Research Work

Four aspects can be emphasised in this respect :

(*a*) For the analysis of foreign policy-making in third world states, a conceptual framework—stemming from these actors' situation—is elaborated.

(*b*) This conceptual framework does not remain an abstract, theoretical schema, but it is confronted with empirical data throughout the study.

(*c*) Some research problems and concepts which intrigued political scientists have been singled out, and ways to operationalise and apply them have been suggested. For example, (i) rather than lumping together Saudi Arabia and Cuba, how do we classify their non-aligned behaviour and eventually establish a typology among non-aligned states ? (ii) how do we investigate the impact of third world foreign policy on the contemporary international system and see whether it has tended to increase or decrease international tension?

(*d*) Even for the non-specialist, the work offers something, I feel, on the level of pure information. For example, (i) no work has been published on the relationships among all non-aligned states analysed as an international subsystem. Through Chapter V we know the degree of regular (diplomatic) communication among non-aligned states. (ii) We know how Jordan's non-alignment, for instance, is to be situated in comparison with Ethiopia's, or Senegal's with Indonesia's. (iii) Through investigation of historical material in indigenous languages we know that as early as 1881 a "third world" Prime Minister, Mahmud Sami El-Barudi Pasha, of pre-colonial Egypt, prescribed a form of non-alignment for his country.

But after all is said and done, a researcher faces several research problems during his work. What are the main ones that need to be explicited here, and how did I cope with them?

V. Research Problems Encountered and Solutions Adopted

(*a*) The subject proved very wide. Non-alignment itself is an international movement that has been going on for at least twenty years and now embraces as many as 75 full member states. In order to attenuate this problem, restraints have been imposed as regards time periods, countries considered in detail, and number of variables to be measured and analysed. For instance, the specific aspects of Latin America's non-alignment could not receive detailed attention for two main reasons: (i) the analysis of the historical-cultural context of the Western hemisphere, with a superpower at its centre, would have complicated a subject already intricate enough; (ii) but this complexity resulting from emphasis on these Latin American specificities would not be compensated for by immediate equivalent payoffs. For, Cuba apart, Latin American countries have not yet manifested great salience in the non-aligned subsystem. For instance, their membership increase between the second and third Non-Aligned Summits was 300 per cent (*i.e.* from 1 to 4 members), but their share in the overall membership was still very modest: 7.5 per cent. Though their membership increased between the third and fourth Summits by 75 per cent (from 4 to 7 members), they still represented only 9.3 per cent of the overall membership. Latin America, however, should occupy a prominent place in an analysis which aims to investigate, primarily, the role of the forces of intrusion in the third world subsystem.

A second restraint is that in operationalising and measuring diplomatic heterogeneity among non-aligned states, data-collection and the ensuing quantitative analysis centred on the degree of diplomatic representation with "cold war-divided" countries. A second necessary step, at present, is to procure data on other indicatos *(e.g.* military and trade relationships with the superpowers) and even to devise new indicators (*e.g.* number of high-level visits to different capitals). Thirdly, sometimes I made a point of raising questions, [11] even those that did not permit an immediate, precise answer, for I felt that singling out the question is tantamount to fighting half the battle (*e.g.* What are the non-aligned states' own operational criteria of membership in their subsystem ?).

These self-imposed limitations were not allowed, however, to endanger the main objective : a systematic, holistic view of both the bases of third world foreign policy and of the structure and functioning of the non-aligned international subsystem.

(*b*) A second research problem was bias in the data sources, a problem which could affect the reliability of the work's conclusions. For data sources about third world actors tend to be of modest quality, low credibility, and sometimes even incorrect. For instance, a well-known columnist of a standard information source, C. L. Sulzberger of the *International New York Herald Tribune,* has an error margin of about 20 per cent in reporting membership in the recently-convened Non-Aligned Summit (Algiers, September 1973). He reported the number of members attending as "some sixty" instead of 75, and affirmed that Saudi Arabia did not attend, while its foreign minister was congratulating the Algerian government on the Conference's success and when the country's delegation was headed by King Faisal in person. Moreover, a generally used and important source of information such as *Europa Yearbook* was sometimes confined to reporting that there existed "diplomatic relations" or "diplomatic recognition" between state "A" and state "B" without specifying the rank of diplomatic representation. As we shall see in the scaling scheme applied in chapter V, such low level information was given the weight of 1 (*i.e.* equating unspecified diplomatic relations with diplomatic recognition). Similarly, one of the techniques I am using for the analysis in chapter VI is events data. This technique, however, is vulnerable to serious biases in terms of either volume, or content, or both. Discussions by Rosenau and others during the IXth World Congress of the International Political Science Association (Montreal, August 1973) indicated

[11] For an emphasis on "theory as a set of questions" in International Relations, see Stanley Hoffmann (ed.) : *Contemporary Theory in International Relations,* Englewood Cliffs, Prentice Hall, 1960 ; also by Hoffmann : *The State of War,* New York, Praeger, 1965, especially pp. 3-22.

that the overlap between the chronology of events in the Middle East reconstructed from the *New York Times* and the *Middle East Journal* was only 9.7 per cent, mainly because the *New York Times* did not report as many events about the Middle East as the *Middle East Journal.* Similarly, the *New York Times,* the *Asian Recorder* and *Deadline Data* together reported only 26 per cent of India's diplomatic interactions gathered from documents contained in the *Indian White Paper* for the same period. The same thing happened when the comparison of data sources on four Middle Eastern states was effected. The result was that "only one-third of the events in this region appeared in more than one of the nine sources". But not only is there a danger of bias as far as volume is concerned, but also as regards content. Thus it was found that global sources of data (*e.g. New York Times, Deadline Data),* tend to report hostile relations of nations, specially of the strong states, more extensively than friendly interactions. This data bias results in a biased picture where conflict is more emphasised than cooperation and large states are depicted as more active than small ones.

In trying to procure the most reliable and greatest amount of information possible, I followed three principles : (i) Research efforts were concentrated, at this stage, on analysing "active" *(i.e.* identifiable) foreign policy behaviours since it is in these that the bases of foreign policy are more explicited ; (ii) the use of multiple data sources : global, regional and national *(e.g. New York Times* and *Le Monde, Middle Eastern Affairs* and *El-Nahar,* and *Al-Ahram)* ; (iii) I tried to procure as much information as possible from sources within third world states themselves since there is a general complaint about the hazards of relying mainly on "foreign sources" on the "third world". But the scrutinisation of "indigenous sources" was not to be attained at the expense of a "balanced view". For instance, in discussing the February 4, 1942 incident (British tanks besieging the Royal Palace in Cairo and giving ex-King Faruq the choice between abdication and acceptance of the Egyptian Prime Minister designated by London), we have counted not only on the data collected and analysed by the Centre of Historical Studies and Research in Cairo, but also on the diaries of Lord Killearn who was then Britain's High Commissioner in Egypt and the man who engineered and addressed the ultimatum to ex-King Faruq. I myself translated Arabic (and French) material, whether novels and other literary material, findings by Arab sociologists and social psychologists, or the quotations from Nasser's speeches and press interviews. When an Arabic name or word has a form which is precise and generally accepted in English I have normally used it. Otherwise, I transliterated it in an accessible form.

Though in the concluding remarks the confrontation of the findings with both the null hypothesis and the outcome of the 4th Non-Aligned Summit supports this study's conclusions, and thus justify the endeavour,

I am nonetheless conscious of the risks inherent in attempting a conceptual mapping. For a conceptual mapping is something of an adventure —an effort to probe in a tentative way some unknown, neglected, but nevertheless promising, research areas. Some conceptualisations, of course, turn out to have great payoffs, but some end up with little return. Risks may even be greater here since this is an epoch of "team research" efforts and collaborative work rather than of the individual scholar, especially in investigating such a wide phenomenon as third world foreign policy-making. The breadth of the topic, however, is justified since some scholars working on more limited items of research face the risk of becoming like the "blind men" in the story of the Blind Men and the Elephant. A conceptual mapping, then, helps us to keep the whole "Elephant" in view. [12] And, after all, it is mainly by attempts at explicitness and systematisation that researchers discover the inherent limitations and proceed to cope with them. We hope that our experience will incite others to pick up where we left off.

Bahgat KORANY.

---

[12] Holt, Robert, and Turner, John : *The Political Basis of Economic Development : An Exploration in Comparative Political Analysis,* Princeton, Van Nostrand, 1966, pp. 1-4.

PART ONE

International Relations Paradigms and the Study of Non-Alignment

CHAPTER ONE

The 'Classical Paradigm'[1] and the Study of Non-Alignment

1.

In 1946 the contemporary international system numbered 59 national actors and in 1970 the membership has risen to 127. This membership increase of more than 100 per cent is due—largely—to the decline of colonial empires and the emergence—instead—of Afro-Asian states. Reacting against their recent colonial past, the leaders of most of these states insisted on the 'demonstration' of their newly-won independence and the playing of a distinctive international role. They tried to achieve this end by rejecting formal incorporation in, or subordination to, any of the then

[1] We are using "classical" rather than "traditional" because it seems to be less value-laden and thus does not prejudge the issue. Moreover, this is the labellation the adherents to this school prefer for themselves. And by its present usage is not meant the study and criticism of the 'classics' of international relations such as the works of Hobbs, Grotius, Kant and "other great thinkers of the past who have turned their attention to international affairs". Rather, 'classical' is used to designate "the approach to theorizing that derives from philosophy, history and law, and that is characterized above all by explicit reliance upon the exercise of judgement and by the assumptions that if we confine ourselves to strict standards of verification and proof there is very little of significance that can be said about international relations, that general propositions about this subject must therefore derive from a scientifically imperfect process of perception or intuition, and that these general propositions cannot be accorded anything more than the tentative and inconclusive status appropriate to their doubtful origin". Bull, Hedley : "International Theory : The Case for a Classical Approach", *World Politics,* XVIII (1966), pp. 361-378.

The word 'paradigm' seems to be less easy to dispense with. The Oxford dictionary defines it as "a pattern, exemplar, example". The word has been popularized among social scientists following Thomas Kuhn's treatment of the philosophy of science in his *The Structure of Scientific Revolutions.* Chicago, Chicago University Press, 1962, 2nd edition, 1970. Though the notion of paradigms is central to Kuhn's argument on the cumulative growth of scientific knowledge, he does not provide a single unequivocal definition. In an attempt to elucidate Kuhn's conception of a

existing blocs. This new actors' dissociation from East-West military alliances came to be known as non-alignment. [2]

The first official declaration of a policy of non-alignment came with Nehru's appointment as the Vice-President and Member-in-Charge of External Affairs of India's first national government (known as the Interim Government) constituted on the 2nd of September 1946. In a declaration on the all-India radio on 7 September, Nehru stated new India's foreign policy orientation of non-alignment and its opposition to systemic bipolarization as such. Nehru said :

> "We propose, as far as possible, to keep away from the power politics of groups, aligned against one another, which have led in the past to world wars and which may again lead to disasters on an even vaster scale." [3]

---

paradigm, Margaret Masterman counts no less than 21 different senses in which he uses the term, but argues that these fall into 3 main groups : (*a*) metaphysical or philosophical paradigms, which are general comprehensive ways of looking at the subject matter, or "world views" ; (*b*) sociological paradigms *i.e.* "set(s) of scientific habits" shared by particular research communities ; and (*c*) construct paradigms : concrete examples of successful research that serve as models for further scientific endeavours.

Among International Relations scholars, the paradigm concept seems to be used to classify academic work on the basis of two criteria : (*a*) a substantive criterion : the scholar's fundamental assumptions about the way the world is structured, and his set of legitimate research problems ; and (*b*) a methodological criterion : the scholar's techniques for conducting research and his criteria for concept-validation.

Beside Kuhn's book, see for instance : Lijphart, Arend : "The Structure of the Theoretical Revolution in International Relations", an *unpublished paper submitted to the ECPR Workshop on "Models of International Relations"* (Mannheim, Germany, April 1973). Masterman, Margaret : "The Nature of a Paradigm", Imre Lakatos and Alan Musgrave (eds.) : *Criticism and the Growth of Knowledge,* London, Cambridge University Press, 1970, pp. 61-66. Handelehman, John ; Vasquez, John ; O'Leary, Michael, and Coplin, William : "Color it Morgenthau : A Data-Based Assessment of Quantitative International Relations Research", *Research Studies No. 11,* International Relations Program, Maxwell School, Syracuse University, 1973.

[2] There is no consensus on one labellation to designate this posture among the non-aligned actors themselves. Consequently, the term non-alignment covers Egypt's "positive neutralism", Afghanistan's "equal friendship", Morocco's "non-dependence", Senegal's "non-suivisme", Jordan's "active neutrality", Nigeria's "independent view", Guinea's "active formal neutralism", Malawi's "discretional alignment and neutralism" ... See Crabb, Cecil, Jr. : *The Elephants and the Grass : A Study of Non-Alignment.* New York, Praeger, 1965, pp. 4-5. This indicates why non-alignment has proved difficult to define briefly and in specific terms. The Yugoslavs have tried to solve this problem by preaching—in vain it seems—the adoption of a "positive" and a "uniform" labellation like "active peaceful coexistence" and the codification of its principles.

[3] Jawaharlal Nehru's *Speeches,* Vol. I (September 1946 - May 1949), Government of India, Ministry of Information and Broadcasting, p. 2.

With the accelerating pace of decolonisation, the number of adherents to non-alignment grew. Thus as early as 1948, Burma's Prime Minister stated that "of the three great ... powers, the U.K., the U.S.A. and the U.S.S.R. ... Burma should be in friendly relations with all the three". In 1950, he explicitly declared that Burma did not desire "alignment with a particular power bloc antagonistic to other opposing blocs". [4] This was the same stand adopted by Indonesian leaders, and in a few years time "Asian neutralism"—as Panikkar called it—became a characteristic of the contemporary international system. [5]

2.

The exposition of factual aspects describing the rise of non-alignment is not controversial, it is the attempt to analyse the determinants of non-alignment that seems inadequate.

2.1. The general trend that pervaded the literature purported—implicitly or explicitly—to explain [6] non-alignment by attributing a relationship of causality between non-alignment and the bipolar East-West conflict. Thus a scholar explicitly states "neutralism, or non-alignment, as the neutrals (sic) all prefer to call it, is primarily a response to the Cold War, and only in part a product of rising nationalism ... *Afro-Asian neutralism is a function of bipolarity*". [7]

Explaining small states' foreign policy in a non-empathetic way results in defining non-alignment as nothing but equidistance between the Superpowers. Thus P. Kannelopoulos—the Honorary Chairman of the 4th International Conference on World Politics (Athens, September 1962) and the then Deputy Prime Minister of Greece—described the policy of non-alignment as "an adherence to an abstraction that is in fact utopian. Neutrality (sic)", he continued, "must be advantageous to neither side or both.

---

[4] Nayar, Parameswaran: "Growth of Non-Alignment in World Affairs", *India Quarterly,* XVIII (1962), pp. 28-58.

[5] Panikkar, K. M.: "The Twentieth Century in Asia and World Politics", *India Quarterly,* XII (1956), pp. 245-256. Even Pakistan's policy makers followed a policy of non-alignment before being motivated by their dispute with India to participate in SEATO and CENTO.

[6] One may question even the labellation 'explanation' for such an attempt. See, for instance, Kaplan, Abraham: *The Conduct of Inquiry,* San Francisco, Chandler Publishing Co., 1964, pp. 327-370; Popper, Karl: *The Logic of Scientific Discovery,* London, Hutchinson, 1968.

[7] Lefever, Ernest: "Nehru, Nasser and Nkrumah on Neutralism", in Lawrence W. Martin (ed.): *Neutralism and Non-Alignment,* New York, Praeger, 1962, pp. 93-121 (emphasis added).

A middle position that directly or indirectly favors only one of the two sides, by definition cannot be called neutrality . . . Neutrality implies a lack of resistance, and such passivity can only serve the aggressor" [8] (meaning the Communist states).

Apart from the use of neutrality and non-alignment interchangeably [9] and the value judgments that are at the basis of Kannelopoulos' statements, he shares with Lefever the same frame of reference, which has been expressed academically through the "Power Paradigm" or the "Realist School" in international politics. The name that is most associated with this dominant paradigm is Hans Morgenthau. When he published the first edition of his *Politics Among Nations* in 1948 the work was considered "unprecedented and attractive" in a number of respects. [10]

(*a*) Morgenthau captured and synthesized in one volume the ideas on international politics which an entire generation was attempting to express. Though "other scholars such as E. H. Carr, Harold Nicolson, Frederick Schumann and Nicholas Spykman (were) writing before him, and Frederick Dunn, George Kennan and Kenneth W. Thompson (were) writing about the same time as Morgenthau . . . it was *Politics Among Nations* which became the *one* most important book in the field. Not surprisingly it outsold all other textbooks on international relations during the fifties". [11] Moreover, *Politics Among Nations* has been translated into such 'third world' languages as Arabic, Turkish and Swahili.

---

[8] Kannelopoulos, Panayotis : "Neutrality - Utopia or Reality ?", in Kurt London (ed.) : *New Nations in a Divided World,* New York, Praeger, 1964, p. xiii.

[9] In spite of the varied labellations, all non-aligned actors agreed—already at their 1st Summit—with Guinea's Foreign Minister that non-alignment "is an essentially active policy". Nkrumah found passive neutrality unrealistic in the contemporary international system. The three official sponsors of the First Summit—Tito, Nasser and Sukarno—reiterated in their public speeches that non-alignment, as an active policy, is different from neutrality and that it does not mean equidistance. Sukarno, in particular, stated at length his view on the basic meaning of non-alignment. See the *Official Report of the Conference of Heads of State or Government of Non-Aligned Countries,* Belgrade, 1961 (to be referred to hereafter as *B.C.R.).* Moreover, the coding and processing of about 50,000 of the speeches of some non-aligned leaders in three summit conferences show that "the term non-alignment is used with great frequency in the speeches delivered at the three Conferences, while the word 'neutralism' is rarely mentioned and *neutrality never appears*". Choucri, Nazli : "The Perceptual Base of Non-Alignment", *Journal of Conflict Resolution,* XIII (1969), pp. 57-73 (emphasis added). This is why it is not a coincidence that such 'classic' neutrals as Sweden and Switzerland never attended non-aligned gatherings.

[10] Handelman et al. : "Color it Morgenthau . . .", *op. cit.*

[11] *Ibid.*

(*b*) By departing from the inter-war mode of diplomatic narration and from the emphasis on international law and organization, Morgenthau has set the tone for most of the 'grand' theoretical activity ever since. [12] He committed himself to bringing order into a mass of seemingly unconnected material and thus proved the value of generalization. Thus he attempted to show that states in their interaction follow a regular pattern (*e.g.* the search for power).

(*c*) By providing a set of concepts and propositions, and by claiming that his 'theory' could account for all relevant behaviour, he mapped out "legitimate topics of research" [13] for future scholars.

2.2. *The Power Paradigm and the Explanation of Non-Alignment*

2.2.1. In 1957 Morgenthau attempted an 'explanation' of Afro-Asian non-alignment. [14] What is typical of the Morgenthau treatment is his failure to distinguish between the foreign policy orientation of the newly-independent actors and legal neutrality. Thus under the subtitle "Three types of neutral*ISM*" he says that "the effects of . . . (post-war) developments upon neutral*ITY* as a viable legal and political status are of course beyond doubt". [15] This is perhaps why he cannot view non-alignment except as a function of the balance of power, since for Morgenthau "there exists . . . an intimate relationship between the politico-legal status of neutrality and the balance of power". [16] Consequently, Morgenthau disregards completely Afro-Asian actors' emphasis on the distinction between the withdrawn, passive neutrality and the involved, self-assertive non-alignment. For the non-aligned actors differentiate between neutrality as a *legal* concept which assumes the *legality of war* as an instrument of national policy and the *political* concept of non-alignment which claims to be anti-war and has as its objective to prevent war between the blocs. [17]

---

[12] Holsti, K. J.: "Retreat from Utopia: International Relations Theory, 1945-1970", *Canadian Journal of Political Science,* IV (1971), pp. 165-178.

[13] Handelman et al.: "Color it Morgenthau . . .", *op. cit.*

[14] Morgenthau, Hans: "Neutrality and Neutralism", *The Yearbook of World Affairs,* 1957, pp. 47-75.

[15] *Ibid.* (emphasis added).

[16] *Ibid.*

[17] ". . . non-alignment is not neutrality . . . Non alignment is not the sanctimonious attitude of the man who holds himself aloft—'a plague on both your houses' . . . Non-aligned policy is not a policy of neutrality without its own colour: being non-aligned does not mean becoming a buffer state between the two giant blocs. Non-alignment is active devotion to the lofty cause of independence, abiding peace . . .". Kahin, Georges: *The Asian-African Conference,* Bandung, Indonesia, 1955. New York, Cornell U.P., 1956. As quoted in Choucri: *op. cit.* But see also footnote 9 above.

According to the non-aligned actors, this war-prevention [18] component of their policy is dictated by the characteristics of the contemporary international system, and especially the evolution of warfare technology. In fact, Morgenthau realises the balance-of-terror aspect of the system, but either fails to relate it to the rationale of non-alignment or draws conclusions different from those of the non-aligned actors. For instance, Morgenthau rightly remarks that "the technology of warfare had progressed to a point at which the protection of geographic location was largely eliminated". [19] This is as empirically valid as his truism that "before the atomic fall-out and bacteriological contamination all men and all nations, big and small, neutrals and belligerents, are equal". [20] Up to this point, Morgenthau and the non-aligned Afro-Asians are in complete agreement, but his conclusion is diametrically opposed to theirs. "Under these conditions", Morgenthau says, "they ("nations of the second and third rank") have no chance to remain neutral either in 'cold' or 'hot' war since it is their fate, decided by others, to belong to one or the other bloc". [21] Thus the balance of terror that *did* act as one of the determinants of Afro-Asian non-alignment *should* be—according to Morgenthau—a determinant of Afro-Asian participation in bloc alliances. We see here one of the problems of the 'power paradigm'. Morgenthau's conclusion is empirically at complete variance with the Afro-Asian foreign policy orientation it purports to explain.

Four years later Morgenthau came back to the subject. This time he aimed to establish a classification scheme that purported to discern between one variety of "neutralism" representing nothing more than "escapism pure and simple", another characterised by "moral indifference" to global issues, and still a third that amounted to a "surreptitious alignment with the Soviet bloc." [22]

Leaving aside the value judgments and the 'Dullesian' overtones, Morgenthau's classification rests upon some underlying conception of an 'ideal' or 'pure' type of neutralism which serves as the standard to designate and measure the 'deviant' types. Yet typically, this standard is never explicitly set forth. But it seems that Morgenthau's implicit standard of measurement and evaluation is traditional-legal neutrality.

---

[18] For a detailed treatment of this aspect of non-alignment, see, for instance, Lyon, Peter: *Neutralism,* Leicester U.P., 1963, pp. 62-67.

[19] Morgenthau: "Neutrality and Neutralism", *op. cit.*

[20] *Ibid.*

[21] *Ibid.*

[22] Morgenthau, Hans: "Critical Look at the New Neutralism", *New York Times Magazine,* August 27, 1961, pp. 25, 76-77. As summarized by Crabb: *op. cit.,* pp. 20-21.

2.2.2. Georg Schwarzenberger—another influential exponent of the "Power Paradigm" [23]—is a step ahead of Morgenthau. He realises that the word neutralism or non-alignment—unlike neutrality—"is still a newcomer to the vocabulary of international relations". [24] Consequently, "its meaning cannot yet be taken for granted". Thus, in order to avoid "inarticulate associations" with "related terms", Schwarzenberger devotes some space to distinguish between neutralism or non-alignment and other expressions such as isolationism, non-commitment, neutrality, neutralisation, non-involvement. But of course, his frame of reference is the same. In analysing non-alignment, he places himself directly and at the start in a balance of power framework based uniquely on the structure of the dominant subsystem : the bipolar East-West conflict. He explicitly states that his object is "to examine the scope and limits of neutralism as a pattern of international strategy in the specific context of the present phase of nuclear stalemate between the two world camps". Indeed, he realises —and even admits explicitly—that taking the dominant subsystem as the only variable accounting for the emergence of Afro-Asian non-alignment is not adequate. "It must be remembered", Shwarzenberger says, "how much the leaders of non-committed nations themselves are conditioned by the emotional liability of their own political environment at home and the personal rivalries in the political movements on whose loyal support their political and sometimes even their physical existence depends". [25] But this admission is not allowed to influence his analysis in the slightest form, and he goes on to present five possible models of neutralism as "a strategy of international policy in an environment of power politics" :

1. $B \longleftrightarrow R \,//\, Y$: B and R are antagonistic actors and Y is standing passively aside. The empirical referent of this model is the policy of neutralised Switzerland before 1914 and during the first World War.

2. $B \leftarrow Y \rightarrow R$: B and R are still antagonistic but Y this time is more involved for it acts as a 'balancer'. The empirical referent of this model is British policy in Europe before 1914.

3. $B + Y \longleftrightarrow R$, and

4. $B \longleftrightarrow Y + R$

In both these models, Y went a step forward in its involvement and aligned itself with one of the antagonists against the other. The empirical referent of this model is Italian policy prior to and during the first World War.

---

[23] See his 614-page volume : *Power Politics : A Study of World Society,* London, Stevens and Sons Ltd (3rd edition), 1964.

[24] Schwarzenberger, Georg : "The Scope for Neutralism", *The Yearbook of World Affairs,* London, 1961, pp. 233-244.

[25] *Ibid.*

5. B + R ⟷ Y : Here the two antagonists B and R aligned themselves against Y. Schwarzenberger evokes the three partitions of Poland during the 18th and 19th centuries to support his thesis that "neutralism presupposes the willingness of other states to respect or, at least, to tolerate such a policy". [26] Empirically, however, Afro-Asian non-alignment has emerged in the face of opposition—and even resistance—on the part of the two Superpowers. [27] Consequently, Schwarzenberger's claim to explain Afro-Asian non-alignment through the application of examples taken from European history seems to be unsubstantiated. This only raises the question of how 'Eurocentric and time-bound' the explanatory function of the 'Power Paradigm' is. This, in its turn, brings us to the objections levelled against this paradigm.

3. Objections to the 'Power Paradigm'

3.1. To the exclusion of everything else, it identified 'power' as the explanatory basis of international politics. [28] Inis Claude expresses this point very explicitly :

> "However one may resolve the question of priority to be assigned to the maintenance of peace, it is clear that the problem of the management of power in international relations looms as the central issue of our time. Power exists in states. It may be used in competitive

---

[26] *Ibid.*

[27] The blocs' reaction to non-alignment was at the beginning hostile. India's failure to get a seat in the Security Council in 1947 was symbolic of opposition to non-alignment. Soviet analysis of India's orientation after independence was that "Congress leaders have made a deal with Anglo-American imperialism and Indian reactionaries to fight their own people", and that Nehru was directing his country's affairs "with the support of warmongers and trying to cut off the Indian people from their natural allies and liberty-loving people". For details of the early Soviet attitude toward newly-independent India, see Kapur, Harish : *The Embattled Triangle : Moscow - Peking - New Delhi,* Delhi, 1973, Abhinav Publications, pp. 99-107. Similarly, in the Western bloc the *New York Times* described Nehru as "a great disappointment", and as late as June 1956, John Foster Dulles defined non-alignment as the "fallacy" that "a nation can buy safety for itself by being indifferent to the fate of others". He qualified this conception as "obsolete . . . immoral and short-sighted". Martin, Lawrence : "The Emergence of the New States", *Neutralism and Non-Alignment, op. cit.,* pp. xi-xxi.

[28] As late as May 1973, Morgenthau emphatically and consistently affirmed : "power is the core of both national and international politics". Since power—according to Morgenthau—cannot be quantified in the same sense that wealth in economics—for instance—can, it follows that quantitative studies of politics are "apolitical". "New Trends in the Study of International Politics", *Lecture at the Graduate Institute of International Studies,* Geneva, 22nd May, 1973.

struggle producing intolerable destruction. It may be used unilaterally, producing enslavement and degradation of its victims. In short, both survival and freedom, both existence itself and the higher values that enrich existence, are implicated in the problem of power . . ." [29]

Claude's position is a continuation of a trend of thought. Schuman has affirmed the general proposition that "all politics is a struggle for power. People with power relish the joy of commanding others to do their will". Consequently in international politics "foreign policy is an expression of a state's will-to-power". [30]

Hans Morgenthau is equally explicit. As a logical consequence of his main assumption of an 'aggressive' human nature and "man's sinfulness", he believes that "international politics, like all politics, is a struggle for power. Whatever the ultimate aims of international politics, power is *always* the immediate aim". [31]

3.1.1. It is true that the power paradigm directs attention to some main variables in the explanation of international phenomena (*e.g.* capabilities such as natural resources, technological level available, military resources ... etc.) which account for an actor's position in the international system. But because of "its undue emphasis on power and struggle, it (the paradigm) conceals other aspects of international politics which are also important. If some types of relationships can be described as struggle, surely Anglo-American relations are not, for the most part, adequately characterized by this term." Moreover, even in situations where power and struggle are the dominant note of interaction, capabilities or 'elements of power' do not always explain how effective a state will be in its external relations. For an actor can be very well endowed with the 'elements of power' and still not achieve its objectives against a weak and/or a small state. Consequently, "while the approach does explain a limited range of phenomena and helps to emphasize the importance of one variable—power—in international politics, it is burdened with its own oversimplicity, lexical definitions, unexamined assumptions, and Hobbesian view of international relationships". [32]

---

[29] Claude, Inis (Jr.): *Power and International Relations,* New York, Random House, 1962, pp. 5-6.

[30] Schuman, Frederick: *International Politics,* New York, McGraw-Hill, 1958 (6th edition). Chapter VI and VIII, but see also pp. 674-679.

[31] Morgenthau, Hans: *Politics Among Nations,* New York, Knopf, 3rd edition, 1960, pp. 27-38.

[32] Holsti, K. J.: *International Politics: A Framework for Analysis,* Englewood Cliffs, N.J., Prentice-Hall, 1967, p. 15.

The result is rigidity in analysis and attempts to make contemporary phenomena fit into a framework which is a "highly embellished ideal-type of 18th and 19th century international relations". [33]

In anticipating this objection, Morgenthau based his answer on the permanence of human nature :

> "Human nature, in which the laws of politics have their roots, has not changed since the classical philosophies of China, India and Greece endeavored to discover these laws. Hence novelty is not necessarily a virtue in political theory, nor is old age a defect . . . The fact that a theory of politics was developed hundreds or even thousands of years ago . . . does not create a presumption that it must be outmoded and obsolete . . . To dismiss such a theory because it had its flowering in centuries past is to present not a rational argument but a modernistic prejudice that takes for granted the superiority of the present over the past . . ." [34]

In spite of our agreement with Morgenthau that in academic matters no *a priori* superiority of the present over the past should be the rule, Hoffmann's argument that "it would be very dangerous in the long run to continue to work in our field with a model that does not fit" [35] is particularly valid. In other words, the argument that "whatever (conceptual framework) has been, must continue" [36] is valid only if the framework's empirical referent is the same, that is if the social reality that the 'theory' purports to explain has not changed. [37]

[33] Stanley Hoffmann (ed.): *Contemporary Theory in International Politics,* Englewoods Cliffs, N.J., Prentice-Hall, 1960, pp. 32-35.

[34] Morgenthau : *Politics Among Nations, op. cit.,* pp. 3-13.

[35] Hoffmann : *Contemporary Theory in International Politics, op. cit.,* p. 36.

[36] Moreover, Morgenthau's basic assumption of "man's sinfulness" and a permanent 'aggressive' human nature is still questioned and controversial since it has not been proven to *be a general law universal both in time and space.* It is more accurate to regard 'aggressive' political behaviour, domestically and internationally, as rooted not in a "sinfulness of man but in a context, a constellation, a *situation* to which men respond". Discrimination between the inherent or instinctive aspects of an actor's behaviour, and the *situational* one is an important task. However, "reactions to shifting situations are scarcely considered by the theory". *Ibid.,* pp. 32-36 (emphasis added).

[37] Indeed, we are here applying the criteria Morgenthau himself has chosen to evaluate any "theory of international politics". "The test by which such a theory must be judged", Morgenthau said, "is not *a priori* and abstract but empirical and pragmatic. The theory . . . must be judged not by some preconceived abstract principle or concept unrelated to reality . . .", *Politics Among Nations, op. cit.,* p. 3.

3.1.2. Yet the contemporary international system is not a continuation[38] of even the inter-war system immediately preceding it. For example:

(*a*) post-war communication and transportation developments greatly changed the character of international relations and stimulated different forms of integration. Thus contrary to the premises of the "realist" school which accepts the nation-state as the basic unit of the international system, the number of international organizations has reached 1,900 in 1964 (not including international business enterprises), 180 of which are intergovernmental ;

(*b*) the number of "basic actors" has more than doubled. The change is not only quantitative, but qualitative too. The contemporary international system is no longer Euro-centered, for the multitude of actors have varying cultural contexts and new problems (*e.g.* decolonization, economic development . . .) ;

(*c*) nuclear weapons had revolutionary effects on the strategic and diplomatic fields and modified the role of violence as an instrument of international relations, at least among the superpowers. Consequently adjustment and steering[39] replaced the "struggle for power" as the most important facet of their foreign policy formulation and behaviour (*e.g.* the 1962 Cuban crisis, the SALT talks).

Yet the 'power paradigm' has not incorporated these changes in its analysis. This 'fallacy of continuity' resulted in some "oddities"[40] as far as non-alignment is concerned :

(*a*) No adequate discussion of the actor's specific ends is included. As has been mentioned above, the 'theory' has taken the relatively homogeneous 18th and 19th century international politics (*i.e.* only a particular historical pattern) as the "norm for a scientific system". Yet when this basis of analysis is applied to a "heterogeneous"[41] international system—like the contemporary international system—the neglect of ends is a "fatal mistake".[42] When this mistake is made with non-alignment, the result is

---

[38] Alger, Chadwick : "International Relations", *International Encyclopedia of the Social Sciences,* VIII, New York, The Macmillan Company and the Free Press, 1968, pp. 61-69.

[39] For a detailed account of this argument as well as a criticism of the "Power Paradigm", see Burton, John : *International Relations : A General Theory,* London, Cambridge U.P., 1965, pp. 31-151.

[40] For a treatment of these oddities, see Hoffmann : *Contemporary Theory . . ., op. cit.,* pp. 32-35.

[41] The term is Raymond Aron's. See his *War and Peace Among Nations : A Theory of International Relations,* New York, Praeger, 1966 (This is a translation of the 1962 French edition), pp. 373-404.

[42] Hoffmann : *Contemporary Theory . . ., op. cit.,* pp. 32-35.

undue emphasis on non-aligned actors as a monolithic homogeneous group. Thus Saudi Arabia and Cuba are eggs in the same basket.

(*b*) Differing domestic pressures and processes of foreign-policy making are ignored.

(*c*) The treatment is essentially a function of the 'balance of power'. As a result, emphasis was mainly put on 'tangible power factors', and since non-aligned actors did not rank very high on this basis, they were normally treated as negligible factors in the play of big-power politics. This 'big-power bias' could be justified in the age of European 'power politics' when the international system was dominated by events in this continent ; and when other areas in the world were politically irrelevant and incapable of generating system-wide demands or 'disturbances' (*e.g.* dependent peoples). [43]

3.2. A second major criticism of the power paradigm is that the definition of its basic concept—Power—is far from clear. [44]

Because the 'realist school' wanted its 'theory' to be "timeless" and its "struggle for power" as "universal in time and space", [45] this led to ambiguities and controversies. As Kenneth W. Thompson—a leading 'realist' —has observed : "much of the literature of international politics is a dia-

[43] Consequently, instead of theories of international politics essentially based on major actors' behaviour while treating smaller actors as the object rather than the subject, a "set of questions" should be directed toward "explorations into the typical models of thinking and behaviour" of the smaller actors. For a criticism of International Relations from this angle, see for instance Huopaniemi : *op. cit.;* Rothstein : *op. cit.,* pp. 1-8.

[44] The 'power' concept seems to be inherently controversial. For among sociologists, for instance, there is no consensus on the definition of power : "in the entire lexicon of sociological concepts, none is more troublesome than the concept of power". Bierstadt, Robert : "An Analysis of Social Power", Lewis Coser and Bernard Rosenberg (ed.), *Sociological Theory,* New York, The Macmillan Company, 1957, p. 152. Though Max Weber explicited his definition of 'power' as "the possibility of imposing one's will upon the behaviour of other persons" (which influenced Morgenthau's definition), many interpretations have grown—with greater or lesser variations—out of Weber's thought. Consequently, some scholars distinguish between power and influence, others use both interchangeably, and still others use influence as a component of power. Thus a sociologist turned political scientist defined "power's" presence as when the actions of one actor "are capable of changing, in greater or lesser degree, the actions of the second (national actor) either by coercion or by influence. Power, in its coercive aspect is always a latent force". Lagos, Gustave : *International Stratification and Underdeveloped Countries,* University of North Carolina Press, 1963, p. 96.

[45] Morgenthau : *Politics Among Nations, op. cit.,* pp. 25-34.

logue, explicit or not, between Morgenthau and his critics . . .". [46] One of the controversies is around the definition of the basis of the paradigm ; 'power' itself.

3.2.1. With authors like Machiavelli or Hobbes, the concept of power "has usually seemed to imply abusive coercion on behalf of the coercer . . . and thus carry with it a certain misanthropy towards life". [47] In the public mind it refers to the ability to win an international war. This is the meaning given to the term by the Sprouts : ". . . it should be emphasised that in American popular usage, the term power tends more often than not to denote military power, or at least to connote some idea of coercion or threatened coercion which is the essence of military power". [48] This is also the definition Inis Claude gives the term : "I use the term power to denote what is essentially military capability—the elements which contribute directly or indirectly to the capacity to coerce, kill and destroy." [49]

Reduced to military capability, the "power" approach suffers from the defects of any single-variable explanation, whether the explanatory variable is "power", "ideology" or any other. At best its 'explanation' is one-sided, and needs to be completed by the investigation of other variables determining political behaviour.

3.2.2. Moreover, reducing power to the place of a mere instrument contrasts with Morgenthau's above-mentioned statement of power as "the immediate aim". In fact, Morgenthau excludes the military aspect from his definition of [political] power :

> "Political power, however, must be distinguished from force in the sense of the actual exercise of physical violence. The threat of physical violence in the form of police action . . . or war is an intrinsic element of politics. When violence becomes an actuality, it signifies *the abdication of political power* in favor of military or pseudo-military power. In international politics, in particular, . . . the actual exercise of physical violence substitutes for the psychological relation between two minds, which is of the essence of political power, the physical relation between two bodies, one of which is strong enough to dominate the other's movements. It is for this reason that in the exercise of physical violence the psychological elements of the political relationship is lost, and that we must distinguish between military and political power." [50]

[46] Thompson, Kenneth : "American Approaches to International Politics", *Yearbook of World Affairs,* London, 1959, p. 222.

[47] Easton, David : *The Political System,* New York, Knopf, 1953, pp. 115-124.

[48] Sprout, Harold and Margaret : *Foundations of International Politics,* Princeton, Van Nostrand Company, 1962, p. 141.

[49] Claude : *op. cit.,* p. 6.

[50] Morgenthau : *Politics Among Nations, op. cit.* (emphasis added), pp. 25-35.

Since Morgenthau excludes the military aspect from his definition of (political) power, [51] he considers "power . . . a special value ; it is a possession but not in a tangible form like money or real estate". [52] In a much-quoted statement he emphasizes the relational aspect in the definition of power. "Political power", Morgenthau says, "is a psychological relation between those who exercise it and those over whom it is exercised. It gives the former control over certain actions of the latter through the influence which the former exerts over the latter's mind". [53] Thus power here is synonymous with "control", "man's control over the minds and actions of other men". [54] But are [political] power and control exactly the same ? They do not always go hand in hand. For example, a country with massive resources might arouse anxiety and fear in a neighbouring country which results in the latter's attempt to reduce the possibilities of future control by the powerful neighbour. Thus "here the power in hand tends to offset the power to control". [55]

The result of Morgenthau's failure to define his concept operationally is that political power as a mere social fact (as in the case of the lobbyist or the legitimate authority of the U.S. president) is always considered to be the same—however different its source and nature may be.

In fact, Morgenthau's definition of power is even more general than the "political power" of the lobbyist or the U.S. president. Morgenthau says : "Statesmen and people may seek freedom, security, prosperity or power itself. They may define their goals in terms of a religious, philosophic, economic or social ideal. They may hope that this ideal will materialize through its own inner force, through divine intervention, or through the natural development of human affairs. They may also try to further its realization through non-political means, such as technical co-operation with other nations or international organizations. But whenever they strive to realize their goal by means of international politics, they do so by striving for power." [56]

3.2.3. Power is thus synonymous with the field of international politics itself. It is a catch-all term, a "hasty effort to account for everything at once", [57] a variable that includes almost every other thing. Conse-

---

[51] McClelland, Charles : *Theory and the International System,* New York, Macmillan, 1966, p. 70.

[52] *Ibid.,* p. 68.

[53] Morgenthau : *Politics Among Nations, op. cit.,* pp. 25-34.

[54] *Ibid.*

[55] McClelland : *op. cit.,* p. 70.

[56] Morgenthau : *Politics Among Nations, op. cit.,* pp. 25-34.

[57] Hoffmann : *Contemporary Theory . . ., op. cit.,* p. 29. Note, for instance, this definition of power as provided by one of the pillars of the power paradigm, Georg Schwarzenberger : "Power can be . . . defined", he said, "as the capability of forcing

quently, an unpublished Ph.D. thesis found out that in international relations textbooks alone, 'power' is used in 17 different ways. [58] Moreover, because the concept covered as distinct variables as "power as a potential and power in use, power as a sum of resources and power as a set of processes", [59] all these variables remained hidden rather than being allowed to see the light. The result is that—as we have mentioned above—differences in the actor's historical experience, in the structure of a society, the formation and personality of foreign policy decision-makers as well as other societal or national characteristics are not singled out to see their effect on foreign policy attitudes and behaviour. For instance, questions such as 'why a decision-maker uses a certain quantity of power rather than another, and handles it in a certain way' are left unanswered. The result is that the paradigm's empirical referent "comes out oversimplified, for we get a somewhat mechanistic view of international affairs in which the statesman's role consists of adjusting national power to an almost immutable set of external givens". [60] Moreover, the weight put on the power concept makes it collapse under the burden. [61]

---

one's own will on others, irrespective of the reasonableness of the demand, and with political, economic and military pressure as the ultimate means of achieving this object". See "Beyond Power Politics", *Yearbook of World Affairs,* London, 1965, pp. 223-235.

[58] Sullivan, Denis: *Towards an Inventory of Major Propositions contained in Contemporary Textbooks in International Relations,* Ph.D., Dissertation, Northwestern University, 1963, as quoted in Alger: *op. cit.*

[59] Hoffmann: *Contemporary Theory ..., op. cit.,* pp. 29-38. In the field of political science proper, David Easton condemned as early as 1953 this "breadth of definition" of the concept of power which treats equally "the hierarchical arrangement of relationships within a criminal band or in a respectable fraternal club". *The Political System, op. cit.,* pp. 115-124.

[60] Hoffmann: *Contemporary Theory ..., op. cit.,* pp. 29-38.

[61] In criticising Morgenthau, Aron said: "The first pages of that classic, *Politics Among Nations,* offer an equally classic example of conceptual confusion arising from the use of a term such as 'power', which, depending on the paragraph or even the sentence one is reading, means either the end or the means of politics and which, finally, is of no use. If 'power' is defined in Weber's way, which is moreover the common way, as the ability of agent A to get agent B to submit to his will or to obey his orders (or, more precisely, the good fortune of agent A to achieve submission and obedience), then all social life is a question of power to some extent; power is obviously essential for collective action in any field whatsoever. Setting up power, thus defined, as the unique and highest goal of individuals, parties, or nations does not constitute a theory in the scientific sense, but instead amounts to a philosophy or an ideology. In any event, it is not a proposition that can be proven false; thus it cannot even be considered a scientific hypothesis." Aron, Raymond: "What is a Theory of International Relations", John Farrell and Asa Smith (eds.): *Theory and Reality in International Relations,* New York, Columbia University Press, 1967, pp. 1-23. Also *Peace and War, op. cit.,* pp. 595-597. Consequently, the 'power' concept becomes too general to be useful, and because it can mean everything, it can mean nothing at the same time. As an example of this conceptual confusion, the

4.

The paradigm's oversimplications [62] are, then, responsible for its failure to account for non-alignment :

---

paradigm's proposed pattern of inter-state interaction—"the balance of power"—is used, at least verbally, in eight different meanings: distribution of power, equilibrium, hegemony, stability and peace, instability and war, power politics generally, universal law of history, a system and guide to policy-making. See Haas, Ernest : "The Balance of Power : Prescription, Concept or Propaganda", *World Politics,* Vol. V (1953), pp. 442-477. Morgenthau alone uses the term in four different senses : "(*a*) as a policy aimed at a certain state of affairs ; (*b*) as an actual state of affairs ; (*c*) as an approximately equal distribution of power ; and (*d*) as any distribution of power". *Politics Among Nations, op. cit.,* p. 157, footnote 1. Morgenthau is, indeed, conscious of the problem for he says "whenever the term (balance of power) is used without qualification it refers to an actual state of affairs in which power is distributed among several nations with approximate equality". Thus balance of power —according to Morgenthau and if not otherwise indicated—means equilibrium. But he goes on afterwards to refer—without any qualification—to the possibility that a certain group of states might gain "a decisive advantage in the overall European balance of power", and that the Central Powers believed in 1914 that "the balance of power favored them". *Ibid.,* pp. 192, 209. Here balance of power is used in the sense of distribution of power rather than equilibrium. This inconsistency in usage makes the researcher wonder—whenever the term recurs—in what sense it is used this time. This "philological, semantic and theoretic confusion ... (of) the focal concept in several quite distinct theories of international relations" confirms what A. F. Pillard said almost 50 years ago. "The balance of power", Pillard said, "may mean almost anything, and it is used not only in different senses by different people, or in different senses by the same people at different times, but in different senses by the same person at the same time." As quoted in Claude : *op. cit.,* p. 12.

[62] Thus the often-quoted concept or "pseudo-theory" of "national interest" has been criticized as too simplistic to be meaningful. "Let us take the formula", Aron suggested, "sometimes presented as theoretical, according to which states act according to their 'national interest'. The formula is just as meaningless as ... (the) postulate that Meredith's character Beauchamp, who drowns while trying to save a child, finds more satisfaction in sacrificing his life than in saving it at the expense of someone else's death. Likewise, whatever the diplomacy of a state may be, nothing prevents one from asserting after the fact that it was dictated by considerations of 'national interest', as long as 'national interest' has not been strictly defined." Aron : "What is a Theory of International Relations ?", *op. cit.* Also *Peace and War, op. cit.,* pp. 91-92. Other scholars have doubts about the analytic utility of the national interest concept. See Modelski, George : *A Theory of Foreign Policy,* London, Pall Mall, 1962, pp. 70-72. Moreover, a review of International Relations literature indicates "serious limitations in the concept as an analytic tool" leading to its "failure". This is why the national interest (concept) has not sparked research or otherwise lived up to its early promise as an analytic tool. All the approaches to it suffer from difficulties which defy resolution and which confound rather than clarify analysis. Consequently, "as political inquiry becomes more systematic and explicit, the concept is therefore likely to be used less and less". Rosenau, James : "The National Interest", *The International Encyclopedia of the Social Sciences, op. cit.,* vol. XI, pp. 34-40.

(*a*) analytically any foreign policy is to be viewed as a process of interaction [63] wherein numerous variables enter to contribute to the 'definition of the situation' and the choice of the response. In singling out the bipolar East-West conflict as the main "input" in a non-aligned orientation and/or behaviour, this paradigm was logically deficient as it resulted in one-sided 'explanation' of foreign-policy making in new states ;

(*b*) this indicates why the paradigm's 'explanation' was *empirically* falsified. For instance, whereas Morgenthau prescribed alignment, the Afro-Asian actors chose non-alignment. But this is not all. For when the adherents to this paradigm proposed a relationship of causality between the bipolar East-West conflict (A) and non-alignment (B), one is entitled to expect that 'B' would not only vary in the same direction as 'A', but also generally to the same degree. Yet empirically we see the reverse. With the decline of bipolarity and the growth of centrifugal forces within the blocs, not only did non-alignment continue to exist but also the number of non-aligned actors was constantly on the increase : from 25 full members + 3 observers at the 1st Non-Aligned Summit Conference, to 47 full members + 10 observers at the 2nd Summit and to 52 full members + 9 observers at the 3rd Summit.

[63] Modelski : *A Theory of Foreign Policy, op. cit.*

CHAPTER II

The Evolving Paradigm and the Study of Non-Alignment

It was as a reaction to the methodological-conceptual deficiencies of the dominant paradigm in International Relations that a "protest movement" [1] was triggered off which aimed to evolve an alternative paradigm in the field. One of the cornerstones of this "scientific approach" [2] to the analysis of international phenomena is "systems theory". This international systems analysis is a good starting point for (*a*) it explicits the general bases of the alternative paradigm ; and (*b*) it provides a summary description of the environment or 'systemic setting' within which non-aligned actors interact.

This last point is basic, for it is generally agreed that global structural features, whether of alliances or domination, "set limits upon the actions of states and policy-makers no matter what their ideological persuasion, the state of domestic opinion or individual ideals". [3] Consequently, the

[1] Dahl, Robert: "The Behavioral Approach in Political Science: Epitaph for a Movement to a Successful Protest", *American Political Science Review,* LV (1961), pp. 763-772.

[2] This is how an advocate of the 'classical paradigm' qualified the evolving paradigm. For his definition of the latter, see Bull: *International Theory . . ., op. cit.* But see also Kaplan's answer in Kaplan, Morton: "The new Great Debate: Traditionalism vs. Science in International Relations", *World Politics,* XIX (1966), pp. 1-21. The evolving paradigm has been difficult to define briefly yet comprehensively, but Easton provided an inventory of seven of its essential bases. Easton, David: "The Current Meaning of Behavioralism", in James Charlesworth (ed.): *Contemporary Political Analysis,* New York, The Free Press, 1967, pp. 11-32. A voluminous literature is available on the debate between the advocates of the different paradigms. See for instance Heinz Eulau (ed.): *Behavioralism in Political Science,* New York, Atherton Press, 1969 ; Michael Haas and Henry Kariel (ed.): *Approaches to the Study of Political Science,* Scranton, Chandler Publishing Co., 1970 ; Klaus Knorr and James Rosenau (ed.): *Contending Approaches to International Politics,* Princeton, Princeton University Press (paperback edition), 1970.

[3] Holsti: *International Politics, op. cit.,* pp. 13-29. And Holsti continues: "... the external environment ... may have profound effects on the general orienta-

macro-framework of 'systems theory' provides "the best approach for delineating the *main* features and characteristics of international political processes over a relatively long period of time". [4]

Since this particular macro-framework has proved popular in International Relations recently, we will start with a brief historical note on its origins, review some basic definitions offered by a number of International Relations scholars, and then explicit our main variables. The remaining and biggest portion of this part of the chapter is devoted to a summary application of these variables to post-war international politics, *i.e.* the environment within which non-aligned actors interact.

Though functional in expliciting the systemic setting of non-alignment, international systems analysis can account for *only a part* of the conditions underlying the policies of different non-aligned actors. For one cannot explain the non-aligned actors' behaviour by reference only to the environment (the system), but rather one must emphasize primarily the domestic variables that affect policy-making (*e.g.* internal political pressures, economic and social needs, psychological determinants . . .). Indeed, 'systems theorists' admit this serious limitation of their mode of analysis and suggest shifting to the micro-level-of-analysis [5] : *i.e.* the actor- (and/or individual-) oriented. [6] Consequently the decision-making model [7] is

---

tions of a state toward the rest of the world". Thus the major characteristics of any international system can be used as *one set of variables* to help explain the typical actions of that system's component political units. This is the same view of Singer, David : "The Global System and its Subsystems : A Developmental View", in James Rosenau (ed.) : *Linkage Politics : Essays on the Convergence of National and International Systems,* New York, The Free Press, 1969, pp. 21-44. Systemic influences on actors' foreign policy orientation and/or behaviour are even more significant in the case of system-dominated smaller members which is the case of the majority of non-aligned actors.

[4] Holsti : *International Politics, op. cit.,* pp. 15-29.

[5] The oft-quoted treatment of this problem in International Relations is Singer, David : "The Level-of-Analysis Problem in International Relations", *World Politics,* XIV (1961), pp. 77-92.

[6] In our usage 'actor-oriented' will have to deal with both the national or state variables and the policy-makers' since (*a*) when we say 'states' behave, we really mean that policy-makers are defining purposes, choosing courses of action and utilizing national capabilities to achieve objectives in the name of the state. This is an important advantage in the decision-making model which emphasised the 'psychological environment' and perceptual orientation of the decision makers ; and (*b*) in most non-aligned and less-developed actors generally, the motivations, ideals, perceptions, values or idiosyncracies of their policy-makers are a key variable in the analysis of these actors' foreign policies. We will discuss this in greater detail later.

[7] Though international systems analysis and the decision-making model work on different levels-of-analysis and have different foci of research interest, both are typical representatives of the ferment going on in International Relations, they aspire to act as the cornerstone of the 'scientific' evolving paradigm and both are notable

singled out to consider its appropriateness to the analysis of policy-making in non-aligned actors. In spite of its methodological-conceptual superiority and potential operationalization, the discussion of this influential model reveals some of its limitations for our topic. Consequently, we conclude by expliciting two basic assumptions.

Let us start then by seeing why the "system" concept is so used in political and social science generally.

1. "System" Conceptualisation Concept

1.1. A bird's'eye view of different studies in the social sciences from Talcott Parsons' *The Social System* [8] to David Easton's *A Systems Analysis of Political Life* [9] and passing by Morton Kaplan's *System and Process in International Politics* [10] indicates the popularity of the "system" concept among researchers of different approaches and disciplines. This popularity is due to researchers considering the concept as the shortest cut to establishing a solid theoretical foundation for an "interdisciplinary" integrated approach. How? Mainly because the "system" concept goes

---

for their heavy borrowing from other disciplines. An example applying international systems analysis and the decision-making model in one volume is the sixth volume of the International Yearbook of Political Behaviour Research : David Singer (ed.) : *Quantitative International Politics,* New York, The Free Press, 1968. This volume is also a typical illustration of the "opening" of International Relations toward other disciplines. The 14 authors and co-authors of the 10 papers are political scientists and historians working together. The combined references drawn from journal articles amount to 130, but only 25 (19 per cent) of these journal articles are to be found in periodicals devoted to International Relations (*e.g.* World Politics, International Studies Quarterly, International Organizations . . .). Other quotations are from sociology (18 per cent) and psychology (15 per cent), but the highest number of quotations (26 per cent) is from interdisciplinary social science journals not devoted only to international politics (*e.g.* Journal of Conflict Resolution, Behavioral Science, General Systems Yearbook, International Social Science Bulletin . . .). See also Alger, Chadwick : "Trends in International Relations Research", in Norman Palmer (ed.) : *A Design for International Relations Research : Scope, Theory, Methods and Relevance,* Philadelphia, American Academy of Political and Social Science, 1970, pp. 7-29.

[8] Parsons, Talcott : *The Social System,* New York, The Free Press, 1951.

[9] Easton, David : *A Systems Analysis of Political Life,* New York, Wiley, 1965.

[10] Kaplan, Morton : *System and Process in International Politics,* New York, Wiley (Science edition), 1964.

against the "rigid compartmentalising of disciplines", [11] helps cross-flows between various fields of research, thus linking "all the sciences, natural and social" [12] and hence can lead to "the unification of science and scientific analysis". [13]

1.2. But precisely because of the attempts by different students of different disciplines to apply the system concept, and because of the origins and history of "systems theory" generally, [14] we are bound to have several definitions. Engineers, for instance, concentrate their attention on systems as "functionally related aggregates of technological devices" (*e.g.* a car). Physiologists single out "functionally related portions of living organisms" (circulatory, digestive, nervous systems). [15] Whereas economists insist that their discipline has used "a systematic treatment since almost its very beginning" [16] (*e.g.* the physiocrats, the neo-classicists) ; in sociology Talcott Parsons explicits his definition of a social system as the system "of interaction of a plurality of individual actors oriented to a situation and where the system includes a commonly understood system of cultural symbols". [17] Thus Parsons insists on the "relational scheme", the *inter*action among the individual actors. [18] This insistence on interaction is shared by political science, for Easton—for example—defines the political system as those interactions "through which values are allocated for a society". [19]

---

[11] McClelland : *Theory and the International System, op. cit.*, p. 92.

[12] Easton, David : *A Framework for Political Analysis,* Englewoods Cliffs, N.J., Prentice Hall, 1965, p. 26.

[13] Young, Oran : *Systems of Political Science,* Englewood Cliffs, Prentice Hall, N.J., 1968, pp. 14-15.

[14] Whether "Systems Theory" is only a product of the 20th century and especially the post-war period, or—on the contrary—can be traced back to 1651 and Thomas Hobbes' *Leviathan* is still a controversial question. For the different positions, see Young, Oran : *Systems of Political Science,* Englewoods Cliffs, Prentice Hall, N.J., 1968, pp. 14-15, and Spiro, Herbert : *World Politics : The Global System,* Homewood, The Dorsey Press, 1966, ch. III. This controversy is not unrelated to what was said about the theory of international relations as being "both very old and very young". It depends whether we are talking about a philosophical theory or an empirical one. See, for instance, Hoffmann, Stanley : *The State of War,* New York, Praeger, 1965, ch. I.

[15] Rapoport, Anatol : "General System Theory", *The International Encyclopedia of the Social Sciences, op. cit.*, vol. XV, p. 453.

[16] Mitchell, William : "Political Systems", *ibid.*, p. 473.

[17] Parsons : *op. cit.*, p. 5.

[18] *Ibid.*, pp. 3-4.

[19] Easton : *A Systems Analysis, op. cit.*, p. 21.

In the field of international politics proper, scholars use increasingly the term "international system" and offer their own definition. But because the attempt at application of the model provided by 'systems theory' is still relatively new, agreement on terms and propositions is not easily achieved. [20] That is why we have to start by looking at the definition offered by general systems theory. In the first volume of the General Systems Yearbook, Von Bertalanffy defined system as "a set of elements standing in interaction". [21] In the same volume, Hall and Fagen defined it as "a set of objects together with relationships between the objects and between their attributes". [22] But M. Kaplan was the first to face the task of elaborating a "unified theory" of international politics based on 'systems theory'. Before presenting his six "models" of different international systems, *Kaplan* gave the following definition : "A system of action is a set of variables so related, in contradistinction to its environment, that describable behavioural regularities characterize the international relationships of the set of individual variables to combinations of external variables". [23] In spite of his attempt at explicitness and clarity, the repetition of the word "variables" (defined five pages later) makes the definition look awkward and not as clear as Kaplan might have hoped. But Kaplan's was a pioneering attempt to conceptualize the international phenomena in systemic terms, and he must be given merit for emphasising the distinction between the system and its environment.

Stanley Hoffmann, for his part, talked directly about the international system (and not systems in general) and defined it as "a pattern of relations among the *basic units* of world politics, characterized by the scope of the objectives pursued by those units and of the tasks performed among them as well as by the means used to achieve those goals and perform those tasks". [24] Hoffmann's definition is not very different from *Aron's,* who defined the international system as "l'ensemble constitué par les unités politiques qu'entretiennent les unes avec les autres des relations régulières et qui sont toutes susceptibles d'être impliquées dans une guerre généralisée". [25] Both Hoffmann and Aron have the merit of being clear,

---

[20] E. Haas : *Beyond the Nation-State, op. cit.,* pp. 51-53.

[21] Von Bertalanffy, Ludwig : "General Systems Theory", in Ludwig von Bertalanffy and Anatol Rapoport (eds.) : *General Systems,* Yearbook of the Society for General Systems Research, I (1956), pp. 1-11.

[22] Hall, A. D. ; Fagen, R. E. : "Definition of System", *ibid.,* pp. 18-29.

[23] Kaplan, Morton : *System and Process, op. cit.,* p. 4.

[24] Hoffmann : *The State of War, op. cit.,* p. 90.

[25] This is Aron's original definition as it appeared in the 1962-French edition (p. 103) and which the 1966-English edition translated literally as "the ensemble constituted by political units that maintain regular relations with each other and that are all capable of being implicated in a generalized war". *Peace and War, op. cit.,* p. 94.

but both suffer from concentrating on states (Hoffman's "basic units" and Aron's "unités politiques") as the most important (only ?) actors. They give the impression that other entities cannot be actors (*e.g.* the Church in the Middle Ages) whereas in fact they can sometimes be more important than the nation-state (*e.g.* the U.N. Secretary-General has more weight on the international scene than, say, Dahomey ; the British Petroleum Company is more influential in the Middle East than the government of Yemen). *H. Spiro* considers the 'system' mainly from the point of view of the researcher as the *assumption* that *"more or less* regular relationships can be discerned among various aspects of politics, and between the phenomena he (the researcher) describes as political and certain other phenomena not so described". [26] The emphasis here is on what is called the *analytical* system, *i.e.* perceived by the observer and subjectively defined. *Charles McClelland* defined 'system' simply as "an ensemble of parts or subsystems capable of changing from one state to another". [27] Though the idea of structure and elements in interaction is implied, the stress here is on change or transformation in the system. He introduces also the idea of a complex and hierarchical order (*i.e.* the relationship between the system and the subsystems).

1.3. One can go on quoting different authors and definitions (*e.g.* Hassner, Rosecrance, Scott, Rosenau), but they would offer little not mentioned by others. In spite of the different stresses, the common elements in a definition of a system seem to include :

(*a*) a group of elements or objects, constituting the units or components of the system,

(*b*) that these units have some common properties or attributes (as shown by Bertalanffy's use of the word 'set'),

(*c*) that these units interact for a certain period of time and on a regular basis to establish a pattern of relationships,

(*d*) that the sum of interactions is something greater than the mere addition of all separate actions of the units, *i.e.* the system as a whole has "got something" which its components separately have not got. [28]

---

[26] Spiro : *op. cit.* (emphasis added).

[27] McClelland : *Theory and the International System, op. cit.*, pp. 20-21.

[28] Mackenzie, W. J. M. : *Politics and Social Science,* London, Penguin Books, 1967, p. 100.

2. **Variables**

2.1. *Structure of the System*

Three elements would determine the system's pattern of relationship :

(*a*) The distribution of capabilities : whether characterized by relative evenness or, on the contrary, unevenness.

(*b*) The characteristic configuration : bipolar, multipolar, unipolar.

(*c*) The hierarchy within the system : "dominant" and "subordinate" subsystems (*e.g.* the East-West as compared with the Somali-Ethiopia conflict subsystem).

2.2. *Components or Members of the System*

The actors [29] can be of different types : sub-national (*e.g.* the Palestinians in Jordan or Lebanon), national, transnational (*e.g.* the Zionist Movement), universal (*e.g.* the U.N.). Moreover, they can adopt different objectives (*e.g. status quo* or revolutionary-oriented).

2.3. *The Boundary of the System*

This involves dealing with the system's environment, distinguishing between it and the system itself. A system's environment is all that exists or is perceived as existing outside of that system. [30] This definition would make it relatively easy to draw the line between a national (sub-)system or an international one (*e.g.* the South-East Asia subsystem), on the one hand, and their respective environments on the other. This, however, raises the thorny problem of expliciting consensual criteria for system delimitation.

---

[29] For the definition of systemic components as actors, see Scott, Andrew : *The Functioning of the International Political System,* New York, Macmillan, 1967, p. 37.

[30] James Rosenau (ed.) : *International Politics and Foreign Policy,* New York, The Free Press (revised edition), 1969, pp. 71-76. The boundary issue is especially important when we are dealing with subsystems rather than the global system. For if we say that the environment of the global system is, for instance, outer space, this is neither operationally significant nor empirically useful, since outer space is becoming more and more part of the international system.

2.4. *Interaction Among the Components*

Interaction is the basis of the system, for without a continued interaction there can be no system. All 'systems theorists'—in spite of their different views on other questions—are unanimous on this point. That is to say—as was clear in our definition of a 'system'—continued interaction gives a certain distinct character *to the whole,* which is different from the mere sum of the units. [31] For instance, in a simplified dyadic relationship on the international scene, the two actors are the primary source of action. But if their interaction continues over a period of time (and it has to, otherwise it cannot be taken as a system), "each actor may be influenced by the past experience of interacting, and on this basis it can be said that the interaction itself is a source of behaviour". Thus, "from past experience with interaction, the actors may anticipate what will happen next and each may act according to the anticipation". [32]

(i) Interaction differs in *form :* it can be direct and indirect, governmental and non-governmental. [33] It can also be :

(*a*) direct governmental : *e.g.* economic collaboration, diplomatic contacts, and warfare ;

(*b*) direct non-governmental : *e.g.* tourism ;

(*c*) indirect governmental : when decision-makers in one component or subsystem are influenced by certain practices or experiences in other components or subsystems (*e.g.* industrialization in the new states, or the adoption of a certain type of planning, the drive toward regional integration among some new states after the success of the Western European experience) ;

(*d*) indirect non-governmental : the "demonstration effect" accross national boundaries, through novels, television, cinema films and private correspondence (*e.g.* the spread of the "American way of life" or the increasing importance of "the revolution of rising expectations" in the new states).

(ii) Interaction differs, secondly, in *content :* it may be either collaborative or conflicting. Admittedly, it is very rare to find either of these two in its pure form, and the usual pattern of interaction is a mixed collaboration-conflict one. Consequently when one talks of collaborative or conflicting interaction, one is designating the dominant traits of the interaction.

---

[31] Piaget, Jean : *Le Structuralisme,* Paris, Presses Universitaires de France (Que sais-je ? No. 1311), 1968, p. 8.

[32] McClelland : *Theory and the International System, op. cit.,* p. 18.

[33] Scott : *op. cit.,* ch. VII.

(iii) Interaction differs, thirdly, in *intensity :* it can vary from the maximum to the minimum end of an activity-passivity scale. Because interaction is not distributed evenly in the international system, the intensity of interaction among the actors of the West-European subsystem, for instance, is higher than among the actors of the African.

2.5. *Regulation in the System*

Regulation is "the process by means of which a system attempts to maintain or preserve its identity over time as it adapts to changing circumstances". [34] In fact, the system's ability to contain disruptive forces is crucial to its survival. That is why many writers concentrated their greatest attention on problems of change, failure and transformation in systems. Crucial determinants of systemic regulation include :

(i) The presence of 'consociational' norms [35] in the system : for instance, if agreement and collaboration persist for a certain time at a relatively high level of interaction, "selected features of a common 'system culture' may sometimes be produced, including common culture traits, common forms of behaviour, common norms and a system ideology" [36] (*e.g.* nowadays, the non-acceptance of gunboat diplomacy or the slave trade).

(ii) Various institutional and/or informal devices to settle major conflicts.

(iii) Other *regulatory devices :*

(*a*) For instance, in the late 19th century Euro-centred international system, the environment—making colonisation available—provided a safety valve to decrease the pressure of the conflict in Europe. Is there 'a colonisable environment' to siphon off major conflict in the contemporary international system ?

(*b*) With nuclear weapons war's gain/cost ratio has changed. Consequently, when actors are not faced with the surrender/annihilation alternative, they are amenable to regulation-promoting compromises (*e.g.* the Cuban crisis). Can deterrence be considered a regulatory mechanism ?

---

[34] Kaplan : *System and Process, op. cit.*, p. 89.

[35] For the usage of this concept in the field of "development politics", see Apter, David : *The Political Kingdom in Uganda : A Study in Bureaucratic Nationalism,* Princeton, Princeton University Press, 1961, pp. 24-25. For a more recent usage in the field of comparative politics generally, see Lijphart, Arend : "Consociational Democracy", *World Politics,* XXI (1969).

[36] Scott : *op. cit.,* ch. VII.

3. The Contemporary International System

Actors in the field of international politics are engaged in a process of regular and frequent interaction which form the (contemporary) international system. This interaction process can range theoretically along a continuum from the complete conflict to the complete co-operation end of the scale. It is precisely this value-free aspect of international systems analysis which is to be welcomed (*e.g.* the word 'system' itself denotes a neutral concept). For many years the world has been labelled "the family of nations", the "international society" or the "world community" when the world was not organized in actual fact on familial, societal or communal lines, nor did it possess the coherence and unity these terms imply.

3.1. *The Structure of the System*

Towards the end of the Second World War, on the 25th of April 1945, "advancing units of the American and Russian Armies met in the middle of Europe, along the banks of the Elbe River, near the German town of Targau". [37] Symbolically, this event heralded the division of Europe and the attempt to divide the world between the two 'Superpowers'.

In July of the same year, the Americans successfully tested the first nuclear weapon in the history of mankind and followed this up by dropping two atomic bombs on Hiroshima and Nagasaki in August. Japan surrendered immediately. [38] In 1949 and 1953, the USSR exploded its atomic and hydrogen bombs respectively.

The events which marked the end of the war gave the contemporary international system the structure designated "loose bipolar" [39] or "diffuse-bloc", [40] based on nuclear deterrence.

---

[37] Lucaks, John : *A History of the Cold War,* New York, Garden City, Doubleday and Company, 1961, p. 17.

[38] Calvocoressi, Peter : *World Politics Since 1945,* London, Longmans, p. 3.

[39] For details about this "model's" characteristics, see Kaplan : *System and Process, op. cit.,* pp. 36-42. For a slightly empirical—in addition to a theoretical—discussion of the model, see Kaplan, Morton : "Bipolarity in a Revolutionary Age", in Morton Kaplan (ed.) : *The Revolution in World Politics,* New York, Wiley and Sons, 1963, p. 252.

[40] Holsti : *International Politics, op. cit.,* pp. 76-78, 92-94.

3.1.1. *Bipolarity,* though a direct result of World War II, was prophesied as far back as 1830, when De Tocqueville wrote :

> "There are on earth today two great peoples, who, from different points of departure, seem to be advancing toward the same end. They are the Russians and the Anglo-Americans." [41]

The process bringing the USA and the USSR to the forefront of world politics was accelerated by the two world wars. The first brought a reluctant USA to the centre as the dominant actor in the Western hemisphere. The war contributed to the USSR's emergence too as a world superpower ; first through the October Revolution which broke the restraints imposed by Czarist tradition and thus prepared for its industrial and technological expansion, and secondly by the Versailles Conference which dismembered two of the five empires which constrained Russia's extension.

But the first World War, however, did not lead to *bipolarity.* In 1920, although the USA was the only truly world power, it declined to play this role, as can be seen in the refusal by Congress to allow American membership in the League of Nations, and favoured instead the return to isolationism or "normalcy". The Soviet Union, on the other hand, with its ideals of world revolution, yearned to play that world role but did not have the capabilities to do so. When both of them became "active world powers after 1945, it was as implacable rivals", [42] and the bipolar pattern was facilitated by Germany and Japan being in ruins, by the decline of colonial empires, and by the weakening of England and France as major powers.

3.1.2. But if De Tocqueville prophesied the advent of bipolarity, he could not foresee the invention of nuclear weapons. These weapons gave the contemporary international system its uneven military capability distribution—the superpowers with their absolute weapons and the rest of the world without them, with some in-betweens : *e.g.* Britain, France, China. Thus, though there arose a clear distinction—at least in one domain—between two categories of states, an unoperationalized category of "middle powers" still constitute a problem since some countries are difficult to classify [43] (*e.g.* India).

Related to this is the problem of the *ranking of national actors.* Difficulties arise because the criteria for classification are still controversial, the more so in a rapidly-changing system like the contemporary one. Is

---

[41] From "De la Démocratie en Amérique" as quoted in Halle, Louis : *The Cold War as History,* London, Chatto and Windus, 1967, ch. II.

[42] Lyon : *Neutralism, op. cit.,* p. 23.

[43] Holsti : *International Politics, op. cit.,* pp. 73-76.

it military capability ? It is the USA that has the greatest military capability, but this does not mean that it exercises the greatest proportional influence in all international issues (*e.g.* Nehru's India during the Korean war), or in all relationships (*e.g.* the war in Vietnam). Three criteria are suggested to classify national actors in the stratified international system :

(*a*) a national actor's level of technology, which allows it to impose certain views and influence certain issues in the system. Indeed, technology is increasingly coming to represent a subtle kind of 'colonialism' by creating technological dependence on the part of some actors toward others [44] ;

(*b*) an actor's immediately available military capabilities, a factor which is obviously related to first criterion ; and

(*c*) the reputation an actor "can generate abroad through its day-to-day diplomatic conduct and political, economic and social behaviour at home" (*e.g.* Sweden and Switzerland perceived as neutral and having the highest standard of living). [45]

Though nuclear military capability confers a certain status (*e.g.* China, France), the ranking of national actors depends on what *issue* we are dealing with (*e.g.* on the decolonisation issue, Algeria, compared with South Vietnam or Ivory Coast), or on the *subsystem* one is investigating (*e.g.* in the Communist subsystem, the ranking might depend on a state's —or a party's—adherence to a particular doctrinal line or even on the revolutionary careers of its leadership). Thus in the contemporary international system, which is complex and rapidly-changing, no single and permanent variable for the ranking of states is sufficient.

Related to the ranking of national actors, is the presence of a corresponding ranking of international subsystems, whether they are geographical subsystems, [46] ideological subsystems [47] (*e.g.* the Communist subsystem), or issue subsystems (*e.g.* the East-West Conflict). [48]

---

[44] Skolnikoff, Eugene : "The Implications of Science and Technology for International Relations", *a one-year seminar* given at the Graduate Institute of International Studies, Geneva, 1969-1970. See also his *Science, Technology and American* Foreign Policy, Cambridge, Mass., the M.I.T. Press, 1967.

[45] Holsti : *International Politics, op. cit.,* p. 73.

[46] Binder, Leonard : "The Middle East Subordinate International System", *World Politics,* X (1958), pp. 408-429. Brecher, Michael : "The Subordinate State System of Southern Asia", *World Politics,* XV (1963), pp. 213-235. Zartman, William : "Africa as a Subordinate State System in International Relations", *International Organization,* XXI (1967), pp. 545-564. W. Thompson : *op. cit.*

[47] Modelski, George : "The Communist International System", *Research Monograph,* No. 9, Princeton University, Center of International Studies, 1961.

[48] These are "more or less" rather than mutually exclusive "either ... or ..." classifications.

To take this last subsystem as an example, World War II resulted in the prevailing influence of the USA/USSR relationship which took the shape of an East-West bipolar conflict. It is true that other patterns of relationships (*e.g.* the North-South subsystem) were imposing themselves more and more. Yet the USA/USSR relationship has continued to be a 'dominant subsystem' since the world cannot remain indifferent to the worsening of their relations or the possibility of a nuclear clash, and the settlement of the Berlin or German problem depends on their collaboration. Thus, one feature of the contemporary international system has been the apparent dominance of one of its issue subsystems. Besides the dominant subsystem, there are numerous 'subordinate' subsystems. [49] They are 'subordinate' mainly for two reasons :

(1) In the 'subordinate subsystem', the level of capabilities is relatively inferior to that of the 'dominant subsystem'.

(2) There is generally more intensive and influential penetration of the 'subordinate subsystem' by the 'dominant subsystem' rather than the reverse.

3.2. *Components or Members of the System and their Main Characteristics*

Compared with the international systems of the 18th and 19th centuries, the contemporary international system reflects basic differences :

(i) *The change in actors :* from a few, mainly European sovereign nation-states as the major actors in international relations to the emergence of non-European countries such as the USSR, USA, [50] China, plus a host of poorly-defined newly-independent Afro-Asian states. These are in addition to "international" (*e.g.* blocs) and universal actors (*e.g.* the U.N.). These latter actors are different from the "basic actors" as they do not possess the independent means of enforcing their policies or decisions through the threat or use of force. [51]

(ii) *The great diversity* (of size, population and socio-economic conditions) among national actors in spite of their common characteristics of territorial and national independence. Thus "the Soviet Union covers one eighth of the world's land surface, six states—Canada, the U.S., the Soviet Union, Brazil, China and Australia—comprise over half of the world's

[49] For some examples, see footnote 46 above.

[50] Some scholars consider these two 'superactors' European in culture and/or stock. See Halle : *op. cit.*

[51] Holsti : *International Politics, op. cit.,* pp. 72-73.

land territory. On the other hand, there are political units—Luxembourg, Lebanon, Singapore and Trinidad for example—smaller in size than some metropolitan areas in the U.S.". [52]

Population variations are even more striking ; the Maldive Islands—a U.N. member—have less than 100,000 inhabitants. Several countries have fewer than one million inhabitants while China has over 700 million. Consequently "the physical and population differences between the USSR and Togo are infinitely greater than the differences between Athens and one of the smaller city-states in Greece or between Prussia and Schleswig-Holstein in the 18th century". [53]

Diversities in economic, social and political conditions are also great among the national actors, for we have :

(*a*) A group of highly industrialized actors with relatively 'established' political systems, high literacy rates, social mobility between classes and high density of communication media (*e.g.* Scandinavian countries and North America).

(*b*) A group of actors with illiteracy problems, relative political instability, low agricultural productivity and censored mass media (*e.g.* Spain, Greece).

(*c*) A third group, constituting the majority of the world population, is characterized by high illiteracy rates, poor communications, population explosion, poverty, little social mobility, and life conducted on a tribal or village basis, military rule and/or charismatic leadership, where the state itself does not correspond to either ethnic, linguistic or religious distinctions but constitutes a geographical expression (*e.g.* most African states South of the Sahara).

(*d*) A group of "those few states whose predominant socio-economic and political conditions are comparable to those found in 18th century Europe. These comprise the territories ruled by dynastic families as private realms", [54] though they are being threatened more and more by the impact of social change and modernization (*e.g.* Saudi Arabia, Haiti, Sheikdoms of the Arabian peninsula).

(iii) *A change in objectives :* from being limited and pursued with limited means through traditional procedures, to unlimited objectives, both in "substance and in geographical scope", pursued at a time when the traditional procedure no longer commands consensus and there is a

---

[52] *Ibid.*

[53] *Ibid.*

[54] *Ibid.*

[55] Spiro : *op. cit.,* pp. 12-13.

drive toward the elaboration of new methods [55] (*e.g.* Parliamentary diplomacy). Resource mobilisation has attained an unprecedented level and military force has changed from being at a low level but widely used, to being overabundant but rarely used among the major actors.

3.3. *The Boundary of the System*

What characterises the contemporary international system is its evolution from being Euro-centred to being global. It is true that even in the last century the field of the international system was widened through the scramble for the colonisation of extra-European territories (*e.g.* the partition of Africa), and it appeared that what had started as a European system was becoming a global system. [56] But the driving forces were still the European actors who were extending their European 'balance of power' abroad and almost every move in Africa or Asia was judged according to its repercussions on European equilibrium. Thus "Germany's first major intervention in the Far East—its participation in the protest of the European powers against the Treaty of Shimonoski in 1895—was undertaken with the purely European objective of weakening Russian pressure on the German Eastern frontier". [57]

Therefore, it was only too true—as the Russian General Dragomirov said—that "Far Eastern affairs are decided in Europe". [58]

After 1945, on the contrary, the protagonists were (at least partly) extra-European, using the old continent as their arena of conflict, and very often deciding for it.

Along with the post-war subordination of Europe in the contemporary international system, most of its colonial empire collapsed and there arose instead several dozen new actors, wishing to play an active role on the international scene. To increase their influence they try to form their own constellations and act collectively (*e.g.* the Afro-Asian group, the non-aligned conferences . . .). The emergence of new states as participants in the contemporary international system led to the emergence of new topics and concepts (*e.g.* decolonisation). Moreover, with trade, diplomatic communication, travel and occasional 'subversion', all involving about 130 actors, issues of conflict are not provoked mainly in Europe but in Africa, Asia and Latin America, and involve primarily such actors as the USA, USSR and China rather than the traditional big European powers (England, France, Germany, Austria-Hungary, Turkey). Thus the geo-

---

[56] Barraclough, Geoffrey: *An Introduction to Contemporary History,* London, Penguin Books, 1967, pp. 93-124.

[57] *Ibid.*

[58] *Ibid.*

graphical boundaries of the system have been extended to the whole world, and the number of participants has trebled in the last 50 years. [59]

A third important element in the widening of the field of interaction in the contemporary international system is the 'revolution in science and technology'. This led, obviously, to the 'shrinking' of the world. For apart from its visible effects in the military domain, technology—through improved printing machinery, ultra-rapid means of transport and the modern apparatus of electronic communication [60]—increased contacts among world areas. Moreover, the increasing use of global technology (*e.g.* satellite communications) demands efforts of coordination and even the elaboration of international agreements among the participants (*e.g.* on air transport, weather broadcasting and at present the containing of environmental pollution). [61]

3.4. *Interaction among the System's Components*

Rapid and continuing contacts—both intergovernmental and private—have increased substantially within the system. "In the early 1800's less than a dozen American diplomats worked in Paris to protect and promote the interests of the U.S. and its citizens in France". [62] At present, several hundred are needed to fulfil these functions.

International *trade* statistics show the scope of the increasing interaction. In 1938, world imports were worth $25,400 billion and exports $23,500 billion. The corresponding figures for 1967 were $227,100 billion and $217,400 respectively, an increase of about 1000 per cent. [62] As for *communication,* kilometres flown by civil aviation amounted to 1,940 billion in 1953 and rose to 5,290 billion in 1967. The number of letters greatly increased too. In 1953, Belgians for instance, received from abroad 73,492 and sent 84,120 letters. In 1967 the corresponding figures were 205,110 and 172,484. [63]

Personal contacts soared too. In 1948, "149,000 people entered Austria, 14 years later 5.5 million visited that country. Japan had fewer than 30,000 visitors in 1948 but almost 250,000 by 1962". The origin and direction of this flow of private contacts is equally significant, because they are related to the international political situation. For instance, U.N.

---

[59] Holsti : *International Politics, op. cit.,* p. 68.

[60] Sprout, Harold and Margaret : *Foundations of International Politics,* Princeton, Van Nostrand Co., 1962, p. 523.

[61] Skolnikoff : *op. cit.*

[62] Holsti : *International Politics, op. cit.,* pp. 78-82.

[63] *Ibid.* and the United Nations *Statistical Yearbook,* 1967, New York, United Nations, 1968.

figures show that private contacts tended to follow in the early phase of this system an intra- rather than inter-bloc trend. For whereas 14,000 Americans visited Australia in 1962, only 40 Hungarians went to that country. This shows that interaction between these two countries was confined to formal diplomatic and commercial channels. [64]

Besides the overall increase in interaction, new forms appeared while other ones acquired a new significance. For instance, there are the contacts between experts through the meetings of technical international organizations (*e.g.* ILO, WHO). There is also the interaction between scientists who consider themselves an international group, and contact through journals and meetings. Given the relative ease of their exchange of ideas, there is a growing interdependence and some scientists talk in terms of a "scientific community". [65]

Because of this multi-form and increasing interaction in the internationl system, the traditional distinction between domestic and international politics is blurred. What happens internally becomes easily and quickly known internationally and affects international relations (*e.g.* the internationalization of many internal conflicts).

This blurring of the distinction between internal and international politics led to varied techniques of *informal access* (*e.g.* overt information programmes, covert psychological warfare programmes, militant parties and political organizations), different from formal inter-governmental interaction through diplomats and soldiers. To be sure, informal penetration is not unique to the contemporary international system, because there are isolated examples of its use in different eras of history. But what characterizes the contemporary international system is the greater dependence on this means of international influence. "The range of techniques used is greater. The human and material resources devoted to it are greater. The objectives pursued by means of informal penetration are broader. In addition, the techniques can be used in combinations never before available and can be used in novel ways in conjunction with the techniques of formal relations." [66] A national actor might depend on informal access techniques only (*e.g.* Maoists in countries not having diplomatic relations with China) or use a combination of formal and informal techniques (*e.g.* Nasser's Egypt or Castro's Cuba).

Consequently, internal disorders and civil wars become international events (*e.g.* the Congo crisis), and informal interaction constitutes one of the factors which can lead to the transformation of the international system (*e.g.* the spread of revolutionary ideas, and the acceleration of 'modernization' and social change).

---

[64] *Ibid.*

[65] Skolnikoff : *op. cit.*

[66] Scott : *op. cit.,* ch. XIII.

3.5. *Regulation*[67] *in the System*

Though, according to an observer,[68] the contemporary international system suffers from increasing disturbances (*e.g.* instability in many new states, the commitment by some actors to revolutionary goals on the international scene, technological innovations), while regulatory mechanism is not increasing accordingly, the system has managed to continue since the end of the war. I shall limit myself here to dealing with two factors which seem to have played an important role in the systemic regulation during the different crises.

3.5.1. The first one, *deterrence,* imposes itself since it is one of the most (if not the most) salient characteristics of the system since its advent in 1945. The Hiroshima and Nagasaki bombs had an explosive power of 20,000 tons of T.N.T. Sixteen years later, the USSR experimented with a bomb whose explosive capacity amounted to 61 megatons (61,000,000 tons of T.N.T.), more than all the explosive power fired during the last war.[69] The Soviet Union indicated that future nuclear testing would include bombs with 100 megatons.[70] Moreover, President Kennedy asserted some years ago that "nuclear stockpiles contain the equivalent of ten tons of T.N.T. for every human being on earth and they are continuing to grow".[71] The Pentagon, for its part, affirmed that in the case of a nuclear war, with the present delivery systems, about 149 million Americans and 100 million Russians would perish.[72]

As a result, some scholars believe that a total war between the superpowers is "unthinkable" and Clauswitz's well-known statement that "war is the continuation of policy by other means" has to be qualified in this context ; consequently, the superpowers are collaborating to transform the "nuclear technical peace" into a political one. They saw this all too clearly at a 'moment of truth' during the 1962-Cuban missile crisis, which forced each to moderate its position rather than to face a nuclear showdown. It is not coincidental that the Cuban crisis was the beginning of

---

[67] For a detailed discussion of this key variable in the maintenance of the system, see McClelland : *Theory and the International System, op. cit.,* pp. 33-60 ; Hoffmann : *The State of War, op. cit.,* pp. 92-96 ; Kaplan : *System and Process . . ., op. cit.,* pp. 89-106 ; and Scott : *op. cit.,* pp. 216-229.

[68] Rosecrance, Richard : *Action and Reaction in International Politics : International Systems in Perspective,* Boston, Little Brown, 1963, p. 304.

[69] Holsti : *International Politics, op. cit.,* p. 349.

[70] General Gallois : "Les conséquences politiques de l'évolution des armements" in Leo Hamon (ed.) : *L'élaboration de la politique étrangère,* Paris, Presses Universitaires de France, 1966, pp. 179-201.

[71] Holsti : *International Politics, op. cit.,* p. 349.

[72] *Ibid.*

the 'thaw' in Soviet-American relations, and that American mass media started talking about a 'new era' in the relations between the two superpowers. Only one year afterwards, the test-ban treaty was signed, to be followed by such measures as the non-proliferation treaty and the present talks on the limitation of strategic armaments.

3.5.2. The second factor to be examined as far as regulation in the system is concerned is the role of non-alignment. Its choice is justified because the non-aligned actors usually claim a regulatory or a stability function performed by their policy in the system. In fact, at one of their first big gatherings—the Conference of Afro-Asian States, Bandung 1955—two principal 'theories' of international politics were in opposition : that of the non-aligned and that of the states aligned with the West.

The non-aligned point of view was advocated by Burma's U Nu, Egypt's Nasser and especially India's Nehru. They stated that the existence of two rival military blocs not only increased tension in the system but in fact threatened its maintenance. Consequently, if every state joined one or the other of the two conflicting blocs, rigid bipolarity would increase and war might become inevitable. Hence, one had to create in Afro-Asia an "area of peace", [73] whose "mobilization of the moral violence of people" [74] against "situations of strength" and military alliances would introduce an element of systemic flexibility, act as a bridge-builder and a communication channel, and mediate to reduce the level of conflict. Their practical means of action were the consolidation of the universal actor—the U.N.—and strengthening the application of the principles of peaceful coexistence [75] as norms governing the functioning of the international system.

The 'theory' of the actors allied to the West was mainly expounded by the representatives of Turkey, Iraq, Iran and the Philippines. These states agreed with the non-aligned in their diagnosis of the international system. They expressed, like the non-aligned, their desire to contribute to the reduction of conflict and to systemic regulation, but they differed with them as to the means of achieving this goal. For instance, while the non-aligned actors proposed remaining aloof from both the two blocs, the actors allied to the West believed that it was more 'realistic' to take all preventive measures in the form of military pacts to frustrate the "aggressiveness" of the Communist bloc. Their starting-point was that newly-independent states should not trust the Communists who were aiming at

---

[73] Das, M. N. : *The Political Philosophy of Jawaharlal Nehru,* London, Allen & Unwin, 1961, especially pp. 189-242.

[74] The phrase is Sukarno's at the Bandung Conference.

[75] The reference is to the Panchsheel, first listed in the Agreement on Trade and Intercourse between India and China relating to Tibet, issued in Peking on the 29th of April, 1954.

"world supremacy". The concept of peaceful coexistence was nothing but a device by the Communists to drug their victims till they became ripe for "Communist revolution". That is why small states had no choice but to join defensive military pacts with the anti-Communist bloc.

It is the claim of non-aligned actors that their foreign policy orientation and/or behaviour is conflict-reducing that should be emphasised in this context. Of course, their contention is not to be taken as a statement beyond refutation, but rather as a "working hypothesis". Indeed there are writers who argue that the non-aligned actors are only producers of conflict and "dividers". Others believe that their regulatory credentials are low, for example H. Kissinger says : "It is not clear why nations said to be in need of assistance in almost all respects of their national life, many of which have difficulty organizing their own countries, should be presumed to be able to act with more wisdom in relation to the whole gamut of international relations." [76] Still others see the intensity of the internal problems of non-aligned states as an obstacle to an active role in the system. As Kripalani argues "the underdeveloped Asian-African countries which have recently achieved freedom have so many political, economic and social problems of their own that they feel they must confine their attention to the solution of these rather than dabble in partisan international politics". [77] Lefever shows the limitation of their mediatory functions: "The contribution of the neutrals to the preservation of international peace and stability is severely limited. Their efforts to mediate big-power disputes are effective only when the big powers are willing to compromise their differences. If the willingness is present, an agreement can be reached through normal diplomatic channels, without mediation." [78]

Though these arguments are 'wisdom' rather than empirically-based generalisations, they caution us against accepting the conflict-reducing role of non-aligned actors as anything more than a 'working' hypothesis which has to be less broadly formulated in order to be falsifiable. This will be done later for we have now to discuss the applicability of international systems analysis to our study of non-alignment.

4.

As mentioned above, the usefulness of international systems analysis lies in its function as an organizing macro-framework that could give in a relatively ordered and brief form the general pattern of the environment

---

[76] Kissinger, Henry : *The Necessity for Choice,* New York, Garden City, Doubleday, 1962, p. 346.

[77] Kripalani, A. : "For Principled Neutrality", *Foreign Affairs,* LIX (1959), p. 56.

[78] Lefever : *op. cit.,* p. 118.

or setting of non-alignment. It can also inspire some hypotheses as to the influence of non-alignment on the contemporary international system.

As far as our topic is concerned, however, the payoffs of international systems analysis are undermined by some limitations :

(*a*) The main justification of borrowing 'models' inspired by General Systems Theory is the hypothesis of isomorphism, *i.e.* that biological and social organizations have the same structure and that generalizations that describe and explain the behaviour of one organization can be used to describe and explain the behaviour of another. [79] Thus Bertalanfy, for instance, thinks it significant that growth curves are exponential for "pounds in a banking account, (for) radium atoms, molecules bacteria, or individuals in a population". [80] In his examination of General Systems Theory, Roger Buck [81] called statements like those of Bertalanfy the 'so what type'. That is once we have found that pounds in a bank account and molecules fit the same curve, the next question is : so what ? Even when this question is answered satisfactorily, it still remains to apply this satisfactory answer to political analysis. [82] At the moment, however, we are still far away from this state of affairs for "it is not unfair to say that students of politics have produced no real isomorphisms between living organisms and political systems". [83] Consequently, at present the usefulness of international systems analysis is limited to its function as an organizing macro-framework. [84]

---

[79] Stephens, Jerome : "An Appraisal of Some Systems Approaches to the Study of International Systems", *International Studies Quarterly,* XVI (1972), pp. 321-351.

[80] Von Bertalanfy, Ludwig : *General Systems Theory,* New York, Braziller, 1969, p. 82.

[81] Buck, Roger: "On the Logic of General Behavior Systems Theory", in H. Feigl and M. Scriven (eds.) : *Minnesota Studies in the Philosophy of Science,* Vol. I, Minneapolis, University of Minnesota Press—as quoted in Stephens : *op. cit.*

[82] In fact, on this specific point "some critics maintain that, in actuality, there are not very many significant isomorphic relationships and that systems theory's demand for isomorphisms sometimes leads to a practice of forcing things into 'boxes' in which they do not belong". This is, however, an empirical question that cannot be answered *a priori* or purely deductively. Young : *Systems of Political Science, op. cit.,* pp. 24-26.

[83] Stephens : *op. cit.*

[84] This is why some advocates of International Relations Theory intend the 'international systems analysis' to act as a "conceptual framework", an "organizing device" rather than a full deductive theory. "Any theory", Holsti affirmed, "should have axioms, propositions and formal hypotheses which can be verified both logically and empirically. This kind of theory has not yet been developed in most of the social sciences, perhaps least of all in the field of International Relations." Consequently, the objective of the evolving paradigm, at least in its early phase, is a "relatively modest theoretical activity which defines concepts, establishes taxonomies

(*b*) A second limitation concerning the general applicability of international systems analysis to our topic is related to emphasis on the "essential rules" necessary for the maintenance of an international system. That is "those rules which describe general relationships between the actors of a system or which assign definite systemic role functions to actors independently of the labelling of the actors".[85] It was in this context that some scholars of International Relations criticized 'system's tyranny',[86] *i.e.* the discussion of systems as if they have a will of their own : the implicit God. That is why Kaplan's emphasis on the system's essential rules, for instance, leads to the neglect of domestic determinants of the non-aligned actor's behaviour and his 'system of action' leaves out the forces of change operating within or across actors. In other words, international systems analysis will be functional when we are treating non-alignment as a general orientation, as an international subsystem. But when we want to analyse non-alignment as a specific foreign policy behaviour, international systems analysis' reductionist tendency would entail "a loss of such vital elements as institutions, culture, and the action of individuals as autonomous variables rather than social atoms".[87]

Indeed, in 1968[88]—*i.e.* about 11 years after the publication of *System and Process*—Kaplan concurred with this criticism but argued that his international systems analysis is destined for a certain level-of-analysis : the macro-level. That is if one, for instance, wanted to account for the U.S. decision to cross the 38th parallel in Korea, the international system-oriented or macro-level-of-analysis would not be enough to explain all aspects and thus the researcher has to shift to another level-of-analysis appropriate to the specific problem,[89] *i.e.* in this specific example of U.S.

---

and suggests some of the variables which affect behavior at the international level —in short activity which creates some order out of our immense field of knowledge". Holsti : *International Politics, op. cit.,* pp. 17-18.

[85] Kaplan : *System and Process, op. cit.,* p. 9. For the "essential rules of the balance of power model", see pp. 23, 129, of the "loose bipolar model", pp. 38-39, of the "tight bipolar", p. 44, of the "universal", p. 47.

[86] Hoffmann : *Contemporary Theory, op. cit.,* pp. 40-50.

[87] *Ibid.*

[88] Kaplan (ed.) : *New Approaches to International Relations, op. cit.,* pp. vi-vii.

[89] This is also the view of Oran Young who believes that the usefulness of "systems theory" is highlighted in macro- rather than in micro-analysis, because of its capacity in classifying and analysing large aggregates of data. Young : *Systems of Political Sciences, op. cit.,* pp. 21-23. In other words, "systems theory" is geared toward holistic analysis, *i.e.* it concentrates on "patterns of interaction among actors in international systems in contrast to the internal political relationships or processes of individual actors". Young, Oran : *A Systemic Approach to International Politics,* Center of International Studies, Princeton University, 1968. Not all "sys-

intervention in Korea one has to shift to the actor-oriented or micro-level-of-analysis.[90]

This is what Glenn Paige did when researching the U.S. decision to intervene in Korea[91]: he applied the actor-oriented decision-making model.

5. The Decision-Making Model[92] and the Study of Policy-Making in Non-Aligned Actors

Snyder and his colleagues exposed their ideas first in their privately published paperback format distributed in 1954, a study which offered an outline of categories for the collection and processing of data on foreign

---

tems theorists", however, agree on this limitation of their mode of analysis. McClelland, for instance, contends that "systems theory" allows the shift in levels of analysis, and uses a matrix technique to support his argument. McClelland: *Theory and the International System, op. cit.*, pp. 93-94.

[90] This *analytical* distinction in terms of levels-of-analysis between (international) system-oriented and actor-oriented research is at the basis of the boundary-drawing operation between International Relations and Foreign Policy Analysis. As Quincy Wright suggested: "the adjective 'foreign' implies *the point of view of one nation* . . ." 'Systems theorists', however, warn against deducing from this distinction that International Relations is only the combination of different foreign policies, since—in terms of general systems theory—International Relations is *more* than the mere sum of its parts. Hartley Clark, in a different context, put it more concretely: "approaching the study of International Relations by way of comparative foreign policy", he believed, "is like approaching the study of sex by way of the comparative study of the male and female. Vital background, yes, but it is the study of the interaction between male and female that crowns the study of sex". (*The American Political Science Review,* LXIV (1970), p. 975.) For the general discussion of this problem, see for instance: Fifield, Russell: "The Introductory Course in International Relations", *The American Political Science Review,* Vol. XLII (1948), pp. 1189-1197; Sondermann, Fred: "The Linkage between Foreign Policy and International Politics", in James Rosenau (ed.): *International Politics and Foreign Policy,* New York, The Free Press, 1961, pp. 8-18; and Holsti: *International Politics, op. cit.*, pp. 13-22. This distinction is very significant for both the methodological and substantive issues involved in the treatment of non-alignment, since this latter is both a specific foreign policy behaviour and a common attitude or external orientation of a group of national actors, *i.e.* an international subsystem.

[91] Paige, Glenn: *The Korean Decision,* New York, The Free Press, 1968.

[92] Snyder, Richard; Bruck, H. W., and Sapin, Burton: *Foreign Policy Decision-Making,* New York, The Free Press, 1962. Though the most well-known work in this field, the work of Snyder et al. is not the only one. Joseph Frankel has written an important book: *The Making of Foreign Policy: An Analysis of Decision-Making,* London, O.U.P., 1963. As Snyder et al., Frankel considers the state the princi-

policy decisions. The study was hailed as a breakthrough in foreign policy analysis, and before its publication in book form in 1962, excerpts from it had been widely reprinted and the study was soon cited in different works ranging from treatment of disturbed communication to publications on judicial behaviour. [93]

In addition to the decision-making model that it elaborated, the study's popularity was due to its "explicit concern with a number of issues in methodology and the philosophy of science that were current in American political science in the 1950's". [94] Some important difficulties common to research in International Relations are cited and discussed, for instance "the absence of a frame of reference for relating the several aspects of the field ; the random nature of the search for important variables ; the tendency to construct entire systems of explanation around single factors (for example, power) ; the lack of a clear definition of purpose and the consequent tendency for policy, empirical, value, and scientific questions to be thoughtlessly thrown together in the same investigation ; the failure to make explicit the assumptions and concepts employed in research ; the habit of confusing analytic and concrete structures ; the preoccupation with questions that are not stated in researchable form . . .". [95]

An illustration of the popularity and enormous impact of the decision-making model is that the phrase was used not only in standard textbooks on International Relations and related subjects, but was also appropriated in the everyday language of both the politician and the layman. Moreover, historical material was studied in terms of this approach. [96]

---

pal decision-making unit in world politics. As the Sprouts, he makes the distinction (essential for theory-building) between the external environment (*i.e.* institutional restraints on decision-makers) and the psychological one (the determinants of elite perceptions), but he does not integrate the two. He divides *the sequence* of decision-making into three stages (predecisional, formulation of the decision and its implementation). But since the feedback is not incorporated in the analysis, the model remains static. See also Brecher, Michael et al. : "A Framework for Research on Foreign Policy Behavior", *op. cit.*

[93] Robinson, James : "Decision-Making : Political Aspects", *International Encyclopedia of the Social Sciences, op. cit.*, IV, pp. 55-62. Also Snyder et al. : *op. cit.*, p. vi.

[94] Robinson : *op. cit.*

[95] McClosky, Herbert : "Concerning Strategies for a Science of International Politics", *World Politics,* VII (1956), pp. 281-295.

[96] Zinnes, Dina ; North, Robert, and Koch, Howard (Jr.) : "Capability, Threat and the Outbreak of War", in Rosenau (ed.) : *International Politics and Foreign Policy* (1961), *op. cit.*, pp. 469-483. For a comment on the Stanford project, see Jervis, Robert : "The Costs of the Quantitative Study of International Relations", in Knorr and Rosenau (eds.) : *Contending Approaches to International Politics, op. cit.*, pp. 177-218.

5.1. The assumption of Snyder and his colleagues is that "the nation-state is going to be the significant unit of action for many years to come",[97] and thus strategies of action and commitment of resources will continue to be decided at the national level. Consequently, action in International Relations can be best understood by focusing on the "decisions" of these basic actors, and a strategic focus for research is the point at which the inputs are transformed into outputs, through the decision-making process. Thus rather than concentrating primarily on ends or forms of foreign policy, the authors are concerned with the process of foreign policy itself. In fact, decision-making itself is defined as "a *process* which results in the selection from a socially defined, limited number of problematical, alternative projects of one project intended to bring about the particular future state of affairs envisaged by decision-makers".[98] This selection or choice process is determined by certain variables which can explain how and why the actors behave in the international system as they do, and which embrace a wide range of concepts and disciplines, *e.g.* economy, psychology, sociology, besides—of course—political science. The following diagram indicates easily the diversity and multiplicity of variables to be analysed. (See table following page.)

In order to reduce the inherent complexity in investigating a big number of psychological, social, economic and political variables, the authors suggested a way of handling the possible influences on decision-making. They elaborated three clusters of variables which are "the three major determinants of action".[99]

The exposition here is oversimplified for the sake of clarity and communication, for each of these "major determinants" is in itself a complex cluster of variables with potential ramifications and expanding proliferation. For from these "major determinants" one would deal with "a host of questions concerning such matters as the general setting in which a decision is made ; the actors' perceptions of their roles and the actual authority they are free to exercise ; the information, attitudes, and beliefs they bring to the decision-making event ; the actors' views of the alternative choices and consequences ; the actual and perceived goals of the organization and its actors ; the personality, skills, and needs of the decision-makers ; and dozens of other matters of a similar order".[100]

---

[97] Snyder et al. : *op. cit.*, pp. 60-74.

[98] *Ibid.*, p. 90. In fact their approach represents an early example which stresses the distinction between structures and processes. Young : *Systems of Political Science, op. cit.*, p. 63.

[99] Snyder et al. : *op. cit.*, pp. 105-137. (The three clusters of variables are spheres of competence, communication and information ; and motivation.)

[100] McClosky : *op. cit.*

TABLE 1. *Variables of the Decision-Making Model*

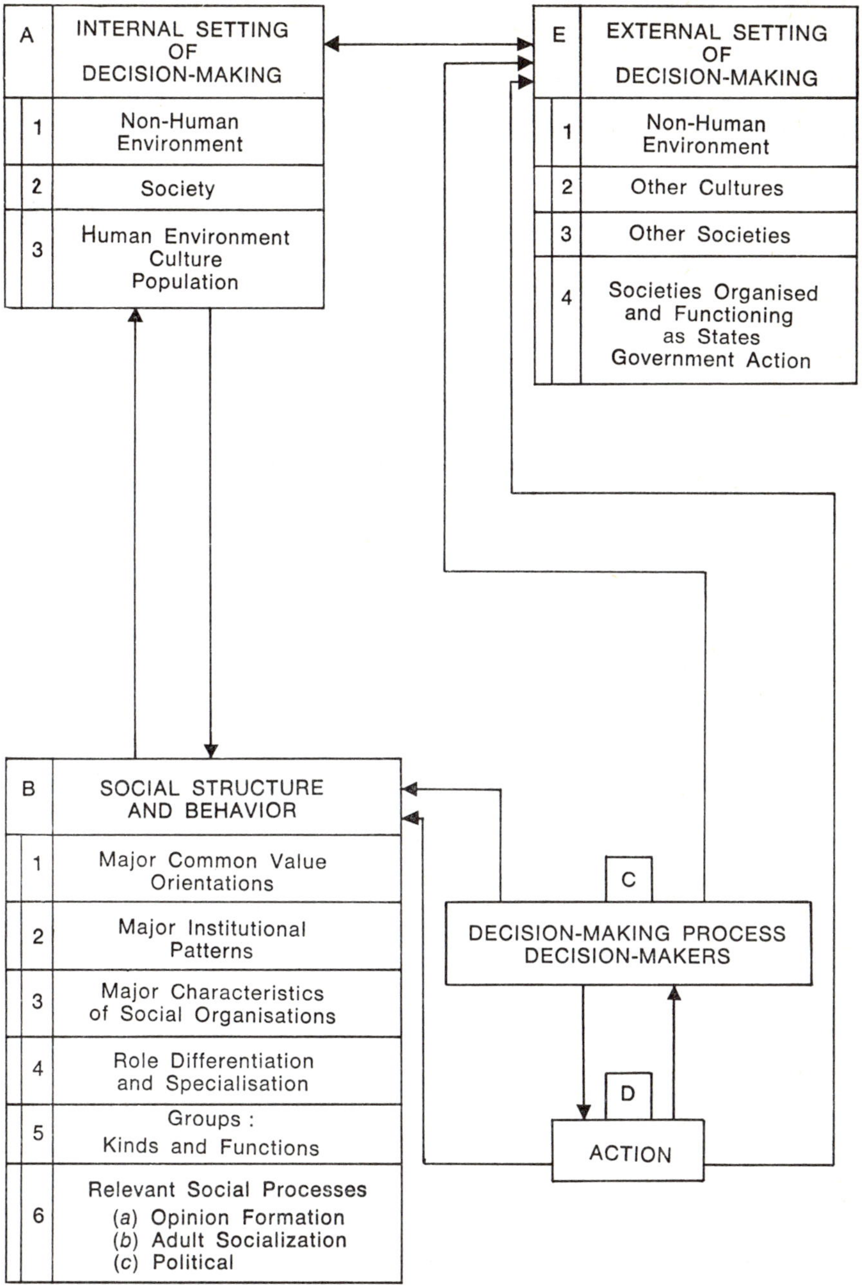

5.2. Though lacking in parsimony as a model, the continued impact of the decision-making model almost twenty years after its exposition is due to its pioneering aspect but also to some of the *advantages* which it offered by providing a scheme rich in concepts and constructs :

(A) The study proposed uniform and comparable categories for the collection of data, thus making comparative foreign policy research feasible.

(B) The authors explored in depth the crucial psychological environment which conditions the response of the decision-makers.

(C) They provided in rigorous conceptual terms an analysis of the decision-making process.

(D) Because of the importance the authors attached to methodological-conceptual issues, they avoided such problems as the reification of the state. [101] As the authors themselves state "we need to . . . rid ourselves of the troublesome abstraction 'state'. It's one of our basic methodological choices to define the state as its official decision-makers—those whose authoritative acts are, to all intents and purposes, the acts of the state. *State action is the action taken by those acting in the name of the state.*" [102] Such a stand has permitted the authors to combine many assets :

(*a*) operationally, they have given form and substance to such a widespread—but controversial—concept as that of "national interest" and have indicated the way to discern and investigate it. "The key to the explanation of why the state behaves the way it does", the authors state, "lies in the way its decision-makers as actors define the situation. The *definition of the situation* is built around the projected action as well as the reasons for the action" [103] ;

(*b*) methodologically, by identifying the state with its top political officials they have reaped the benefit accruing from combining two levels of analysis : the individual and the collective entity. They thus

[101] "The description and explanation of national behavior has also suffered from the common fallacy of misplaced *concreteness* or *reification,* examplified chiefly by the subtle transformation of the word 'state' from a proper analytical abstraction into a symbol allegedly standing for a concrete entity—that is an object or system having an existence of its own apart from real persons and their behaviors". Snyder et al. : *op. cit.,* p. 39.

[102] *Ibid.,* p. 65.

[103] *Ibid.,* pp. 60-74.

attempted to link, at this early stage of theoretically-oriented foreign policy research, the gross characteristics of states to the individual's behavioural attributes in a unified model ;

(*c*) conceptually, their dual level of analysis has enabled and facilitated the borrowing of some basic organizing concepts from two pioneering social sciences : sociology and psychology. These borrowed concepts acted as a source of enrichment for a young potentially empirical political science. As the authors themselves assert "explicit mention must be made of our employment of action analysis and of some of the vocabulary of the now well-known Parsons-Shils scheme". [104]

This last point might be a source of weakness. For as the authors themselves are perfectly aware "as new schemes of social analysis are developed (mostly outside of political science) there is a great temptation to apply such schemes quickly, one result being the use of new words without comprehension of the theoretical system of which they are a part". [105]

5.3. This brings us to the model's *limitations :*

(A) The number of variables is simply overwhelming : the political subsystem, the economy, the actors, the perceptions, the motivations, the values, the goals, the communication problems ... Thus, though we have a single framework, almost everything is treated as a variable and no constants are specified. [106] This inordinate complexity explains why in almost two decades only one study that purported to apply this model has been published, [107] and in spite of the heavy investment of time, skill and financial resources few testable hypotheses seem to have emerged. [108]

(B) The decision-making model offers no help on how to limit the number of variables, and even if the researcher manages to do this on his own, the model does not indicate any guideline on how to proceed in carrying out research even then. [109]

---

104 *Ibid.*

105 *Ibid.*

106 McClosky : *op. cit.*

107 Paige : *The Korean Decision, op. cit.*

108 Brecher et al. : *op. cit.*

109 Weinstein, Franklin : "The Uses of Foreign Policy in Indonesia", *World Politics,* XXIV (1972), pp. 356-382.

(C) The model does not provide the means of analysing the relationship among the variables that are listed. [110] This is the task of Paige's empirical study on the Korean decision which "does describe some relationships, but at the same time remind us that the Snyder framework is really designed for the analysis of policy-making in complex organizations". [111] Since he was dealing with the U.S., Paige rightly emphasized the significance of organizational relationships and communication networks. Such categories, however, would be difficult to apply in the analysis of actors which do not have the same level of organizational complexity, structural differentiation and formalized, identifiable communication networks as the U.S. This is why some foreign policy analysts expressed doubts as to the immediate applicability of the decision-making model to developing countries. "Some observers", James Rosenau said, "... question whether the foreign policy behaviour of non-Western, unindustrialized societies can be explained through the use of a model which is geared mainly to the large-scale decision-making systems of the industrialized West." [112]

(D) Even if all, or at least most, of these problems are overcome, it would still be quite difficult to amass the needed data [113] to produce a study as detailed as Paige's study of the U.S. decision on the Korean War. In developing countries, the press—for instance—is less widespread, less technically developed and in some cases more 'guided' than in many of the developed actors. This makes it very hard to get detailed accounts of decisions. [114] Nor is this problem going to be solved with the passage of time ; on the contrary, it might be aggravated because of "the scantiness of documentary materials and the inadequacy of archival facilities". [115]

(E) Optimistically assuming that all these difficulties are solved and that we found the same organizational complexity and the formalised com-

---

[110] *Ibid.*

[111] *Ibid.*

[112] Rosenau : *International Politics and Foreign Policy* (revised edition), 1969, *op. cit.*, p. 171.

[113] Written material—even if easily available—might not be enough to reveal the exact membership of the decision-making group.

[114] Weinstein : *op. cit.*

[115] *Ibid.* Moreover, "content analysis of written communications, for example, would have an imperceptible statistical base when dealing with a state which has traditionally not made very much use of written materials". Said, Abdul : "The Impact of the Emergence of the Non-West upon Theories of International Relations", Abdul Said (ed.) : *Theory of International Relations,* Englewood Cliffs, Prentice Hall, 1968, pp. 93-107.

munication networks as prescribed by the model, and that we could and did investigate them, nonetheless the effort would be so back-breaking that we would be detracted from investigating and analysing the interaction among the "permanent" domestic determinants, the external pressures and the personality variables.

(F) Worse still, we would realize that the decision-making model is destined—as indeed its labellation indicates—for the analysis of a "once-and-for-all" decision rather than the wider process of foreign policy-making. In other words, the *possible* pay-offs might not compensate the exorbitant research effort deployed. This is an important criterion of applicability in any researchable model.

6. Two Basic Assumptions

6.1. *The Complementarity of levels-of-analysis*

Because of methodological-conceptual consciousness, students of International Relations are about to create a false dilemma: the *choice between* international system-oriented and actor-oriented frameworks. This false dilemma is not unknown to students of social theory. "There are two different approaches to the study of social phenomena", Cohen states. The first may be called "holistic", the second "atomistic". "The 'holistic approach' has tended to treat societies or social wholes as having characteristics similar to those of organic matter or of organism ; it also stresses ... the *'systemic'* properties of social wholes." On the other hand, "the atomistic approach ... stresses the importance of understanding the nature of *individual units* which make up the social wholes". [116] Thus though one has to be aware of the properties and *analytical* distinctions between the different levels of analysis, [117] one need not consider them mutually exclusive. On the contrary, they can be rendered complementary [118] as the following *analytical* distinctions show.

[116] Cohen, Percy : *Modern Social Theory,* London, Heinemann, 1968, pp. 13-14.

[117] Singer : "The Level-of-Analysis Problem", *op. cit.*

[118] This is also the position adopted by Holsti in his "Framework for Analysis" of "International Politics". "Which level-of-analysis (international system, national actor or individual policy-maker) should we employ as the most useful perspective from which to explain or understand politics among nations ?", Holsti asked. After stating that "each makes a contribution, but each fails to account for certain aspects

The international system as a level-of-analysis	*The actor as a level-of-analysis*
Advantages :	
1. Instead of atomising the world or considering it a sum of actions, it emphasises its wholeness. It thus allows us to "focus upon the actions of nations as the components of the system, upon the structure and functioning of the system which results from the interaction of nations, or upon the environmental factors which condition both the actions of nations and the operation of the system". Consequently, we have *comprehensive description.*	1. The study in depth of individual actors would lead to detailed explanation and awareness of their differentiation. Because of the analysis of the actor's goals, motivations, purpose, perception, modes of decision-making . . . this level has a high *explanatory* capability. Consequently, generalizations—through comparison—would be adequately documented and more valid.
2. It is precisely because of this comprehensiveness that it has an integrative capacity. The systemic level offers a mapping function and an organizing device, not only in the use of both macro- and micro-analysis but also in the use of different analytical techniques (*e.g.* communication, decision-making . . .).	
BUT	*BUT*
Disadvantages :	
1. It can lead the observer to exaggerate the impact of the system on the actors and discounts the influence of the actors (especially small states) on the system.	1. It can lead to the exaggeration of differences and the overlooking of existing uniformities. The result is that one would over-differentiate and contrast the peculiarities, rather than compare and generalize.

of reality that must be considered", he reached the (inevitable ?) conclusion that "therefore, all three levels of analysis will be employed at different times, depending upon the type of problem which must be analysed". Holsti : *International Politics, op. cit.*, pp. 16-17 (emphasis added).

The international system as a level-of-analysis	*The actor as a level-of-analysis*
2. It is based on the assumption of high uniformity among national actors. Thus by concentrating on the whole, very little room is allowed for individual characteristics of national actors. We have seen that Morgenthau is led to "assume that (all) statesmen think and act in terms of interest defined as power". Since actors are treated as a sort of "black box", their domestic variations and national peculiarities are neglected and, consequently, we are left with a highly homogenized image of the actors in the system. These two above-mentioned points explain the limited *explanatory capability* of the systemic level.	2. If any general picture emerges, it would tend to be atomised and in need of an integrative (macro) framework.

6.2. *The complementarity of conceptualization and Empirical Relevance*

Our summary treatment of the dominant and evolving paradigms in International Relations indicates that a time-bound and/or culturally enthnocentric frame of reference prevailed and still prevails in theory-building. This frame of reference is irrelevant to a conceptual treatment of non-alignment. The irrelevance of the classical paradigm speaks for itself when we quote the frame of reference explicited by Wolfers :

> "... The stage is preempted by a set of states, each in full control of all territory, men and resources within its boundaries. Every state represents a closed, impermeable and sovereign unit, completely separated from all other states." [119]

[119] Wolfers, Arnold : "The Actors in International Politics", in A. Fox (ed.) : *Theoretical Aspects of International Relations,* Notre-Dame, Indiana, University of Notre-Dame Press, 1959, pp. 83-107.

Apart from the 'state-as-sole-actor' hypothesis incorporated in this proposition, the paradigm is inapplicable to non-aligned actors in two respects :

(*a*) States are supposed to be well-defined, territorially-determined entities in which the political process proceeds autonomously, isolated from external influences and based on an internal consensus concerning both domestic and external orientation. [120]

(*b*) Consequently, foreign policies of states are explained mainly in terms of the external stimuli, *i.e.* that originate in the international system, as Morgenthau did in his treatment of non-alignment. Thus not only has the internal political process an autonomous character, but so does the international political process too. Accordingly 'the balance of power theory"—as developed by Morgenthau, for instance—maintains that situations of equilibrium are the natural outcome of the forces inherent in the international system. [121] Similarly Kaplan's 'balance of power model'—in spite of his extended list of "international actors", his use of 'systems theory' and cybernetic vocabulary—shares the same assumption. That is why a recent research project affirmed that though "Kaplan proclaimed his work as a break with traditional theory . . . it can best be viewed as an elaboration of the Morgenthau paradigm . . . Kaplan refined the Morgenthau concept of the balance of power . . . (but) kept the basic assumptions . . . (and) provided a new language in which to express the Morgenthau paradigm". [122]

---

[120] Leurdijk, Henk : "From International to Transnational Politics : A Change of Paradigms ?". *An unpublished paper submitted to the "Models of International Relations" Workshop of the ECPR* (Mannheim, Germany, 1973).

[121] Morgenthau : *Politics among Nations, op. cit.,* pp. 167-204. As we said in the first chapter, the result of this paradigm is a mechanistic view of the international system where the actions of the national actor are predetermined.

[122] Handelman et al. : *op. cit.,* especially p. 26. The other model we have discussed—the decision-making model—has also been accused of working on the basis of Morgenthau's basic assumptions. Consequently, this model's variables and new concepts—in spite of their methodological refinement—"were employed as independent variables. Their function was to fill in the gaps in Morgenthau's paradigm. They could be used to generate new propositions about international behavior and thereby elaborate the paradigm. But the paradigm itself was not challenged. The three fundamental assumptions Morgenthau had made about International Relations were kept. The unit of analysis was still the nation and there was still the belief that domestic politics were fundamentally different from international politics. Most importantly they did not question Morgenthau's purpose for the field or his definition of international relations—the struggle for power and peace. The dependent variable in the scheme was the foreign policy decisions of national decision-makers. But what foreign policy decisions were worthy of study ? As the authors moved from theory to research the answer became clear : conflict behavior. The first and main use of the framework was to study the Korean war." *Ibid.*

What is the logical result—as far as non-aligned actors are concerned—of maintaining "a rigid distinction between national and international political systems in the face of mounting evidence that the distinction is breaking down" ? [123] The logical result is a tendency among International Relations scholars to view "nation-states as essentially monolithic units whose value systems and internal processes are of secondary importance for understanding their external conduct". [124] Because the decision-making model was actor-oriented and has provided a long inventory where almost everything is treated as a variable and no constants are specified, it is more advanced in avoiding the 'actor-as-billiard-ball' defect. But it faced the problem of unresearchability and inapplicability as far as non-aligned actors are concerned, [125] since it assumed that the model can equally apply to the USA and Togo, Sweden and Ghana, Austria and Indonesia which would be treated as "interchangeable eggs in the same basket". This is related to the bigger problem of the conceptualization of an international system of symmetrical relations, where problems of inequality, underdevelopment and dependence are to be neglected, as is the 'perception' of non-aligned actors of the international system. [126]

While building on the payoffs of the different frameworks but attempting to cope with their limitations, an operational model for the analysis of non-aligned actors' foreign policy has to be based on :

(*a*) the asymmetry of relations in the international system : how the position of the 'underdogs' is correlated with their perception of the international system and how this perception affects their foreign policy orientation and behaviour ;

---

[123] Rosenau, James : "Pre-Theories and Theories of Foreign Policy", in Barry Farrell (ed.) : *Approaches to Comparative and International Politics,* Evanston, Northwestern University Press, 1966, pp. 27-93. For more elaboration on this subject by Rosenau himself, see James Rosenau (ed.) : *Linkage Politics, op. cit.* This book is a collection of 12 papers attempting to link the conceptual frameworks of both Comparative and International Politics, and is based on Rosenau's model.

[124] Hanrieder, Wolfram : "International and Comparative Politics : Toward a Synthesis ?", *World Politics,* XX (1968), pp. 480-494.

[125] Some students of International Relations attribute this inapplicability to other actors of models 'made in the USA' to the preeminence of Euro-centric and American perspectives in the field. "It has thus been", Van Benthem van den Berg said, "the perspective of a controlling center in the network of international relations, which has determined the intellectual interests of the discipline." As quoted in Leurdijk : *op. cit.*

[126] Similarly, other scholars have wondered very recently "whether the basis on which theorizing in international politics proceeds needs revision, whether the *horizontal* analysis of international relations needs to be replaced, or at least supplemented, by a *vertical* analysis" where "we take as a starting point a system of states whose relations are based on subordination and supremacy". *Ibid.* (emphasis added).

(*b*) the investigation of how the psycho-societal variables that constitute the essence of these actors being 'developing or less developed' (*e.g.* problems of social change and national integration) affect their foreign policy orientation and international behaviour ; and

(*c*) the complementarity of different levels-of-analysis since the *empirical* dichotomy of intra-international politics processes is increasingly questioned. In other words, the moving from one level of analysis to the other should not affect the unity of the whole.

CHAPTER III

An alternative: the Situation-Role Model

The elaboration of an alternative model is to be based on our two principal assumptions :

(*a*) it must embrace the three [1] levels-of-analysis, and

(*b*) emphasise the psycho-societal key attributes of non-aligned actors.

In other words, the model will take as its focus of conceptualization, not the frame of reference [2] of other (developed) actors, but the perspective and the *specific situation* of these (developing) non-aligned actors.

1.

It is here that situation-role analysis, as developed in sociology, anthropology and social psychology, can be of immense help in the field of comparative foreign policy analysis. As early as 1950 a sociologist, Robert Bales, took as the starting point of his Interaction Process Analysis [3] the assertion (following Parsons) that all empirical observations can be described under two heads ; namely, *action,* which includes interaction, and the *situation,* in which the action takes place. Similarly, in 1953, a political scientist, David Easton, referred to "situational analysis" when he

---

[1] The exact number of levels-of-analysis one can use in International Relations is not yet accepted by everyone. Singer talks about two levels : the intra-national (domestic) and the extra-national (international). North et al. favour six levels of analysis ranging from the individual to the supra-national, and Galtung seems to go even further. Hveem, Helge : "Foreign Policy Opinion as a Function of International Position", *Co-operation and Conflict,* VII (1972), pp. 65-87. For the merits of adopting three levels of analysis, see Holsti : *International Politics, op. cit.,* pp. 15-17.

[2] For a discussion of 'the frame of reference' in the field of foreign policy analysis, see Synder et al. : *Foreign Policy Decision-Making, op. cit.,* pp. 26-35.

[3] Bales, Robert : *Interaction Process Analysis,* Reading, Mass. Addison-Wesley, 1951.

started his "Inquiry into the State of Political Science".[4] Easton remarked then that few scholars use the concept of "situation" explicitly and "yet the ideas underlying it constantly appear". The present state of foreign policy analysis is not dissimilar to the state of Political Science at the time Easton was writing. For indeed the "situation-role" construct cannot be ignored since it consists of those variables (psychological, societal, systemic or environmental) that shape and condition the actor's foreign policy. But perhaps, as Easton again said, "because the point is so obvious ... it is often neglected".[5] Yet explicit commitment to "situation-role" analysis and an awareness of its different issues will promote interdisciplinary investigation and conceptualisation, and serve to bring foreign policy analysis into closer integration with the other social sciences.[6]

1.1. Put simply, this "situation-role model" stipulates that the orientation or behaviour of the non-aligned actor is a function of the situation it confronts. In other words, we are no longer interested in adopting single-variable explanation, but in substituting for it the concept of social situation which emphasises the interdependence of numerous variables. As Snyder et al. expressed the same idea : " 'Situation' is an analytical concept pointing to a pattern of relationships among events, objects, conditions and other actors" around a focus which is the center of interest for the policy-makers (and hence for the researcher).[7]

1.2. Yet this seemingly straigthforward definition does not eliminate all the conceptual problems, for a controversy has arisen among social scientists[8] as to whether this "situation" is internal or external to the actor ; that is subjective or objective :

(*a*) *The emphasis on the 'subjective' situation :* This is particularly advocated by psychologists. Their argument is that the policy-maker (or

---

[4] This is the sub-title of Easton's *The Political System, op. cit.*

[5] *Ibid.,* pp. 192-193.

[6] This interdisciplinary property seems to be the objective of Bales when he suggested in 1950 that all (social science) generalizations must identify both the concrete action and the situation of the action, whether the ultimate concern is personality, social system or culture. He hoped that by setting out to observe and record data on action and situation, an interdisciplinary bridge would be established among the social sciences. Similarly, Easton believed that the clarification of the 'situation' concept constitutes a precondition of political theory, since the concept serves as a guide to select the significant variables and the important data. Easton, *The Political System, op. cit.,* pp. 198-199.

[7] Besides Snyder et al., other foreign policy analysts express the 'situation' concept without using the same terminology. Thus "it (the world perspective) is a rough single-concept description of how the foreign policy milieu of an actor relates itself ... to the environing world". Hveem : *op. cit.*

[8] Historians cannot be neatly classified into a conceptual category.

foreign policy elite) acts "not on the basis of surrounding forces but on the basis of the (subjective) integration he has fashioned".[9] As early as 1953, David Easton examined this problem for political science when he discussed the view which argues

> "that the *most* significant kind of data is psychological. Policy is to be understood in the light of the kind of people who act in political life, not as a result of the kind of institutions or structures through which they act. Those committed to psychology have insisted that to explain political activity, even the institutional patterns, political science must turn to the motivations and feelings that individuals bring to political life or acquire through the political process itself. This group has stressed the study of what is often loosely called political behaviour in contrast to political institutions. For this reason we call the group behaviouralists, so long as we do not confuse their views with that of strict, and now antiquated behaviourism."[10]

(*b*) *The emphasis on the 'objective' situation:* This is advocated mainly by sociologists. This mode of conceptualisation seeks illumination from studying "the confluence of outer forces that act upon" the actor. In other words, "causation is seen as residing to a greater or lesser degree behind and beyond" the actor.[11] The justification, sociologists indicate, seems to be related to operationalisation for "we can only imagine what structuring" of the situation takes place in the actor's phenomenal field, "but actually we can only *know* for certain the outer (*i.e.* 'objective') situation".

As for political scientists, Easton advocates this point of view. He considers only the 'objective' aspects of the 'situation', which he calls situational data, whereas the internal aspects of the situation he calls psychological data. Thus he says :

> "As a determinant of policy, the situation by implication has been conceived to be quite distinct from, and more significant than, the

---

[9] As expressed by Allport, Gordon : "Prejudice : A Problem in Psychological and Social Causation" in Talcott Parsons and Edward Shils (eds.) : *Toward a General Theory of Action,* New York, Harper & Row, 1962, pp. 465-488.

[10] Easton : *The Political System, op. cit.,* ch. 6 (emphasis added).

[11] Allport : *op. cit.* Advocates of this view cite this example to support their contention : the pupils of a rural school of South Africa were not making satisfactory progress in learning English. A supervisor of the English language programme visited the school and asked the native teacher to give a demonstration lesson. Thereupon the teacher began his lesson, but only after saying to the group in their vernacular : "Come now, children, put away your things and let us spend an hour wrestling with the enemy's language". This, then, was the *situation* in which the learning was supposed to proceed. We can imagine what structuring took place in the students' phenomenal field, but actually we can only *know* for certain the outer situation.

kind of people who acted in the situation. What is thus meant by situational as *contrasted* with psychological data will become apparent in due course." [12]

Thus, rather than emphasising the interdependence between personality variables and societal variables in shaping the actor's behaviour, Easton considers them opposed or "contrasted". This attitude is more explicitly expounded in the way Easton defines the components of the "situational data". "The situational", he says, "refers to those determinants which shape activity *in spite of* the kind of personalities and motivations in the participants. There are at least three separate categories of situational data to be identified : (1) the physical environment ; (2) the non-human organic environment ; and (3) the social environment or patterns of human activity flowing from social interaction". [13] But he soon realises the impasse, and in order to complete his explanation, he is soon forced to include the 'internal situation' or 'psychological data' as Easton calls it.

> "We can appreciate", he says, "the independent influence of situational data on activity if we look at the role that a fourth and final element, the personality, plays in the situation. I am not denying here the obviously indubitable, that how a person reacts to a given set of so-called objective circumstances is conditioned in part by the kind of person he is. A party leader who is stable and free of severe internal tensions will clearly be able to evaluate his surrounding circumstances, such as the strength and tactics of his opponents, more reliably than a leader who is riddled with frustrations and a deep sense of persecution. *Identical situations* will elicit quite *divergent responses* from each of these leaders. Each will *define his situation differently* in terms of the predispositions of his personality." [14]

1.3. What is our position toward this presumed polarisation ? We suggest that this is a false dilemma, as false as the polarisation of "holistic" versus "atomistic" frameworks in modern social theory, [15] or "systemic" versus "actor-oriented" levels of analysis in the evolving paradigm of International Relations. In other words one *does not have to choose between* 'subjective' and 'objective', 'internal' and 'external' components determining the "definition of the situation" but one *can emphasise* one component rather than the other depending on (*a*) *what* issues in (*b*) *which* situations we are investigating. For it is difficult to "generalize about which factors are most important in each situation, since policy-makers

[12] Easton : *The Political System, op. cit.*, p. 152 (emphasis added).

[13] *Ibid.*, p. 194 (emphasis added).

[14] *Ibid.*, p. 196 (emphasis added).

[15] Cohen : *Modern Social Theory, op. cit.*, pp. 13-15.

seldom draw up careful lists assessing the relative weight of each component of the 'definition of the situation' ".[16] We can then reiterate our definition of the "situation-role" construct provided at the beginning of this section and express it, as did the social psychologist Kurt Lewin,[17] in equation form :

$$B = F (A \cdot E)$$

where behaviour (B) is a function (F) of the interaction between the actor (A) and his environment (E). In this equation, then, both the actor and the environment are viewed as two interacting (sets of) variables since they are considered "a constellation of interdependent factors".[18] In other words, our model will not solely emphasise 'objective' external events but also the "meanings" which actors assign to them. Thus psychological factors—rather than being considered constants—are regarded as important variables.[19]

1.4. *An Anthropological Treatment of the "Situation" Concept in the Research on Colonialism*

An example can indicate the payoffs of this mode of conceptualisation in two respects :

(*a*) by showing the model's applicability to the analysis of one of the key attributes of non-aligned actors : the "colonial situation" ; and

(*b*) by drawing this example from an anthropologist's treatment (after having already discussed the views of sociologists, political scientists

[16] Holsti : *International Politics, op. cit.,* p. 157.

[17] D. Cartwright (ed.) : *Kurt Lewin's Field Theory in Social Science,* New York, Harper and Brothers, 1951, especially chapter 10.

[18] Many others—in addition to Lewin—express the same idea. Note this example from 'political psychology' : "Politics is a matter of human behavior, and behavior ... is a function of both the *environmental* situations in which actors find themselves and the *psychological predispositions* they bring to those situations". Greenstein, Fred : *Personality and Politics,* Chicago, Markham Publishing Co., 1969, p. 7. Similarly two social scientists "primarily concerned with the application of hitherto neglected sociological theory to international relations" accept as the basis of their analysis that "the definition of the situation consists of mutually interactive components drawn from within" and from outside. Nettl, J., and Robertson, Roland : *International Systems and the Modernization of Societies,* London, Faber, 1968, p. 75. Their "actor-in-situation approach" (*ibid.,* p. 65) is the same as that of the decision-making model-builders who approached their analysis of "state-action from an actor-situation point of view".

[19] For a detailed diagramatic form of this definition, see Smith : *op. cit.*

and social psychologists), we can then indicate the function of this mode of conceptualisation as a meeting point among different social scientists, *i.e.* the model's interdisciplinary function. [20]

The "Colonial Situation"

The main attack of Balandier's analysis is against those researchers who dealt with the colonial intrusion and social change in an atomistic way. For instance, trying to explain the colonial relationship in terms of the coming of monetary economy and wages, the diffusion of "modern" education, the action of the missionaries . . . rather than taking this colonial-colonised relationship as *a whole.* For since "colonialism, in establishing itself, imposed on subject peoples a very special type of *situation",* [21] it follows that :

> ". . . any *present-day* study of colonial societies striving for an understanding of current realities and not a reconstitution of a purely historical nature, a study aiming at a comprehension of conditions as they are, not sacrificing facts for the convenience of some dogmatic schematization, can only be accomplished by taking into account this complex . . . the *colonial situation."* [22]

Thus in emphasising this multifaceted aspect of the colonial phenomenon political scientists will benefit from the contributions of other social scientists by integrating other variables (*e.g.* economic, psychological, sociological) into their own explanation. Moreover, rather than being merely synchronic in their analysis, social scientists can then draw on the essential historical dimension. For the historian

> ". . . makes us understand how, in the course of time the colonial power implanted itself in the heart of its colonial societies. Acting in this manner he furnishes the sociologist with the first and indispensable frame of reference. He reminds the sociologist that the history of a colonial people has developed as a result of a foreign presence while at the same time he elucidates the different aspects of the latter's role and influence." [23]

And Balandier implies that "situating" colonial societies in relation to this dual history, with its socio-psychological aspects, is almost the only way to understand this "single complex", this "totality".

---

[20] Balandier, Georges : *Sociologie actuelle de l'Afrique noire,* Paris, Presses Universitaires de France, 1963 (2nd edition), pp. 3-39. Also the translation in Immanuel Wallerstein (ed.) : *Social Change : The Colonial Situation,* New York, Wiley, 1966, pp. 34-62.

[21] As in Wallerstein, *op. cit.,* p. 34.

[22] *Ibid.,* p. 35.

[23] *Ibid.*

2. *The Situation-Role Model and the Analysis of Foreign Policy-Making*

As in the above anthropological treatment, and with other social scientists, the application of the 'situation-role model' emphasises the totality of the foreign policy-making process. Holsti expressed the idea very explicitly when he said that

> "the 'definition of the situation' would include all external and domestic, historical and contemporary, conditions which policy-makers consider relevant to any given foreign policy problem. These might include important events abroad, domestic political needs, social values or ideological imperatives, state of public opinion, availability of capabilities, degree of threat or opportunity perceived in a situation, predicted consequences and costs of proposed courses of action, and the time element or 'requiredness' of a situation."

Many of these 'components' in the actor's "definition of the situation" [24] can be treated explicitly and in greater detail to concretise our basic assumption on the complementarity of levels of analysis.

2.1. *The 'International System' Component*

2.1.1. It has already been noted that the general foreign policy *orientation* of national actors *(e.g.* alliance versus non-alignment) is a function of the international system, for instance of its structure (unipolar, bipolar, multipolar). This is simply a shorthand way of saying that the policy-makers in non-aligned actors perceived major structural characteristics of their external environment in approximately the same way and adopted strategies and policies that orient their states' policies to fit this systemic structure.

2.1.2. But the general foreign policy orientation of non-aligned actors is conditioned not only by the systemic structure, but also by the norms governing the function of the system, whether these norms are declaratory (*e.g.* the "set norm" of the equality of states) or operative (*e.g.* the "enforced norm" of the banning of the slave trade). These systemic norms—which transcend purely local or national norms—exercise their

---

[24] For an elaboration of the actor's "definition of the situation" concept, see for instance: Banton, Michael: *Roles: An Introduction to the Study of Social Relations*, London, Tavistock Publications, 1965, pp. 135-137; Frankel: *The Making of Foreign Policy, op. cit.*, pp. 183-185; Holsti: *International Politics, op. cit.*, pp. 155-191.

subtle impact on the actors' foreign policy objectives, as the analysis of historical international systems shows. [25] For instance,

> "in the eighteenth century the doctrine of divine right and the values associated with royal authority were accepted by the European upper classes irrespective of nationality ; hence, certain external objectives and actions relating to the preservation or extension of royal authority were highly valued. If dynastic prestige was a goal to which all monarchs aspired, then the various methods of achieving status, such as alliances and marriages, were also considered legitimate." [26]

In the contemporary international system the systemic norms mostly emphasised by the non-aligned actors are independence from the politico-military blocs, equal status among members of the international system, economic development . . . On these systemic determinants of non-alignment, there has been consensus among these actors (as we shall see in greater detail later) ; and this indicates that the 'systemic component' in its 'definition of the situation' has acted as a given, a parameter. This is certainly what Sukarno, for instance, meant when he reminded his colleagues that non-aligned actors had come to adopt non-alignment without *prior* consultation or coordination. [27]

2.1.3. In fact, the treatment of non-aligned actors as an international subsystem indicates that this consociational 'systemic component' acted as a very important determinant in delimiting the subsystem's boundaries and in performing an integrative function among its members. In other words, differentiation among non-aligned actors arises not so much at the general foreign policy orientation level (as the consensus in their voting behaviour on colonial and racial discrimination questions shows) but rather at the behavioural level, *i.e.* when the general orientation of non-alignment is operationalised and translated into a specific international behaviour *(e.g.* Egypt's relations with the U.S.A. versus Tunisia's, Algeria's relations with the U.S.S.R. versus the Ivory Coast's). And the differentiation is—logically—the most pronounced when the specific international behaviour is not so much *influenced* by the (relatively consociational)

---

[25] See, for instance, Rosecrance : *Action and Reaction in International Politics : International Systems in Perspective, op. cit.*

[26] Holsti : *International Politics, op. cit.*, p. 171.

[27] See Sukarno's speech as published in the official report of the 1st Summit : *The Conference of Heads of State or Government of Non-Aligned Countries,* Beograd, Publicisticko-Izdavacki Zavod, 1961.

'systemic component', but rather *conditioned* by a predominant 'national component' and/or *dominated* by an imposing (top leadership's) 'personality component' [28] in the 'definition of the situation'.

2.2. *The 'National' Component*

We have already seen that both the 'Power Paradigm' and 'International Systems Analysis' tended to overlook the importance of this component and to adopt a mechanistic view of international interaction based either on each actor's immutable 'search for power' or on the system's impersonal "needs" and its "essential rules". Many foreign policy objectives, however, are formulated to fulfil *primarily* internal social needs and satisfy specific pressure groups or domestic forces. Thus a national actor bargains for a special tariff agreement to benefit one of its industries, and intervenes diplomatically or even militarily to protect one of its enterprises abroad *(e.g.* the 1956-Suez intervention).

2.2.1. An actor's *geographic location and topographical features* [29] are very important variables in the 'definition of the situation', because they are the least changing (especially in non-aligned actors) and that is in spite of scientific-technological advances. For

> "while modern technology can alter the political and economic significance of geographic characteristics, many of these characteristics still influence policies by providing opportunities or by placing limitations on what is feasible in both domestic and foreign policy programs. A country's size, population, distribution of natural resources, climate, and topography will have an important bearing on its socioeconomic development, needs vis-a-vis other nations, and access to other areas of the world. These conditions also have the greatest relevance to military and defence policies. Topographical features create avenues for invasion and suggest the best lines of defense ; economic characteristics and distribution of natural resources determine a nation's self reliance or dependency on others in wartime as

---

[28] Lyon starts his treatment of the neutralist doctrine by suggesting that "it may help to understand some of the characteristics of such [*a*] ... doctrine when we remember who the leading neutralist 'ideologues' are, what roles they perform, what aims and aspirations they have in common". Lyon : *Neutralism, op. cit.,* p. 59.

[29] For a conceptual treatment of the man-milieu relationship, see, for instance, Sprout, Harold and Margaret : *The Ecological Perspective on Human Affairs, with Special Reference to International Politics,* Princeton, N.J., Princeton U.P., 1965. For a recent example of empirical research on the relationship between environment and political behaviour, see : Holt, Robert, and Turner, John : "Insular Polities" in Rosenau James (ed.) : *Linkage Politics, op. cit.,* pp. 199-236.

> well as during peace ; and climate imposes restrictions on the types of warfare that can be conducted in a particular area or the kinds of agricultural products that can be grown." [30]

2.2.2. Though this does not mean that different policy-makers interpret the significance of these geographical-topographical determinants in the same way, or adopt the same means to promote foreign policy objectives, a policy-maker is forced to relate his country's international behaviour to its immediate and potential *capabilities* [31]*(e.g.* military forces, transportation facilities, diplomatic personnel). However, foreign policy objectives that demand capabilities beyond the actor's potential *(e.g.* a non-aligned actor's demand for an alteration in systemic or subsystemic structure) are not altogether dropped but are still adhered to, at least symbolically.

2.2.3. Diplomatic historians and students of International Relations point to another variable in the 'national component' when they quote examples about the influence of *organisational values, needs and traditions (e.g.* military organisations, foreign offices, intelligence services) on foreign policies. A notorious historical example showing the influence of lower grade personnel on the formal policy-making authority which led to a major conflict is the case

> "in 1914 when German military and diplomatic officials took steps to goad Austria into war against Serbia, and deliberately kept the Kaiser uninformed of their own activities as well as of several British diplomatic moves aimed at reducing tensions and preserving peace". [32]

The values of these bureaucrats and civil servants are bound to influence the formal policy-making process if only through their interpretation of other actors' "messages" or through their organisational sources of information and briefing. For instance,

> "the American State Department in any one day receives about 1,300 cables from American diplomatic and consular officials abroad providing information, requesting directions, or seeking permission to make certain decisions in the field. But of the large number of communications the Secretary of State will read only 20 to 30—about 2 per cent of the total. The State Department also sends out approximately 1,000 cables daily, many of which elucidate objectives and provide directions on policies designed to implement them ; of these

---

[30] Holsti : *International Politics, op. cit.,* p. 174. Holsti goes on to substantiate his argument by citing the examples of Britain and Japan.

[31] Wilkinson, David : *Comparative Foreign Relations : Framework and Methods,* Belmont, California, Dickenson Publishing Co., 1969, pp. 33-71.

[32] Holsti : *International Politics, op. cit.,* p. 181.

> the Secretary of State may see only six, while the President will have only one or two of the most important communications referred to his office." [33]

Though these are routine and non-vital happenings, a decision made on a misleading basis can lead to an international crisis, or a major foreign policy failure *(e.g.* the failure of Cairo's policy in the "Syrian region" of the U.A.R.). Since top policy-makers are generally concerned only with suggesting the general objectives and not with their specifics, values and traditions of lower policy-making organisations and officials will continue to influence policy. As Frankel's analysis of *The Making of Foreign Policy* stated,

> "the higher the position of the decision-maker, the more remote he is from the original sources of information. Compression of information invariably involves the omission of subtler points and simplification, and the further it proceeds the more does it involve separation from the operational environment and the possibility of its complete misinterpretation."

And the study substantiates its proposition by giving the example of

> "President Eisenhower . . . [who] refused to become acquainted with news directly and dispensed even with the one-page summary for every twenty-four hours period which Truman had used. He relied on John Foster Dulles to draw his attention to anything important." [34]

Though most non-aligned actors do not have the same degree of elaborate organisational networks, bureaucratic complexity and structural differentiation as other 'developed' actors, different organisations *(e.g.* the military) [35] still influence the policy-making process in these "praetorian" societies. [36]

2.2.4. All these foreign policy determinants are relatively more easy to identify and measure than other variables of the 'national component' such as the influence of *'national historical experience'* or of domestic

---

[33] Testimony of Secretary of State, Dean Rusk, to a Senate Sub-committee, as reported in *ibid.,* p. 183.

[34] Frankel : *The Making of Foreign Policy, op. cit.,* pp. 96-97.

[35] The importance of the military in 'third world' societies is apparent in this statement of President Senghor, made after an abortive coup against his government. "After God", Senghor said, "it is above all to our armed forces that I must express the gratitude of the nation". For a recent treatment of this subject, see First, Ruth : *The Barrel of a Gun,* London, Penguin African Library, 1972.

[36] For a treatment of the 'praetorian' society in the field of 'developmental politics', see Huntington, Samuel : *Political Order in Changing Societies,* New Haven, Yale U.P., 1968, pp. 192-264.

public opinion. To take the historical variable first, a common variable among non-aligned actors is their colonial "inheritance situation". [37] This "colonial relationship" [38] has imposed a very special type of variable in the 'national component' which explains not only the non-aligned actors' past reaction as "dependent peoples", but also conditions their post-independence behaviour. For colonialism implied not only political subjugation or economic exploitation, but also cultural degradation and psychological humiliation. [39] Nkrumah has expressed these multi-faceted effects of the "colonial relationship" very explicitly :

> "The stage opens with the appearance of 'missionaries' and anthropologists, traders and concessionaires, and administrators. While the 'missionaries' with 'Christianity' perverted implore the colonial subject to lay up 'his treasures in Heaven where neither moth nor rust doth corrupt', the traders and concessionaires and administrators acquire his mineral and land resources, destroy his arts, crafts and home industries." [40]

This explains why

> "the social effects of colonialism are more insidious than the political and economic. This is because they go deep into the minds of the people and therefore take longer to eradicate. The Europeans relegated us to the position of inferiors in every aspect of our everyday life. Many of our people came to accept the view that we are an inferior people." [41]

Because of the deep-rooted influence of this variable, a Sukarno—through his 'theory' of "New Emerging Forces"—would insist that the basic task of non-alignment is to fight the "forces of domination". Similarly, a Nasser—in a key statement—would link explicitly Egypt's past colonial experience with its present policy of non-alignment.

2.2.5. As for the influence of *domestic public opinion* on foreign policy, its importance lies in its function as a summary indice of the psycho-societal state of 'the people'. But, unfortunately, there seems to be consensus that

---

[37] Nettl and Robertson : *International Systems and the Modernization of Societies, op. cit.,* pp. 63-129.

[38] Worsley, Peter : *The Third World,* London, Weidenfeld and Nicolson, 1967 (2nd edition), pp. 21-31.

[39] For a passionate expression of these psychological-cultural effects of colonialism, see the works of Frantz Fanon, for instance, *Les Damnés de la Terre,* Paris, Maspero, 1966.

[40] Speech at the Conference of Independent African States, Accra, 15 April 1958.

[41] Nkrumah, Kwame : *Africa Must Unite,* London, 1963, p. 32.

> "probably no aspect of the study of international politics or foreign policy is more difficult to generalize about than the relationship of public opinion to a government's external objectives and diplomatic behavior"

and consequently,

> "more research on this area, particularly in *non-Western countries,* needs to be completed before students of international relations can offer generalizations with much confidence". [42]

This undeveloped stage of the study of the relationship between public opinion and foreign policy is not surprising, given the vague and diffuse character of the "public opinion" concept itself. Consequently, if there is here "a broad field of future research"—especially as far as "non-Western countries" are concerned—it is imperative that some conceptual-methodological refinements be made first.

To start with, such extreme and unconfirmed general hypotheses suggesting, for instance, that : (*a*) "foreign policy goals and diplomatic behavior are merely a response to domestic opinions" or (*b*) "public attitudes are virtually ignored as important components of a definition of the situation", should be discarded—at least at the beginning. Empirical examples do not confirm either absolutely and/or on all occasions. Indeed, "some government officials have claimed frankly that their decisions could not be influenced by fickle public attitudes", but there are also examples where "officials yielded to public pressures despite their own preferred policies".

The second conceptual-methodological refinement is that the simple direct correlation between public opinion and foreign policy has to be qualified by breaking down the very general "public opinion" concept into its constitutive parts and by distinguishing between (*a*) *who* is expressing opinions concerning (*b*) *what* issues in (*c*) *which* situations. [43]

For various studies concluded their analyses of public attitudes by the proposition :

> "the vast majority of population—even in highly literate societies—is unknowledgeable, uninterested and apathetic with regard to most issues of world affairs." [44]

Other studies substantiated this proposition by showing that even in the U.S.

---

[42] Holsti : *International Politics, op. cit.,* pp. 176-181 (emphasis added).

[43] *Ibid. ;* Rosenau, James : *Public Opinion and Foreign Policy,* New York, Random House, 1961, pp. 35-41.

[44] Holsti : *ibid. ;* Rosenau : *ibid.*

"the sustained efforts made by the government, the foundations, the universities and some private individuals to educate the public in foreign affairs have not been successful". [45]

This is why scholars of "public opinion and foreign policy" divide the people—for purposes of analysis—into a small "attentive" minority (ranging from 1 per cent to 15 per cent in "Western" actors) which is closely correlated with higher education, urban domicile, higher income, male sex . . ., [46] and the "mass public" or "inattentive" majority (about 70 per cent or more of the population) which "can be characterized on *most* issues as apathetic, uninformed and non-expressive". In certain circumstances, however, these people "can display considerable interest in some issue areas and, if properly mobilized, can express great hostility or loyalty to foreign nations or their political leaders". [47]

Because most of the empirical findings are—as we indicated above—based on research done in "Western" actors (especially the U.S.) they cannot—given the existing structural and cultural differences—be easily generalized to apply to non-aligned actors. But what is called in public opinion studies the "Mood Theory" [48] *(i.e.* the general notions, attitudes or predispositions about what is appropriate and inappropriate in foreign policy orientation and behaviour) is very applicable to our research topic. Though this "public opinion mood" can be, as Caspary said, "permissive" and provides "a blank check for foreign policy adventures", it can also be restrictive and prescribe limits within which foreign policy can be oriented and carried out. An example from "colonial wars" can clarify this point. If we compare the termination of the French colonial war in Indo-China with its continuation in Algeria, we find that "Mendes-France was given an opportunity to find a settlement because the (French) people had become tired of the prolonged war in Indo-China, (whereas) for a long time public opinion obstructed a solution of the Algerian problem even under de Gaulle's subtle leadership". [49] Similarly, one of the very few

---

[45] Frankel: *The Making of Foreign Policy, op. cit.*, p. 72.

[46] In their "Inventory of Scientific Findings" about "Human Behavior", Berelson and Steiner offer this proposition :

"The higher a person's socio-economic and educational level—especially the latter—the higher his political interest, participation and voting turnout."

"Men are more active politically than women . . . Urban residents are somewhat more active politically than rural residents, especially with regard to national affairs."

Berelson, Bernard, and Steiner, Gray : *Human Behavior : An Inventory of Scientific Findings,* New York, Harcourt, Brace & World, 1964, pp. 423-424.

[47] Holsti : *International Politics, op. cit.*, p. 177.

[48] Caspary, William : "The 'Mood Theory' : A Study of Public Opinion and Foreign Policy", *The American Political Science Review,* LXIV (1970), pp. 536-547.

[49] Frankel : *The Making of Foreign Policy, op. cit.*, p. 74. And another analyst adds : "In the nineteenth and early twentieth centuries in the United States, the pre-

surveys of public opinion in non-aligned actors resulted in the finding that of a sample of 49 Egyptian professionals in 1951, 25 (more than 50 per cent) respondents considered relations with Britain their main problem and this led to their strongly nationalistic view of the international system.[50] One can explain in this case why essentially non-militant, pre-1952 Egyptian governments adopted a 'hard line' on Anglo-Egyptian relations, refused participation in Common Defence Organizations and indeed showed a tendency toward a de-facto non-alignment. When Nasser came to power, he could not disregard this 'public opinion mood'. Other examples could be quoted, but a proposition remains valid : while 'public opinion mood' might not prescribe exact policies or responses, it establishes limits beyond which few policy-makers would normally dare to act. As we shall see in the next chapter, the choice of non-alignment seemed to be in accordance with 'public opinion mood' and managed to bring together divergent political forces within the non-aligned actor's domestic system.

There is, however, one important point that needs to be mentioned concerning the relationship between public opinion and foreign policy : namely that this relationship is not 'one-way', as some recent findings have shown.[51] In other words, policy-makers—especially in non-aligned (developing) actors—do not only respond to public pressures but also orient these pressures and make public opinion perform a supporting function.[52] The exact influence-ratio between the policy-maker and the 'people' depends on such variables as the degree of societal and political

---

dominant public mood was isolation and indifference to European affairs. In the 1950's, it was a mood of pronounced fear of, and hostility toward, the Soviet Union ... Such moods, while not suggesting concrete foreign policy objectives, at least *set limits* around the theoretical policy alternatives of policy-makers. The Prime Minister of neutral Sweden could not, for example, announce one day that he had concluded a military alliance, unless large segments of the population also believed that neutrality was outmoded, ineffective or incompatible with some value such as national survival ...". Thus "on the major questions of a country's general orientation to the rest of the world, war and peace, and general style of diplomacy, everyone has opinions and is likely to express them when challenged. When the *scope* of public opinion is so broad, it is likely to have great influence on the alternatives which policy-makers regard seriously". Holsti : *International Politics, op. cit.,* pp. 178-179.

[50] Kendall, Patricia : "The Ambivalent Character of Nationalism among Egyptian Professionals", *Public Opinion Quarterly,* XX (1956), pp. 277-292.

[51] Verba, Sidney et al. : "Public Opinion and the War in Vietnam", *The American Political Science Review,* LXI (1967), pp. 317-333.

[52] "Because of superior knowledge and access to information, governments occupy a position from which they can interpret reality to the population and actually create attitudes, opinions, and images where none existed before. While independent communications media may express differing views, a prime minister or president can be very persuasive by virtue of his political prestige and exper-

system differentiation [53] (*e.g.* mobilisation versus reconciliation systems), [54] the degree of autonomy of the communication media, [55] and the degree of 'charisma' in the leadership authority. [56] This last factor points out the importance of a key component in the non-aligned actors' 'definition of the situation' : the leadership's personality variable. This brings us to our third level-of-analysis.

2.3. *The 'Personality'* [57] *Component in the 'Definition of the Situation'*

2.3.1. Observers and statesmen group actors as diverse as India, Malawi, Saudi Arabia and Algeria into one category labelled 'third world' or developing, because the members of this category share some common attributes such as similar positions in the international system, and the similar structure of their social (sub)system. These *common attributes*

---

tise ... Thus, what many people know of, or feel about, a critical situation abroad and its own government's actions and responses to it may originate from the government itself—from press conferences, parliamentary debates, or political speeches. As much as they respond to public opinions, governments also help create those opinions. Public opinion, rather than controlling or restricting policy choices, may serve primarily to support government actions". Holsti : *International Politics, op. cit.,* p. 180.

[53] "Mob pressures often come to bear in societies in which political institutions are rudimentary or non-existent and where public opinion is not well articulated. In the Middle Eastern, African, and Asian cities, the illiterate masses of unskilled urban workers, unstable in their divorce from their rural origins and unhappy in their wretched living conditions, and the students, aware of the shortcomings of their societies but incapable of providing answers to their problems, form a public opinion vastly different from that found in Western democracies." Frankel : *The Making of Foreign Policy, op. cit.,* p. 79.

[54] For the analysis of these two types of political systems in the context of 'modernisation', see Apter, David : *The Politics of Modernization,* Chicago, The University of Chicago Press, 19965, pp. 357-422.

[55] "A person whose sources of information on the outside world are restricted to a government-controlled newspaper must have considerable initiative and access to unusual resources in order to develop attitudes and opinions contrary to those prescribed for him by his government." Holsti : *International Politics, op. cit.,* pp. 180-181.

[56] "It has often been observed that information or propaganda emanating from a reliable or prestigious source has more impact on opinions than information dispersed by less credible sources." Hovland, C. I., Janis, I. L., and Kelley, H. H. : *Communication and Persuasion,* New Haven, Yale U.P., 1953, pp. 19-55, as reported in *ibid.*

[57] There is general agreement among psychologists that the term "personality" refers "to an *inferred* entity rather than to a directly observable phenomenon. 'Per-

are correlated with their *common foreign policy ortientation* (non-alignment). But one need not be a specialist on African politics to notice the wide differences between, for instance, Guinea and the Ivory Coast in their foreign policy behaviour (as distinguished from foreign policy orientation). The leader's *'personality'* variable—as manifested in his state's role conception [58]—is adopted here as a means to account for *behavioural specificities* within the non-aligned subsystem.

---

sonality' refers to a construct that is introduced to account for the regularities in an individual's behavior as he responds to diverse stimuli". Greenstein : *Politics and Personality, op. cit.,* p. 3. For a classical and more detailed treatment of an inventory of definitions in the study of personality, see Allport, Gordon : *Pattern and Growth in Personality,* London, Holt, Rinehart and Winston, 1963 (1937), pp. 22-30.

[58] Standard textbooks in Sociology and Social Psychology deal with the concept. Banton, Michael : *Roles, op. cit.,* gives a detailed treatment with short, but useful bibliography. Rochblave-Spenlé, Ann-Marie : *La notion de rôle en psychologie sociale : étude historico-critique* (Paris, P.U.F., 1962) gives a detailed analysis of the role concept. The recent explicit advocacy for the application of the role concept in foreign policy analysis is Holsti, K. J. : "National Role Conceptions in the Study of Foreign Policy", *International Studies Quarterly,* XIV, 3 (1970), pp. 233-310. See also the comment of the social psychologist C. W. Backman on the application of role theory in International Relations, pp. 310-320 in the same issue. It can be claimed that Kautilya, in describing the six types of foreign policy in the ancient Hindu world applied a role approach. See Modelski, George : "Kautilya : Foreign Policy and International Systems in the Ancient Hindu World", *The American Political Science Review,* vol. LVIII (1964), pp. 349-360. More related to our concerns is the study by Lyon : *Neutralism, op. cit.,* which distinguishes between the 'active' neutrality of Sweden and the 'passive' neutrality of Switzerland, as well as the different national role conceptions adopted by the policy-makers of similarly 'non-aligned' countries like Afghanistan, Egypt, India ... Though "traditional", this study is more informative in this aspect than M. Kaplan's *System and Process, op. cit.,* which is based on one country-one role approach. In other words, Kaplan's loose bipolar model does not make a place for an actor to be non-aligned and perform an integrative function on the global systemic level, while at the same time perform a revolutionary anti-status quo role in the regional (sub)system. As Holsti rightly says : "most of the literature on non-alignment similarly ignores the possibility that while a state may be non-aligned with respect to cold-war issues, it may very well be a bloc leader or some other type of role player at the regional level". Holsti in "National Role Conceptions ...", *op. cit.*

For instance, a difference exists between Nehru's conception of India's role and Sukarno's conception of Indonesia's role. For a discussion of the latter, see Modelski, George (ed.) : *The New Emerging Forces,* Canberra, The Australian National University, 1963. Not only implicitly, but also explicitly third world policy-makers have used a national role conception. An example is this quotation from Nasser : "For some reason", Nasser said very early in his political career, "it seems to me that within the Arab circle, there is a role, wandering aimlessly in search of a hero. And I do not know why it seems to me that this role exhausted by its wanderings, has at last settled down, tired and weary, near the borders of our country and is beckoning *to us* to move, to assume it as nobody else can do so." *The Philosophy of the Revolution* (the Arabic edition), Cairo, 1954, p. 62 (emphasis added).

The following table [59] is an *indicator* of these specificities of non-aligned behaviour within the general orientation. The top leadership's policy statements *(e.g.* official statements and foreign policy reviews around mid 1960s) are plotted on an 8-point scale of role conceptions ranging from the most moderate (isolate: 0) to the relatively most militant (bastion of the anti-colonial revolution : 7). The number of times stating the role conception is multiplied by this role conception's weighted value on the scale. These weighted values are then summed into the weighted total, an indicator of differences among non-aligned actors as to the degree of their involvement and militancy : *e.g.* Egypt's score of 260 versus Nepal's 18, Indonesia's 80 versus Niger's 12 and India's 66 versus Cambodia's 6 (see table following page).

Thus the treatment of the 'personality' component in the 'definition of the situation' attenuates the oversimplification in lumping non-aligned actors together as one uniform entity. Moreover, this procedure paves the way toward a typology of behavioural patterns within the non-aligned group.

In addition to this function of the 'personality' component, the treatment of its influence on the foreign policy-making process in non-aligned actors seems to be justified by other—but reinforcing—premises. [60]

2.3.2. Epistemologically, political behaviour is a human activity, and since men are the prime actors in this activity, "their personalities are important contributors to the character of their political participation". [61] In other words, political participants are "something considerably more than can be indicated by the impersonal categories students of politics ordinarily use to explain political behavior—as more than . . . creatures of situation, members of culture, and possessors of social characteristics . . ." [62]

2.3.3. Methodologically, the personality variable links the global systemic to societal determinants of foreign policy, since foreign policy-makers occupy the middle position linking the international system to the national (sub)system. Thus one of the endemic methodological problems

---

[59] The table is based on the definitions offered and data collected by Holsti. For a treatment of these two issues, see Holsti : "National Role Conceptions . . .", *op. cit.* By using a weighting methodology and tabulating some of the data, I have tried to adapt some of Holsti's concerns to the problems at hand.

[60] See, however, an inventory of possible "objections to the study of personality and politics" in Greenstein : *Personality and Politics, op. cit.*, pp. 33-63.

[61] Wolfenstein, Victor : *The Revolutionary Personality : Lenin, Trostsky, Gandhi*, Princeton, Princeton U.P., 1967, p. 3.

[62] Greenstein : *Personality and Politics, op. cit.*, p. 1.

TABLE 2. *A Typology of Moderate-Militant Patterns Among 29 Non-Aligned Actors*

State	Years	Bastion of Anti-Colonial Revolution	Weighted Value (7)	Regional Leader	Weighted Value (6)	Active Independent	Weighted Value (5)	Liberator Supporter	Weighted Value (4)	Regional Sub-system Collaborator	Weighted Value (3)	Independent	Weighted Value (2)	Internal Development	Weighted Value (1)	Isolate	Weighted Value (0)	Weighted Total
1. Burma	64-68											2	4	2	2	6	0	6
2. Cambodia	64, 65-67											3	6			2	0	6
3. Ceylon	65-67									1	3	8	16	1	1			20
4. Congo (Braz.)	65-68							3	12	1	3	1	2					17
5. Congo (Kin.)	65-68							2	8	1	3							11
6. Egypt	63, 65-67	10	70	13	78	4	20	20	80	4	12							260
7. Ghana	66-68									2	6	5	10	1	1			17
8. Guinea	65-68	2	14					5	20	6	18							52
9. India	66-68			1	6	7	35	5	20			2	4	1	1			66
10. Indonesia	66-67	3	21			8	40	2	8	1	3	1	2	6	6			80
11. Iraq	66-68							3	12	6	18	7	14	1	1			45
12. Ivory Coast	65-67							1	4	1	3							7
13. Kenya	65-67	1	7							3	9	4	8					24
14. Kuwait	65-67							3	12	2	6	4	8					26
15. Laos	64-68											3	6			3	0	6
16. Lebanon	65-67									3	9	5	10					19
17. Liberia	57-59, 65-68							3	12					6	6			18
18. Mali	65-68							1	4	5	15	2	4					23
19. Morocco	65-68							1	4	7	21	1	2					27
20. Nepal	64-67							2	8			5	10			1	0	18
21. Niger	64-66, 68									4	12							12
22. Senegal	65-68									5	15	2	4					19
23. Singapore	66-67									1	3	2	4	4	4	3	0	11
24. Sudan	65-67			1	6			3	12	4	12	2	4					34
25. Syria	66-67							2	8	4	12	3	6					26
26. Tanzania	65-67							3	12	3	9	4	8	1	1			30
27. Tunisia	65-67					1	5			4	12	2	4	2	2			23
28. Uganda	65-68									1	3	3	6	3	3			12
29. Zambia	64-67					2	10	2	8			5	10					28

in both natural and social sciences (micro-macro linkages) [63] seems to be cared for ; and this is without having to choose between "Durkheimian unwillingness to explain 'social facts' psychologically" and various "reductionist failures". [64]

2.3.4. Operationally, the "personality" component helps us not only to avoid the reification of the state but to account for such a widespread —but controversial—concept as the "national interest". Our position here is the same as that of the decision-making model which explains state behaviour by the way its policy-makers define the situation. [65].

2.3.5. Empirically, the importance of the "personality" component lies not only in the fact that other foreign policy determinants *(i.e.* the systemic and the national) are mediated by the policy-makers' images, attitudes, values, beliefs, doctrines and ideologies [66] but also in the characteristics of the political (sub)system of most non-aligned actors. In these actors, a 'charismatic' [67] leader tends to play a monopolistic part in the policy-making process, with little possibility that he will be contradicted by other high officials. Hence, in these actors, the relative influence of the 'personality' component in foreign policy-making is accrued.

The review of the literature confirms this proposition. For instance, though Choucri accepts other determinants of non-alignment *(e.g.* alliance formation as such, strategic location, national capability, diplomatic sta-

---

[63] For a detailed discussion of this micro-macro linkage problem in economics, see Kuznets, Simon : "Parts and Wholes in Economics" in Daniel Lerner (ed.) : *Parts and Wholes,* New York, The Free Press, 1963.

[64] Greenstein : *Personality and Politics, op. cit.,* p. 24.

[65] As Snyder et al. stated : "We need to ... rid ourselves of the troublesome abstraction 'state'. It's one of our basic methodological choices to define the state as its official decision-makers—those whose authoritative acts are, to all intents and purposes, the acts of the state. *State action is the action taken by those acting in the name of the state."* Snyder et al. : *Foreign Policy Decision-Making, op. cit.,* p. 65.

[66] Holsti : *International Politics, op. cit.,* pp. 157-169.

[67] For the treatment of 'charisma' as expounded by Max Weber, see Weber, Max : *On Charisma and Institution-Building,* edited by Shmuel Eisenstadt, Chicago, The University of Chicago Press, 1968. Also Freund, Julien : *The Sociology of Max Weber,* New York, A Vintage Book, 1969, especially pp. 218-245. For an application of the concept to Afro-Asian leadership, see Apter, David : "Nkrumah, Charisma and the Coup", *Daedalus* (1968), pp. 757-793 ; Willner, Ann and Dorothy : "The Rise and Role of Charismatic Leaders", *Annals of the American Academy of Political and Social Science* (1965), pp. 77-89 ; Lacouture, Jean : *Quatre hommes et leurs peuples : le sous-développement et le sur-pouvoir,* Paris, Seuil, 1969. For a treatment of 'charisma' linking it to the general 'situation' of the new states, see Rustow, Dunkwart : *A World of Nations,* Washington D.C., The Brookings Institution, 1967, pp. 135-170. For a recent criticism of "conceptual stretching" in the study of 'Charisma', see Cohen, D. L. : "The Concept of Charisma and the Analysis of Leadership", *Political Studies,* XX (1972), pp. 299-305.

tus), she states that "in the last analysis, however, the *perceptual orientation* of the national leadership may well be the most significant determinant of a state's alignment or non-alignment". [68] This is confirmed by Shaw's analysis who qualifies foreign policy decisions in African and Asian states as "presidential decisions". [69] Moreover, detailed analyses of many new states have emphasised this 'personalised' aspect of the policy-making process, and link it not only to present societal characteristics of non-aligned actors, but also to their age-old cultural traditions and religious precepts. Thus, for instance, it was found that Islamic constitutional theory emphasises as its "sole important proposition" the personal qualifications of the ruler. Therefore, "most Islamic constitutional lawyers, in speaking of political leadership, emphasised specific personal qualifications. This emphasis was closely connected throughout Islamic history with military ability and prominence. There was rarely any serious discussion of checks to be placed upon the ruler, so he came to be accepted as the law-maker, dispenser of justice and chief executive". [70] If the leader combines with these personal qualities effective control over the sources of physical force *(i.e.* military leadership) his position is even stronger. These factors, then, help to explain why "the type of leadership has always been more important in Arab-Islamic societies" *(e.g.* Kassem in Iraq, or Qathafi in Libya) "than the type of political institutions", and why "a charismatic leader is more important in Egyptian politics than the mechanisms, checks and balances that loom large in Western political practice". [71] Precisely, the pattern of policy-making in Nasser's Egypt can be cited as a revealing example. Indeed there was a National Assembly, but it only recorded "its approval of (foreign) policies already decreed by the executive", and indeed there was a cabinet, but cabinet status was not the most important criteria for collaboration in policy-making ; for President Nasser continued "to make policy in consultation with a core of Free Officers closest and most loyal to him, and presently in executive positions, but *not necessarily with their real participation*". [72] Moreover, President Nasser was "not constitutionally responsible to any institutional checks upon his authority". [73]

---

[68] Choucri, Nazli : "The Perceptual Base of Non-alignment", *op. cit.*

[69] Shaw, Timothy : "African States and International Stratification : The Adaptive Foreign Policy of Tanzania", a paper submitted to *The Colston Symposium* on "Foreign Relations of African States", University of Bristol (England), April 1973.

[70] Vatikiotis, P. J. : "Foreign Policy of Egypt" in Macridis (ed.) : *Foreign Policy in World Politics* (2nd edition), 1962, *op. cit.*, pp. 335-361.

[71] *Ibid.*

[72] *Ibid.* (emphasis added).

[73] *Ibid.* And Vatikiotis adds : "The record and the proceedings of the First National Assembly (1957) in Egypt indicate that this body did not exercise any legislative function, but merely approved decisions already made by the executive-in-council".

While this hypothetical positive correlation between a 'personalised' policy-making process and an Arabic-Islamic culture merits further testing, we must nonetheless agree that this 'personalised' policy-making process is not limited to Arab-Moslim members of the non-aligned subsystem. For it was found that *International Relations in the New Africa* [74] follow the same pattern.

> "In few African states", Zartman affirmed, "does the opposition have access to national symbols or an opportunity to organise public opinion to the point where it becomes necessary for the group in power to defend itself with a particular foreign-policy action. The unit of interest referred to here is purely personal. Summit meetings enhance the local prestige of the party-government leader (they may thus also enhance his value as a central symbol for nation-building). Good relations are based most firmly on personal friendships drawn from common experiences in school, politics, labour unions or exile. Rapprochement is more frequently reached in terms of this common past than in terms of national interests. If there is no common past, rapprochement is contingent upon a personal meeting of the heads of state. An alliance functions when heads of state meet ; when they do not—even if lesser figures do—the alliance is often considered to be foundering. Bad relations are revealed through nasty comments about the head of state—not about the state itself and sometimes not even about the rest of the government." [75]

Looking at the actual decision-making process we find that it

> "derives from this situation and is focused on the president and the presidency. The declarations of the president become the national ideology, consecrated into "-isms" formed on the leader's name—such as Bourgibism, Nkrumahism, and ben Bellaism. Specific, even minute decisions are made by the President . . . His anger and his ardor, his whims and his convictions become the mood of his country's policy, and his friendships and acquaintances mark its limits. When the chief is absent—he must attend conferences and take vacations—or occupied with other problems, the progress of African relations awaits his return, for there is no alternative person or institution qualified to handle them. It is therefore necessary to deal with problems seriatim, so that long-term or sustained action in one field, such as African relations, is not possible and projects progress slowly. On the other hand, because of the personal nature of decisions, the roles and influence of all other groups and institutions changes are also possible. Within this pattern of relations and decisions, the roles and influences of all other groups and institutions work through the presidency and must be seen primarily as modifications of the rule of centralised personalised power." [76]

---

[74] This is the title of William Zartman's book : *op. cit.*

[75] *Ibid.,* pp. 53-54.

[76] *Ibid.,* p. 65.

Nor is the pattern of a 'personalised' foreign policy-making process reversed, as one might imagine, in those non-aligned actors which still apply substantially a form of the Western democracy model. Thus in the Indian multi-party political system which is supposed to check and restrain personal monopoly of the foreign policy-making process, Nehru remained supreme.

> "The influence of a Foreign Ministry varies widely from one state to another", Michael Brecher remarks. "Nowhere does one man dominate foreign policy as does Nehru in India. Indeed, Nehru is the philosopher, the architect, the engineer and the voice of his country's policy towards the outside world. This does not mean that he is entirely a free agent. It does mean, however, that he has impressed his personality and his views with such effect that foreign policy may properly be termed a private monopoly. . . .
>
> The decision to remain in the Commonwealth was, in the last analysis, Nehru's. India's Asian policy and the initiative for the Asian Relations Conferences in Delhi in 1947 and 1949 derive entirely from Nehru. So do the doctrine of peaceful coexistence (the Panch Sheel) and India's policy towards China and the Soviet Union. It was Nehru, too, who intervened with an offer of mediation in both Korea and Indo-China. Even in the execution of policy his role has been decisive—through his widespread travels which have taken him to China (1954), Russia (1955), the United States (1949 and 1956), South-East Asia (1950 and 1955), Japan (1957), many countries in Europe, and Great Britain (almost annually since 1948, usually for the Commonwealth Prime Ministers' Conference). He is then, Minister, chief policy planner and roving Ambassador . . ." [77]

It is because of the importance of this 'personalised' policy-making process in these countries that it is more apt to talk about "situation-role model", rather than simply "situational analysis".

2.4. Though there are other methodological-conceptual issues in the model that can still be elaborated upon, none is perhaps more significant than the ranking among the different components. Since the "definition of the situation" is the basis of foreign policy orientation, which component (systemic, national, personality) is the most crucial in defining the situation ? Within a certain component which variable is the most relevant *(e.g.* within the national component, is it historical influence, public opinion mood or geographical-topographical characteristics) ?

---

[77] Brecher, Michael : *Nehru : A Political Biography,* London, Oxford U.P., 1961, pp. 216-217. See also his more recent treatment of policy-makers' images as a (the ?) determinant of foreign policy—significantly entitled : *India and World Politics : Krishna Menon's View of the World, op. cit.*

2.4.1. The problem of the relative importance of the different components and variables is not a purely academic one, for pragmatic policy-makers must debate the issue. In fact, some policy-oriented controversies over the mainsprings of—for instance—Soviet foreign policy [78] illustrate the problem :

(i) some observers of Soviet politics give priority to "ideological imperatives" and argue that "all middle-range and long-range objectives and the diplomatic strategies used to achieve them are deduced from Marxism-Leninism" ;

(ii) other observers have emphasised "the persistence of purely 'national' themes in Soviet foreign policy" and insist that "the Soviet Union is primarily continuing Tsarist foreign policies, albeit under Communist slogans" ;

(iii) a third category of observers emphasise "the contemporary leadership qualities and role" as a more important component than ideology or traditional policies in Soviet external relations ; and

(iv) still a fourth type of explanation is that "the leadership is increasingly concerned with fulfilling domestic needs and responding to consumer demands. Thus, domestic needs and expectations will loom as important components of any definition of the situation". [79]

2.4.2. The review of the literature analysing the external relations of non-aligned actors reflects the same uncodified diversity.

(i) There are studies which emphasise the personality component, *i.e.* the idiosyncratic sources of policy-making. Thus one of the very few complete studies published recently on the foreign policy of a non-aligned state (Ghana) decides to begin "with an examination of Nkrumah's role, for Ghana's foreign policy was from the first his in character and stamp. It was most significantly a reflection of Nkrumah's characteristics and desires, of his perceptions of how the international system worked and of his reaction to external events." Consequently, the author affirms, "Ghana's foreign policy was Nkrumah's and a reflection of his moods and ambitions ». [80] Other scholars have generalised this conclusion to apply to *International Relations in the New Africa.* Accordingly, the different conflicts and feuds between Mali and Ivory Coast (1958-1960), Guinea and Ivory Coast (1958-1960), Upper Volta and Ivory Coast (1961), Ghana

[78] Holsti : *International Politics, op. cit.,* pp. 184-185.

[79] *Ibid.*

[80] Thompson, Scott : *Ghana's Foreign Policy, 1957-1966,* Princeton, Princeton U.P., 1969, pp. 415-421.

and Ivory Coast (1957-1964), Ghana and Togo (1957-1963), Mali and Senegal (1960-1963), Morocco and Algeria (1962-1964) and Tunisia and Algeria (1962-1963) were "either caused or prolonged by personal reactions of pride and anger usually felt by the head of a state". [81]

(ii) There is the opposite tendency that emphasises the 'national' component or the more 'permanent' variables shaping foreign policy *(e.g.* size, geographical location, historical and cultural background, industrial and military capabilities . . .). A representative sample of this tendency is the study on the foreign policy of Burma, [82] which has emphasised such "permanent" determinants as the religious-cultural (Buddhism), the historical *(e.g.* "colonial-capitalist experience"), geographical *(e.g.* closeness to China), the societal *(e.g.* problems of national unity), and the economic (economic underdevelopment). Similarly, in the study of Cambodia's foreign policy, [83] variables of the 'national' component such as *historical* feuds with both Thailand and Vietnam, *geographical* contiguity to these two "traditional enemies", and Cambodia's search for security are brought out to account for its brand of neutrality.

2.4.3. Though all the above interpretations are at least partly valid since the different variables listed *(e.g.* ideology, traditional policies, personal idiosyncracies, domestic determinants . . .) are all relevant to the foreign policy-making process, the question about the relative importance of each component in different circumstances remains unanswered. Indeed, some theorists of International Relations are grappling with the problem. [84] Thus Rosenau, for instance, has based his "Pre-Theory" of foreign policy on 5 sets of variables : the idiosyncratic, role, governmental, societal and systemic sets of variables. He then goes a step further to assess the relative influence of the variables by ranking them according to three criteria : size of the country (large versus small), state of the economy (developed versus underdeveloped) and type of political system (open versus closed). [85] The following table summarises both Rosenau's foreign policy variables as well as their rankings.

---

[81] Zartman : *International Relations in the New Africa, op. cit.,* p. 54.

[82] Johnstone, William : *Burma's Foreign Policy,* Cambridge, Mass., Harvard U.P., 1963.

[83] Smith, Roger : *Cambodia's Foreign Policy,* Ithaca, N.Y., Cornell U.P., 1969. Also included in this category is Phillips, Claude, Jr. : *The Development of Nigerian Foreign Policy,* Evanston, Northwestern U.P., 1964.

[84] See, for instance, Kaplan : *System and Process . . ., op. cit.,* pp. 54-75.

[85] Rosenau, James : "Pre-Theories and Theories of Foreign Policy" in Barry Farrell (ed.) : *Approaches to Comparative and International Politics, op. cit.,* pp. 27-93.

TABLE 3. *An Abbreviated Presentation of Rosenau's Pre-Theory of Foreign Policy, in Which Five Sets of Variables Underlying the External Behaviour of Societies are Ranked According to Their Relative Potencies in Eight Types of Societies*

Geography and physical resources	Large Country				Small Country			
State of the economy	Developed		Underdeveloped		Developed		Underdeveloped	
State of the policy	Open	Closed	Open	Closed	Open	Closed	Open	Closed
Rankings of the variables	Role Societal Govern-mental Systemic Idiosyn-cratic	Role Idiosyn-cratic Govern-mental Systemic Societal	Idiosyn-cratic Role Societal Systemic Govern-mental	Idiosyn-cratic Role Govern-mental Systemic Societal	Role Systemic Societal Govern-mental Idiosyn-cratic	Role Systemic Idiosyn-cratic Govern-mental Societal	Idiosyn-cratic Systemic Role Societal Govern-mental	Idiosyn-cratic Systemic Role Govern-mental Societal
Illustrative examples	U.S.	U.S.S.R.	India	China	Holland	Czecho-slovakia	Kenya	Ghana

We notice that in the category of actors that interest us here *(i.e.* the "underdeveloped"), Rosenau hypothesises that the personality component is the most important in *all* circumstances, for it occupies the first place whether the "underdeveloped" actor is large or small, an open or closed polity. In fact, a few pages later in the same article he states his hypothesis explicitly by saying that "the potency of an idiosyncratic factor is assumed to be greater in less developed economies" than in developed ones because there are "fewer of the restraints which bureaucracy and large scale organization impose in more developed economies". [86]

2.4.4. But Rosenau's hypothesis remains untested. This is only logical since historical information has not been processed to provide systematic, comparative analyses of foreign policies in different actors. Suggesting untested hypotheses [87] is the stage at which *Holsti,* too, stops. He remarks very realistically that

> "making foreign policy decisions and formulation of goals and objectives involve complex processes in which values, attitudes, and images mediate perceptions of reality provided by various sources of information. The resulting images or definitions of the situation form the reality and expectations upon which decisions are formulated. The components of any definition of a situation will vary with conditions in the system, internal political structure, degree of urgency in a situation, and political roles of policy-makers, but most definitions of a situation include estimations of capabilities, domestic reactions, and national role. How important each component may be in a given situation is difficult to predict . . ." [88]

2.5. In other words, in the absence of data-based studies, the primacy of a certain component in the actor's foreign policy-making process remains an empirical question. Thus at this stage we reemphasise the multivariate character of the proposed model by showing in matrix form the complementarity of the multi-level components in the choice of non-alignment.

Analytically, the determinants of an actor's non-alignment can be divided into internal or domestic variables, *i.e.* within the actor's boundaries ; and external, *i.e.* in its regional subsystem or in the global system. Moreover, these foreign policy determinants can be *general* to all or the majority of non-aligned actors, or *particular* to one or a limited group of them.

---

[86] *Ibid.*

[87] Holsti : *International Politics, op. cit.,* p. 186.

[88] *Ibid.,* p. 187.

TABLE 4. *An Illustrative Situation-Role Matrix of the Multi-Level Determinants of Non-Alignment*

Specificity Dimension	Spatial Dimension	
	External Situation	Internal Situation
General	1. Systemic Bipolarity 2. Cold War conflict	1. Historically newly-independent 2. Economically developing 3. Politically prismatic 4. Geo-culturally Afro-Asian
Particular	1. Arab-Israeli conflict for Arab actors 2. Contiguity to China for some Asian states 3. Western policies in South Africa and Rhodesia for some black African states	1. Leadership's national role conception and enactment 2. Intra- and/or inter-elite conflict and regime stability

The external/internal and general/particular dimensions can give us the following combinations of non-alignment determinants :

1. general external *(e.g.* the global systemic setting) ;
2. general internal *(e.g.* common structural characteristics of non-aligned actors) ;
3. particular external *(e.g.* some regional issues) ; and
4. particular internal *(e.g.* need to disarm the internal opposition).

We are thus far ahead of, for instance, the power paradigm's univariable 'explanation' of non-alignment. In addition to the multivariate emphasis, the matrix has the following advantages :

1. it provides a scheme for incorporating and classifying in a manageable form the varieties of non-alignment determinants observed and described in the literature [89] ;
2. consequently, it does not limit non-aligned behaviour to prescriptions of a given position *(e.g.* equidistance) that are supposed to apply to all non-aligned actors in all circumstances. Nor does it identify characteristic non-aligned behaviour with the policy of a non-aligned actor

[89] For a treatment of the gamut of motives determining non-alignment, see Crabb, Cecil, Jr. : *The Elephants and the Grass : A Study of Non-Alignment,* New York, Praeger, 1965, pp. 39-77 ; Lyon : *Neutralism, op. cit.,* pp. 89-177 ; Jansen, G. H. : *Afro-Asia and Non-alignment,* London, Faber, 1966, pp. 115-140 ; John Burton (ed.) : *Non-Alignment,* London, André Deutsch, 1966.

(*e.g.* Egypt, India, Yugoslavia). It can thus indicate that the choice and practice of non-alignment is a function of (*a*) a combination of different determinants in different non-aligned actors ; and/or (*b*) a varied combination of the same determinants [90] ;

3. the matrix can thus permit us to treat non-alignment both as an individual actor's foreign policy *behaviour (e.g.* of Ghana, Indonesia, Syria) ; and as an international *orientation* of a group of actors, *i.e.* an international subsystem. Thus, the more the determinants in square 4 are emphasised, the more behavioural specificities tend to prevail. Inversely, the more the shared determinants in squares 1 and 2 are emphasised, the greater the consensus among non-aligned actors and the higher the cohesion potential in their subsystem. [91]

2.6. *The Place of the Proposed Model in International Relations Theorisation*

The whole of this part has tried to address itself to some specific deficiencies in the field of foreign policy analysis, especially as far as non-aligned actors are concerned.

The alternative proposed here is based on a sort of empathy, for it takes as its starting point the frame of reference of non-aligned actors and aims to focus conceptualisation on components of their 'situation'. Moreover, the proposed model offers a way to build upon the contributions of other approaches to foreign policy analysis, while helping to minimise their drawbacks.

For instance, apart from the fact that the decision-making model is taxing for the researcher, and might not be very applicable in the case of non-aligned actors, its results might not in the end compensate the researcher's heavy investment or his aspirations for a cumulative knowledge contributing to theory-building. Indeed, decisions as the unit of analysis and the dependent variable might lead—because of their unique characteristics—to "reconstructed history with emphasis on the actions of unique individuals operating within unique organisations, in a unique set of historical circumstances". [92]

That is why the situation-role model [93] advocated here is more useful, for it can claim to contribute not only to the development of foreign-policy

---

[90] *Ibid.*

[91] These are "more-or-less" rather than "either ... or" propositions.

[92] Holsti : "National Role Conceptions ...", *op. cit.*

[93] See the 'linkage' between 'role' and 'situation' as explicited in Allport : *Pattern and Growth in Personality, op. cit.*, pp. 165-196.

analysis, but also to that of International Relations, and this is in two ways :

1. Students of International Relations are mainly interested in the structure and functioning of past and contemporary international systems, and they use a mode of systems analysis to meet their concerns. But this mode of analysis "tends to regard behavior as a reflection of the characteristics of a social system containing a series of impersonal processes which are external to the actors and constrain them".[94] In emphasising a situation-role analysis, students of foreign policy are attracting attention to the fact that the assumption of interchangeability among the actors of the international system is—beyond a certain point—dysfunctional. In this way the student of foreign policy is contributing to balance the picture offered by the student of international systems, and that is by seeking to underline the fact that the actor does not merely react to the "machine-like character", or "mechanical laws" of the system, but that rather it has its own objectives, its own perception of "reality" and both determine its means-end formula.

2. The treatment of this means-end formula would not be primarily (as the decision-making model advises) through the detailed inquiry into "the decision-making processes of a single government in one brief, atypical scene (usually crisis situation)", which would not, in any case, be of much interest to the student of the theory of International Relations.[95] The latter's interest is international systems, and he is thus concerned with "the *typical* behaviour of all states over a considerable period of time, changes in critical variables and the totality of foreign policy decisions and actions conceived as resulting in identifiable interaction patterns".[96] A situation-role model, through its emphasis on the actor's general orientation and type of commitments as well as its behaviour, attains a level of generality appropriate for both foreign policy frameworks and international systems studies. Thus in foreign policy analysis, it can be used to account for the dependent variable : the actor's *output* (*i.e.* his foreign policy orientation and/or behaviour) which is—for the student of international systems—one *input* or independent variable in international systems analysis.[97]

With such necessary "linkages" and refinements, we hope to move from a semi-eternalised tradition of "heuristic" abstraction on to the conceptual questions and empirically-based answers which would bring us nearer to a cumulative science of International Relations.

---

[94] Silverman, David : *The Theory of Organisations,* London, Heineman, 1970, p. 141.

[95] Holsti : "National Role Conceptions . . .", *op. cit.*

[96] *Ibid.* (emphasis added).

[97] *Ibid.* (emphasis added).

PART TWO

Non-Alignment as a Foreign Policy Orientation

CHAPTER IV

Some common Systemic-National Components in the Afro-Asians' 'Definition of the Situation' and Non-Alignment as an International Orientation[1]: Observed Correlations

In applying the proposed model, a basic question in current International Relations theorisation has to be faced : whether the application would aim at an *inclusive* inventory of (sets of) variables or a *selective* one. We have opted for the second solution. This option is justified since :

(*a*) the decision-making model has resulted in an overcrowded and almost unresearchable taxonomy, rather than "a map of factors accurate and concise enough to guide the researcher to the important points", [2] and

(*b*) by attempting to be inclusive, the suggested "pre-theories and theories of foreign policy" [3] have missed the distinction between such basic problems to non-aligned actors as those of social change, and others not so basic, since all are equally buried amid a host of other "non-governmental" variables.

[1] For the definition of this term in sociological theory, see Parson and Shils (eds.) : *Toward a General Theory of Action, op. cit.* For an example of its treatment in International Relations by a sociologist, see Lagos : *op. cit.* Some International Relations students have equated it with "fundamental strategy". Thus Holsti states : "... by orientation we mean a state's general attitudes and commitments toward the external environment, its fundamental strategy for accomplishing its domestic and external objectives and aspirations. A nation's general strategy or orientation is seldom revealed in any one decision, but results from a series of cumulative decisions made in an effort to adjust objectives, values and interests to conditions and characteristics of the domestic and external environments." Holsti : *International Politics, op. cit.*, p. 198.

[2] Hveem, Helge : *op. cit.*

[3] Rosenau : "Pre-Theories and Theories ...", *op. cit.*

1. **The systemic component**

In chapter two, we have dealt with the payoffs of 'systems theory' as far as foreign policy analysis is concerned. Moreover, in the preceding chapter we have mentioned how environmental or systemic variables are considered a "given", a parameter in the choice of the non-aligned actors' foreign policy. Consequently, we will confine ourselves here to treating the "systemic component" primarily in its subjective aspect (the psychological as opposed to the operational environment) *i.e.* as the non-aligned actors perceive it ; for on the basis of this perception they choose their foreign policy objectives and general orientation.

1.1. This international system is perceived as "a great social system composed of different groups interacting". These "national groups *occupy various positions* within the (international) social system". [4] Consequently their perception of the general structure and functioning of the system is influenced by their position in it ; and theirs is a position of demanders of "aid", of economic dependence and, frequently, of political subordination. [5] This relationship of subordination-superordination, dependence-dominance or periphery-centre is typical of a system of *social stratification.* [6] What determines and/or changes the position of an actor in this stratified system ? Sociological theory on social stratification divides the criteria determining the actor's position into two categories : (*a*) objective material criteria (*e.g.* material wealth), and (*b*) subjective criteria (*e.g.* deference, esteem). Adapting these sociological formulations

---

[4] Lagos : *op. cit.,* ch. I (emphasis added). For further application of the stratification concept to the international system, see also Horowitz, Irving : *Three Worlds of Development : The Theory and Practice of International Stratification,* New York, Oxford U.P., 1966. A student of International Relations talks about the "cobweb" model ; see Burton, John : *World Society,* London, Cambridge U.P., 1972 ; and a sociologist writing on International Relations bases his analysis on an "octopus" paradigm : Jenkins, Robin : *Exploitation,* London, Paladin, 1971. Note also this statement by Nehru : "remember", he cautioned members of parliament in 1950, "... the world has many countries. Some of them are called great powers by virtue of their influence. They are nations with great resources behind them and inevitably play a significant part in the world's history to-day ... The most relevant fact at the moment is that *there are some great nations in the world with concentrated power in their hands that influence all other nations*". Nehru : *India's Foreign Policy, op. cit.,* pp. 52-53 (emphasis added).

[5] Thus, the basic problem of inequality tends to be perceived in terms of states rather than in terms of classes. As the sociologist Bendix has pointed out, the "class differences in underdeveloped areas have remained subordinate to the more decisive conflict between these areas and the industrialized countries". Lagos : *op. cit.,* p. 6. Among 'third world' leaders, both Sekou Touré and Sukarno tended to transfer the class-conflict concept to the international systemic level.

[6] See footnote 4, above.

to our specific concerns as students of foreign policy analysis, we can decide on three criteria that determine the actor's position in the international system :

(1) Level of socio-economic development : this criteria can be easily translated into measurable indicators *(e.g.* size of GNP, economic ranking, literacy rate, physicians per one million . . .).

(2) Level of military capabilities *(e.g.* technological advance, percentage in world military expenditures . . .).

This is as far as the material criteria are concerned, but there remains a third (subjective) criteria [7] which is

(3) Prestige : defined as essentially "a sentiment in the minds of men that is expressed in . . . (intergroup) interaction". Prestige is thus the image that one has of an actor, when this image is associated with a positive evaluation, *i.e.* imbued with social esteem, honour or admiration. [8]

Though a national actor might occupy the same position on each of these three ranking criteria, this need not be the case. In fact, the relative positions of the international actor on each of these scalar criteria might well not coincide. That is why it is the sum of the distinct positions that the actor occupies on each of these ranking criteria that determines its general ranking position in the international system—its status-set. [9] In other words, the status-set is the result of adding distinct positions on the objective-material criteria (socio-economic development and military capability which establish a "measurable" scale of social differentiation among international actors, *e.g.* big versus small, developed versus developing, rich versus poor) and the subjective one *(i.e.* social ranking of the international actor according to the prestige that is conferred on it by the system's members).

1.2. Applying these theoretical formulations to the position of non-aligned actors within the stratified international system, there is a point to be emphasised. The norms of the international system *(e.g.* as incorporated in international law or in the U.N. Charter) bestow *(formal)* equal

[7] According to some sociologists, this subjective criteria represents a synthesis of all the other (objective-material) criteria of ranking. Thus, for instance, in the international system an actor might possess and even increase its objective criteria of status, yet because there is no degree of conformity between its international behaviour and the value orientations that happen to be predominant in the specific international system, the actor suffers a loss of esteem, deference or prestige (*e.g.* France during the Algerian war, the U.S. on the Vietnam issue, South Africa). The converse can also be true.

[8] Lagos : *op. cit.,* p. 132.

[9] Robert Merton defined the status-set as "the complex of distinct positions assigned to individuals both within and among social systems", *Social Theory and Social Structure,* New York, The Free Press (revised edition), 1957, p. 380.

status on all members of the system : developed and developing, big and small, rich and poor. Yet looking at the ranking of newly-independent actors along the easily measurable, material criteria of stratification, we find that they occupy a low status. Moreover, if the discrepancy between their formal and real status is not halted, it will end by affecting the third criteria of the status-set, *i.e.* prestige. In other words, the continuation of this discrepancy will result in a process of atimia—the deterioration or loss of status. Thus the fear of atimia, the need for recognition, [10] and the awareness of underdevelopment constitute crucial variables of their 'definition of the situation', as evidenced by such instances as :

(1) The emphasis on "underdevelopment" appears almost constantly in official declarations and statements of these actors.

(2) The use of this term is not limited to official governmental circles, but is used in the press and by political organizations, which indicates that it has penetratd the polity's political culture and its language of political communication.

But

> "if prestige is represented by an image of admiration, esteem and honor, how can the underdeveloped nations, which are the "retarded" nations in the international system, be accredited prestige in a world dominated by the values of wealth and power, when by definition they do not possess such attributes ? How can their condition of underdevelopment, characterized by subordination and dependence within the international system, awaken admiration and social recognition by other nations . . ." [11]

1.3. That is why the elevation of status should be based on sources other than the slow and gradual process of socio-economic development and/or military capability. Hence our hypothesis that these newly-independent actors aimed to raise their status by means of a foreign policy orientation of national self-assertion through non-alignment. This foreign policy orientation may raise status in two ways.

1.3.1. *Exploitation of the bipolar systemic structure to increase the actor's influence :* indeed "when the scales are evenly balanced", Nehru said, "even a single country can make a difference". The example of

---

[10] In the first international conference organised by Asians and entitled Asian Relations Conference (Delhi, March 1947), Nehru expressed this need for recognition : "For too long", he said, "have we of Asia been petitioners in Western courts and chancelleries ... That story must now belong to the past ... We do not intend to be the playthings of others." See Brecher, Michael : *Nehru,* London, Oxford U.P., 1961, p. 129.

[11] Lagos : *op. cit.,* p. 138.

Yugoslavia in the late 1940's can clearly illustrate how the adoption of non-alignment can effect the actor's status, and this is without a change in its own economic or military capability. [12] In adopting this position the non-aligned may be indulging in a reperformance of the "balance of power" scheme, and Nehru betrayed himself in the above quotation and also in declaring in April 1954 : "When the opposing forces are fairly evenly matched, then it is possible to make our weight felt in the balance." Moreover, a scholar has recently based all his research on this hypothesis. [13] But whatever the name given to the practice that permitted this outcome, the end result is that an underdeveloped actor could find itself "a factor to be contended with" in the international system, as Egyptian decision-makers emphasised. As Nasser himself expressed it when welcoming Nkrumah in Cairo in 1958 :

> "If we are tied to one of the blocs, we would be a weightless appendage whose word does not have any influence. An independent policy based on non-alignment and positive neutralism will, on the contrary, make of our countries a great force permitting an independent say. Such a position would be met with respect from all over the world." [14]

Nehru was equally explicit :

> "We counted for something ... though *actually we need not have counted for much* ... The fact of the matter is that inspite of *our weakness in a military sense,* because we are obviously not a great military power, we are not an industrially advanced power, India even to-day counts in world affairs ... Because we count ... everything we do becomes a matter for comment and many people do not like our counting so much ..."

---

[12] This position is similar to that of the third party in a two-party political system. Talcott Parsons has developed this argument, but more closely related to our concerns, see Fayez Sayegh (ed.) : *The Dynamics of Neutralism in the Arab World,* San Francisco, Chandler Publishing Co., 1964, part I.

[13] Rana, A. : *A Framework for the Analysis of India's Foreign Policy Strategy in the Nehru Period.* A Ph.D. dissertation submitted to the Graduate Institute of International Studies, 1973, pp. 26-128, 152. Another scholar has remarked: "... Inasmuch as she (India) sought to get her status and prestige enhanced and exerted her influence through these endeavours, and tried to preserve her weight for keeping the balance, even though in favour of peace, her non-alignment ... was a calculated projection for power and a move, with a difference, of power politics." Mallik, Deva : *The Development of Non-Alignment in India's Foreign Policy,* Allahabad, Chaitanya Publishing House, 1967, p. 49.

[14] *Nasser' Speeches,* vol. II, Cairo, Information Department, n.d., pp. 133-135 (Arabic edition).

If, on the other hand, the newly-independent, underdeveloped actor joined one of the East-West blocs

> "... We are not respected by any party, we may get some petty benefits, but ultimately even these may be denied us."

Consequently,

> "If you give it (non-alignment) up, there is no other policy for this country to adopt with the slightest advantage ... Therefore, purely, from the point of view of opportunism, if you like, a straightforward honest policy, an independent policy, is the best." [15]

And if the size of aid given by the two superpowers can be used as an indicator of the international weight of a newly-independent, developing actor, India and Egypt received the greatest amount of Soviet aid among all newly-independent underdeveloped actors ($1011 and $1022 million respectively with the mean being $902 million, the standard deviation 2555 million, the range $16,235 million, and the number of states 44). Moreover, U.S. economic aid to Egypt amounted to $945 million and to India $4893 million (compared with the amount given to the fellow-member of the Western alliance system, Pakistan, $2360 million). [16]

If the number of diplomats received in the national capital is another indicator of influence and (high) ranking, Egypt received 559 diplomats, India 530, compared to Pakistan's 321. Even actors plotted higher on material criteria of ranking received less. For instance, Switzerland, Sweden, Denmark, Czechoslovakia, received 315, 287, 231, 321, respectively. [17]

1.3.2. *Conformity with the norms of (international) system-maintenance :* non-aligned actors search to raise their status by stating that their foreign policy orientation is almost the only course that could help in the establishment of peace during the cold war era. At Bandung Nehru asked: "If all the world were to be divided up between these two big blocs, what would be the result ?", and he went on to answer :

> "The inevitable result would be war. Therefore every step that takes place in reducing that area in the world which may be called

---

[15] Nehru, Jawaharlal : *India's Foreign Policy,* Delhi, Minister of Information and Broadcasting, 1961, pp. 30, 36-37 (emphasis added), as quoted in Rana : *op. cit.,* pp. 148-149.

[16] Dates for U.S. aid are 1958-1963 and for Soviet aid 1954-1955-1965. For greater details, see Charles Taylor, Michael Hudson et al. (eds.) : *World Handbook of Political and Social Indicators,* New Haven, Yale U.P. (2nd edition), 1972, pp. 360-365.

[17] Alger, Chadwick, and Brams, Steven : "Patterns of Representation in National Capitals and Intergovernmental Organizations", *World Politics,* XIX (1966-1967), pp. 346-363. Dates for all data are 1963-1964.

the unaligned area is a dangerous step and leads to war. It reduces that objective, that balance, that outlook which other countries *without military might* perhaps exercise." [18]

Thus non-alignment reduces the tension-maintaining, strait-jacket aspect in the international system and introduces structural flexibility. Moreover, by keeping contacts with both blocs in the early phase of the bipolar international system, and by accepting aid from both superpowers, non-aligned actors could show in practice the values of peaceful competition between the blocs as an alternative to mutual suicide. Not surprisingly, they insisted—as Tito expressed it—that they represented "the conscience of the world" and constituted—as Nehru repeated—an "area of peace".

The representation of non-aligned actors in the Disarmament talks, [19] the suggestion of Egypt's Marechal Amer as the third man in Krushchev's troika project, participation of non-aligned actors in the U.N. peace-keeping operation, [20] and non-aligned India's role in the Korean conflict (which was disproportionate to its socio-economic and military capabilities) are all indicators of non-alignment as a status-raising orientation in this respect. As Nehru again explicited :

> "... Progressively, people see that within the United Nations things are done far from the idealistic, moral way, or in terms of the underdog, the smaller nations, or the Asian nations. Therefore, more and more of these people try to find someone else ..." [21]

That is why

> "... We have laboured to the best of our ability for world peace. We realize that our influence in such matters can only be limited, because we are not in possession of, nor have we the capacity to possess weapons like the modern nuclear weapons. Still our influence has not been negligible. *This is not because we ourselves are influential but because we do believe that what we have said in regard to peace has found an echo in people's minds and hearts in all countries* ... Inspite of governmental policies, the people have appreciated what we have said and reacted to it favourably ..." [22]

---

[18] Emphasis added. Sukarno talked about "the mobilisation of the moral violence of people" to express the same idea.

[19] Ahmed, Samir : *The Neutrals and the Test Ban Negotiations : An Analysis of the Non-Aligned States' efforts between 1962 and 1963,* New York, Carnegie Endowment for International Peace, Occasional Paper No. 4, 1967 ; Crabb : *op. cit.*

[20] *Ibid.,* pp. 112-134.

[21] Nehru : *India's Foreign Policy, op. cit.,* p. 34.

[22] *Ibid.* (emphasis added).

2. **The National Component**

It would have been very useful to deal with each of the four domestic variables listed in square 2 of the matrix, and try to correlate them with the adoption of non-alignment. But since this is too vast a job to be handled adequately in the space available here, we have chosen one of these variables characteristic of the general internal "situation" of non-aligned actors : their prismatic political system. [23] Its choice has been governed by various calculations :

1. It is the variable that falls most within the competence of a political scientist (as the "economically less developed" variable would be for the economist).

2. The prismatic political system can act as a "summary variable", for it is linked to the other domestic variables and thus its treatment will shed light on the others too. For instance, one cannot treat the problem of the prismatic political system without considering the process of social change. And one cannot deal with this latter without treating the effects of the "colonial intrusion" which disturbed these societies. Moreover, the process of social change and the resultant prismatic political system are both affected by the rate of economic development and in turn affect it. Lastly, one cannot deal with the political system in rapidly changing societies without mentioning their "search for identity" as Afro-Asian states.

Three Basic Arguments :

1. The process of social change (as the process of social persistence) is a characteristic of societies ;
2. this process of social change implies conflict between the persistent and the 'becoming' which will on occasions lead to a state of 'social disorganisation', [24] and

[23] For an elaboration on this theme, see the works of Fred Riggs, especially : *Administration in Developing Countries : The Theory of Prismatic Society,* Boston, Houghton, Mifflin, 1964 ; especially pp. 206-240 ; "The Theory of Political Development" in James Charlesworth (ed.) : *Contemporary Political Analysis,* New York, The Free Press, 1967, pp. 217-250 ; "The Dialactics of Developmental Conflict", *Comparative Political Studies,* I (1968), pp. 197-226 ; "System Theory : Structural Analysis Reconsidered", in Michael Haas and Henry Kariel (eds.) : *Approaches to the Study of Political Science,* San Francisco, Chandler, 1970.

[24] In their monumental work, *The Polish Peasant in Europe and America* (Boston, Gorham Press, 1918-1920), W. Thomas and F. Znaniecki defined social disorganisation as "the decrease of the influence of existing social rules of behavior upon individual members of the group". See Madge, John : *The Origins of Scientific Sociology* (London, Tavistock, 1963, pp. 52-88) for a very insightful analysis.

3. that the process of social disorganisation and conflict is singularly acute in Afro-Asian non-aligned actors.

These three basic arguments make the adoption of non-alignment the functional response to the psycho-societal situation of Afro-Asian actors. We take these arguments one by one.

2.1. *The Universality of the Process of Social Change*

The observation of different societies—even the so-called 'stagnant' ones—shows that fluctuation, transformation and mutation are an inherent aspect of social reality. This universality of the process of social change has justified its separate treatment as a sub-discipline in sociological theory.

Yet it is precisely the process' generality and universality that create difficulties in its conceptualisation. If considered as a subfield of inquiry, social change appears to occupy "a kind of no man's land between sociology and history". [25] Thus when we consider it as the "systematic study of variations in social life", it is not very different from the definition of sociology as a whole. If social change is viewed—on the other hand—as the study of the "unfolding of man's social arrangements through time, it appears to be indistinguishable from social history." [26] This overlapping —leading to difficulties in conceptualisation—is manifested in the sociologist's complaints about the lack of a theory of social change. [27] But rather than reviewing the arguments and counter-arguments about the theory of social change, I shall limit myself to two objectives :

(*a*) Methodologically, I will not dwell on individual cases of social change or the comparative applicability of particular historical generalisations, but deal mainly with "ideal-type" constructs following Max Weber's example [28] ;

---

[25] Giner, Salvador : *Sociology,* London, Martin Robinson, 1972, pp. 264-287.

[26] *Ibid.*

[27] Cohen : *Modern Social Theory, op. cit.,* pp. 174-236.

[28] According to Weber "an ideal type is formed by the one-sided accentuation of one or more points of view and by the synthesis of a great many diffuse, discrete, more or less present and occasionally absent concrete individual phenomena, which are arranged according to those one-sidedly emphasised viewpoints into a *unified analytical construct*" (emphasis added). It thus seeks perfection of a logical and not a moral order, to stress what is characteristic, distinctive, or 'typical'. Such generic terms as christianity, Islam, feudalism, capitalism, democracy, nation-state, industrial society are ideal-types which—in their *conceptual purity*—rarely exist in reality. This is why ideal-types, in themselves, are neither absolutely true nor absolutely false, but simply—like any other analytical tool—useful or useless. For a

(*b*) Substantively, I shall not deal with the effects of social change in the different societal sectors except in so far as they affect the structure and functioning of the national system as a whole.

But before proceeding any further, it is important to state the meaning of 'social change' as it is used here. Social change can be defined as "the observed difference between the earlier and the later states of a given area of social reality, or rather *what happens between these two moments in time. Thus, change is not the final observed modification but the processes leading toward it.*" [29]

But since social change is defined as a process, it should have—like any other process—sources and consequences. As for the sources or mechanisms which produce change, one notices that social theorists have emphasised on the whole, since the 18th century, single-variable explanation of social change, and that those theories emphasising the primarily endogenous sources of change (*e.g.* the technological theory, the economic theory, the conflict theory, the malintegration theory) are more dominant in the literature than those emphasising exogenous sources (*e.g.* the cultural interaction theory, the adaptation theory, and also the ideational theory). [30]

As far as Afro-Asian actors are concerned this can already be a weakness in the sociological literature on social change. For in any treatment of Afro-Asian non-aligned actors, a big part of the analysis should be devoted to the influence of the 'colonial relationship' [31] on the structure and functioning of these societies, leading in many cases not only to change in the social system but also—through an intensive cumulative process—to change of the system. [32] This brings us to our second argument : the consequences of this (continuing) process of social change and its impact on the political (sub)system—whose agents plan and direct foreign policy.

---

succinct discussion of Weber's methodology, especially the ideal-type, see for instance : Aron, Raymond : *Main Currents in Sociological Thought,* London, Penguin, vol. II, pp. 185-259, but especially pp. 202-210 ; Fletcher, Ronald : *The Making of Sociology : A Study of Sociological Theory,* London, Nelson's University Paperbacks, 1972, vol. II, pp. 411-439 ; Freund, Julien : *The Sociology of Max Weber.* The French edition was published by P.U.F. in 1966, but the references here are to the 1969 Vintage Book edition, pp. 59-70.

[29] Giner : *op. cit,* p. 264 (emphasis added).

[30] Cohen : *op. cit.,* pp. 174-208.

[31] Worsley : *The Third World, op. cit.,* pp. 21-31.

[32] For the conceptual issues, see Smelser, Neil : *Essays in Sociological Explanation,* Englewood Cliffs, Prentice Hall, 1968, pp. 192-280 ; and Wiseman, H. : *Political Systems : Some Sociological Approaches,* New York, Praeger, 1966. The statement in the text does not—of course— prejudge the question of 'internal dynamism' of pre-colonial Afro-Asian societies, but only aims to emphasise the "cultural shock"

2.2. *Social Change and Social Disorganisation*

The colonial intrusion, then, has resulted in imported political and economic institutions as well as foreign attitudes and ideas. These two effects have injected (into Afro-Asian societies) *elements of instability* which they have never experienced before. Consequently, it is impossible for most of these societies—should they so desire—to return (purely and simply) to their own former varieties of social organisation. It is this 'falling between two stools' which some students of "Comparative Politics" and "Political Development" have labelled the "transitional process", [33] and which a prominent authority in the field has described in a very telling way :

> "Old forms of belief and social practices endowed with sanctity are often dismissed with cruelty and carelessness by those in positions of power. A cheerful confrontation of the future may easily be replaced by deep-rooted despair. For many, modernization is like hurtling

---

or the "social disturbance" caused by the colonial intrusion. As a black African has noticed "our societies were like a clock, and the coming of colonialism has upset them". Geiger expressed the same idea when he stated that the colonial intrusion into the "traditional" societies of Afro-Asia "has introduced ... novel influences that are not simply inconsistent with, but have been actively eroding and disintegrating, its memorial institutions, attitudes and behavioral norms". For a detailed treatment of these imported factors of social disorganisation (*e.g.* rapid population explosion, market economy, Western forms of government and administration, foreign law practices), see Geiger, Theodore : *The Conflicted Relationship : The West and the Transformation of Asia, Africa and Latin America,* New York, McGraw-Hill, 1967, ch. II, but especially pp. 57-68.

[33] This is the labellation that seems to dominate most of social science literature dealing with problems of political change and development. See, for instance, Geiger : *op. cit.,* pp. 84-125, 134-137, and whose chapter II is entitled "The Nature and Outcome of the Transitional Process in Asia and Africa" and starts with a "model of the Transitional Process". See also Hagen, Everett : *On the Theory of Social Change,* Homewood, The Dorsey Press, 1962, whose part II (pp. 185-261) is entitled "The Transition to Economic Growth". Some writers use the term "transition" even in the titles of their books, *e.g.* Harvey Kebschull (ed.) : *Politics in Transitional Societies : The Challenge of Change in Asia, Africa and Latin America,* New York, Appleton Century Crofts, 1968. Some writers do not use the labellation itself, but use the concept. For instance Rustow : *op. cit.,* especially pp. 148-170, and whose chapter IV (pp. 105-135) treats both "Blends of Tradition and Modernity" and "The Problem of Sequence" in political "modernisation". Indeed the implicit assumption of a "transition process" is at the basis of diacronic studies on "sequences" and "stages" of "political development", whether they are of the 'conservative' type (*e.g.* Shils, Edward : *Political Development in the New States,* The Hague, Mouton, 1962) or of the 'radical' type (*e.g.* Moore, Barrington, Jr. : *Social Origins of Dictatorship and Democracy,* London, Penguin, 1969). This "transition process" approach is one of the main points raised in some of the literature critical of present "modernization theory" ; see for instance : Bernstein, Henry : "Moderni-

through a tunnel at frightening speed without knowing what waits at the other end. Fear creates serious political problems. Hence, it is not surprising that in modernizing societies the mood fluctuates between an exciting sense of new freedom and hope in the future and a fearful, cynical, or opportunistic view." [34]

2.2.1. This social disorganisation can be dealt with at both the individual (elite) level and the societal level (with the process of socialisation constituting a link between the two levels). [35] For in Afro-Asian societies, the so-called national "culture paradigm" that is supposed to be transferred to the individual during the socialisation process is not free from inconsistencies. Naturally, these inconsistencies and incompatibilities in the 'national' culture paradigm would affect the individual's sense of identity and his learning of roles to be played in social groups and institutions. Of course, Western societies themselves face seemingly similar problems of alienation, anomie and identity-crisis ; but the dimension of the problem is quite different in Afro-Asian societies. For in Western societies, whatever the inconsistencies and the conflicting roles in the culture paradigm may be, they are still "parts of a single culture, share a common history and have developed *organically* within the same social system". [36] This is different from the 'situation' of Afro-Asian non-aligned societies, which (generally) contain "two sets of paradigms, roles, values and standards" : one is indigenous, familiar and deep-rooted and the other alien, imported and, in many cases, half-assimilated. [37]

But this state of affairs would not only affect the individual's sense of identity but also the group's and social cohesion generally, since the culture paradigm is supposed to be the "directive system" which guides people on how to perceive, feel, interpret, think and perform in the desired

---

sation Theory and the Sociological Study of Development", *Journal of Development Studies* (1971), pp. 141-161 ; Frank, André : *Sociology of Development and Underdevelopment of Sociology,* London, Pluto Press, 1971 ; and Mazrui, Ali : "From Social Darwinism to Current Theories of Modernization", *World Politics* (1968), pp. 69-83. Other writers use the labellation "transitional" to emphasise the possibility of "breakdowns" during the transformation process of 'third world' societies ; see for instance : Halpern, Manfred : "The Revolution of Modernization in National and International Society" in Robert Jackson and Michael Stein (eds.) : *Issues in Comparative Politics,* New York, St. Martin's Press, pp. 39-60.

[34] Apter : *Politics of Modernization, op. cit.,* p. viii.

[35] From the point of view of sociologists, socialisation involves the internalisation of the distinctive values and the cultural concepts and norms that are at the basis of the preservation and transference of relationships and institutions among generations. From the point of view of psychologists, this internalisation is part of the psychological process of personality formation.

[36] Geiger : *op. cit.,* p. 89 (emphasis added).

[37] *Ibid.*

ways—what Nelson called "cue sets". [38] The instability of these cue sets —due to the heterogeneity and inconsistency in the culture paradigm— pushes the Afro-Asian societies toward the inconsistency-instability end of Nelson's scale. The results of this "situation" for Afro-Asian societies is clear since

> "societies which tend toward the inconsistent-unstable-incongruous end of the scale are bound to suffer from crises of identity, excessively conflicted motivations and attitudes within individuals and groups, ambivalent behavior, apathy and depersonalisation". [39]

This problem of (diffuse) identification is felt almost in daily life by the individual in Afro-Asian societies, since he is participating

> "in a growing number of contrasting and often conflicting old and new social units—on the one hand, the traditional extended family, village, tribe, caste and sect ; and on the other hand, the modern nuclear family, productive enterprise, trade union, political party, social club and atomized urban mass". [40]

The members of the new elite groups (*e.g.* political leaders, government administrators, entrepreneurs, managers, professionals and intellectuals) are the most severely affected by these conflicting cues and roles included in the 'national' culture paradigm. A look at an 'ideal-type' process of personality-formation and role-determination of the Afro-Asian elites would illustrate these severe effects [41] :

(*a*) Most of them have been born and have grown up in some variant of extended family, even though they have spent a big part of their lives in the town rather than in the countryside. Affective personalised kinship relationships were characteristic of their social context, and the individual is accustomed to the warmth and emotional security provided by the extended family and the various lineage affiliations.

(*b*) Through school education (especially in the pre-independence period) or study abroad they have been exposed to another culture paradigm which contests for their loyalty. Moreover, they support their nuclear families through various activities in the "modern sector" with its impersonal institutions based on (Western) legal concepts. They have come to feel that the achievement of a higher standard of living and upward social mobility depend on their personal performance in this "modern sector", and on their effort to advance these Western-based institutions. Moreover, the new authorities they work under were the colonial

---

[38] Nelson, Benjamin : "Actors, Directives, Roles, Cues, Meanings, Identities", *The Psychoanalytic Review,* LI (1964), pp. 135-160.

[39] Geiger : *op. cit.,* p. 91.

[40] *Ibid.,* pp. 88-99.

[41] *Ibid.*

head or are the Western-educated indigenous elite who direct the new impersonal institutions of society.

(*c*) Consequently, inconsistencies are bound to arise in their value orientations between, for instance, the "exclusive tribal or caste brotherhood" and the "imported religious and political concepts". Thus because they have been habituated as children to recognise "without question the authority and example of the traditional head of the household (father, maternal uncle, older brother or cousin) and of the other elders of the village, tribe, caste or sect with which their family is traditionally affiliated", they continue—as adults—

> "to acknowledge, or to feel uncomfortable in denying, the traditional family obligations of mutual sharing of output or income, of defending and advancing relatives' interests, and of according these claims a priority that overrides even their own self-interest. They are expected to provide jobs for relatives regardless of their employment qualifications and to divert often substantial portions of their own earnings or capital . . . to help parents, brothers, uncles, cousins and other relatives to live better, to start a business, to send their children to school, to pay their taxes and fines, and in other ways to share freely with anyone who falls within the degrees of kinship recognized by custom." [42]

(*d*) In many cases, individuals are incapable of handling these conflicts without passing through different degrees of tension. Although very few studies on the psychiatric disorders that can result from this value conflict and role-strain have been conducted in the field, the little evidence at hand indicates

> "a high percentage of the particular kinds of psychiatric illnesses that could be expected in such circumstances : psychosomatic headaches and gastrointestinal symptoms, neuroses of the anxiety and depressive types, and schizophrenic psychoses". [43]

But most people try to meet this value-conflict and role-strain by trying to compartmentalise their lives, and where they fail to do so they accustom themselves to live with social ambiguities and inner conflict. Thus examples are not rare of

> "Asian cabinet ministers who consult astrologers before making important decisions ; African presidents and prime ministers who use witchcraft to protect themselves and defeat their rivals ; high government officials and managing directors of private companies who propitiate local spirits and deities when modern bridges, power plants

[42] *Ibid.*, p. 93.

[43] *Ibid.*, p. 95.

and factories are dedicated—these and many similar phenomena ... are ways of relieving the anxieties and accepting the ambiguities of living simultaneously in two worlds." [44]

However, in either compartmentalisation of lives or living with inner conflict, a psychic effort is required, and a personal and social price has to be paid for the search of identity.

2.2.2. *Empirical Findings on the Psychic Dimension of Social Change and Value Conflict :* One of the first and most well-known field studies —at least in English—about a non-aligned Afro-Asian state is Lucian Pye's on *Burma's Search for Identity.* [45] Pye investigates primarily the related search for both individual and collective identity by analysing the attitudes of various members of Burma's intellectual and political elite toward Burmese politics and society. The 79 interviews (34 with administrative officials, 27 with politicians and 18 with "observers and critics of the political scene such as journalists, educators and businessmen") put in evidence the value-conflict and role-strain ensuing from the malintegrated culture paradigm based on primary socialisation in "indigenous traditions" and their secondary acculturation to 'alien' *(i.e.* colonial or generally Western) values. Since these findings are "suggestive of comparable effects of similar processes at work in other formerly colonial countries", the implication is that the empirically-based "sketches" are generalizable to other Afro-Asian non-aligned actors and thus justify some comment.

Two representative samples of conflict-torn elites are interviewed and analysed : the administrator and the politician. The administrators are those who "first realized that they were at home neither with their own people nor with the British". [46] They were the first to be in close contact with the British colonial authorities, to be acculturated to their values and thus became "a group who had some deep and disturbing questions about what they really wanted to be". This close contact with the imported colonial culture had as a result the psychic isolation of being deprived from belonging to either of the two creative communities (the indigenous and the alien) and brought into question their identity. [47]

---

[44] *Ibid.*

[45] Pye, Lucian : *Politics, Personality and Nation-Building : Burma's Search for Identity,* New Haven, Yale U.P., 1962.

[46] *Ibid.,* p. 223.

[47] *Ibid.,* p. 230. The parallel case of Edward Atiyah (1903-1964) is equally interesting for he has left a public record, *An Arab Tells His Story* (1946), of how he oscillated between two worlds. In this book, Atiyah describes how—growing up in the Anglo-Egyptian Sudan and studying at Victoria College—it became "my lot to adopt England ... the spirit and prestige of England : her kings and heroes,

The other sample of the elite—the politician—faces the same problem of the search for identity Though the politicians' social origins are far less homogeneous than the administrators', the problem is still there ; for, as one member of the political elite confessed :

> "I don't care much for being with Burmese who have studied abroad or even with those who have graduated from Rangoon University. When I listen to them I find I have little to say and I begin to wish that I were back with the village type of Burman. I must also confess that when I am with the villagers, I can feel just as left out." [48]

This explains perhaps the uncomfortable position of some Burmese politicians which causes them to vascillate between opposite images of themselves. At times they think of themselves as legitimate members of the modern or Westernized community, and at other times they see themselves as pure Burmese, as this significant quotation reveals :

> "I had never given any thought to what it meant to be a Burmese. I must have filled in countless forms in which I called myself a 'Burmese Buddhist', but it did not have much meaning ... In my second year at the university, I met this young Englishman who was very keen on learning all about Burma. He had read more about Burmese history than I had, and he knew much more than I did about the old days of the Burmese kings. I remember telling some of my friends at the university some of the things he had taught me about Burmese history, and they all said that it was foolish to think about such things, for we should be looking to the future and to a modern Burma which would be much better. My English friend was most interested in learning about Burmese customs. He was always asking me questions about why the Burmese do all the things they do. Sometimes I didn't know, sometimes I just couldn't explain it to him.
>
> Then one day, I still remember very clearly, he got quite angry with me when I could not answer his questions and could only laugh at the customs he wanted to know more about. He said 'Don't you

---

armies, fleets and victories ; her history and literature ...". At the end of his three years at Oxford, he saw himself "as a product of the British liberal tradition ...". He went out to Khartoum to teach at Gordon College and found himself segregated from the British staff ; after Victoria College and Oxford "I was flung back at one bound into a world of group barriers ... in which I, despite my long and passionate struggle to assimilate England and be assimilated by her, was consigned to that side of the fence on which I was born ... (and) I wanted to assert my identity as a Syrian". See Elie Kedouri (ed.) : *Nationalism in Asia and Africa,* London, Weidenfeld, 1970, pp. 87-88.

[48] Pye : *Politics, Personality and Nation-Building, op. cit.,* p. 251.

know anything about your own beliefs ; *what kind of a Burmese are you ?' The question really bothered me. You can't imagine how awful it was.*" [49]

Another type of politician would change this intermediary position between two worlds into an advantage by transforming this inner conflict of values into a sense of freedom to choose among alternative models for the future of his country . He tends to believe that it is possible to select the best ways from both the old and the new and in this fashion ensure that the Burmese *(i.e.* independent, non-aligned) way will remain the best way. In this case, it can be argued that non-alignment projects in the international system the actor's search for an independent identity away from either bloc. In addition, the insistence in many non-aligned actors on an indigenous form of socialistic development *(e.g.* Indian, Asian, Arab, African, Islamic socialism) is a part of the same search for an independent identity.

This 'search for identity' argument would be more strongly supported if the interview-based findings drawn from non-aligned Burma's case are confirmed by empirical research about other non-aligned actors and thus the generalizability assumption of the identity problems in newly-independent Afro-Asian societies is justified. The 'checking process' would be even more reliable if findings were arrived at by 'indigenous' social scientists who confront lesser linguistic barriers and cultural bias in the conduct of their research.

We can check the findings of the Burma study by considering the field work on problems of Sudanese identity or national character. [50] These problems—we are told—are not only specific to the Sudan but also to "other countries existing in the same situation". Here too, then, there is implication of generalizability. The interviews were conducted in the first part of 1959 by fourth year university students in Khartoum, under the guidance of a Sudanese social psychologist working in the field. Moreover, Dr. Saber—the ex-undersecretary of the Sudanese Ministry of Social Affairs who afterwards became the head of the Social Science Department in the Training Centre for the Development of the Arab World (Sers El-Layyan, Egypt)—helped in the interpretation of the qualitative findings. But not only did well-known national academic 'authorities' participate in the research project, but also the findings were published in eleven articles

---

[49] *Ibid.*, pp. 258-259 (emphasis added). See, for other profiles of the politician, *ibid.*, pp. 267-282.

[50] Dessouki, Kamal : "An Exploratory Study of the Sudanese Identity" in Lewis Melika (ed.) : *Readings in Social Psychology in Arab Countries,* Cairo, National Editing & Publication House, vol. I, 1965 (in Arabic), pp. 207-220. See also Diab, Lotfi : "Domination and Social Distance Among Near-Eastern Students in American Universities" in *ibid.*, pp. 220-231.

in Sudan's newspaper *El-Zamman* in September-December 1959. Consequently, other sociologists and social psychologists had the possibility to evaluate the research project and/or contest the findings. All these factors are bound to lessen bias in the findings and increase confidence in their reliability. [51]

Though many of the questions dealt with in the study are interesting, the most relevant is the one concerned with the individual's early socialisation process and his subsequent feelings toward the values inculcated into him in childhood. In the Sudan, the study tells us, the result of the socialisation process is that

> "individual self-evaluation is not based on his talents and potential, but on his feeling of 'belonging' to a group which protects him ... The early socialisation of the child has as a result the subordination of the 'ego' to the group's identity and the individual's strict conformity to rigid traditions and group values which govern social behaviour."

Briefly, the group's approval is the prime objective of the individual's social behaviour, and the group's interest comes before his own, for he has identity only through the group (whether it is a village, a tribe, an ethnic group, an extended family . . .).

Once the individual moves to the town or abroad for work or education (as most of the elite do), he feels certain "uprootedness, marginality and aggressiveness" and begins to reflect on his own identity. An internal conflict then starts to appear, for instance concerning some of the backbreaking social obligations to be performed toward the original group. [52]

Thus a

> "characteristic feature of the Sudanese identity is this perennial conflict between personal identity and group values, where it is unlikely that the ego will have the upper hand. The result of this internal conflict between the 'ego' and group demands, the 'new' that the individual aspires to and the 'old' that the group represents, leads to inhibition and inertia on the individual level."

---

[51] The findings' reliability is even more accrued since the researchers used the "stop watch" technique, which uses the length of time necessary for answering a question as a measure of value-conflict and role-strain, namely the quicker the answer by the interviewed, the lesser conflict he feels on the subject.

[52] For instance, anyone from the same tribe is a "brother", and can thus come to the capital to share with his 'urban brother' his living, whether this latter has the means or not. For a revealing text (in English) of these socio-psychological problems, see the novel by the Sudanese Tayeb Salih : *Season of Migration,* translated from the Arabic by Denys Johnson-Davis, London, Heineman (African Writers Series), 1970.

At the societal level, there might be 'splits' or 'discontinuities' in the national system that add to the racially- or geographically-based disintegrative aspects *(e.g.* secession attempts in the South of the Sudan), and renders the problems of social change singularly acute in Afro-Asian non-aligned actors. This brings us to our third basic argument.

2.3. *Acuteness of the Process of Social Disorganisation and Political Strain*

The 'ideal-type' domestic 'situational' component of an Afro-Asian non-aligned actor is

> "one exposed to modernity, disrupted socially from the traditional patterns of life ; confronted with pressures to change their ways, economically, socially and politically ; bombarded with new and 'better' ways of producing economic goods and services ; and frustrated by the modernization process of change, generally, and the failure of ... [the] government to satisfy ... [the people's] ever-rising expectations, particularly". [53]

As we have stated explicitly in our first basic argument, this "modernization process of change" is universal both in time and space. But there are two (interdependent) characteristics peculiar to the process in non-aligned societies :

(*a*) Because of increased communication in the global system and a "demonstration effect", *the rate of change in these societies is very fast.* If we take Cyril Black's variable—"consolidation of modernizing leadership"—and use the time-length necessary for its achievement as a measure of the rate of change, indeed this rate of change is very fast in non-aligned societies. [54] For instance, in England (Black's first modernizer) the "consolidation of modernizing leadership" stretched from 1649 to 1832, *i.e.* 183 years ; and in the U.S. (Black's second modernizer) this process stretched from 1776 to 1863, *i.e.* 89 years. But for 13 countries which entered this phase of "consolidation of modernizing leadership" during the Napoleonic period, the average time-length was only 73 years. Among non-aligned actors, Egypt took 30 years, India 28 and Indonesia 27. Nor are these states untypical examples, for 21 of the 26 states which began this "consolidation of modernizing leadership" during "the first quarter of the

---

[53] Huntington, Samuel : *Political Order in Changing Societies,* New Haven, Yale U.P., 1968, p. 46.

[54] Black, Cyril : *The Dynamics of Modernization,* New York, Harper Torchbook Edition, 1967, pp. 67-94.

20th century and had emerged by the 1960's, the average was only 29 years". Data collected by Deutsch confirms this acceleration in the rate of social change, and he, in fact, explicits that

> "during the 19th century the principal indicators of social mobilisation in modernizing countries changed at about the rate of 0.1 per cent per year, while in 20th century modernizing countries they change at about the rate of 1 per cent per year". [55]

(*b*) *Simultaneously rather than sequentially,* the non-aligned actors meet the "crises" of social change, national integration, centralisation of authority, economic development, political participation, social welfare . . .

2.3.1. Thus given that this dislocating "modernization process of change" in the non-aligned actors is not only singularly rapid but also all-pervasive, should we not ask with Riggs : "May not some 'transitional' conditions turn out to be relatively permanent" rather than "a temporary stage between a particular past and a predictable future state ?" [56]

Deutsch's 8-indicator operationalisation of this "modernisation process of change" (Deutsch prefers calling it "social mobilization") confirms Riggs' doubts. For the original images of "mobilisation" imply, in fact, two distinct images : (i) the stage of uprooting from old habits, traditions,

---

[55] Deutsch, Karl : "Social Mobilization and Political Development", *American Political Science Review,* LV (1961), pp. 493-514.

[56] Riggs : *Administration in Developing Countries, op. cit.,* p. 4. This shows the serious drawbacks of present "modernisation theory" as pioneered by Gabriel Almond's and James Coleman's neo-classic *The Politics of the Developing Areas* (Princeton, Princeton U.P., 1960). Not only has the assumption of unilinear development toward (Western) 'democratic modernity' been belied by the seeming eternalisation of the "transitional stage", but also the 'system-maintenance' bias inherent in structural-functional analysis has been invalidated by the empirical dynamics of underdevelopment. For instance, the growing population coupled with the incapacity of present economic performance to cope with the new context (*e.g.* Frank's Development of Underdevelopment) has materialised the warning that unsatisfied rising expectations (turned into rising frustrations) lead to mass unrest, political instability and violence.

Some quotations are revealing in this respect. "During the years I was in the State Department", George W. Ball said in *The Discipline of Power,* "I was awakened once or twice a month by a telephone call in the middle of the night announcing a *coup d'Etat* in some distant capital with a name like a topographical error." "It was not a coup", colonel Alphonse Alley of Dahomey said, "we only relieved two quarrelling Presidents of their duties." First, Ruth : *The Barrel of a Gun. Political Power in Africa and the Coup d'Etat,* London, Penguin African Library, 1972. Moreover, it was recently estimated that the average of cabinet shuffles in the Central African Republic was one every month. "La République de Bokassa", *Jeune Afrique,* No. 606, 19 August 1972.

patterns of relationships and social commitments ; and (ii) the induction of these "uprooted" persons into alternative patterns of group membership, organisation and commitment. In this sense Mannheim suggested the image of

> "large numbers of people moving away *from* a life of local isolation, traditionalism and political apathy and moving *into* a different life of broader and deeper involvement in the vast complexities of modern life, including potential and actual involvement in mass politics". [57]

But this "*de*mobilisation from . . . *re*mobilisation into" two-stage cycle cannot—in the case of societies—take place overnight as it is relatively the case with the drafting of soldiers. In other words until their remobilisation into the new patterns of social commitment and roles, people stay demobilised and in a state of 'ambivalence' and uncertainty—as we have seen from the findings on the individual's search for identity. This timelapse between "demobilisation from" and "remobilisation into" is the period full of tension, frustration and conflict. This climate of social disorganisation favours the disintegrative factors in the political (sub)system, especially if the volume of people's demands exceeds the capacity of the political system to satisfy them. [58]

2.3.2. Though social theorists might differ in predicting and diagnosing the forms or consequences of political conflict, yet there seems to be consensus on this point : once there is a gap between demands and the capacity of the political (sub)system to cope with them, "rising expectations" turn into rising frustrations leading to systemic strain and favouring political instability. Any political system—and a newly-born one especially—has a certain capacity (at least during a specified interval of time) to consider a certain volume of demands. When demands exceed this empirically determinable limit, there is a demand input overload. [59]

---

[57] As in Huntington : *op. cit.*, pp. 42-49. In this sense, soldiers are demobilised *from* their homes and families and mobilised *into* the army in which they then serve.

[58] As we shall see in detail later in this chapter, this want/get gap is common in situations of fast social change. See Deutsch : "Social Mobilization . . .", *op. cit.*

[59] This is similar to traffic movement in an airport. The traffic control tower can handle only a certain amount of messages or demands during a specific time interval. If messages from aircrafts are viewed as demands being made upon the controllers, the traffic system would break down if so many messages were coming through—during any specified interval of time—that the controllers could not process them under the prevailing structure and operating rules. For a detailed analysis, see Easton, David : *A Systems Analysis of Political Life, op. cit.*, pp. 58, 65-66.

In addition to its elaboration in Easton's "systems theory", [60] the correlation between the want/get gap and political instability is supported by Daniel Lerner's theorem [61] :

$$\frac{\text{social satisfactions}}{\text{social expectations}} = \text{systemic frustration}$$

Moreover, the correlation has been empirically confirmed by the Feierabends' findings. [62] Recently, it has been restated in a theoretical-empirical study [63] :

> "the heightened drive for social and economic change and development was *directly* related to the increasing political instability and violence that characterized Africa, Asia and Latin America in the years after World War II".

Last but not least, the chain of social change—rising demands—systemic strain [64] seems to be confirmed by "overwhelming" historical evidence from the experience of the West. Kornhauser states that

> "the *rapid* influx of large numbers of people into newly developing urban areas invites mass movements".

---

[60] *Ibid.* Also Easton, David : *A Framework for Political Analysis, op. cit.*

[61] Lerner, Daniel : "Modernization" in *International Encyclopedia of the Social Sciences,* New York, Macmillan, 1968, vol. X, pp. 386-395. See also his : *The Passing of Traditional Society,* New York, The Free Press, 1958.

[62] Feierabend, Ivo and Rosalind (with Frank Scanland III and John Chambers) : "Level of Development and International Behavior" in Richard Butwell (ed.) : *Foreign Policy and the Developing Nation,* Lexington, University of Kentucky Press, 1969, pp. 135-189.

[63] Not only is political instability hypothetically correlated with socio-economic change, but also *the degree* of instability is related to the *degree* of change. That is, "the *higher* the rate of change toward modernity, the *greater* the political instability". Huntington, *op. cit.,* pp. 45-49 (emphasis added). Huntington adds : "the faster the enlightenment of the population, the more frequent the overthrow of the government". In his study of Ceylon, Wriggins touched on this problem and stated that "increase in the number of students graduating in the indigenous languages satisfied some ambitions but contributed social pressures among the articulate educated middle classes". Wriggins, Howard : *Ceylon : Dilemmas of a New Nation,* Princeton, Princeton U.P., 1960, pp. 119, 245, as quoted in *ibid.* See also W. Howard Wriggins : "Impediments to Unity in New Nations : the Case of Ceylon", *The American Political Science Review,* LV (1961), pp. 313-320.

[64] For a very recent discussion (both of theory and of data) of this social change-instability correlation, see for instance : Gurr, Ted : "The Revolution - Social Change Nexus : Some Old Theories and New Hypotheses", *Comparative Politics,* V (1973), pp. 359-393 ; Feierabend, Ivo ; Feierabend, Rosalind, and Nesvold, Betty : "The Comparative Study of Revolution and Violence", *ibid.,* pp. 393-425 ; Tilly, Charles : "Does Modernization Breed Revolution ?", *ibid.,* pp. 425-449. An example from India might clarify how unemployment can easily lead to riots and systemic stress. In April 1958, the Calcutta fire brigade advertised 100 vacant posts for firemen for

Moreover, the Scandinavian experience shows that whenever

> "industrialization occurred *rapidly* introducing sharp *discontinuities* between the pre-industrial and industrial situation, more rather than less extremist working-class movements emerged".[65]

In addition,

> "the combined rate of change on 6 of 8 indicators of modernization (*e.g.* primary and post-primary education, rise in standard of living, infant mortality, urbanisation, literacy . . .) for 67 countries between 1933 and 1962 correlated .647 with political instability in those countries between 1955 and 1961".

Perhaps economic development can solve this dilemma of rising demands/increasing political instability correlation in these rapidly changing societies of today, since economic development is supposed to increase the capacity of the political subsystem to satisfy the rising level of expectations. Many economists do not think so, and in fact they emphasise the thesis of "Rapid Growth as a Destabilising Force",[66] at least beyond a certain subsistence level.[67] Rapid economic growth, it is suggested,[68] creates :

A. an increased number of people whose traditional social grouping (family, class, caste) are disrupted, and thus increases "the number of individuals who are *déclassés* . . . and who are thus in circumstances conducive to revolutionary protest » ;

---

a salary of 55 rupees ($11) per month, and fixed a date for interviews. On that day, about 10,000 to 12,000 persons turned up. Unable to cope with the situation, the authorities cancelled the interviews and declared that recruitment would not take place that day. Furious and frustrated, the crowd resorted to violence. The police reacted with sticks and tear gas. Furniture was broken, windows and doors smashed and 150 persons arrested. Weiner, Myron : *The Politics of Scarcity,* Chicago, Chicago U.P., 1962, p. 190. The situation is aggravated when large numbers of the unemployed are educated (estimated at 5 out of the 14 million unemployed in India in the early 1960's). "In general", Huntington says, "the higher the level of education of the unemployed, alienated or otherwise dissatisfied person, the more extreme the destabilising behavior which results. Alienated university graduates prepare revolutions ; alienated technical or secondary school graduates plan coups ; alienated primary school leavers engage in more frequent but less significant forms of political unrest." *Op. cit.,* p. 48. The relationship between literacy and the political subsystem is not confined, of course, to the search for jobs. There is, for instance, the very crucial issue of political participation.

[65] Kornhauser, William : *The Politics of Mass Society,* New York, The Free Press, 1958, pp. 143-145, as quoted in Huntington : *op. cit.,* p. 45.

[66] This is the title of Mancur Olson Jr.'s article : *Journal of Economic History,* XXIII (1963), pp. 529-552.

[67] Rapid economic growth seems to be compatible with political stability (rather than destabilising) at two extremes of economic development : the relatively high level and the very low one.

[68] Olson : *op. cit.,* and Huntington : *op. cit.,* pp. 49-50.

B. *nouveaux riches* who ask for the political power and social status corresponding to their new economic position ;

C. alienation, as a result of increasing geographical mobility and upsetting of social ties *(e.g.* the lumpenproletariat), and thus favours the rise of violent political protest ;

D. additional sources of social tension and unrest by widening the gap between the rich and those whose standard of living is declining, in relative if not in absolute terms ;

E. popular discontent as a result of restrictions on consumption in order to promote investment ;

F. increased literacy, education, and exposure to mass media, resulting in rising aspirations that cannot be satisfied at once ;

G. conflicts over distribution of investment and consumption which exacerbate ethnic and regional conflicts ;

H. increased "capacities for group organization and consequently the strength of group demands on government, which the government is unable to satisfy".

Thus historians, political scientists, sociologists, psychologists and economists seem to confirm the plausibility of the J-curve proposition.[69] Indeed, this proposition provides the basis for a more comprehensive explanation of systemic strain and instability, since it synthesises the different hypotheses advanced in the literature *(e.g.* Plato and Aristotle ver-

---

[69] The J-curve hypothesis is a partial synthesis of the two seemingly contradictory theses on the courses of political instability and revolution : the theses of Plato and Aristotle that poverty leads to political instability and systemic breakdown, and that of the comparative historical studies by, for instance, De Tocqueville and Brinton suggesting that political conflict leading to systemic breakdown is preceded by significant increase in economic development. The hypothesis accepts the suggestion—drawn from historical material—that systemic breakdown can be preceded by a long-term increase in economic development followed by a short period of sharp reversal. This would not abate the want/get gap which Olson rightly emphasised, and hence people will resent their poverty (which is perceived as increasing). The diagramatic formulation would make the argument more concrete :

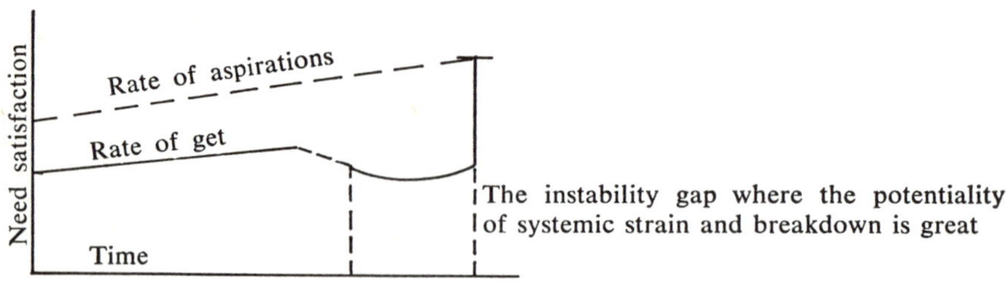

For the full analysis, see : Davies, James : "Toward a Theory of Revolution", *American Sociological Review,* XXVII, 1 (March 1962).

sus De Tocqueville and Brinton) and also attempts to combine the individual-psychological level with the collectivity-sociological level. The analysis, based on this proposition, however, has a shortcoming. It can typically emphasise the quantity of demands causing the want/get gap and overlook differences in quality and content of the various demands. In other words, a demand for better health conditions, better education, higher salary can be equated with system-threatening demands such as for a change of government or ethnic autonomy which is a common menace given the linguistic-ethnic fractionalisation of these societies as the following table shows.

TABLE 5. *Ethnic and Linguistic Fractionalisation in Some Non-Aligned Actors* *

Country	Roberts	Muller	Atlas Narodov Mira
1. Tanzania			.93
2. Congo (Kinshasa)	.88	.89	.90
3. Uganda	.82	.92	.90
4. Cameroon		.89	.89
5. India	.75	.84	.89
6. Nigeria	.82	.91	.87
7. Chad	.64	.68	.83
8. Zambia	.81		.82
9. Mali	.84		.78
10. Indonesia	.71	.77	.76
11. Guinea	.81	.83	.75
12. Niger	.83	.74	.73
13. Sudan	.49	.59	.73
14. Senegal	.78		.72
15. Ghana	.65		.71
16. Togo		.80	.71
17. Nepal		.48	.70
18. Central African Republic			.69
19. Ethiopia	.70	.84	.69
20. Upper Volta	.66	.62	.68
21. Afghanistan	.67	.71	.66
22. Congo (Brazzaville)			.66
23. Dahomey	.66	.84	.62
24. Morocco	.50	.38	.53
25. Burma	.53	.43	.47
26. Algeria	.48	.40	.43
27. Singapore	.41	.59	.42
28. Iraq	.39	.32	.36
29. Cambodia	.24	.30	.30
30. Lebanon	.12	.18	.13

* Fractionalisation varies from 0 (complete absence) to 1 (complete fractionalisation), and the indicator shows the probability that two randomly selected persons from one country will not speak the same language.
Dates for the data are 1960-1965.
Sources are: For the first column: Roberts, Janet: "Sociocultural Change and Commu-

2.4. Precisely, because of the prevalence of ethnic-linguistic heterogeneity in non-aligned actors, secessionist movements and the demand for ethnic autonomy are some of the most serious threats to the integration, and indeed survival, of the national system. Coupled with the index of ethnic-linguistic fractionalisation in non-aligned actors, the analysis—then —points out the primacy of the task of societal integration : how to build and/or consolidate a coherent system out of the multiplicity of fragmented societies that characterise the domestic situation of many non-aligned actors ? One of the propositions of the *Theory of Political Integration* is that the integrative cultural homogeneity and value-consensus can be effected through the forging of a "mature political culture" which in turn can be created through "social communication" among the various parts of the fragmented social system. [70] This social communication process would take place with the acceleration of the process of social change or mobilisation which entails "the breaking down of physical barriers between people and facilitating a greater flow of goods and services between the different parts of the country, educating the masses, developing urban centers and the mass media". But we have seen that this massive transformation of social relationships and individual values is disruptive and can lead to disintegrative political movements. Thus we face a paradox. For to increase its political integration the new state must undertake social mobilisation. Yet social mobilisation is essentially disruptive of the political order in the short run.

The threats of disruption are even increased when 'political malintegration' coincides with 'societal malintegration'. [71] That is when political cleavages coincide with ethnic cleavages. In this case, conflicts become

---

nications Problems", in Frank Rice (ed.) : *Study of the Role of Second Languages in Asia, Africa and Latin America,* Washington, D.C., Center for Applied Linguistics of the Modern Language Association of America, 1962. For the second column : Muller, Siegfried : *The World's Living Languages : Basic Facts of their Structure,* Kinship, Location and Number of Speakers, New York, Ungar, 1964. For the third column : *Atlas Narodov Mira,* Moscow, the N.N. Miklukho-Maklaya Institute of Ethnography of the Academy of Sciences, Department of Geodesy and Cartography of the State Geological Committee of the U.S.S.R., 1964. As quoted in *World Handbook, op. cit.,* pp. 271-275.

[70] Ake, Claude : *A Theory of Political Integration,* Homewood, The Dorsey Press, 1967, pp. 96-98.

[71] Consequently, "disunity rather than unity is the spirit of the new nations". Among the various barriers impeding the integrative process are :

(*a*) *Racial heterogeneity :* of the 7.5 million and 2 million in Malaya and Singapore respectively, almost 2.8 million and 1.3 million are Chinese.

(*b*) *Religious animosities :* though religious heterogeneity exists in many European countries, they do not lead to the dislocation of millions of people and the slaughter of thousands of hundreds—as happened between India and Pakistan. The founder of Pakistan expressed this religious barrier to national integration : "To yoke together", Jinnah said, "two such nations under a single state . . . must lead to growing discontent and final destruction of any fabric that may be so built up for the

additive rather than criss-crossing and a bureaucratic conflict in the civil service, for instance, can precipitate a generalised civil strife.[72] This "politics of retribalisation"[73] is the serious danger in "plural" societies.[74]

---

government of such a state." Not all religiously divided nations experience the torture, mutilation, assault, conversion by force, extermination en route that took place in the Indo-Pakistan case, but divisions between the Moslems and Christians of Lebanon hamper its integration.

(*c*) *Regional differences:* especially divisive when they are accompanied by uneven distribution of resources and wealth (*e.g.* Sumatra versus Java in Indonesia). The Indonesian case seems to be repeated in Africa. "Regionalism is understandable" in Africa, Wallerstein said, "because ethnic loyalties can usually find expression in geographical terms. Inevitably some regions will be richer (or less poor) than others, and if the ethnic claim to power combines with relative wealth, the case for secession is strong."

(*d*) *Tribalism:* some tribes are not small ethnic groups but big nations (*e.g.* the Hausa in Nigeria is over 10 million) and the tribe is thus "still the psychological, economic and political reality to many, for it is the social organisation most familiar to many". In Nigeria, both the Hausa and Fulani constitute 27 per cent of the population, whereas the Ibo constitute 17 per cent and the Yoruba 16 per cent. In Mali, the biggest ethnic group (the Banbarra) constitutes 27 per cent of the population and is followed by the Fulani (12 per cent) and the Songhai (5 per cent). Liberia does not have less than six principal ethnic groups (Mandingo, Gissi, Gola, Kpelle, Kru, Greboes), and the Ivory Coast's principal ethnic groups are five (Agni, Kru, Mande, Baole and Dan).

(*e*) *Linguistic diversity:* an important indicator of malintegration since it emphasises impediments to communication. In India, for instance, there are 12 major languages—each of which is spoken by more than a million people. Then there are an additional 24 tribal languages or dialects, each spoken by more than 100,000; plus 63 non-Indian languages, of which English is the most well-known. Linguistic diversity is no less a problem in some African countries. For example, the 2 million people of Dahomey speak six different languages and dialects; and the 0.5 million population of Gabon speak 40 different languages and dialects. See: Emerson, Rupert: *From Empire to Nation,* Cambridge, Mass., Harvard U.P., 1960, pp. 141-143; Lloyd, C.: *Africa in Social Change,* London, Penguin, 1967, pp. 331-343; Spanier, John: *World Politics in an Age of Revolution,* New York, Praeger, 1967, pp. 151-196; Wriggins: "Impediments to Unity in the New States", *op. cit.*

[72] This cross-pressures hypothesis which states that "politically relevant divisions which cross-cut each other contribute to the mitigation and regulation of conflicts" has been developed, or its validity attested to, by such highly respected social scientists as Bentley, Truman, Kornhauser, Lipset, Key, Parsons, Deutsch, Lane, Almond, Rokkan and Huntington among others. For a detailed discussion, see: Nordlinger, Eric: *Conflict Regulation in Divided Societies,* Cambridge, Harvard University, Center for International Affairs, 1972, pp. 88-117.

[73] Mazrui, Ali: "Violent Contiguity and the Politics of Retribalisation in Africa", *Journal of International Affairs,* XXIII (1969).

[74] The notion of "plural society" was first enunciated in the context that interests us here by J. S. Furnival in his *Colonial Policy and Practice* (London, 1948, pp. 303-312). In his attempt to elaborate a broader model of societal relations, M. G. Smith refined Furnival's concept in his two volumes: *The Plural Society in the British West Indies* (Berkeley and Los Angeles, 1965) and—with Kuper—*Pluralism in Africa*

Briefly, the problem of societal and political integration in non-aligned actors is reduced to two interrelated parts of a basic question : if social change or mobilisation is inevitable, rapid and all-pervasive in non-aligned actors, what kind of policy can enable the political system to neutralise and/or reduce the disintegrative short-run effects of this process ? In other words, what are the factors favouring the minimum of political stability necessary to contain or balance the disruptive effects of social mobilisation ?

2.4.1. The different conceptual approaches to political integration agree that the political system undertaking social mobilisation maximises its capacity to carry out the process while keeping the society together by either the use of maximum force for systemic control *(i.e.* coercion) or by increasing the bases of consensus and legitimacy *(e.g.* make the spirit of citizenship predominate over "primordial attachments"). [75] This is based on the equation of a "developmental framework" as

$$C = F + L$$

where C (control) is held constant and F (force) and L (legitimacy) are interdependent variables inversely proportional to one another. [76] Thus at the time of independence, for instance, legitimacy of "national government" is not usually in question, [77] as the following figure shows

(Berkeley, 1969). Smith emphasises "cultural discontinuities and separateness" in these plural societies which are "defined by dissensus and pregnant with conflict". See also : Horowitz, Donald : "Multiracial Politics in the New States : Toward a Theory of Conflict", paper delivered at the *Annual Meeting of the American Political Science Association,* September 1969 ; Rothchild, Donald : "Ethnicity and Conflict Resolution", *World Politics,* XXII (1970).

[75] Greetz, Clifford : "The Integrative Revolution : Primordial Sentiments and Civil Politics in the New States" in Clifford Greetz (ed.) : *Old Societies and New States : The Quest for Modernity in Asia and Africa,* New York, The Free Press, 1963, pp. 105-158.

[76] Consequently, "the relative proportions of legitimacy and force vary in a given political system depending on leadership performance, as well as a multitude of other internal and external factors". Dekmejian, Hrair : *Egypt under Nasser : A Study in Political Dynamics,* Albany, State University of New York Press, 1971, pp. 2-17. The dialectical L-F relationship is supposed to distinguish between developed political systems (*e.g.* Great Britain) and 'emerging' or 'prismatic' political systems (*e.g.* Syria). In the first category "$L > F$ and continues to increase, C increasingly becomes dependent on L ; the resultant trend would be toward stability". In the 2nd category, "component $F > L$, and continues to increase, C becomes more and more dependent on F, creating a condition of increasing instability". *Ibid.* Our 'testing' case study of Egypt will deal with these issues.

[77] Both Algeria and the Congo were notable exceptions.

Figure 1

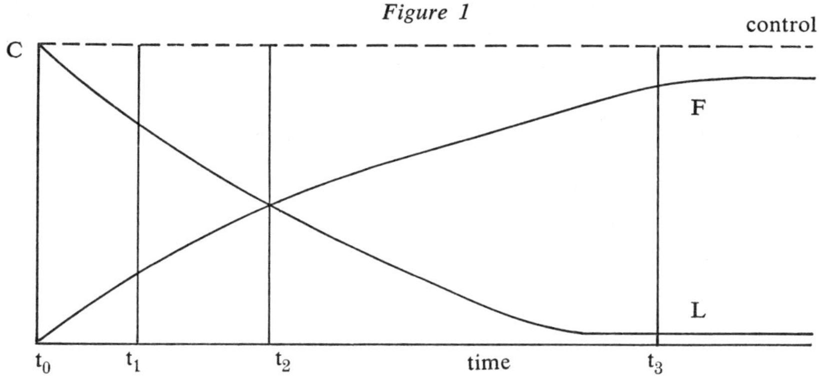

where t_o is time of independence.

At t_o $C = L, F = o$
(Realistically "o" can never be reached.)

But since legitimacy and consensus are not constants, once the "colonial enemy" of the "national front" has disappeared and the further in time the "historical day" of independence, the more disintegrative elements (political and societal) tend to strain the system. Thus taking deaths from domestic violence [78] as a measure of this domestic conflict variable, Indonesia—for instance—had 13,00 deaths in 1950, 22,00 in 1951, 15,00 in 1952, 45,00 in 1955, 50,00 in 1956, 41,00 in 1957, 14,000 in 1959, 48,00 in 1960, 50,000 in 1965, 525,000 in 1966. The population of about 3 million in Rwanda suffered 21,000 deaths in 1964 and a further 50,00 in 1966. In 1960, the year of its independence, the Congo (Kinshasa) had 12,00 deaths to be followed by 23,00 in 1961, 11,00 in 1962, 36,00 in 1963 and 40,00 in 1964. Neighbouring Cameroon had 10,000 deaths in 1964. The story of Nigeria is too recent to be forgotten, but the figures can be recalled : 11,00 in 1964, 42,00 in 1966, 37,00 in 1967—and the Biafra secession attempt was to continue for at least a further three years. Iraq had 23,00 deaths in 1959, followed by 14,00 in 1963 and a further 20,00 in 1966.

This prevalence of domestic conflict—threatening the very survival of the system—explains why in the above figure the curve of legitimacy and consensus tends to decline and that of force to rise. Yet a look at this table showing the size of internal security forces in some non-aligned actors [79] (as a measure of the capability of state authorities to impose themselves by force) indicates that the agents of the political system cannot maintain the system by mere coercion—even if they wanted to.

[78] This measure records the number of persons reportedly killed in events of domestic political conflict. Hudson and Taylor : *World Handbook of Political and Social Indicators, op. cit.*, pp. 110-116.

[79] *Ibid.*, pp. 42-47.

TABLE 6. *Size of Internal Security Forces of Some Non-Aligned Actors* *

Country	Total	Per Thousand Square Kilometer	Per Thousand Working Age Population	Notes	Date	Source
1. Libya	12,000	7	14.0	b	1966	
2. Egypt	100,000	100	6.6	c	1963	3
3. Algeria	36,000	15	5.7	c	1966	
4. Jordan	5,000	51	5.1	b	1965	
5. Iraq	16,616	37	5.0	b	1965	2
6. Cambodia	12,000	66	4.1	c	1965	3
7. Ghana	16,500	69	4.0	b	1966	
8. Tunisia	9,600	59	4.0	b	1966	
9. Syria	9,800	53	3.8	b	1965	
10. Zambia	6,134	8	3.7	b	1965	
11. Cameroon	10,700	23	3.5	b	1966	
12. Morocco	24,000	54	3.5	b	1966	
13. Somalia	5,000	8	3.5	b	1966	
14. Afghanistan	21,000	32	2.7	c	1965	1
15. Congo (Kinshasa)	21,000	9	2.4	b	1966	
16. Senegal	4,500	23	2.3	b	1966	
17. Indonesia	130,000	87	2.2	b	1965	
18. Lebanon	3,250	313	2.2	b	1965	
19. India	504,016	158	2.1	b	1965	1
20. Central African Republic	1,530	3	1.9	b	1966	
21. Ceylon	9,812	150	1.6	b	1964	1
22. Sudan	10,000	4	1.5	c	1964	
23. Chad	2,500	2	1.4	c	1966	
24. Guinea	1,900	8	1.1	b	1966	
25. Burma	13,000	19	1.0	c	1961	1
26. Mali	1,600	1	.7	b	1966	
27. Nigeria	24,000	26	.7	b	1966	
28. Upper Volta	1,800	7	.7	b	1966	
29. Rwanda	750	29	.4	b	1966	
30. Tanzania	1,350	1	.2	b	1966	

* These data were selected from a variety of possibilities by Hudson and Taylor who graded them A (reliable), B (good) or C (questionable).

Sources of the data are: S. H. Steinberg (ed.): *The Statesman's Year-Book, Statistical and Historical Annual of the States of the World for the Year 1966-1967,* London, Macmillan, 1966; Annual governmental fiscal and statistical reports; Gurr, Ted: *New Error-Compensated Measures for Comparing Nations,* Research Monograph, No. 25, Princeton, Center of International Studies, 1966, pp. 111-126; Nonannual governmental and statistical reports. If the source is not noted in the source-column, this means that the data is drawn from: *The Military Balance, 1965-1966* (London, Institute for Strategic Studies, 1965); *The Military Balance, 1966-1967* (London, Institute for Strategic Studies, 1966); Wood, David: *The Armed Forces of African States,* Adelphi Papers, No. 27 (London Institute for Strategic Studies, 1966); or Wood, David: *The Military Strength of Israel's Arab Neighbors* (London, Institute for Strategic Studies, 1965). *World Handbook, op. cit.,* pp. 42-48.

To the extent, then, that the governments of these "modernising" societies work to maintain viable political systems, and to the extent that force or coercion is not capable by itself to control permanently the system, these governments have only one alternative. The alternative is to reinforce the other basis of societal consensus and systemic control : legitimacy. Yet there is another paradox here. For we have seen that at this stage in the "political development" of these newly-independent and rapidly-changing systems, the symbols of legitimacy *(e.g.* strong political institutions, 'rules of the game', spirit of citizenship rather than 'primordial attachment') are not yet firmly established. This might explain the prevalence of another phenomenon in non-aligned actors : personalised and/or charismatic [80] political leadership *(e.g.* the Bourguibas, the Nassers, the Nehrus, the Nkrumahs, the Sukarnos . . .) which tries to act as the rallying point and a symbol of consensus in the emerging political system.

2.4.2. The influence of charismatic leadership on societal integration can be seen from this more than two century-old statement of Montesquieu :

> "At the birth of societies, it is the leaders of the common wealth who create the institutions ; afterwards it is the institutions that shape the leaders". [81]

If Americans pride themselves of having "a government of laws and not of men" and "People's Democracies" look forward to a stateless society, in the emerging political systems of non-aligned actors it is suggested that "wise and firm leadership alone can make the difference between steady progress and early ruin". This 'survival' and integrative function of charismatic leadership in newly-independent states [82] explains the renewed interest in Max Weber's analysis of political authority and its applicability to the emerging political system. Weber exposed his theory of charisma in the following way :

> "The term 'charisma' shall be understood to refer to an extraordinary quality of a person, regardless of whether this quality is actual, alleged or presumed. Charismatic authority hence shall refer to a rule over men ... to which the governed submit because of their

[80] See footnote 66 (chapter III) for sources on this increasingly important subject in the treatment of emerging political systems.

[81] *Considérations sur les causes de la grandeur des Romains et de leur décadence,* 1734, ch. I, as quoted in Rustow : *A World of Nations, op. cit.,* p. 135.

[82] It has not been sufficiently emphasised that illiteracy has its part in the exaggerated personification of authority which exists in most of Afro-Asian states. Simply because, for someone who cannot read, a man is more easily grasped than a program. Illiterate communities are attached to oral manifestation, and the Sukarnos, the Nassers and the Nkrumahs were good orators whose words were—thanks to the radio—communicated to even isolated villagers. Tucker, Robert: "Theory of Charismatic Leadership", *Daedalus* (1968), pp. 731-756.

belief in the extraordinary quality of the specific person. The legitimacy of charismatic rule ... rests upon the belief in magical powers, revelations and hero worship."

Weber gave this definition in his treatment of the three types of political authority (traditional, charismatic and legal-rational), one of which is necessary to hold the political system together. And

"since Weber's threefold distinction among types of legitimate authority is meant to be exhaustive, one may infer that the charismatic element is more prominent the weaker the traditional and rational-legal elements. This is the chief reason Weber's concept is so widely applicable in situations of decolonization, where both traditional and rational-legal elements of authority are suddenly dissolved and the entire weight of legitimacy may come to rest on a single leader and his personal reputation." [83]

In other words, charismatic leadership itself is a function of a certain domestic situation, for there is "a need for personal leadership at times of rapid and fundamental transition such as the birth of a new state" or the emergence of a political system [84]. The reason is simple : if systemic control based on legitimacy and consensus is to be achieved in times of rapid and all-pervasive social change, man must be tied to the political system either by his devotion to the institutions or to the leader. And since the institutions are in flux and the legitimacy of the government or the state itself is in question, the need is greater to achieve consensus on persons.

"At moments when the entire order of political institutions is to be changed—as in the attainment of independence or generally the founding of a new state—the entire burden of legitimacy is on the person of the leader in the transition." [85]

---

[83] Rustow : *op. cit.,* p. 152. Whether the leader has 'really' a divine gift or grace is not the most important thing according to Weber. It is the subject's perception that counts. Thus "as beauty is said to be in the eye of the beholder, so the leader's charisma is in the mind of the follower". It is the relational property of charisma that has been confused in the literature. *Ibid.,* pp. 150-152.

[84] With social mobilisation and "the rapid intake of hitherto non-political men into the developing political parties, and the consequent conflicts between local and party loyalties, there lacks [even] within the parties, and even more so among the masses, a consensus on the legitimate means and ends of political activity. It is in such situations, *where norms are poorly defined,* that the emergence of the charismatic leader is facilitated. Such a status gives its holder considerable freedom in formulating the policies of his party, for these are not expected to be related to specific interest groups. Loyalty to the charismatic leader is an emotional one, with a high expressive content. He is expected to maintain the degree of pomp and ceremony that characterized the rulers of many traditional African Societies." Lloyd : *Social Change in Africa, op. cit.,* pp. 220-221 (emphasis added).

[85] Thus Weber's hypothesis can be summed up in the formula

$$\text{Political legitimacy} = \begin{array}{c}\text{Traditional}\\ \text{legitimacy}\end{array} + \begin{array}{c}\text{Legal}\\ \text{legitimacy}\end{array} + \begin{array}{c}\text{Charismatic}\\ \text{legitimacy}\end{array}$$

Thus the overall consensus and legitimacy necessary for systemic viability can be maintained if an increase in legitimacy of, and consensus around, rulers compensates for the loss of legitimacy of institutions and vice-versa. And Robert Tucker confirms : charisma is just part of the "situation" of the new state, whereas some psychologists insist that charisma arises in situations in which people—as Erickson suggested—become "charisma hungry". [86]

An empirical example from the history of the first and biggest non-aligned actor (India) can indicate the validity of the preceding theoretical analysis. For instance, though the attachment of the masses to the "Mahatma" does not need any detailed comment, a specific incident can show both his charismatic influence and its effect on the nascent Indian system. During the communal riots that marked the birth of the Indian political system, he went to India's largest city and began a fast in protest against communal disturbances. Consequently, serious rioting was averted in the city, and this made lord Mountbatten describe Gandhi as "the one man boundary force who kept the peace while a force of 50,000 strong was swamped by riots".

The successor Gandhi chose—Nehru—had a charisma of a different kind. He acted as the meeting-point between so many views and loyalties which otherwise would have been divergent and threatened the viability of the newly-born political system. The old and orthodox elements were attached to him because he was Gandhi's nominee and represented—after the death of Patel—the only link with the past. The young and "leftist" intellectuals had considered him their man since the late 1920's for he was the only one among the known leaders who found virtue in planning. The advocates of free enterprise supported him because he was committed to

---

"To obtain the same amount of political legitimacy, any decrease in one of the terms must be compensated by an increase in one or both of the others. The mathematical expression makes it clearer, perhaps, than does Weber's text that the personal legitimacy accorded to rulers (just like the legitimacy of institutions) is a matter of degree and hence subject to variations, whether gradual or sharp, over time. Charisma (or rather *charismatic situations)* are an ideal type—a matter not of either-or but of more or less." Rustow : *op. cit.,* pp. 152-159 (emphasis added).

[86] According to Erickson, some of the factors that make people "charisma hungry" are : (*a*) fear : *e.g.* imminence of nuclear destruction ; (*b*) anxiety : due—for example—to an "identity-vacuum" or the condition of not knowing just who or what they are. This is to be related to our treatment of problems involved in the search for identity during the process of rapid social change ; (*c*) existential dread : the distress that people experience under conditions in which rituals of their existence have broken down. The charisma of a leader is successful to the extent of meeting these 'situational needs'. The charismatic leader is saying in effect : "I will make you safe" or "I will give you identity" or "I will give you rituals". In the application of his scheme to Gandhi, Erickson affirms that the Indian people were given a new collective identity. Tucker : *op. cit. ;* Spanier : *op. cit.,* pp. 251-254.

rapid industrialisation of the country. The British-educated civil servants respected and followed him because he was even more an Englishman than they were. Because of his artistocratic origins he had the halo of a modern prince who had sacrificed wealth and leisure to gain independence, and this made him a continuing symbol of the freedom struggle for his country. He thus benefited from, and gave justification for, the tradition of hero-worship. At the age of 40 he was elected President of the Congress Party, thus becoming the youngest ever to hold this position. His popularity was so well-established and the people's admiration for him so great that he was largely awaited wherever he went. Even in Tamil-speaking Madras, a huge gathering listened to him speaking in Hindi—a language very few understood in that part of India. No one wanted a translation, as if his voice and the chance to see him were enough. [87]

2.4.3. But a 'great man theory of history' should not be exaggerated and the consensual integrative function of charismatic leadership should not be overemphasised. It was after all Nehru's party—the prestigious Congress—that was increasingly losing votes in face of organised opposition in state elections. For instance, in 1952 the organised opposition got 32 per cent of the votes. This figure rose to 35 per cent in 1957 and in 1962 to 40 per cent. [88] Some observers can interpret this decline in support and consensus as directed against the Congress Party's 'establishment' rather than against the charismatic leadership of Nehru himself. But it is equally true that after the 1962 border conflict with China, not only was Nehru's leadership questioned but also his policy was criticised. Moreover, the overthrowing of such charismatic leaders as Nkrumah and Sukarno are empirical indicators of the insufficiency of personalised systemic control. And though Nasser himself was not overthrown after his (mis) handling of the 1967 war, his leadership was increasingly questioned too.

These examples indicate that the charismatic *personality* of the leader —as the basis for consensus and integration in the emerging political system—is not enough by itself. Charismatic leadership's contribution to systemic maintenance depends on whether the leader's *policies* are perceived by his followers as responding to the 'general situation' of the newly-independent state or not. In other words,

> "the followers' attitude . . . (empirically rather than by definition) is influenced not so much by specific personal qualities common to all

---

[87] Brecher : *Nehru, op. cit.,* p. 23.

[88] Morris-Jones, W. H. : *The Government and Politics of India,* London, Hutchinson (2nd edition), 1967, pp. 148-190. Chopra, Pran : *Uncertain India,* Bombay, 1968, pp. 246-248.

> charismatic leaders, but rather *by the magnitude and improbability of the results he obtains. No results, no belief; no belief, no charisma.*" [89]

Here lies our hypothesis: a non-aligned foreign policy orientation is a function of the specific psycho-societal needs of Afro-Asian states.

2.5. *Non-Alignment and the Psycho-Societal Situation of Afro-Asian States: an Observed Correlation*

It was mainly because of the characteristics of this national component of the "situation" that some students of foreign policy analysis started attracting attention to "State-Building as a Determinant of Foreign Policy in the New States". [90] This hypothetical internal political system/foreign policy correlation is based on the observation that.

> "the demands of state-building in former colonies overwhelm all others. Inevitably, they impinge on foreign policy. The foreign policy of a new state cannot be understood exclusively in the light of domestic necessities; but unless the omnipresent task of state-building is allowed to illuminate the objectives and motives of foreign policy, *it cannot be understood at all.*" [91]

As the data on linguistic-ethnic fractionalisation and deaths from domestic violence served to indicate, the legal-formal structure of the state is there but the actual nation is still "the pattern of our hopes" as Nkrumah once expressed it. If (as the Organisation of African Unity, for instance, advises its 43 members) the Pandora box of boundary redemarcation is not to be opened, new states have to continue as the

> "administrative units [established] under colonialism [which] frequently bore little relation to the distribution of ethnic or linguistic groupings, or even to the logic of geography".

Consequently, this achievement of "juridical recognition far in advance of their [the new states'] capacities to perform as states"

> "is the *salient fact* to hold in mind when analysing the foreign policy of a new nation. For, frequently, *foreign policy is recruited to the state-building task*—or is intimately affected by the immensity of that task." [92]

---

[89] Rustow: *op. cit.*, p. 151 (emphasis added).

[90] Good, Robert: "State-Building as a Determinant of Foreign Policy in New States" in Martin: *op. cit.*, pp. 3-13.

[91] *Ibid.* (emphasis added).

[92] *Ibid.* (emphasis added). A specialist of African politics equally hypothesises: "Foreign policy may be used as an instrument of internal policy to bolster the image of the national leader at home or as a mechanism to create internal political integra-

2.5.1. For the foreign policy field offers opportunities to emphasise the actuality of the new nation-state : its existence and integrity are confirmed by such symbols as U.N. membership, recognition of foreign governments and attendance at international gatherings. And if foreign policy is to project and/or enhance the national identity, non-alignment presents positive assets for the newly-independent state :

> "Before independence, a colony was related to the external world only through the foreign office of its metropole. It participated in the international community only by proxy. Once independent, it wants to pick up its own franchise, speak with its own voice and *demonstrate* its own capacities." [93]

Consequently, for some students of new states, "non-alignment means an uninhibited voice, an independent role and a sense of uniqueness". [94]

These last three words—"a sense of uniqueness"—attract attention to an important psycho-societal basis of non-alignment : non-aligned actors' negative identification with either of the Cold War blocs and their insistence on an independent national identity in the international system. This insistence on an independent national identity has the advantage of rallying divergent domestic forces. This "linkage" is authoritatively illustrated in this statement from Nehru's speech to his Afro-Asian colleagues at the 1955 Bandung Conference :

> "Has it come to this that the leaders of thought who have given religions and all kinds of things to the world have to tag on to this kind of group or that, and be hangers on of this party or the other, carrying out their wishes and occasionally giving an idea ? . . . It is an intolerable thought to me that the great countries of Asia and Africa shall have come out of bondage into freedom only to degrade themselves in this way . . . I will not tie myself to this degradation . . . and become a camp-follower of others."

For not only is the "tying to" one bloc degrading, but it is also disruptive of the political system. If Nehru, for instance, becomes the "camp-follower" of one side in the Cold War, the political opposition would not

---

tion and solidarity." Cowan, Gray : "Political Determinants" in Vernon McKay (ed.) : *African Diplomacy : Studies in the Determinants of Foreign Policy,* New York, Praeger, 1966, pp. 119-145. See also Spanier : *op. cit.,* pp. 249-288.

[93] Good : *op. cit.* (emphasis added). Formal independence without an independent foreign policy can be analogous to the state of Togo's ex-President, Sylvanus Olympio, upon release from a Vichy French prison during World War II : "The jailor told me 'You are free'. But what kind of freedom was it when the jail was in the desert, hundreds of miles from my home, and there was no gasoline for the truck we were to travel in ?"

[94] *Ibid.* For the newly-independent, malintegrated state which is very attached to its independence but is also aware of the threats to it, even the idea of 'interdependence' is suspect as presenting the danger of renewed control of the strong over the weak.

only try to discredit him by accusing him of bringing the country back to "bondage", but also this opposition might become the "camp-follower" of the other side in the Cold War, thus adding to the strains in the country's emerging political system. Hence our hypothesis : a non-aligned foreign policy orientation performs an integrative function in the prismatic political system of third world societies.

For in addition to ethnic heterogeneity and societal strain due to the rapid and all-pervasive process of social change, the emerging political system sees the "national front" that led it to independent birth disintegrating. [95] For instance, the study of the 14 French and English-speaking states of West Africa shows that

> "at the threshold of the constitutional advance towards self-government and national independence, the nationalist movements of the various West African territories were usually divided into several factions, sometimes organised as political parties, sometimes as cliques around an individual leader. In some cases, the divisions coincided with personal rivalries for leadership in the national movements ; in others, ethnic divisions formed the basis . . . The most significant divisions, however, were those which reflected differences in ideology. *These differences were often latent in the earlier stages,* but became apparent as the factions began to develop a party organisation and direct their appeal to the masses." [96]

Three contrasting "ideal-types" would seem to characterise political forces in the emerging political system :

(*a*) The strong traditionalist, nativistic societal elements, whose approach to the new state's foreign policy orientation is ideologically atavistic. Its leaders might still resent the vanishing of "many of the old traditions, patterns of authority and ties of family life". Whether it is the Northern People's Congress in Nigeria, Darul Islam in Indonesia, Jan Sangh in India or the True Whig Party in Liberia, they had varying degrees of influence depending on the specific conditions of the social system. [97] We shall see the trouble that the strongly-based Moslem Brethren *(El-Ikhwan El Muslimin)* caused for Nasser, not only at the birth of his regime but even after its firm establishment.

(*b*) At the other end of the continuum there are the various left-wing groups. They mistrust 'Western capitalism and colonialism' and profess

---

[95] Crabb : *The Elephants and the Grass, op. cit.,* p. 57. Also Nayar : "The Growth of Non-alignment in World Affairs", *op. cit.*

[96] Lloyd : *Social Change in Africa, op. cit.,* p. 221 (emphasis added).

[97] Morris-Jones : *op. cit.,* pp. 148-191 ; Lloyd : *op. cit.,* pp. 214-244 ; Mintz, Jeanne : *Mohamed, Marx and Marhean : The Roots of Indonesian Socialism,* London, Pall Mall, 1965, p. 101.

open admiration for certain features of the Soviet and/or Chinese experiences, and generally advocate closer relations with the "Socialist Camp". Though neither in Egypt nor in sub-Saharan African states were the Communist parties—for instance—as strong as in Indonesia or India, anti-Western and socialist ideas were becoming increasingly widespread. [98]

(*c*) The third trend is represented by the 'centralist' forces which are mainly composed of the non-communist, Western-educated nationalist elite. They generally provided the 'national leadership' in the national liberation movements and continued to manage the state's affairs immediately after independence. The Nehrus, the Nassers and even the Nkrumahs are prominent examples. [99]

Thus political disintegration is added to both ethnic fractionalisation and societal disruption to increase the threats to systemic viability. It is in this 'situation' that

> "Non-alignment ... more than any other conceivable approach to foreign relations ... serves to hold these disruptive political forces in check and to make possible that degree of political unity which is the minimal price for internal stability and national survival." [100]

Thus non-alignment performs an integrative function since it constitutes a "broad national front" behind which extremely divergent sections of the population are able to come together [101] :

(*a*) Communist and other left-wing groups support non-alignment as long as the 'Eastern Camp' does not reject it (which the U.S.S.R. stopped doing after Stalin's death), and because non-alignment signifies refusal of integration in Western pacts, made possible friendly relations with socialist countries and was dedicated to the promotion of revolutionary anti-colonial struggle.

(*b*) Pro-Western elements favour non-alignment because it would permit contacts and friendly ties with the West while (i) leaving the new state free to *choose* what it wishes to take from the West in material assistance and in ideological inspiration, and (ii) permits such elements to reconcile their affinity with the West with the necessity to prove their independence from it in policy-formulation.

---

[98] Paul Sigmund (ed.) : *The Ideologies of the Developing Nations,* New York, Praeger, 1963, pp. 3-4.

[99] This is one of the factors that might help to explain why the early foreign policy of these leaders leaned more to the 'West'. See, for instance : Thompson : *Ghana's Foreign Policy, op. cit.,* pp. 28-119 ; Lyon : *Neutralism, op. cit.,* pp. 121-130 ; Sayegh (ed.) : *The Dynamics of Neutralism in the Arab World, op. cit.,* pp. 163-224 ; Abdel Malek, Anouar : *Egypt : Military Society : The Army Regime, the Left, and Social Change under Nasser,* New York, Vintage Book, 1968, pp. 222-246.

[100] Crabb : *op. cit.,* p. 62.

[101] Nayar : *op. cit.,* p. 51.

(*c*) The ultranationalistic and atavistic elements support non-alignment because it signifies the absence of foreign domination in policy-making and permits the nation to define the external role that best accords with its own traditions. [102]

2.5.2. This "accordance with its own traditions" is the more credible when it is coupled with "Indian", "Arab" or "African Socialism" as a part of a general 'third road' (*i.e.* independent) orientation :

> "African socialism has a function for the African political leaders as they find themselves involved in the world conflict. It permits them to distinguish themselves from both the East and the West. It accomplishes this by delineating their role in the international arena as an independent one. *Thus African socialism becomes equated with neutralism and other ideologies that reject political domination by either East or West.*" [103]

This non-alignment/'nationalised socialism' complex is part of these actors' general refusal to follow somebody else's 'book of rules' and insistence on an independent identity : 'Asianness', 'Arabness' or 'Africanness'. [104] At the Bandung Conference Nehru expressed this insistence on an independent identity when he asked : "Are we copies of Europeans, Americans or Russians ?" Then he, himself, went on to answer this question by linking non-alignment to the expression of an independent identity : "If I join any of these groups, I lose my identity, I have no identity left". Senghor expressed the same insistence on an independent identity in his justification of an *African Socialism :*

> "No, an ideology which was thought out for others and by others; and which, moreover, denied the values of our civilisation, of our *collective personality,* such an ideology we cannot adopt without adapting it. Otherwise we negate our selfhood and accept passively depersonalisation : our non-being." [105]

---

[102] Crabb : *op. cit.,* pp. 58-65.

[103] William Friedland and Carl Rosberg, Jr. (eds.) : *African Socialism,* Stanford, Stanford U.P., 1964, p. 91 (emphasis added).

[104] A scholar affirmed : "The assertion of an African form of socialism also enables the political leaders to pursue foreign policies of non-alignment." Lloyd : *op. cit.,* p. 278.

[105] Senghor, Léopold : *Pierre Teilhard de Chardin et la politique africaine,* Paris, Seuil, 1962, p. 26 (translation and emphasis added). This combination of "nationalised" socialism internally and non-alignment externally would then seem—as a specialist in the sociology of African political systems expressed it—to fulfil two functions : "First, the members of the new elites seek an ideology which will provide them with an identity. As individuals they have experienced both the life of traditional African society and that of the industrial Western world. All have rejected at least some of the values of the former and consequently experienced reproof from

2.5.3. This affirmation of an independent identity is more popular and appealing when the "mass political religion" [106](*e.g. African* personality, *Arab* socialism) demonstrates the continuity of the present society with the past and when individuals are made to feel that they are products of lives lived before theirs within the context of the nation. [107] This is precisely a dominant characteristic of African socialism, "for part of the search for identity consists of discovering ostensible roots of African socialism in indigenous society". Thus Senghor affirmed that through the study of African civilisation

> "we would learn that we had already realized socialism before the coming of the European". [108]

A question might come to the mind : if both non-alignment and a form of 'nationalised' socialism are two sides of the same integrative function affirming an independent identity, and if the 'nationalised' socialism has been linked to indigenous roots and traditions of African, Arab or Asian societies, is non-alignment not to be linked also to indigenous roots and traditions ? Indeed, Indian and other scholars have affirmed linkages

---

their elders or feelings of guilt. In accepting the technology of the West and acknowledging its superiority, they feel drawn towards declaiming the superiority of Western values, too. In their uncertainty they seek for guiding principles, defining the relationship between African and Western society ... Secondly, the elites seek to legitimize their rule. They have attained political power, as politicians and civil servants, by virtue of their education and by the ballot box, neither of which existed in traditional society. No traditional sanctions, therefore, exist by which the new leaders may justify their rule, although some have, after their accession to power, sought to assume the traditional symbols of chieftancy. The elite must thus espouse a doctrine that purports to explain and justify its leadership, converting political power into authority. And the ideology must find acceptance not only among the elite but also among the masses. For the alternative to a general acceptance of the legitimacy of government is rule by coercion." Lloyd : *op. cit.,* p. 270.

[106] The expression is Apter's in his article in Geertz (ed.) : *Old Societies and New States, op. cit.* ; see also his *Politics of Modernization, op. cit.,* pp. 267-270.

[107] Among the various African traditional values that are cited as precursors of present-day African socialism are communal ownership of land, egalitarian character of traditional African society or the low degree of its social stratification, the prevalence of group (rather than individual) psychology that resulted in the extensive network of social obligations and cooperation. For a detailed treatment of this point, see the papers submitted to the "Colloquium on Policies of Development and African Approaches to Socialism" (Dakar, 3-8 December 1962). See also : Zollberg, Aristide : "The Dakar Colloquium : the Search for a Doctrine" in *African Socialism, op. cit.,* pp. 113-127 ; Friedland, William : "Basic Social Trends" in *ibid.,* pp. 15-35 ; Kopytoff, Igor : "Socialism and Traditional African Societies" in *ibid.,* pp. 53-63 ; Thomas, L. : *Le socialisme et l'Afrique,* Paris, Le Livre Africain, 1966, especially vol. 1.

[108] Senghor, Léopold : *African Socialism,* New York, American Society for African Culture, 1959, p. 32.

between India's old culture, or principles of Buddhism, on the one hand, and, on the other, non-alignment as a foreign policy orientation. [109] Similarly, in the Arab subsystem, some analysts have claimed that non-alignment as a foreign policy orientation has its origins in the *Qur'an.* The '*sura*' of the *Qur'an* which says "*wa laqad khalaqnakum omattan wasat*" (We have created you an intermediary community) was quoted to prove this contention. [110]

This contention may or may not be true, and we will deal in detail with the bases and evolution of this policy as practiced by the precursor of "Arab Non-Alignment" : Nasser's Egypt. But before seeing how a *particular situation,* the Egyptian 'situation', led to a *specific behaviour* within the general spectrum of non-aligned orientation, we have to see first how some *shared situational determinants* led to the *grouping of the non-aligned actors together* as an international subsystem.

[109] See, for instance : Brecher, Michael : *The New States of Asia,* London, O.U.P., 1963, pp. 111-123 ; Jansen : *op. cit.,* pp. 115-124 ; Rana : *op. cit.,* pp. 206-260 ; Zinkin, Taya : "Indian Foreign Policy : An Interpretation of Attitudes", *World Politics,* VII (1955), pp. 179-209.

[110] Saab, Hassan : "The Philosophy of Neutralism in the Arab Mind" in Sayegh (ed.) : *The Dynamics of Neutralism in the Arab World, op. cit.,* pp. 105-111. More recently, another Arab scholar implied the correlation between present-day neutralism and cultural-Islamic history when he said : "The attitude (*i.e.* neutralism or non-alignment) evolved partly as a legacy of Islamic history and partly as the product of post-war circumstances." Khadduri, Majid : *Political Trends in the Arab World : The Role of Ideas and Ideals in Politics,* Baltimore, The Johns Hopkins Press, 1970, p. 273.

CHAPTER V

Non-Aligned Actors as an International Subsystem

1. Repeatedly and intuitively, labellations designate non-aligned actors as a *bloc, region,* or *group.*

1.1. Yet the non-aligned actors do not constitute a bloc. In their first meeting as early as 1954, both President Tito and Prime Minister Nehru repudiated in their final communiqué the "erroneous conception which has become prevalent in some quarters" of the creation by the non-aligned actors of a "third bloc". The two leaders stated that "this is a contradiction in terms because such a bloc would involve them in the very system of alignments which they regard as undesirable". [1] Similarly, at the First Summit Conference of Non-Aligned Countries (Belgrade, 1961), Nasser expressed the non-aligned position on the subject as follows :

> "I believe . . . we all agree that there should not be in the method of our approach, in the resolutions we reach or in the effects it may leave on world public opinion, that which might insinuate directly or indirectly that the states following a policy of non-alignment are by their activities creating a third world bloc. We live in a world suffering from the strife between two blocs and we cannot imagine that a third bloc should enter the arena and increase the tension of this strife instead of easing it." [2]

Not only do public declarations argue against the labellation "bloc", but also their collective international behaviour does not warrant it. An example is their discordant and opposed views toward a seemingly straightforward issue : the 1960 Congo Crisis. [3] We shall see this later in the chapter when we deal with the subsystem's structure.

---

[1] Rubinstein, Alvin Z. : *Yugoslavia and the Non-Aligned World,* Princeton, Princeton U.P., 1970.

[2] Choucri, Nazli : "The Perceptual Base of Non-Alignment", *op. cit.,* p. 70.

[3] On the Congo and non-aligned states, see, for instance : Crabb : *op. cit.,* pp. 59, 86, 121, 181. Good, Robert C. : "The Congo Crisis : A Study of Postcolonial Politics" in Martin : *op. cit.,* pp. 34-64.

1.2. To designate non-aligned actors as a region is not the most appropriate term either. Though the majority of non-aligned actors are situated in Afro-Asia, not all states in these two continents are non-aligned (*e.g.* the Asian members of both CENTO and SEATO). Moreover, interaction among non-aligned actors is not based solely on their geographical affinity, for it cannot be ignored that states like Cuba, Cyprus, Guyana, Trinidad and Tobago, and Yugoslavia are full non-aligned members. In addition, the definition of the term region has not been confined sometimes to geographical criteria. "Region" has been defined in terms of isolation or separateness (*e.g.* Africa South of the Sahara), of assumed sociophysical homogeneity and loyalties or patriotism on the part of its inhabitants (*e.g.* the Arab world), of an *ad hoc* problem (South-East Asia), or for reasons of administrative convenience to effect control over an area (*e.g.* the Middle East during the second World War). All this shows that the "region" concept can be vague, changing, and without an accepted operational definition. [4]

1.3. The generally used term in talking about non-aligned actors is "group". This designation is basically correct, for the term 'group' is often used too generally and can thus denote all ranges of 'togetherness'. But precisely because of its general applicability and use, its utility is limited. Moreover, the term 'group' is not very illuminating in expliciting the factors that bring the non-aligned actors together or take them apart. Nor does the term 'group' explicit the "linkage" of the non-aligned 'feeling of togetherness' to the structure and functioning of the contemporary international system.

This latter problem is dealt with when we use the term 'subsystem', and thus treat the non-aligned actors' coming together as linked to the global international system, *i.e.* as a 'partial international system' as Stanley Hoffmann preferred to call it.

2. **Subsystem Theory**

Empirical Relevance and Conceptual Non-Additivity

The demise of colonial empires and the rapid growth of new actors with their own level of political consciousness and distinctive patterns of interaction (whether conflict or collaboration) emphasised the relevance of a "political discontinuities" [5] model for the contemporary international

[4] Russett, Bruce M.: *International Regions and the International System,* Chicago, Rand McNally, 1967.

[5] Young, Oran: "Political Discontinuities in the International System", *World Politics,* XX (1968), pp. 369-392.

system, and hence the emphasis on a distinct analysis of international subsystems. Indeed, the first published use of the term was a reaction by a Middle East specialist [6] to Kaplan's analysis of the global system.

As was mentioned in chapter 2, Kaplan emphasised the bipolar model as an explanation of the structure of, and interaction in, the contemporary international system. Binder questioned the empirical extension of this bipolar model to all actor interactions and contended that Kaplan's model contained a "great power" bias and that its validity was limited in explaining less-than-great power behaviour. [7]

The payoffs and the potentiality of subsystem conceptualisation seem to be gaining at present increasing support among International Relations analysts, as manifested by the great mass of literature that seems to be developing around the subsystem concept. [8] A survey of this literature shows, however, that not only are different labellations *(e.g.* subordinate international subsystem, subordinate state subsystem, international regions . . .) used to identify the same object of analysis (the subsystem construct), but also that there is "conceptual disparity" as far as the contents of the various definitions are concerned. This is why we will start with stating our used definition of the concept, which will at the same time explicit some of the main variables of the non-aligned international subsystem that are going to be this chapter's focus of analysis.

2.1. An international subsystem is an *identifiable pattern of relations* (conflict and/or collaboration) among *political units (e.g.* states, international organisations, empires, blocs . . .) of the global system who *perceive themselves as interdependent* and interact with *frequency* according to *regularised* processes. [9]

Though an international subsystem need not be limited to states as its main components, this is indeed the case in the non-aligned subsystem. It is essentially an intergovernmental rather than a societal subsystem. But the proposed definition tries to confront a basic thorny problem in subsystem conceptualization : boundary delineation that serves to distinguish

---

[6] Binder, Leonard : "The Middle East Subordinate International System", *World Politics,* X (1958), pp. 408-429. Also W. Thompson : "The Regional Subsystem", *op. cit.*

[7] *Ibid.*

[8] See our bibliography, and also the more detailed bibliography in *ibid.* Moreover, the 70th annual meeting (1974) of the American Political Science Association is announcing a panel on "Foreign Policy and the International System : Theoretical Dimensions of the Subordinate System".

[9] See also Holsti : *International Politics, op. cit.,* p. 27, and Kaiser, Karl : "The Interaction of Regional Subsystems", *World Politics,* XXI (1968), p. 86.

the subsystem from its environment.[10] On this issue of boundary delineation, subsystem analysts seem to be divided between those who insist on the "objective" (*e.g.* geographical) boundary line and those who emphasise the "subjective" boundary line. The view adopted here is that these criteria of subsystem boundary demarcation are not mutually exclusive.

For instance, both the level of interaction within the subsystem (*i.e.* frequent regularised interaction) and the self-identification of the members as constituting a subsystem (*i.e.* perceived interdependence) are important criteria. The subjective boundary delineation is—as we shall shortly see—especially applicable in dealing with the non-aligned international subsystem.[11]

2.2. The application of subsystem conceptualization to non-aligned actors involves some difficulties ; for instance :

1. There is a problem of data availability on the non-aligned actors' interaction with each other. This problem seems to be inherent in the nature of non-alignment "which defines the position of its adherents

---

[10] *Ibid.* A subsystem could—but need not necessarily—be synonymous with geographical regions. It can be chosen to denote ideological (*e.g.* the Communist subsystem), political and/or military (*e.g.* Nato), financial (*e.g.* the group of ten), or organizational ties (*e.g.* the British Commonwealth, the Francophonie). Thus the subsystem concept includes not only geographical regions, but also groupings not based on geography. The relationship between the international system and its subsystems is a relationship of inclusion. The international system is the most comprehensive, spatially and not functionally speaking. Consequently, nation-states and also other socio-political systems can be (international) subsystems since they are actors in the global system ; but with some differences. For instance, usually

(*a*) international subsystems are more decentralized than nation-states, *i.e.* their components have more autonomy than those of nation-states ;

(*b*) international subsystems are (at least formally) more horizontally organized, *i.e.* relationships among their component units are not as hierarchical as among the units in states or nations (*e.g.* formally, all states, big and small, rich and poor, are equal in the General Assembly) ;

(*c*) international subsystems, compared with nation-states, have a "rather low level of institutionalization".

See Young, Oran : *A Systemic Approach to International Politics,* Princeton University, Center of International Studies, 1968, pamphlet 33, pp. 7-8. But other scholars have emphasized the similarities between international systems and subsystems, on the one hand, and nation-states or domestic political systems on the other. See, for instance : Alger, Chadwick F. : "Comparison of Intranational and International Politics", *American Political Science Review,* LVII (1969), pp. 406-419 ; Masters, Roger D. : "World Politics as a Primitive Political System", *World Politics,* XVI (1964), pp. 595-619 ; Riggs, Fred W. : "International Relations as a Prismatic System", *World Politics,* XIV (1961), pp. 144-181.

[11] "Political cultural identity" is the first in the 4-bases treatment of Africa as an "international subsystem". See Shepherd, George W. : *Non-aligned Black Africa: An International Subsystem,* Lexington, Heath Lexington Books, 1970, p. 9.

toward the great powers" but "does not attempt to prescribe the relations of neutralist countries with each other". In fact, "the doctrine neither seeks to, nor does it, guide Morocco's relations with Algeria, Ghana's with the Ivory Coast, Egypt's with Iraq or India's with Burma". [12]

2. Not only does Crabb's statement suggest that non-aligned actors lack the 'rules' or 'norms' for the establishment of a closely-integrated subsystem, but also he hints at the delineation of the subsystem's boundary on the basis of a small/great power dichotomy. Of course not all non-aligned actors are small powers *(e.g.* India) and not all small powers are non-aligned *(e.g.* The Philippines). We will deal with the problematical issue of the subsystem boundary later. For Crabb—unintentionally—uncovers a basic difficulty : how—in dealing with the non-aligned subsystem—to avoid using interchangeably the activities non-aligned actors undertake as 'third world members' and those they undertake in their non-aligned status. Shepherd—the first and only author of a book applying explicitly systems analysis to Africa—tried to solve this dilemma by suggesting that "the third world exists as a (sub)system only in an issue-area context. It has none of the features of an integrative problem-solving system of the non-aligned African subsystem. The various Afro-Asian conferences that have been held reflect the issue-area character of this system and not these other features. The membership of the third world group has been very fluid so that no identity has been established. Even the polar states, such as India and Ghana, can no longer be identified as spokesmen for this group. The third world does not caucus as a group at the United Nations. The major unifying theme is a point of view on colonial and racial issues." [13] Still, Shepherd's distinction is operationally neither convincing nor clear-cut. The problem is becoming even more complex for two reasons :

(*a*) the loosening of bipolar structure in the global system strengthens the North-South, rather than the East-West dichotomy and hence makes 'third world' states and non-aligned actors more overlapping and interchangeable ; and

(*b*) this overlapping and interchangeability are increasing at the moment with the growing recruitment of 'third world' states to the membership of the non-aligned subsystem, and thus the 'watering down' of the formal boundary of non-alignment.

An attempt to meet these problems systematically is (1) operationalize the concept of the non-aligned subsystem : *i.e.* specify the criteria necessary for its identification ; (2) explicit the subsystem variables and apply

[12] Crabb : *op. cit.,* p. 13.

[13] Shepherd : *op. cit.,* p. 127.

them to the formally and avowedly non-aligned activities : *i.e.* non-aligned summit conferences. The overall gatherings are :

1. June 1961 : Cairo Preparatory Meeting, 20 members with 1 observer.
2. September 1961 : Belgrade First Summit Conference, 25 members with 3 observers.
3. March 1964 : Colombo Preparatory Meeting, 23 members.
4. October 1964 : Cairo Second Summit Conference, 47 members with 10 observers.
5. July 1969 : Belgrade Consultative Meeting, 44 members with 7 observers.
6. September 1969 : New York Consultative Meeting, 53 members with 6 observers.
7. April 1970 : Dar-es-Salaam Preparatory Meeting, 51 members with 3 observers.
8. September 1970 : Lusaka Third Summit Conference, 53 members with 12 observers.
9. September 1971 : New York Consultative Meetings, about 53 members with 5 observers.
10. August 1972 : Georgetown Conference of Foreign Ministers, 58 members with 10 observers.

2.3. *Criteria for Identifying a Subsystem*

2.3.1. Raymond Aron has explicited three criteria :

1. That the subsystem, though obviously linked to the dominant pattern of relationship in the global system, has its autonomous pattern of relationship. Thus in "the Near East, despite the armistice signed by Israel and its neighbours, a state of war officially subsists. The Arab states have not 'recognized' the state created by the Jews . . . The equilibrium of local forces is a decisive factor in the situation. Yet this regional equilibrium cannot be envisaged without considering global conditions." [14]

[14] Aron : *Peace and War, op. cit.*, pp. 389-395.

2. But what if a state of war does not exist permanently in time and space and thus the local equilibrium of military forces cannot be used to identify a subsystem ? Aron then suggests his second criterion : states or peoples' spontaneous experience of solidarity of their destiny ; that is when they "observe a difference between what is happening inside and what is happening outside their geographical historical zone". [15] To illustrate this second criterion, Aron gives the example of the Cuban revolution and the effect both on the U.S. and on Latin American states of "the exploit of this bearded David standing up to a Goliath armed with dollars". And Aron continues : "Why did the earth shake in Latin America, after the Cuban revolution and not after the Chinese one ? The reasons are simple, eternal : neither the means of transport nor the means of destruction have suppressed the human significance of distance, the mutual reinforcements of historical relationship and spatial proximity. What Fidel Castro has done other men in Brazil or Peru may also dream of doing. In any case, all the peoples of Latin America feel that the Cuban experiment is instructive, that it suggests a possible path. Revolutions accomplished far away, by people of other races, do not provoke the same passions. Humanity is perhaps one, but the peoples have not a clear awareness of their unity." [16]

3. A third criterion in identifying a subsystem results from "the very rivalry of the two superpowers, from the stake which it constitutes in each part of the world, and from the manner in which it is carried on by each power". And in order to concretize the criterion, Aron gives an empirical example—not from the Middle East or Latin America but this time from Europe. "Europe", Aron says, "does not constitute a subsystem merely on account of the equilibrium between the two coalitions or on account of the awareness of a common civilization : the direct impact of the two superpowers and the constitution of military blocs make Europe a subsystem or, if one prefers, a theater of diplomatic operations with a certain autonomy." [17]

---

[15] *Ibid.*

[16] *Ibid.*

[17] Aron gives also a different example : "... the situation emerging in Africa ... Neither the United States nor the Soviet Union is, in military terms, present in Africa. The United States does not aim at the same goal there as in Asia or in South America : the neutrality of the states is enough, and the commitment of the Western side seems futile or dangerous. The Soviet Union applies its usual techniques : propaganda, education of militants in special schools, invitations to students, moral or material aid ... But even when it achieves its goals and one of the African republics declares itself a 'people's republic', the result is not the equivalent of the Sovietization of a European nation ... In Africa each of the superpowers has as its main objective to keep out the other ..." *Ibid.*

Aron's criteria of subsystem identification raise problems of operationalization, [18] and Aron admits it for he says, for instance, that his "second criterion is not easy to use". [19] Two points, however, have to be stressed:

1. The delineation of the subsystem is geographically-based, even though Aron does not always say this explicitly. Thus he talks about "the regional [20] subsystem" or about "other regions, what one would call subsystems". [21] It is true that Aron realizes that delineation can be "of an economic or ideological character. In Japan, for instance, in the early 1950's, Tokyo seemed closer to Washington, to London or even to Paris than to Peking. . . . Established within the network of alliances and bases woven by the maritime power, Japan communicated more readily with the Anglo-Saxon world than with nearby China . . ." [22] But this is a "paradox", a "temporary rupture" and anyhow "seems to be in the process of attenuation, if not of disappearing". [23]

2. The delineation of the subsystem is also based on the 'subjective' feeling of the participants, their self-identification as constituting a subsystem. After mentioning the example of Europe to concretise his third criterion, Aron adds: "The (European) actors feel more vitally affected by what happens inside than by what happens outside the regional ensemble". [24] This 'subjective' element in subsystem delineation is even clearer in his second criterion and is emphasized when Aron quotes the example of the Cuban revolution to substantiate this second criterion. For, compared to the Chinese revolution, the greater impact of the Cuban revolution on Latin America is not to be explained by geographical proximity only, but also by 'socio-psychological nearness'. Geographical proximity, the 'objective' criterion of subsystem identification, and 'socio-psychological nearness', the 'subjective' criterion, are mutually reinforcing. There is the implication of a positive correlation, since "in certain regions the geographical, racial and historical solidarity" is put together, and since China—Aron says—is not only the geographical neighbour of Japan, but also "the hearth of the culture it (Japan) had received . . .". [25]

---

[18] This is in addition to the lack in expliciting the subsystem variables.

[19] *Ibid.*

[20] Aron uses 'region' in the accepted geographical sense. We will respect the convention.

[21] *Ibid.*

[22] *Ibid.*

[23] *Ibid.*

[24] *Ibid.*

[25] *Ibid.*

2.3.2. Both the 'objective' (geographical) and 'subjective' (feeling of the participants) criteria of subsystem identification are adopted by another 'subsystem theorist'. But Michael Brecher's [26] list includes six "conditions of subordinate [27] system's existence" :

1. Delimited scope, with primary stress on a geographic region.
2. Objective recognition by most actors as constituting a distinctive community, region, or segment of the global system.
3. Self-identification as such.
4. The subsystem should at least have three actors.
5. Units of power relatively inferior to units in the dominant system.
6. More intensive and influential penetration of the subordinate system rather than the reverse.

To clarify intensity of interaction within a subsystem, Brecher quotes the example of Arab-Israeli relations within the Middle East subsystem, where interaction is so high that domestic developments in one of the members affect "the internal and frequently the external affairs of others as well as the power and psychological equilibria of the Near East Case". Firstly, Israel would react violently to a basic change in Jordan's or Lebanon's domestic politics. Secondly, though no formal relations exist between Israel and the Arab states, interaction is high at several levels : military (three wars and continuous clashes), diplomatic (moves in the international system : in Africa, the U.N. and different gatherings). Brecher mentions also the "striking homogeneity" in the pattern of values among the Arab members : common culture, history, language and religious tradition, as well as other traits they share with Afro-Asian states : common experience of foreign domination, goals of economic development and political stability, and attachment to nationalism and symbols of independence.

Brecher's first criterion of subsystem identification is the geographical delineation, which is relatively easy to use and in fact seems to receive consensus among subsystem theorists—as we have seen in Aron's case. With Aron, Brecher shares the attempt to combine 'subjective' and 'objective' criteria in the identification of a subsystem—as his criteria two and

[26] Brecher, Michael : "The Middle East Subordinate System and its Impact on Israel's Foreign Policy", *International Studies Quarterly,* XIII (1969), pp. 985-998.

[27] Cantori and Spiegel defined a "subordinate system" as consisting of one state, or of two or more proximate and interacting states which have some common ethnic, linguistic, cultural, social and historical bonds, and whose sense of identity is sometimes increased by the actions and attitudes of states external to the system. Louis Cantori and Steven Spiegel (eds.) : *The International Politics of Regions : A Comparative Approach,* Englewood Cliffs, Prentice Hall, 1970, p. 8.

three show. As for criterion four, one wonders why Brecher insists on a minimum of three actors [28] to identify a subsystem—an insistence that few subsystem theorists would share with Brecher. The reason is simple : the insistence on three actors as a minimum would exclude areas such as Soviet-American, Sino-Soviet, Anglo-French or Egyptian-Israeli relations from being treated in systemic terms, *i.e.* interactionally. [29] Brecher's fifth and sixth criteria attract attention to the hierarchical ranking among system and subsystem, or among subsystems. On this point, however, Brecher uses ambiguous terminology, for one is left uncertain about whether Brecher intends the hierarchy between a subsystem and the global system, or the hierarchy between two distinct subsystems, or he intends the hierarchy to apply in both cases.

2.3.3. While emphasizing this element of hierarchical ranking, Deutsch avoids this terminological ambiguity by explicitly identifying the subsystem in relation to the global system. [30] While expressed in a formalized way, like Aron, Deutsch offers three criteria for the identification of a subsystem. In order that subsystem "A" can be considered as such in its relation to (the system) "B" :

1. "A" has to be entirely contained by "B" ;
2. "A" has to be numerically or quantitatively smaller than "B" ;
3. In the case of opposition or conflict between "A" and "B", "A" has to be theoretically subdued.

Deutsch's first criterion emphasizes the relationship of inclusion between the global system and a subsystem. This criterion is true by definition as the prefix 'sub' in the term 'subsystem' indicates, and as labellations like Hoffmann's 'partial international system' more explicitly show. Deutsch's second criterion emphasizes the smaller size of the subsystem, and the hierarchical aspect is even more clear in the third criterion.

---

[28] The minimum of three actors is also insisted on by Shepherd, but differently from Brecher he is speaking only of a non-aligned subsystem rather than providing a general definition of a subsystem, Shepherd says "a non-alignment subsystem is a group of three or more non-aligned states that form a functioning political system". Shepherd : *op. cit.*, p. 9.

[29] Some scholars tried to specify 'interaction' and distinguish it from 'relationship'. Thus "when two or more entities behave vis-à-vis one another, and there is a sequence of at least two discernible acts such that the first can 'reasonably' be interpreted as partly responsible for the second, we may speak of *interaction.* Before and after, as well as during, a given interaction sequence, the entities continue to be related in some fashion, however distant and remote."

Singer, J. David : "The Global System and its Subsystems : A Developmental View" in Rosenau (ed.) : *Linkage Politics, op. cit.*, p. 37.

[30] Deutsch, Karl W. in : *Colloque sur la démarche scientifique dans l'étude des relations internationales,* Genève, Dotation Carnegie, 17-18 novembre 1968.

3. **Application of Subsystem Theory to Non-Aligned Actors**

In the light of the criteria of subsystem identification offered by the different 'subsystem theorists', we must now consider whether the hypothesis that non-aligned actors have constituted a distinct entity from the other two blocs or subsystems is valid or not.

3.1. In applying the criteria mentioned above by Aron, Brecher and Deutsch, it follows that non-aligned actors do constitute a subsystem. The reasons justifying this statement are :

1. Non-aligned states are a multiplicity of actors which enjoy certain autonomy vis-a-vis each other but are related since the basis of their interaction is the espousal of a common set of foreign policy norms : non-alignment. Some students of non-alignment affirm that the common features go even beyond and deeper than foreign policy orientation. "... Most of the leading neutralist 'ideologues' ", says Lyon, "share a wide range of strikingly similar national and personal problems, that they are facing these problems at approximately the same time, that these similarities tend to give something of a common character, even an international aspect to neutralist doctrine. For these 'ideologues' are not only prominent figures in international politics, they nearly all spring from the Western-educated intelligentsia of their countries. They are all, in a sense, both producers and consumers of anti-colonial and nationalist revolution, and have to act as the chief spokesmen—at home and abroad—for their generally new, poor, ex-colonial states." [31]

2. The empirical existence of a certain pattern of relationships based on regular interaction through periodic summit conferences and consultations at the U.N. This distinguishes between the non-aligned actors constituting a subsystem and any multiplicity of entities having no regular interaction with each other.

3.2. Though these arguments supporting the presence of a non-aligned subsystem seem to be justified, they will be even more so once counter-arguments that might question the presence of a non-aligned subsystem are falsified. For on the surface of it, little might support the hypothesis that non-aligned countries can be treated as a subsystem :

1. For even if one agreed that there is an 'esprit de corps' among non-aligned actors, one also sees that their non-alignment does not mean a uniform policy for all its adherents on all occasions. But this counter-

[31] Lyon : *op. cit.*, p. 60.

argument is based on the erroneous assumption of equating 'subsystem' with uniformity or harmony. If this were indeed the meaning of a subsystem, there would not have been any studies treating conflict-torn, geographically identifiable areas in 'systemic' terms. Yet both Binder and Brecher have treated the Middle East, for instance, as a subsystem.[32] Moreover, conflict precisely seems to be a reason advanced by Bernard Gordon for considering South-East Asia a subsystem, a "political region" as he calls it. "The second factor", Gordon says, "which makes South-East Asia a 'region' is the widespread incidence of conflict, along with some attempts at cooperation, in the area. Both conflict and cooperation are forms of communication . . ."[33]

2. That the broad similarity in approach toward the contemporary international system and the common reaction a Nasser, a Nehru or a Sukarno shared toward East-West bloc affiliation does not seem to have resulted in an institutionally identifiable structure binding the non-aligned actors together. But the low level of institutionalization and the weakness in formal organizational links characterize other regionally-based, geographically-identifiable subsystems, *e.g.* South-East Asia. Moreover, the non-aligned subsystem—as we shall see in detail—is driving toward increasing formalization of its structure.

3. A related counter-argument might point out the absence of enforcement mechanism among non-aligned actors. But this weakness exists in generally-accepted subsystems, characterized by an advanced level of institutionalization *(e.g.* Arab subsystem, Africa).

These aspects do exist in the non-aligned subsystem, but they can be cited as imperfections : evidence of its weakness rather than its non-existence. Moreover, the imperfections may also be indications of the subsystem's growth or decay, rather than its absence.[34] This is why Shepherd in his application of subsystem theory to Africa focuses—not upon traditional institutions of authority—but quotes as the first basis of a non-aligned subsystem "political cultural identity" and fifth basis "non-subordination to an external power".[35]

---

[32] Binder : *op. cit.* Brecher : "The Middle East . . .", *op. cit.*

[33] Gordon, Bernard : "A Political Region of South-East Asia" in Cantori and Spiegel : *op. cit.*, p. 132.

[34] Shepherd : *op. cit.*, p. 23.

[35] *Ibid.*, p. 9. The five bases of a non-aligned subsystem as Shepherd elaborated them, correspond to the components of non-alignment. These components are : (*a*) diplomatic independence ; (*b*) military disengagement ; (*c*) economic diversification ; (*d*) ideological and cultural self-identification. *Ibid.*, p. 8.

4.

Once the hypothesis of non-aligned actors constituting a subsystem is accepted, the problem of how many and which *variables* to single out for detailed analysis must be decided. Of course, we can take the same variables as for the global international system, though this is not necessary. For the variables are best chosen as a function of the particular points that are relevant for any particular chapter. However, the different definitions of a system and/or a subsystem show consensus on four basic variables : boundaries, components or members, interaction processes and structure. Not only are these variables treated at length here, but a fifth variable—regulatory mechanism in the non-aligned subsystem—is included.

4.1. *The Subsystem Boundaries* [36]

4.1.1. As we have seen, most subsystem theorists have emphasized primarily geographical delineation, whether the author was dealing with Africa, [37] the Middle East, [38] or South-East Asia. [39] A geographical boundary is indeed very important for it is 'objectively' identifiable, but it should neither be taken as a *sine qua non* condition of subsystem presence, nor should it be taken as the sole boundary.

It is, indeed, true that the greatest majority of non-aligned actors are situated in Africa and Asia, yet some actors in these two continents are not non-aligned (*e.g.* Pakistan). Others, though declaredly non-aligned, have never attended these non-aligned summit conferences (*e.g.* Upper Volta, Ivory Coast). Moreover, interaction among non-aligned actors is not solely based on their geographical affinity, for it cannot be ignored that Cuba, Cyprus, Guyana, Trinidad and Tobago, as well as Yugoslavia are not within the Afro-Asian geographical region.

4.1.2. When a non-aligned actor, for instance, shows more concern with what befalls an Afro-Asian fellow actor than with what happens to a European, a boundary is indeed there but it is not solely geographical.

---

[36] The formal definition of boundary (or "boundary condition") as stated in general systems theory, for instance, is : "a line area, or statistical measure that separates two completely distinguishable classes of things thereby serving as a determinant of inclusion and exclusion". Young : *A Systemic Approach . . ., op. cit.*, p. 109.

[37] Zartman, William I. : "Africa as a Subordinate State System in International Relations", *International Organization,* XXI (1967), pp. 345-364.

[38] Binder : *op. cit.* Brecher : *The Middle East . . ., op. cit.*

[39] Brecher : "The Subordinate State System of Southern Asia", *op. cit.*

Common history as ex-colonies, and present socio-psychological characteristics also contribute to boundary-delineation. This is the 'subjective' boundary line that both Aron and Brecher have emphasized, and the "common ethnic, ... cultural, social and historical bonds ..." that Cantori and Spiegel have included in their definition of a subsystem. These two authors, in fact, do not limit themselves to the geographical boundary. They affirm that "indigenous political relationships (antagonistic and cooperative), geographic factors, and social and historical backgrounds help to define a subordinate system". And again they say : "Within the boundaries of a subordinate system, there is a complex interaction between political, social and geographic factors. It is this interaction which is most important in defining the limits of a subordinate system." [40]

Holsti also emphasizes this plural aspect of the subsystem boundary. "Any international (sub)system", Holsti says, "has identifiable boundaries —geographic, cultural, or issue lines ..." [41]

An indicator of this subjective, less material but important boundary line is the reaction of India's top leadership to events taking place almost at the same time in both Egypt and Hungary (October-November 1956). India's reaction to the Anglo-French "aggression" in Egypt was prompt condemnation "of Anglo-French behaviour suggesting their retreat to past colonial ways and was in full sympathy with Egypt, fraternal in relations with her and sharing her anti-colonialism, non-alignment and opposition to the great power military pacts and alliances". Briefly, in Suez, India "was prepossessed with an anti-colonial complex". As for Hungary, "her pre-possession lay in her hope that de-stalinization, left unintercepted, would lead to de-polarization in world politics". [42] Summarizing India's different stands toward these two simultaneous issues, as well as outside reaction to the Indian government's position, a standard study on non-alignment confirms the above interpretation. India "herself", Lyon says, "came to support her neutralist friend Egypt, with whose plight she had a great deal of sympathy. Mr. Nehru's initial public reaction to the Hungarian Revolution was vacillating and then rather evasive. This caused a great annoyance in the Western world and among a sizeable [43] segment of Indian opinion, and he was accused of *applying double standards,* either

[40] *The International Politics of Regions ..., op. cit.*

[41] Holsti : *International Politics ..., op. cit.*

[42] Mallik, *op. cit.,* p. 182. See also *Nehru's Speech* in Lok Sabha, November 19, 1956.

[43] In his public statements, Krishna Menon—India's chief delegate at the U.N. at the time and a close collaborator of Nehru—agreed that "the reaction against India's policy on Hungary in the U.N. was not confined to those ... [who] would ... [be] ... consider[ed] traditional critics, people hostile to India in the U.S. and elsewhere. Within the country itself [*i.e.* India] there was very substantial criticism from a wide

as between Suez and Hungary questions, or as *between Asian (sic) and European questions.*" [44] We do not need to dwell on Nehru's justifications of the two positions at Lok Sabha, for the important indicator for us is Nehru's condemnatory tone as far as Suez was concerned and his emphasis on 'mediatorial' efforts as far as Hungary was concerned.

Nehru's reaction was, then, not only dictated by geographical factors, but also by socio-psychological affinity : an anti-colonial drive and a feeling of "togetherness" among underdogs, *perceived* as common victims of a "certain configuration of power" at the global systemic level. It is this *common perception* of the contemporary international system, their "definition of the situation" that is at the basis of their common attitudinal orientation toward the system's key members and issues.

The socio-psychological boundary line is even clearer in the public statements and press interviews of Krishna Menon—India's chief delegate at the U.N. at the time and Nehru's friend. [45] For Menon, Hungary was essentially a Cold War question. "In the Hungary question", Menon affirmed, "the U.S.—the U.K. too—was most shame-facedly using the U.N. as an instrument of the Cold War." In fact, Hungary was used because "the American desire was only to give the one side a grand slam in the Assembly. That is the background." In this situation, Menon continues, "you cannot expect us to take the same line as the prosecutors did, to make the U.N. a forum for the Cold War". In this case the affair is basically a case of Western "interventionism . . . It really means that the U.S. is to decide when there is to be an election anywhere . . . Secondly,

---

section of the public, from Parliament, political parties, from the Press, etc.". Menon's explanation of this phenomenon is interesting, for he remarks that everyone of these critics, including the Indians, have as their source of information *Western news agencies* and thus have only these agencies version. "They get it [information] from the Western news agencies", Menon insisted, ". . . they don't read the U.N. papers to which I have referred. The articulate people here are our political opposition. They would try to discredit the Prime Minister or to attack me and also show up that I am a particular friend of the Prime Minister . . ." Brecher : *India and World Politics, op. cit.*, p. 93.

[44] Lyon : *op. cit.*, pp. 126-127 (emphasis added).

[45] Menon's view is very important because he was more than a normal chief delegate at the U.N. He himself explained in public how he used very often to act independently without returning to his Foreign Ministry or to the Prime Minister for instructions. "When I wanted instructions", Menon said, "I sent a telegram to the Prime Minister suggesting how and what should be done ; in fact, *more or less informing him what our instructions should be.* He would usually send a telegram back and say, 'I generally agree with your analysis. You must use your discretion'. *No representative functioned in the way I did. I functioned as a Foreign Minister at the U.N.* and the Americans and other people knew it. Sometimes, to gain time, I would say, 'I want time for instructions', which I was entitled to say. And they often laugh." Brecher : *India and World Politics, op. cit.*, p. 93 (emphasis added).

to the U.S. Hungary was a Cold War affair, although the issue was being debated on other ostensible grounds." [46]

The main distinction that needs to be stressed, as far as the difference between Suez and Hungary is concerned, is that "we took the view that ... you could not talk of her [Hungary] as a colony". And again the distinction between European and Afro-Asian issues is stated more straightforwardly when Menon says: "You hear a great deal about rescuing *foreign* (*i.e.* European) women [in Stanleyville, the Congo, December 1964] but what about all the Africans killed by the *foreigners?* ... What about the Indian troops who were killed in Katanga?" [47] Thus whereas Africans and Indians are called by their names, K. Menon uses the labellation "foreigners" to designate Europeans and North Americans—or the non-Afro-Asians. The latter are the 'insiders' and the former are the 'outsiders'.

This socio-psychological boundary is even clearer when Menon is dealing with Suez. [48] "The Egyptians", Menon emphatically says, "... are ... like us." [49] The common identification among Afro-Asians is implicitly emphasised when Menon angrily repudiates the British unfavorable image of the ex-colonized (which is—of course—insulting for *both* Indians and Egyptians): "The British banked on the idea that the Egyptians would never be able to take ships through the Canal. But that was one of the fictions that had built up. More ships passed through the Canal during the period of the interregnum than during any corresponding length of time before, which angered the British very much." [50] And again more explicitly "The British spoilt all ... because they still thought of the Egyptians as 'natives'." [51] In this case, the boundary line is drawn between the Hungarian question, an essentially European *(i.e.* "foreign") conflict of Cold War politics and the Egyptian question, an Afro-Asian issue *(i.e.* an "in"-concern) of common anti-colonial war. "For myself", Menon asserts, "I anticipated this war [Suez], but the Prime Minister never believed—there is no harm in saying so—that the British would send troops. He had great faith in British common sense. I said to him 'You

[46] *Ibid.*, pp. 85-97.

[47] *Ibid.*, p. 91.

[48] Menon's treatment of Suez is even more significant because, beside representing his country at the U.N., he was its delegate at the London Users' Meeting to discuss the issue after Nasser's nationalization of the Canal. Moreover, he used to move between London and Delhi proposing settlements, phone Nasser from London to discuss compromises ... For details, see *ibid.*, pp. 62-77.

[49] *Ibid.*, p. 71.

[50] *Ibid.*, pp. 62-63.

[51] *Ibid.*, p. 66.

don't know them as well as I do . . . You don't take into account their imperial methods—it's in their blood; the British will invade them.' "[52] This is why "when British troops landed in Egypt, Nehru was the *most shocked man.* He said 'what is the use of my talking about changes in the world, it's like the old [*i.e.* colonial] days'."[53]

To sum up, then, the subsystem boundary between Afro-Asian, non-aligned and Cold War or "foreign" issues, should not be limited only to geographical demarcation, but should also emphasize the participants' socio-psychological distinction between "out" and "in" concerns, negative and positive identification.

There might be objections to the sample : that Nehru's or Menon's drawing of the subsystem boundary—even though their country is the biggest and first non-aligned actor and that they personally contributed significantly to the conceptualization and exercise of non-alignment—cannot be taken as a solid basis for generalization. But two points can be emphasized in this respect :

1. In the First Non-Aligned Summit Conference (Belgrade, September 1961), India was accused by some of its fellow-participants of being too internationalist. Nehru, in fact, advocated—both in the conference discussions and in the final communiqué—paying more attention to Cold War rather than to colonial issues. In other words, if anything India was accused of 'conservatism' as far as the emphasis on "colonial questions" was concerned,[54] and hence Nehru's and Menon's emphasis on the boundary line acquires an added significance.

2. A quantitative study applying the perceptual distinctions—established by some studies in psychology—to the way Afro-Asian non-aligned actors evaluate each other and the way they evaluate Cold War protagonists seem to confirm the subsystem boundary as drawn in Nehru's and Menon's statements.[55] Through the use of automated content analysis, measurement of perceptual orientation from speeches and addresses by major non-aligned leaders[56] (50,000 words approximately) in three sum-

---

[52] *Ibid.,* p. 66.

[53] *Ibid.,* pp. 65-67 (emphasis added).

[54] We will discuss this aspect in detail when we treat the subsystem's structural heterogeneity.

[55] Choucri : *op. cit.*

[56] Choucri has chosen only three leaders : Nehru, Nasser and Sukarno, because India, Egypt and Indonesia were accepted as "key states in their respective areas, and their behavior inevitably affects the configuration of their regional systems. At the global level each has achieved a measure of renown for its official refusal to align in the Cold War conflict. These three were among the earliest nations to adopt a non-aligned position and were instrumental in developing the rudimentary tenets of this policy." *Ibid.,* pp. 61-62.

mit conferences [57] confirms the hypothesis of positive evaluation (*i.e.* togetherness) of Afro-Asians and ambiguity or indifference toward Cold War powers (the summary indice indicates a "negative evaluation of .560 toward Cold War powers"). [58]

4.1.3. This positive evaluation, common identification or spirit of 'togetherness' among Afro-Asian non-aligned states, acting as the subsystem's 'subjective' boundary between the "ins" and the "outs", is conditioned—as Nehru's and Menon's reactions show—by these states' past as ex-colonies and their common present as new actors. Thus their *common* position in the international system *(i.e.* the systemic component of their *common* 'definition of the situation') resulted in a *common* attitudinal orientation to systemic bipolarization ; non-participation in *formal* East-East alliances, or non-alignment.

When the blocs were well-defined, semi-closed entities, the refusal to participate in East-West blocs constituted the *formal* materialization of the boundary. Admittedly this formal concretization of the (subjective) boundary was based on a 'community of negativeness'.

But this 'community of negativeness' constituted a common meeting point grouping national variations in the practice of non-alignment, as a computer-based analysis proved. "There are", Choucri states, "many conflicting interpretations in both academic and official circles as to how various groups in the international system are viewed by the non-aligned states. There is also considerable question as to whether historical contacts with the Western nations have affected present evaluation, and whether Communist policies in adjacent areas have had any significant impact on the 'third world'." The summary indices resulting from the testing of the hypothesis about non-aligned actors' evaluation of East and West Cold War participants show a negative score of .561 for the West and .540 for the East (with number of sources 495 and 210 respectively). [59]

---

[57] The three Conferences are : Bogor (1954), Bandung (1955) and Belgrade (1961).

[58] Choucri : *op. cit.,* pp. 66-67. There is another significant empirical finding in the study which has to be mentioned in this respect, and that is how the three non-aligned Afro-Asians evaluate aligned Afro-Asian actors : do they evaluate them in the same terms as the non-aligned ones or do they evaluate them in the same way they evaluate aligned Western or Eastern members ? The result of computation indicates that the non-aligned leaders do not seem to differentiate between the allied and non-aligned states of Asia and Africa : both are viewed favorably regardless of foreign policy orientation. According to the summary indices, aligned states are viewed as negative in a score of 272 and the non-aligned in a score of 275. These empirical findings indicate that the Afro-Asian 'spirit of togetherness' is based on an Afro-Asian 'common situation' and is not radically affected by subsequent differences in foreign policy orientation.

[59] *Ibid.,* p. 64.

In spite of its 'negativeness', [60] this formal concretization of the (subjective) boundary helped to bring and maintain together the non-aligned actors in the 1950's and early 1960's. But because this formalization was effected in relation to the blocs (formalization = non-participation in East-West alliances), once the bipolar division became looser, and the East-West blocs tended to become less closed and monolithic, the *formal* aspect of the boundary separating alignment from non-alignment was blurred. Indeed, for some non-alignment appeared "as obsolete as the Cold War". [61] This need not necessarily be the case, for if the formal aspect of the boundary has been blurred, both the geographical and socio-psychological aspects of the boundary are still there. As if to support this view, an international symposium of academicians and statesmen mainly from non-aligned actors believed that "the term non-alignment is not adequate, especially not at the present phase of international developments. In this respect, two things are particularly obvious : first, that the term narrows and limits its substance, its historical role, that is, the lasting quality of non-alignment ; and second, that it does not center on the

---

[60] As the term non-alignment itself shows, the formal aspect of the boundary was essentially negative : rejection of Cold War-defined identification and control. Though negative labellations can sometimes be more specific than positive ones (*e.g.* "Thou shalt not steal" compared with "Do unto others as you would like others to do unto you") the term non-alignment still hid more than it revealed. But its adoption was dictated by the global systemic structure (bipolarity) in which it arose, and thus the term was used as a residual category in relation to the two existing blocs. This was clear in the first official declaration of non-alignment when Nehru was appointed Member for External Affairs and Commonwealth in the Government of India in September 1946. Nehru said : "We propose ... to *keep away* from the power politics of groups ..." (emphasis added). In retrospect, this negative connotation introduced an element of flexibility in the boundary line and gave each non-aligned actor (as long as it did not subscribe formally to the Superpowers' blocs) the freedom to practice its non-alignment and shape its specific foreign policy behavior without losing subsystem membership. Moreover, with the increasing pressures for bloc participation, non-aligned actors felt that they were facing a common danger. This elicited similar reactions which helped to regroup them together and promote the 'feeling of togetherness'. Consequently, common situational features and similar foreign policy attitudes tended to suppress differences and predominate over divergences.

But with the increasing looseness of the bipolar pattern, the boundary of the subsystem became blurred and heterogeneity among subsystem members tended to be more apparent. This decline in subsystem cohesiveness was aggravated by an increase in "an indiscriminate membership ... [which] merely devolve[d] the policy and blur[red] its distinctiveness". Jansen : *op. cit.*, p. 375. But this did not mean that non-alignment as a foreign policy—rather than as an international subsystem—had declined. This is the mistake the 'power school' has committed : it confused between non-alignment as an international subsystem (*i.e.* the systemic level of analysis) and non-alignment as a state's foreign policy (the actor level of analysis).

[61] Ljubivoje Acimovic (ed.) : *Non-alignment in the World of Today,* Beograd, 1969, p. 27.

objectives of this policy but on its means, and that it is not adequate even in this respect." [62]

To conclude, a common geographical and socio-psychological situation conditioned a common perceptual orientation toward the East-West conflict and fostered a 'feeling of togetherness' among newly-independent actors. This common perceptual orientation and this 'feeling of togetherness' manifested themselves in rejection of East-West bloc membership. As long as the blocs remained well-defined, this rejection of bloc-membership acted as the formal aspect of the subsystem boundary. But once this simplicity in global systemic structure tended to disappear, the formal aspect of the boundary separating the aligned from the non-aligned was undermined. Moreover, heterogeneity within the non-aligned subsystem tended to be more apparent. This heterogeneity was always there, because it seems inherent in non-alignment as such and in the diversity of the subsystem components. This brings us to our second variable : components or members of the subsystem.

4.2. *Components or Members*

4.2.1. By definition the subsystem is composed of all actors that are declaredly non-aligned, yet this criterion of membership is not as easy to apply as it would appear. Since non-alignment is not operationalized beyond non-participation in formal East-West military alliances, there is no unanimity on other uniform criteria to identify and classify a non-aligned actor. What is 'really and objectively' a non-aligned actor and what is not, constituted a basic problem in some cases for the sponsors of the First Summit Conference. Before the convening of the main gathering, the problem had to be settled by a Preparatory Conference held in Cairo (June 1961).

From the very start, there were two opposing groups in the conference [63] :

1. The 'exclusivists' who adopted a strict definition of non-alignment and aimed at limiting the number of the non-aligned countries to be invited. This tendency was mainly represented by the militant Casablanca group, supported by Cuba, Indonesia and Yugoslavia.

---

[62] *Ibid.,* pp. 36-37. What this, in fact, boils down to is that as long as the socio-psychological common situation (*i.e.* the bases that gave birth to non-alignment) exist, non-alignment itself would continue to exist—though its expression and character might change and develop in response to different global systemic configurations (*e.g.* degrees of bipolarity).

[63] Jansen : *op. cit.,* p. 285.

2. The 'inclusivists' who embraced a broader point of view and sought a more flexible definition of non-alignment (applying to any country which was not a member of a big power bloc). Even India went so far as to suggest drawing the distinction between "military alliances which were objectionable and agreements for military training concluded between ex-colonies and former rulers which could be condoned". [64]

This latter group, which wanted to invite all shades of non-aligned states to the conference, was represented by most Asian countries, supported by Ethiopia and Sudan and led by India :

But first non-alignment had to be defined, and so a subcommittee was constituted and charged with this task. After eleven hours of discussion, it produced a five-point definition of non-alignment.

To be invited to the non-aligned conference, countries had to meet the following requirements [65] :

1. To follow an independent policy based on peaceful co-existence with other countries of different political and social ideologies or to show trends towards such a policy.
2. Always to support popular liberation movements.
3. Refusal to join any bilateral treaty with any regional defence bloc, if that would mean involvement in East-West conflict.
4. Refusal to join any collective military pact that would involve implication in current East-West disputes.
5. Refusal to have on its territory any foreign military bases set up with their own consent. [66]

These five points were drawn in general terms which left room for flexibility in interpretation. For example, the first condition 'to follow an independent policy . . .' is too general and even ambiguous. The points concerned with alliances and bases are negative prohibitions. [67] The second item is the clearest perhaps, and much stress was laid upon it. This constituted a straightforward Afro-Asian anti-colonialism.

Thus the definition was general, and at this level of generality the non-aligned actors did come together. But this general level made of membership a recurrent issue in non-aligned conferences.

To start with, sovereign independent statehood does not seem to be a *sine qua non* of membership in the non-aligned subsystem. At the First

---

[64] *Ibid.*

[65] Lyon : *op. cit.,* p. 181.

[66] *Ibid.*

[67] Jansen : *op. cit.,* p. 286.

Non-Aligned Summit Conference, the Algerian Provisional Government was invited as a full member. Similarly, at the Second Non-Aligned Summit Conference Angola, a Portuguese colony, was invited and attended as a full member. [68] At the Third Non-Aligned Summit, South Vietnam attended as an observer, and was represented by the foreign minister of the Provisional Government. [69] Prince Sihanouk's delegate, however, was not accepted as a representative of the Kingdom of Cambodia—a full member of both the First and Second Non-Aligned Summit Conferences. But full membership was restored to the Kingdom of Cambodia at the Georgetown Conference of Foreign Ministers of Non-Aligned Countries.

4.2.2. This lack of 'impersonal', well-defined and institutionalized criteria of membership can, indeed, give rise to serious problems. An example of such problems is what is called "The Tshombe Affair" : the refusal to let the then Prime Minister of the Congo-Kinshasa (Republic of Zaire) occupy this state's seat at the Second Non-Aligned Summit. In this case, neither the membership of the state itself (the Congo) nor its government in power were in question. What was questioned was the *person* of the prime minister. Tshombe was—as some delegates pointed out—legally appointed by the Congolese President of the Republic and hence—it was argued—should be permitted to attend the Conference. This emphasis on 'correct and universal' legalistic procedures made some observers and even statesmen question the right of the Conference members to "intervene in the Congo's right to send its representative to the conference". Dean Rusk—U.S. Secretary of State at the time—refused to discuss this question specifically ; he nonetheless said : "It is of some concern, some importance, that in an international meeting delegates undertake to determine who shall represent a government invited to the meeting, because if that principle were followed very far it could go a very long way to a great many complications in the very structure of international affairs". [70] This legalistic 'universal' aspect of Tshombe's representativeness was debated in the Political Committee of the Second Summit. Press reports indicated that three members were in favour of accepting the credentials of the legally-appointed Prime Minister and against the

---

[68] Angola was dropped from the membership of the Third Summit in Lusaka.

[69] Mrs. Nguyen Thi Binh, Foreign Minister of the Provisional Government of South Vietnam, said in an interview in Dar-es-Salaam : "We hold that the participation of the Provisional Government in the Non-aligned Conference would strengthen the positive role played by the non-aligned countries." For in taking a stand on the participation of the Provisional Government, Mrs. Binh emphasized, the Conference members "illustrate their position in regard to national liberation against imperialism and also their position with regard to non-alignment". *New York Times*, September 7, 1970.

[70] *New York Times*, October 9, 1964.

principle of inviting a certain State's delegate in person (*e.g.* President Kasavobou).[71] The Political Committee, however, backed the decision of the Conference sponsors (Mrs. Bandaranaika, Presidents Nasser and Tito) to send a cable to Kasavobou—President of the Republic—to ask him to represent the Congo *in person.* How did the Conference sponsors explain this? Nasser's semi-official spokesman and his *alter-ego*—Mohamed Heikal—discussed the issue in detail. He started by the legal aspect: "Did the non-aligned states attending the Cairo Conference", Heikal asked, "have the right to send to the Congolese President objecting to Tshombe's presence; since the Congo was a full member of the First Non-Aligned Summit and also of the Preparatory Committee which addressed invitations for the Second Summit in Cairo? . . . Is not the objection to the formation of the Congolese delegation considered an interference?"[72] Heikal is not very interested in emphasizing a legalistic answer, but in one which "is related to the nature of the Non-Aligned Conference itself". The answer Heikal gives is worth quoting in detail, not only because of his closeness to Nasser, his influence in the Arab world and in other non-aligned circles,[73] but also because it sheds light on the nature of the non-aligned subsystem as such. "That conference", Heikal affirms, "is different from the African or Arab Summit Conferences. These latter are international organizations. Every state therein has, by the right of pertaining to the region, full unconditional membership and unlimited representation." The implication here is that membership in the non-aligned subsystem is not limited to geographically-based criterion, and this confirms our point about the necessity of a (subjective) socio-psychological boundary for the subsystem in addition to geographical location. This is indeed explicit in Heikal's next sentence. "The

[71] Nehru, if he were still living, would have rallied most probably to the side of 'legalism'. For when Nasser told Tito that Tshombe was being held in a guest house in Cairo and would not attend the 2nd Summit, Tito's first reaction was to ask: "I wonder what Nehru would have said if he had been with us." Tito knew that Nehru would have questioned the legality of Tshombe's arrest. Heikal, Mohamed: *Nasser: The Cairo Documents,* London, New English Library, 1972, p. 242.

[72] *Al-Ahram,* October 9, 1964. *Egyptian Mail,* October 10, 1964. On this point of interference and non-interference in domestic affairs the *Guardian* had this comment: "Though many proposals call for a ban on interference in the internal affairs of individual states, the treatment of Tshombe is a mockery of the non-interference item." But the *Guardian* added: "Leaders who oppose him said their object was not to interfere in Congolese affairs but to assure success of the Conference. They maintain that Tshombe's presence would have a disruptive effect." The *Guardian* October 7, 1964. In fact, some leaders insisted that if Tshombe were admitted they would not attend the Conference.

[73] In 1972, Heikal has been described by the *New York Herald Tribune* as one of the most influential journalists in the world. His 'biography' of Nasser does not only reveal the intimate friendship between the two men, but Heikal's close relationship with other world leaders (*e.g.* Tito).

Non-Aligned Conference", Heikal continues, "also differs from the Afro-Asian Summit Conference, for the latter is a conference of a certain geographic area. Every international entity which is situated inside this geographic area has the right to participate without complications or questioning." However, "... non-alignment is not an expression of a geographic area, but an expression of an idea ... and a reflection of a principle. The adherence to the idea and to the principle equals exactly the right of pertaining to the non-aligned group, or in other words equals the membership of a non-aligned conference ... Consequently, it is possible to say to a President : 'Your representative whom you sent to sit with us does not represent either the idea or the principle. Hence, please send someone else.' " Heikal moves afterwards to the specific issue of Tshombe and asks : "Can Tshombe represent the idea and the principle ?" In answering Heikal quotes Ben Bella who qualified Tshombe as "a mobile museum of everything that the non-aligned states stand against and fight". And Heikal continues : "Those behind Tshombe are those behind foreign occupation, neo-imperialism, who loot the people's wealth, those who practise coups and plotting, and use mercenaries ... The imperialists' logic to its agents was as follows : would words cost money ?! If the fashion nowadays is non-alignment, well put on this showy dress. Thus non-alignment too has been forged.

Moreover, the presence of Tshombe beside other non-aligned leaders would have caused confusion and pushed people to wonder whether this is really non-alignment and what its criteria are. Besides, imperialism wanted to realize some specific objectives :

1. by attending the Conference Tshombe would obtain forgiveness and indulgence which would wipe out all his crimes, and
2. his presence could be a fetter to those who want to speak about old and new imperialism, the looting, small wars ..."

To sum up, then, the Tshombe affair's importance was that "it drew the attention of others to the fact that the membership of non-alignment is not a taken-for-granted membership card or a permanent seat ...".[74]

It is true that from a purely practical point of view, Tshombe was a *persona non grata*[75] at the Conference and was thus to be excluded, but

[74] *Al-Ahram,* October 9, 1964, and *Egyptian Mail,* October 10, 1964.

[75] The Chinese News Agency, *Hsinhua,* reported on October 8, 1964 the declaration of Algeria's President : "Under no circumstances will I sit with Tshombe under one roof", Ben Bella said. The *Egyptian Gazette* summarized, in detail, the disruptive effects on the 2nd Summit of Tshombe's presence. After stating that Nigeria, Senegal and Liberia objected to inviting President Kasavobou *in person* for this goes against legal norms, the paper continued : "Legalities must, of course, be given the

still no specific criteria of the subsystem membership are explicited. Heikal's lengthy treatment implies that these criteria are complex and in the last analysis may be decided by the members themselves—according to the merits of the specific case rather than on the basis of operational, 'legalistic and universal' rules. But who and how to decide whether an actor is eligible for membership or not? And what is to be done when two or more of the existing members evaluate the credentials of a potential new member differently?

4.2.3. The fact that there are not clearly-set answers for these important questions did not prevent subsystem membership from rising substantially. In the First Summit at Belgrade, there were 25 full members (plus 3 observers). In the Second Summit, the number of full members rose to 47 (plus 10 observers), an increase in full participation of 88 per cent. In the Third Summit, full membership rose to 53 (plus 9 observers), a further rise in full participation of almost 13 per cent.

But the change in full membership was not limited to quantitative terms only, but to the qualitative too, as the following table shows.

TABLE 7. *Evolution of Continental Membership Within the Non-Aligned Subsystem*

Conference	Asians	Africans	Latin Americans	Europeans	Total
First Summit	11	11	1	2	25
Second Summit	15	29	1	2	47
Third Summit	15	32	4	2	53

From the data in this table, some points have to be reiterated as far as quantity and quality of full membership is concerned:

1. European membership seem to be stabilized without change in absolute numbers. Cyprus and Yugoslavia stayed as the two European

fullest consideration but also must other aspects. The plain truth is that the presence of Mr. Tshombe could serve no useful purpose and would only hinder the normal progress of the Conference. Since he is *persona non grata* with the majority of the Heads of State and Government and the countries they represent, he could not present the Congo's case with any conviction nor would his views and opinions on any other question carry much weight", and so it is essential that the Congo be represented by someone who can command respect. After reviewing Tshombe's history in Katanga, the Congo and Africa, the paper continued: "Yet the Congo should be represented at the Cairo Conference, and since Mr. Tshombe has obviously made himself ineligible, President Kasavobou is the logical alternative." *Egyptian Gazette*, October 6, 1964.

full members without any addition or substraction. But with the increase in overall membership from one conference to the other, the percentage of European membership was bound to decline from 8 per cent at the First Summit to 4.25 per cent at the Second Summit and to approximately 3.9 per cent at the Third Summit.

2. This percentage decline in European membership is not very different from the pattern of Asian membership. It is true that from the First Summit to the Second Summit, the absolute number of Asian members has increased (from 11 to 15 : a rise of approximately 36.35 per cent). Yet inspite of this increase in absolute numbers, Asian members' percentage at the Second Summit represented approximately 32 per cent of total membership, compared to 44 per cent at the First Summit. At the Third Summit absolute Asian membership remained quantitatively unchanged at 15, though some Asian states were added as new members while others did not attend. Thus Malaysia and Singapore attended for the first time to replace Burma and Saudi Arabia—original members of both the First and Second Summits. Yet with the increase of overall membership in the non-aligned subsystem from 47 members at the Second Summit to 53 at the Third Summit, Asian percentage of membership had to decline from approximately 32 per cent to approximately 28.5 per cent.

3. Latin American members have increased both in absolute numbers and in percentage of the total, especially between the Second Summit and Third Summit : from 1 to 4 members, a rise of 300 per cent. The percentage increase of their representation in the overall membership is less remarkable : 4 per cent at the First Summit, declined to approximately 2.1 per cent at the Second Summit in order to rise to approximately 7.5 per cent at the Third Summit.

4. African membership registered a great rise in membership both in absolute numbers and in percentage of their representation in the total (the percentage increase applies mainly to the evolution between the First and Second Summits). Eleven African states attended the First Summit, their number more than doubled and became 29 at the Second Summit—a net rise of approximately 163.7 per cent, and this increase in membership continued in the Third Summit to reach 32 members—a further net rise of approximately 10.3 per cent. In spite of the fact that African actors like, for instance, the Ivory Coast, Malagashy Republic or Upper Volta never attended Non-Aligned Summit Conferences, and that Malawi attended only the Second Summit but did not come to the Third Summit in neighbouring Lusaka, the percentage of African representation in the subsystem's overall membership also rose : from 44 per cent at the First Summit

to approximately 61.77 at the Second, and decreased slightly to reach 60.4 per cent at the Third Summit.

4.2.4. Is this change in one variable, *i.e.* membership, bound to affect other subsystem variables, *e.g.* interaction or structure ? Intuitively at least, one would expect that the Indian member with its more than 500 million population, GNP of $49,220 million, industrial base and scientific capacity (*e.g.* publishes about 470 scientific journals [76]) would not always perceive all issues and problems in exactly the same way as Lesotho or Botswana (population 910,000 and 611,000 [77] ; GNP $49 million and $34 million respectively ; number of scientific journals : 0 for both [78]). This is already clear as far as the degree of their involvement in the international system is concerned, if we measure the degree of this systemic involvement through the two indicators of (*a*) membership in international organizations and (*b*) diplomatic representation (*i.e.* number of diplomats sent or received and number of missions abroad). India is a member in 58 international organizations, [79] sent 467 diplomats, received 530 and had 64 missions abroad. [80] Corresponding data for Lesotho and Botswana are not available. [81] But if we take the corresponding data about another African actor which is structurally similar to Lesotho and Botswana—say Gabon (population 480,000 [82] ; GNP $130 million, and number of scientific journals 0 [83]), the comparison will still be valid. Gabon was a member of 33 international organizations, [84] sent 10 diplomats, received 23 and had 4 missions abroad. [85]

But how, then, does this change in membership affect other subsystem variables, for instance, regular interaction ? This brings us to our third variable.

---

[76] Hudson and Taylor : *World Handbook ..., op. cit.*, pp. 306, 322.

[77] *Review of International Affairs,* XXI (September 20, 1970). Documentation on the Lusaka Conference, pp. 11-39.

[78] Hudson and Taylor : *World Handbook ..., op. cit.*, pp. 310-312, 324.

[79] *Ibid.*, pp. 354-356. Data are for 1965.

[80] Data are for 1963-1964. Alger, Chadwick W. and Brams, Steven J. : "Patterns of Representation in National Capitals and Intergovernmental Organizations", *World Politics,* XIX (1967), pp. 646-663. Also Hudson and Taylor : *World Handbook ..., op. cit.*, p. 357.

[81] Most probably because of the recent date of political independence.

[82] *Review of International Affairs,* XXI (September 20, 1970), p. 11.

[83] Hudson and Taylor : *World Handbook ..., op. cit.*, pp. 310-312, 324-325.

[84] *Ibid.*, pp. 354-356. Data are for 1965.

[85] Alger and Brams : *op. cit.* Also Hudson and Taylor : *World Handbook ..., op. cit.*, pp. 357-359.

4.3. *Interaction*

4.3.1. As was explicitly reiterated in the chapter on the global system, *regular interaction* is a *sine qua non* of system (and subsystem) existence. Interaction itself does not connote any positive or negative value, and as in any subsystem interaction among members of the non-aligned subsystem is not always at the pure conflict or pure cooperation end of the interaction continuum. There are famous and repeated examples of conflict, and indeed armed conflict, among the subsystem members : *e.g.* the U.A.R.-Saudi Arabia-Yemen military clashes in the mid 1960's, the Algeria-Morocco border conflict of 1963-1964, the Somalia-Kenya-Ethiopia skirmishes, the Indonesia-Malaysia confrontation, the recent Uganda-Tanzania fighting. Among some non-aligned actors, there are also other forms of interaction : movements of people across political frontiers such as between Uganda and the Sudan, Vietnam-Laos-Cambodia, Angola and the Congo, Guinea and Senegal. Though these are regular forms of (informal) interaction, we are going to concentrate here on such aspects of interaction as diplomatic representation and other indicators for which data are accessible.

4.3.2. Thus looking at diplomatic representation among black African states in only one geographical region (West Africa)—and thus neutralising the effect of geographical distance—the pattern of regular interaction, through diplomatic representation, is not fully intense. The following table will give a clear picture. [86] (See table following page.)

Though the table speaks for itself, some points can be mentioned to illustrate the (weak) pattern of interaction through permanent diplomatic representation. Mauritania, for instance, has permanent diplomatic representatives in Senegal and Ivory Coast, *i.e.* in only 16.7 per cent approximately of the total. The percentage is the same for both Togo and Dahomey, but with a difference. Togo sent to its fellow-members in the region only one ambassador, whereas its other permanent diplomatic representative was of the rank of chargé d'affaires. As for Dahomey, both the two permanent diplomatic representatives it sent were of the chargé d'affaires rank. Ivory Coast sent 3 permanent diplomatic representatives, all at the ambassadorial level, *i.e.* ambassadors in 25 per cent of the overall capitals of the West African geographical region—but its ambassador in Liberia represented it in Sierra Leone, and its permanent representative to Senegal is staying in Ivory Coast rather than in Dakar. Upper Volta got the same score as Ivory Coast : permanent diplomatic representation at the ambassadorial level in 25 per cent of the region's members. Those two countries are

[86] Data are based on Zartman : *International Relations . . ., op. cit.*, p. 71.

TABLE 8. *Diplomatic Representation Among 13 Western African States (1964)*

			U.A.S.				ENTENTE						
From to	Mauritania	Senegal	Mali	Ghana	Guinea	Liberia	Ivory Coast	Upper Volta	Niger	Dahomey	Sierra Leone	Togo	Nigeria
Mauritania		PR					A						
Senegal			A	A	A	A					A[4]		A
Mali		A		RM[7]	RM	A	A	A	D		A[3]		A[7]
Guinea	A[1]	A	RM[7]		RM[7]	A	A[7]	A[2]	A[5]	A[5]	A[7]	A	A
Ghana	A	A	RM	RM		A	A	A	C	A	HC	C	HC
Liberia		A	A	A	A		A				A	A	A
Ivory Coast		PR[2]			A	A					A[4]		A
Upper Volta			PR		A		A						
Niger					A	A	D			D	A[4]	D[6]	A
Dahomey					C								C
Sierra Leone		A[3]		A	HC	A							HC
Togo					A								C
Nigeria		A	A	A	HC	A	A		C		HC	C	

Codes used: A Ambassador
HC High Commissioner (Commonwealth members)
RM Resident Minister (among members of Union of African States - U.A.S.)
C Chargé d'afafires
D Delegate
PR Permanent Representative
[1] Resident in Senegal
[2] Resident in Ivory Coast
[3] Resident in Guinea
[4] Resident in Liberia
[5] Resident in Togo
[6] Resident in Dahomey
[7] Withdrawn in 1964 for reasons of economy

surpassed by Sierra Leone: 33.3 per cent. Guinea, Niger and Senegal have the same score of 41.7 per cent, inspite of different distribution of permanent representatives. Mali (50 per cent) would have scored more if it had not withdrawn its permanent diplomatic representative in both Guinea and Nigeria. Liberia is relatively active, for it scores 66.7 per cent, and comes immediately before Nigeria (75 per cent), the biggest state not only in the Western African region but in the whole continent. Nigeria, however, did not send as many permanent diplomatic representatives as Nkrumah's Ghana which is the state to score 100 per cent. Ghana's top score is not only quantitative but also qualitative, for its permanent diplomatic representative was usually of top rank (ambassador, high commissioner or a resident minister in the members of the Union of African states : Guinea and Mali), with only two chargé d'affaires to Niger and Togo. [87]

Now if we—rather than neutralising geographical distance—allow it to intervene, and consider in the same year (1964) regular interaction through diplomatic representation (indicator : member of embassies) among non-aligned actors of two different geographical regions : for instance, Southeast Asia and black Africa, what would the picture be like in this case ? The pattern is one of virtual absence of regular interaction through permanent diplomatic representation, as the following table shows [88] :

TABLE 9. *Embassies of Southeast Asian States in some Black African States (1964)*

From To	Ethiopia	Guinea	Mali	Niger	Nigeria	Senegal	Sudan
Burma							
Cambodia							
Indonesia		+					+
Malaysia							

The results of the table would not be very different if we were to consider the number of embassies of these African actors in the above-mentioned Southeast Asian capitals. For if we consider the overall number of diplomats sent and received by our sample of black African states as well as the sum of their missions in the global system in the same period (1963-1964), [89] this pattern of weak interaction through permanent diplomatic representation can be easily inferred.

[87] The tabulated data might contain some bias. For instance, some actors might practice sending on special envoys when important contacts are necessary and so interaction might be higher than the data indicate. Though this should not invalidate our conclusion since our indicator is permanent diplomatic representation, there is another reason that might diminish the data's potential bias. Many of the ambassadors have "long absences—a habit encouraged by presidential example" (*ibid.*, p. 72) and some actors are too small to send permanent diplomatic representatives in every capital. Consequently, these two potential sources of data bias—running in opposite directions—will tend to diminish the data's potential overall bias.

[88] Von der Mehden, Fred : "Southeast Asian Relations with Africa", *Asian Survey*, V (1965), pp. 341-349.

[89] Dates for all data are 1963-1964. See Alger and Brams, *op. cit.* Also Hudson and Taylor : *World Handbook ..., op. cit.*, pp. 357-359.

TABLE 10. *Diplomatic Representation of Fifteen Non-Aligned African Actors*

Rank compared to other world national actors (No. 119)	States	Diplomats sent	Diplomats received	Missions abroad
35.5	Ghana	212	242	42
52.5	Sudan	93	123	27
55.5	Nigeria	151	232	26
58.5	Ethiopia	81	129	25
64.	Liberia	54	99	23
64.	Senegal	72	163	23
78.	Mali	55	115	18
81.	Guinea	63	158	17
91.	Ivory Coast	39	not known	12
97.	Upper Volta	19	not known	10
102.	Dahomey	19	not known	8
102.	Niger	15	not known	8
	Sierra Leone	35	50	8
111.	Mauritania	11	26	5
111.	Togo	16	45	5

Nkrumah's Ghana is very activist (ahead of Nigeria in ranking by 20 points), and this confirms our data about regular interaction in the West African region. Otherwise, the picture that evolves is one of weak diplomatic interaction. For one can almost certainly surmise that Mauritania's or Togo's 3 missions (*i.e.* 5 minus the two missions sent by these two states to their Western African fellow members) would be distributed among Paris, New York and perhaps other 'developed' capitals before being sent to Colombo, Kaboul or even Nairobi. But in order to be sure that our inference is empirically justified, we should compute the complete data about the overall pattern of diplomatic representation among all the subsystem members that attended the last Non-Aligned Summit (Lusaka, 1970). Admittedly there would be some differences, since the computation for the overall interaction is based on data as for 1970. Mauritania, for instance, had at least 8 embassies at that time in non-aligned capitals, as the matrix of full diplomatic interaction shows. [90]

To grasp easily the matrix's information about both the *overall pattern* of diplomatic interaction in the subsystem and the *degree* of interaction of each subsystem member with the rest, a complete interaction scale has been elaborated. The methodology used is straightforward weighting

[90] See appendix I.

based on both the rank and directness of diplomatic representation. The weighting code is as follows :

1. Direct ambassadorial level	5
2. Indirect ambassadorial level : *e.g.* exchange of ambassadors but through another country	4
3. Direct diplomatic representation : *i.e.* lower than ambassadorial level	3
4. Indirect diplomatic representation : *i.e.* both lower than ambassadorial level and through another country	2
5. Other diplomatic relations (*e.g.* recognition)	1

Ideal complete diplomatic interaction on this scale would, for each of the 53 full members of the 3rd Non-Aligned Summit, involve scoring 520 points—that is a non-aligned actor sending to, and receiving from, its 52 fellow subsystem members a direct ambassador : in an equation form $[(5 + 5) \times 52]$. In the table that follows the subsystem members are arranged in a descending hierarchical order. The first column shows the score computed on the basis of the rank and residence of diplomatic representatives to each subsystem member. The second column applies the same computation procedure to the diplomatic representatives sent by this member to its fellow subsystem members. In the third column the two scores are summed to show this member's index of diplomatic interaction. Lastly, in a fourth column, the index of interaction of each member in the whole subsystem has been computed in the form of a percentage of the ideal complete-interaction scale.

The absence of 'normal distribution' in the interaction pattern is too obvious to be commented. The asymmetry is shown by the fact that the sum of Egypt's, India's and Yugoslavia's interaction score is higher than the combined interaction score of Afghanistan, Chad, Congo (People's Republic), Yemen, Zambia, Sierra Leone, Central African Republic, Burundi, Trinidad and Tobago, Cyprus, Singapore, Nepal, Laos, Gabon, Republic of South Yemen, Jamaica, Rwanda, Guyana, equatorial Guinea, Botswana and Lesotho (21 subsystem members). Moreover, as late as 1970 when these data were compiled, there were still large areas of non-interaction, for instance : (1) Afghanistan did not have any diplomatic representation in sub-Saharan Africa. In the whole of Africa it had an ambassador in Cairo and unspecified diplomatic relations with the Sudan. (2) Ceylon had full diplomatic relations only with Ghana in sub-Saharan Africa (probably because of common membership in the Commonwealth), and unspecified diplomatic relations with the Sudan. For the whole of Africa we only find another ambassador (Cairo). (3) Cyprus did not have any ambassador in sub-Saharan Africa, and unspecified diplomatic relations with the Congo Democratic Republic and the Sudan. If we take the whole of Africa we find only one ambassador in Cairo. (4) As for Nepal, no diplomatic representation whatsoever is indicated between this state and any sub-Saharan African state. If we take the whole of Africa, there is only the ambassador in Cairo who also represents Nepal in Algeria. [91] The other side of the coin is true too, for many sub-Saharan African states do not have permanent diplomatic representation with their Asian fellow members (*e.g.* Burundi). Botswana, for instance, does not have any diplomatic representation in the pioneering capitals of the non-aligned core sector : Cairo, Delhi or Belgrade. But perhaps these states are small and not very active subsystem members. Yet an actor like Tanzania—which was the host to the Preparatory Conference of the 3rd Non-Aligned Summit—had diplomatic representation only with India in Asia. Moreover, Zambia—who received the 3rd Summit in its capital—did not have any permanent diplomatic representation with any Asian state as late as 1970.

This pattern of weak interaction through regular diplomatic representation might explain why controversial issues in the non-aligned subsystem are more easily settled through geographically-based (sub-)subsystems. Thus in the controversy over the acceptance of Tshombe's credentials as representative of the Congo at the 2nd Summit in Cairo, it was officially the African actors—members of the O.A.U.—that met and decided not to

TABLE 11. *Interaction Index of all Members in the Non-Aligned Subsystem* *

Group	Group Interval	Rank	Country	Receiving Score	Sending Score	Interaction Index	Per cent
1	80-70	1	Egypt	198	190	388	74.6
2	70-60	2	India	128	205	333	64.0
		3	Yugoslavia	145	181	326	62.6
	60-50						
3	50-40	4	Algeria	120	118	238	45.8
		5	Lebanon	103	129	232	44.6
		6	Ethiopia	124	104	228	43.8
		7	Morocco	103	113	216	41.5
		8	Sudan	94	118	212	40.8

[91] *Europa Yearbook* (1970) states that Nepal has diplomatic relations with 42 countries—but does not give further specifications.

TABLE 11 *(continued)*

Group	Group Interval	Rank	Country	Receiving Score	Sending Score	Interaction Index	Per cent
4	40-30	9	Ghana	85	116	201	38.7
		10	Nigeria	98	86	184	35.4
		11	Guinea	67	116	183	35.2
		12		93	78	171	32.9
		13	Congo (Zaire)	100	70	170	32.7
		14	Iraq	80	85	165	31.7
		15	Senegal	87	71	158	30.4
5	30-20	16	Mali	57	97	154	29.8
		17	Indonesia	48	93	141	27.1
		18	Cameroon	87	52	139	26.7
		19	Jordan	62	67	129	24.8
		20	Syria	58	69	127	24.4
		21	Kenya	88	37	125	24.0
		22	Kuwait	61	64	125	24.0
		23	Liberia	56	62	118	22.7
		24	Libya	54	63	117	22.5
		25	Cuba	50	60	110	21.2
		26	Ceylon	58	49	107	20.6
		27	Tanzania	80	27	107	20.6
6	20-10	28	Somalia	50	50	100	19.2
		29	Mauritania	48	50	98	18.9
		30	Uganda	74	16	90	17.3
		31	Malaysia	58	30	88	16.9
		32	Afghanistan	51	34	85	16.3
		33	Chad	47	36	83	16.0
		34	Congo (People's Rep.)	55	23	78	15.0
		35	Yemen Arab Republic	35	31	66	12.7
		36	Zambia	29	36	65	12.5
		37	Sierra Leone	33	28	61	11.7
		38	Central African Republic	34	27	61	11.7
		39	Burundi	30	30	60	11.5
7	10-0	40	Trinidad and Tobago	19	30	49	9.4
		41	Cyprus	34	14	48	9.2
		42	Singapore	22	26	48	9.2
		43	Nepal	6	34	40	7.6
		44	Laos	21	17	38	7.3
		45	Gabon	13	24	37	7.1
		46	Republic of South Yemen	18	10	28	5.4
		47	Jamaica	13	10	23	4.4
		48	Ruanda	9	14	23	4.4
		49	Guyana	15	5	20	3.8
		50	Equatorial Guinea	14	5	19	3.7
		51	Botswana	10	9	19	3.7
		52	Lesotho	0	14	14	2.7
		53	Swaziland	0	0	0	0.0

allow Tshombe to occupy the Congo's seat in the Conference.[92] Similarly, when the controversy arose over whether the delegate of Sihanouk or of Lon Nol should represent Cambodia, the issue was sent to the Asian members to meet and take a decision.[93]

There is, however, an area where interaction is not according to geographically-based criteria,[94] but rather to adherence to non-alignment. Moreover, the forms of this interaction go beyond the establishment of direct and top-rank diplomatic representation, periodic consultation and coordination of diplomatic action to embrace such areas as common economic projects and even the accordance of mutual commercial preferences. This is the *core sector*[95] of tripartite interaction among Egypt, India, Yugoslavia.

4.3.3. *The Core Sector.* Not only does this triumvirate occupy the three first positions in the subsystem interaction scale (388, 333, 326 are the top total scores for Egypt, India and Yugoslavia respectively), but also their interaction can be traced back to 1950-1951. At that time, all three were members of the Security Council,[96] and contacts used to take place —especially during the discussion of the Korean question—among Dr. Aleš Bebter, Dr. Mahmoud Fawzi and Sir Benegal Rau, representatives of Yugoslavia, Egypt and India respectively.

Two years earlier, Yugoslavia had been ex-communicated from the Cominform, was therefore in the position of not being able to be integrated in either bloc and thus became non-aligned.[97] During the discus-

[92] Swaran Singh—India's Foreign Minister—commented on the Tshombe issue by saying that many *Africans* refused to work with him. And the Hindu added: "*Asian* countries attending the Conference thought the question whether Tshombe was to attend or not was *an African affair and they stayed out of it*". *Hindu,* October 13, 1964 (emphasis added).

[93] "The *Asian group* is to hold a meeting to decide on Cambodia's admission." *Daily Telegraph,* September 6, 1970 (emphasis added).

[94] For instance, at the closing session of the 2nd Summit, Shastri spoke for Asia, President Aref (of Iraq) for the Arab world, and Sekou Touré for Africa. Also after the 3rd Summit, Prime Minister Tun Abdel Razek—the delegate of the newest member in the non-aligned subsystem (Malaysia)—suggested, before leaving Lusaka, the organization of 'regional' meetings of non-aligned states, *e.g.* Asian members in Asia, Arab members in an Arab capital ...

[95] The core sector can be defined as consisting of "a state or group of states which form a *central focus* of the international politics within a given region" or a subsystem. For more elaboration on the concept of "core sector" as well as the relation between the core sector and the peripheral sector, see Cantori and Spiegel (eds.): *The International Politics of Regions, op. cit.,* pp. 20-25 (emphasis added).

[96] The Yugoslav Embassy in New Delhi, for instance, was opened on April 20, 1950 and India accredited a permanent ambassador to Yugoslavia in October 1954. Rubinstein, *op. cit.,* p. 47.

[97] For details, see *ibid.,* pp. 3-21.

sion of the Korean question, the Yugoslav foreign minister came to emphasize in the U.N. what can be considered the "conceptual underpinnings of non-alignment" : opposition to Great Power hegemony and rejection of permanent commitment to either bloc, insistence upon the equality of large and small states as well as the latter's right to play an independent and enlarged role in the international system, cooperation among states with different social and political structures [98] . . . As Edward Kardelj —Yugoslav Foreign Minister—expressed his country's position in the General Assembly in 1950 :

> "The people of Yugoslavia cannot accept the assumption that mankind must to-day choose between the domination of one great power or another. We consider that there is another path . . ." [99]

Such a foreign policy orientation was already adopted by Indian decision-makers and was also debated in Cairo at the time.

Consequently, like both India and Egypt, [100] Yugoslavia had doubts about the merits of carrying the Korean war across the 38th parallel.

> "The aim of the Security Council's action had been to prevent the alteration by force of a given situation, and not to use armed force to change the *de facto* situation existing at the beginning of hostilities, which would establish a precedent to justify any intervention in a country's internal affairs." [101]

Dr. Joze Vilfan—Yugoslavia's ambassador in India (1952-1953)—worked closely with the Indians in helping to arrange the truce in Korea, and thus initiated the period of Indo-Yugoslav consultation and coordination. [102] At the same time, "the Yugoslav and Egyptian delegations in the

---

[98] *Ibid.,* p. 29.

[99] United Nations, General Assembly, *Official Records,* 5th Session, p. 69—as quoted in *ibid.*

[100] For details about non-aligned actors' behaviour during the Korean crisis, see the last chapter.

[101] United Nations, General Assembly, *Official Records,* 5th Session, p. 39, as quoted in Rubinstein : *op. cit.,* p. 30.

[102] Personality variables of officials also played a role in the initiation of the core sector. Thus "an astute, empathetic and humane person, Dr. Vilfan, quickly earned the respect of the Indians. During his first Summer in New Delhi, when air-conditioning was not yet standard Embassy equipment, he encountered the oppressiveness of the Indian plain. Most of the foreign missions left New Delhi for the highlands to escape the hot season, as had been the custom during the British period. Detecting an underlying unhappiness among the hypersensitive Indians, to whom such behavior smacked of the colonial tradition, Vilfan and his wife remained in New Delhi. The incident itself was of minor importance, but it helped to distinguish Vilfan in Indian eyes. It was also symptomatic of Yugoslav sensitiveness to the fragile egos of the new nations and to the small matters that often condition the outlook on the substantive issues of international affairs . . ." *Ibid.,* pp. 47-48.

Security Council conferred frequently and agreed on many issues" regarding the Korean conflict, while concurrently India and Egypt were involved in the work of the newly-emerging Arab-Asian group. [103]

This collaboration and consultation among the three states was followed by the exchange of visits among high officials. [104] Thus Tito was invited to visit India in December 1954. He stayed in India from December 16, 1954 to January 3, 1955, then went to Burma before returning to India to stay from January 20 to 25. Not only was Tito's trip his first visit to the newly-independent Asian states who pioneered non-alignment, but also on his way back he met Nasser on February 5, 1955—apparently on Nehru's suggestion. [105] At that time Nasser was preparing for his first trip outside Egypt [106] to attend the Bandung Conference in April ; he was in conflict with the British over the Baghdad Pact, and with the Americans who would not supply the weapons Egypt needed unless it accepted alignment. [107] The first Nasser-Tito meeting took place in the Suez Canal, when Tito's yacht Galeb—the Seagull—was passing through, and when it reached Suez Nasser went on board and sailed with Tito to Lake Timsah. On the whole the meeting was cordial, "but it lacked the warmth of their future friendship. They did not quite click. They were feeling one another out. Nasser was rather put off by what he considered the excessive protocol [108] with which Tito was surrounded. Nasser still had ideas about the austerity of Communism and he was rather taken aback by Tito's way of life. Tito wore the uniform of a Field-Marshal ; Nasser that of a Colonel. Indeed, they discussed world affairs, but nothing important occurred. It was essentially a reconnaissance meeting between the two men." When Tito returned to Egypt on an official visit in December of the same year, the atmosphere of their meeting was different. For in the meantime Nasser was still opposing strongly the British over the Baghdad Pact, still determined to demonstrate his independence and had contracted the Soviet arms deal to prove it. This time the two leaders "clicked immediately

---

[103] Hovet, Thomas : *Bloc Politics in the U.N.*, Cambridge, Mass., Harvard U.P., 1960, p. 79.

[104] For instance, a Yugoslav goodwill mission headed by a member of the Federal Executive Council, Rodoljub Colakovic, visited India from December 14, 1952 to January 12, 1953. Rubinstein : *op. cit.*, p. 47. Also, in August 1953, the first Egyptian military mission visited Yugoslavia and toured Army units and factories. *Ibid.*, pp. 51-52.

[105] Heikal : *Nasser : The Cairo Documents, op. cit.*, p. 229.

[106] This was Nasser's first trip abroad, apart from his service in the Sudan before the coup d'Etat.

[107] Nasser's speeches from February 1955 tended to emphasize this point. *Nasser's speeches*, vol. I.

[108] Heikal : *Nasser : The Cairo Documents, op. cit.*, p. 229.

and the concept of non-alignment emerged as a power in the world from their meeting".[109]

Tito's two trips then in 1954-1955 initiated the frequent exchange of visits among the three 'high priests' of non-alignment. For instance, between 1959 and 1964, Nehru came to Belgrade 3 times : July 1955, July 1956 and September 1961 ; Nasser came 5 times in the same period : July 1956, July 1958, June 1960, August 1961 and May 1963.[110] But the number of times they met was, of course, higher. For instance, during the period 1955-1968, Nasser and Tito met at least more than twenty times[111] and Nasser's biographer affirms that—in fact—the number of Nasser-Tito meetings totals more than 30 times.[112] Even if we adopt the 'conservative' figure, it indicates "a frequency of personal contact not approached by the leaders of any other two countries".[113]

The *First Tripartite Meeting,* however, was at the Yugoslav island of Brioni in July 1956. Tito had invited Nasser for a tour of the Yugoslav republics and perhaps also to gain Nasser's support for more coordination among non-aligned states and more involvement in the contemporary international system—for Nehru was usually reluctant to provide any semblance of organized non-aligned grouping. Nehru, in fact, did not join Nasser and Tito out of conviction but rather to return Tito's state visit to India and was consequently irritated when some press correspondents called the Tripartite Meeting a conference.[114] At the personal level, Nehru—the Cambridge-educated Brahmin aristocrat—was different from Tito—the national Communist—and from Nasser—the inexperienced 38-year old military leader. At the state level, Indian decision-makers were conscious of their country's weight in the contemporary international system and its mediatorial credibility—as the Korean War had shown. In fact, at the conclusion of the Brioni tripartite talks, Nehru was reluctant to issue a formal communiqué. To an Egyptian correspondent who asked him whether a statement would be announced, Nehru retorted irritably "whenever two or three people get together you (the Press) call it a conference".[115]

---

[109] *Ibid.,* p. 230.

[110] Rubinstein : *op. cit.,* p. 93. At the end of September 1955, both the Egyptian and Yugoslav governments agreed to raise their mutual diplomatic representation from legation to embassy. *Ibid.,* p. 241.

[111] *Ibid.,* p. 229.

[112] Heikal : *Nasser : The Cairo Documents, op. cit.,* p. 237.

[113] Rubinstein : *op. cit.,* p. 229. Both Nasser and Tito developed a "'pattern of consultation that has resulted in their meeting twice a year". *Ibid,* p. 246. For instance, Nasser "never went to Moscow without calling on Tito". Heikal : *Nasser : The Cairo Documents, op. cit.,* p. 237.

[114] *Ibid.,* pp. 231-232.

[115] Rubinstein : *op. cit.,* p. 242. Also Lyon : *op. cit.,* p. 126.

But an official communiqué was given on July 19 at the end of this First Tripartite Meeting. The communiqué declared, *inter alia,* that "the three Heads of Government consider that these contacts and exchange of views should be continued and stimulated . . ." Therefore, by emphasizing the importance of direct contacts and consultations, "the conclusions of the Brioni meeting", a semi-official Yugoslav publication believed, ". . . provided an incentive to hold regular consultations from time to time among the non-aligned countries, in the form either of personal contacts or of exchanges of messages on the most important problems of international policy. This meeting may therefore be considered a preliminary step in the preparation of the active role of the non-aligned countries" and a step in holding "a great international conference of non-aligned countries . . .". Not only was a First "great international conference of non-aligned countries" held in Yugoslavia itself, but a Second and a Third were held in Cairo and Lusaka respectively. More importantly, however, the Brioni tripartite talks established the pattern of close contacts and consultations among the three pioneers of non-alignment. For instance, "one of the most important aspects of the talks was an effort by the three men to judge how Krushchev would run the Soviet Union and how his policies would affect the rest of the world", and although it was not announced at the time, "the possible world effects of de-stalinization was the second most important subject, after non-alignment, discussed at Brioni". In this respect, Tito was very functional. Not only was he in Moscow five months before the Brioni Meeting (*i.e.* February 1956) and thus could "tell both Nehru and Nasser about Krushchev's famous speech attacking Stalin and the start of the de-stalinization process", but also he "knew about virtually everything that happened in the Soviet bloc". This pattern of coordination and information exchange continued for "Tito used to send Nasser and Nehru copies of reports that were of interest to them. He would write on them 'interesting reading' and sign them." [116]

But not only did the Brioni Tripartite Meeting establish a pattern of close contacts and coordination [117] and seal the friendship among the three men but it also mapped out the future of the policy of non-alignment and initiated the tradition of tripartite meetings. For five years after the Brioni Meeting, the three 'high priests' of non-alignment met again together, *this time in Cairo.* The occasion was the secession of the 'Syrian Region' from

---

[116] Heikal: *op. cit.,* p. 233.

[117] For intense communication through letters and other contacts, see the long list mentioned by Heikal as well as long extracts from these letters. *Ibid.,* pp. 238-240, 242-243. Another example of the Nasser-Tito close coordination and friendship "was the voyage that Tito undertook to Africa and Asia for two months in 1958 when, at Nasser's request, *he represented Egypt as well as Yugoslavia*". *Ibid.,* pp. 236-237 (emphasis added).

the U.A.R. on September 28, 1961 and the severe setback this caused for Nasser's attempts to achieve Arab Unity. Feeling "his grief deeply", Tito wrote to Nasser on October 8, and together with Nehru arranged to meet about a month after the secession in Cairo where "like any other close friends, they sat reminiscing and discussing their problems". [118] This Second Tripartite Meeting proved the strength of personal bonds in the core sector and indicated that "defeat for one was defeat for them all, victory for one was victory for them all". [119]

But it was the *Third Tripartite Meeting in New Delhi,* [120] also five years after the Second, that proved to be the most significant in the institutionalization of the core sector. It was this tradition of tripartite and periodical consultations that made some non-aligned states suspect a leadership claim. [121] Though official sources in Delhi indicated that these meetings were no substitute for general non-aligned conferences and that they were only in the nature of consultations between states which have similarity of views, some non-aligned actors have told the three 'pioneers' not to refer to the Delhi Tripartite Meeting as either the "Non-Aligned Conference" or the "Summit" meeting. To dissipate doubts about the triumvirate's leadership claim, press reports indicated that Nasser was to meet with Nyrere and Haile Selassi. [122] Similarly, a top official of the External Affairs Ministry in India declared : "We do not claim to be leaders, nor are we participating in the tripartite meeting to establish our leadership claim. We are meeting to exchange views on world problems with like-minded nations." [123]

"World problems" were indeed discussed : deploring the Vietnam War and the arms race, opposition to colonialism and neo-colonialism "in all

---

[118] *Ibid.,* p. 227.

[119] *Ibid.,* p. 228.

[120] Though it was India's turn to have the Tripartite Meeting in its capital, there was also the occasion of Mrs. Gandhi's assuming the premiership. Thus "when Indira Ghandi took over the leadership of India after Shastri's death in 1966, Tito and Nasser rallied to their old friend's daughter and travelled to India to show their solidarity with her in the troubles which she faced immediately she assumed power. They were no longer three musketeers but they never forgot that they had once been three." *Ibid.,* p. 243.

[121] Those who suspected this tripartite leadership claim could perhaps find a supporting argument in such occurrences as, after the 2nd Summit, the first to sign the Final Declaration was Tito, followed by Nasser, then Shastri. *Hindu,* October 12, 1964.

[122] *Hindu,* October 2, 1966.

[123] Mrs. Gandhi has already said in a press interview that the newspapers created "difficulties" by giving particular names to the Tripartite Meeting. *Hindu,* October 2, 1966. On the other hand, some observers perceived the Tripartite Meeting as "rather like a reunion of *three leading actors* from a play whose run has ended". *The Times,* October 21, 1966 (emphasis added).

their forms and manifestations . . ." [124] However, the significance of this Third Tripartite Meeting was—as Nasser expressed it in the final press conference [125] that the three leaders held together—that "we three have had intimate relations for a long time, and we want to develop those close relations and contacts". [126] And—something new [127]—it was in the economic realm that "close relations and contacts" were developed. About 40 per cent of the Final Communiqué was devoted to economic issues. [128] According to Prime Minister Indira Gandhi "perhaps the most outstanding result of the meeting" was the collective approach "to the economic challenges to non-alignment and peaceful coexistence". [129] Consequently, the three leaders decided [130] to join in an effort "to expand the area of mutual cooperation, increase trade exchanges among themselves, pool technical and scientific experience and undertake joint endeavors to develop mutually beneficial patterns of trade and development". [131] Thus about two months later (December 12-15, 1966), the Ministers of Economy

---

[124] Rubinstein: *op. cit.*, p. 217.

[125] All three leaders noted in their Press Conference that the Tripartite Meeting was concluded on U.N. Day and called on non-aligned states to strengthen the world organization. *New York Herald Tribune,* October 25, 1966.

[126] *Hindu,* October 25, 1966. As if to support Nasser's statement of "intimate relations for a long time", the *Hindu* greeted the Delhi Tripartite Meeting by publishing a long article tracing the history of Indian-Egyptian relations, links of trade and ideas and showing how these links were cut off by the intrusion of "Western imperialism". However, the Indian paper continued, in 1928 the Indian Congress supported the Arab fight for freedom and in 1939 an Egyptian delegation attended the Congress session in India. *Hindu,* October 21, 1966.

[127] Discussing economic cooperation was not that new. For instance, in October 1964 in an interview with the Middle East News Agency in Cairo after attending the 2nd Summit, Prime Minister Shastri declared that the volume of trade exchange between Egypt and India amounted to 10 million Egyptian pounds each way. Every effort was being made to widen the scope of trade exchange so as to include new products. Investigations were being made of the potentialities of technical co-operation. In fact, an Indian mission had visited Cairo a few days before the Prime Minister's arrival and had signed an agreement in connection with a programme for the manufacture of a supersonic aircraft. The agreement provided that aircraft frames were to be built in India, while the Egyptians would supply the engines. Shastri also noted that the two delegations had also worked in close co-operation in international conferences. *Egyptian Gazette,* October 13, 1964. It was, however, the emphasis on closer and institutionalized economic co-operation that seemed new. Thus after the Delhi Tripartite Meeting, Nasser stayed for two days after Tito's departure. He conferred with Mrs. Gandhi without any aides and strengthening of economic relations and trade was believed to be the topic. *Hindu,* October 26, 1966.

[128] For the full text of the Final Communiqué, see *International Politics* (Cairo), III (1967), pp. 247-249.

[129] Rubinstein: *op. cit.*, p. 217.

[130] *Ibid.*

[131] *Ibid.*

of the three states met in New Delhi "in conformity with the resolutions of the Non-Aligned Tripartite Meeting" and "agreement was achieved on the measures required to increase economic and technical cooperation among the three non-aligned states".[132] The three Ministers of the Economy established "three *ad hoc* working groups : one to negotiate tariff preferences, payment procedures, and measures for expanding trade ; another to consider possibilities for economic specialization; and the third to investigate the establishment of a joint shipping company".[133] Working parties studying mutual trade preferences continued meeting alternatively in the three capitals during 1967. After their third meeting in Delhi, the "Tripartite Agreement" was signed on the 23rd December 1967. On the same day the Agreement was signed (*i.e.* more than three months before it came into force on April 1st, 1968[134]) it was announced that both Egypt and Yugoslavia had accepted to reduce by 50 per cent tariffs and customs duties imposed on 77 Indian products exported to the two countries.[135]

However, what concerns us more here is the significance of this Tripartite Agreement in the core sector[136] on the subsystem as a whole. In this respect, two points can be emphasized :

1. It is a truism to state that less developed countries trade very little among themselves. The 1969 Pearson Report found that the average of mutual exports among less-developed countries amounts to a maximum of 20 per cent of the total, with distinct variations in the different geographical regions. One of the important reasons for this anomaly is the historical legacy of colonial rule, where the colony and the metropolitan state were conceived as economically complementary. Consequently, steps that try to break the continuation of 'the colonial pattern' of economic

[132] *International Politics* (Cairo), *op. cit.,* p. 428.

[133] Rubinstein : *op. cit.,* pp. 217-218.

[134] Article XII of the Agreement stipulated that after its ratification by the competent authorities in the three states, the Agreement would come into force on April 1st, 1968. April 1st was chosen because it is the beginning of the Indian fiscal year. The text of the Tripartite Agreement has been deposited at GATT, but can also be consulted in the *Indian Journal of Law,* IV (1968), p. 298.

[135] The review *International Politics* (Cairo) evaluated the total number of "products" as 500 rather than only 77. But according to a talk with an economic expert participating in this question, the publication has counted products and subproducts. See *International Politics* (Cairo), IV (1968), p. 465. Moreover, in July 1969 a protocol expanding the Tripartite Agreement was signed in Cairo. It increased the list of (exempted) products by 57.

[136] Other aspects of intense interaction in the core sector that could be dealt with are, for instance, mutual impact in the formulation and execution of development plans. For illustrations of this mutual impact in both domestic and foreign policies, see Rubinstein : *op. cit.,* pp. 234-284.

exchange would tend to lessen non-aligned actors' economic dependence on non-subsystem members, increase interaction among them and consolidate their subsystem. [137]

2. When less developed countries fostered their economic cooperation, they primarily did this among the members of a geographical region (*e.g.* East Africa). But the diversity of natural resources and difference in the levels of development are more characteristic of actors when they are members of different geographical regions, and hence their economic complementarity is heightened. One of the important characteristics of the Tripartite Agreement is that it is concerned with economic exchange among members not only of different regions, but also of different continents. Consequently, the three signatories of the Tripartite Agreement have created the *precedent* [138] of establishing closer economic cooperation among less developed countries on bases other than geographical proximity or regional membership. In this specific example, the tripartite initiation of closer and formal economic coordination was based on the three actors' adoption of a common foreign policy orientation : non-alignment.

In spite of the core sector's pioneering precedent in institutionalization, geographical caucusing and heterogeneity still affect the structure of the subsystem. This leads us to the fourth variable.

4.4. *Structure*

4.4.1. Since non-aligned actors declaredly reject 'power politics', [139] one would expect that the classical bases of military capabilities would not determine the pattern of their relationships. In fact, exceptions like India

---

[137] From the start, the three non-aligned actors thought of their 'pioneering' efforts as part of finding solutions to the general economic 'situation' characterizing less developed states. This is clear in the text of the Final Communiqué ending the 1966 Delhi Tripartite Meeting. See text in *International Politics* (Cairo), 1967, *op. cit.* Moreover, the report of the Working Party on the commercial arrangements between India, Egypt and Yugoslavia—working within the framework of GATT (L/3032 - 25 June 1968)—said : "Dès le début, les trois pays ont considéré que leurs efforts s'inscrivent dans le cadre plus vaste des efforts tentés par les pays en voie de développement dans le domaine de l'expansion des échanges et de la coopération économique . . .", p. 8.

[138] *Annuaire français de Droit international,* 1969, p. 629.

[139] Burton developed this argument at length. See Burton, John : *International Relations : A General Theory,* especially pp. 141-151 and 228-243, but also passim. Among non-aligned leaders, Nehru was very vocal in condemning 'power politics', whether in his speeches or in other declarations. See, for instance, his speeches of March 8, 1949 at the Constituent Assembly, October 3, 1950 at the 11th session of the Institute of Pacific Relations (Lucknow). See also Karanjia, P. K. : *The Mind of Mr. Nehru,* London, George Allen & Unwin, pp. 81-95.

apart, the dominant structural pattern of the majority is more or less *egalitarian weakness* in the level of military capabilities. Again if we take the sixteen actors of North and West Africa, we find that "the classical elements of state power are noticeably weak. Area is especially illusory, for the largest states—Algeria, Niger, Mali, Mauritania—are largely desert and—except for spots in the Algerian and Mauritanian Sahara—poor desert at that. Population figures must be tempered by considerations of illiteracy, heterogeneity, underemployment, ruralism, poor integration and apathy ; the 55 million people of . . . Nigeria represent both problems and potential—but not [actual] power. Military strength is low both in absolute and in relative terms, and is further depleted by domestic preoccupations, inefficiency and difficult terrain. Economic development is the goal" but not yet the reality of these African states. [140]

There is no claim implied here that there is absolute evenness in the "classical bases of state power". For a brief look at data on population, GNP, degree of urbanization, military manpower, and scientific capacity would indicate variations among non-aligned actors. [141] What is claimed here is that there is not among the subsystem members that unevenness in the level of "classical bases of state power" that characterizes the global system : *e.g.* possession of 'unlimited' (military) means to unlimited objectives.

Nor is it claimed that the egalitarian weakness in the "classical bases of state power" excludes variations in the degree of interstate influence. For though in sub-Saharan Africa, for instance, no state depends on the other absolutely for food or raw materials, variations in the degree of inter-state dependence among non-aligned actors can come from such a classical tangible element as the geography of communications. Thus land-locked states (*e.g.* Mali, Niger, Zambia) have to depend on coastal states which control their outlets to the sea. Indeed at both the 2nd and 3rd Non-Aligned Summits, some of these states tried to bring this issue to discussion. [142]

4.4.2. However, variations in the degree of such inter-state influence does not lead to a pattern of domination. For states with ports—*e.g.* Guinea, Ivory Coast, Liberia, Senegal, Sierra Leone, Dahomey, Ghana,

---

[140] Zartman : *International Relations in the New Africa ..., op. cit.,* pp. 61-62.

[141] For data, see Hudson and Taylor : *World Handbook ..., op. cit.,* pp. 38-42, 219-222, 295-299, 306-314, 322-326.

[142] Thus in his speech to the 2nd Summit, President Kaunda, for example, asked that the Conference pass a recommendation asking the U.N.—or one of its specialized agencies—to arrange an "international convention which will grant or give the land-locked countries the right of transit and free access to the sea . . .". Kaunda's speech to the 2nd Summit Conference of Non-Aligned Countries, *Review of Inter-*

Togo—and those through whose territories pipe-lines pass—*e.g.* Syria—need to depend on "a hinterland area for the full commercial use of their port facilities".[143] Thus interdependence among non-aligned actors is preferred to their dependence on outside states—especially states which are their arch-enemies. An example of this dependence of non-aligned actors on their worst enemies is the pattern of relations between Zambia and Rhodesia. Before the beginning of the 3rd Summit in Lusaka, the Zambian authorities had to give permission for the import of 1,500 tons of coal from Rhodesia to operate the special thermal power station so that villas for the heads of delegations at the newly-built Conference Centre would not be plunged into darkness should Rhodesian authorities switch off Zambia's main source of power from Kariba. Moreover, it was reported, most of the public and private messages sent out by delegates and the non-aligned press depended largely on South Africa's communications systems in Johannesburg.[144]

This dependence, however, did not prevent—on this specific issue of South Africa—the attenders of the 3rd Summit from recommending "to all non-aligned countries to refrain from entering into diplomatic, economic or relations of any other nature with South Africa and . . . to all such non-aligned countries as may be maintaining such relations with South Africa to break them forthwith".[145] But shortly afterwards sources from Ceylon's Plantation Ministry felt that it would be "next to impossible" for the Island to comply with the Lusaka resolution. South Africa annually buys about 30 million pounds of best quality Ceylon tea and is the Island's fifth largest tea customer (tea represents about 65 per cent of Ceylon's foreign exchange earnings). This was the same stand taken by the two newest African members of the non-aligned subsystem—Swaziland and Lesotho—which said they could not do without their heavy dependence on South Africa.[146]

national Affairs, XV (November 5, 1964), p. 46. Also *Egyptian Gazette,* October 8, 1964. Similarly in Katmandu and before embarking to attend the 3rd Summit, the Nepalese Finance Minister—Gahendra Bahadur Rajbhandari—hinted that his country will raise the question of uninterrupted transit facilities to the land-locked states at the Non-Aligned Summit. He replied to a question by saying that "certainly we shall try to use all forms to achieve our objectives and solve our problems". In fact, Nepal had been trying to secure free and uninterrupted transit facilities through India for its trade. *Dawn,* September 5, 1970.

[143] Zartman : *International Relations in the New Africa, op. cit.,* p. 62.

[144] *Daily Telegraph,* August 26, August 27, and September 3, 1970.

[145] The Final Declaration of the 3rd Summit : "Resolution on Apartheid and Racial Discrimination", Clause 11. *Review of International Affairs,* XXI (September 20, 1970), p. 31.

[146] *The Guardian,* September 14, 1970.

Thus a manifestation of structural heterogeneity was not the prevalence of a net domination-dependence dichotomy among subsystem members, but rather the opposition over 'vital subsystem interests'. [147] For some issues perceived as 'vital' by some could not be promoted by their subsystem fellow-members, and if anything the perceived 'vital' interests of the former were undermined by the latter.

4.4.3. This first cause of structural heterogeneity is similar to, but not identical with, the second : opposition over 'particularistic demands' or 'national interests'. [148] For instance, before leaving Baghdad to attend the 2nd Summit, President Aref emphasized—in his message to the Iraqi people—the importance of the Conference for "the Arab cause". Support for 'the Arab cause' was not to be taken for granted, since about half the Conference members had diplomatic and economic relations with Israel, and many sub-Saharan African states—for instance—received important 'technical aid' from Tel-Aviv. Consequently, when the Arab states managed to make the 2nd Summit condemn "the imperialistic policy pursued in the Middle East" and decide to "endorse the full restoration of all the rights of the Arab people of Palestine to their homeland . . .", Ceylon, Chad, Liberia, Nigeria, Senegal, Tanzania, and Togo contested parts of the resolution and "gave way after a fierce tussle in the final stages of the Conference". [149] Nepal and Burma, however, maintained reservations to the end, as they also did, together with Jamaica and Singapore, in the recent Georgetown Conference (August 1972). [150] Another example of opposition over 'particularistic demands' was the clash between Sukarno's Indonesia and India over Malaysia. This opposition however was linked to ideological differences, for to the Indians Sukarno symbolized the "Chinese adventurist line" and for the Indonesians India was supporting the imperialist base" of Malaysia.

---

[147] Ceylon itself severed diplomatic relations with Israel—a move that pleased its Arab fellow-members. But as a result, Ceylon was threatened with a Jewish boycott of its tea. *Dawn,* September 15, 1970. Also *Hindu,* September 15, 1970.

[148] For instance, before leaving Nicosia to attend the 2nd Summit, President Makarious declared that in his meeting with the Conference delegations, he would hope to explain the Cyprus problem and seek their support. Their attitude, he added, would greatly influence the Cyprus problem at the U.N. General Assembly. Though a 'particularistic demand', this would not cause much division among the members compared to the Arab states' demand for support on the Palestinian question.

[149] Seale, Patrick : *Overseas Foreign News Service* (referred to hereafter as : *O.F.N.S.),* October 12, 1964.

[150] *The Georgetown Declaration,* the Action Programme for Economic Co-operation and Related Documents : Conference of Foreign Ministers of Non-Aligned Countries, Georgetown, Guyana (August 8-12, 1972), pp. 39-40, 47.

4.4.4. Ideological divergences can be cited then as a third cause of structural heterogeneity. As early as 1960 and on a seemingly straightforward question—the Congo crisis [151]—this third cause of structural heterogeneity manifested itself in an acute form as the following table shows. (See table following page.)

These ideological divergences took a 'bipolar' form and were at the basis of the cleavage between the 'inclusivists' and the 'exclusivists' at the 1961 Cairo Preparatory Meeting. [152] The 'inclusivists' were those who wanted to enlarge the scope of the *First Non-Aligned Summit* and were thus in favour of inviting additional countries. India, for instance, suggested—beside the 19 states attending the Preparatory Conference—inviting Lebanon, Jordan and Malaya from Asia and Nigeria, Sierra Leone, Tunisia, Upper Volta, Togo, Kenya and Tanganyika from Africa. [153] The 'exclusivists' wanted to keep non-alignment 'pure'. Thus Ghana, Guinea and Mali—for instance—evaluated the non-alignment credentials of potential new African members in terms of their policies regarding the Congo crisis. [154]

This inclusivists/exclusivists bipolarization at the Cairo Preparatory Meeting reappeared at the main gathering of the First Summit between the 'moderates' and the 'militants'.

The *'MODERATES'* were particularly represented by U Nu, Makarious, Haile Selassi and Mrs. Bandaranaika—with Nehru as their spokesman and leader. For this school of thought non-aligned action was essentially mediatory. The Soviet atomic explosion intentionally timed on the eve of the 1st Non-Aligned Summit justified these leaders' contention that East-West tension was increasing. Consequently, they believed that as world peace was seriously threatened, all other problems such as—to quote Nehru—"imperialism, colonialism, racialism and the rest" [155] should

---

[151] Good: "The Congo Crisis", *op. cit.*

[152] Jansen: *op. cit.*, pp. 278-290. The 'inclusivists' were mostly the "older Asians": India, Burma, Afghanistan and Nepal, with support from the Sudan and Ethiopia. The 'exclusivists' were the "Younger Africans": Ghana, Guinea, Mali and the other members of the Casablanca Group supported by other 'radicals', *e.g.* Cuba.

[153] The head of the Indian delegation—R. K. Nehru, the then Secretary-General of the Indian Foreign Ministry—favoured extending the scope and broadening the basis of non-alignment. Consequently—as said before—India was ready to consider as non-aligned those countries that had military agreements with ex-colonial rulers. Jansen: *op. cit.*, p. 285.

[154] Egypt's "real criterion was the extent of cooperation extended by various states to the Casablanca Group . And Cuba, ... took her decisions according to the reaction [Latin American] nations had displayed to the Bay of Pigs invasion". *Ibid.*, p. 287.

[155] Nehru's speech at the 1st Summit, *Official Report of the Conference of Heads of State or Government of Non-Aligned Countries, Belgrade, 1961* (referred to hereafter as *B.C.R.*).

TABLE 12. *Core Positions of the Non-Aligned States concerning the Basic Issues in the Congo Crisis*

	RADICALS	MODERATES	CONSERVATIVES
	Ghana, Guinea, Indonesia, Mali, Morocco, U.A.R.	Ethiopia, Liberia, Libya, Nigeria, Somalia, Sudan, Togo, Tunisia, India and other non-aligned Asian states except Indonesia.	Cameroun Republic, Chad, Congo (Braz.), Dahomey, Gabon, Ivory Coast, Malagasy Republic, Mauritania, Niger, Senegal, Upper Volta.
Who is the "enemy" ?	Western "neocolonialists" and their African "puppets".	Belgium, African and non-African interventionists, and irresponsible Congolese leaders.	Communist "imperialists" and their African "acolytes". (Several "conservative" states would subscribe to the more complex view of the "moderates".)
How to organize the Congo ?	Establish a strong centralist government under "genuinely nationalist" régime closely affiliated with Pan-Africanist aspirations.	Preserve the legal and territorial integrity of the Congo ; support the legal Government and uphold the institutions of the Presidency and Parliament ; pursue constitutional changes in strict accord with due process.	Establish a decentralized government consistent with the diversity of the country ; affiliate with the Brazzaville group.
What role should the U.N. play ?	Strong U.N. intervention should be an adjunct to the "legitimate" régime ; short of this, no significant or legitimate role at all.	Expand U.N. authority for the maintenance of law and order, assist in evacuating foreign personnel, in creating a dependable Congolese army insulated from politics, and in establishing the requisite conditions for constitutional government.	A minimal role limited to banning foreign intervention and under no circumstances involving interference with Congolese settlement of the problem.
How should the problem of direct aid or intervention be solved ?	All direct aid necessary to defeat the "imperialist plot" against the Congo and to unify the Congo under a "genuinely nationalist" régime.	No foreign intervention ; all aid through the U.N.	No foreign intervention.

occupy a secondary position. "If war comes", Nehru affirmed, "all else for the moment goes." The delegates should not forget, he maintained, that the primary objective of non-alignment was peace and that was why the non-aligned states refused "military blocs, military alliances and the like". Therefore, if the delegates confined themselves to the practice of "passing long resolutions and making brave declarations, and then going home and allowing the world to drift to disaster", [156] the whole Conference would be "little short of tragedy". That is why in order to live up to their responsibility and "to meet the demands made by humanity" on the Conference, the representatives of non-aligned states should focus attention on the urgent problem of peace and war, especially when this problem is related to all other matters. For "it is war or the fear of war that has led to the Cold War. It is the Cold War which has resulted and is resulting in the old imperialism and the old colonialism hanging on wherever they exist because they deem it advantageous". [157]

But many Africans, for instance, would not accept Nehru's contention that East-West peace comes before fighting colonialism.

This *'MILITANT'* trend—mainly represented by the radical Casablanca Group, supported by Cuba and led by Sukarno—had a 'combative' view of non-alignment. They saw it as the expression of a new force in the contemporary international system, one which did not need to accept only the task of mediation, but which could stand up and address the world as an imposing group . They saw the Conference, therefore, as a chance to affirm their basic values, whether people listened or not. Hence their willingness to dwell on the colonial question and their reluctance to give priority to the detailed problems of diplomatic negotiation involved in trying to reduce the Cold War tensions.

If Nehru's attitude could be interpreted as India "losing its revolutionary spirit", [158] Sukarno's speech—reflecting the militant tendency—represented the opposite ideological pole. For him, the ideological East-West conflict was not "the real source of international tension and strife", but the root problem was "a conflict which cuts deeper into the flesh of man, and that is the conflict between the new emergent forces for freedom and justice and the old forces of domination, the one pushing its head relentlessly through the crust of the earth which has given it its lifeblood, the other striving desperately to retain all it can trying to hold back the course of history". [159] Ideological conflict, he believed, does not need to be decided through "nuclear weapons and napalm bombs" on the battle-

[156] *Ibid.*

[157] *Ibid.*

[158] *Hindu,* September 1, 1961.

[159] Sukarno's speech, *B.C.R.*

field, but through "bulldozers and antibiotics" and on "the construction site". In Europe, for example, the world has several countries of different social systems, but they coexisted in the past and they coexist now. Whereas, the trouble spots in South Africa, Algeria, Congo, Angola, Cuba, Tunisia are "the consequence of the desire for domination". Accordingly, "in every single case the cause, the root of international tension is imperialism and colonialism and the forcible division of nations", add to this neo-colonialism, or colonialism in "a new cloak".[160] The 'militants' believed that "there may be no nuclear war as yet, but that in a colonial war, as in Angola, Algeria, Tunisia ... ordinary bombs can kill many Asians and Africans ... and to be killed by an ordinary bomb or an atom bomb, there is no difference".[161]

But Nehru still insisted that he did not want to "waste time on secondary matters—on colonialism we are all agreed and our attitude on that subject is known". U Nu of Burma advised his colleagues not to be too passionate about the evils of past colonial powers, but to obey the golden rule "forgive and forget"[162] when the "goals are attained". Otherwise, new problems are created and the world would move to a "tragic division ... on the basis of colour".[163]

But such 'militant' leaders, as Sukarno or Nkrumah, were not in agreement with U Nu's appeal. In fact, the 'Militants' felt that their non-alignment was an integral part of the ongoing struggle against all forms of imperialism and colonialism. They also suggested that the former colonial powers tried to create trouble in the newly-liberated countries. That is why Sukarno held imperialism to be "the root of international tension" and asked the delegates to see that colonialism is "eradicated completely and irrevocably" within not more than two years or even less.[164] Nkrumah, typically, was more specific and urged the "end of all forms of colonialism by 31st December 1962".[165]

In the drafting committee the heated discussion continued between the 'Militants' on the one hand and the 'Moderates' on the other.[166] The first

---

[160] Most of Sukarno's speech is an exposé of the radicals' belief in the domination of the world scene by the struggle between the old forces of imperialism and the new emerging forces (*B.C.R.*, pp. 25-40).

[161] Declaration of the vice-chairman of President Sukarno's Supreme Advisory Council. *Dawn* (Pakistan), September 5, 1961.

[162] *B.C.R.*, p. 70.

[163] *Ibid.*

[164] *Ibid.*, p. 33.

[165] *Ibid.*, p. 104.

[166] Jansen : *op. cit.*, pp. 300-307.

group wanted to include a specific date for the end of colonialism, while the latter considered this "unreal and demagogic".[167] After much wrestling with terms, the Conference asked for "... immediate, unconditional, total and final abolition of colonialism ... in all its forms and manifestations".[168]

The ideological bipolarization in the subsystem continued at *the 2nd Summit,* but was influenced by changes that occurred at the global systemic level : *e.g.* decline of a simplified image of East-West bipolar structure, the direct channels of communication established between the superpowers, the 1962 Sino-Indian military conflict as well as China's increasing influence on the structure of—and interaction in—the contemporary international system.[169]

Sukarno's Indonesia, aided by Cuba, Algeria, Guinea, Ghana and also other African states like Congo (Brazzaville), Mali and Tanzania, still reflected the militant pole. Thus even though the agenda of the 2nd Summit was approved at its Preparatory Conference (Colombo, March 1964), a sub-item about "concerted action for national liberation of dependent countries" as well as a separate item on self-determination were introduced.[170] Then Indonesia, backed by Cuba, Guinea and Algeria wanted to list the 'new emerging forces' as a new item, but this was refused after a one-hour discussion. Then the same group attempted to give colonialism a separate heading so that "the Conference's main task would be to concentrate on the elimination of colonialism and not on peaceful coexist-

---

[167] *Ibid.,* p. 301.

[168] *B.C.R.,* p. 257.

[169] "The old model of international alignment, always oversimplified, [became] ... dangerously misleading. That model showed a big area coloured white, another coloured black (or red), and all the rest coloured grey. The idea was to enlarge the boundary line round your own colour. That may still be the idea, but in fact the map is still made up of innumerable colours. Even the Communist world is a patch work ... The unreality of the old model is most obvious in Southeast Asia ...", *The Guardian,* October 3, 1964.

In *Al-Ahram,* Heikal too reviewed at length the characteristics of the international system emphasizing the balance-of-terror aspects and then coming full circle to the U.S.-U.S.S.R. rapprochement. This rapprochement, however, "does not put an end to non-alignment, but rather requires adaptation of the methods applied by non-aligned states". *Al-Ahram,* October 2, 1964 ; *Egyptian Gazette,* October 3, 1964. What Heikal is saying is that—in spite of environmental or systemic changes—non-alignment is still viable and valid. This was a point insisted upon by Nasser in his opening speech in the session of the 5th October 1964. See *Report on the Second Conference of Non-Aligned Countries,* Cairo, October 1964 (hereafter referred to as *C.C.R.). Review of International Affairs* (hereafter referred to as *R.I.A.),* XV (November 5, 1964).

[170] *Hindu,* October 4, 1964.

ence".[171] This was met by strong opposition from India and Yugoslavia, joined by the Sudan, Uganda and Tunisia—and thus the 'militants' ' proposal was rejected. The 'militants' did succeed, however, in pushing the item of peaceful coexistence from the first position accorded to it by the Colombo Preparatory Meeting down to the fourth rank. Thus by relegating "peaceful coexistence to a back place"[172] they still managed to give "priority in the Conference work to anti-colonialism".[173]

But this ideological bipolarization did not come to an end once the Conference's agenda was settled, and it continued in the 'general debate' and also in the drafting political committee.

The 'general debate' started by Nasser's opening speech (5th October), who was followed—in the 2nd session (6th October) by Sukarno and Tito. Comparison of the three speeches indicates that Nasser and Tito were somewhat 'allied against' Sukarno. In spite of Nasser's insistence on colonialism's economic exploitation,[174] for instance, both he and Tito could be qualified as optimists in their judgement on the evolution of the contemporary international system. They believed that the system witnessed less tension, strengthened its self-maintenance mechanism, promoted and consolidated the role of emergent states.[175]

Sukarno vigorously combatted this view.[176] According to him, this optimism is based on a lop-sided perception of the international system, for such "progressive changes" (the phrase is Tito's) as have occurred (*e.g.* improved American-Soviet relations) have in no way improved the cause of non-aligned states. Imperialism has grown stronger and more

---

[171] *Ibid.*

[172] *Ibid.*

[173] See the official Conference agenda in *C.C.R.*, p. 6.

[174] Nasser's speech in *C.C.R.*, pp. 11-15.

[175] For instance, Tito affirmed: "I believe we share a common conviction that the situation to-day is somewhat better than it was at the time of the Belgrade Conference, that the development of international relations during that period was basically positive and that our first gathering gauged correctly the general interest and the trends of international events ..." Tito's speech, *C.C.R.*, pp. 20-24.

[176] Thus Sukarno said: "Originally ... peaceful coexistence was a term related to the war of ideologies, that is the war between the capitalist and the Communist ideologies. Even for the Agenda of our First Non-Aligned Countries Conference we spoke of—and I quote—'Peaceful coexistence among States with different political and social systems' ...

Well, Sisters and Brothers, you probably know what I think about ideological wars! Already in Beograd I remarked that 'ideological conflict need not lead to tension. It must not lead to tension'. Oh, no! In our age, ideologies will not create a big power conflict leading to world conflagration." Sukarno's speech, *C.C.R.*, pp. 17-20.

vicious, and the old colonial powers are out to extend their former domination. There is a "new era of confrontation", [177] Sukarno stated—seeking to enlarge his own policy of confrontation with Malaysia into a confrontation between the non-aligned states and the "imperialists". Sukarno's criticisms were all directed against the West, and though, unlike the Chinese, he welcomed the unfreezing of hostility between Moscow and Washington, like them he insisted that the guarantee of world peace today is not that of keeping the superpowers from attacking each other but to achieve unity for the developing countries.

This perception led Sukarno to question the meaning of peaceful coexistence itself. [178] For it was not a question of how nations with different ideologies could dwell peacefully together, he maintained. "Today", Sukarno affirmed, "the problem of security is no longer a problem directly related to the big Powers. [179] They can take care of themselves." Indeed "the grave ... problem of security ... now resides in security connected with the struggle for independence and in the security of the developing nations once independence has been won. Because all else is useless when our security is under serious threat, this is *the most important* matter for our attention, with all other political and economic items of our agenda subservient to it ...". [180] Sukarno then went on "to throw out some questions to show you in what directions my thoughts turn". He asked his "Sisters and Brothers" to

> "look at the military bases scattered all over the world ... Those foreign bases ... are said to be for the purpose of containing alien ideologies. But that is nonsense! ... They are used against the

[177] In his heavily-guarded Heliopolis Palace (because of lack of all quarantine documents and/or until the Conference Committee decided his fate), Tshombe—through T.V.—saw Sukarno referring not only to "confrontation" with Malaysia but also to Katanga when he favoured "confrontation" with old colonial powers which are trying to "preserve their interests by provoking secession of one part of the old colonial territory from the rest under the pretext of self-determination". *Ibid.* Also *The Guardian,* October 7, 1964.

[178] "An oriental Goldwater", Tito is reported to have said about Sukarno. *New York Times,* October 3, 1964.

[179] Sukarno's speech, in *C.C.R., op. cit.* And Sukarno reminded his "Sisters and Brothers": "... See what came to pass after the crisis over Berlin at the time of our First Conference in Beograd! From that Conference we expressed our great concern, from that Conference we sent envoys to Moscow and to Washington. Today ... it is certain that the protagonists of the conflicting ideologies have discovered ample reasons to live side by side, without trying to wipe each other off the face of the earth. They are reaching an accommodation if only because they feel mutually protected by their huge arsenals of nuclear deterrents." *Ibid.*

[180] *Ibid.* (emphasis added). For a general treatment of what can be called Sukarno's theory of international relations, see George Modelski (ed.): *The New Emerging Forces. Documents on the Ideology of Indonesian Foreign Policy,* Canberra, Australian National University, 1963.

newly-developing countries ... to preserve the interests of the old imperialist order. They are used as the paramount vehicle of imperialist interests in the newly-developing countries."

Consequently, military bases, like racial discrimination and economic subservience, are only symptoms of the same basic disease :

> "[the] question of domination of race by race ... of nation by nation for the sake of preserving, of strengthening, of promoting and extending the interests of the dominator."

Therefore

> "in this matter of domination lies the source of our weakness. Here in this matter of the persistent determination of the forces of the old order to maintain their privileges, their interests, their power in the world, lies the source of our division. This is the question about which we must concentrate our attention. This is the question upon the solution of which we must concentrate our energies." [181]

This was also Nkrumah's perception. After listing four "major causes of tension in the world", [182] he affirmed :

> "To my mind, the overriding cause of tension in the world to-day lies in the second of the four classes of tension I have defined, namely the difficulties placed in the path of development of the emergent and developing nations by the imperialist and neo-colonialist powers. Thus we in Africa are threatened by two dangerous forces. The first is the desire of foreign powers to penetrate Africa, and establish new forms of colonialism through the vicious system of economic imperialism. The world is witnessing the intrigues of this system in their classic form in the Congo and Southern Rhodesia.
>
> The second threat to the new Africa is the danger of ultra-right trends in neo-colonialism, which I would designate as fascist imperialism." [183]

The 'optimists' or 'moderates' were not unconcerned about "old imperialism and neo-colonialism", but their great concern was still over the danger of unpremeditated nuclear war and their desire was to consolidate the uneasy truce between the superpowers. Though they believed that the non-aligned actors have to carry on the struggle against the remnants of colonialism and consolidate the independence of the new states, they wanted the 2nd Summit to work for the promotion of the 'peaceful coexistence' objectives. Tito especially wanted to lead the non-aligned states in what he called "a conference for the consolidation of peace through international cooperation", and condemned all attempts at dividing peoples along racial lines. In his sharpest attack on the 'militant' position, Tito

---

[181] Sukarno's speech in *C.C.R., op. cit.*

[182] Nkrumah's speech in *C.C.R., op. cit.*, pp. 32-34.

[183] *Ibid.*

criticized those who thought it possible "to accept peace and coexistence in one area while defending one's interest by force and pressure . . ." and by "invoking ideological or other motives supporting Cold War conditions".[184]

Thus while Sukarno—like the Chinese—championed putting in opposition peaceful coexistence and liberation struggle, arguing that the latter is impossible so long as the former is the principal objective of non-aligned states, Nasser but especially Tito and India's Shastri perceived the two objectives as complementary and not antagonistic. This vital distinction was succinctly summed up by Tito in the phrase : "It is obvious that there can be no peace without freedom but under the present conditions it's also true that there can be no freedom without peace."[185] Conse-

[184] Legum, Colin : *O.F.N.S.*, October 7, 1964.

[185] It was probably for this that the Chinese News Agency—*Hsinhua*—attacked Tito. The Hsinhua report about the 2nd Summit is a very significant indicator of China's interpretation of non-alignment and is worth quoting at length. Dealing with the "struggle between two lines for guiding the course of the Conference", the Hsinhua Cairo correspondent continued : "One was the line stressing the struggle against imperialism, colonialism and neo-colonialism which was followed by most of the participating countries, and the other was a line of so-called peaceful coexistence propagated by India and Yugoslavia, which in fact aims at liquidating the struggle against imperialism and colonialism. During the discussion of the draft agenda for the 2nd Summit, many delegates maintained that priority should be given to the liberation of countries still dependent, and to the elimination of imperialism, colonialism and neo-colonialism.

"One delegate said : 'if we are silent and indifferent to African liberation, we could hardly call ourselves non-aligned'. Another African delegate said that when the peoples of countries still dependent were dying in fighting for independence to talk about peaceful coexistence would be meaningless. However, the Yugoslav delegate insisted on making 'peaceful co-existence' the most important item on the agenda. Failing to put forward any reasonable argument to back his proposition, he merely reiterated that he 'cannot understand' the amendment presented by Guinea, explicit and clear as it was to everybody else. His stand won the 'unreserved' support of the Indian delegate . . ."

After explaining how the 'militants' managed to put "self-determination and liberation struggle" issues on top of the Agenda, and relegate peaceful coexistence to the fourth place, *Hsinhua* continued : "Many delegates pointed out that disputes among Afro-Asian and Latin-American countries [on the one hand], and opposition to imperialist occupation of territories [on the other] were questions of categorically different nature.

"The principle of settling disputes without the threat or use of force was only applicable to the former but absolutely not to the latter. As a result, the Foreign Ministers Conference resolved that the item 'settlement of disputes without the threat or use of force in accordance with the principles of the U.N. Charter and particularly the right of self-determination' as proposed by the Colombo Preparatory Conference should be divided into two separate items, *i.e.* 'respect for the right of peoples to self-determination and condemnation of the use of force against the exercise of this right' and 'settlement of disputes without the threat or use of force in accordance with the principles of the U.N. Charter." *Hsinhua,* October 8, 1964.

quently, in the very first and second points of his speech, Prime Minister Shastri—like Nehru at the 1st Summit—dealt with "nuclear disarmament" which came "first and foremost", followed by "peaceful settlement of border disputes", and only in the third rank came "freedom from foreign domination . . .". [186]

After the 'general debate', the bipolarization continued in the drafting committee. At one stage, the 2nd Summit's Political Committee was confronted with five full drafts on peaceful coexistence, self-determination, and even the definition of non-alignment itself, from India, Yugoslavia, Egypt, Ghana and of course Indonesia. As was expected, Indonesia's draft was the most militant and went so far as to declare that there could be no peaceful coexistence with old colonial powers while they had even indirect influences in developing parts of the world. [187] As expected, India, Yugoslavia and also Egypt objected. [188] After lengthy discussions, the Political Committee had to break up so that foreign ministers could take over from the officials. Finally compromises had to be found through meetings between heads of delegations themselves—especially Sukarno and Shastri. [189]

To conclude : a shared colonial past, common problems of economic underdevelopment, psycho-societal issues of social change and nation-building and a similar position in—and perception of—the contemporary

---

[186] Shastri's speech, *C.C.R., op. cit.,* pp. 36-39.

[187] *The Guardian,* October 9, 1964.

[188] Though Nasser emphasized the history of Western exploitation and was criticized by Western observers for "exaggerating" it, his role in the Conference was basically nearer to the 'moderates'. For instance (*a*) he held back Algeria's President—Ben Bella—from fully endorsing the Sukarno policy line. *The Guardian,* October 9, 1964. (An interesting indicator : the speech that received the greatest coverage by the Chinese News Agency—*Hsinhua*—was Sukarno's, and Ben Bella's came second.) (*b*) Though Malaysia failed to secure official representation at the 2nd Summit, it sent a 3-man delegation as unofficial observers at the Conference—and this was after Nasser had sent a note urging Malaysia's presence at the Conference "in one form or another". *The Sunday Times,* October 4, 1964. In order to counteract the Indonesian efforts, the team brought with them 7 large bags of documents, films and tape recordings to show journalists and diplomats. *Straits Times,* October 6, 1964. Another indirect reflection of Nasser's sympathies in the Indonesian-Malaysian dispute is a 4-page supplement about Malaysia which appeared on the last day the Conference was meeting (October 10, 1964) in the semi-official *Al-Ahram.* See also Tunku Abdul Rahman's message to Nasser : *Straits Times,* October 15, 1964.

[189] To resolve the bipolarization between their divergent approaches, "confrontation of opponents" versus "peaceful methods by conciliation", Swaran Singh—India's Foreign Minister—and Subandrio—Indonesia's Foreign Minister—met at least twice. *Hindu,* October 2, 1964 and October 4, 1964. Four days later an official spokesman of the Indian delegation declared that Prime Minister Shastri held a meeting with President Sukarno. *Egyptian Gazette,* October 9, 1964.

international system did not hide or always attenuate manifestations of heterogeneity in the subsystem's structure. These manifestations—opposition over perceived 'vital subsystem interests', [190] estrangement over the satisfaction of 'particularistic demands' and especially different ideological perspectives even as for the basic tasks of non-alignment—can be traced back to 'specific situation' differences that arise when such disparate and varied actors come together. For instance, not all their elites have the same formation, not all of these actors are exactly at the same level of development, not all of them have acquired political independence at the same time or even in the same way, and—of course—not all of them have the same regional-local problems. Yet the non-aligned subsystem managed to achieve self-maintenance and none of the three Summit Conferences, for instance, broke up before achieving its business and publishing its Final Communiqué. How were the cleavages controlled and managed ? What was the regulatory mechanism involved ? This brings us to our fifth and last variable.

4.5. *Subsystem Regulation and Institutionalisation*

4.5.1. In reporting from Cairo about the 2nd Summit, Colin Legum has—unintentionally—hinted at how structural heterogeneity might act sometimes—surprisingly enough—as a factor of *regulation* to keep the subsystem together. "With 20 of the 47 participants", Legum said, "having direct national interests for which they sought support—the Arab League members over Palestine, Indonesia over Malaysia, India over

[190] The opposition between 'universalistic' or 'subsystem interests' and 'particularistic demands' is not always as clear-cut as this treatment—for analytical purposes—emphasizes, for delegations depict the two categories sometimes as not unlinked. The Arab states, for instance, had a resolution on the 'Palestinian Cause' as part of the general resolution on colonialism and racial discrimination. Similarly, resolutions on such 'subsystem interests' as self-determination was linked to 'particularistic demands'. Thus both India and Somalia, for instance, had reservations on this "universal principle"'s application, but for diametrically opposed reasons. Somalia's reservation was that existing boundaries should not be regarded as final and inviolable, whereas India asked that the right of self-determination should not apply to parts of territories (*i.e.* within the same domestic political system). Moreover, India linked the non-aligned actors' 'universalistic' demand for general disarmament and opposition to nuclear armaments with its 'particularistic demand' to send a mission to China to dissuade it from developing nuclear weapons. Similarly, Cyprus' Foreign Minister found that the *general* resolutions of the 2nd Summit are a great support for *Cyprus*' demands for self-determination and unconditional independence.

China, Cyprus over Turkey—it was perhaps inevitable that there should have been *a great deal of horse-trading in the lobbies.*" [191]

What this statement implies is that the subsystem members feel a common need for mutual support. This common need creates interdependence which in turn facilitates flexibility on conflict issues and helps to cement together the subsystem. There is, however, another aspect of conflict-regulation which the above statement suggests. As long as the conflict issues and the different manifestations of heterogeneity are not superimposed or mutually reinforcing, but rather cross-cutting, conflicts are softened and their regulation is facilitated. This is the cross-cutting divisions proposition, very influential among some sociologists and political sociologists. [192] This hypothetical proposition briefly states that "divisions which cross-cut each other contribute to the mitigation and regulation of conflicts . . .". [193] The proposition was first stated by the sociologist George Simmel who reasoned that the criss-crossing of antagonistic groups "serves to 'sew the social system together' by cancelling each other out, thus prevent[ing] disintegration along one primary line of cleavage". [194] Lipset supported this proposition by arguing that when a significant proportion of the actors is pulled by conflicting forces, "its members have an interest in reducing the intensity of political conflict . . .". [195]

How does this proposition—formulated by sociologists and political sociologists—apply to the non-aligned subsystem?

In talking about interaction in the subsystem, the data suggested that in addition to the general pattern of weak interaction there is a tendency to form geographically-based configurations which might create "discontinuities" [196] in the non-aligned subsystem. Moreover, in dealing with the subsystem structure, we concluded that cleavages occurred over the application of 'vital subsystem interests', 'particularistic demands' and the 'ideological orientation' of non-aligned actors. Hitherto, empirical findings indicate that the "discontinuities" and/or cleavages are not always mutually reinforcing or additive but criss-crossing, and thus do not lead to the disintegration of the subsystem. For instance, African actors—members of the O.A.U.—might group themselves *(e.g.* over South Africa) with

---

[191] Legum, Colin: *The Observer,* October 11, 1964 (emphasis added).

[192] For more details about this proposition, see above: ch. IV, footnote 72; and Nordlinger: *op. cit.,* ch. VI, but especially pp. 93-104. Nordlinger offers some qualifications for the proposition. See also my review of Nordlinger's book in *Annals of International Studies* (Geneva), III (1972), pp. 237-241.

[193] Nordlinger: *op. cit.,* p. 93.

[194] As quoted in *ibid.*

[195] Lipset, Seymour: *Political Man,* Garden City, Doubleday, 1958, p. 31.

[196] Young: "Political Discontinuities in the International System", *op. cit.*

their own (geographical) subsystem—an aspect of interaction discontinuity. But this situation does not become a permanent facet for on an aspect of structural heterogeneity—the 'ideological orientation' of the non-aligned subsystem—these African members would not stay as a caucus, but will look for different 'allies' or like-minded members in either the 'militant' or 'moderate' (sub-)subsystems, which is not primarily a geographical caucus. Consequently (through this caucusing on an 'ideological orientation basis), instead of 'isolated islands' of like-mindedness and one-sided integration transforming interaction "discontinuities" into complete non-interaction, we end up by cross-factors of interdependence among the members of the general non-aligned subsystem.

Similarly, the Arab actors—members of the Arab League—do act as a coherent caucusing group on one of their 'particularistic issues' (their conflict with Israel). But again this Arab caucusing does not go so far as to lead to their complete separation from the other subsystem members or—for instance—to the threat of abandoning the non-aligned subsystem if their 'particularistic demands' (perceived as 'vital') are not satisfied. For on other issues, the Arab states do not remain united as a caucusing or a (sub-)subsystem. For instance, in the case of geographically-based interaction, only the Arab actors situated in Africa have the right to attend the meetings of the O.A.U., while the Arab actors of West Asia do not. Similarly, on another issue of intra-subsystem cleavage (ideological orientation), there is among them the same bipolarization as within the general subsystem. Consequently, they are encouraged to look for 'allies' among respectively like-minded members ; and they might support the views of those who do not usually support them on their 'particularistic demands'—the Arab-Israeli conflict *(e.g.* Saudi Arabia and Nepal or Liberia). Thus the Arab (sub-)subsystem is prevented from *acting always* as an integrated 'isolated island' of intense interaction or a permanent caucusing group and can in fact contribute to a general 'feeling of interdependence' in the non-aligned subsystem. [197]

Let us take an empirical example, the Algerian-Moroccan border conflict, which will serve to illustrate two points : (*a*) how an Arab actor —Morocco—was reluctant to go to the Arab League for fear of being put in a minority because of the influence of Algeria's 'ideological' friends ; and (*b*) a formal institutionalized case of conflict-regulation among two non-aligned actors.

---

[197] Thus, in its editorial comment on the 3rd Summit, the Malaysian newspaper *Straits Times* states : "Admittedly there are many issues on which they [the non-aligned actors] differed. This is only natural for non-alignment does not presuppose ideological or political conformity ... *That the differences are many does not detract from the fact that such unity as exists is formidable." Straits Times,* September 12, 1970 (emphasis added).

The Algerian-Moroccan Border Conflict of 1963 [198]

This is one of the typical conflicts likely to erupt between pairs of countries in the non-aligned subsystem (especially in Africa). The immediate cause of the 1963 conflict between Algeria and Morocco was the demarcation of borders, with the possible transfer of territory from one country to another. As with almost all border conflicts resulting from colonial legacies, the stakes were not considered to be high, nor were core interests perceived to be in peril.

In this specific conflict, Morocco took the initiative in making demands and then in taking concrete measures to support them. Though military force was used for a short while, the overall level of violence was low. The danger of a generalized conflict was not very credible ; nor was the possibility of bloc actor's involvement.

In this type of conflict (between a pair of non-aligned states) any other actor in the system, at least theoretically, can intervene as mediator. But evidence seems to show that bloc actors were reluctant to mediate, and were even opposed to a discussion within the U.N. for fear of "cold war" intrusion. In fact, Morocco wanted to refer the conflict to the U.N., but it was advised by some of the bloc actors to seek an "African" mode of settlement.

Given the nature of the conflict-issue, the protagonists were not intransigent ; rather they were ready to accept mediation and a quick termination, especially since the "legitimacy" of border conflicts in Africa was not generally accepted. After an initial period of hesitation, the African states came to the conclusion that opening the "borders dossier" would be very disruptive to the stability of the African continent and consequently were opposed to a "rediscussion" of the border issue.

Fighting broke out on October 8, 1963 in the Hassi Beida area and subsequently spread to other border areas. Following news of fighting, a number of non-aligned countries tried to intervene as mediators.

President Bourgiba sent messages to King Hassan II and to President Ben Bella on October 12, calling for a cease-fire and a meeting between the three countries (Algeria, Morocco and Tunisia) to be held in Bizerta. The same proposal was repeated on October 15. But for one reason or another, and in spite of acceptance (at least in principle) of the Bourgiba

---

[198] For factual information, see Wild, Patricia Berko : "The Organization of African Unity and the Algerian-Moroccan Border Conflict", *International Organization,* XX (1966), pp. 18-36. Touval, Saadia : "The Organization of African Unity and African Borders", *International Organization,* XXI (1967), pp. 102-127, *Kessing's Contemporary Archives,* XIV, 1963-1964. Evan Luard (ed.) : *The International Regulation of Frontier Disputes* (especially ch. I and IV), London, Thames & Hundson, 1970.

proposal, the Conference never met. We may presume that Bourgiba, appearances notwithstanding, was not totally acceptable to Algeria as mediator.

Other mediatory efforts were made (by Syria on October 16, and by Irak on October 18), but both offers came to nothing. This is not surprising if we remember the "pro-Algerian" stand of both countries.

The Arab League tried to pose as mediator and adopted, in its meeting in Cairo on October 20, a resolution moved by the U.A.R. This resolution :

(*a*) invited Algeria and Morocco to withdraw their troops to prefighting positions ;

(*b*) set up a mediation committee composed of representatives from Lebanon, Libya, Tunisia, and the U.A.R., as well as the Secretary-General of the Arab League ; and

(*c*) requested Algeria and Morocco to help the Committee in its work.

Though both parties expressed no objection to receiving the proposed mediation committee, Morocco manifested a *de facto* opposition which killed the proposal. The fact that the Arab League (because of Egyptian influence ?) was viewed as sympathetic to Algeria, explains the Moroccan attitude. The same charge of sympathy can be levelled against Nasser and explains the failure of his mediatory offer, made on October 20.

Haile Selasie, who was on an official visit to Morocco starting on October 17 (after which he went to Tunisia), tried to intervene. He suggested a meeting on "neutral" territory to settle the conflict. Algeria and Morocco accepted the idea in principle, but differed on the meeting place. No progress was made until October 26, when the Emperor left for Paris.

Then on the same day (October 26) Modibo Keita of Mali proposed that Hassan II, Ben Bella, Haile Selasie and himself should meet in Bamako on October 29. As Keita and Selasie were perceived as "truly impartial", the proposal was accepted and the Conference was held in Bamako on October 29-30. Agreement was reached on the following points :

(*a*) a cease-fire, effective from November 1st ;

(*b*) a Commission of Algerian, Ethiopian, Malian and Moroccan officers to determine a demilitarized zone ;

(*c*) Ethiopian and Malian officers to watch over security in this zone ;

(*d*) the convocation of an extraordinary meeting of the Foreign Ministers of the *Organization of African Unity* in order to set up an arbitration committee whose task would be to determine responsibility for the outbreak of hostilities, study the border question and make proposals for a settlement ;

(*e*) an end to hostile propaganda by Algeria and Morocco.

The O.A.U. Council of Ministers met from November 15-18, 1963, and decided to set up a special mediation committee (at this time the Commission of Mediation, Conciliation, and Arbitration, foreseen by article 19 of the Addis-Ababa Charter, was not yet set up), composed of Ethiopia, Ivory Coast, Mali, Nigeria, Senegal, Sudan and Tanganyika. The actual work of the committee took place in Bamako on January 23-27, 1964. Meanwhile, relations between the protagonists had improved, especially after the meeting between Hassan II and Ben Bella during the Cairo Arab Summit Conference of January 1964 (to discuss the diversion of the waters of the river Jordan by Israel). Consequently, the border conflict subsided mainly as a result of mutual efforts by the parties concerned.

Two factors seem to have been important in containing the conflict and in facilitating third-party mediation. The first was the low stakes of the conflict itself, not only for the parties directly concerned, but also for potential outside "abettors". The second factor was the numerous mediatory efforts made by fellow non-aligned states, which exercised a kind of "moral pressure" on the protagonists to terminate the conflict as soon as possible.

The regulatory intervention [199] in the Algerian-Moroccan border conflict, however, begs an important question. Was the mechanism of conflict-regulation among these two non-aligned members initiated by primarily self-identified *non-aligned* OR *African* members? To some people this question might seem pointless and in fact "splitting hairs" since article III, item 7 of the Charter of the O.A.U. stated the African states' "affirmation of a policy of non-alignment with regard to all blocs". In other words, it might be said African states are, by definition, non-aligned actors. The question, however, is still important, for it needs to be decided whether the 'conflict regulators' acted primarily as non-aligned or as African states. It is clear that it was the institutionalized conflict-regulation mechanism of the O.A.U. that was essentially involved, and this indicates what answer can be given to this question. But it might be objected that the regulatory mechanism of the O.A.U. was chosen because it was the only alternative, *i.e.* there was not any institutionalized conflict-regulatory mechanism for the non-aligned subsystem as such.

4.5.2. Precisely, this brings us to another question : why has there not appeared—apart from the core sector—an institution formalizing the presence of the non-aligned subsystem ? Because of its importance, this issue was discussed by non-aligned actors as early as their *1st Summit*. At the Conference, some non-aligned leaders were convinced that if the non-

---

[199] For a general discussion of the regulatory function of non-alignment, see : Korany, Bahgat and Tawfik, Nagy : "Non-alignment : Its Conflict-Reducing Function in the International System", *Annals of International Studies,* III (1972), pp. 47-85.

aligned actors were to exercise an effective mediatorial role and to serve 'world peace', there should be a necessary minimum of coordination in views and of concerted action among members of the non-aligned sub-system.

By 1960, particularly in the Congo crisis, the disunity of the non-aligned members was amply displayed. Not only did the members express different points of view, but there was a total absence of any collective action.

To guarantee that clear-cut and sharp divisions would not take place among the non-aligned actors, some delegates were eager to achieve a minimum coordination on an agreed strategy for the future. Almost all the delegates agreed with Nehru that a formation of a non-aligned bloc would be a "contradiction in terms" and that the Conference was not supposed to herald in a third bloc. However, there were *three cross-currents* concerning the question of coordinated strategy of the non-aligned sub-system.

One point of view was represented by India which felt that if the non-aligned actors tried to form a bloc, they would deny their basic value ; hence India's hesitation before accepting even the invitation to Belgrade.

But some delegates represented a different position. Bourguiba of Tunisia—for example—favoured meetings among non-aligned "Ministers of Foreign Affairs, Finance, Development, Education, and Information" [200] so that the non-aligned states "can give each other mutual assistance, strengthen our unity", [201] coordinate policy, widen "the circle of uncommitted countries" and achieve a "moral striking force". [202]

Nasser and Tito occupied a middle position. They agreed with Nehru that the world did not need another bloc to drift to war, for "it is sufficient to have only one bloc—not two or more—for the war to break out". [203] But they aspired to the formation of a loose club that might attract nations to its ranks. This loose association should, for instance, hold consultations in the U.N. before crucial votes to coordinate the non-aligned approach towards political problems. [204]

The Conference's Final Communiqué echoed the dominant trend among delegates when it stated that "the non-aligned countries . . . do not wish to form a new bloc and cannot be a bloc". [205]

At the 2nd Summit, the Cultural Sub-Committee submitted a 5-point project including general principles of cultural, scientific and educational

---

[200] *B.C.R., op. cit.* Bourguiba's speech.

[201] *Ibid.*

[202] *Ibid.*

[203] *Ibid.*, p. 20.

[204] *New York Times,* September 3, 1961.

[205] *B.C.R., op. cit.*, p. 256.

cooperation as well as means of realizing this cooperation.[206] Yet the Final Communiqué of the Conference could only state "that participating countries should adopt measures to strengthen their ties with one another in the fields of education, science and culture",[207] and so the concept of formalizing the non-aligned subsystem was avoided. Though Tito at the end of this 2nd Summit thought that "we [non-aligned members] have done a big job" and that the "non-aligned countries have emerged after the Conference stronger and more united and now *they should pursue all international actions collectively*", he still observed that the cohesion of the non-aligned states had, so far, not been at the required level.[208] Though interested in more coordination and cohesion among the non-aligned actors, Tito did not welcome some proposals advocating that foreign ministers of non-aligned states should have *regular* meetings. "It is better we meet 'ad hoc', when it is needed", Tito said and added that "all statesmen with whom I have talked had the same opinion about that question." The reason for a consensus on refusing the institutionalization of the non-aligned subsystem was that "we have the U.N. for regular meetings, otherwise *such permanent meetings would lead towards creating the third bloc, which we do not want*".[209]

This fear of giving the impression of constituting a third bloc was at the basis of Nehru's reluctance to participate in even the most elementary forms of coordination or association among non-aligned actors, whether at the Brioni Tripartite Meeting of 1956 or at the 1st Summit of 1961. We have seen that to press correspondents who called the Brioni Meeting a conference, Nehru retorted that they talk as if the non-aligned states constitute another bloc while "we are against all blocs". Similarly, before Belgrade Nehru had his objections. This is why "it was only on the 9th August, a mere three weeks before Belgrade [Summit Conference], and three and half months after receiving the invitation that Mr. Nehru reluctantly accepted".[210] And the acceptance was conditional : "There should be no suggestion that a Third Bloc was in process of formation."[211]

Yet, not only was a 1st Summit convened, but also a 2nd and a 3rd. And it was at this *3rd Summit*, more than six years after Nehru's death, that the biggest step was taken toward institutionalization. In fact, the Final Communiqué approved a "resolution on the strengthening of the

---

[206] *Egyptian Gazette*, October 6, 1964.

[207] The Final Communiqué of the 2nd Summit. See *C.C.R.* in *Review of International Affairs*, November 5, 1964, *op. cit.*, p. 88.

[208] *Hindu*, October 13, 1964 (emphasis added).

[209] *Straits Times*, October 14, 1964, quoting the Yugoslav News Agency Tanjug (emphasis added).

[210] *Ibid.*, p. 289.

[211] *Ibid.*, p. 281.

role of the non-aligned countries" which merits much more emphasis than it has hitherto received. For this resolution speaks of "the Conference of Non-Aligned Countries, meeting at its *third regular session* at Lusaka, Zambia from 8 to 12 September 1970". [212] As is clear the words "third regular session" are to be interpreted as deliberate on the part of non-aligned members to emphasise both continuity with preceding Summits and a tendency toward formalization of structure. This interpretation is warranted when we look at another more explicit part of the resolution which states:

> "Considering the numerous statements of Heads of State and delegations during the general debate at the present session, urging the pressing need to ensure the continuity and increase the effectiveness of the role of the non-aligned countries by ensuring the implementation, through *appropriate machinery,* of the decisions, resolutions and directives of the conference*s* of non-aligned countries",

and the resolution continues:

> "Considering that the foregoing makes clear the need for appropriate implementation machinery of a flexible character, while at the same time having no financial implications, to *provide for continuity,* maintain contacts between member States and ensure the implementation of the decisions of the conference*s* of non-aligned countries,
>
> (1) entrusts its *Chairman* with the function of taking all necessary steps to maintain contacts among member States, *ensure continuity,* and carry into effect the decisions, resolutions and directives of the Conference of Non-Aligned Countries,
>
> (*a*) Requests all representatives of the non-aligned countries in the United Nations and its specialized agencies and in all international bodies to co-ordinate and harmonize their efforts ..." [213]

It might be an exaggeration to take at face value such press reports as "Third World nations set up headquarters" or "Zambia Chief heads permanent secretariat", [214] but the 3rd Summit—compared to the preceding two—showed a marked tendency toward institutionalization and formalization of structure. And if anything, the Conference of Foreign

---

[212] Final Communiqué of the 3rd Summit, *L.C.R., Review of International Affairs,* XXI (September 20, 1971), p. 34 (emphasis added).

[213] *Ibid.* (emphasis added).

[214] *Christian Science Monitor,* editorial, September 15, 1970. Another observer stated that "the Conference discussed among other things the possibility of setting up of a machinery for consultations among member nations whenever any of them faced a threat to its independence and integrity. There was also considerable support for the idea that members of the non-aligned club should meet every year at the level of senior officials if not of Foreign Ministers ..." Arora, V. K.: "The Lusaka Conference" in *Foreign Affairs Report,* XIX, Nos. 9-10-11 (September, October, November 1970), p. 80.

Ministers of Non-Aligned Countries—held in *Georgetown* (August 8-12, 1972)—went even further in emphasizing the drive toward institutionalization. To start with, the Georgetown Declaration (item 5) emphasized continuity by "recall[ing] that in September 1970 the Third Conference of Heads of State or Government of Non-Aligned Countries agreed at Lusaka on *concerted action* required to implement the principles of non-alignment". [215] Then item 40 of the same declaration stated that the participating countries undertook :

> "(i) to endeavour by all means to translate into action the principles of non-alignment as a basis for international relations. Having in mind that Zambia is the current coordinator of the non-aligned movement, the Foreign Ministers decided to extend the mandate of the Preparatory Committee and entrust it with the task of assisting the Government of Zambia in coordinating all further activities, particularly in the preparations for the next Summit ;
>
> (ii) to pursue, in concert with each other, solutions to current problems affecting the Non-Aligned Countries by consultations at all levels, including bilateral, sub-regional, regional and inter-regional consultations and arrangements, depending upon the issue involved . . . [216]

And item 42 is even more explicit for it states that

> "The Conference also adopted an Action Programme for Economic Cooperation among Non-Aligned Countries which identified *institutional arrangements for such cooperation and coordination . . .*" [217]

Consequently, under the subtitle "Institutional Arrangements for Economic Cooperation and Coordination" this "Action Programme for Economic Cooperation Among Non-Aligned Countries" stated in its items 38 and 39 :

> "38. Non-Aligned Countries should, in the interest of continuity and without prejudice to the possible need for a Permanent Secretariat, establish the necessary machinery for the execution of these decisions and recommendations. To this end, they decided that the Ministers of Non-Aligned Countries should meet every two years to consider the following :
>
> (i) the development of cooperation among Non-Aligned Countries ;
>
> (ii) international cooperation for the economic development of the developing countries.

---

[215] Item 5 of the NAC/FM/CONF. 1/21. *The Georgetown Declaration of the Conference of Foreign Ministers of Non-Aligned Countries,* p. 4 (emphasis added).

[216] *Ibid.,* p. 15.

[217] *Ibid.,* p. 16 (emphasis added).

39. To ensure the proper follow-up of the implementation of the above actions, four member countries, selected on a regional basis, should be responsible for the following :

(i) trade, industry, and transport among the Non-Aligned Countries and other developing countries ;

(ii) technology, know-how and technical assistance among the Non-Aligned Countries and other developing countries ;

(iii) financial and monetary cooperation among the Non-Aligned Countries and other developing countries ;

(iv) international cooperation for the economic development of the developing countries.

40. In accordance with the decision of the Heads of State/ Government at Lusaka in 1970, the host country of a preceding Summit Meeting shall coordinate all the activities outlined above." [218]

This drive for institutionalization and formalization of structure was followed to its logical conclusion by the adoption of the "Resolution on Coordination". This resolution, after extending the mandate of the Preparatory Committee that assists the Government of Zambia, the then coordinator, in coordinating all further activities in the preparation of the next (4th) Summit, proposes to the next Summit Conference :

"A. September Meeting of Non-Aligned Countries

A meeting of Non-Aligned Countries at a Ministrial level shall be held in the last week of September, as deemed necessary and desirable from 1974, at the United Nations Headquarters a few days after the opening of the General Assembly, to coordinate participants' approaches to the matters of common concern.

B. Standing Committee of Non-Aligned Countries

To consider the desirability of creating a Standing Committee composed of seven Non-Aligned Countries which shall be elected every year by the September Ministrial Meeting on the basis of geographical distribution and of rotation. Its main task will be to review all preparatory work of the yearly September Ministrial Meeting and any other matter they consider necessary to bring to the notice of the yearly Foreign Ministers' Meeting." [219]

4.5.3. At least two questions need to be raised at this point : the reasons for this change toward institutionalization, and the consequence of this change *(i.e.* institutionalization) on the non-aligned subsystem.

---

[218] *Ibid.,* pp. 27-28.

[219] *Ibid.,* p. 45.

As for reasons, an *analytical* distinction can be made between those belonging primarily to the non-aligned subsystem as such and those inherent in the subsystem's environment : the contemporary international system. The distinction is far from clear-cut and is not always easy to discern since by definition there is interaction between the subsystem and its environment, but this distinction is still useful for explanatory purposes. Two reasons have been selected on these two different levels :

(1) *Change in subsystem membership :* this change is not limited to quantitative terms but to changes in composition too. Not only has Nehru [220]—the most adamant opponent to even elementary forms of institutionalization—disappeared, but also there was the rise of 'younger African members' [221] whose emphases were not necessarily coinciding with those of the 'older Asians'. The scene of the opening session of the 3rd Summit illustrates both this change in membership and its effect on the Conference's deliberations. For "slowly the infectious rhythm of a Zambian freedom song, with its refrain, *'let's go forward together with one heart',* filled the . . . Mulungushi Hall. Kaunda led the song in a clear, sure voice and was joined, first hesitantly, then enthusiastically by the . . . monarchs, presidents, princes and prime ministers clapping in unison." That was the way the 3rd Summit started : the African majority (32 members out of 53 or 60.4 per cent compared to 11 out of 25 at the 1st Summit or 44 per cent of total membership) intended to exercise their weight according to their size. Consequently they "set the pace and pulled with them the leaders from Asia, Latin America and the Middle East". As a result "the face of non-alignment born in Belgrade [Summit] in 1961 as a reaction—largely by European and Asian neutrals—to the power struggle of the Cold War has changed ... Tito—father of non-alignment—remained quietly in the background". [222] Both the creation of the post of Chairman

---

[220] In comparing between the 1st Summit (at Belgrade) and the 2nd Summit (at Cairo), Jansen implied that the difference is due to Nehru who was present in the former but absent in the latter. "Second Belgrade", Jansen says, "might have achieved the level of First Belgrade if a second Nehru had emerged. He was much missed at Cairo, and there were many moving tributes to his memory. There was also much speculation as to who would succeed him as the unacknowledged leader of the non-aligned world. Though this occasioned some sidewards glancing between the main contenders for the role, the large void left by Jawaharlal Nehru is still empty." Jansen : *op. cit.,* p. 391.

[221] "The great absentee from [the 1st Summit at] Belgrade was the new Africa. That continent had not really been adequately represented at Bandung, where its special problems had been rather overlooked. Since Bandung twenty-five independent African states had emerged, and of these only six were at Belgrade . . ." *Ibid.,* p. 289.

[222] *New York Times,* September 13, 1970 (emphasis added).

and the appointment of President Kaunda to the chairmanship is an illustration of this change in subsystem membership. [223]

(2) *An environmental variable :* in talking about the (formal) boundary of the non-aligned subsystem, we proposed that in the early phases non-aligned actors were brought together by their opposition to the Cold War and its universalization to the subordination of everything else, as well as by their need for 'mutual protection and reassurance' against Superpower pressures "to stand up and be counted". With the increasing 'looseness' in systemic bipolar structure, some bases of integration within the non-aligned subsystem were expected to decline. This is, in fact, what happened. There was even talk about the end of non-alignment itself, since it became "as obsolete as the Cold War". [224] The 'non-alignment-as-anachronistic' hypothesis was so widespread that the conferees at the 2nd Summit had to face it from the very start. "From various parts", the host to the Conference affirmed in his opening speech, "come those who tell us that the policy of non-alignment has exhausted its role, through the changes which occurred in the international situation, particularly with regard to the Cold War and the blocs policy". And he continued : "We have to ask ourselves here, and in the light of the historic and human responsibility we shoulder, 'Is this true ?'." In his answer to this question, Nasser gave two "facts : (*a*) the policy of non-alignment is not a Cold War trade ; and (*b*) the changes in the situation of world blocs have *no bearing*

[223] As late as 1970, Mrs. Gandhi reaffirmed the view held by Nehru that it was a right decision not to institutionalize non-alignment. "Once you are in a bloc you are imprisoned. That is not the idea of non-alignment. Even those who are in blocs want to be more flexible." *The Times of India,* October 12, 1970. Moreover, after the approval of the "Resolution on Coordination" (NAC/FM/CONF. 1/RES. 8) at the Georgetown Conference of Foreign Ministers of Non-Aligned Countries (August 1972), the Delegation of Burma reserved its position on the ground that it considered it "... inopportune and impractical to institutionalize the Non-Aligned Movement". The Georgetown Declaration : *op. cit.,* pp. 45, 48. These 'Asian' declarations came at a time when President Nyrere had been working on a plan for closer cooperation among the non-aligned states to promote economic links among themselves. Legum, Colin : *O.F.N.S.,* August 21, 1970.

[224] "... [the] essence [of non-alignment] lies in the rejection of this [Cold War] dilemma and in keeping clear of bloc politics. *This is what brought the non-aligned together, but for the same reason as the Cold War slackens, non-alignment must become weaker, since little remains that unites these countries.* ... As soon as the factor of the Cold War disappears, the various national interests and contradictions among the non-aligned countries themselves intensify ... This is why non-alignment as a product of the Cold War and as a phenomenon which developed within this framework necessarily becomes as obsolete as the Cold War." Ljubwoje Acimovic (ed.) : *Non-Alignment in the World of Today,* Beograd, Institute of International Politics and Economics, 1969, p. 27 (emphasis added).

on the policy of non-alignment". [225] Though one can accept the first "fact", the second is hardly substantiated empirically.

For with the decline of an 'integrative function' formerly performed by Cold War threats and Superpower pressures for bloc affiliation, [226] an alternative basis of integration [227] is needed to counterbalance the increasingly-perceived heterogeneity. The 'integrative' factor that is increasingly emphasized at the moment is the *economic component of the non-aligned actors' common situation,* whether this economic component is related to internal aspects of economic development, or to questions of international trade and aid.

4.5.4. The inclusion of 'economic questions' in the non-aligned subsystem is not, in itself, new, but it is the different emphasis that is noticeable. At the *First Summit,* delegates mentioned—either in the public debate or in the lobbies—the necessity of equitable terms of trade, efforts to eliminate excessive fluctuations and to end restrictive practices, the desirability of convening an international conference to discuss economic cooperation among developing countries, means to improve world economic machinery ... But the aspect that received wide consensus was the widening gap between poor and rich countries, especially after the formation of economic blocs by technologically advanced states. The Conference resolution talked about the need for "the immediate establishment and operation of a U.N. Capital Development Fund", and recommended that in order to cope with the adverse effects of economic blocs *(e.g.* E.E.C.) the non-aligned states should strengthen their economic cooperation. [228] However, and in spite of Tito's efforts, [229] the Conferees stayed at the level of general recommendations to "close ... the ever-widening gap", [230] but failed to enunciate the specific modalities. If the number of

---

[225] *C.C.R., Review of International Affairs,* November 5, 1964, *op. cit.,* p. 12 (emphasis added).

[226] Because of Yugoslavia's 'defection' from the Communist bloc, "Krushchev was always highly suspicious of Nasser's friendship with Tito, and one day when Krushchev and Nasser were together the Russian saw a picture of Nasser and Tito kissing one another on the cheek in greeeting. 'I know you are friendly with Tito', said Krushchev, 'but do you believe him ?' The President replied : 'Yes I do believe him. I like him very much.' Krushchev would have none of it : 'He is a hypocrite. Whenever he kisses you he gives one cheek to you and the other to the Americans.' Nasser defended Tito and then went on to ask Krushchev : 'Why do you tolerate me being non-aligned while you will not accept Tito's non-alignment ?' Krushchev was blunt ... 'Because', said Krushchev, 'if Tito succeeds he will affect our bloc, but if you succeed you will affect the other bloc.' Heikal : *Nasser : The Cairo Documents, op. cit.,* p. 236.

[227] Rosecrance : *Action and Reaction ..., op. cit.,* pp. 220-232.

[228] *B.C.R., op. cit.,* p. 260.

[229] See Tito's Speech at the 1st Summit in *B.C.R., op. cit.,* pp. 153-170.

[230] *Ibid.,* p. 260.

words devoted to an issue in the Final Communiqué is an indicator of this issue's salience to the participants, 293 words approximately were devoted to economic issues at the 1st Summit. [231] This lack of salience of economic issues justified the convening of a special Economic Conference in Cairo ten months after the 1st Summit. [232]

Thus when the *2nd Summit* was held, the difference in emphasis on economic issues was noticeable. Already in the opening speech, the host to the Conference asked for the eradication of the "fateful disparity" in living standards among the world's peoples and proposed that less-developed states revise the prices of their raw materials to meet the higher cost of manufacturized goods from industrialized countries. [233] This early emphasis on economic issues led some observers to compare between the 1st and 2nd Summit, remarking that whereas "[la Conférence de] Belgrade s'est contentée de constater les inégalités de niveau de vie existant entre les peuples sans proposer de solutions pour y remédier, . . . [la Conférence du] Caire consacre une grande partie de son exposé à cette question. Certes, les pays non alignés ne font que définir les grandes lignes de nouveaux rapports économiques internationaux qu'ils désirent voir s'instaurer. Cependant leurs revendications sont aujourd'hui plus précises." [234] Other reports affirmed that "la Yougoslavie demande à la Conférence . . . la priorité pour les questions économiques", [235] and still others stated that in the 2nd Summit the economic issue "is as important as the political one". [236] These reports are confirmed by our indicator of salience : the number of words devoted to economic issues in the Final Communiqué rose from 293 at the 1st Summit to 923 at the 2nd—a net increase of 215 per cent. [237]

By April 1970, President Nyrere—the host to the Preparatory Meeting of the *3rd Summit*—made economic issues the centre of his speech :

> "The real and urgent threat to the independence of almost all non-aligned states thus comes not from the military but from the economic power of the big states. It is poverty which constitutes our greatest danger and to a greater or lesser extent we are all poor." [238]

---

[231] See the Final Communiqué of the 1st Summit.

[232] On the 1962-Cairo Economic Conference, see, for instance, Jansen : *op. cit.*, pp. 308-319.

[233] Opening Speech, *C.C.R., Review of International Affairs,* November 5, 1964, *op. cit.*

[234] *Le Commerce du Levant* (Beirut), October 17, 1964.

[235] Eric Rouleau in *Le Monde,* October 6, 1964.

[236] *Egyptian Mail,* October 10, 1964.

[237] See the Final Communiqué of the 2nd Summit in *C.C.R.*

[238] *The Nationalist* (Dar-es-Salaam), April 14, 1970, as quoted in Willetts, Peter : "Towards a Theory of the Phenomenon of Non-Alignment", unpublished paper sub-

If anything, the 3rd Summit itself—when it was held in September of the same year—reiterated this emphasis on economic issues. [239] For it attached greater status to its resolutions on "Non-Alignment and Economic Progress" by separating them from the Conference's 14 resolutions and signing them out as a "Lusaka Declaration". [240] In quantitative terms, the number of words devoted to economic issues attained 2158 words, a net increase of 133.8 per cent from the 2nd Summit and 636.5 per cent from the 1st Summit. [241]

The proposition that the 'economic component' is increasingly emphasized as performing an alternative 'integrative function' in the non-aligned subsystem is confirmed when we look at the Yugoslav-sponsored "International Symposium" on non-alignment. After stating the proposition of "economic development as *the strongest cohesive factor* in the non-alignment movement", it reiterated : "... the problems of economic development are the most genuine and the *strongest bonds* between the non-aligned countries. It is therefore urgent that the activity of the non-aligned is focused on economic aspects". [242] The publication implies a positive correlation between increasing emphasis on economic issues and more subsystem coordination and formalization. "In addition", the publication continues, "non-aligned states must try to create various mechanisms to defend their interests. It is especially necessary to work to unify the conditions of investment and trade, since small and medium-sized countries are in daily competition for credits and for markets, in which they are left to themselves and are therefore compelled to make concessions. It is therefore vital that non-aligned countries should create some means to defend their national economies through mutual consensus." [243]

The views screened in this Symposium are important indicators since among its 34 participants, 28 (or 82.3 per cent) were university professors,

---

mitted to the ECPR Workshop on 'Models of International Relations' (Mannheim, Germany, April 1973), p. 5.

[239] The host's opening speech is significantly entitled : "Economic Development and Social Justice". See *L.C.R., Review of International Affairs,* September 20, 1970, *op. cit.,* p. 18.

[240] *Ibid.,* pp. 26-29.

[241] The *ratio* increases of economic issues to others in each Final Communiqué of the three Summits would not be that high, since each Final Communiqué was longer than its precedent : 5-6 pages for the First Summit, 10-11 pages for the Second, and 12-13 pages for the Third.

[242] *Non-Alignment in the World of To-Day, op. cit.,* p. 74 (emphasis added).

[243] *Ibid.*

ambassadors or other top diplomats and also politicians coming from developing states.[244] But not only because of its semi-authoritative nature, but also because it links the past and present of the non-aligned subsystem that this Symposium's summary of the discussion is worth quoting in some detail :

> "To understand the prospects of non-alignment it is necessary to bear in mind the difficulties and problems it is facing today. It is true that this policy is no longer as effective as it used to be and that the non-aligned countries are no longer united in their efforts. There are two things to be underlined in this connection. Firstly, it was not difficult for the non-aligned states to act jointly when they were passing moral judgements on the big powers which were the sole actors on the world scene. But when problems began to arise between the non-aligned countries themselves, then different values and approaches set in. The non-aligned countries were not prepared for such contingencies. The second point is that after political independence many states did not visualize the complexity of the situations they would have to face. After a few years of independence the economic realities accumulated with all their difficulties and complexities, and many of the non-aligned countries were not able to cope with them. This led to setbacks, especially in Africa, and above all to internal instability and changes of government. Economic problems became dominant in those countries, but non-alignment failed to give them priority.
>
> All this suggests several conclusions that might be drawn in connection with the future of non-alignment. Firstly, a more adequate and stronger economic concept must be developed as part of the non-alignment platform. *This would bring new enthusiasm and solidarity to the movement.* Secondly, it would be useful to set up machinery or perhaps adopt some leading principles and guidelines to help solve disputes which might arise among the non-aligned. Such a mechanism could study and prepare various forms and formulas of mediation, conciliation, arbitration and similar models for the settlement of disputes. Thirdly, it might be also useful to open a research centre which would collect information and study the problems falling within the sphere of non-alignment, and could at the same time offer assistance in making plans for joint action."[245]

[244] There were, for instance, 3 ambassadors, an Assistant Minister at the Ministry of Foreign Affairs, an Assistant Secretary of State for Foreign Affairs, Chairman of the Commission for International Affairs of the (Yugoslav) Socialist Alliance, Member of the Central Committee of the (Tunisian) Socialist Destour Party . . . For the complete list of the 34 participants, see *ibid.*, pp. 11-13.

[245] *Ibid.*, pp. 75-76 (emphasis added).

Thus the trend in the non-aligned subsystem is toward more emphasis on the 'economic component' of the 'general situation' of non-aligned actors and a drive toward more institutionalization. But what is the consequence of this trend? Would the non-aligned subsystem become fully institutionalized and emerge as an integrated bloc?

4.5.5. There are limits to the degree of integration that can be established among the non-aligned actors. The reasons seem to be the following:

1. The basing of the subsystem's integration on economic issues would lead to interchangeability among non-aligned and third world states. [246] In other words, the *formal* aspect of the boundary (non-participation in East-West military alliances) would be—if not dropped altogether—at least increasingly blurred. Consequently, not only would the identification of a non-aligned subsystem be rendered more difficult, but also operational criteria of inclusion in—and exclusion from—the subsystem membership would be more difficult to discern. An illustration of this possibility can be quoted from the recent Georgetown Declaration on "The Action Programme for Economic Cooperation" of the Conference of Foreign Ministers of Non-Aligned Countries (August 1972). Item 11 of this Action Programme stated:

> "Developing countries not belonging to the Non-Aligned Group and which are major producers (of primary commodities) should be encouraged by Non-Aligned Countries to join producers' associations set up by the Non-Aligned Countries." [247]

2. Nor would increasing institutionalization lead overnight to a general unified international behaviour among the subsystem members, for their heterogeneity goes much deeper as the part on structure meant to show. [248]

---

[246] For attempts to define this widely used term—the 'Third World'—see for instance: Horowitz, Irving: *Three Worlds of Development: The Theory and Practice of International Stratification,* London, O.U.P., 1966, pp. 3-39; Lacouture J., and Baumier, J.: *Le poids du tiers monde,* Paris, Arthaud, 1962, ch. I; Miller, J. D. B.: *The Politics of the Third World,* London, O.U.P., 1966, pp. 10-15; and Worsley, Peter: *The Third World,* London, Weidenfeld (2nd edition), 1967.

[247] It is possible that non-aligned and (aligned but) third world states will combine their efforts only in some issue-areas. For a recent discussion of the concept of "issue-area" in the theory of international relations, see Rosenau, James: "Foreign Policy as an Issue-Area" in James Rosenau (ed.): *Domestic Sources of Foreign Policy,* New York, The Free Press, 1967, pp. 11-51. Even if the coordination between the two groups would be limited to some specific issue-areas, the non-aligned subsystem's formal boundary will still be blurred.

[248] One can deal with different aspects of heterogeneity, *e.g.* the diverse motives behind the adoption of non-alignment. Thus "a rapid sweep through the wide gamut of motives of the non-aligned reveals that this policy is a capacious house of many

3. Nor can one assume that the increasing recruitment of members within the non-aligned subsystem would lessen this heterogeneity. In fact, if the past experience of the subsystem offers any clue, the hypothesis of an inverse relationship between rising membership and declining integration seems to be more plausible than that of a rising membership/rising integration positive correlation.

Consequently, with or without institutionalization a certain degree of heterogeneity will prevail in the subsystem, and this heterogeneity will set limits (that are conditioned by the issue-area) on the level of integration which could be achieved among subsystem members. We have dealt at some length with *verbal* heterogeneity in this chapter and it might be useful to conclude it by measuring non-verbal or behavioural heterogeneity. Our operationalization of heterogeneity is based on the original definition of non-alignment as enunciated by Nehru in 1946 : "... to keep away from the power politics of groups, aligned against one another ..." [249] Moreover, this definition has been reaffirmed 24 years later by Nyrere when he said that non-alignment was "a refusal to be party to any *permanent* diplomatic or military identification with the Great Powers". [250]

The question then is whether non-aligned actors apply this definition of non-alignment in a uniform or semi-uniform way. Is there, for instance, an accepted mode of (diplomatic) behaviour around which the majority cluster ? Or are there variations, and if so how wide are they ? The

---

mansions, the central meeting point of a great variety of national interests that reach the same end from exactly opposite directions. For example, anger with the two blocs brought some countries such as the Arab states, to non-alignment : the absence of hostility to anyone was the motive of others, such as India. The politico-geographic squeeze of large neighbours forced Nepal, Laos and Cambodia to non-alignment : whereas their position of strategic 'openness' furnished the impulse to Indonesia and India. The proximity of a great power makes non-alignment the path of safety for Afghanistan : while the remoteness of the powers makes this policy possible for Ghana. India's vastness pushes it towards non-alignment : for Lebanon it is its smallness. A free choice of non-alignment was made by most of Afro-Asia, but it was dictated to a few, Cambodia and Laos. Varied markets for its numerous primary products made non-alignment an economic necessity for Indonesia, and because they were tied to limited markets for their few crops it was equally a necessary policy for Burma and Ceylon. Because they did not wholly favour either of the two sides in the Cold War, most of the Afro-Asian countries turned to non-alignment as the third course, but Yugoslavia did so perforce", because it could not wholly fit with either side. Jansen : *op. cit.,* pp. 126-127. This is why President Kaunda—the host to the 3rd Summit—qualified non-alignment in his opening speech as "a child of many fathers", or *"unity in diversity".* See *L.C.R., Review of International Affairs,* September 20, 1970, *op. cit.,* pp. 18-21 (emphasis added).

[249] *Nehru's Speeches,* vol. I, *op. cit.,* p. 2.

[250] *The Nationalist* (Dar es Salaam), April 14, 1970 as quoted in Willetts : "Towards a Theory of the Phenomenon of Non-Alignment", *op. cit.* (emphasis added).

degree of dispersion will indicate the measure of behavioural heterogeneity.

The *methodology* used is similar to the one applied in measuring interaction within the non-aligned subsystem, and the coding scheme is exactly the same. An index of diplomatic heterogeneity [251] has been designed by attaching numerical weights to patterns of diplomatic representation between each non-aligned actor (which attended the 3rd Summit) and each of the four countries that split into two opposed political systems coinciding with the East-West dichotomy, namely: China, Germany, Korea, Vietnam. [252] The data about diplomatic representation are coded on the basis of the following scheme of weighting:

	Sent	Received
1. Direct ambassadorial level	5	5
2. Indirect ambassadorial level	4	4
3. Direct diplomatic representation	3	3
4. Indirect diplomatic representation . . .	2	2
5. Unspecified diplomatic relations	1	1

If each non-aligned actor sent an ambassador to, and received one from, each of the 8 political systems, there would be 16 possible diplomatic links establishing a scale of 80, *i.e.* $(5 \times 16) = [(5 + 5) \times (4 + 4)]$. To distinguish between diplomatic representation with the 'Eastern' and the 'Western' political systems, a '+' sign has been given to the former and a '—' sign to the latter. Consequently, the 80 point scale will range from '+ 40' (the position occupied by an actor which sends an ambassador to, and receives one from, each of the 'Eastern' political systems) to '— 40' (the position occupied by an actor which sends an ambassador to, and receives one from, each of the 'Western' political systems). The median position on this scale, *i.e.* '0', would occur in two cases: (1) when a non-aligned actor is diplomatically inactive and diplomatic representatives were neither sent to, nor received from, any of the 8 political systems (*e.g.* Swaziland); and (2) when the non-aligned actor is active, but its diplomatic representation score with the 'Western' political systems is

[251] Hveem, Helge, and Willetts, Peter: "The Practice of Non-Alignment" in Ali Mazrui (ed.): *The Horizons of African Diplomacy,* Nairobi, East African Publishing House, forthcoming. I am grateful to Mr. Willetts for discussing the Index with me in two personal meetings: at the University of Essex, Summer 1972, and in April 1973 at the "Models of International Relations" Workshop of the ECPR (Mannheim). I am using different data and weighting code and this might explain some differences in placing different actors on the scale.

[252] There might be some bias in the indicator, since Taiwan and China were not of equal weight. But on the other hand West Germany was much more active diplomatically than East Germany. Since there is one potential bias on each side, they will tend to balance each other and do not seriously distort the validity of the indicator.

exactly balanced by its diplomatic representation score with the 'Eastern' political systems *(i.e.* the 'minuses' and 'pluses' cancel themselves out, *e.g.* Ceylon).

TABLE 13. *Heterogeneity Index of Non-Aligned Diplomatic Behaviour*

Non-Aligned Actor	'Eastern' Political System (+)			'Western' Political System (—)			Index
	Sent	Received	Total	Sent	Received	Total	
Afghanistan	5		5	5	5	10	— 5
Algeria	10	15	25				+ 25
Botswana				4	9	13	— 13
Burundi	1		1	5	5	10	— 9
Cameroon				5	18	23	— 23
Central African Republic				5	8	13	— 13
Ceylon	5	5	10	5	5	10	0
Chad	1		1	5	14	19	— 18
Congo (Zaire)		4	4	5	14	19	— 15
Congo People's Republic	11	14	25	5	5	10	+ 15
Cuba	8	20	28				+ 28
Cyprus				5	10	15	— 15
Equatorial Guinea	1	1	2				+ 2
Ethiopia				5	10	15	— 15
Gabon				14	15	29	— 29
Ghana				3	5	8	— 8
Guinea	16	20	36	5		5	+ 31
Guyana				4	5	9	— 9
India	5	3	8	6	5	11	— 3
Indonesia		5	5	5	1	6	— 1
Iraq	9	6	15				+ 15
Jamaica				4	11	15	— 15
Jordan				10	18	28	— 28
Kenya				5	10	15	— 15
Kuwait					5	5	— 5
Laos	3	8	11	9	7	16	— 5
Lebanon				4	9	13	— 13
Lesotho				4	7	11	— 11
Liberia				5	14	19	— 19
Libya				5	5	10	— 10
Malaysia				13	15	28	— 28
Mali	15	15	30	4	5	9	+ 21
Mauritania	10	14	24	5	1	6	+ 18
Morocco	5	5	10	9	13	22	— 12
Nepal	5	5	10	5	5	10	0
Nigeria				5	6	11	— 11
Rwanda				5	10	15	— 15
Senegal		1	1	5	19	24	— 23
Sierra Leone					11	11	— 11
Singapore					5	5	— 5

TABLE 13 *(continued)*

Non-Aligned Actor	'Eastern' Political System (+)			'Western' Political System (—)			Index
	Sent	Received	Total	Sent	Received	Total	
Somalia	1	7	8	5	5	10	— 2
Sudan	11	5	16				+ 16
Swaziland							0
Syria	12	16	28				+ 28
Tanzania	10	13	23	5	5	10	+ 13
Trinidad and Tobago					5	5	— 5
Tunisia				5	6	11	— 11
Uganda		3	3	5	10	15	— 12
U.A.R.	15	20	35				+ 35
Yemen Arab Rep.	6	13	19				+ 19
South Yemen Rep.	6	5	11		5	5	+ 6
Yugoslavia	8	14	22	5	5	10	+ 13
Zambia	6		6	5		5	+ 1

1. For the details of the data see the complete matrix on Diplomatic Interaction, appendix.
2. Algeria, the Congo People's Republic and Mali not only had diplomatic relations with North Vietnam rather than with South Vietnam but they also recognized the Revolutionary Provisional Government of South Vietnam as the only legitimate authority.
3. At the time the data was compiled (1970), the majority of Arab States were suspending their diplomatic relations with West Germany because of its arms shipments to Israel in the mid-1960s. This helps to explain the absence of any minus scores in the case of some Arab States (*e.g.* Algeria, Iraq, Sudan, Syria, U.A.R., Yemen).

The table is a useful *indicator* of not only the heterogeneity of diplomatic behaviour in the non-aligned subsystem, but also as a means of situating different non-aligned actors on the scale relative to their fellow-members. For instance, Guinea is very far on this scale from culturally-similar and geographically-near Gabon *(i.e.* an index of '+ 31' versus an index of '— 29', respectively) for they are separated by 60 points. [253]

Consequently, this behavioural heterogeneity will tend to make the level of integration to be attained and the agreement on a consensual international behaviour (as distinguished from a general orientation)

[253] Consequently, one can predict that on some subsystem political issues, Gabon's position would coincide with that of Jordan or Malaysia (— 28) rather than with that of Algeria or Egypt (+ 25 and + 35 respectively).

limited. The result is that each non-aligned actor will tend to practice its non-aligned international behaviour in a specific way. As a scholar of the *Politics of the Third World* has expressed it :

> "It is likely that non-alignment will survive in something like the same way as monarchy survives in Britain, as a frequently useful but not essential aspect of policy, which would be difficult to dispose of but is not permitted to stand in the way of necessary action when a government is convinced that action must be taken." [254]

One might or might not agree with this statement, but this begs the question of how non-alignment has been practiced as a specific foreign policy behaviour. This introduces the next part.

---

[254] Miller : *Politics of the Third World, op. cit.*, p. 106.

PART THREE

Non-Alignment as a Foreign Policy Behaviour

CHAPTER VI

Social Change, Systemic Strain and the Integrative Function of Foreign Policy

1. A Methodological note: on the Case-Study Approach and Aggregation

In their enthusiasm for cumulation, the establishment of general laws or "if . . . then" propositions, some social scientists—especially those who employ advanced quantitative techniques—have tended to overlook the contribution of case-studies to theory-building. The purpose of this methodological note is to reemphasise the role that the case-study approach can still perform by being complementary to the systematic correlational analyses aiming at general laws. In other words, the nomothetic-idiographic dilemma might prove to be a fake one, since the case-study approach can perform three important functions in social science theory-building:

1. The case-study can stimulate hypotheses about possible regular correlations. Indeed, most of the hypotheses tested at the moment in general correlational studies are *originally generated* in case-study material.

2. A case-study *can test in greater depth* inferences suggested in general correlational studies. In this case repeated case-studies can provide a solid basis for acceptance or rejection of the hypothesis and/or suggest important refinements.

3. If the correlation between two variables (*e.g.* social change and instability) has been solidly verified, a case-study approach could then go a step further to *investigate the precise causal relationship* between the independent and dependent variables. [1]

---

[1] But, of course, "all these uses of case studies ... assume further correlational analyses at a later state. Without iteratively shifting back and forth, without later correlational analyses building upon the hypotheses suggested, or supported by the case studies, one is only a little better off than without any case studies at all." Russett, Bruce: "International Behaviour Research", in Michael Haas and Henry Kariel (eds.): *Approaches to the Study of Political Science,* Scranton, Chandler Publishing Co., 1970, pp. 425-444 (emphasis added).

For all these significant functions that the case-study approach can perform, it is important to emphasise that *both* case-studies and general correlational studies

> "... *are critical to the development of scientific knowledge* either for its own sake or as reliable advice to the policy-maker ; neither one alone is satisfactory. Some scholars may prefer to work solely with one approach or the other. One may be better suited for a particular person's temperament, or he may have such a comparative advantage in the skills of one approach over the other that it is not productive for him to attempt both. Other analysts will find it easier to shift back and forth and may enjoy doing so. In any case, a recognition of the basic symbiosis between the two is essential to the long-run health of the research process." [2]

2. The Social Change Process

In his first book after the coup d'état, the *Philosophy of the Revolution,* Nasser depicts in a very metaphoric but telling way the process of social change that hit Egypt :

> "Our modern awakening ... began with a crisis. In my opinion our case very much resembled that of a sick man who spent a long time in a closed room. The heat in that closed room became so intense that the man was in anguish. Suddenly a violent storm blew, smashing all windows and doors, and strong currents of cold air began to lash the body of the sick man who was still perspiring. The sick man needed a breath of air. Instead, a raging hurricane assailed him, and fever began to devour his feeble body. This was exactly the case of our society ... *a society not yet crystallised ... still in a state of ferment and agitation.* It is not yet stabilised in its gradual development compared with other people who passed before on the same road." [3]

Nasser then goes on to point out the adverse effects of this speedy process of social change :

> "Undoubtedly this state of affairs is responsible for the lack of a strong *united* public opinion in our country. The difference between an individual and another is vast, that between a generation and another is vaster still."

To underline his point, Nasser gives the example of

> "an average Egyptian family—one of the thousands of families which live in the capital of the country. The father, for example, is a tur-

[2] *Ibid.*

[3] Nasser, Gamal Abdel : *The Philosophy of the Revolution,* Cairo, The National Publication House, n.d. but 1953-1954, pp. 42-43 (emphasis added).

> baned fellah, a thorough-bred country-fellow. The mother is a lady of Turkish descent. The sons and daughters attend schools respectively following the English and French educational systems. *All this is in an atmosphere where the thirteenth century spirit and twentieth century manifestations intermingle and interact.*" [4]

As with most Egyptians, this speedy process of social change does not leave Nasser's mind in peace : "I see all this and feel in my heart that I know the cause of this bewildering perplexity torturing our minds and this astounding confusion destroying our very existence." [5]

Then comes a note of hope : "I then say to myself 'surely our society will crystallise ; surely it will be satisfied ; surely be *welded into a strong homogeneous whole.*" [6]

But first : "It is required that we strain every nerve *to hold our ground during this period of transition.*" [7]

This holding of "our ground during this period of transition" (*i.e.* social integration) is not, however, guaranteed since Egypt is going through a period—again as Nasser expressed it—characterised by "the disintegration of values, dislocation of beliefs, dissension and conflict among both classes and individuals." [8]

2.1. A relatively unused—but crucial—source that analyses this value-conflict and role-strain is modern Egyptian literature. [9] Because of the capacity of the novelist, the poet or the playwrighter to catch—so to speak—the spontaneous reaction of the different classes, analyse their dispersed

[4] *Ibid.*, pp. 43-44 (emphasis added).

[5] *Ibid.*

[6] *Ibid.* (emphasis added).

[7] *Ibid.* (emphasis added).

[8] Nasser continues to diagnose Egypt's difficult 'situation'. "And between these two milestones", Nasser explains, "we find ourselves today destined to go through two [simultaneous] revolutions [*i.e.* a political one and a social one]—one [the political] calling for unity, solidarity, self-sacrifice and devotion to sacred duty, while the other [*i.e.* the social] imposes upon us, against our will, disunity, dissension, and nothing but envy, hatred, vindictivism and egoism." *Ibid.*, p. 27.

[9] For a treatment of this "cultural shock" problem in 19th century Egypt, see, for instance : 'Awad, Lewis : *Tarikh El-Fikr El-Misri El-Hadith* (History of Modern Egyptian Thought), Cairo, Kitab Al-Hilal, 1969, especially pp. 8-204 ; Abdel-Malek, Anouar : *Idéologie et renaissance nationale, l'Egypte moderne,* Paris, Anthropos, 1969 ; Louca, Anouar : *Voyageurs et écrivains égyptiens en France au XIXe siècle,* Paris, Didier, 1970. This volume has an excellent "essai de bibliographie systématique", pp. 269-331. A more general treatment is : Abdel Malek, Anwar : *Dirasat fi El-Thakafa El-Wataniyya* (Studies on National Culture), Beirut, Dar El-Tali'a, 1967 ; Ahmed, Gamal : *The Intellectual Origins of Egyptian Nationalism,* London, O.U.P., 1960.

and seemingly unconnected behaviour (which reflects anxiety and internal conflict) the artist is somehow capable of grasping the spirit of the age.

Literature—ranging from the works of Taha Hussein ("dean of Arab literature") to the trilogy of Naguib Mahfouz—analysed these strains (of change) as arising from conflict between the cultures of the 'spiritual East and materialist West' and/or collision between the 'old and the new'.

2.1.1. *Reaction to Western Civilisation :* A very early example of this "thorny problem, *i.e.* our relation with Western civilisation", [10] is *Hadith 'Eisa bin-Hisham* (Tales of Eisa bin-Hisham) by Mohamed El-Mwailhy. [11] Mwailhy started publishing his novel as early as 1898 in the newspaper *Misbah El Sharq* and finished its publication in 1900. Consequently, the novel treats the social problems of Egyptian society in the second half of the 19th century. The novelist dreamt that he was walking in El-Imam El Shafdi district (where a cemetery of Cairo is), when one of the tombs opened suddenly and Menaikly Pasha—who had died in 1850—arose. The novelist and the Pasha wanderd in the different districts of Cairo, and the Pasha was surprised by the new ways that had invaded the country since his death less than 50 years earlier. The Pasha then decided to get into direct contact with this new invading civilisation, and thus went on a trip to Paris.

In addition to the social criticism characterising the novel, it is an early example analysing the social conflict between the forces of 'modernisation' and advocates of Westernisation, on the one hand, and the defenders of 'traditionalism' and 'authenticity' on the other.

Tawfiq El-Hakim [12] in both *'Asfour Min El-Sharq* (A Sparrow from the East) and in *'Awdat El Roah* (translated into French as *L'Ame retrouvée)* dwells on the same subject. He shows the internal conflict of an Egyptian student in Paris who oscillates between the 'idealism' of his platonic love and the 'realism' that is to be applied in treating French girls. The main character expresses sadness for the deterioration of the East and its satellisation by the West. Hakim's emphasis is more on the return to an 'authentic' Egyptian identity (*i.e.* pharonic) and away from European materialism (and also from Bedouin anarchism or Turkish arrogance).

---

[10] Shukry, Ghali : *Muthakkarat Thaqafa Tahtader* (Memoirs of an Agonizing Culture), Beirut, Dar el-Tali'a, 1970, p. 252.

[11] El-Mwailhy, Mohamed : *Hadith 'Eisa bin Hisham* (Tales of Eisa bin Hisham), Cairo, Kitab El-Sha'ab, 1969, 3 volumes.

[12] With Taha Hussein (the "dean of Arab literature"), El-Hakim is one of the most prominent figures in both Egyptian and Arab literature. His *'Awdat El-Roah* had a direct influence on Nasser's thinking, as seen, for instance, in *The Philosophy of the Revolution, op. cit.*, pp. 43-44. El-Hakim, Tawfiq : *'Asfour Min El-Sharq* (Sparrow from the East), Cairo, Maktabat El-Adab, 1938 ; *'Awdat El-Roah* (The Restored Soul), Cairo, Maktabat El-Adab, 1933.

Similarly, in *Mellim El-Akbar,* 'Adel Kamel [13] analyses the personality of Khaled, the son of Ahmed Khurshid Pasha (an ex-judge and high civil servant in the Ministry of the Interior). Khaled—as many of the sons of beys and pashas—went to continue his studies in the metropolis—Britain. He then goes on a European tour and "his mind started working and contemplating his experiences. This mental effort was accompanied by serious psychological crises".

But one of the important novels that analyses this crisis of acceptance/rejection of Western civilisation is *Qandil Om Hashim* [14] (the Oil Lamp of Hashim's Mother) by Yehia Haqqy. In this novel, the writer is no longer satisfied with stating the socio-psychological conflict of 'spiritual East versus materialist West', but goes a step fruther to illustrate the collision and the crisis. This is why the movement in the novel is fast.

In one line the writer tells us that Ismail—the main character in the novel—went to Europe and stayed for seven years : "the boat has gone, seven years have elapsed and the boat has come back". But the boat brought back a different person—both physically and psychologically. Physically, he went "a fat, flabby person with a big tummy, where laziness mingled with rural naïveté" and came back "elegant, handsome, agile ... jumping down the staircase of the boat". Psychologically, he was reacting against his Egyptian environment and had big hopes and ambitions to change and even recreate it.

The change was essentially generated by his relationship and repeated discussions with his English girl-friend, Mary, the symbol of Europe (to be contrasted later with his relationship with his cousin, Fatma El-Nabawiya, who, with her traditional Egyptian name, symbolised his homeland). Through Mary, Ismail discovered European civilisation with its heuristic ethos and achievement and individualistic drive. She jolted him in his long-established beliefs and lectured him on the fact that life is not a mere routine, but an unending process of change. A revealing example is her blaming him for his addiction to helping the poor, his insistence on supporting his weak patients and his attachment to altruism. [15] "You are not Jesus Christ", she said, "these are drowning people who are looking for a hand to hold; if they find it, they will pull it down with them. These

[13] Kamel, 'Adel : *Mellim El-Akbar,* Cairo, Lagnat El-Nashr Lilgami'yyin, 1945.

[14] Haqqy, Yehia : *Qandil Om Hashim* (The Oil Lamp of Hashim's Mother), Cairo, Selselat Eqraa'. Haqqy is an important man of letters who has worked as a diplomat and was later in charge of the Supreme Council of the Arts.

[15] According to the senior expert of Egypt's National Centre for Sociological and Criminological Research, altruism and sacrifice are among the "positive social values" of the Egyptians. See Ewais, Sayed : *Hadith 'An El-Thakafa* (A Discussion of Culture : Some Cultural Facts in the Contemporary Egyptian Society), Cairo, Maktabat El-Anglo, 1970, pp. 71-121.

oriental sentiments are rejected and hated." [16] Ismaïl's inner self has been dislocated, his oriental values have been shaken and he came to believe that religion is a form of superstition to lull the people. Consequently, the individual acquires his worth in imposing himself on and challenging the community rather than in being contained by it.

The change was enormous and could have led to Ismaïl's psychological collapse, but he tried to pull himself together and to think of his homeland. He tried to think of excuses for his compatriots to explain their state of "physical and cultural underdevelopment". He thought that he had finally reached a solution, combining the 'best' of European civilisation with its individualism and achievement ethos with the basic oriental values of his psycho-societal environment.

But once back in his old house in the popular district of Saïda Zainab, he was appalled by its aspect of 'underdevelopment' ; and he reverted again to the crisis of swinging between his original rural character and his acquired background of Western culture. The crisis manifested itself in his relationship with his cousin, Fatma, the future wife chosen for him by the elders and the symbol of his origin. As soon as he saw her at the door, he was amazed and repeated irritably : "Is this the girl I am supposed to marry ?" This limited rejection is part and parcel of a more generalised one ; for Ismaïl withdrew from his environment and thought of going back to England. This, however, was not immediately feasible, and so he went to live in a guest-house run on European lines and symbolised by its Greek landlady. [17]

We do not need to continue the story, for—as usual—it ends happily. But what is important is the author's emphasis on this value-conflict and role-strain which an Egyptian political scientist called very recently "mental homelessness" due to the 'schizophrenia and intellectual dualism' that characterise the present Egyptian elite. [18]

2.1.2. *The Old versus the New :* Though this overlaps the conflict of the 'East versus West', the two are not exactly identical. Not only can the new come from sources other than the West, but also in the West itself there is the conflict between the old and the new, since social change is a continuous process.

---

[16] *Qandil Om Hashim, op. cit.,* p. 31.

[17] When Ismaïl went to this Europeanised guest-house, he was disappointed for he saw another aspect of Europe unknown to him : the fat, exploiting and miserly landlady type who accepted his presents but nagged at him for staying up late at night in his room and using up a lot of electricity.

[18] Hilal, 'Aly : "Thawrat Yolyo wa Qadaya fi El-Manhag" (The July Revolution and some Methodological Issues), *Al-Ahram,* 29 September 1973.

Our sample this time is the Arab historian Costantine Zuraiq who is not only concerned with Egypt's 'situation' but generalises it to include the whole Arab subsystem. In his book, significantly entitled "We ... and History" [19] Zuraiq states that the stage through which the Arabs are going is part of the great transformation from a medieval heritage toward a modern civilisation and mentality. But this transformation is not an easy straightforward process, for in its way there are restraints, both external (*e.g.* imperialist forces) and internal (*e.g.* illiteracy, fanaticism), and hence the inevitability of strain and conflict. The conflict with the internal restraints is especially serious for the forces of 'modernisation' [20] have to come to grips with such counter-forces as 'traditionalism', based—for instance—on a theological 'explanation' of causality rather than on critical evaluation or empirical investigation.

Zuraiq returned later to the same topic of the conflict between the old and the new. He reiterated his former views about the three pillars of modern civilisation : evidence to be sought in the natural world, faith in individualism, and rationality as the base of excellence. Though not overlooking the "contradictions, strains, confusions and disturbances" in modern civilisation, he is advocating its dynamism and its capacity to dominate nature. In fact, the underdevelopment of the Arabs—he thinks—is due to their incapacity to dominate their natural resources, the fragility of their economic and social systems, and the loss of inherited social-individual values coupled with their refusal to adopt alternatives from other sources. It is this state of 'underdevelopment'—in its varied dimensions—that is the real cause behind social diseases and political setbacks. For it is this state of underdevelopment that is responsible for the colonisation and satellisation of the Arabs, the poverty and ignorance of their great majority as well as the "Palestinian disaster". [21]

In his *A Discussion of Culture : Some Contemporary Cultural Facts about Egyptian Society* [22] the Egyptian sociologist, Sayed 'Ewais, is equally explicit about this disharmony and conflict between the old and the new. His empirical findings indicate that the Egyptian society—in its fast process of socio-cultural change—has some of its segments lagging behind

[19] Zuraiq, Costantine : *Nahn ... Wa El-Tarikh* (We ... and History), Beirut, Dar El-'Elm (2nd edition), 1963, also on the same subject : Wahby, Mohamed : *Azmat El-Tamadion El-'Arabi* (Crisis of Arab Civilisation), Beirut, Dar El-'Elm, 1956.

[20] For a treatment of 'modernisation' as seen by Arab scholars, see for instance : Abou-Zaid, Hekmat : *El-Takayyof El-Egtema'i fi El-Rif El-Misri El-Gadid* (Social Adaptation in the New Egyptian Countryside), Cairo, Maktabat El-Anglo, n.d. ; Saab, Hassan : *Tahdith El-'Aql El-'Arabi* (Modernisation of the Arab Mind), Beirut, Dar El-'Elm, 1969.

[21] Zuraiq, Costantine : *M'ana El-Nakba Mogaddadan* (The Renewed Meaning of Disaster), Beirut, Dar El-'Elm, 1967.

[22] *Op. cit.* (see footnote 15 above).

and suffering from what 'Ewais calls "cultural isolation". [23] In addition to this socio-cultural dichotomy within the districts of the same town [24] (let alone the city-country gap), [25] this mixture of the old and the new is within the same family and even within the behaviour of the individual. For instance, the owner of an expensive brand new car (a symbol of the new technology) will still put "*suras* of the *Qur'an*" and citations from the prophet's sayings on it to prevent the evil eye and road accidents. A family which has a fridge, a television set, a telephone and all other modern technological equipment will still on a certain day, at a certain time (*e.g.* Friday lunch time) wander in the house spreading incense to defeat the evil eye, to dismiss the devil and/or to cure a disease. [26]

2.2. These contradictions [27] are part of the 'Egyptian situation' that the new military elite inherited when it came to power. But to the then-existing problems were added new ones due to the new elite's commitment to accelerating the process of social change. [28] For Nasser believed that the way out of Egypt's "gruelling ordeal" characterising the "period of transition" is through revolution. He expressed this belief explicitly in the second part of *El-Mithaq* (National Charter) significantly entitled "On the Necessity of Revolution". "Experience has proved and proves every day", Nasser asserted, "that revolution is the *only* road by which Arab struggle

---

[23] According to the Islamologist Gibb, this "uneven distribution of social changes" is due to two factors : (*a*) variation in the force and duration of the external pressures ; and (*b*) variation in the desire of the people to accept them and their aptitude to assimilate them.

Consequently, "the contrast and the clash between the old and the new are quite obvious in everyday life" : traditional versus modern dress for both men and women, secular versus religious education, the donkey versus the aeroplane. Gibb, H. : "Social Change in the Near East", in *The Near East : Problems and Prospects,* edited by Philip Ireland, Chicago, University of Chicago Press, 1942, as quoted in Berger, Morroe : *The Arab World Today,* Garden City, Doubleday, 1962, pp. 389-435.

[24] See 'Ewais' quantified data about the popular *Boulaq district* in "the capital of Africa and its bride" (*i.e.* Cairo), *op. cit.,* pp. 63-67.

[25] For empirical examples of this city-country gap in the Egyptian context, see *ibid.,* pp. 215-217.

[26] *Ibid.,* pp. 58-59.

[27] An aspect of these contradictions is the general crisis of secularisation versus religious faith or "Mecca versus mechanisation'. See Berger : *op. cit.,* pp. 414-421. As we stated in chapter IV, part of the contradiction is due to the process of socialisation. One of the rare studies on socialisation of Egyptian children, especially in the countryside, is 'Ammar, Hamed : *Growing Up in an Egyptian Village,* London, Routhledge & Kegan Paul, 1954.

[28] This accelerated process of change is illustrated, for instance, by the change in the governing elite itself. The military who took over the political system were members of the first generation of officers not to be admitted to the military aca-

can cover its transition from the past to the future . . . and bridge its transition from its present state to its aspired state". [29] This acceleration of the process of social change can, perhaps, be conveniently indicated through this table emphasising the contrast between the pre-military and the military regimes. [30]

TABLE 14. *The Social Change Process in Pre-Military and Military Regimes*

Variables	Pre-military	Military
	1. *Social Processes*	
Communication	limited to elites and periphery	attempt to extend to whole society
Voluntary organizations	permits existence, makes some effort to control, organizations based either on religion or kinship	destroys or co-opts; creates mass organizations, substituting politics for kinship and religion; nationalizes loyalties, permits nothing between family and state unless controlled by latter
Education	emphasis mainly on liberal professions; foreign schools permitted	greater emphasis on primary education and on science and technology; foreign schools nationalized
Status of women	traditional subordination altered slightly	greater freedom through education and occupational mobility
Social structure and standards	loose, many differences; individual closely bound to family and other groups and to locale	greater individual freedom from family and all non-political associations but deliberate effort to produce national uniformity of "acceptable" behaviour

demy on purely "ascriptive" criteria. In fact, Nasser himself came from the middle or lower middle class and was thus bound to bring with him social ideas opposed to those espoused by the 'established order'. Nasser used to take pride in his modest social origin and identify himself with the low strata of society. Similarly, El-Sadat renders periodical visits to his village and does not fail to appear in his *Galabiyya* —the traditional dress of the fellah. See, for instance: El-Sadat, Anwar: *Révolte sur le Nil,* Paris, Amiot, 1957; Stephens, Robert: *Nasser: A Political Biography,* London, Allen Lane, 1971; St. John, Robert: *The Boss,* London, Arthur Barker, 1961; and Lacouture, Jean: *Nasser,* Paris, Seuil, 1971.

[29] Nasser goes on to explain at length why revolutionary change is the only way of social change. See the *National Charter, op. cit.,* pp. 11-12 (emphasis added).

[30] Berger: *op. cit.,* pp. 393-396. Methodologically, the two compared types of regimes are "ideal types", since empirically neither is the change so abrupt nor is the dichotomy so clear-cut.

TABLE 14 *(continued)*

Variables	Pre-military	Military
	2. *Economic Processes and Policies*	
Organization	loose controls, private enterprise dominant	extensive controls, claims of socialism
Industry	small but growing	great emphasis on industrialization
Agriculture	large holdings	land reform, state-controlled cooperatives
Ownership	private, with considerable foreign interests	nationalization in two senses: transfer of foreign property to native control, and state's acquisition of private property and creation of new assets by state
Prices	few controls	increasing control, mainly of food staples
	3. *Political Processes and Programs*	
Nationalism of dominant elite	strong but mixed with older loyalties	intensified, less influenced by other loyalties
Participation	masses left largely quiescent	goads, exhorts, draws in masses
Freedom : meaning	Western sense : individual liberty	Synonymous with national independence
Freedom : incidence	some freedom resulting from competition for power among (1) foreign interests, (2) native elite in office, (3) new more nationalist native elite seeking power	no challenge to native ruling elite permited
Class distinctions	form basis of regime's policies	emphasis on "social justice", "economic" democracy and appeal to "classless" society
Parties	several	one, or a mass political organization not called a party
Legislation	by parliament, with strong executive	rule by decree of leader or cabinet ; parliament, when existing, plays a largely supporting function
Representative character	not "representative", in sense that rulers are traditional elite	more "representative" in sense that rulers' origin is middle or lower class
Rule of law	slow, uncertain growth	reversal of direction
Public administration	civil service tends to be personal appendage to ruler ; little effort at reform	efforts to introduce modern bureaucratic structure

Since the process of social change entails strain and conflict, it is a logical inference that the level of social dislocation and socio-political conflict rises with the acceleration of this social change process by the new military elite. [31] And to this conflict we now turn.

3. **Data Analysis of the Systemic Strain**

The main sources of the events data are *Middle Eastern Affairs, Al-Ahram, Bourse Egyptienne* and also the *Keesings Archives*. Given the length of the data sheets, they have not been included as an appendix to the present chapter which will itself be devoted to a detailed analysis of the data.

3.1. But before embarking on the analysis of the data, there are a few points that must be dealt with :

(i) There may be some 'data errors' due to the sources. Though I have tried to check and counter-check the different types of information recorded, there may still be some loopholes, especially since press censorship was very frequently exercised by the new regime during the period under analysis (*e.g.* the Nasser-Naguib split was only revealed three full days after Naguib had been boycotting the meetings of the Revolutionary Command Council). But on the whole the question of potential "source errors" was not allowed to affect the general trend the data indicate.

(ii) Some objections might be raised against singling out a certain type of data to emphasise (overemphasise ?) certain types of events (*i.e.* the high level of conflict in the 1952-1954 Egyptian political system and the struggle of the new regime for legitimacy). But—to take an already classical metaphor—if we are interested in a certain tree or type of tree in a forest, singling it out is the way to identify its properties. Though we do not need to overlook the fact that this tree is part of the forest, we have—nonetheless—to concentrate our efforts on it in order to anatomise and analyse it.

(iii) But this raises a third type of objection—which is, in fact, the opposite of the last one : why include some data of the 'forest' along with data of the 'tree-type' ? That is, data not destined to test our main point

[31] An illustration of the military elite's commitment to accelerate social change is the fact that Nasser attributes the failure of the 1919-nationalist revolution to its neglect of the social change dimension. *The National Charter, op. cit.,* pp. 21-27.

about the high level of conflict, but data that show—on the contrary—some reconciliation attempts within the polity (*e.g.* visiting and revisiting among some members of the new regime and leaders of the "ancien regime" especially those of the popular Wafd party, releasing Ahmed Hussein—head of the Socialist Party—who was received twice by Nasser himself . . .). All this, it might be alleged, either confuses the picture or weakens the main contention about the high level of conflict. The answer to this objection is two-fold :

(*a*) In providing data to support his hypothesis, the researcher should not fall into what is known, euphemistically, as data-cleaning : putting only the data that emphasises a certain hypothesis and neglecting or ignoring contrary data—allegedly for the sake of clarity. The big danger of this practice—especially if it is exaggerated—is the creation of a discrepancy between the image of the 'situation' one tries to communicate and the empirical referent of this 'situation'.

(*b*) Though the 'reconciliation attempts' within the Egyptian political system might at first glance go against the hypothesis of a high level of conflict in the period under analysis, these reconciliation attempts—if taken in the period as a whole and placed in the context of the total social system (*i.e.* looked at both diacronically and syncronically) indicate the contrary. For since *El-Dubbat El-Ahrar* (The Free Officers) did not have a political organisation with grass roots among the masses, they could not afford to alienate *simultaneously* all the other political organisations (*e.g.* the Wafd, *El-Ikhwan* . . .).

3.2. This last point brings us to the analysis proper of the data. In chapter IV we have discussed the 'developmental framework' which is based on a varied combination of force (F) and legitimacy (L) to maintain control (C) and was symbolised by the equation : $C = F + L$.

The period under analysis started with sieges of the royal palaces, broadcasting building and ministries, deposition of King Faruq and the arrest of the pillars of the 'ancien regime'. So at that time in the political system, the "force" component was the keynote of the junta's control of the system. For if *El-Dubbat El-Ahrar* had got rid easily of the traditional-legal bases of formal legitimacy and had removed the old political forces, they were not yet clear about what to replace them with. Hence, the long road in the search for the 'legitimacy' component of political control.

3.2.1. To start with *El-Dubbat El-Ahrar* had neither an operational political programme nor even an elementary mass political organisation to start preparing this programme for a new political system. Beyond certain general objectives related to the evacuation of the British occupation forces and the "purging of the country from corruption", they had a very naive image about political action in the Egyptian political system. Nasser, better than anyone else, revealed this naïveté :

> "I admit I fell, after July 23, a prey to fits during which I accused myself, my colleagues and the rest of the Army of folly and madness for what we did on that day.
>
> Before July 23, I imagined that the whole nation was on the alert. I thought it only awaited the leaders to storm the strongholds of oppression, to follow them in close orderly ranks on the Holy March to the Great Goal.
>
> I had imagined our role to be [that of] a commando advance-guard, lasting only a few hours, after which the Holy March of the whole nation, advancing in close orderly ranks to the Great Goal, would follow. I felt I could even hear the terrific and tremendous uproar caused by these great masses advancing in close orderly ranks to the Great Goal. So strong indeed was my conviction that I felt in my inmost soul that this was a reality, not a mere flight of imagination.
>
> But the facts I faced after July 23 took me by surprise.
>
> The leaders had accomplished their mission. They stormed the strongholds of oppression, dethroned the despot and stood awaiting the Holy March in close orderly ranks to the Great Goal.
>
> They waited long, however.
>
> The masses did come. But how different is fiction from facts !
>
> The masses did come. But they came struggling in scattered groups. The Holy March to the Great Goal was halted, and the picture in those days looked dark, dastardly and foreboding.
>
> It was only then that I realised, with an embittered heart torn with grief, that the vanguard's mission did not end at that hour, but it had just begun." [32]

3.2.2. Yet, Nasser himself continues, the vanguard was "unprepared". Consequently, in the early hours of 23rd July, Naguib confided to his friend—the journalist Ihsan Abdel Qeddous—that *El-Dubbat El-Ahrar* would not take the government since the constitution did not permit it. Instead they were thinking of summoning the old parliament. Thus the intention was legalism, respect of the existing pattern of 'multi-party democracy', and the guarantee of continuity. Consequently, a respectable, well-known politician, 'Aly Maher Pasha, was asked to form the first cabinet. But he did not stay very long in power, for on the 5th September he reshuffled his cabinet, and only two days later he finally resigned definitively. In fact, throughout the month of August relations between *El-Dubbat El-Ahrar* and 'Ali Maher continued to deteriorate. Differences of opinion appeared concerning the definition of a foreign policy (Maher did

[32] Nasser : *The Philosophy of the Revolution, op. cit.*, pp. 21-22.

not hide his inclination to associate Egypt with the Western coalition, in return for evacuation and financial aid); agrarian reform (Maher, encouraged by the Army's representative on the Regency Council, Rashad Mehanna, wanted to fix the ownership ceiling at 500 feddans instead of 200); the relationship between the old political parties and the new regime (Maher had spent about 40 years in the multi-party political life of the 'ancien regime' and the word 'purging' did not have exactly the same connotation for him as was intended for it by *El-Dubbat El-Ahrar).* Since opposition was so basic Maher had to leave sooner or later, and an article in the magazine *Rose el-Youssef* asking : "who governs ? 'Aly Maher or the Army ?" exploded the crisis. On the 7th September, then, he was replaced by Naguib, only a few hours before the military police arrested 50 prominent personalities of the 'ancien regime' (*e.g.* the ex-premiers Naguib El-Hilali and Ihrahim 'Abdel Hadi), friends or colleagues of the ex-premier 'Aly Maher. [33]

With Naguib at the head of the cabinet, formal and effective sources of authority in the Egyptian political system tended to coincide, at a time when the level of societal conflict was manifestly rising. For though the first cabinet had stayed in power less than 45 days, it had decreed that all civil servants should account for the sources of their increased income since 1939, and in fact, had appointed seven "purification committees" to investigate corruption in governmental departments. Thus the clash with the old Egyptian bureaucracy (or at least its superior segments) was initiated. The first cabinet also discredited the traditional social stratification order by abolishing the Ottoman civil titles of 'Bey' and 'Pasha', hence unleashing the influential users of this old order against the new one which was as yet not well-rooted. There were even attempts at overthrowing the new regime, since the former governor of the capital was accused of "plotting against the government" and was arrested.

3.2.3. In collision with influential traditional interests, going against the 'norms' of an established social order, in conflict with relatively well-organised political forces, the new regime could count on "the people" —*i.e.* the underprivileged classes—since it was "in the name of the people" that the army movement had started. Yet it was a prominent segment of "the people"—*i.e.* the workers—that initiated the first violent, bloody crisis of the "white revolution". On the 12th August (20 days after the coup d'état) at 7 p.m. a group of trade-union workers, employed in the National Misr Company, started a riot in the textile mills of Kafr El-Dawwar, the Delta industrial town about 20 kilometers from Alexandria. They asked, "in the name of the army", for the removal of three members

[33] Lacouture, Jean et Simone : *L'Egypte en mouvement,* Paris, Seuil, 1962, p. 158.

of the management, occupied the factories and, to react against police firing, set on fire two factories. It was precisely the army which was dispatched from Alexandria in the early morning of August 13 to deal with the workers' procession : the result was 9 dead, 25 wounded and 200 workers arrested. On August 14 a military court—headed by one of *El-Dubbat El-Ahrar,* col. Abdel Moneim Amin—was convened and 5 days later it hanged Khamis and Bakri, the presumed two leaders of the riot.

Though it had managed to protect 'public order', the new regime found its political position weakened, since it added left-wing elements to the list of hostile political organisations. For after hailing "the movement of the people", the Egyptian communists [34] then issued tracts denouncing "la dictature militaire qui — épargnant Farouq, les féodaux, les traîtres et les concussionnaires — ne tachait ses mains que du sang des ouvriers". [35] Press censorship was reimposed and—after the rounding up by the army of about 50 persons in Cairo and Alexandria—General Naguib issued a warning to all classes of society "and particularly the working class" that any attempt at disorder would be punishable as high treason. On September 9, Premier Naguib himself was appointed the Military Governor-General and on the same day the land-reform bill—limiting land ownership to a maximum of 200 feddans for each individual owner and 300 for each family—was published. [36]

---

[34] For a treatment of communism in Egypt, see, for instance : Agwani, M. S. : *Communism in the Arab East,* Asia Publishing House, 1969, especially pp. 44-45 ; El-Bishri, Tareq : *El-Haraka El-Siassiyya Fi Misr* (Political Movement in Egypt, 1945-1952), Cairo, El-Hayyäa El-Misriyya, 1972, pp. 416-456 ; Laqueur, Walter : *Communism and Nationalism in the Middle East,* London, Routledge and Kegan, 1956, pp. 31-63 ; Morquos, Elias : *Tarikh El-Ahzab El Shyu'yya Fi El-Watan El-'Arabi* (History of Communist Parties in the Arab Homeland), Beirut, Dar El Tali'a, 1964, pp. 54-139.

[35] Lacouture : *L'Egypte en mouvement, op. cit.,* p. 157.

[36] This seems to have been devised by the new political elite after they had taken power, with the objective of giving the movement "an economic and social basis". Under the supervision of one of *El-Dubbat El-Ahrar,* Gamal Salem, two leftist economists, Ahmed Fouad (an old friend of Nasser) and professor Rashed El Barawi (translator of Marx into Arabic) prepared the bill. *Ibid.* At the time the land reform law was issued, the king possessed 55,000 feddans, Prince Yussef Kamal, 16,000 and was followed by the Badrawis' 9,000. For statistics concerning land distribution in pre-July, 1952 Egypt, see *The U.A.R. Statistical Yearbook,* Central Agency for Public Mobilisation and Statistics, June 1970, p. 54. These statistics are of limited utility because they take as their ceiling 200 feddans, thus grouping together those who owned 201 feddans and those who owned 10,000 or 15,000. But the statistics clearly show that whereas 94.3 per cent of the landowners owned 35.4 per cent of the total owned area, 0.1 per cent owned 19.7 per cent. For a recent comprehensive treatment of the rural problem in Egypt, see : 'Oda, Mahmud : *El-Qarya El-Misriyya Bina El-Tarikh Wa 'El El-Egtema'* (The Egyptian Village between History and Sociology), Cairo, Maktabat Sa'ïd Raäfat, 1972 ; and El-Shihawi, Abdel

3.2.4. This bill limiting landownership erupted into an acute crisis too, this time with the big landowners and the rural bourgeoisie—including the still popular Wafd party. For already on the 6th of September—before the change of cabinet—the landowners had conferred with the ex-Premier, 'Aly Maher, about the proposed land-reform law and published their objections to it. Their attacks were seconded by the Wafd party, whose leaders were among the first people to be adversely affected by the limits imposed on landownership. Thus before the regime had time to recover from the repercussions of the bloody clash with the working class and the Communist attacks, the 'new order' found itself heading for a clash with the old one. The number of *leading* persons arrested by the army between 7th and 11th of September reached 57, an average of just less than 15 arrests daily. But on September 13, the violent conflict with the landlords erupted at Maghagha in the Minya Province of Southern Egypt. 'Adley Saleh Lamloum—a farmer deputy and the oldest son of a rich, feudal family—refused to accept the land-reform law. When representatives of the 'new order' went to examine the family ownership and redistribute the property exceeding the new law's limit, Lamloum released his dogs and fired at the 'intruders'. With the help of supporters, Lamloum organised raids against the police of Maghagha. After the arrival of reinforcements and the surrounding of his 'headquarters', 'Adley 'bey'—the son of the completely illiterate M.P.—was arrested and deported to Cairo for trial. [37] The incident showed the lengths to which landlords were ready to go to defend their privileges.

The protracted conflict in the emerging political system can be easily followed in the events data. Consequently, rather than continuing with the chronological order, we can more usefully analyse the conflict *systemically,* namely through the relationship between the organised political forces [38] and the new regime in their contest for systemic control.

Khaleq : *Roäya Gadida Lilmasäala El-Zera'yya* (A New Vision of the Agricultural Problem), *El-Kateb,* XII (August 1972), pp. 23-38. For a useful treatment of the "Land Problem" in English, see Abdel Malek, Anwar : *Egypt : Military Society,* New York, Vintage Books, 1968, pp. 50-86. (The book was originally published in French by Seuil in 1962.)

[37] Lamloum was not sentenced to death but only to imprisonment, and thus the conflict with 'the right' was not compensated by a rapprochement with 'the left', for "des tracts communistes eurent beau jeu d'opposer le cas Lamloun au cas Khamis, l'homme à la carabine et l'homme aux mains vides". Lacouture : *L'Egypte en mouvement, op. cit.,* p. 158.

[38] For a useful treatment of the organised political forces in the pre-1952 political system, see : El-Bishri : *op. cit.* ; Landau, Jacob : *Parliaments and Parties in Egypt,* Tel-Aviv, Israeli Publishing House, 1953 ; Ramadan, Abdel 'Azim : *Tatawor El-Haraka El-Wataniyya Fi Misr* (The Evolution of the Nationalist Movement in Egypt, 1918-1936), Cairo, Dar El-Kitab, 1968 ; Vatikiotis, P. : *The Egyptian Army in Politics,* Bloomington, Indiana U.P., 1961.

3.3. *The Conflict with the Wafd*

The Wafd [39] was not just a political party among others, for when the new regime decreed the abolition of political parties and the confiscation of their funds, 90,000 Egyptian pounds of the 95,000 confiscated belonged to the Wafd. To say that it was the biggest political party is not enough, for the gap separating it from the parties that followed behind was really wide.

3.3.1. Since its appearance under the leadership of the prestigious Sa'ad Zaghlool at the time of the 1919-revolution, the Wafd had been identified with the Egyptian 'nationalist' point of view in the triangular conflict between the king, the British and the nationalist forces. The king wanted to continue his autocratic rule, the British wanted to preserve their post-1882 preponderant position in Egypt, and the Wafd pursued the dual aim of trying to limit the monarchy's autocracy in the Egyptian political system while at the same time securing independence for the country.

In this triangular contest, the Wafd's two contestants resorted to coercion to settle their differences with the party. The British counted on gunboat diplomacy, based on ultimatums backed by their military occupation force to carry out their demands. The monarchy resorted to what were virtually royal coups d'état through violations and suspensions of the 1923-constitution. Thus the Wafd was kept out of power between 1930 and 1936, when it had won a substantial electoral victory. In the following ten years (1936-1946), the cabinet was given to lesser political parties (*e.g.* the Sa'adists, the Liberal Constitutionalists, the Union Party . . .). Consequently, inspite of its popularity and impressive showing at the polls, the Wafd was permitted by the Royal Palace and/or the British to govern for only seven years between 1923 and 1952. [40]

But the Wafd still grouped within its ranks nationalist forces among the landowners, the rising capitalist class, many religious leaders and affluent lawyers. Though its base was narrow, the party proved capable —through the manipulation of the nationalist symbols—of successfully mobilising mass support among certain important segments of Egypt's

---

[39] The word 'Wafd' (*i.e.* delegation) was coined for the party when Egyptian nationalists were collecting people's signatures to enable a 'wafd' to go—in the name of the Egyptian nation—to defend the country's case for independence before the 1919-Versailles Peace Conference. The only complete work published in English on the Wafd is Quraishi, Zaheer: *Liberal Nationalism in Egypt: Rise and Fall of the Wafd Party,* Delhi, Alwaz Publishers, 1967.

[40] Abdel Malek: *Egypt: Military Society, op. cit.,* p. 19; Dekmejian: *op. cit.,* pp. 18-20; Stephens: *op. cit.,* p. 27.

population—peasants, bureaucrats, students, small businessmen and the urban masses. [41] This enabled it to initiate riots and engage in semi-revolutionary mass agitation.

The British—the source of effective authority in the country—understood this aspect in the working of the Egyptian political system. But their problem was that they

> "sought to keep the Wafd out of power so long as the Wafdist terms for independence and for a treaty were unacceptable to Britain, but at the same time the Wafd was the only power in Egypt with which a durable treaty acceptable to a freely-elected parliament could be negotiated. The king and the governments he formed from minority parties or from courtiers might be willing to compromise on the Wafd's demand for complete British withdrawal from Egypt and the Sudan, in order to retain British support for their domestic position, but they could not impose such agreements on Egypt against the revolutionary will of the Wafd." [42]

This analysis indicates not only the Wafd's heavy weight in Egypt's political system, but also its social importance. For the Wafd party denoted a 'state of mind' and expressed an important 'moment' of Egypt's history. Perhaps this 'moment' was already outdated and gone, but only a few grasped the significance of this or were even aware of it. The Wafd party was, then, both a special form of demagogy and a certain dynamic nationalist conception of the state, identified with parliamentarism and the whole process of liberal thinking.

---

[41] In a certain sense, the Wafd was identified with a lot of things that made it popular: it was dedicated to the principle of (multi-party) parliamentary democracy, "to the promotion of greater justice in the daily life of the country, and the evidence of this lies in the great work achieved in the area of education under the direction of Taha Hussein, the establishment of the right to a job, the creation of the Farm and Cooperative Credit Bank in 1930 to provide assistance to the small landowners in particular". But this did not mean that the Wafd leaders envisaged "carrying revolution to the heart of the social structure, ... achieving a better distribution of the land, ... doing any damage to the upper middle class ...". Abdel Malek: *Egypt: Military Society, op. cit.*, p. 19.

[42] Stephens: *op. cit.* This British appreciation of its rival's weight (the Wafd) explains incidents such as the one on February 4, 1942 when British tanks surrounded the royal Palace and forced Faruq to choose either abdication or the formation of a Wafd government. In British opinion, it was only a Wafd government which could keep the country "safe" (*i.e.* on the side of the Allies) while Rommel was advancing in North Africa. See: Anis, Mohamed: "Hadeth 4 Fabriar" (The 4th February-Incident), *Al-Ahram,* 6 September 1973; and *The Killearn Diaries* 1934-1946: The Diplomatic and Personal Record of Lord Killearn (Sir Miles Lampson), High Commissioner and Ambassador to Egypt, edited and introduced by Trefor Evans, London, Sidgwick & Jackson, 1972, pp. 194-241.

3.3.2. Hence, the conflict with the Wafd was serious. This is why, perhaps, *El-Dubbat El-Ahrar* moved cautiously. Already on the morning of July 23, Nasser discussed with his Wafdist friend, Ahmed Abul Fath,[43] (editor-in-chief of the influential newspaper, *El Misri*) the form of the emerging political system and the possibility of summoning the Wafd-dominated, 1930-parliament. On the 3rd of August, a meeting was organised between, on the one hand, Nasser, Gamal Salem and Khaled Mohei Ed-Din, and, on the other, Fouad Serag El-Din, the very influential Secretary-General of the Wafd. But the two sides were separated not only by differences over the form of the emerging political system but also over their respective conceptions of the whole social system, a precursor of their imminent conflict over the land-reform law.[44] Consequently, on September 9, the Naguib cabinet approved a bill on the "reorganisation of political parties". Since these political parties—the bill said—were based on personalities rather than principles, they should drop all members suspected of corruption and offer real platforms with alternative policies. Naguib gave the parties thirty days to "reorganise" themselves.

Though some of the Wafd leaders (*e.g.* the Party's Secretary-General) were ousted, the popular leader of the party—Nahas—refused to submit to "any mortal force". "Allah only could remove me", the old Pasha said. He was backed by the Party lieutenants : "no Nahas, no party", the slogan went. But since this constituted a challenge to the new government's determination to prevent Nahas from continuing to lead the party, the Wafd finally decided to register under new leadership. The Party's council, however, voted (November 8, 1952) to keep Nahas as the Party's honorary president. But when the Wafd at last went to register—with other political organisations—under a new leadership, they learnt that all political organisations had to be "purged". Consequently, the many lawyers that swelled the Party's ranks decided to fight the case of the constitutionality of the law on the purging and reorganisation of political parties before the State Council, Egypt's highest judicial body (November 11, 1952).

Perhaps because of the Wafd's capacity to marshal "mass support" and since *El-Dubbat El-Ahrar* movement was declared a "thawra" (revolution), the cabinet issued a decree giving Premier Naguib absolute power, effective as of July 23 (November 13, 1952). Naguib was vested with the full sovereignty of the nation, and the cabinet's measures were deemed

[43] Abul Fath was of the 'left wing' group in the Wafd, a friend of Nasser before the coup and the brother-in-law of El Dubbat El-Ahrar member Tharwat 'Okasha, who later became the Minister of Culture. After his break with Nasser, Abul Fath wrote a violent attack against the regime: Abul-Fath, Ahmed: *L'affaire Nasser,* Paris, Plon, 1962.

[44] Stephens: *op. cit.,* p. 118.

acts of sovereignty not subject to court decisions. Consequently, the Wafd was prevented from fighting its case before the State Council. Thus while the Wafd—backed by other political organisations—could marshal popular support, it lacked the effective means of (physical) force. *El-Dubbat El-Ahrar*—on the other hand—possessed the means of (physical) force but lacked the mass political organisation that could marshal popular support. There was, thus, a stalemate in the Egyptian political system.

3.3.3. Moreover, the economic situation was deteriorating. Purchases by Britain—the main customer for cotton (the basis of Egypt's economy)—dropped from 35 million Egyptian pounds in 1951 to 5.7 million in the first 10 months of 1952. It was estimated that this cotton 'bubble' had cost the Egyptian government in all some 30 million Egyptian pounds. While Britain attributed this drop in cotton purchases to commercial reasons, the Egyptian authorities and the press accused Britain of intransigent colonialism and the intention—as Naguib himself was reported saying—to ruin Egypt by an economic blockade. [45] But the 'fellahin' of Egypt would not easily grasp the niceties of sophisticated economic arguments and they started remembering—not without melancholy—the 1951-soaring cotton prices, associating them with the Wafd's economic policies rather than with the Korean War. Some urban masses too—who were not accustomed to press censorship or restriction of individual liberty—started talking, not without nostalgia, about the chief politicians "called Nahas Pasha, Makram 'Ebeid, 'Abdel Fattah El-Tawil . . .". [46]

The situation was even worse, for no legal or quasi-legal means had yet been devised to manage conflict and maintain the system. [47] In this system under stress, Naguib was reported to have become a tired man, and steps were taken towards political detente. An administrative tribunal was permitted to sit in on the hearings of the Wafd's case to include Nahas as its honorary president, and 'Abdel Fattah El Tawil as founder member of the reorganised Wafd Party ; but these hearings were to take place *in camera*. Virtually all political prisoners—including the Wafd's Secretary-General, Serag Ed-Din—were released. Naguib had two meetings with Nahas, who declared that he would withdraw his resignation of the Wafd's leadership. There were even rumours that the 'Pasha' might take part in an all-party national front for the purpose of "achieving national objectives" and drafting a new constitution.

But a truce with the Wafd could not result in a solid detente, let alone collaboration. For since *El-Dubbat El-Ahrar* were bent on putting on

---

[45] Moreover, customs receipts which were expected to provide 46 per cent of the revenue of 1952-1953 were seriously down on the previous year.

[46] Lacouture : *L'Egypte en mouvement, op. cit.*, p. 227.

[47] Gordon, Morton : *Comparative Political Systems : Managing Conflict*, New York, Macmillan, 1972 ; Nordlinger : *op. cit.*

trial politicians and officials accused of nepotism and corruption, they were bound to clash—sooner or later—with many of the Wafd's personalities. Thus press censorship was reimposed more vigorously (28th December, 1952), while 800 high Egyptian officials 'resigned' or were dismissed as part of "the purging of the government". Cairo University and all its faculties—except those of medicine and Arab studies—were closed and 123 students were arrested.

3.3.4. The stress on the political system increased because *El-Dubbat El-Ahrar* seemed also to be in conflict with other (organised) political forces. For from 17th November onwards, General Naguib's speeches contained frequent denunciations of false rumour-mongering and rebuttals from *El-Ikhwan El-Muslimin* (The Moslem Brethren) that the "Qur'an should be made the legal basis of government". The systemic strain continued to increase, for on January 16, 1953, the Minister of National Guidance broadcasting over all the Egyptian radio network—in the name of the Prime Minister—declared that a plot to overthrow the new regime had been discovered. [48]

In order to attenuate systemic strain, the new military regime had to devise means to increase the 'legitimacy component' in the equation of systemic control. This could be done either by *El-Dubbat El-Ahrar* putting their means of coercion and physical force, at the disposal of those relatively mass-based, well-organised political forces who would then govern, or—alternatively—by keeping their monopoly of physical force while trying to marshal diffuse popular support by creating their own political organisation. The latter solution was adopted, for a new mass organisation "above all political parties"—the Liberation Rally—was created. [49] Simultaneously, all political parties—and above all the Wafd [50]

---

[48] According to the authorities the plot was prepared by the ex-Secretary-General of the Wafd, Serag Ed-Din ; Prince 'Abbas Halim ; and dismissed regent and luminary Moslem Brethren member, Col. Mehanna. But whatever the plot's origin, the measures taken by the government marked the reversal of Naguib's policy of seeking an accommodation with the old political forces and the frank continuation of rule by *El-Dubbat El-Ahrar* for at least a "3-year transition period". See the 11-article declaration of Major-General Naguib "Commander-in-Chief of the Armed Forces and Leader of the Army Revolution" entitled "Government During the 3-Year Transition Period", *Middle Eastern Affairs,* IV (1953), p. 105.

[49] The Liberation Rally—as a mass organisation—was an addition to the list of political organisations which emerged from, and testified to, the disintegration of the party system in many countries after the Second War. For more information on the Liberation Rally, see its proclamation document : "Charter and Aims of the Egyptian Liberation Organisation", *Middle Eastern Affairs,* IV (1953), p. 104.

[50] This formal abolition of the Wafd did not put an end to its influence in the political system. Even as late as the late sixties, press reports and eye-witnesses affirmed that the funeral of "Nahas Pasha" was transformed into a "popular demonstration" on behalf of the old Wafd Party.

—were abolished. Only one very influential organisation managed to escape being abolished, on the basis that it was not a political organisation but a religious one. This was the all-too-strong *El Ikhwan El-Muslimin.*

3.4. *El-Dubbat El-Ahrar and the Moslem Brethren* [51]

The preoccupation of the Wafd and the minority parties with political authority in the pre-revolutionary political system left vast areas of social thought and politicised action neglected. The majority of Egyptians are usually attached to their Islamic religion [52] yet it was precisely this religion that needed adaptation in the face of the fast process of social change. Thus in addition to the political confusion of the pre-revolutionary system, there was the less apparent, but more serious, problem of 'social loss' among many of the intelligentsia and opinion leaders, due to the erosion of the traditional Islamic value system. [53] But in order to deal with this problem [54] involving "nothing less than the creation of a comprehensive national philosophy to guide the subsequent transformation of Egypt", it was imperative to have an effective political leadership capable of presiding over the efforts of ideology-formation and consensus-building, *i.e.* the necessary elements for the "forging of a new synthesis of thought". But due to its "inability to hold power and the self-centered orientation of its [socially] narrow-based leadership, the Wafd did not fulfil this key role in

[51] The two important studies in English on this organisation are: Harris, Christina: *Nationalism and Revolution in Egypt: The Role of the Moslem Brotherhood,* The Hague, Mouton, 1964; and Mitchell, Richard: *The Society of the Moslem Brothers,* New York, O.U.P., 1969. *El-Ikhwan*'s declaration that it was a religious association rather than a political organisation was a mere formality in order to enable *El-Ikhwan* to escape the law abolishing political parties. Already on October 8, 1952, fifteen groups had registered with the Interior Ministry as political parties and *El-Ikhwan* was one of them.

[52] The function of religion in society has been treated mainly by social scientists other than political scientists; see for instance Robertson, Roland: *The Sociological Interpretation of Religion,* Oxford, Blackwell, 1970; Roland Robertson (ed.): *Sociology of Religion,* London, Penguin, 1969. On the social significance of Islam, see: Levy, Reuben: *The Social Structure of Islam,* Cambridge, Cambridge U.P., 1957. On the importance of religion in the life of Egyptians, see 'Ewais: *op. cit.;* and Sha'lan, Ibrahim: *El-Sha'b El-Misri min Amthalehi El-'Ammiyya* (The Egyptian People through its Popular Proverbs), Cairo, El-Hayäa El Misriah Lilkitab, 1972.

[53] This is the problem treated by Harris who emphasised the tension within the Islamic community in face of the growing secularisation, tracing the problem to the 19th century with Al-Afghani and 'Abduh. Harris: *op. cit.*

[54] "The gates to Igtihad that had been opened by Sheikh Mahamed Abduh in the late 1800's remained open with no national consensus in sight." Dekmejian: *op. cit.,* p. 18. See also Hourani, Albert: *Arabic Thought in the Liberal Age 1878-1939,* London, O.U.P., 1970 (paperback edition), pp. 103-193.

the Egyptian political system. As a result the emerging nationalist ideology was not supplemented with a comprehensive creed of societal change." [55]

3.4.1. This situation of political immobility and "social search" accounted for the speedy and phenomenal success of *El-Ikhwan* from a small reformist society founded about 1928 [56] by an unknown schoolteacher, to the status of the mass revivalist movement attained in the late forties and early fifties. The increasing weight of *El-Ikhwan* lay in its response to the socio-psychological needs which the political parties had so clearly failed to satisfy. [57] Moreover, it offered its followers the new formula of the unity of thought and action, that is a "total ideology" not satisfied with only indentifying the ills of society but also "prescribing measures to remedy them". In addition to offering an indigenous doctrine based on Islamic fundamentalism (*e.g.* "the Qur'an is our constitution"), and its advocacy of "total social, economic and political reform", the organisation also proceeded to "demonstrate these in their own subsidiary enterprises. The Brethren provided each follower with specific tasks and duties thereby creating in him the esprit de corps of the indoctrinated believer who was also a participant with vested interests." [58]

---

[55] Dekmeijian : *op. cit.*, p. 18.

[56] Whereas Dekmeijian states that *El-Ikhwan* was founded in 1928, Lacouture *(op. cit.)* fixes 1929 as the date, El-Bishry *(op. cit.)* believes that it was 1927 and Sadat gives 1930 *(Révolte sur le Nil, op. cit.)*. Like Dekmeijian, Harris *(op. cit.)* favours 1928.

[57] Dekmeijian : *op. cit.*, p. 19. The satisfaction of some deeply-felt socio-psychological needs among the Egyptian masses is singled out and emphasised by Lacouture as a cause of *El-Ikhwan*'s speedy rise in the whole system. Thus an important factor of *El-Ikhwan*'s success is "l'adéquation saisissante de (ses) thèmes de propagande et de cette organisation avec l'état de la société urbaine égyptienne à partir des années 1940. Alors s'agglutina autour des villes une manière de prolétariat mi-agricole, mi-artisanal, qui tenta de trouver sa pitance dans le halo des concentrations industrielles gonflées par la guerre. L'abrogation des capitulations en 1937 avait révélé aux masses misérables que l'Européen n'était plus tout-puissant. Pendant la guerre, les trafics de ravitaillement et la suroccupation de l'Egypte par des armées alliées avaient entraîné une profonde démoralisation qui fit vaciller les traditions de ce peuple, brusquement confronté à un alcoolisme exhibitionniste (sic) et à des formes de prostitution déconcertantes pour des Orientaux. A ces masses misérables, sous-alimentées, démoralisées et exaspérées par la soldatesque étrangère, le Banna et ses lieutenants firent entendre un message de revanche et d'espoir, suffisamment vague pour rameuter (sic) les groupes les plus divers, suffisamment lyrique pour agir comme stupéfiant, suffisamment fidèle aux enseignements religieux pour apparaître une bouée où pouvaient se raccrocher ces masses désintégrées et démoralisées. Et suffisamment nourri d'égalitarisme social pour séduire ces diverses catégories de déshérités." Lacouture : *L'Egypte en mouvement, op. cit.*, p. 231.

[58] Dekmejian : *op. cit.*, p. 19.

This well-established socio-psychological function gave *El-Ikhwan* a strong hand [59] in the functioning and/or breakdown of the Egyptian political system.

1. In the 3-year period from the end of the Second World War to the Palestinian War (1945-1948), and if only by violence, *El-Ikhwan* made its strong influence felt through the following: the attempted assassination of Nahas Pasha (December 6, 1945 ; April 25, 1948 ; then November 1948) ; the assassination of the Finance Minister, Amin 'Othman (January 5, 1946) ; the dynamiting of the Metro film theatre (May 6, 1947) ; the assassination of the Deputy-President of the Court of Appeals of Cairo, Ahmed El-Khezindar. The proclamation of the state of Israel and the defeat of Arab armies unleashed the organisation's violent reaction against Jews in Cairo and led to their repeated dynamiting of Jewish business and residential areas (*e.g.* Cicurel, Oreco and the 'Ads Stores in July 1948 ; Benzion, Gattegno and the Ma'adi Company in August ; Haret El-Yahud or the Jewish district, in September, leading to 20 dead and 61 injured ; the explosion in Galal Street, in November, and the discovery of a jeep loaded with explosives in Cairo, also in November). [60]

This rapidly growing influence of *El-Ikhwan* made them look as if "they were preparing for a revolutionary seizure of power. The government had hitherto feared to take action against them because of public sympathy for the courageous performance of their volunteers in Palestine. But the situation in Cairo had begun to frighten the Egyptian ruling class." [61] Consequently, after the November riots, Mohamed Fahmy El-Noqrashy Pasha—the Prime Minister—ordered *El-Ikhwan's* dissolution. On December 4, 1948, General Selim Zaki, the police-chief in Cairo who prided himself on being trained in the Tsarist Okhrana, was killed in his armoured command car under the walls of the School of Medicine, which the police was besieging. About three weeks later, on 28 December, it was the turn of the Prime Minister to be assassinated, and this time in the elevator of the Ministry of the Interior itself.

2. Another indicator of *El-Ikhwan*'s influence was their penetration —both on the level of thought and of action—of the secret society of *El-Dubbat El-Ahrar* before the latter's coup. At least six years before the

[59] Already in 1947, *El-Morshed* appeared to be the master of the urban masses, claiming to be backed by one million effective members. In the key sector of the rising intelligentsia, it was estimated that among the students of Cairo University —for instance—*El-Ikhwan* monopolised 30 per cent. Lacouture: *L'Egypte en mouvement, op. cit.,* p. 27.

[60] Abdel Malek: *op. cit.,* p. 27.

[61] Stephens: *op. cit.,* p. 89.

1952-coup, there were contacts—through Anwar El-Sadat—between *El-Dubbat El-Ahrar* and *El-Morshed* or Supreme Guide, Hassan El-Banna [62] (assassinated in 1949). Moreover, many of *El-Dubbat El-Ahrar* members (*e.g.* Baghdadi, 'Amer and Nasser himself) had contacts with *El-Ikhwan* and they collaborated together in Palestine. Consequently, the prominent members of the new regime were—directly or indirectly—influenced by *El-Ikhwan*'s thinking and propaganda. Nasser himself, in attempting the unsuccessful assassination of Siry Amer referred to in the *Philosophy of the Revolution,* was—knowingly or unknowingly—under the influence of *El-Ikhwan*'s way of thinking and means of action. Then there was, of course, Abdel Moneim Abdel Raouf—one of the first members of *El-Dubbat El-Ahrar*'s committee—who was nothing less than the head of *El-Ikhwan*'s movement in the army. [63] *El-Ikhwan* themselves claimed that at least a third of *El-Dubbat El-Ahrar* was attached—more or less closely—with the Organisation. [64]

3.4.2. It was because of *El-Ikhwan*'s weight, socially and politically, that *El-Dubbat El-Ahrar* invited—as early as the morning of July 23, 1952—one of *El-Ikhwan*'s young leaders, Hassan 'Ashmawi, to the Revolutionary Command Council headquarters. 'Ashmawi was asked to communicate the Junta's invitation to the Morshed, El-Hodeiby, who was spending the Summer holiday in Alexandria. [65] But the Morshed's visit took place only 4 days later, after preparing *El-Ikhwan*'s 'white paper', which explicited a new cabinet's program based on the Qur'an as a constitution, the list of 5 or 6 ministers from the Organisation's ranks, and the demand for *El-Ikhwan*'s right of veto on all legislation connected with Islam within the new cabinet.

Not only did *El-Ikhwan* leaders overestimate their influence in face of the new masters of the system, but they were also misinformed on the psychology of *El-Dubbat El-Ahrar.* These young officers were horrified at the prospect of an organised political force of the 'ancien regime' trying to monopolise the benefits and appropriate the victory of the new regime. They had made this clear to Fouad Serag El-Din, the Wafd's Secretary-General, and they would make it clear to *El-Ikhwan.*

---

[62] El-Bishri : *op. cit.,* p. 472. El-Sadat : *Révolte sur le Nil, op. cit.,* pp. 64-70, 141-155. El-Sadat gives the date of his first meeting with El-Morshed as 1941.

[63] Already in 1951, Abdel Raouf suggested incorporating the whole organisation of *El-Dubbat El-Ahrar* within *El-Ikhwan* to work under the latter's general directives. El-Sadat, Anwar: *Qissat El-Thawra Kamela* (The Complete Story of the Revolution), Beirut, Dar El-Qamous, n.d., p. 47.

[64] Lacouture : *L'Egypte en mouvement, op. cit.,* p. 234.

[65] Le "Guide suprême de la Confrérie — Hassan El-Hodeiby — lequel, en villégiature à Alexandrie avait répondu avec bienveillance qu'il envisagerait d'honorer ces jeunes gens de sa visite." *Ibid.,* p. 153.

When, a month and a half after the coup d'état (*i.e.* in September), the Maher cabinet resigned, *El-Ikhwan* asked for two ministries in the new cabinet ; one for Mounir El-Dalla and the other for Hassan 'Ashmawi. But *El-Dubbat El-Ahrar* retorted by according them only one ministry [66] to be headed by a man of their choice, Hassan El-Baqoury. [67] *El-Ikhwan* exercised pressure on El-Baqoury to refuse the Ministry of Waqfs (Religious Endowments), and when he finally accepted the post, he was 'excommunicated' from the Organisation.

But the definitive break was yet to come, for the two rivals still needed each other politically. *El-Ikhwan* knew that if *El-Dubbat El-Ahrar* unleashed their unequalled physical force against the Organisation, they would disperse its organised means of action for at least some time to come. *El-Dubbat El-Ahrar,* on the other hand, were engaged in conflict with other influential forces (*e.g.* the Wafd), and if they could not guarantee *El-Ikhwan*'s support, they could at least have their silence. [68] Moreover, an open conflict with *El-Ikhwan* would not only have necessitated prior solid popular support, but would also have created divisions within the new regime's base of systemic control (*i.e.* the army) and even among *El-Dubbat El-Ahrar* themselves. Thus the conflict between the two sides remained latent. Consequently, when a law abolishing all political parties was decreed on January 16, 1953, *El-Ikhwan* was allowed to escape the abolition on the pretext that it was a religious association rather than a political organisation.

But in September 1953, while Major Salah Salem—the spokesman of *El-Dubbat El-Ahrar*—declared the discovery of a new plot against the regime, there were rumours about trouble between the government and *El-Ikhwan* and also disagreements within the Revolutionary Command Council. [69] In fact, a state of emergency was proclaimed. The system was obviously under stress, and Squadron leader Hassan Ibrahim announced that ex-king Faruq (who was attacking the regime from abroad) might

---

[66] Be'eri seems to be wrong in saying that *El-Ikhwan* were offered 3 ministries, for if this were the case differences between the two sides would have been limited to *what ministries* and might have been easier to settle, since both parties had reasons for avoiding a strong break. Be'eri, Eliezer : *Army Officers in Arab Politics and Society,* New York and London, Praeger and Pall Mall, 1969, p. 113.

[67] El-Baqoury was an old class-mate of Nasser.

[68] On January 20, 1953—for instance—General Naguib ordered the formation of a "Revolutionary Tribunal" to try persons endangering "national security". At the same time 213 persons, including 48 communists, were arrested.

[69] The intra-organisation and inter-organisation conflicts could be related, since conflicts between the new regime and *El-Ikhwan* were bound to create divisions within the ranks of the two bodies. There were *El-Ikhwan* sympathisers within the *El-Dubbat El-Ahrar* association, and similarly there were "moderates" and "radicals" within *El-Ikhwan* organisation.

be tried in absentia. The systemic strain should have been so high as to create threat-perception, even from outside, for an American freighter carrying U.S. government-denoted wheat for Jordan was fired on by Egyptian guns in the Gulf of Aqaba. On September 21, 1953, a number of former politicians were arrested : Karim Thabet (Faruq's press adviser) and Hafez 'Afifi (former Chief of the Royal Cabinet). The leader of the Wafd Party, Nahas, and his wife were put under house arrest. Moreover, some employees of the War Ministry and other persons were tried and hanged for "spying for foreign interests".

This context of systemic strain was not the appropriate moment for a bloody clash with *El-Ikhwan*. Instead, attempts at rapprochement needed to be encouraged. Thus Ibrahim 'Abdel Hadi (the leader of the Sa'adist Party under whose premiership *El-Ikhwan*'s popular Morshed, Hassan El-Banna, was assassinated in 1949) was tried before a revolutionary tribunal on a 6-count indictment, including 'complicity in murder'. He received nothing less than the death sentence. [70] Moreover, Premier Naguib chose that time to embark—with some of his colleagues—on the pilgrimage to Mecca.

But would a common front [71] and a sharing of political authority be achieved between *El-Dubbat El-Ahrar* and *El-Ikhwan* ? They collaborated together before the coup (if only through common members) and both had the common objective of evacuating the British from Egypt. Yet after the coup, *El-Ikhwan*—a body with a record of activities extending over a quarter of a century, well-entrenched grass roots, cadres, martyrs and martyrdom, and a mass appeal strengthened if anything by the new regime's ostentatious praying movement and its pilgrimages—constituted a serious rival source of political influence. If they wanted to escape the danger of being absorbed by *El-Ikhwan*'s definite plans (or at least claims) and resolute leaders, *El-Dubbat El-Ahrar* had to eliminate the challenge and/or find an alternative mass base outside of (and perhaps different from) *El-Ikhwan*. [72]

3.4.3. Thus, it was almost inevitable that sooner or later misunderstanding—leading to violent, bloody clashes—should arise between the two rival contenders for the monopoly of systemic control. On January 7, 1954, the cabinet approved the appointment of Sheikh Abdel Rahman Tag as Rector of Al-Azhar Islamic University, to replace Sheikh Khedr Husein.

---

[70] Abdel Hadi asked for mercy, and given his old age, his death sentence was commuted to life imprisonment.

[71] But even if this expected rapprochement with *El-Ikhwan* did not materialise, this act of 'piousness' would at least increase support for the new regime among strong believers and widen the regime's base of legitimacy.

[72] Thus the establishment of the liberation Rally to work as the new regime's mass organisation.

On 12 January, fighting erupted at Cairo University between *El-Ikhwan* supporters and supporters of *El-Dubbat El-Ahrar.* [73] At least four of the pro-new regime students were wounded. The following day (January 13) troops and the police surrounded *El-Ikhwan*'s offices at dawn and began a round-up, arresting 78 leaders, including *El-Morshed* or Supreme Guide (El-Hodeiby) himself. This was only the first instalment. The government dissolved the Organisation, [74] and this was followed by the proclamation of a nation-wide state of emergency on the 14th of January while the police and the army troops continued to arrest about 400 more of *El-Ikhwan* leaders. In an official communiqué, the new regime charged *El-Ikhwan* with seeking to impose its will on the government ; and that when this move had failed they had turned to "outright subversion" ; that the Organisation's leaders had tried to sow dissension among army officers and the police and had achieved some success with the latter. Moreover, the official communiqué named British personnel who—it was said—were in contact with *El-Ikhwan*'s leaders. Only the first round was over.

Because of *El-Ikhwan*'s socio-psychological function, its mass support and its influence on the political system, the government instructed newspapers and radio stations to attenuate the subject of mass arrests among *El-Ikhwan* leaders and members. [75] These arrests and liquidation attempts would not put an end to systemic strain and fissures, at least for some time to come. [76] Not only would *El-Ikhwan* shed doubt on the "reality" of

[73] The clash between *El-Ikhwan*'s supporters and the new regime's supporters was symbolised by the following slogans respectively : "God is great, praise to God" versus "God is great, glory to Egypt". The fighting was provoked by *El-Ikhwan*'s members who held a meeting on the University campus to commemorate *El-Ikhwan* students who had been killed during the winter of 1951-1952 in the anti-British struggle in the Canal zone. The audience was overexcited by an inflammatory speech of Nawab Safavi, head of the Persian Fedayin Islam (who was later shot in Tehran in 1955 after organising various assassination attempts) and the members denounced Nasser as "a dictator and a lackey of imperialism". Be'eri : *op. cit.,* pp. 113-114 ; Lacouture : *L'Egypte en mouvement, op. cit.,* p. 236.

[74] *El-Ikhwan* was dissolved on the grounds that it was engaged in political activities in violation of an arrangement whereby the regime permitted it to continue only as a social and religious group. See the statement of the Revolutionary Command Council on *El-Ikhwan*'s dissolution, *Middle Eastern Affairs,* V (1954), pp. 94-100.

[75] In a speech to the Arab Socialist Union in December 1968 Nasser gave the figure as 18,000, as quoted in Stephens : *op. cit.,* p. 136. Moreover, attempts were multiplied to discredit *El-Ikhwan,* for a special emphasis was put on *"El-Ikhwan*-British Embassy collusion".

[76] Hostility toward Nasser and the new regime was not limited to the Egyptian political system. For when some of *El-Ikhwan*'s leaders were tried and sentenced to death later (December 1954), anti-regime mass demonstrations took place in many Arab and Moslem countries—especially after Friday prayers. Even general strikes were proclaimed in mourning for the hanging of *El-Ikhwan*'s leaders.

independence accrued to Egypt by the Anglo-Egyptian Agreement which Nasser negotiated and signed ; not only would they resort to bombing and the blowing up of bridges to express their protest, [77] not only would they shoot at Nasser (while giving a public speech on 26 October 1954), [78] but they also caused the most serious fissure in the system : the public split and the mutual attempt at liquidation within the highest governing apparatus (the Revolutionary Command Council) and within its basis of systemic control : the Army itself.

3.5. *The Army and Systemic Control*

Lacking a political organisation to mobilise and channel mass support, the new regime's systemic control rested on the army. This structure of authority was in the form of a pyramid. At the top there were Nasser and the members of the RCC (Revolutionary Command Council). [79] This RCC was based on a larger group, *Gama'it El Dubbat El-Ahrar* (Society of Free Officers), which grouped approximately 250 members and was the initiator of the coup d'état. The basis of this authority pyramid was the army itself, with its 2,000 officers and 100,000 men monopolising unequalled centralised force in Egypt's political system. [80]

---

[77] See *Al-Ahram,* for instance 7th and 8th August, 1954.

[78] The carpenter Mahmud 'Abdel Latif (*El-Ikhwan* member) fired six shots at Nasser from a range of a few feet. Every bullet missed its mark, but two men beside Nasser were hit. Stephens : *op. cit.,* pp. 135-136. Even though this assassination attempt gave the new regime the occasion to unleash the whole repressive police apparatus against *El-Ikhwan* all over the country (leading to mass arrests and the setting on fire of many of their dispersed centers), the organisation was not finally and completely liquidated. In August 1965, Nasser declared that "as many as 400 people had been arrested as a result of the discovery of another alleged plot by the Muslim Brothers to kill him and other leading ministers." *Ibid.,* p. 372.

[79] The composition of the Officers' Committee that was the source of authority after the coup was not made public and apparently it was not fixed. Lacouture talked of ten members (*L'Egypte en mouvement, op. cit.,* p. 180), as did El-Sadat (*Qisat El Thawra, op. cit.,* pp. 43-44), whereas R. Crossman talked about "Egypt's nine just men" in the *New Statesman* (17 January 1953), and Stephens spoke of "the 13-man executive committee of the Free Officers" (*op. cit.,* p. 111). In January 1953, half a year after the coup, the Officers Committee labelled itself the Revolutionary Command Council (RCC) and still the names were not made public. But when Egypt was proclaimed a republic on 18 June 1953, for the first time twelve names appeared as signers of the Proclamation as well as a collective photo. See *Al-Ahram,* 19 June 1953. The RCC was officially abolished in June 1956, when its presence alongside the government was deemed unnecessary. The RCC members were transferred to the cabinet and civilianised, thus *formally* the military control of the political system had come to an end.

[80] Lacouture : *L'Egypte en mouvement, op. cit.,* p. 180 ; Be'eri : *op. cit.,* pp. 92-93.

3.5.1. In the literature on the intervention of the military in emerging political systems, it is generally assumed that the military are—socially—a homogeneous group and have—politically—uniform ideas. Beyond a certain point, this assumption is questioned here.[81] For as early as June 1953, about the same time the *Philosophy of the Revolution* was written, Nasser was explaining in *Al-Ahram* why no precise political programme of the new regime had been drawn up before the coup. The reason is that they wanted to avoid a split in the army movement. As Nasser himself explained :

> "The political ideas of the Free Officers differed, according to their temperaments and the family or social milieu from which they came . . . What we all wanted was to purge the army, rid the country of foreign occupation and establish a clean, fair government which would work sincerely for the good of the people. Once in power, we found ourselves faced with the difficult problem of establishing a political, social and economic programme. It was necessary to improvise. We did our best. The divergence of political ideas then obliged us to separate from those who did not agree to apply the majority decisions of the Council of the Revolution and then those of the Government we set up."[82]

Thus once army officers took over the political system, cracks in their united front—as Nasser stated—could not be delayed for long.[83] The first clash was with Colonel Rashad Mehanna, the Army's representative in the three-member Regency Council (a nomination that made the public credit him with a key role). His attraction to *El-Dubbat El-Ahrar* dated back only to 1951,[84] when he joined their circle and was supported by them in January 1952 in the election to the Committee of the Officers' Club. Though not a very trustworthy member of *El-Dubbat El-Ahrar,* he was informed of the plans because of his prominent position in the army and his status as a colonel in the influential artillery division. It was probably this prominent position in the army and his characteristic personal ambition that made him think of himself as replacing the king in the Regency

[81] In fact the data on the social background of Egyptian officers show that "the composition of the Egyptian officer class in the last years of the monarchy was, from the point of view of social and family origin, rather varied". For the data on Egyptian officers, see Be'eri : *op. cit.,* pp. 483-496, but also pp. 293-351.

[82] As quoted in Stephens : *op. cit.,* pp. 112-113.

[83] Immediately after the military take-over, at least 300 high army leaders were dismissed and Major 'Abdel Hakim 'Amer was promoted to a "lewa" (full General) to be at the head of the army—a move that would not please many senior officers.

[84] On the social origins and career of Mehanna, see Be'eri : *op. cit.,* p. 110 ; Stephens : *op. cit.,* pp. 118-120 ; Lacouture : *L'Egypte en mouvement, op. cit.,* p. 120. For an important source of the RCC's image of Mehanna, see El-Sadat : *Révolte sur le Nil, op. cit.,* pp. 215-217, and also *Qisat El Thawra, op. cit.,* pp. 57-59, 117-120, 133-135.

Council. Moreover, his belonging to a wealthy family might explain his opposition to some *basic* social policies of *El-Dubbat El-Ahrar.* Thus he criticised the new regime's agrarian reform project and joined the civilian Prime Minister, Ali Maher, who wanted to raise the ownership maximum limit in the Land Reform Law to 500 instead of 200 feddans.

Thus on 14 October, less than three months after the coup, General Naguib announced the RCC's decision to dismiss (with a pension of 1,500 Egyptian pounds) the Army's representative on the Regency Council, Colonel Mehanna. In addition to accusations of favouritism, overstepping the limits of his office, opposition to the government's land reforms, Mehanna was accused of making a bid to revive the Caliphate in collusion with elements of *El-Ikhwan,* with which he was closely associated. [85] The official communiqué stated that Colonel Mehanna had summoned Premier Naguib on the previous day and told him in a stormy interview that he was not disposed to be a rubber stamp for decisions of the RCC but expected to be taken into prior consultation. [86]

The immediate result of Mehanna's dismissal was the dissolution of the three-member Regency Council. Bahei Ed-Din Barakat, the second member of the Council and the elder statesman, [87] resigned in protest against the procedure employed in dismissing Mehanna. On October 19 —five days after Mehanna's announced dismissal—a former commander of the Frontier Corps and his assistant were arrested on charges of desertion and inciting soldiers to rebel. On October 21, censorship was imposed on newspapers which "publish matter harmful to the public interest and security" as well as on all incoming and outgoing telegrams and telephone conversations. On January 16, 1953, the Minister of National Guidance declared that a plot to overthrow the new regime had been discovered. Among the numerous arrests announced the following day, Mehanna figured together with Lieutenant-Colonel Mohamed Damanhuri—a member of *El-Dubbat El-Ahrar* who had held the important post of Governor of the Western Desert. [88] The importance of the incident is shown by the fact that the RCC itself (presided by Nasser in person) sat as a court-martial to try Mehanna, Damanhuri and 23 other officers. Mehanna was

[85] In *Al-Ahram* of October 2, 1952, Mechanna's declarations were very close to the sentiments and ideology of *El-Ikhwan.* Lacouture : *L'Egypte en mouvement, op. cit.,* p. 160.

[86] This was at a time when the European press treated him as the key figure in the Army movement after Naguib. *Ibid.,* p. 161.

[87] He had been invited by Faruq to form a government at the end of June 1952, less than a month before the coup. *Observer,* 3 August 1952.

[88] Officially both Mehanna and El-Damanhuri were arrested for attempting—around the 14th January 1953 and with the help of other persons—to stir up a rebellion in the army. Lacouture : *L'Egypte en mouvement, op. cit.,* p. 161.

sentenced to life imprisonment on the charge of leading the plot, and Damanhuri was sentenced to death, a sentence later commuted to life imprisonment. Though the prominent Egyptian historian 'Abdel Rahman El-Raf'i [89] (considered by some specialists as "the semi-official historian of the regime" [90]) called this conflict the most dangerous conspiracy since the Revolution took place, internecine conflict among members of the new political elite continued. This intra-elite conflict culminated in the 1954-systemic crisis of the Nasser-Naguib public break.

3.5.2. *The Nasser-Naguib Break :* Although it became public only in February 1954, the Nasser-Naguib split had been in the offing for some time. As Nasser admitted in his June-1953-declaration to *Al-Ahram* quoted above, there was no operational political programme agreed upon or even elaborated. Consequently, consensus among the members of the new elite was limited to wide generalities. As early as October 1952, press reports affirmed that (though General Naguib enjoyed the filial respect of his young colleagues), "each member of the new regime had his own views and this—no doubt—is why the Junta meetings consume so many hours". [91] Consequently, the Nasser-Naguib break can be related to *long term* as well as *immediate* sources.

As for the *distant sources of the conflict,* a noticeable fact is the age difference between Naguib and the other *Dubbat Ahrar* members (*e.g.* Naguib was born in 1901, Nasser in 1918). The fact that Naguib at the time of the coup was 51 years old, while the age range among RCC members was 32-37, made them belong to different generations, especially in a social system going through a fast process of change. In fact, it was partly Naguib's advanced age—in a Moslem nation and an oriental cultural system where old age is associated with wisdom, experience and respectability—that made *El-Dubbat El-Ahrar* choose him as the public leader of their movement. [92] But such a 'necessary' choice in accordance with the values of the Egyptian social system turned out to be a handicap after the coup, especially when the expected differences of appreciation became

[89] El-Raf'ï, 'Abdel Rahman : *Muqaddimat Thawrat 23 Yulio* (The Preliminaries of the 23 July Revolution), Cairo, El-Nahda, 1959, p. 94.

[90] Be'eri : *op. cit.,* p. 111.

[91] Peter Calvocoressi and Kostanze Isepp (eds.) : *Survey of International Affairs,* 1952, London, Royal Institute of International Affairs, O.U.P., 1955, p. 216.

[92] The planners of the coup—headed by Nasser—felt that they needed a figurehead of suitable status and maturity. General Naguib, a non-member of the Officers' Committee, was invited to join them—according to El-Sadat—only at three o'clock in the morning of 23 July to perform the role of figure-head. El-Sadat : *Qisat El-Thawra, op. cit.,* pp. 51-80. Several reasons favoured his choice : (i) he was dissatisfied with Faruq's regime ; (ii) he carried the weight of senior army rank ;

contradictions during periods of crisis demanding immediate decisions. Naguib himself expressed very clearly the linkage between this difference in age and difference in political attitudes :

> "Abdul Nasser believed, with all the bravado of a man of thirty-six, that we could afford to alienate every segment of Egyptian public opinion, if necessary, in order to achieve our goals. I believed, with all the prudence of a man of fifty-three, that we would need as much popular support as we could possibly retain. I further believed that it would be better to sacrifice, or at least delay, the attainment of some of our objectives in order to ensure the attainment of others." [93]

Moreover, under the 'ancien regime' Naguib was saluted with the title of 'Bey' which made him—whether he accepted it or not—part of that regime. [94] His distinguished red cap of 'Lewa' (General) separated him from the rank and file of the Egyptian army—to which *El-Dubbat El-Ahrar* belonged. This 'objective' situation was bound to create outlook differences between 'Naguib Bey' and an activist Nasser who tried to assassinate Serry 'Amer, or an explosive Sadat who was sacked from the army after being accused of collaboration, in 1942, with German military command in Libya against the British occupation in Egypt. Consequently, Naguib differed with the majority of the RCC members on even the general structure and form of the emerging political system. For while Naguib—for instance—believed in gradual transition to a parliamentary government, Nasser and the majority of the RCC members came to believe in the necessity of tightening "the Revolution". Whereas those young officers were convinced of the merits of a "mobilisation political system" [95] : *i.e.* Egyptians arrayed under one commander like a fighting army to overcome their economic underdevelopment, defeat their external enemies and purge their political system ; Naguib favoured a "reconciliation system" : broadly-based leadership and a system representing diverse

---

(iii) he had a high reputation as a commander of a unit which had displayed particular bravery in the Palestine War ; and (iv) compared to other senior army officers (*e.g.* Mehanna) he was not regarded as politically ambitious.

[93] Naguib, Mohamed : *Egypt's Destiny,* London, Gollancz, 1955, p. 216., as quoted in Stephens : *op. cit.,* p. 124.

[94] Lacouture quotes Naguib's position when the British Occupation forces surrounded the royal Abdine Palace in February 1942 and imposed Nahas Pasha as a Prime Minister on the legitimate sovereign : "S'il avait démissionné ce jour de février 1942 . . . ce n'était . . . [que] pour affirmer sa fidélité à une monarchie humiliée. Son fils aîné s'appelait Farouk." Lacouture : *L'Egypte en mouvement, op. cit.,* p. 169.

[95] Apter : *The Politics of Modernisation, op. cit.* ; Apter, David : "System, Process and the Politics of Economic Development", in Robert Jackson and Michael Stein (eds.) : *Issues and Comparative Politics,* New York, St. Martin's Press, 1971, pp. 77-93.

interests, opinions and forces 'regulated' by a father-figure, as Naguib was then considered by the masses of Egyptians. [96]

This brings us to Naguib's character and the third difference between him and Nasser. Naguib did not seem to be firm enough to qualify as a 'revolutionary', for already in 1953 there were rumours in the cafés and streets of Cairo that Naguib had disapproved of the arrest of one ex-minister or the condemnation of another. To an ambassador of a European country he revealed his sorrow for the "unfair" sentence imposed on the Secretary-General of the Wafd Party, Serag Ed-Din. [97] But there is an incident which serves as an indicator of the man's character. Several days "after the coup, on one of his trips through Cairo, he passed the military prison where the former army chiefs were kept. He told his driver to stop, visited the prisoners and promised them that a fair trial would be held and that those whose innocence could be proved would be released. With simplicity and gentle ways he won over the masses. In the government and the RCC he regarded himself as being foremost among equals." [98]

The last two sentences—confirming Naguib's towering mass popularity which encouraged him to insist on an equivalent share in political authority [99]—are crucial in accounting for the *immediate causes* that brought about the systemic crisis and accelerated the break. The crisis had arisen largely because Naguib, having occupied the posts of both Prime Minister and President, and aware of an increasing personal popularity, wanted his formal titles to coincide with effective authority. He was no longer satisfied with a figure-head position.

---

[96] The way the coup was planned and effected helped to hide the gap between Naguib and *El-Dubbat El-Ahrar.* For "une révolution sanglante, radicale, terroriste, à la française ou à la russe, l'aurait irrémédiablement 'collé' aux jeunes ... ou décapité. Mais ce passage à blanc de l'autocracie à la régence, puis de la régence à la république autoritaire permettait toutes les liaisons, les rappels d'amitiés anciennes, le bon-garçonisme égyptien aidant, et surtout celui de Mohamed Naguib." Lacouture : *L'Egypte en mouvement, op. cit.,* p. 169. This is why the treatment of Naguib's character is significant.

[97] *Ibid.,* p. 170.

[98] Be'eri : *op. cit.,* p. 114.

[99] Naguib's great popularity was perhaps due to publicity but was certainly also due to his paternal, photogenic charm. This popularity compensated to some extent for the lack of organised political support in the country. Consequently Naguib felt that he was entitled to "real" as opposed to titular leadership. When the republic was declared, he refused to turn the premiership over to Nasser and keep only the Presidency. But since there were already differences over policy and there was no meeting of minds on a detailed operational programme, frictions grew increasingly. When the split became public, the communiqué of *El-Dubbat El-Ahrar* in fact said : "General Naguib was beset by a psychological complex from which we suffered much, though we all made an effort to present him to the world as the actual leader of the revolution", and had resorted to the practice of staying at home to force the RCC to accept his demands. *The Times,* 26 February 1954 ; El-Sadat : *Quissat El Thawra, op. cit.,* pp. 168-189 ; Stephens : *op. cit.,* p. 123.

Thus in August 1953, Naguib decided to go on the pilgrimage to Mecca, a move that might lead to a rapprochement with *El-Ikhwan* and, anyhow, would guarantee more success with the Moslem masses. Though the Vice-President, Nasser, managed to send two 'loyal' RCC members to accompany Naguib, this latter took with him his friend, colonel Ahmed Shawqi, who was not then on very good terms with Nasser. [100] Naguib's particularly warm talks with king Sa'oud—as well as his pan-Islamic public speeches and declarations on Mount 'Arafat—made Nasser suspect the presence of [personal] political calculations behind the whole visit. Consequently on Naguib's return to Cairo, Ahmed Shawqi was "asked to resign all his posts". [101]

In these series of immediate causes of the Nasser-Naguib break, reference should be made again to *El-Ikhwan*. We have mentioned the bloody clashes with *El-Ikhwan,* the arrest of its leaders and the banning of the Organisation. But what was not mentioned is that the decision to outlaw *El-Ikhwan* had been taken and proclaimed without consulting Naguib, who was then President of the RCC, Prime Minister and Commander-in-Chief of the armed forces. [102] Naguib reacted very firmly, for rather than asking for the right to be consulted and to effectively participate in the decision-making process, he insisted on the right of veto on all decisions of the RCC. Unless satisfied, he would resign. Consequently, on February 23, 1954, in a letter to the RCC Naguib declared : "I can no longer

---

[100] Ahmed Shawqi was a prominent Free Officer who commanded the 13th Battalion which captured the General Staff on the night of 22-23 July 1952. After the coup he was appointed Commander of the Cairo military district. He was born in 1907, son of a pasha from Ali Maher's family, and was not characterised by strict observance of Islamic precepts. His well-known indifference to religion made Nasser suspect him of having political motives in accompanying Naguib to Mecca. Be'eri : *op. cit.,* p. 112 ; Lacouture : *L'Egypte en mouvement, op. cit.,* p. 170 ; Wheelock, Keith : *Nasser's New Egypt,* London, Stevens, 1960, p. 139.

[101] This resignation heralded the Nasser-Naguib public clash, not only because of the timing in Shawqi's dismissal, but also because of the affinity in the (liberal) ideas that both Shawqi and Naguib shared.

[102] Nasser, it seems, was aware of a certain political activity within *El-Ikhwan*'s organisation, and even a "terrorist preparation", discovered by an unexpected explosion in an explosives deposit in the house of *El-Ikhwan* engineer, Fayez, at Heliopolis. This might explain Nasser's decision to seize the chance to cripple the Organisation. The non-consultation of Naguib could be explained in this specific case by the 'certainty' of Naguib's contacts with *El-Ikhwan.* In fact, Lacouture states : "Il est certain que ... Naguib était alors en relation avec les 'Frères', par l'entremise de son aide de camp, le capitaine Mohamed Riad. Jusqu'où allaient ces contacts ? Il ne semble pas qu'ils aient pris un tour très politique, et ils devaient se limiter à des déclarations communes d'amitié, au cas où ..." Lacouture : *L'Egypte en mouvement, op. cit.,* p. 171 ; Be'eri : *op. cit.,* pp. 112-113. But the exclusion of Naguib from *El-Dubbat El-Ahrar*'s decision-making process was a part of the general RCC-Naguib conflict. For there are other examples when Naguib felt that his authority

carry out my duties in the manner that I consider best calculated to serve the national interests." [103]

The date was well-chosen not only to increase the stress on the system but in fact to threaten its maintenance. Relying not only on his increasing popularity in Egypt and the fact that his resignation was separated by only about a month from the bloody conflict with *El-Ikhwan,* Naguib was also counting on his key position in dealing with the Sudan. For a week later Naguib was to leave for Khartoum to inaugurate the new parliament, and this trip was to be the symbol of Egyptian-Sudanese union. Thus "se priver de l'ami des Soudanais en un pareil moment, c'était pour l'Egypte se priver d'un atout maître". [104]

The RCC was summoned for a meeting on February 25, and Naguib's resignation was made public. Immediately his removal was known, huge masses of people filled Cairo's streets in big demonstrations in Naguib's favour. [105] Though there is no doubt about Naguib's personal popularity

---

was completely overlooked. Thus on February 22, 1954 in a speech at the Indonesian Club, Naguib strongly attacked Pakistan in connection with its pact with Turkey, though the semi-official newspaper, *El-Gomhouriyya,* had taken a moderate line on the question. It seems that Nasser censored the speech for the press, and this was one of the immediate, direct causes for Naguib's resignation. Carol Bell and F. C. Benham (eds.) : *Survey of International Affairs,* 1954, London, Royal Institute of International Affairs, Oxford U.P., 1957, p. 186.

[103] Naguib : *Egypt's Destiny, op. cit.,* p. 213, as quoted in Stephens : *op. cit.,* p. 124.

[104] Born in Khartoum of a Sudanese mother, Naguib forged many friendships in the Sudan during his term of service there. The Sudanese reacted to his resignation as well as to rumours about his trial in October by sending an official delegation to Cairo to ensure Naguib's personal safety. One would think that the Nasser-Naguib conflict played no small part in the Sudanese decision not to vote for the union with Egypt. Lacouture : *L'Egypte en mouvement, op. cit.,* p. 171 ; Stephens : *op. cit.,* p. 125.

[105] "Indeed, in terms of milieu, personality, and performance, General Naguib possessed considerable charismatic potential." Dekmejian : *op. cit.,* p. 25. Naguib's "charismatic potential" explains why his simple disappearance was not enough to make people channel their support to the RCC, and so an attempt to destroy Naguib's popularity was initiated. A spokesman described him as "a vain dictator addicted to self-indulgence and some immoral tastes". But since these accusations were contrary to Naguib's image as the quiet, paternal leader of the new regime, opposition in the army and street demonstrations took place. The RCC members were conscious of the problems that Naguib's disappearance would cause, for on February 26, Salah Salem—Minister of National Guidance and Spokesman of the RCC—declared to the hastily assembled foreign correspondents : *"En dépit du choc que cette décision créera dans l'opinion,* nous avons dû nous séparer de Naguib qui aspirait à la dictature, critiquait publiquement et auprès des étrangers les décisions de la majorité et, ne songeant qu'à bâtir sa propre popularité, jouait le double jeu et prenait des contre-assurances avec l'opposition." Lacouture : *L'Egypte en mouvement, op. cit.,* pp. 171-172 (emphasis added).

among the Egyptian masses at that time, what attracted attention was that these demonstrations

> "were *organised* by the remaining cadres of Wafdists and the left-wing groups who, with the Muslim Brothers, could still bring masses of students and workers onto the streets. This united front of the Brotherhood, the left and the Wafd aimed to use Naguib's popularity in the hope of forcing the junta to restore political parties, parliament and freer press." [106]

In other words, the Nasser-Naguib conflict led to the establishment of a united front of the system's main political forces (which the new regime was trying to liquidate) and their mobilisation of their grass-root organisations to rally the masses for a decisive blow against the new elite.

But was this erosion of popular *support* and questioning of the new elite's legitimacy a new crucial element in the elite's systemic control? After all, *El-Dubbat El-Ahrar* took over the political system by extra-legal means and—as Nasser admitted—did not possess (either before or immediately after the Army Movement) an organised mass support. [107] The new elite's systemic control counted in the first place on the possession of unequalled organised force through the Army, so why would they not continue the same process during the Nasser-Naguib conflict?

Yet the important characteristic of this conflict is that the new elite could not make use of their unequalled organised force, because it was no longer unequalled or united. In other words, the army—the basis of the new regime—was divided; and fissures existed even within the highest organ of systemic control itself: the RCC. For the "red major", Khaled Mohieddin, [108] the youngest member of the RCC, organised—through his influence in the Armored Corps—a part of the army in favour of Naguib. The action of Khaled Mohieddin had a significance both political and military for the elite's capacity for systemic maintenance. The political significance was related to the requirements of support and legitimacy in Egypt's prismatic system, for Khaled's action marked the *formal* entry of the fourth contending political force—the left [109]—against the

---

[106] Stephens: *op. cit.*, p. 125 (emphasis added).

[107] *The Philosophy of the Revolution*, *op. cit.*, pp. 21-22.

[108] Though 31 years old, Khaled was a veteran Free Officer for he was one of the first five founder members of *El-Dubbat El-Ahrar's* Committee. He was a Marxist and may have been a member of the "Democratic Movement for National Liberation". He had previously opposed the abolition of political parties and urged a quicker return to a form of parliamentary life "through the election of a constituent assembly". Be'eri: *op. cit.*, p. 115; Stephens: *op. cit.*, p. 125; El-Sadat: *Qissat El-Thawra*, *op. cit.*, pp. 43-44, 122.

[109] There is not enough space to deal with the Egyptian Left in detail since preference—on the basis of immediacy rather than potentiality of influence in the emerging political system—was given to the other two political forces (the Wafd and

new elite. The military significance was related to the minimum basic requirement of (coercive) control in the system, since Khaled—through his influence in the army—made about 40 Armored Corps officers rebel on hearing of Naguib's resignation.

Nasser sent the influential Salah Salem to calm the Armored Corps and to explain that Naguib—the "advocate of liberalism"—wanted to be a "dictator". In the meantime the Armored Corps had managed to rally to them some officers from other divisions and they insisted on Nasser's presence in person to justify the decision to exclude Naguib. Nasser went to face a stormy meeting.[110] There were rumours that Nasser was isolated and in danger of being detained[111] at the Cavalry barracks.[112] Nasser gave in :

> "To avoid the split spreading through the army and destroying the power basis of the revolution—and perhaps to escape from an awkward personal situation at the cavalry barracks—Nasser persuaded the Council of the Revolution to adopt a compromise. Khaled Mohieddin was to become premier and Naguib was to be asked to come back as President."[113]

El-Ikhwan). There is not as yet a published study which treats the Egyptian Left in detail. Laqueur's book (*op. cit.*) is a very well-known study, but in addition to being elementary, it is outdated. A more recent study is that of Agwani (*op. cit.*). Suitable material can be found in Lacouture (*L'Egypte en mouvement, op. cit.*, pp. 240-256) and Mahfouz, 'Afaf El Kosheri : *Socialisme et pouvoir en Egypte,* Paris, Librairie générale de droit et de jurisprudence, 1972, pp. 41-88. The are some relevant studies in Arabic : El-Bishri (*op. cit.*), Morqos (*op. cit.*) and Ramadan (*op. cit.*). Also important is the two-volume study by Rifa'at El-Saïd : *Tarikh El-Haraka El-Ishtrakiyya Fi Misr* (History of the Socialist Movement in Egypt 1900-1925), Beirut, El-Faraby, 1972 ; and *El-Yasar El-Misri* (The Egyptian Left 1925-1940), Beirut, El-Tali'a, 1972.

[110] When Nasser was 'summoned' to talk *in person* with the rebel officers "il vint faire face à un auditoire pour la première fois hostile à l'homme du 23 juillet. 'Tu n'as pas le droit ... Tu préfères le pouvoir à l'armée ... Tu es grisé par la puissance. Ce n'était pas là ce que tu nous avais promis. Où est la libération ? Tu as substitué notre autocracie à celle de Farouk : seul Naguib rassurait le peuple'" said the army officers. Lacouture : *L'Egypte en mouvement, op. cit.*, p. 173 ; Stephens : *op. cit.*, p. 125.

[111] When Nasser was busy arguing with the rebel officers "on vint le prévenir que, de même que le soir du 23 juillet, les auto-mitrailleuses encerclaient le bâtiment mais qu'il était, cette fois-ci, à l'intérieur du piège ... que c'était son ami Khaled qui avait pris cette mesure". Lacouture : *L'Egypte en mouvement, op. cit.*, p. 173. Khaled, though, maintained in a personal conversation with Stephens in March 1968 that "the cavalry corps were not preparing a coup and Nasser was never in danger of arrest, though some of the officers present may have tried to make Nasser think their tanks had the barracks surrounded". Stephens : *op. cit.*, pp. 125-126.

[112] "Il [Nasser] remonta en voiture, comme désarticulé, et ne put qu'avec peine franchir les barrages d'auto-mitrailleuses postés par Khaled. Il n'avait pas le mot de passe ..." Lacouture : *L'Egypte en mouvement, op. cit.*, p. 173.

[113] Stephens : *op. cit.*, p. 126.

But the intra-elite conflict over systemic control [114] was by no means over, for it was then the turn of Nasser's and RCC partisans in the army to react. The possibility of intra-army fighting was very near. In fact, the day after Nasser gave in at the cavalry barracks

> "intelligence officers under instructions from Nasser took Naguib away from his home, first to the artillery headquarters near Al Maza airport on the outskirts of Cairo and then, when this was surrounded by demonstrating soldiers, out to a hiding place in the desert. At the same time sections of the Free Officers who had rejected the compromise [of Naguib's coming back as the President with Khaled Mohieddin as Prime Minister] and supported Nasser had begun to organize counter-action against the cavalry corps. The cavalry barracks were surrounded and were overflown by aircraft. While demonstrations continued in the streets and an official delegation flew to Cairo to urge Naguib's release and safety, a new compromise was proposed. Naguib should return as President but with Nasser as premier instead of Mohieddin. Naguib again accepted." [115]

On the surface, then, this compromise of 28 February seemed to effect a division of political authority since Naguib—according to a spokesman for the young officers—returned to the Presidency after accepting the limitations of authority implied in the post. Yet 24 hours later, the spokesman said : "He [Naguib] discovered, or certain circles discovered for him, that he should have full powers and full control over the state." [116]

Consequently for a few weeks it was very difficult to localise the source of ultimate authority in the political system. Nasser declared in an interview that "Naguib was *purely* the President of the Republic and had no vote in the RCC". [117] As if to confirm this, a decree on March 7 named Nasser the Military Governor of Egypt. [118] But on the following day, Naguib resumed his previous positions of Prime Minister and RCC chairman and Nasser was relegated to his old post of Deputy-Prime Minister.

---

[114] Even though he was supported by sections of the army, the impact on Nasser of the incident at the cavalry barracks was enormous. After the incident, he was described as "un Nasser brisé, résigné, bouleversé par l'opposition qu'il avait entendu s'exprimer brutalement, la veille, lui qui croyait entraîner sinon le pays, du moins l'armée, d'un seul élan". Lacouture : *L'Egypte en mouvement, op. cit.*, p. 173. Thereafter, a priority in Nasser's strategy was to control the army as the first step in the control of the political system.

[115] Stephens : *op. cit.*, p. 126.

[116] *New York Times,* 28 March 1954. But the conflict over systemic control was already in process at the time when mass enthusiasm for the emotional public reconciliation had just started ; for evidence see the eye-witness account of Lacouture : *L'Egypte en mouvement, op. cit.*, pp. 174-175.

[117] *Le Populaire,* 6-7 March 1954, as quoted in *Survey ... 1954, op. cit.*, p. 187 (emphasis added).

[118] *Al-Ahram,* March 8, 1954.

A week later, on March 15, Naguib was also reinstated as the Military Governor.[119]

In spite of having almost all the odds against him, Nasser did finally manage to win the contest for systemic control. Nasser's strategy—which was initiated when Naguib was in Khartoum—can be summarised in three tactics :

1. Reconquer the Army, the source of unequalled organised force and hence the base of the regime's (coercive) systemic control. Thus Nasser

> "made use of his ten days as Prime Minister to carry out a quick purge of pro-Naguib elements in the army, especially the cavalry corps. Khaled Mohieddin was sent on a 'special mission' to Europe which was a prelude to his dismissal from the Council of the Revolution and exile for two years. Sixteen other cavalry officers were arrested and three months later tried and sentenced to prison terms."[120]

2. Deprive Naguib of his supporters, especially those who were capable of channelling organised mass support. This is the interpretation that can be given to the indictment of two members of Egypt's most prominent publishing family, Hussein and Ahmed Abou El-Fath, who owned the influential newspaper *El Misri,* two English and three French dailies in Cairo and Alexandria. Moreover, Nasser ordered the arrest of "several hundred people" accused of trying to exploit the Nasser-Naguib conflict to bring about a counter-revolution. For example, "prison sentences were imposed on twenty-two civilians alleged to be Communists . . .". At the same time, Nasser "also tightened his hold on the trade unions and other workers' organizations by appointing one of his loyal Free Officers, Major Kamal el-din Hussein, to be Minister of Social Affairs".[121]

3. But while Nasser was exploiting the time to eliminate pro-Naguib potential opposition organisers, and to prepare his own forces, he

> "had been letting Naguib have his head. His aim was not only to gain time but also to let Naguib work himself eventually into an untenable political position. Nasser saw clearly that, whether Naguib intended it or not, a return to parliamentary life on Naguib's terms would mean the end of the army movement and probably of most of

---

[119] Not only was Naguib accumulating symbols of systemic control, but he was moving away from the continuation of rule by *El-Dubbat El-Ahrar* to the reinstallation of a parliamentary system, and there was talk about the election of a Constituent Assembly in June 1954 to revise and approve a draft constitution and to act as parliament until the constitution was enacted and parliament elected. Thus the basic disagreement within the political elite on the general shape of the emerging political system continued unabated.

[120] Stephens : *op. cit.,* p. 126.

[121] *Ibid.*

> what it had set out to achieve. The public, like Naguib, might mistakenly think that it could have both the fruits of revolution and a return to the old party system. Nasser's plan was to make it plain that they had to choose one or the other."[122]

Consequently, on March 25, the RCC majority voted to issue a communiqué announcing the restoration of political parties and stated :

> "The Revolution Command Council will transfer sovereignty to a constituent assembly on July 24, 1954, with a declaration that the revolution is ended ; the political parties dissolved by the military regime may re-form immediately ; the Revolution Command Council will not form a new political party ; all citizens will enjoy full political rights ; the election for a constituent assemby will be free and direct ; no assemblymen will be appointed ; the immediate task of the constituent assembly, which will meet on July 23, will be the election of a President of the Republic."

But Naguib was hanging himself by allowing the return to the previous 'liberal' model of politics. For once the army saw the prospect of its being eased out of government and the discredited politicians of the ancien regime restored, it would rally behind the RCC to force a showdown and the defeat of Naguib. This was exactly what happened. A group of young officers calling themselves "Terrorist Free Rebels" issued a proclamation opposing the elections scheduled for July 1954 and threatening to kill Naguib and other RCC members if the way was paved to return the ancien regime politicians. Even the pro-Naguib officers in the army—who engineered his return—were reported to be irritated by some aspects of the return to civilian control.

The Cairo crowds and trade unions descended into the street to support the "continuation of the Revolution". A transport strike and then a general strike were put into operation with success both in Cairo and Alexandria. There were no trains, trams, buses or taxies ; and banks, offices, shops and petrol stations were closed. The whole country was certainly divided :

1. On Naguib's side were the upper and middle classes, the political parties, *El-Ikhwan,* most of the press and the University students.
2. On the side of the RCC were the Liberation Rally, trade unions, the Cairo crowd and, most important, the army.

King Sa'oud—who was in Cairo then—tried to bridge the division. But Naguib gave in, since a spokesman on his behalf declared that he had "bowed to the will of the people". He even collapsed while bidding farewell to King Sa'oud and was declared ill for some weeks. On April 18

[122] *Ibid.,* p. 128.

Nasser became the Prime Minister while Naguib was kept in the (honorary) post of President. Later in the year it was declared that Naguib was associated with *El-Ikhwan*'s attempt on Nasser's life, the plot against the regime, but he was saved from public trial by Sudanese intervention.

One can say that Nasser's and the RCC's battle for (coercive) systemic control was won. Nasser's continuation with the signature of the Anglo-Egyptian Evacuation Agreement (October 1954) in spite of *El-Ikhwan*'s strong opposition and bloody attacks, then his crushing of this opposition, are indicators of this (coercive) systemic control.

3.6. Nevertheless, quantitative analysis confirms our conclusion that the three-year period 1952-1954 was one of high conflict and systemic strain. If we take some of the accepted indicators in the literature [123] to measure conflict within the Egyptian political (sub)system, the findings are [124] :

1. *Protest demonstrations :* for the three-year period 1952-1954, the total number amounted to 17, with an annual mean of 5.67, whereas 1955 did not witness any protest demonstrations, and the total for the twelve-year period 1956-1967 was 5, and thus an annual mean of .42.

2. *Riots :* the total for the three-year period 1952-1954 was 16 with an annual mean of 5.33 ; the year 1955 did not witness any and the total for the twelve-year period 1956-1967 was 3 riots and thus an annual mean of .25.

3. *Deaths from domestic violence :* in the three-year period 1952-1954, the total number of deaths amounted to 316, with an annual mean of 105.33 ; no deaths from domestic violence are mentioned for 1955 and the total for the twelve-year period 1956-1967 was 23 persons with an annual mean of about 1.92.

4. *Governmental sanctions* to neutralise or eliminate a perceived threat amount, for the three-year period 1952-1954, to 143, with an annual mean of approximately 48 ; the year 1955 witnessed only 2 governmental sanctions, and the total for the twelve-year period 1956-1967 was 170, with an annual mean of about 14.17.

5. *Armed attacks* by (internal) organised groups totalled, for the three-year period 1952-1954, 158 attacks with an annual mean of 52.67 ;

---

[123] See, for instance : Rummel, Rudolph : "Dimensions of Conflict Behavior Within and Between Nations", *General Systems Yearbook,* VIII (1963), pp. 1-50 ; and Tanter, Raymond : "Dimensions of Conflict Behavior Within and Between Nations, 1958-1960", *Journal of Conflict Resolution,* X (1966), pp. 41-56.

[124] *World Handbook ... op. cit.,* pp. 88-124.

whereas no armed attacks are mentioned for the year 1955 and the total for the twelve-year period 1956-1967 was only 4, and thus an annual mean of .33.

Moreover, events data show that this three-year period of high conflict and systemic strain (1952 - January 1955) witnessed the uncovering (according to governmental sources) of *6 plots* against the new regime, the (declared) *political hanging* of at least 17 persons, a nation-wide *strike,* an assassination attempt on Nasser's life, and a national *state of emergency* was declared twice. Moreover, the constitution of *military tribunals and/or public political trials* amounted to no less than 15 cases ; (declared) *political arrests* among leaders of political parties, army officers, student leaders . . . amounted to at least 1487 persons ; and even 5 prominent leaders of *El-Ikhwan* were deprived of their Egyptian nationality. *Press censorship* was imposed during most of the period (for instance it was ended on March 6, 1954 after almost two years to be reimposed on March 30, 1954) ; the Council of the Press Syndicate was announced resolved and the Middle East News Agency was suddenly closed ; and 6 newspapers and magazines (including the widely-circulated Wafd's newspaper *El-Misri)* saw their licences revoked. The bureaucracy itself was not left untouched by the political conflict, for 800 high civil servants were dismissed as well as 40 university professors (including the deans of the faculties of Law, Medicine and Commerce). Last but not least, the period under analysis witnessed seven *cabinet turnovers.*

But, by the end of 1954, *El-Dubbat El-Ahrar*—headed by Nasser—were in a stronger position in the political system than they had ever been before ; Naguib was retired and under house arrest ; *El-Ikhwan* was severely crippled as an organisation with its *Morshed* in prison and some of its leaders even deprived of Egyptian nationality ; the leftists and all old party organisations were not only dissolved but also their leaders could not—even in their purely personal capacity [125]—participate in the system ; and dissidents in the army were solidly disposed of so that the army would stay solidly behind the new political elite.

---

[125] I am referring to the decrees of *"'azl Siassi"* (deprivation of all political rights). An example is the declaration of April 14, 1954, by the Minister of National Guidance, Salah Salem. After a joint meeting of the cabinet and the RCC he stated: "The RCC has decided that all members of the Wafd, Liberal Constitutional and Sa'adist Parties who held ministerial office between February 6, 1942 and July 23, 1952 will be deprived of all political rights, banned from public office, and will be barred from becoming members of syndicate boards and other organisations for a period of 10 years." Efforts for (coercive) systemic control went so far as to establish censorship on Friday sermons in all mosques throughout Egypt. The sermons were to be written under the supervision of the Ministry of Waqfs (Decree of September 13, 1954).

4.

But as Nkrumah is supposed to have said : "You can do everything with bayonets, except sit on them." The new regime, then, had to try to increase the 'legitimacy' or 'support' [126] component in its systemic control. Here intervenes our hypothesis on the integrative function of non-alignment. For while 1954 witnessed *El-Dubbat El-Ahrar*'s victory in systemic control based largely on the marshalling of coercion, 1955 may be regarded as the consolidation of this systemic control—but this time the new regime was increasingly based on rising support and legitimacy. The sources of this support were the two (interdependent) elements of charismatic appeal and national self-assertion through non-alignment. [127] In fact "almost inadvertently the military began to discover a new base for legitimacy—the leader's popular appeal. This appeal was generated by Nasser's phenomenal success in the international arena during 1955 and 1956." [128]

Landmarks in this period such as his leadership of the "Arab nationalist trend" against the "colonialist" Baghdad pact, his emergence as a "third world" leader at the Bandung Conference, his arms deal with the Socialist bloc resulting in the break of Western monopoly of arms sales, his nationalisation of the Suez Canal Company, and successful resistance to the "tripartite imperialist aggression", constituted bases of Nasser's rising charisma :

1. Nasser's success in these foreign policy moves brought him popularity not only among Egyptian masses but also among Arab masses. [129] Consequently, instead of anti-Nasser street demonstrations in Damascus, or protest cables from Baghdad, or nation-wide anti-Nasser strikes in Jordan, big portions of Arab masses rallied behind Nasser and sometimes even against their national governments.

2. An indicator of the acceptance and support the new regime enjoyed in Egypt itself is that the Egyptian masses tended to model their political

---

[126] Easton : *A Framework for Political Analysis, op. cit.;* and *A Systems Analysis of Political Life, op. cit.*

[127] Legitimacy was the more assured by this foreign policy since basically divergent political forces could be held together in their desire for "complete independence". Consequently, by adopting a non-aligned foreign policy, Nasser could channel this consensus and support in favour of the new regime. An illustration is the telegramme Nasser received—just before the Bandung Meeting—from a group of Egyptian communists who had been arrested and imprisoned. The message praised Nasser as the man who had set Egypt on the road towards 'positive neutralism'. *Le Monde,* September 2, 1961. This is why, perhaps, a member of the Revolutionary Command Council insisted : "We have invented positive neutralism."

[128] Dekmejian : *op. cit.,* p. 39.

[129] This Arab mass support can be illustrated by the fact that Western states suspected any nationalist move in any corner of the Arab subsystem as organised and directed by Nasser. An example from Jordan is King Hussein's decision on March 1,

culture [130] on that of Nasser. In this respect, a recent study confirms that in the 1955-1956 period Nasser's "own personal message ... brought about a substantial normative change in the belief system of Egyptians. Increasingly, Egyptians began to look at themselves as Arabs, thus sharing and adopting their leader's belief system ..." [131]

And what is a better proof of the people's acceptance of a leader and his new regime than their integration of his own value system into their own belief system.

From 1955 then, the new elite's systemic control tended to be increasingly based on rising mass support and legitimacy, derived from Nasser's charisma coinciding with his 'positive neutralism'. The (1955-1956) charisma-neutralism correlation is confirmed by the following graphs, [132] where the lines measure the direction of both variables.

Figure 2. *Nasser's Charismatic Ascendancy*

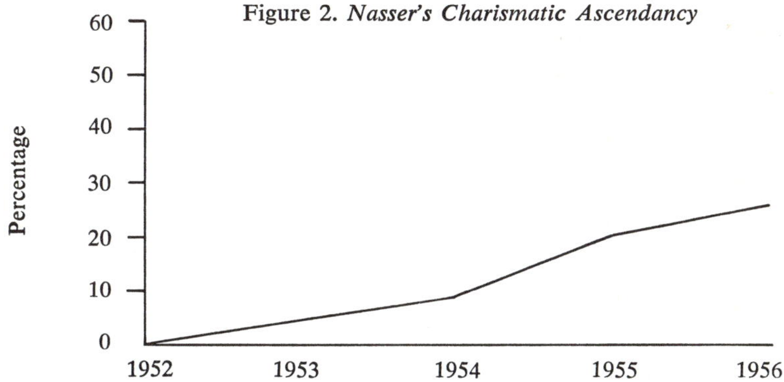

1956 to dismiss General Glubb, the legendary British Commander of the Arab Legion (1931-1956). This decision coincided with the visit to Cairo of the British Foreign Minister, Selwyn Lloyd. Lloyd thought that Nasser had so timely organised the whole affair to humiliate Great Britain and mock him in their talks. But "Nasser's account was that he heard the news after he had left Lloyd that evening and thought at first that Glubb had been withdrawn by the British Government. This, he considered, was a sensible British move and he told Lloyd so when he saw him the next morning before Lloyd flew off. Lloyd thought Nasser was making fun of him and was angry." Stephens : *op. cit.,* p. 180. See also the vivid account given by Heikal in : *Nasser : The Cairo Documents, op. cit.,* pp. 84-87.

[130] For the concept of political culture see, for instance, Lucian Pye and Sidney Verba (eds.) : *Political Culture and Political Development,* Princeton, Princeton U.P., 1965 ; Pateman, Carole : "Political Culture, Political Structure and Political Change", *British Journal of Political Science,* I (1971), pp. 291-307 ; Wilkinson, David : *Comparative Foreign Relations : Framework and Methods,* Belmont, Dickenson Publishing Co., 1969, pp. 90-101 ; and Wiseman, H. : *Political Systems : Some sociological Approaches,* New York, Praeger, 1966, pp. 21-47.

[131] Dekmejian : *op. cit.,* p. 40. For a relevant and systematic treatment of the Arab concept in Egypt, see : Sayegh, Anis : *El-Fikra El-'Arabiyya fi Misr* (The Arab Concept in Egypt), Beirut, 1959.

[132] Dekmejian : *op. cit.,* pp. 112-114. The indicator measuring Nasser's charisma is his centrality in the media.

Figure 3. *Rise of Positive Neutralism (Yearly Index)*

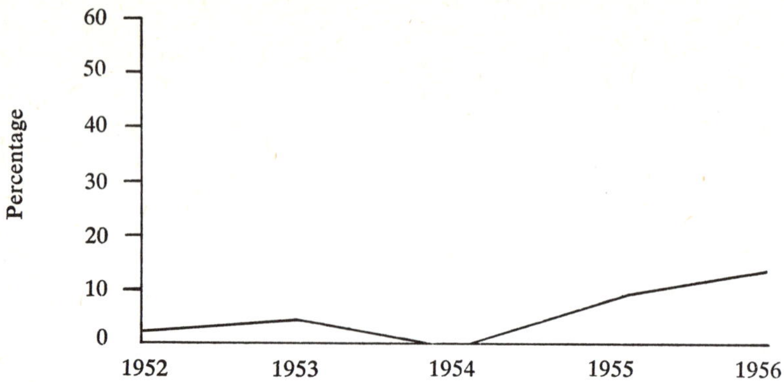

From the mid-1950's, then, the new regime saw its 'legitimacy' component rising—as the 'conflict data' for 1955 indicate. This rising legitimacy and support are correlated with the adoption of a foreign policy that appealed to "the people". As Nasser himself admitted after attending the Bandung Conference and visiting some Asian countries :

> "My visit to India was the turning point in my political understanding. I learned and recognized that the only wise policy for us consisted in adopting positive neutralism and non-alignment. On my return home, the reception that greeted this policy convinced me that it was the sole possible policy that could attract the broadest support of the Arab people." [133]

But a basic question is why this foreign policy of "positive neutralism and non-alignment" could "attract the broadest support among the Arab people", *i.e.* could rally divergent political forces and thus play an integrative function in the conflict-torn prismatic political system. As Nasser's statement suggests, positive neutralism and non-alignment was the policy in conformity with the "public opinion mood", perhaps because it is "the sole possible policy" that responds to the multi-variable national 'situation' of the Afro-Asian actor. All these aspects can be analysed further in attempting to trace the linkage of the historical, economic and geocultural 'situational' variables to the choice of Egypt's non-alignment and the pattern of its evolution.

[133] Abdel Malek : *Egypt : Military Society, op. cit.*, p. 227.

CHAPTER VII

Other 'Situational' Variables and the Pattern of Egypt's Non-Aligned[1] Behaviour

1. The Function of the other Situational Variables

1.1. *The Historical Variable*

1.1.1. The function of history in ideology-formation and rule-legitimation in developing political systems has not received the emphasis equal to its importance. [2] Its importance was reiterated by Nasser in *El-Mithaq*

---

[1] As indicated in chapter one, footnote 2, non-aligned actors do not use a uniform labellation to designate their foreign policy orientation and/or behaviour. This is why some analysts attempted a distinction between non-alignment and neutralism (*e.g.* Lyon, Peter: "Neutrality, Neutralism, Non-Alignment", a *paper submitted to the Seventh World Congress of the International Political Science Association,* Brussels, 18-23 September 1967), but the attempt was not condoned in later analyses. Egyptian policy-makers used to insist on calling their foreign policy "positive neutralism", which provoked Krishna Menon's comment: "positive neutralism" is as contradictory as a vegetarian tiger. Toward the late 1950s Nasser himself used to talk about "positive neutralism" and "non-alignment" interchangeably, and at present the term non-alignment is increasingly used on its own. Some third world leaders use other labellations to designate their foreign policies (*e.g.* Morocco's "non-dependence", Senegal's "non-suivisme" ...). I am using throughout the term non-alignment to cover all the different labellations which denote non-participation in the East-West military alliances. I insist only—following non-aligned actors—on the distinction between this foreign policy and the legal (Swiss-type) neutrality.

[2] "After the defeat of June 1967, ... I felt that there is no other way to understand the present than by studying Egypt's modern history. This modern history which starts officially and effectively about 200 years ago when Egypt entered into direct relationship with European civilisation through Bonaparte's expedition in 1798 ... All intellectuals are unanimous that the series of Egyptian—and Arab—failures in the 1948, 1956 and 1967 confrontations with Israel are due to the cultural roots latent in our national history. Without grasping and remedying these roots, no success can be guaranteed in the future." Awad, Lewis: "Our National History", *Al-Ahram,* 5 October 1973.

(National Charter) in dealing with the conditions that helped the revolutionary national struggle to succeed. [3] Moreover, a survey of Egyptian official documents reveals the frequency and intensity of symbols derived from the society's history which are linked to contemporary policy outputs. [4]

In *The Philosophy of the Revolution,* Nasser could hardly emphasise more the conditioning of the present psychology of the "people" by Egyptian history : "We have often been", he remarked, "the invaders' passage way and the adventurers' target." Then he reiterates the linkage with the present : "So numerous were the circumstances through which we lived that it would be impossible to explain the factors latent in our people's souls unless these circumstances are taken into account." [5]

Thus the historical experience of non-aligned actors—especially their colonisation—affects foreign policy both through its societal-psychological repercussions and also directly through the memories of past subjugation. As Nasser asserts in the *National Charter :* "Our homeland will continue to feel for a long time the bitterness of the humiliation it was subjected to during this crisis period which witnessed colonialism's disdain of our struggle."

These memories of the past explain the suspicions and apprehensions of the present. For when colonialism was on the defensive, it resorted to "common defence" and "alliance" treaties as another name for a "colonial pact" legalising the presence of occupation forces.

Iraq, for instance, got its legal independence in 1932, and joined the League of Nations as a sovereign state. But because a "common defence treaty" was a condition for the granting of this legal independence, no material change took place for the Iraqi people since British occupation forces were still there and Iraq continued as part of the British "sphere of influence" in West Asia. [6]

---

[3] *El-Mithaq* (National Charter), Cairo, Information Department, n.d. (but was read by Nasser before the Congress of Popular Forces in May 1962), p. 9.

[4] El-Sadat : "Le poids du passé", in *Révolte sur le Nil, op. cit.,* pp. 13-29, also Nasser's *Speeches.*

[5] Nasser : *The Philosophy of the Revolution, op. cit.,* p. 38.

[6] Similarly, when Iraq was incorporated in the Baghdad Pact in 1955, "within a short time ... events revealed that Iraq's formal alignment with the West added new fuel for a subsequent nationalist eruption, that was to alter profoundly the country's internal and external policies. Nuri-es-Said was widely regarded by Arab nationalists as a pliant tool of London and Washington, a political puppet who accepted Western directives even when these ran directly counter to the mainstream of Arab nationalist demands."

When the army coup d'état took place on July 14, 1958, Nuri was searched out and found disguised in women's clothes. He was killed and his body dragged through the streets of Baghdad. The new regime adopted non-alignment, justifying

Egypt underwent the same process as Iraq when an Egyptian "national front" signed the 1936 Anglo-Egyptian "Friendship and Alliance" Treaty. Egypt was unanimously admitted to the League of Nations, but for the man in the street the British occupation forces were still in the country as before. Hence occupation treaties and "common defence" treaties tended to amount to exactly the same as far as the presence of occupation forces was concerned. This explains why even pre-1952 governments refused participation in the "Allied Middle East Command" by which the British base at Suez was to be an "Allied" base [7]; and the Arab countries were to put their territory, armies, transport and other facilities at the disposal of a (foreign) high command. It was this word 'command' that struck the psychology of colonised Egyptians.

1.1.2. Nor did the British offer to abandon the 1936 Anglo-Egyptian Treaty (governing the status of British occupation forces in the Suez Canal zone) in return for Egyptian participation in Western defence schemes facilitate matters. On the contrary, it confirmed doubts among many sectors of Egyptian public opinion about the "equality equation" between the 1936-'occupation' Treaty and the 1951-"Alliance" proposals, since the British were ready to exchange one for the other.

Nasser confirmed this 'colonialism-cum-alignment' equation in explaining his repeated refusals of alliance-membership in this way :

> "I feared alignment with any outside power because I know the Arab history and the Arab people. For hundreds of years they had been accustomed to look upon their governments with fear and suspicion as the agents of foreign powers, as governments which took their orders from [foreign] ambassadors." [8]

---

it officially in the following way : "Prior to the Revolution, the Iraqi foreign policy was merely a part of the imperialist design elaborated abroad and handed over to the prime ministers of the old regime for execution. These were tools for carrying out a policy that had nothing in common with the interests of the country. Neither did Iraq have . . . any say in defining its foreign relations. It was necessary, therefore, that the *liberated Republic* of Iraq should decide upon a new policy ; one derived from the native land and in accord with the desire of all Arab people" (emphasis added).

That is, non-alignment, as defined in this official declaration, is a form of national self-determination in foreign policy matters. Crabb : *The Elephants and The Grass, op. cit.*, pp. 47-48. See also Dissouqi, Mohamed : "Thawrat Rashid 'Ali El-Kilani wa El-Qawmiyya El-'Arabiyya" (The Revolution of Rashid Ali El-Kilani and Arab Nationalism), *El-Siassa El-Dawliyya*, Cairo, VI (1970), pp. 586-602.

[7] Cremeans, Charles : *The Arabs and the World : Nasser's Arab Nationalist Policy*, New York, Praeger, 1963, pp. 137-139.

[8] A declaration to Keith Wheeler, *Life* magazine, July 14, 1959. *Nasser's Speeches, op. cit.*, Vol. II, pp. 454-464.

It was this suspicion that made members of the new regime consider the talk about common "defensive" arrangements or "alliance" schemes, during the Anglo-Egyptian negotiations to evacuate Egypt, as just another pretext to prolong British occupation. Consequently, the new elite insisted that "first, Egypt had to be independent, fully and completely, without foreign troops on its soil. Then, but not until then, it might consider a defense agreement". [9] In September 1954, about a month before the conclusion of the Anglo-Egyptian Evacuation Agreement, Nasser declared:

> "We must not sit down and write a confession that we are on the side of the West. In spite of everything, we must be on that side because we are far away from the Russians. If there is a government here that wants to be on the side of the Russians, I don't think it can be this government." [10]

1.1.3. Once the Evacuation Agreement on the Suez Base was signed (October 1954), the U.S. and Britain renewed their attempts to guarantee Egyptian participation in Western defence schemes. But it seems that the two Western powers and the new Egyptian regime had divergent conceptions of the post-Evacuation Agreement policies. The British conception, for instance, was that the Evacuation Agreement granted Egypt sovereign rights over the Suez Base area. This was thus a recognition by the West of Egypt's full independent status which had been its insistent demand. Thus the satisfaction of this demand removed the barrier against Egypt's participation in Western alliance schemes.

As for the new Egyptian regime, it did not seem to have rejected a priori a form of cooperation with the West, as Nasser's above-mentioned declaration to the *U.S. News and World Report* insinuated. Even such an anti-Nasser leader as Anthony Eden stated after his first and only meeting with Nasser: "Nasser declared that his interest and sympathy were with the West." [11] But there was the crucial question of timing. For the new Egyptian regime could not accept—even if it intended to—membership in Western military pacts against a distant Soviet 'enemy' or unidentifiable "communist subversion" so soon after the conclusion of the Evacuation Agreement which had nearly cost Nasser his life. Thus Nasser needed to prove that the independence he obtained from Britain was not nominal but real. Consequently, the new regime had to "practice" and "demonstrate" this independence, especially since Egypt had been deprived of this independence for centuries and there were previous examples of "fake" independence (*e.g.* 1936). On the contrary, if Nasser had accepted immediate membership in Western alliance schemes, he would have confirmed all the

---

[9] Cremeans: *op. cit.*, p. 139.

[10] *U.S. News and World Report,* 3 September 1954.

[11] Eden, Anthony: *The Memoirs of the Rt. Hon. Sir Anthony Eden,* Vol. III (Full Circle), London, Cassell, 1960, p. 221.

accusations about his "pro-Western tendencies" and the "fakeness" of the independence agreement. Briefly, Nasser wanted to show that there is a difference—as a spokesman of a new African state said—between *having* and *exercising* independence. [12] This "exercising" of independence could be put in evidence by the regime's refusal of formal alignment which presented the danger of the renewed control of the strong over the weak, and meant a renewed loss of voice and identity. [13] Consequently, Nasser—as his latest biographer affirms—"hoped for a respite of a year or two before having to review Egypt's foreign policy in the light of her newly-gained independence and before considering any *formal* ties with the West". [14]

1.1.4. This important aspect in the psychology of ex-colonised peoples has not been grasped by former colonial powers. For in answer to Nasser's argument of "bad timing", Eden commented : "I was familiar with this plea, it is never the right time for some." [15]

Thus the prominent figure of Anglo-Saxon policy could not wait, and decided to go ahead with his "common defence" schemes by guaranteeing Iraq's—rather than Egypt's—membership. This step was to constitute a landmark in Egypt's "positive neutralism"—as we shall see when dealing with its pattern—for it confirmed Egyptian mistrust (stemming from its colonial past) of a new form of colonialism-cum-alignment with a big foreign power. And it was this conditioning of post-independence behaviour by past colonial experience that prompted a scholar of non-alignment to assert that "the whole of neutralist doctrine could be described as a quest for distinctive intellectual expression of independence and starts from the assumption of a given independent statehood". [16]

Quantitative content analysis of speeches and official statements of non-aligned actors in the middle of the 1960's confirms Lyon's qualitative remark, for the emphasis on defining non-alignment as 'independence' was the aspect that enjoyed the greatest consensus among them. Thus out of the foreign policy statements of 33 non-aligned Afro-Asian states under analysis, those states who thought of non-alignment as primarily an "independent role" amounted to 26 or 79 per cent (in round figures), whereas those who emphasised the "mediatorial role" too were only 8 states or just less than 25 per cent. [17]

---

[12] Crabb : *op. cit.*, pp. 39-48. Also Sayegh in *The Dynamics of Neutralism ...*, *op. cit.* ; Good in Martin : *Neutralism and Non-Alignment, op. cit.*, pp. 3-13.

[13] *Ibid.*

[14] Stephens : *op. cit.*, p. 145.

[15] Eden : *op. cit.*, p. 221.

[16] Lyon : *Neutralism, op. cit.*, p. 72. Crabb : *op. cit.*, pp. 39-65. Good in Martin : *Neutralism and Non-Alignment, op. cit.*, pp. 3-13.

[17] Holsti in *International Studies Quarterly, op. cit.*

This linkage between a recent colonial past and the adoption of non-alignment might also help to explain some of the characteristics in the emergence and evolution of the non-aligned subsystem. For instance :

1. That Egypt (and other non-aligned actors) fought for the adoption of non-alignment with the same passion reminiscent of national liberation wars.

2. That both the first and second points in the five-point official definition of non-alignment by the First Non-Aligned Summit Conference were "to follow an independent policy" and "always to support popular liberation movements".

3. That the strongly anti-colonial members (*e.g.* Algeria, Egypt, Ghana, Guinea, Indonesia . . .) have come to be the active non-aligned actors.

1.2. *The Economic Variable*

1.2.1. Empirically, a high correlation seems to exist between the state of economic underdevelopment and the adoption of non-alignment since none of the non-aligned Afro-Asian actors are "developed", and the majority of underdeveloped states seems to be regrouped within the non-aligned international subsystem. [18] Moreover, a founder member of the Free Officers' Association Committee and the youngest member of the Revolutionary Command Council, the "red Major", Khaled Mohieddin, confirmed this correlation. "Positive neutralism", he remarked in the 1957-Afro-Asian Peoples Solidarity Conference, "is the policy the newly-independent states follow to build their economies". And Nasser, after attending the 15th session of the United Nations General Assembly, concurred :

> "We the states which had adopted the policy of non-alignment and positive neutralism wanted to show to the peoples of the globe that the world has the place not only for the Western and Eastern blocs but also for those [non-aligned] states which preferred building their homelands and making up for what they had missed in the ages of steam and electricity." [19]

Moreover, Dr. Abdel Razzak Hassan explicited in *Al-Ahram :* "The basic driving force behind a policy of non-alignment is the economic 'situation' of these [non-aligned] peoples." [20]

---

[18] See the treatment of the economic variable as a basis of the regrouping of non-aligned actors in chapter V.

[19] Nasser's *Speeches, op. cit.,* Vol. III, pp. 244-250. See also *El-Mithaq, op. cit.,* chapter VII.

[20] *Al-Ahram,* 8 October 1964.

1.2.2. It is not our purpose to review the different theories of economic development and apply them to the state of affairs prevalent in Egypt. The essential point to be emphasised in this context is the vulnerability of countries like Egypt, a vulnerability that stems from the combination of three circumstances :

(*a*) the vital role played by exports of primary commodities in the economy ;

(*b*) the high degree of concentration on a very limited number of primary commodities among the exports ;

(*c*) the generally high degree of instability that characterises the markets for these primary products.

This instability cannot disappear unless a structural change in the economy takes place—a long-term process. A goal of foreign policy, then, is to mitigate the adverse effects of this instability. Indeed, if Egypt is a member of a certain bloc, committed to it in advance in both political behaviour and economic transactions, it suffers the ups and downs of the bloc's economy. Moreover, it is the mechanism of monopoly-oligopoly that works in this instance, especially as far as the fixing of prices is concerned. If Egypt, however, manages to get out of the monopoly-oligopoly context to act as a seller and/or a buyer in a competitive market, Egypt can sell its products to the highest bidder and buy from the cheapest source. In other words, Egypt can decide freely, basing itself on economic rationality and its own interests, as perceived by its decision-makers. Nehru expressed this way of reasoning when he quoted the saying, "Don't put all your eggs in one basket". This also lessens absolute economic dependence on one country or one bloc, for it is economic dependence which endangers political independence. Consequently, Ali Sabry—Nasser's erstwhile Prime Minister—asserted that "political independence could be maintained . . . if one third of Egypt's exports went to the West, another third to the communists, and the remainder to the 'others'." [21] In fact, even before Cairo's recognition of China in 1956, an agreement was concluded whereby the gigantic Chinese market would absorb part of the Egyptian main export, cotton. Thus only a decade after the 'Revolution' about 51 per cent of Egypt's cotton was being sold to members of the Eastern bloc. [22] Moreover, its exports to other non-aligned actors have risen from 36.5 million pounds in 1962 to 49.8 million in 1963 and in the

[21] Wheelock : *op. cit.*, p. 257. Wheelock adds that "this stratagem reputedly had been recommended to President Nasser by Marshal Tito in 1956".

[22] Lacouture : *L'Egypte en mouvement, op. cit.*, pp. 400-406.

same period its imports rose from 47.7 million to 63.7 million, representing 16 per cent of Egypt's total imports.[23] Consequently, Egypt was becoming less vulnerable to economic fluctuations and to the risks of being dependent on only one or two buyers and/or suppliers.

1.2.3. But the diversification of markets cannot function as a panacea[24] and the real solution remains the diversification of the Egyptian economy within a comprehensive strategy of economic development. This would not only lessen the country's economic and political vulnerability but would also improve the unpalatable status quo.

Yet to 'get started' on the 'take-off' for sustained economic development, outside capital and technicians are necessary. This 'unwelcome' necessity, however, should not be permitted to compromise national independence.[25] Therefore, rather than being tied to one country or bloc, sources of aid have to be diversified and its volume increased. The competition between the 'diplomacy of dollars' and the 'diplomacy of roubles' helped Egypt to gain the maximum from both camps. In fact Nasser's example is very revealing in this respect. Originally, he had to beg the Americans for aid, and although he thought Dulles had promised him $200,000,000, the State Department came later with an offer of only $40,000,000. Even this amount was agreed on after the Egyptian negotiators—according to Abdelhamid Ghaleb[26]—"were treated like children. One day we thought everything was cleared up, then the next day some Pentagon official would lecture us as though we were raw recruits or . . . idiots." This humiliation prompted another member of Nasser's entourage[27] to tell the unofficial American link : "Before very long *you* will be begging *us* to accept the $200,000,000."[28] Nasser seems to have reasoned correctly, for between 1957 and 1965 Egypt received 1,321.1 million Egyptian pounds (excluding military credits).[29] Not only did Americans increase their aid, but also new sources in the Eastern bloc were available.

---

[23] *El-Ahram,* 8 October 1964.

[24] In 1960, the price of cotton was 56 per cent of its price during the base years 1950-1954.

[25] Nasser said : "Tito is a great man. He showed me how to get help from both sides—without joining either." *New York Times,* 3 March 1958, as quoted in Lyon : *Neutralism, op. cit.,* p. 86.

[26] Copeland, Miles : *The Game of Nations : the Amorality of Power Politics,* London, Weidenfeld and Nicolson, 1969, p. 146.

[27] It was Hassan El-Touhami, a member of *El-Dubbat El-Ahrar,* the Secretary-General of the Presidency at the time of Nasser's death, and who is now in charge of the Islamic Conferences.

[28] Copeland : *op. cit.,* p. 147.

[29] Mansfield, Peter : *Nasser's Egypt,* London, Penguin African Library, 1965, p. 163. Mansfield's figures are accepted by Copeland : *op. cit.,* pp. 144-145.

1.2.4. On the whole the balance-sheet of the 1950s and early 1960s was very favourable to the new Egyptian regime. [30] With regard to the Eastern bloc, Egypt held third place in the field of economic assistance. The main projects in heavy and basic industries, and of course the High Dam, were carried out with the financial-technical help of the Soviet Union, Czechoslovakia, East Germany and Hungary. The Eastern bloc represented one third of Egypt's foreign trade (rising from 48 million Egyptian pounds in 1952 to 130 million in 1961). Moreover, the trade volume was (except with China) growing every year, with the balance of trade generally in Egypt's favour. In addition, long-term economic and trade agreements granted Egypt 230 million pounds in credit facilities, and three large loans amounted to a total of 186 million pounds. These commercial credits and loans were combined with "distant maturity dates, low rates of interest (2 per cent or 2.5 per cent for 15 years), loans allocated to the basic projects in the 1960 Five-Year Plan, payment in cotton, training and education of Egyptian engineers and technicians" [31] under favourable conditions, and early delivery dates.

But though Egypt's external dependence became less one-sided, its economic relations with the West continued. Over the seven-year period 1955-1961, Egypt received U.S. aid and loans amounting to $500 million (consisting for the most part in farm surpluses). [32] After Abdel Mon'im Kayssouni's mission to the United States in April-May 1962,

> "Egypt received a $42 million advance from the IBRD, Westinghouse agreed to take part in the construction of a central power station in Cairo ($32 million for thirty years at 2 per cent interest), and General Motors contracted to supply Diesel locomotives ($10 million). A proposal for a second agreement was initiated ; it called for the United States to furnish $450 million in foodstuffs over three years, and $27.5 for the railway system." [33]

Moreover, "the United States, Japan, Great Britain, West Germany and Italy negotiated a joint participation in the projects of the Five-Year Plan". [34]

A closer analysis of all the economic data shows that not only was Egypt's economic position much more balanced, but that by July 1962 Egypt had received about 500 million Egyptian pounds in loans and aid

---

[30] Abdel Malek : *Egypt : Military Society, op. cit.,* pp. 241-243.

[31] *Ibid.*

[32] El-Maraghi, Mahmud : "Al-'hiyad Yaqifu 'Ala Raglayhi" (Neutralism Stands on its Feet), *Rose-El-Youssef,* February 26, 1962, as quoted in *ibid.*

[33] *Ibid.*

[34] *Ibid.*

and had used by the end of 1961 only 27 million. [35] This seems to have prompted Heikal's explicit statement that Egypt's foreign policy behaviour proved to be a successful investment.

1.3. *The Geo-Cultural Variable*

1.3.1. Egypt is the only country which is both African and Asian at the same time. [36] This bicontinental geographical position can perhaps explain why few other countries have been so completely guided by their geographical position. Indeed, many of Egypt's problems of foreign policy "either stem directly from its geographical position or have developed in response to the attitude of foreign powers toward the country's strategic place in the world". [37] The importance of this geographical position was indicated by the pre-1952 government, which emphasised first the " Unity of the Nile Valley", and then came the Arab subsystem in second place. Thus in the House of Representatives on January 16, 1950 ex-king Faruq declared :

> "The nation has decided and is exerting all its efforts to liberate the country. Egypt and the Sudan want to be liberated from all ties restricting their actions in order to regain their ancient glory and assume their rightful place in international life ... My government has found that it is now necessary to concern itself more with the affairs of the Arab World and the Arab League ..." [38]

Equally before the advent of the new regime, Azmi Bey emphasised this geographical position in the U.N. :

> "... Egypt will be in a position to play the international role to which she is entitled by her geographic position ... Along with the states of the Arab League ... Egypt will stand guard over the security of the vulnerable part of the Near East ..." [39]

---

[35] *Ibid.*

[36] Napoleon is supposed to have described Egypt as "the most important country in the world", *The Killearn Diaries, op. cit.*, p. 1.

[37] Choucri, Nazli : *The Role of Egypt in International Affairs : Emergence of the Policy of Non-Alignment,* unpublished M.A. thesis, Stanford University, 1964, p. 116. Indeed, both Napoleon's expedition and the 1882-British occupation were motivated *directly* by Egypt's geographical importance.

[38] *Ibid.,* p. 49.

[39] *Ibid.,* p. 69.

1.3.2. The new regime was not different in its emphasis on Egypt's geographical position.[40] Already in *The Philosophy of the Revolution,* Nasser devoted exactly a third of his book to deal with the impact of the geographical position on Egypt's potential role in the international system. Thus after dealing with the impact of history (*i.e.* "time"), Nasser turned to geography or to "place" as he preferred calling it :

> "I . . . concentrated on time . . . But I feel that place has also its claim, so let me now concentrate on place.
>
> . . . We cannot act as if our country were a part of Alaska in the Far North or as if we were on distant and deserted Wake Island, in the vastness of the Pacific . . . Place . . . imposes upon us its reality.
>
> We should first of all agree upon one thing before we proceed any further, that is to define the boundaries of place as far as we are concerned.
>
> . . . If I am told that our place is limited by the political boundaries of our country, I . . . do not agree.
>
> Had the matter been confined . . . to the political boundaries of our country, the problem would have been easy. We would have locked ourselves up, closing all doors, and lived in an ivory tower, as far away as possible from the world with its problems, wars and troubles that force open the gates of our country and leave their effects upon us, even though we have nothing to do with them."[41]

So at this early stage in his thinking, Nasser decided that Egypt's geographical position forces it—so to speak—to perform a "positive" role, but not "positive neutralism", for the term had not yet been coined. So Egypt's role had—at that stage—to be declared as "positive" because "the era of isolation is over". But even if the word "neutralism" had not yet been added to the decision to be "positive", this "positive" role was the subject of further reflection :

> "As I sit in my study and think of this subject I often ask myself 'What is our positive role in this troubled world and on what scene do we play that role ?' "[42]

But since there is a certain pattern in political interaction for "fate does not play jokes [and] events are not produced haphazardly" ; and since ". . . it is we, and we alone—*by virtue of our position*—who can play

---

[40] This element of continuity between pre- and post-1952 regimes explains our proposed model's emphasis on the relative permanence of the geographical variable in the foreign policy-making process.

[41] *The Philosophy of the Revolution, op. cit.,* pp. 50-51.

[42] *Ibid.,* p. 51.

the [positive] part", [43] Egypt's existing geographical feature has to be the basis of orientation and behaviour :

> "I review our circumstances and find that we are in a group of circles which should be the theatre of our activity and in which we try to move as much as possible.
>
> ... We cannot look stupidly at a map of the world not realising our place therein, and *the role assigned to us by that position.* Neither can we ignore that there is an Arab Circle surrounding us and that this Circle is as much a part of us as we are part of it ; ...
>
> Can we ignore that there is a continent of Africa in which fate has placed us and which is destined to-day to witness a terrible struggle for its future ? This struggle affects us whether we want it or not." [44]

Even during Nasser's first attendance at an international conference (Bandung) and his first visit to India, *Al-Ahram* saw the geographical position as the important factor in the common (non-aligned) foreign policy of both Egypt and India :

> "Thanks to its geographical position", *Al-Ahram* affirmed, "India is a natural link between East and West Asia. Consequently, it is the country that knows best Asian problems and can be most efficacious in solving them.
>
> Egypt's position in Africa is similar to India's in Asia. Egypt is the biggest African country present in the international community, and it is also a natural link between Africa and Asia." [45]

Eight years after "the Army Movement", Nasser—in his first (and only) speech to the United Nations General Assembly—reiterated once more the geographical variable in Egypt's "situation" :

> "There is no problem which concerns our homeland, the United Arab Republic, or which concerns our nation, the Arab nation, or which relates to the two continents, Asia and Africa, *through which the frontiers of our country extend* ... for whose solution we are not ready to accept the Charter of the United Nations and its principles, the resolutions of the United Nations and its recommendations for a just settlement, with the best of good will." [46]

1.3.3. It is perhaps because of this Afro-Asian geographical position that the decision-makers of an actor like Egypt favour a non-aligned foreign policy, and this is for two reasons :

1. The major issues of the East-West conflict are centered in Europe and in the North Atlantic, and are thus the concerns of the rich north.

---

[43] *Ibid.* (emphasis added).

[44] *Ibid.*, pp. 51-52 (emphasis added).

[45] *Al-Ahram,* 13 April 1955.

[46] Nasser's *Speeches, op. cit.,* Vol. II, pp. 228-240 (emphasis added).

As Professor Boutros Ghali expressed it : international relations take place on two levels : (*a*) "relations between the rich countries adopting different social and economic systems. These relations are based on the principle of peaceful coexistence". (*b*) Relations between the developing countries, on the one hand, and each of the blocs of the rich north, on the other. "These relations are governed by the doctrine of positive neutralism . . . Positive neutralism is the foreign policy of proletarian states." [47] Nasser confirmed this by declaring that one of the bases of his policy of positive neutralism and non-alignment was the refusal to subordinate Egypt's "interest" to the issues dividing the rich north. [48]

2. Since the major issues of the East-West conflict are outside Afro-Asia, it is neither profitable for the superpowers nor "conducive to international peace" to have them intervening in purely local conflicts amidst difficult military and political conditions. [49] The 1960-Congo crisis is usually cited to support this argument. [50]

1.3.4. But Nasser in his above-mentioned speech to the U.N. General Assembly suggested that Egypt's position and its links in the Arab subsystem are not purely geographical, but also cultural ; since Nasser talked about "our homeland" (*i.e.* Egypt) and used the term "our nation" to designate the Arab subsystem. Similarly, Egypt's Afro-Asian position denotes not only a geographical concept but also a cultural one, if only through Islam. As Nasser himself emphasised in talking about "the third circle" :

> "Can we ignore that there is a Moslem World to which we are tied by bonds forged not only by religious faith but also by the fact of history ? I said once that fate plays no jokes. It is not in vain that our country lies to the south-west of Asia as part of the Arab World, whose life is intermingled with ours. It is not in vain that

---

[47] Ghali, Boutros : *Dirasat Fi El-Siassa El-Dawliyya* (Studies in International Politics), Cairo, El-Anglo, 1961, pp. 13-39, 90-116. Similarly, the ex-head of the office of President Tito and Yugoslavia's former ambassador to the United Nations affirmed : ". . . the countries of the less developed parts of the world looked upon the cold war as a conflict in another world, a world which was outside their realm of interests and with whose way of life and level of development they could not catch up for a long time to come . . . They therefore could not identify themselves with the cold war." Mates, Leo : *Non-Alignment : Theory and Current Policy,* Belgrade, the Institute of International Politics and Economics, and New York, Oceana Publications, Inc., Dobbs Ferry, 1972, p. 121.

[48] *Al-Ahram,* 10 August 1959.

[49] F. Sayegh : "Anatomy of Neutralism", in Sayegh : *Dynamics of Neutralism in the Arab World, op. cit.,* pp. 1-102.

[50] Good : "The Congo Crisis", in Martin : *Neutralism and Non-Alignment, op. cit.,* pp. 34-64.

our country lies in the north-east of Africa, overlooking the dark continent, wherein rages to-day the most violent struggle between white colonisers and black natives to possess its inexhaustible resources. It is not in vain that Islamic civilisation and the Islamic heritage, which the Mongols ravaged in their conquest of the old Islamic capitals, retreated and sought refuge in Egypt, where they found shelter and safety resulting from the counterattack at Ein Galout in which Egypt repelled the invasion of these Tartars." [51]

Thus the Afro-Asian position, as a cultural concept, favours the insistence on philosophical and ideological independence, and the search for a distinct identity by attempting to revive traditional culture and to emphasise a pre-colonial glorious past. [52] An indicator of Egypt's insistence on a distinct identity is its attempt to elaborate a developmental ideology [53] different from both "Bolschevik-type socialism" and "Manchestrian capitalism". This distinct developmental ideology (*Arab* and Islamic socialism) is used both as a reaction against external pressures and as a manifestation of ideological independence.

In this case, emphasis is put on what is considered the "inherently socialist nature of early Islam". [54] For instance : equality (which Islam has dictated among believers), social justice (through *El-Zakat* or alms

[51] Nasser : *The Philosophy of the Revolution, op. cit.,* p. 52.

[52] As Nkrumah's Government put it when it first suggested the adoption of the name "Ghana" for the future independent Gold Coast state : "It is clear the name GHANA serves the purpose of providing the people of the Gold Coast with a symbol of their *national* unity and a *link* with past history." *Gold Coast Government's Proposals for Constitutional Reform,* Accra, 1953, p. 15. Similarly "Zaïre" or "Mali" are names linked to historical symbols and old African empires.

[53] Equally, Mates states : "The policy of non-alignment ... implies not only political independence and autonomy, but also the search for individual modes of internal development." See *Non-Alignment, op. cit.,* p. 122.

[54] Dekmejian : *op. cit.,* p. 132 ; and El-Sharabassy, El-Saïd : *Mabadï El-Ishtrakiyya Fi El-Islam* (Principles of Socialism in Islam), Cairo, El-Dar El-Qawmiyya, Kutob Thaqafiyya No. 171, n.d. Moreover, a governmental publication states : "... it might be well to point out what makes our socialism basically an Arab socialism and not just socialism as conceived by any other nation. The basic tradition of brotherliness which our religious background gives us emphasises the necessity of providing for all. Alms-giving at certain religious feasts are a necessary part of the formalities, thus providing for the less fortunate in thanks for the good received. The true spirit of this sharing of good fortune became only a symbolic ritual with most of those who were well able to provide much more for the poor. If the true spirit of tradition of helping those less fortunate had been kept, the tradition of hospitality and brotherly sharing which is basic to the Arab would have sufficed. However, through greed this tradition was forgotten except in form only." United Arab Republic, Information Department : *Arab Socialism,* Cairo, 1963, p. 8.

tax), prevention of monopoly (through the unlawful status of usury).[55] These socialistic seeds of the Arab-Islamic context endow Egypt's socialism with historical legitimacy and religious sanction to neutralise (traditional) accusations equating socialism with communism and atheism. Moreover, this socialism's manifest Arabness and its "spiritual bases" in Islam reinforce its distinctiveness from, and superiority over, various forms of foreign ideologies. As El-Sharabassi said : Egypt's ideology is an "Islamic socialism to assert and bolster the slogan of the great Arab revolution : neither Eastern nor Western philosophies but that of the Arab nation".[56] Consequently, "the common historical roots of *Arab* nationalism and *Arab* socialism unite them in the modern context as a distinctly *Arab* ideology".[57]

1.3.5. An illustration of the problems that can arise between a non-aligned actor and one of the blocs because of insistence on this ideological independence and distinct identity is the 1961-controversy between Kruschev and a visiting U.A.R. parliamentary delegation headed by the then chairman of the National Assembly, Anwar El-Sadat. The Soviet Premier came to Arab socialism and stated :

> "We operate on socialist bases. You, the Arabs, now understand this, but you do not understand what socialism which leads to Communism is ... You are like a person learning the alphabet ... You are learning the 'A'. Socialism is the first letter in the alphabet which organizes human society, while 'B' is the beginning of Communism. If you seek socialism you should not say you are against Communism, since you place yourselves in an embarrassing situation and fall into the trap of imperialism."[58]

In insisting on ideological independence, El-Sadat answered Kruschev by stating that the Arabs have rejected capitalism

> "not because we hate it but because we believe it does not suit the nature, conditions, hopes, needs and requirements of our people ...

[55] Dekmejian : *op. cit.,* p. 132. But see especially the detailed discussion that Nasser had with "the Popular Forces" after submitting *El-Mithaq* (The National Charter) in May 1962. Nasser's first distinction between "Arab Socialism and Communism" turns around religion. See Nasser's *Speeches : op. cit.,* Vol. IV, pp. 35-95, but especially p. 89 and 92.

[56] El-Sharabassy : *op. cit.,* p. 6.

[57] Dekmejian : *op. cit.,* p. 57 (emphasis added). For a very thorough and detailed analysis in English, see Sayegh, Fayez : "The Theoretical Structure of Nasser's Arab Socialism", in *Middle Eastern Affairs,* No. 4, edited by Albert Hourani, St. Antony's Papers, No. 17, O.U.P., 1965, pp. 9-56.

[58] "The Sadat-Khruschev Exchange", *The Egyptian Economic and Political Review,* Cairo, May-June 1961, pp. 25-28, as quoted in Cremeans : *op. cit.,* pp. 290-292.

This does not mean that communism, which proved successful in conditions prevailing in other countries, is suitable for successful application in our country."

Then comes El-Sadat's emphasis on both a distinct identity and a potential ideological contribution :

"Our people refuse to be limited to this choice and believe that the ideological scope in the world is bigger than this closed circle. Our people also believe they are capable, without becoming isolated from the world's wealth of ideologies, of participating *creatively* in adding to this wealth." [59]

The interaction between the different variables of the national component in the 'definition of the situation' was explicitly stated in a 1963-publication of the Egyptian government. [60] After discussing the interdependence between Arab socialism and Arab nationalism, it went on to say :

"The fact that Arab socialism is so closely connected with Arab nationalism protects it from being influenced by any outside doctrines to the detriment of its own people."

Then it linked Arab socialism to the Arabs' search for their own identity : " Its concept is basically that of building and protecting the identity of the . . . people as such."

It then unites between Arab socialism and non-alignment or positive neutralism :

"This philosophy [Arab socialism] has also been the basis for the policy of positive neutralism, [since] by . . . not becoming involved in the identities of other systems, it is able to continue in its advancement toward bettering the lives of the people." [61]

---

[59] *Ibid.* (emphasis added).

[60] For instance, this governmental publication said : "Arab Socialism and Arab Nationalism are interchangeable, interacting one upon another. The desire of the Arab people to maintain their own entity as such and the necessity of raising the standard of living for these people in order to maintain this entity in this highly competitive modern world, make socialism and nationalism interdependent upon each other." United Arab Republic, Information Department : *Arab Socialism, op. cit.*, p. 9.

[61] *Ibid.* The last sentence (*i.e.* "bettering the lives of the people") suggests that in addition to its psychological appeal, such a 'nationalised' socialism is economically functional. It is thus thought of as an efficient vehicle for realising "the transition from traditional and subsistence economies to an expanding and developing dynamic system" through government planning. See *El-Mithaq* (The National Charter), *op. cit.*, where chapter VI is significantly entitled "On the Necessity of the Socialist Solution" ; chapter VII on "Production and Society" ; and chapter VIII treating "Socialist Application and its Problems", pp. 49-92. See also Nasser's discussion with the "Popular Forces", Nasser's *Speeches, op. cit.*, Vol. IV, pp. 35-95, and also Paul Sigmund, Jr. (ed.) : *The Ideologies of the Developing Nations,* New York. Praeger, 1963, pp. 11-22.

Equally explicit in emphasising the 'nationalised' socialism/neutralism linkage is Egypt's English-speaking magazine, the *Scribe* : "Socialism and neutralism realize the same aim inside and outside. Socialism is to internal policy what neutralism is to external policy." [62]

We shall see that this "not becoming involved in the identities of other systems" [63] or ideological independence was the predominant element in Nasser's "third road" policy, as practised in what this chapter calls the Third Phase in the pattern of Egypt's non-aligned behaviour. It is precisely this pattern of non-aligned behaviour that we must now consider.

2. The Pattern of Egypt's Non-Aligned Behaviour

2.1. In order to grasp the behavioural pattern of Egypt's "positive neutralism" or non-alignment, two characteristics of this pattern have to be kept in mind :

1. the predominantly nationalist context of Egyptian non-alignment which *mingled with Egyptian nationalism* during British occupation and with Arab nationalism from 1955-1956 ;
2. its primarily pragmatic aspect giving it "the *evolutionary* process through which it came into its own" [64] as we shall see in its different phases.

---

[62] "Arab Socialism : Pilot Experience of Young Nations", *The Scribe* (special issue), Cairo, 1962, p. 23 ; as quoted in Choucri : *Egypt's Role . . ., op. cit.*, p. 140.

[63] On "the specificity" of Egypt's identity, see : Abdel Malek : *Egypt : Military Society, op. cit.*, pp. 353-372 ; Abdel Malek : *Dirassat fi El-Thaqafa El-Wataniyya, op. cit.*, pp. 265-411 ; 'Ewais : *Hadith 'An El-Thaqafa, op. cit.*, pp. 47-275 ; Amin, Ahmed : *Qamous El-'Adat wa El-Taqalid El-Misriyya* (A Dictionary of Egyptian Customs and Traditions), Cairo, Matb't Lagnat El-Taäleef wa El-Targama wa El-Nashr, 1953 ; 'Ayrout, Henri : *El-Fallahoon,* Cairo, Moässat El-Halaby, 1968, especially pp. 150-291 (this book first appeared in French and was published by Payot in 1938, then was republished in 1952 as *Fellahs d'Egypte,* Cairo, Editions du Sphinx. The book has also been translated into English and was published in 1962 as *The Egyptian Peasant*) ; Fouad, Ne'mat : "Shakhssiyyat Misr fi El-Adab El-Sha'bi" (Egypt's Identity in Folk Literature), in *Qiräat fi 'Elm El-Nafs El-Igtma'i fi El-Bilad El-'Arabiyya* (Readings in Social Psychology in Arab countries), *op cit.*, Vol. II, pp. 537-552 ; Rabi', Hamed : "Hawl El-Tahlil El-'Elmi Limafhoum El-Tabe' El-Qawmi El-Misri" (On the Scientific Analysis of Egyptian National Character), in *ibid.*, pp. 519-537 ; Melika, Lewis : "Bin El-Eegabiyyah wa El-Lamobalah : Dirasat Li-Itgahat El-Qarawiyyeen Nahwa El-'Aml El-Gam'i Fi Khams Sanawat" (Between Active Involvement and Indifference : A Study of Villagers' Attitudes toward Collective Work over a Five-Year Period), in *ibid.*, pp. 611-620 ; Hemdan, Gamal : *Shakhssiyyat Misr* (Egypt's Identity), El-Nahda, Cairo, 1967.

[64] Sayegh, Fayez : "Neutralism in the United Arab Republic", in Sayegh : *Dynamics of Neutralism in the Arab World, op. cit.*, pp. 163-224.

2.1.1. *Egyptian non-alignment and Egyptian nationalism:* It might seem paradoxical to state that Egypt's "positive neutralism" or non-alignment has been more organically related to a national context rather than to the issues of the cold war as such. In the late 19th century, Mahmud Sami El-Barudi Pasha, Egypt's Prime Minister before the 1882-British occupation, hoped that Egypt could be declared "a neutral republic like Switzerland".[65] This hope was enunciated when the slogan of *El-Hizb El-Watani* (the Nationalist Party), of which El-Barudi Pasha was precisely a founder member, was "Egypt for the Egyptians".[66] Lutfi El-Sayed —the inheritor of the slogan "Egypt for the Egyptians" in the early 20th century[67]—commented, in the pages of the newspaper *El-Garida,* on the 1911-Italian attack on Tripoli in the following way:

> "This is the occasion to realise what I have always been advocating: Egypt should be for the Egyptians. I have been warning—timidly—that the duty of Egypt in this war is to stick to neutrality. Turkish sovereignty does not either protect or profit Egypt . . . and the only way to get rid of British occupation is through [national] solidarity and self-reliance."[68]

This explains why in the late 1940's Egypt's neutralist overtones contained little reference to the ideological issues or the politico-military antagonisms dividing the cold-war blocs. The fact that the early years of the cold war coincided not only with rising impatience with, and struggle against, British occupation forces, but also with the war in Palestine, accounts for Egyptians' relative unconcern and disinterest in the cold war and the concentration of their attention on matters nearer home. An illustration of Egypt's attitude was its position as a member of the Security Council during the Korean War. Egypt preferred not to vote on the Security Council resolution of 27 June 1950, which asked U.N. members to furnish military or relief assistance to the Republic of Korea. The Egyptian representative announced, on 30 June, that "had he received

---

[65] El-Hadidi, 'Ali: *Abdallah El-Nadim,* Cairo, Maktabat Misr (A'lam El-'Arab, No. 9), 1961, p. 203. Moreover, after the 1882-'Orabi Revolution, one of its leaders, El-Sheikh Mohamed 'Abduh, confided to Blunt: "From the very start of our movement, we were aiming to transform Egypt into a small republic similar to that of Switzerland." Blunt, Wilfrid: *Secret History of the English Occupation in Egypt,* London, 1907, p. 344, as quoted in Mustafa, Ahmed: *Misr wa El-Masäala El-Misriyya* (Egypt and the Egyptian Question 1876-1882), Cairo, Dar El-Ma'aref, n.d.

[66] El-Sayed, Afaf Lutfi: *Egypt and Cromer: A Study in Anglo-Egyptian Relations,* London, John Murray, 1968, pp. 9-20.

[67] El-Sayed, Ahmed Lutfi: *Qissat 'Hayati* (My Life History), Cairo, Dar El-Hilal, 1962.

[68] El-Naggar, Hussein: *Lutfi El-Sayed wa El-Shakhssiyya El-Misriyya* (Lutfi El-Sayed and the Egyptian Identity), Cairo, Maktabat El-Qahira, 1963, p. 128.

instructions when the Council was voting ... he would have abstained from voting". He went on to explain his position by reminding the Council that

> "several cases of aggression against peoples, and violations of the sovereignty and unity of territory of States Members of the United Nations had been submitted to the Security Council, which had not taken any action to end those aggressions and violations as it was then doing in the case of Korea." [69]

The Egyptian representative was here referring to the Western-inspired U.N. failure to give satisfaction to Egypt in both the 1947-Suez conflict with Britain in the Security Council, and in the Palestinian partition.

This nationalist context of Egyptian non-alignment is even clearer when we analyse the few references to non-alignment in the pre-1952 secret tracts of *El-Dubbat El-Ahrar*. Thus the different tracts insist that "freedom and independence should be untouched and complete, without any alliance with imperialism". [70] The tract of March 22, 1952 concludes with the slogans : "Down with imperialism, down with alliance with imperialism ; down with common defence schemes and collective security under the domination of imperialism". Less than 10 days before the coup d'état, the tract of July 14, 1952 asserted "the word of *El-Dubbat El-Ahrar* which is in agreement with the word of the people : ... no alliance, no defence schemes and non-participation in an imperialist bloc, but complete, full independence and freedom, and open, straightforward neutrality". [71]

Given all these formative elements in Egyptian non-alignment, the conclusions of an Arab scholar are confirmed :

> "... Egyptian *non-alignment* ... was waged as a continuation of the struggle for national liberation. And the ... exercise of *positive neutralism* was at once a nationalistic assertion of the right to self-determination and freedom of orientation and a strategy calculated to aid the country during its difficult period of economic development and social modernization. Even when neutralism of the U.A.R. finally developed into a clear attitude toward cold-war issues as such, the initial relationship between neutralism and nationalism persisted, surviving the successive transformations which it had undergone over the years. Neutralism continues until today to be looked upon as an

---

[69] *Yearbook of the United Nations : 1950,* New York, United Nations, 1951, pp. 224-227, as quoted in F. Sayegh : "Neutralism in the United Arab Republic", *op. cit.,* pp. 171-172.

[70] El-Barrawi, Rashed : *Haqiqat El-Inqlab El-Akhir Fi Misr* (The Military Coup in Egypt, 1952), Cairo, Maktabat El Nahda, 1952, pp. 205-210.

[71] *Ibid.,* pp. 200-201.

aspect of nationalism ; its espousal is still proclaimed and defended in relation to nationalism ; and it remains one of the cardinal objectives of the nationalist movement." [72]

2.1.2. *The primarily pragmatic aspect of Egyptian non-alignment and its evolutionary process :* There is nothing to indicate that *El-Dubbat El-Ahrar* had thought out or decided upon an operational and coherent foreign policy programme. The few brief references to non-alignment in their secret tracts indicated a clear conception of what needed to be done, but were vague as to the applicable measures to achieve their goals. Their major immediate objective was the evacuation of British troops and the achievement of "complete, full independence" so that Egypt could occupy its status in the international system. Moreover, in neither Nasser's *The Philosophy of the Revolution* nor in Anwar El-Sadat's *Révolte sur le Nil* are the premises of non-alignment elaborated or non-alignment itself even mentioned. This is why Egypt's non-alignment tended to be—especially before the late 1950's—an *ad hoc* reaction to events governed principally by Egypt's traditional nationalist aspirations :

> "Nasser was thus the first of the . . . *unconcernedly undoctrinaire* neutralists—many African neutralist leaders of the post-1957 period are like this now, their strength and weaknesses, like those of Nasser, depending very much on the nationalist movement they lead." [73]

But while being pragmatic, Egypt's non-alignment displayed an evolutionary process. This pragmatically-based evolutionary process accounts for the problems scholars face in attempting to fix the starting-point of Egypt's non-alignment :

> "Egypt's neutralist policy", Lyon complained, "has no obvious starting point comparable with Yugoslavia's break with the Cominform or India's achievement of independence. For an Egyptian it might be dated from the onset of the Cold War, or from the July Revolution of 1952, or from the conclusion of the Anglo-Egyptian agreement of October 1954 regarding the British evacuation of the Suez base, or from the actual departure of the last of the British troops from Suez in 1956—a few weeks before Nasser announced the nationalization of the Suez Canal Company." [74]

This brings us to our next point : the behavioural pattern of Egypt's non-alignment, which can be divided into 4 phases.

---

[72] F. Sayegh : "Neutralism in the United Arab Republic", *op. cit.*, pp. 165-166.

[73] Lyon : *Neutralism, op. cit.*, p. 150 (emphasis added).

[74] *Ibid.*, p. 138.

2.2. *Expression of Protest and Groping for a Non-Aligned Behavioural Pattern 1952-1955*

The lack of an "obvious starting point" in Egypt's non-alignment is due to another lack : absence of agreement on a certain ideology and/or well-defined operational programme on the part of *El-Dubbat El-Ahrar*. We have seen that Nasser admitted it and stated that this was intentional. The result as far as foreign policy behaviour was concerned, however, is that there was no sharp break between the new regime and the pre-1952 political forces that dominated the Egyptian political system. [75].

We have indicated that during the Korean War, Egypt adopted basically a "non-aligned" position. Moreover, on 8 October 1951, Nahas Pasha—the head of the Wafd government—announced in the Parliament Egypt's decision to abolish the 1936-Anglo-Egyptian Treaty of "Friendship and Alliance". On 14 October 1951, the Egyptian cabinet met and decided to reject the Allied Middle East Command (the substitute for the abolished 1936-Anglo-Egyptian Treaty) submitted the previous day by the ambassadors of Great Britain, France, Turkey and the U.S.A. to Egypt's foreign minister. [76] A secret tract of *El-Dubbat El-Ahrar* expressed its support for the refusal of the "quadrite pact". [77] On 22 and 29 April 1952, Sayed Qutb—the ideologue of *El-Ikhwan*—wrote two articles in the Moslem Brethren's newspaper, *El-Da'wa,* advocating the establishment of "an Islamic bloc distinct from both the Western and Eastern blocs". [78]

2.2.1. *El-Dubbat El-Ahrar* continued to reflect this general anti-alliance (*i.e.* anti-British occupation of the Canal zone) "public opinion mood". The colour of their foreign policy behaviour from July 1952 to the early part of 1955 (*i.e.* the first phase of what Nasser called later "positive neutralism") adopted the same general principles as previous royal cabinets. During this phase the new regime's policy was limited to reactions against Western pressures rather than taking "positive neutralist" initiatives, reactions which purported to withhold support and get concessions rather than to seek a strong international counterweight.

---

[75] As Abdel Malek rightly remarked : "Fathi Radwan and Ehsan Abdel Koddus ... underscored the lack of a general policy and an ideology on the part of the military leadership until 1954. Let us look at *The Philosophy of the Revolution* which bears the date of the same year : there is no mention of positive neutralism or even of neutrality ; there is no definition of principle with respect to relations with the forces that were in conflict for the world." *Egypt : Military Society, op. cit.,* p. 222.

[76] El-Bishri : *op. cit.,* pp. 486-487 ; F. Sayegh : "Neutralism in the United Arab Republic", *op. cit.,* pp. 176-177.

[77] El-Barrawi : *op. cit.,* p. 199.

[78] El-Bishri : *op. cit.,* p. 578.

The bases of this attitude are nicely put in a 1950-article by Salah Ed-Din El-Bitar, a prominent leader of the Arab Socialist *Ba'ath* Party who later became Syria's foreign minister, and who in fact negotiated with Nasser the terms of the Egypto-Syrian union. After discussing the bipolar structure in the international system, El-Bitar analysed the 'Arab situation' : "The Arabs are seeking new social and political forms, but they are not finding the answers they want in either the American or the Soviet system. Moreover, Western imperialism divided the Arab homeland, maintained it in a divided condition, took away Palestine, drove out its people, made it Jewish and continues in its efforts to make Arab lands Jewish. Thus the Arab position must reflect an *attitude toward the West which is in harmony with the lack of Western justice*" (the element of protest). "It must strengthen the Arab case in the U.N., so that the smaller nations will be astonished and ask why the Arabs *so behave* when they are non-communist states . . ." (the withholding of support). "When they learn the answer, the smaller states will press the U.S., the U.K. and France to change their duplicitous policies" [79] (the demand for concessions). Disengagement, then, was an expression of a protest against the unfaithfulness of Western states and a "demand for justice" toward their Arab partners.

The "demand for justice"—according to Cairo—could come from Britain's acceptance of Egypt's nationalist aspirations, but mainly through U.S. pressure. [80] Already in 1947 the Egyptian cabinet believed that a campaign of information in America was of prime importance. Discussion groups and research projects about the bases and technicalities of an information campaign were initiated. A special information bureau was attached to the cabinet, and an American expert was appointed at its head. This American expert became advisor to Nuqrashi Pasha—Egypt's Prime Minister and head of its delegation to submit the country's case against

[79] El-Bitar, Salah : *Arab Policy,* Beirut, 1960, pp. 23-27, as quoted in Binder, Leonard : "Egypt's Positive Neutrality", in Morton Kaplan (ed.) : *The Revolution in World Politics,* London and New York, John Wiley and Sons, 1962, pp. 175-192 (emphasis and brackets added).

[80] Thus Heikal stated : "... growing American involvement in the Middle East ... was looked on with hope by many people in the area. The whole picture of the United States at that time was a glamorous one. Britain and France were fading, hated empires. Russia was five thousand miles away and the ideology of Communism was anathema to the Moslem Religion. But America had emerged from the Second World War richer, more powerful and more appealing than ever. Hollywood was churning out war pictures in which the Americans were the heroes and the others were the villains. Refrigerators, television, all the new instruments of the new life seemed to be coming from America. So the United States wore an aura of success and glamour, shining out above the tarnished failure of the old imperialists, and people were receptive to the idea of the Americans playing a major role in the Middle East." Heikal : *Nasser : The Cairo Documents, op. cit.,* pp. 44-45.

Britain before the Security Council in 1947.[81] As soon as he arrived in New York, Nuqrashi Pasha declared : "I am sure that America will appreciate the Egyptians' efforts to acquire the sovereignty of their country and security of their land." In the American Press Club, the Prime Minister delivered a speech—"prepared by the American Information advisor"—in which he violently attacked communism and the Soviet system and sollicited Western trust in "democratic and anti-communist" Egypt.[82] Four years later, Nahas Pasha assured some members of the Wafd Party after the abolition of the 1936-Anglo-Egyptian Treaty by affirming : ". . . the Americans are on our side . . . The American ambassador is supporting us but this should not be mentioned to anyone . . . I am very sure of this . . . and Salah Ed-Din [Egypt's foreign minister at the time] phoned from Paris to assure us that the British would be forced to leave the Suez Canal zone because there is pressure on England."[83]

Similarly,[84] General Naguib wrote after the coup d'état :

> "I believe the United States is the one power on earth that is capable of dealing with the Arab states on equitable terms. I say this in spite of the partiality that the United States has displayed in the recent past in its dealing with Israel."[85]

2.2.2. A foreign assistance agreement between Egypt and the U.S., valid till June 30, 1954, was signed in Cairo on February 23, 1953, by Egypt's Foreign Minister Fawzi and U.S. ambassador Caffery. But this would not be allowed to jeopardise the new regime's stand on Egypt's constant basic demands for complete evacuation of British troops before the signing of any defence pacts with the West. Thus already on December 10, 1952, Prime Minister Naguib declared that : "Egypt desires to join in an overall alliance for the purpose of defending the Middle East, but *only after her national aspirations have been satisfied*."[86]

---

[81] El-Bishri : *op. cit.*, pp. 144-145.

[82] *Ibid.*

[83] Sabri, Mousa : *Qissat Malik wa Arba' Wizarat* (The Story of a King and Four Cabinets), Cairo, Dar El-Qalam, n.d., pp. 58-59.

[84] Thus "one ironic symptom of America's growing importance in Egypt at that time is that on the night of the Revolution, the leaders of both sides, President Nasser and King Faruq, sent messengers to the American Ambassador, Mr. Jefferson Caffery . . .

So there were connected events which were highly symbolic of America's position and influence at that time. Her representative was the last man to see off the remains of the old regime and the first in contact with the new." Heikal : *Nasser : The Cairo Documents, op. cit.*, pp. 45-47.

[85] Naguib : *Egypt's Destiny, op. cit.*, p. 261, as quoted in Choucri : *Egypt's Role, op. cit.*, p. 136.

[86] *Middle Eastern Affairs,* Vol. IV (1953) (emphasis added), *op. cit.*, p. 31.

Less than a month later, Naguib repeated: "Egypt will never join a Western alliance for the defence of the Middle East *so long as British troops are in the Suez Canal zone.*" [87]

On July 21, 1954, *Al-Ahram* reproduced Nasser's declaration: "No defence scheme would succeed *before* the settlement of the issue on British evacuation from the Suez Canal Zone" (emphasis added).

What we notice in these declarations is that the refusal to participate in Western alliance was not absolute or a general principle, but rather temporary and conditional on the *prior* evacuation of British troops, as the Wafd cabinet insisted in 1951. This is why the leaders of the new regime refused to discuss the issue of participation in the West's common defence schemes while negotiating the evacuation issue. They only accepted to negotiate officially with the occupying state alone and refused to give the impression that Egypt was negotiating with "the West". Consequently the attempt to bring the U.S.A. into the discussion on the Suez Base issue met with a rebuff in order to reject the implied suggestion of joint defence schemes. [88] Thus on March 15, 1953, Prime Minister Naguib declared emphatically: "The U.S. may take part in the Suez talks only to the extent of providing its good offices."

As if to confirm what he said, Naguib followed up his declaration by meeting—separately—with the American and British ambassadors in Cairo. On March 16, the Revolutionary Command Council and the Council of Ministers met jointly to reiterate their rejection of U.S. participation in the Suez talks beyond the extent of good offices. The U.S. had no choice but to accept the new regime's objections, and the American ambassador in Cairo—Jefferson Caffery—declared that the U.S. had no wish to take part in any discussions regarding the Suez question unless asked to do so by both Egypt and Great Britain.

2.2.3. But while Anglo-Egyptian negotiations were not advancing as fast as the new regime hoped, disillusionment with the U.S. started to take place among the new elite. Not only did America not want to anger its ally, Britain, by supporting Egypt's demand for full evacuation, but also Washington indefinitely "shelved" an Egyptian demand for arms. When contacts first started, Washington seemed to respond positively. An Egyptian mission was asked to come to the U.S. to—according to William Forster, the American Assistant Secretary for Defence—"tour military bases, talk to the men responsible for supplying arms and arrange for deliveries". [89] But when the mission went to Washington (Autumn 1952)

[87] *Ibid.*, p. 73 (emphasis added).

[88] *New York Times,* March 26, 1953.

[89] Heikal: *Nasser: The Cairo Documents, op. cit.*, p. 48.

the old idea of an anti-Soviet, Islamic military pact was again linked to the satisfaction of Egypt's demand for arms. As Nasser's alter-ego expressed it :

> "The man who put up the idea was General Olmstead, Director of the foreign military aid programme. He told the mission that the potential of an Islamic pact would be great. It would contain three capitals : Ankara, capital of the most modern Islamic country ; Karachi, capital of the most populous Islamic country ; and Cairo, capital of the most prestigious Islamic country. He went on to say that such a pact, apart from defending the Middle East, could have an enormous impact on Moslems in the Soviet Union and China. Then he shocked everybody by talking about how a fifth column could be created in those countries. It was quite astonishing because it was completely outside the context of the mission.
>
> He pushed aside a curtain covering a big map on the wall of his office. The map was full of pins and flags. He took a pointer and started to demonstrate what the markers stood for and then he pointed to an area where there were few pins and said : 'Gentlemen, we ought to put some pins and flags here. There is a vacuum here.' And he was talking about the area covered by the proposed Islamic Pact . . ." [90]

However, the Egyptian mission tried to continue negotiating the arms purchases without linking this to the issue of mutual security or common defence pacts. Nasser was so confident of success that he told his army men that they would be receiving new weapons soon. But the weapons were not shipped. Then the Egyptian mission was told that :

> "Eisenhower was about to take over from Truman. Nothing could be done until the new President had taken office. But . . . the Egyptian request was already on the desk of the new President and it would be one of the first things he would decide." [91]

But about five months after Eisenhower became officially President, no decision was communicated to Cairo. At last, when Dulles arrived on May 11, 1953 for an Egyptian visit, Nasser asked him about the reason for the delay of the arms shipments. Dulles offered the first explanation :

> "Sir Winston Churchill had telephoned the newly-elected President and urged him not to sell arms to the Egyptians and to start his Presidency by providing weapons which might be used to kill British tommies who had served under Eisenhower during the war.

---

[90] *Ibid.*, p. 49.

[91] *Ibid.*, p. 50, also Heikal : *Nahn . . . wa Amrica, op. cit.*, pp. 68-81.

This plea ... affected Ike deeply ... So Eisenhower decided to do nothing. He did not refuse the arms outright. He just kept the application in the 'pending' file." [92]

2.2.4. Precisely, Dulles' first (and only) meeting with Nasser showed how much the perception of American decision-makers differed from that of the Egyptians. When Dulles arrived at Cairo Airport in May 1953 (only four months after taking over the State Department), he expressed his hope that the Suez problem could be solved by recognition of full Egyptian sovereignty and that "all [could] be arranged, however, so that the important base ... be available ... on behalf of the free world in the event of future hostilities". [93] On the two issues of the meaning of "Free World" and the foreign use of the Canal base, Nasser had wide differences with Dulles. First, the phrase "Free world" had unfortunate connotations for Egypt

> "because we have been occupied by the British to secure the communications of 'the Free World' and so for us 'the Free World' has come to mean imperialism and domination and when you used that phrase this morning it created a bad effect." [94]

Secondly, Dulles and Nasser differed over the target of common defence pacts, over 'who is the enemy ?'. For Dulles it was—without the slightest doubt—the Soviet Union, but Nasser was of a very different opinion.

> "Why ?" Nasser asked astonished, "The Soviet Union is 5,000 miles away and we've never had any trouble with them. They have never attacked us. They have never occupied our territory. They have never had a base here, but the British have been here for seventy years."
>
> "All right", Dulles said, "but under the pact the British who stay here in the base would belong to the pact and they would not be allowed to raise the British flag ; they would be under the flag of the pact."
>
> "If I went", Nasser retorted, "and told my people that the British status here is going to be changed from [that of] occupiers to partners by a change of flag, they will laugh at me.
>
> "They will lose faith in me and other people will rise from the underground and win the confidence of the people. If I stop lead-

---

[92] Heikal : *Nasser : The Cairo Documents, op. cit.*, p. 50. Dulles, however, added : "The question of selling arms to Egypt would be easiest if Egypt could come to an agreement with Britain, especially if this agreement is within a system of collective defence of the Middle East." Heikal : *Nahn ... wa Amrica, op. cit.*, p. 77.

[93] *Documents on International Affairs,* 1953, London, O.U.P., pp. 341-342, as quoted in El-Sayed, Raouf : *The Baghdad Pact in World Politics,* a Ph.D. thesis presented to the Graduate Institute of International Studies (Geneva), 1971, p. 28.

[94] Heikal : *Nasser : The Cairo Documents, op. cit.*, p. 44.

ing my people as a nationalist, then the Communists are going to lead them. They would use my partnership in pacts with you to say that I am a stooge.

"How can I go to my people and tell them I am disregarding a killer with a pistol sixty miles from me at the Suez Canal to worry about somebody who is holding a knife 5,000 miles away? They would tell me, 'first things first'. People must first own their independence before they are really interested in defending it." [95]

2.2.5. Less than a month after Dulles' visit, there was a significant occurrence which went unnoticed by many analysts : Nehru's stop-over in Cairo and his meeting with General Naguib on June 23, 1963. Non-aligned India had then all the prestige accruing from its crucial role in the settlement of the Korean conflict. Moreover, for Nehru non-alignment was more than the mere opposition to the "imperialist pacts" near home, for he was busy emphasising its global dimensions : the promotion of a "third area" and the formation of "an area of peace". [96] This visit certainly—if only indirectly—opened new horizons to the Egyptian regime, situated its resistance to Western pressures for bloc-membership within a wider international movement, and made its *ad hoc* reactions acquire ideological respectability. Thus an Egyptian spokesman indicated after Nehru's visit : "It is possible that Egypt may ally herself with the neutralist bloc of Asian nations *in order to try to put an end to the imperialist occupation of the Suez Canal Zone by Great Britain.*" [97]

In the meantime Naguib was portrayed in India as "Egypt's Gandhi", and a trade agreement with India providing the "most favoured nation" treatment was signed in Cairo on July 8, 1953.

Consequently, British attempts to link the evacuation issue with participation in Western defence schemes ; Britain's negation of Egypt's nationalist aspirations ; what seemed U.S. siding with "its ally Britain" against Egypt ; and the visit of Nehru ("the apostle of neutralism") ; all constituted basic factors in the shaping of what Nasser would call later 'positive

---

[95] *Ibid.,* p. 51. And Nasser continued to stress the integrative function of non-alignment in the prismatic political system : "We believe that our participation in Western military alliances or in any other alliance with foreign countries would not be of any use to the constitution of a solid domestic front. On the contrary it would weaken it." Nasser then concluded by refusing to discuss any common defence schemes *at that time : "Now* we are not thinking of anything except British evacuation ... Once this is achieved and once our people feel they have attained their long-term aspirations ... we can entertain any proposals you want to put forward for discussion." Heikal : *Nahn ... wa Amrica, op. cit.,* pp. 79-80) (emphasis added).

[96] Mallik : *op. cit.,* pp. 128-129.

[97] *New York Times,* June 25, 1973, as quoted in Abdel Malek : *Egypt : Military Society, op. cit.,* p. 226 (emphasis added).

neutralism'. Thus on November 20, 1953, Nasser declared in Minia El-Qamh :

> "Take the U.S., for instance. All the newspapers affirm that it will give us loans and help us to carry out our development projects ; that the U.S. helps the needy countries to raise their health, social, economic and cultural standards.
>
> But here we are fourteen months after the revolution without receiving anything. We no longer believe in these hollow promises and deceptions.
>
> *We should count on ourselves,* and not lead ourselves to believe that our enemy will help us while it is working to weaken us.
>
> The reason is clear : the U.S. is intimately linked with its ally, Britain. Both of them have a common enemy : Russia. The U.S. would not satisfy us if this makes Britain angry. This is why you should never believe that the U.S. will help us, because the U.S. and its ally, England, have the same pre-determined policy. Consequently, *if we want to build a strong country and to have our sons free, we should have self-confidence and practice self-reliance.*" [98]

2.2.6. On December 9, 1953, *Al-Ahram* quoted a government spokesman affirming that Egypt would be neutralist in any eventual conflict as long as its nationalist demands remained unsatisfied. Envoys "were recalled for consultation to help bend foreign policy in a neutralist direction". [99] Thus on January 4, 1954 a special meeting in Cairo of Egyptian ambassadors to the USSR, the U.S., Britain and France, together with the Egyptian members in the Anglo-Egyptian negotiations, discussed the foreign policy of Egypt. The ambassador to Moscow, Aziz al-Misri, [100] a veteran soldier-politician and a prestigious nationalist, explained that "the Soviet Union has always supported national causes . . . Countries do not support one another unless they have mutual interests based on give and take . . . Russia is a great country." [101] On March 10, a trade agreement providing for "most favoured nation" treatment was signed with the USSR. On March 22, a joint communiqué issued simultaneously in Cairo and Moscow said that the Government of the Republic of Egypt and the Government of the USSR had decided to strengthen and promote relations between the two countries and to raise their respective legations to the rank of embassies.

But Western states did not seem to judge these indicators as significant. Thus when the Secretary-General of the Arab League—during his 1954-

---

[98] Nasser's *Speeches, op. cit.,* Vol. I, pp. 73-75 (emphasis added).

[99] *Middle Eastern Affairs,* Vol. V (1954), pp. 59-60.

[100] Khadduri, Majid : "'Aziz 'Ali Al-Misri and the Arab Nationalist Movement", in *Middle Eastern Affairs,* St. Antony's Papers No. 17, *op. cit.,* pp. 140-164.

[101] *Middle Eastern Affairs,* Vol. V, *op. cit.,* pp. 59-60.

winter visit to the U.S.—threatened the Western bloc with Arab indifference and disaffection if not defection, American decision-makers interpreted this as only an attempt at blackmail. [102] Consequently, preparations for the conclusion of the 'Northern tier' project continued and materialised. On April 2, 1953 a Turko-Pakistani alliance was concluded in Karachi. Since this was only a start, and the Western project was destined to persuade at least some Arab states to join in, Egypt's new regime tried to counteract Western pressures. Thus Salah Salem—Minister of Orientation and National Guidance—started in the Summer of 1954 an Arab tour to encourage members of the Arab League to refuse participation in Western alliances. Nevertheless, the refusal of bloc-membership with the West still seemed conditional rather than absolute and a matter of principle.

Thus after one of the deadlocks in the Anglo-Egyptian negotiations, Nasser declared in May 1954 that the Egyptians insisted on unconditional evacuation without linking this issue to common defence of the Middle East. Linking the two was perceived as "a new form of colonialism" since—for the 'people'—alliance with the colonial power would not be *materially* different from occupation by the colonial power. Indeed, *legally* Egypt would sign an evacuation agreement according it *formal* independence, but for the Egyptian citizen foreign troops would still be there occupying a part of the national territory. Consequently, "complete, full independence" should not be negated by *prior* commitment to participate in Western defence pacts nor be subjected to preconceived restrictions in foreign policy matters. Nasser repeated the argument he had used with Dulles a year earlier : "If he entered into a pact *before* the British evacuated the Canal Zone it would look as if he was being forced into it by the pressure of the 80,000 British soldiers in the Suez Canal bases." [103] Consequently, "we are not ready to discuss pacts or any security measures unless we do it of our own free will" [104] he said. Similarly, the big headline of *Al-Ahram* on July 1, 1954 summarised the outcome of Salem's visit to Lebanon by announcing : "Egypt and Lebanon agree to refuse discussing Western defence proposals *before* a solution is found to the Arab cause" (emphasis added).

On July 21, *Al-Ahram* reproduced another declaration by Nasser : "No defence scheme will succeed *before* the settlement of the issue on British evacuation from the Suez Canal" (emphasis added).

---

[102] This is also the opinion of Abdel Malek who says "... the first large commercial transactions with the socialist countries were intended, in the minds of the Egyptian rulers, to force the hand of the West and no more". *Egypt : Military Society, op. cit.*, p. 223.

[103] Heikal : *Nasser : The Cairo Documents, op. cit.*, p. 51.

[104] *Ibid.*

2.2.7. In October 1954, the Anglo-Egyptian Evacuation Agreement was signed in Cairo. Did this guarantee the new regime's readiness to participate in Western defence schemes ? And if not, why did the insistence on a non-aligned position continue, since the new regime's refusals of alliance-participation were conditional and the *sine qua non* seemed to be satisfied ?

Two interpretations can be deduced from the chronology of events and the official declarations or speeches :

1. The new regime had a phased strategy and Nasser's general plan was : get what you can and fight for the rest. In fact, a Lebanese historian quotes the Egyptian leader as saying, after the signing of the Anglo-Egyptian agreement, that since Egypt's historical and first objective had been achieved, its second objective was non-participation in the Western alliance bloc and common defence schemes. [105] Indeed, in *El-Mithaq* (National Charter) Nasser says :

> "Victory over colonialism was not for this great people the end of the road but the beginning of real work. It was the occasion to continue the struggle—from a better position—to guarantee real freedom and to keep it prosperous for ever on this land." [106]

But *El-Mithaq* (National Charter) was prepared in 1962, *i.e.* ten years after Nasser came to power. An important question, then, is whether Nasser had this strategy at the time or whether he developed it in retrospect.

2. The second interpretation of Nasser's refusal to participate in Western alliances immediately after the signature of the Anglo-Egyptian agreement is that the new regime needed a respite during which it could think on Egypt's foreign policy while convincing 'the people' that the 1954-Anglo-Egyptian agreement (unlike the 1936-Treaty which linked independence to Anglo-Egyptian alliance) guaranteed complete independence. [107] This was especially important since tracts were distributed all over the country by—as Nasser admitted—the left (the communists) and the right *(El-Ikhwan)* as well as by "politics-mongers" [108] to refute any gains accruing from the new agreement. Nasser was delivering a public

---

[105] Mahmud, Mustafa : *Abdel Nasser : Qadaya wa Mawaqif* (Abdel Nasser : Issues and Attitudes), Beirut, Publications of Sawt El-'Orouba, 1971, pp. 202-205.

[106] *El-Mithaq, op. cit.,* p. 36.

[107] Nasser said, for instance : "Positive neutralism means independence. In other words I do not yield to one bloc, nor to the influence of any power and I avoid zones of influence." Cremeans : *op. cit.,* p. 278.

[108] See the declarations of Nasser on July 29, 31, August 2, 3, 4, 19, 21, 30, September 5, 19, 20 and October 21, 1954. Nasser's *Speeches, op. cit.,* Vol. I, pp. 188-228.

speech almost every other day to refute anti-regime attacks and convince the people that "this agreement ... has not stipulated any military alliance, any common defence scheme or any other diminishing of our rights ..." [109] and that

> "whereas the 1936-Anglo-Egyptian agreement stipulated a permanent alliance with Britain, the present agreement puts a definitive end to occupation and does not substitute for it any alliance or common defence. For the first time in the history of Egypt, not even one British soldier will stay in the Canal zone." [110]

In this state of affairs, Nasser could not accept participation in Western defence schemes and thus confirm anti-regime attacks on the Anglo-Egyptian agreement and rumours about its "secret clauses". Consequently, he asked for time :

> "We thought that things would not crystallize before the lapse of two years after the British withdrawal from Egypt ; that Egypt would need two years after the evacuation, to think and decide upon the policy it would follow." [111]

In the meantime, Western preoccupation with Middle East defence was not to be neglected, but this defence was to be organised at first by the Arabs themselves and then a little later in contact with the Western bloc. Thus Salem tried to dissuade Iraq from participating in Western alliances by suggesting :

> "Let us call all the Arab countries to a conference and together set up a real defence organization. If Cairo and Baghdad agree to this, all the others will follow. If we, in fact, set up a *purely* Arab pact in this decisive region of the world, with a combined headquarters, a common defence strategy and joint plans for training, for building roads, aerodromes and so on ... then went together to the Western powers and said to them : here is a regional organization ... You have many interests in this area. We want you to help this organization by giving it arms so that it may *repel aggression from any quarter. Our peoples would not be suspicious of a purely Arab organization of this sort.*" [112]

Consequently, both the Egyptian and Iraqi sides recorded in the minutes of their talks their agreement on :

> "... the necessity of reconsidering the Arab Collective Security Pact, with a view to strengthening it and making it a strong, effective

---

[109] *Ibid.,* p. 184.

[110] *Ibid.,* p. 191.

[111] As quoted in R. El-Sayed : *op. cit.,* p. 62.

[112] Salah Salem in a personal interview with Partick Seale, author of *The Struggle for Syria* (London, O.U.P., 1965), p. 203 (emphasis added).

> instrument that will enable the Arab countries to face any danger which may threaten them, and to defend their countries powerfully and efficiently. Each party shall, however, study this question and shall make the necessary contacts with the United States and Britain in this respect. There will be held in the second half of September a further meeting in Cairo between Egypt and Iraq for reviewing the results of the contacts and to resume talks. The two parties will then jointly get in touch with the representatives of Britain and the United States in order to discuss this subject in preparation for its submission to the other Arab states with a view to reaching a general agreement thereon." [113]

Thus whereas *Al-Ahram* affirmed at the end of the Iraqi-Egyptian talks the reaching "of complete agreement and understanding between the two parties on all the topics discussed", [114] Salah Salem declared that *"at this stage* we should pay attention to the consolidation of military and economic force, and the coordination of plans within the Arab area itself rather than outside it". [115] Consequently, contacts with Arab capitals multiplied because "our peoples would not be suspicious of a purely Arab organization". [116] But Britain, for instance, would not wait and we have mentioned how Eden retorted to the demand for a respite by saying : "I know this plea, it is never the right time for some." Thereafter Iraq was courted into participation in the "Baghdad Pact" in February 1955, a year that constituted a crucial milestone in Egypt's non-alignment.

2.3. *The Consolidation of Non-Alignment 1955-1959*

The Baghdad Pact project [117] started formally with the Turco-Pakistani Treaty on April 4, 1953, followed by Anglo-Saxon attempts to incorporate Iraq and Iran into the new "anti-communist" organisation destined

---

[113] *Ibid.,* pp. 61-62.

[114] *Al-Ahram,* 19 August 1954.

[115] *Al-Ahram,* 20 August 1954 (emphasis added).

[116] The former Secretary-General of the Arab League—Abdel Rahman Azzam—supported strongly the new regime's approach to Western defence projects. In a public statement he declared : "The Council of the Arab League adopted in 1947 its first serious resolution : Arab states were not to cooperate with the West [in common defence schemes] *unless their national demands had first been satisfied.* Foremost among these demands were : the achievement of Egypt's nationalist aspirations as regards British evacuation, the solution of the Palestinian problem on the basis of the United Nations resolutions, and the granting of the right to self-determination to the peoples of the Maghreb." *Al-Ahram,* 31 August 1954 (emphasis added).

[117] For a detailed, recent treatment of the Baghdad Pact, see R. El-Sayed : *The Baghdad Pact in World Politics, op. cit.*

to stretch from the Bosphorus to the Indus. Britain was enthusiastic in its welcome of this arrangement, because it offered Britain a new treaty instead of the existing Anglo-Iraqi one which was to expire by 1957. Thus on February 24, 1955, Turkey and Iraq signed their mutual assistance pact, Britain joined on April 5, 1955, followed by Pakistan [118] and Iran in September and November respectively.

2.3.1. Nasser reacted violently [119] to Iraq's 'defection', and this issue was to dominate policies in the Arab subsystem for almost the whole year. Nasser's arguments were diffused through the widely-heard Cairo Radio, which gave them added weight. He also contacted Arab nationalists throughout the subsystem, explaining that Iraq had violated the solidarity of the Arab League in committing itself to outside obligations and threatened to withdraw from the League—a move which would have brought its demise. Nasser's line of attack was simple. He emphasised Pan-Arabism against "imperialism and zionism" and said that the Baghdad Pact was not aimed at the "real" enemy of the Arabs—Israel—but was instead an alliance with those who had created and still supported this "imperialist base" against the Arabs, *i.e.* the Western states.

Not only was the pact unrelated to the Arabs' defence against their "real" enemies, but also it was an "imperialist formula" permitting "imperialist forces" to come back into the Arab world through the backdoor. The appeal of this argument to ex-colonial people was even strengthened when "material evidence" was cited to "prove" its truth. For according to the agreement governing British accession to the Turko-Iraqi pact

> "the airfields in Iraq occupied by Great Britain in accordance with the 1932 treaty were to pass under Iraqi sovereignty ; but the existing facilities of overflying, landing and servicing British aircraft in Iraq were to be maintained and British military personnel would remain in Iraq, under British command, for this purpose, and would enjoy appropriate amenities. Furthermore, the installations on the airfields retained for British use were to remain British property." [120]

---

[118] Egyptian-Indian common opposition to the Baghdad Pact played an important role in bringing India and Egypt closer together. When Nehru visited Cairo in February 1955, an official statement revealed "the existence of an identity of views on the great international questions" between the two countries. As quoted in Abdel Malek : *Egypt : Military Society, op. cit.*, p. 226. On the 30th of March, *Al-Ahram* mentioned the formation of an Indo-Egyptian Friendship Society, headed by Nasser himself with an Egyptian and an Indian as Vice-Presidents. *Al-Ahram,* 30 March 1955. A week later, a friendship treaty was signed between Egypt and India in Cairo and served to popularise the five principles of *Panch Sheel* in Egypt.

[119] One of Nasser's reactions was to form the Cairo-Damascus-Riad military pact, and thus bipolarity seemed to spread into the Arab subsystem.

[120] Geoffrey Barraclough and Rachel Wall (eds.) : *Survey of International Affairs, 1955-1956, op. cit.*, London, 1960, p. 28.

Consequently, as a British analyst summarised the new agreement,

> "the effects of the new agreement were therefore juridical rather than practical ; in other words, although sovereignty and legal ownership passed to Iraq, effective use by Great Britain remained largely undisturbed." [121]

Thus, Iraq's step—as far as the relationship between the Arabs and the Western powers was concerned—meant (Nasser insisted) a return to the old treaty relationships which brought the newly-independent state back into the "imperialist sphere of influence". Instead, an alternative Arab strategy could achieve the Arab nationalist aim of independence by materialising Arab solidarity on the basis of the 1950-Arab League Collective Security Pact. In practice, as Salah Salem expressed it :

1. Efforts have to be focused on arranging and organising the "Arab house", consolidating Arab military and economic capabilities and coordinating Arab efforts and plans. At this stage, no commitments should be concluded with foreign states. This is why Arab states should not participate in the Turko-Pakistani alliance or any other defence arrangements outside the Arab subsystem.

2. This "unification of an Arab policy" (as Turkish newspapers expressed it) would put an end to the Arabs' dispersion of their capabilities and their "wasting of energy" through disunity. Moreover, a 'unified Arab stand' would make of the Arab states a 'weighty' interlocutor, and give them an elevated status in the international system. [122]

And Nasser emphasised why such an "Arab strategy" would appeal to the "masses" *psychologically :* "The Arabs have been colonised for a long time and they are always afraid of falling back again under Western domination." This is why "defence of the area . . . has to spring from the area itself", otherwise the Arabs would not feel that "they are defending their own families, their own children, their own property . . . [but] British or American interests". [123]

---

[121] *Ibid.,* p. 28. This is why "public opinion mood" was provoked in Iraq. Thus El-Gamali was forced to resign on April 19, 1954 because of "an uncooperative parliament and the strong public reaction to his policy towards the Turco-Pakistani Pact". New elections were organised under the supervision of a provisional government. But the new parliament members could still "embarrass any government which sought rapprochement with the West, especially since they had large support from public opinion. In these circumstances the 'strong man' of Iraq had to be brought to power. Nuri as-Said dissolved the parliament and all political parties, held new elections which brought the 'proper' elements to parliament, and several decrees were promulgated to prevent any sort of opposition." R. El-Sayed : *The Baghdad Pact in World Politics, op. cit.,* p. 60.

[122] *Al-Ahram,* July 1st and 6th, August 16th, 19th and 20th, 1954.

[123] Nasser's press interview with Keith Wheeler, *Life* magazine, 14 July 1959. See Nasser's *Speeches, op. cit.,* Vol. II, pp. 454-464.

Consequently, if the Western powers were really interested in having independent states which would provide Middle East defence against "communist danger", they should supply the Arabs with weapons without pressure and without requiring political commitments. Especially they should not insist on retaining the power of command in this field ; this the Arabs themselves were capable of providing without any alignment.

The Baghdad Pact controversy is significant in at least two respects :

(*a*) According to Nasser, he was not only talking for Egypt, but also in the name of a unified Arab strategy. What is characteristic of his speeches at that time is his identification with nationalist Arab aspirations and the transcendence of the interests of individual states and governments.

(*b*) The controversy between the supporters of pro-Western alignment and those of non-alignment was depicted as synonymous with the battle of 'imperialism, zionism and their stooges' against the forces of independence and Arab nationalism. If anyone questioned this equation, the Israeli attack of February 28th on the Egyptian-controlled territory of Gaza (killing 38 people and wounding 31), was to 'prove' that Egypt was paying the price for its opposition to "imperialist" alliances. [124] This 'confirmed' that Nasser—an 'Arab champion'—was the "target of the Arabs' enemies" and this strengthened his position in the Arab subsystem enormously.

2.3.2. But the Israeli attack had another significance for Nasser. It revealed the continuing weakness of the Egyptian armed forces, a situation the army—the basis of the regime's systemic control—could not accept. Nasser needed arms both to strengthen his defences and to maintain the support of the army. This amounted to a review of his whole relations with the 'Great Powers' and was tantamount to a reconsideration of Egyptian traditional international behaviour. Heikal explains his friend's dilemma :

> "He had to get arms from somewhere to face the threat . . .
>
> Nasser tried to buy obsolete arms from Second World War dumps in Belgium. He got a few pieces in Italy. He tried in Sweden, Switzerland and Spain. He tried to get the British to release the eighty Centurian tanks which the Government had contracted to buy before the revolution and which had already been paid for. They sent sixteen and said they would deliver the rest if Egypt would stop attacking the Baghdad Pact.

[124] "Political sources in Khartoum estimate that the Israeli attack is a form of political and military pressure so that Arab states stand on the side of Western pacts or at least attenuate the strong opposition—advocated by Egypt—against the Mendris-Nuri pact." *Al-Ahram,* 7 March 1955.

At the same time our Intelligence Service began to get information about the Israeli arms purchases from France which had started in 1954." [125]

Consequently, it was vital for him to get arms from somewhere. At his first meeting with the new American ambassador, Henry Byroade, Nasser asked him to pass on urgently to Dulles Egypt's need for arms. Dulles, however,

> "was not at all happy with the President at that time because Nasser had announced his intention of going to Bandung for the conference of non-aligned nations and Dulles saw this as a betrayal of his anti-Communist crusade. Non-alignment was a dirty word to Dulles. He tried to convince the President that he ought not to go. But he did not succeed." [126]

2.3.3. Thus coming between the Gaza raid and the approach to the Soviet ambassador for arms was this Afro-Asian Conference at Bandung. It was Nasser's first political trip as a leader of the new Egypt, and the Conference seemed to be of crucial significance in both his political socialisation and Egypt's subsequent international behaviour. A week before the Conference, Cairo's newspaper, *Al-Akhbar,* revealed its significance as seen from Egypt :

> "Whereas every conference held by the Western Powers in the past 150 years has been a conference to divide spheres of influence, or to determine the fate of nations in Africa and Asia, or to establish a balance of power, the nations in Africa and Asia are today—for the first time in their history—in a position to hold their own conference at which there will be no place for the Western countries." [127]

Similarly, *Al-Ahram* analysed the importance of the conference but emphasised its special significance for the "new international personality" of "revolutionary Egypt" as part of the "non-war area". [128] But the conference was also the "historical trip" for Nasser, because it was to be a test for him since "most of the leading political personalities meeting in Bandung [had] already acted on the scene of international politics". [129] And Nasser was determined to be active. He tried to coordinate and unify the Arabs so that the conference members would support the Arab cause (*e.g.* against French colonialism in North Africa). He also proposed the con-

[125] Heikal : *Nasser : The Cairo Documents, op. cit.,* p. 56.

[126] *Ibid.,* pp. 56-57.

[127] *Al-Akhbar,* 10 April 1955 ; as quoted in Choucri : *Egypt's Role ..., op. cit.,* pp. 77-78.

[128] *Al-Ahram,* 10 April 1955.

[129] *Al-Ahram,* 9 April 1955.

vening of a second Afro-Asian Conference in Cairo the following year. [130] Moreover, Nehru praised Nasser who suggested "constructive compromises" when the Committee on World Peace and the one on "Dependent Peoples" faced impasses. [131]

Thus this Conference, coming at a period of self-searching, crystallised the 1952-ideals and made Nasser clearer in his mind about Egypt's policy. For Nasser met leaders of other emerging states who were similarly committed to social and economic development, subject to great power pressures, wary of involvement in great power struggles, and in search of a formula whereby new states could play a role in the international system while continuing their tasks of nation-building and social development. Besides, he was listened to not only as an Egyptian but also as an Arab leader, defending the problems of Palestine and North Africa. Moreover, such terms as "neutralism" and "socialism" did not always have the negative connotations given to them in some Western countries.

2.3.4. Consequently, Nasser left Bandung with a wider and clearer view of both his and Egypt's potential role in the international system, especially since he had established a close association with the leading statesmen in the Asian continent. After the Bandung Conference, Egyptian policy-makers felt that their country's status was rising in a very satisfactory way. For instance, the Soviets calculated that Nasser would emerge as the central figure of the "third world", and that in supporting him they would be able to identify themselves with the cause of the Afro-Asians. [132] Chou En-Lai gave Moscow the chance to manifest its support.

At Bandung, Nehru [133] introduced Nasser to Chou En-Lai "and the two men struck up an immediate rapport". [134] This meeting with Chou had a far-reaching impact, economically and politically. Economically, the vast Chinese market offered an opportunity to lessen Egypt's complete and one-sided dependence on, for instance, Western purchases of its cotton. For when Nasser and Chou were discussing areas of possible Egyptian-Sino cooperation, Chou told Nasser that "China could take all the cotton that Egypt produced simply by ordering every Chinese to lengthen his coat by five centimetres". [135]

Politically, Nasser felt that he desperately needed weapons to protect Egypt from another massive Israeli attack and to guarantee the satisfaction

[130] *Al-Ahram,* 17 April 1955.

[131] *Al-Ahram,* 29 April 1954.

[132] Choucri : *Egypt's Role . . ., op. cit.,* p. 90.

[133] *Al-Ahram* of 17 April 1955 gives very relevant details on Nehru's contribution to the establishment of Sino-Egyptian contacts.

[134] Heikal : *Nasser : The Cairo Documents, op. cit.,* p. 57.

[135] *Ibid.*

of the army. Consequently Nasser asked if Chou thought the Soviet Union would sell arms to Egypt. Chou promised to ask the Russians who, he knew, thought highly of the Egyptian government ; but Chou warned that this would create many complications with the Western powers for Egypt. Nasser, however, maintained that obtaining arms from the Soviet Union was the only course open to him. The Soviet ambassador in Cairo met Nasser on May 21 and this resulted in the Egyptian-Czech arms deal announced on September 27th, 1955, a 'bombshell' amounting to a historic change for two main reasons :

1. From the point of view of the peoples of the Arab subsystem, the arms deal ended their absolute dependence on the West, a dependence which had characterised the Arab 'situation' from the time modern arms had been introduced into the Middle East.

2. From the Western point of view, the change amounted to (*a*) the end of the monopolist advantage the West had long enjoyed as the sole supplier of arms, (*b*) the self-assertion of a rising national actor with which it had henceforth to contend, (*c*) the presence of another counterweight—the U.S.S.R.—the 'bête noire' that the West had tried so long and worked so hard to keep out of the area.

The year 1955 should have been a source of satisfaction to Nasser, for while Soviet arms were flowing into Egypt, British troops were evacuating the country according to the 1954 Suez Base Agreement. The completion of the evacuation in June 1956, together with the third anniversary of the "Revolution", were celebrated with an immense parade of Egyptian troops and units from "sisterly" Arab states, with Stalin tanks rumbling by, and Mig planes roaring overhead. For the first time since the British occupation of 1882 the Egyptian Army—not British forces—was the source of authority in Egypt, providing the country with the strength to run its own show in its own way. [136] Moreover, with the Western offer to finance the High Dam (Nasser's symbol of Egypt's internal development programme), 1955 witnessed the success of "positive neutralism" in obtaining aid "from both sides without joining either".

2.3.5. While 1955 showed Nasser as an Arab neutralist, 1956 showed him—with Nehru and Tito at the Brioni meeting—as one of the neutralist 'philosopher-kings'. There he discussed problems of the global system and got Nehru's and Tito's sympathy for the Arab view which "had thus captured another stronghold and asserted its presence in the world." [137] Not only was Nasser becoming one of the 'big three' in the non-aligned

---

[136] Cremeans : *op. cit.*, pp. 147-148.

[137] Nasser's *Speeches, op. cit.*, Vol. I, p. 549.

subsystem, but during 1956 he also became an Afro-Asian 'hero', heading a small underdeveloped country which was to resist the armed attack of three states—two of which were still Great Powers and ruled over (declining) colonial empires. As Lyon put it very succinctly :

> "The time between the signature of the Anglo-Egyptian agreements on Suez in October 1954, and the nationalization of the Suez Canal Company in July 1956 was seminal in the shaping of Nasser's neutralist policy, and it was during this period that its general character began to unfold. Until 1954 Nasser had been content to speak for Egypt, henceforward he assumed the role of chief spokesman and champion of the 'Arab People'. Nasser's working assumption from 1954 onwards seems to be that all Arabs, all 'true' nationalists in Afro-Asia, are naturally neutralists. If African or Asian states are not neutralist this is due, on this view, to the perversities of governments, not the desires of their subjects. Since 1954 Egypt has become a home in exile for discontented Arab nationalists and for many other dissident nationalists." [138]

Nasser's nationalisation of the Suez Canal Company—in reply to the "humiliating withdrawal" of the Western offer to finance the Aswan High Dam—was typical of this whole foreign policy pattern he was developing. It was a challenge not only to a foreign company, or even to a nation or two, but to the whole system of Western hegemony and, moreover, an assertion of the sovereignty of a newly-independent and developing actor. That is why all Afro-Asian states supported him ; even his arch-enemies in the Arab subsystem could not afford the risk of minimising the significance of his victory. In addition, the two Superpowers found themselves voting together on Egypt's side in the U.N. The significance of this was not lost on Nasser, for in 1947 when the division of Palestine was agreed upon by the U.N., both Superpowers voted identically—but on that occasion it had been against the Arab Case.

However, simultaneous support from both Superpowers could not be maintained for long. Washington refused to release frozen Egyptian funds as long as the compensation issue with the shareholders of the Suez Canal Company remained unsettled. Then on January 5th, 1957, the Eisenhower Doctrine was announced to fill the Middle East "power vaccuum"—a term which Nasser could never accept, since (according to him) Arab nationalism left no vacuum to be filled. Moreover, this doctrine purported to protect the Middle East "against overt armed aggression from any nation controlled by International Communism". But this came at a time when the communist actors were the supporters of Arab nationalism against the "imperialist pressures" and the nearby "Israeli threat".

---

[138] Lyon : *Neutralism, op. cit.,* pp. 141-142.

2.3.6. Like the Baghdad Pact, this created a split among Arab actors and led to heated controversies over Western influence and Nasser's policy of non-alignment. As he did with the Baghdad Pact, Nasser attacked violently the "new imperialism" represented by the Eisenhower Doctrine and the "pro-imperialist" governments which would not refuse it. Once again his policy succeeded, as was proved, firstly, by the dismissal in 1958 of the pro-Western Lebanese President Chamoun after a bloody civil war and, secondly, by the fall of the Iraqi monarchy and the assassination of its Premier, Nuri El-Said, after the "Army Revolution" (July 14th, 1958).

To many, then, Egypt's positive neutralism seemed nothing but anti-Westernism and crypto-communism. It is a fact that by mid-1958 Nasser's brand of neutralism brought him into open conflict with the Western powers more often than with the Soviet bloc. [139] The Soviet Union—unlike the West—did not seem handicapped in its policy in the Arab subsystem by commitments to "vested interests of imperialism and zionism". [140] Moreover, on combatting "Western colonialism and its stooges" in the subsystem, or attacking foreign bases and spheres of influence in Afro-Asia (Nasser's main objectives in this period), he was in complete harmony with Moscow. Up till then Nasser had never met with "Russian imperialism" or "communist danger". Soviet intervention in Hungary coincided with Suez, and Nasser had little chance to consider it.

> "I can say without any reservation", said Nasser in 1958, "that I cannot recall a single incident where they [members of the Soviet bloc] tried to exploit our difficulties. They understand fully that we are an independent people who have our own will and so they respect our dignity and sovereignty." [141]

2.3.7. However, one point of serious discord remained between Cairo and Moscow : the activities of local Communists in Egypt and the Arab subsystem. When this problem was in the offing Nasser gave orders that all branches of the government and the press present Egypt as a strictly neutralist country. He also seemed inclined to abandon the term 'positive neutralism' (with its unfavourable connotations in the West) in favour of

---

[139] This seems to have been inevitable and it was the general pattern in the case of most Afro-Asian states. Since their ex-colonisers were Western states, national liberation movements were naturally directed against the West. For an analysis of non-alignment from the Soviet view, see, for instance : Etinger, Y., and Melikian, O. : *El-Hyad wa El-'Assr El-Hader* (Neutralism and the Contemporary Age), which has been translated from Russian into French as *Neutralisme et actualité,* Moscow, Edition du Progrès, 1965.

[140] F. Sayegh : "Neutralism in the United Arab Republic", *op. cit.*

[141] Nasser's *Speeches, op. cit.,* Vol. II, p. 178.

'non-alignment'.[142] The 'Arab nationalism-communism' controversy became public in 1959, the year following the proclamation of the union between Syria and Egypt. Nasser, then, treated the U.S.S.R. in the same way he had treated the West before, and relations between Egypt and the Soviet bloc came close to a serious breach. "The trouble really started", Nasser said, "when I attacked Syrian Communism, which was my domestic business. I was shocked when the answer came from Krushchev." Then Nasser proceeded to enumerate the things Krushchev did that "convinced me that Moscow had emerged as the protector of communists against Arab nationalism. So I had no alternative but to tell the Russians that we do not want this new type of colonialism."[143]

Mutual press and radio attacks continued until the Summer of 1959. Nasser gave speeches and interviews almost every other day, attacking the communists' attempt to "separate Syria from the U.A.R.", and their intention to establish a "terrorist reactionary dictatorship ... where dependence would prevail ... and we would tow the line of International Communism and receive directives from it".[144]

But both sides were bent on mending the breach, and Nasser believed that "the friendly relations between us and the Soviets cannot se shattered by a single crisis ... They are worth another test."[145]

2.4. *Seasoned Non-Alignment: 1959-1967*

The first phase in the evolution of Egypt's non-alignment was characterised by dependence on the West for historical reasons. This brought on a process of corrective self-extrication which started in 1955. This process seems to have led to an 'inordinate leaning' toward the other side in the late 1950's. This 'inordinate leaning' seemed inevitable because relations with Britain and France were suspended after the Suez attack, and the U.S.A. was imposing a programme of virtual boycott.

2.4.1. The beginning of the third phase[146] witnessed two important happenings: a certain relaxation of Western-Egyptian estrangement, and this coincided with the 'Arab nationalism-communism' controversy.[147]

---

[142] *Daily Telegraph,* 10 October 1957; Wheelock: *op. cit.,* p. 256; Lyon: *Neutralism, op. cit.,* p. 146; Abdel-Malek: *Egypt: Military Society, op. cit.,* pp. 231-235.

[143] Nasser's *Speeches, op. cit.,* Vol. II, p. 417.

[144] *Ibid.,* p. 382.

[145] *Ibid.,* p. 445.

[146] For a different division into phases, see: Sayegh, F.: "Neutralism in the United Arab Republic", *op. cit.*; Heikal, Mohamed: "Igtima' Roasaa El-Dewal Ghyre El Monhaza" (The Meeting of Heads of State or Government of Non-Aligned Countries), *Al-Ahram,* 26 May 1961.

[147] Sayegh, F.: "Neutralism in the United Arab Republic", *op. cit.*

The Egyptian-Western rapprochement was facilitated by, for example:

(*a*) both the death of the 'generalissimo' of neutrophobia, Dulles, and the coming to power of an understanding Kennedy who established direct communication channels with Nasser. [148] This was coupled with military-technological advances which did not make Western-Arab alliances so vital ;

(*b*) pro-Western forces in the Arab subsystem, which acted as an Arab vehicle for Western anti-Nasser projects, were weakened. Moreover, with the conflict between Nasser and the communist-backed regime in Iraq, Egypt's feud with the monarchies of Jordan and Saudi-Arabia was relaxed.

This rapprochement was manifested in, for example :

(*a*) the signing of a compensation agreement between Egypt and the Suez Canal Company ;

(*b*) the re-opening of the British embassy in Cairo ;

(*c*) the removal of restrictions on American economic aid funds and the resumption of technical cooperation activities interrupted since mid-1956 ;

(*d*) the rechannelling of thousands of Egyptian students from Eastern Europe to the U.S.A. [149]

The 'Arab nationalism-communism' controversy, on the other hand, alerted the Egyptian mind to the differences in the ultimate objectives between Egypt and the Soviet bloc and the ideological-organisational challenge represented by communism

2.4.2 The interaction between these two occurrences resulted in

> "a greater balance in the Arab nationalist outlook, coupled with greater balance in the economic, cultural and technological relations of the U.A.R. with the two blocs, [which] led in turn to greater balance in the political expression and orientation of U.A.R. neutralism." [150]

Nasser, then, was bent on distributing his friendship (and suspicions) to both sides evenly, since "power politics is practised by both East and

---

[148] Kennedy took the initiative by sending on May 11, 1961 a long message to Nasser in order to settle the Palestinian question and other pending problems. Nasser answered with a long message on August 11, 1961. See Nasser's *Speeches, op. cit.,* Vol. III, pp. 494-501.

[149] Heikal : *Nahn ... wa Amrica, op. cit.,* pp. 127-128.

[150] Sayegh, F. : "Neutralism in the United Arab Republic", *op. cit.*

West".[151] That is why "we are putting our case before the Asians and Africans at the Neutralists' Conference", to show "that there is a third road for all the countries facing the problems of development after independence".[152]

2.4.3. Nasser continued to put his policy of Arab socialism into practice (*e.g.* the 1961 Socialist Laws), a socialism—as he expressed it in 1962—emanating from a "mind open to all human experiences".[153] But this openness did not mean that Egypt's socialism would necessarily follow "rigid theories which have not arisen out of the nature of national experience".[154] This 'nationalised' socialism was in line with Egypt's insistence on its own identity and ideological independence, as El-Sadat told Khrushchev in 1959. It had as an effect the strengthening of 'seasoned non-alignment' :

1. Since its socialism was based on a "mind open to all human experiences", Egypt had to keep open its channels of communication with all sources committed to socio-economic development.

2. The elaboration of a distinct ideological line for internal development would immunise the country's independence against outside (ideological) temptation and/or incursions.

3. Nasser's insistence on a distinct socialism put him in the ideological company of other prominent third world leaders, as non-alignment put him in their political company.

2.4.4. Egypt's rising international status and Nasser's 'third road' strategy coincided with the increase in the number of independent Afro-Asian states. Cairo became the 'Mecca' of many third world leaders and Nasser returned these visits. With its election to membership of the Security Council in 1961, Egypt was even able to give vigourous expression to this 'third road' strategy. For instance :

1. Nasser participated with other heads of state in the 15th session of the U.N. General Assembly (1960) and co-sponsored the 'initiative of the five' urging the renewal of high-level Soviet-American contacts.

2. Egypt participated in the U.N. action in the Congo and insisted that both colonial presence and Cold War antagonism should be excluded from the internal Congolese conflict.

---

[151] Quoted as coming from "a responsible authority of the U.A.R.", *New York Times,* 7 June 1961, as quoted in Cremeans : *op. cit.,* p. 292.

[152] *Ibid.*

[153] *El-Mithaq* (The National Charter), *op. cit.,* p. 9.

[154] *Ibid.,* p. 37.

3. Cairo was host to the Preparatory Conference of Uncommitted States which gave the official five-point definition of non-alignment.

4. Nasser co-sponsored the 25-member Non-Aligned Summit Conference held in Belgrade in September 1961.

5. Egypt was chosen as a member of the 18-nation Disarmament Committee established by the U.N. General Assembly in 1961.

6. Cairo was host to the 31-nation Third World Conference (July 1962) on the problems of economic development—the precursor of U.N.C.T.A.D.

7. Egypt participated with other non-aligned countries in attempts to reduce the East-West conflict in Cuba (October 1962).

8. Egypt attempted to mediate in the 1962 Sino-Indian conflict through direct contacts with both China and India, by its participation in the Colombo Conference of six non-aligned actors, and through elaboration of proposals and subsequent visits by the Egyptian Prime Minister to both Peking and New Delhi in 1962-1963.

9. Nasser participated in the efforts to end the division of Africa between the 'Casablanca' and the 'Monrovia' groups, efforts which culminated in the convening of the 1963 Addis Ababa Summit and the establishment of the Organisation of African Unity.

10. Between July and October 1964 Egypt was host to the 14-member Arab Summit, the Second African Summit of more than 30 states, and the 47-member Second Summit of Non-Aligned Countries.

11. On April 1st, 1965, Egypt, with 16 other non-aligned actors, called for immediate negotiations to end the war in Vietnam without preconditions.

12. Nasser participated in the 1966 Delhi meeting (with Tito and Mrs. Gandhi), a continuation of the 1956 Brioni meeting and the 1961 Cairo meeting between the three 'philosopher-kings' of non-alignment. [155]

But this balanced internationalist strategy [156] was not to continue for long, for following the 1967 "setback" the long-dreaded Israeli military threat had advanced to little more than one hundred miles from Cairo.

---

[155] For details see the treatment of the "core sector" in the non-aligned international subsystem, chapter V.

[156] Nasser's policy of military presence in the Yemen prevented Anglo-Saxon relations with Egypt from improving as quickly as Nasser expected. But relations with the Soviet Union continued to develop with the building of the High Dam, and relations with France were normalised after the settlement of the Algerian conflict.

2.5. *Non-Alignment versus National Security, 1967-1970*

Strictly speaking, this period is not a centre of our interest since we are primarily concerned with why non-alignment was chosen and how it evolved in its formative years. Moreover, it may be too early to analyse the repercussions of the 1967 war on Egypt, since the country is still experiencing the acute crisis of "the battle of destiny".

2.5.1. But a brief note on Egypt's non-alignment just before Nasser's death is justified on two counts :

(i) Egypt was not the first non-aligned actor to face the apparent dilemma of "non-alignment versus national security". In 1962 India was overrun by Chinese troops, and some political forces within India itself attacked the government for still holding to non-alignment. And while Western weapons flowed into India, Nehru's government tightened its relations with countries like South Korea and the Philippines, and was even accused by some African countries of being lukewarm to the West. The Indian government proclaimed, however, its determination to keep the country non-aligned. It was helped in carrying out its determination by the Soviet readiness to continue with arms delivery, and this made it look as if India had substituted bi-alignment for non-alignment. In the meantime, Indian decision-makers were bent on a reappraisal of non-alignment :

> "The state [of reappraisal] was natural inasmuch as the question of her territorial security assumed a new colour, her economic development was faced with retardation and, consequently, the edges of the constructive dynamism of her foreign policy were bound to lose their sharpness ... India's policy-makers were seized with a kind of heart-searching in respect of non-alignment, examining if there were any lapses or leakages and reassessing it for an overhaul." [157]

Indeed, Nehru himself during one of the debates of Lok Sabha said very explicitly that "the old concept of non-alignment is slowly undergoing a change". [158]

Consequently, Egypt's non-alignment in the 1967-1970 period is of conceptual significance not only in tracing a certain actor's reaction, but also in revealing some of the problems that purport to non-alignment in general. [159]

---

[157] Mallik : *op. cit.*, p. 247.

[158] *Ibid.*, p. 269.

[159] See, for instance, the discussion in the pages of *Al-Ahram* about the necessity of adapting non-alignment to the new context : *Al-Ahram,* 8 July 1969.

(ii) Egypt's non-aligned behaviour in this period would serve to emphasise once more the whole of Nasser's pragmatic approach to international relations.

2.5.2. Put simply, the argument is that there were 'incompatibilities' in the post-1967 non-alignment of Nasser's Egypt, because of :

(*a*) the facilities given to the Soviet fleet in Egyptian ports ;

(*b*) the presence of Soviet military experts in Egypt, estimated by Western press reports as ranging from 15,000 to 30,000 men ; and

(*c*) Egypt's complete and one-sided dependence on Soviet weapons.

Though Egyptian policy-makers insisted that their country was still non-aligned after as before 1967, its international behaviour toward the Superpowers has undergone a change in the post-1967 period. A revealing indicator of the change in Egypt's behaviour is its official attitude toward the entry of the Warsaw Pact troops into Czechoslovakia in 1968.

Cairo at first abstained from taking a declared official position, then very timidly Heikal wrote an article in *Al-Ahram* where he stated that Egyptian policy-makers are *in principle* against any form of foreign intervention in the internal affairs of other countries, but in the *specific* Czechoslovak case they understand the special circumstances of Soviet intervention. Afterwards, Egyptian newsmedia tended either to emphasise Soviet attacks on "counter-revolutionary and reactionary forces" or to overlook the subject altogether. [160] For many observers, this seemed a virtual acceptance of the Soviet case, and this attitude drove a wedge between Egypt and another pioneer non-aligned actor and, in fact, one of Egypt's closest associates in the non-aligned subsystem : Yugoslavia.

The discussion between Tito and Nasser when they met in Aswan is revealing, not only as far as Egypt's attitude is concerned, but also as regards the problems of non-alignment as such. Tito was not at all pleased with the absence of "a violent denunciation" on Cairo's part, and Nasser's "mild reaction" to the intervention, and so at Aswan he told Nasser :

> " 'We are non-aligned, we must state our position on these matters'.
>
> Nasser replied : 'You must see the realities of my situation. Part of my territory is occupied. I cannot be completely non-aligned. No nation which is partly occupied can be completely independent.'
>
> He asked Tito : 'What if my relations worsened with the Soviet Union ? What would happen if I attacked them over Czechoslovakia ? It would mean that my position in the Middle East would be lost completely because the Soviet Union is my only hope of getting

[160] See, for instance, *Al-Ahram* during September 1968.

the arms I need to regain the lost territory. And if that happened, who would benefit from the situation . . . ? The Americans. Do you want them to benefit in the Middle East ?

And Tito replied : 'No'." [161]

Then Heikal significantly comments : "This was one of those occasions when they both felt that the spirit of non-alignment had its hands tied." [162]

2.5.3. In his explanations to his friend, Nasser meant to emphasise very explicitly that he was forced to accept this military dependence on the Soviet Union with all its consequences on Egypt's non-alignment. About nine weeks before his death (on September 28, 1970), Nasser explained the reasons behind his dependence on the Soviet Union. After the 1967-"setback", Nasser said, "the Israeli leaders were expecting a telephone call from Cairo asking for the terms of surrender". When this did not happen, Nasser argued, Israel attempted to force Egypt into submission by air raids deep into Cairo suburbs with the more sophisticated weapons it had just obtained from the U.S.A. and the U.K. Since Egyptian air defence was weak, Nasser said, he had no choice but to remedy his weak position with Soviet help. After a secret visit to Moscow, Soviet ground-air missiles (along with their technicians) were installed in Egypt. As a result, Nasser concluded, "the air raids deep into Egyptian territory, of which Israel used to boast, . . . have stopped". [163] Briefly, Nasser evoked the dictates of necessity [164] and the simple instinct for self-preservation to explain the evolution of his non-alignment after 1967.

But is this "special friendship" [165] and "close cooperation" with the Soviet Union in contradiction with the bases of Egyptian non-alignment ? Heikal does not think so. Speaking not only as Nasser's alter ego, but also officially as the Minister of National Guidance (and this is why his declaration was of double importance) Heikal said :

> "Non-alignment is not passive neutrality . . . [but] a positive stand, . . . a participation in all the issues relating to war and peace. In this sense Egypt is non-aligned . . . [but] non-aligned only in the Cold War ; . . . [that is to say] its stand on any issue is not based on a priori commitment to one of the blocs . . . [but] on our evaluation of the issue at hand . . ."

---

[161] Heikal : *The Cairo Documents, op. cit.,* p. 245.

[162] *Ibid.*

[163] Nasser's speech, 23 July 1970, *Al-Ahram,* 24 July 1970.

[164] This is the same reason Nasser gave for not leaving "the battlefield" to attend personally the Third Summit Conference of Non-Aligned Countries (Lusaka, September 1970).

[165] The Soviet-Egyptian Friendship Treaty was signed after Nasser's death and is thus outside the scope of this chapter.

Applying these general principles to the present situation of Egypt, Heikal said:

> "When we are in a crisis ... when part of our territory is occupied ... non-alignment means opposition to occupation and all that it entails, and the rest of the world should join us in this."

Inevitably in this situation Egypt cannot

> "evaluate on the same footing the U.S.A.—which gives arms to the enemy occupying our land—and another state which gives us the necessary weapons to defend ourselves". [166]

2.6. Be that as it may, the tracing of Egypt's pattern of non-aligned behaviour shows that Nasser was committed to pragmatism and flexibility. As a concept, Nasser's non-alignment had as its principal objective to keep Egypt diplomatically as free as possible from prior commitment to either East or West, so that all issues could be judged on their own merits (as perceived from Cairo) rather than as they fitted into one or the other of the Superpowers' schemes. [167]

At least until June 1967, non-alignment constituted the pillar of his charisma-based rule, and he prided himself on several achievements which tended to answer the needs of newly-independent, economically developing and Afro-Asian Egypt.

1. As far as his country was concerned, Egypt had asserted its identity on the international scene, had become a "factor to be contended with"—a source of national self-respect.

2. Within the Arab "circle", [168] Nasser was identified with the activist assertion of Arab nationalism.

3. Within the "African circle", because of its diplomatic freedom of action, Egypt had formed hundreds of African "freedom fighters". Cairo's "Voice of Free Africa" was broadcasting in at least seven African languages in 1962, and Cairo was the headquarters of national liberation movements from Algeria to Angola.

---

[166] *Al-Ahram*, 13 October 1970. Differently from India, Egyptian policy-makers never emphasised absolute impartiality, for their slogan was: "We are friendly to those who are friendly to us, and hostile to those who are hostile to us."

[167] Maqsoud, Clovis: *Ma'na El-Hyad El-Igabi* (The Meaning of Positive Neutralism), Beirut, Dar El-'Elm, 1960.

[168] The order of mentioning these "achievements" is based on Nasser's own conception of "circles" as expounded in *The Philosophy of the Revolution, op. cit.*, pp. 51-72.

4. Within the 'Third World', Egypt was among both the leaders of non-alignment and the pioneers of Afro-Asian action. For instance, the election of the Egyptian Minister of the Economy to the position of Vice-President of the first U.N. Conference on Trade and Development (U.N.C.T.A.D., Geneva 1964) was a recognition of Egypt's status.

5. Even within the international system generally Nasser prided himself that he had championed an affirmative role for small states, a role which permitted them to gain an international status disproportionate to their existing economic and military capabilities.

CHAPTER VIII

The Personality variable and the Relevance of Typology-Building among Non-Aligned Actors

Part two emphasised the *common attributes* of non-aligned actors (mainly 'systemic' and 'national' components of their general 'situation') that are at the basis of their *common foreign policy orientation.* Part three treated the *peculiarities of a non-aligned actor* (national but also personality components of the particular 'situation') that account for *behavioural specificities* when the common foreign policy orientation becomes the individual actor's international behaviour. But if the use of the proposed situation-role model is to be both conceptually self-sufficient and empirically relevant, it has to provide possible classification criteria that pave the way for typology-building [1] among these non-aligned behavioural specificities. In developing the situation-role model in chapter III, we have suggested the charismatic leader's personality—reflected in his country's national role conception—as a basis of this proposed typology. [2] Two conceptual points need to be treated briefly : 'role theory' [3] itself,

---

[1] Taxonomy and typology-building are a vital part of any (aspiring) empirical science. Since science assumes the orderliness of phenomena and the rational apprehension of this order by man, typology-building and the explication of the rationale for the classification are indeed tantamount to the codification of the existing state of knowledge in a discipline or a subdiscipline. But though typological classification has characterised a considerable part of the social sciences, the notion of types and the method of classification have been subject to methodological and ideological controversies. "Few subjects in taxonomy", Simpson said in 1945, "are understood in more different ways or are more misunderstood than the nature and use of types." Tiryakin, Edward : "Typologies", *International Encyclopedia of the Social Sciences,* XVI, pp. 177-185.

[2] I do not mean, of course, that this is the only strategy for potential typology-building among non-aligned behavioural patterns. There are differences in size and geographical location, in external problems faced by the different actors, in their political culture, in 'national character'. However, the method adopted here is believed to be the most relevant for our purposes.

[3] For bibliographical details on this subject, see chapter III, footnote 57.

especially as applied to non-alignment, and—secondly—the relationship between role-enactment or behaviour and the 'personality' of the role-performer.

1.

The application of the role concept in foreign policy analysis is not as new as it might seem at first glance. We have already mentioned how Kautilya—in the ancient Hindu world—described six types of foreign policy (accommodation, hostility, indifference, attack, protection, and double policy). [4] He correlated specific roles with their sources, *i.e.* the status of the ruler according to him. Thus a king of inferior status is correlated with a role of accommodation, protection or double policy. Superior status, on the other hand, leads to a foreign policy of hostility (*i.e.* a type of cold war) or attack (imperialism). When an international system is dominated by conflict among kings of roughly equal status, the appropriate foreign policy of others is abstention from taking sides, or indifference (in modern terminology : non-alignment).

Contemporary books of international relations have also used role conceptualisation, if only implicitly. Thus whereas Morgenthau dealt with active and passive policies in his *Politics Among Nations,* his discussion of bloc leader, bloc member, satellite, aligned, non-aligned . . . indicates the conceptualisation of foreign policy as a patterned behaviour where an actor occupies a certain position (*e.g.* ally, bloc leader), and thus obeys certain rules and expectations linked to this position (*i.e.* role demands or requisites in the language of "role theory"). Thus in the balance of power analysis, the balancer is expected to perform a specific (*e.g.* integrative) role.

Related more directly to our concerns is Lyon's insightful study on non-alignment. If non-alignment denotes a certain position [5] (*i.e.* formal

---

[4] Modelski : "Kautilya : Foreign Policy and International Systems in the Ancient Hindu World", *op. cit.*

[5] Newcomb defined position as a "unit of social structure". This is similar to Secord and Backman's definition of position as a category of actors "who occupy a specific place in a social structure". This is the accepted definition, for Biddle and Thomas too defined position as a "collectively recognized category of . . . [actors] for whom the basis of such differentiation is their common attribute, their common behaviour, or the common reactions of others toward them" (*Role Theory : Concepts and Research*, New York, Wiley, 1966, p. 29). According to this definition, Biddle and Thomas have posited three criteria for the assignment of actors into a position category : (*a*) A common attribute or several common attributes, *e.g.* in our non-aligned subsystem, we can talk about Africans, Asians, Europeans, Latin Ameri-

non-participation in East-West military blocs) there are certain role-demands associated with this non-aligned position: *e.g.* prohibition against maintenance of big-power troops on the territory of the non-aligned actor, receipt of foreign aid from a variety of sources, "judging issues on their merits", support of the national liberation movements ... and generally the different expectations in the five-point official definition of non-alignment of the 1961-Preparatory Cairo Conference. But since these role-demands are very general and flexible, and although accepted by all members of the non-aligned subsystem, they are not nevertheless interpreted identically or performed in the same way, thus we meet variations in the non-aligned actors' role-enactment.[6] Peter Lyon found no less than six types of role-enactment among non-aligned actors (*e.g.* ranging from the "erstwhile isolationism" of Yemen or Liberia to the "new state neutralism" of Algeria or Ghana). Unfortunately, Lyon has neither explicited the variables that are at the basis of his typology nor codified the criteria that might account for a non-aligned actor's emphasis on some demands of the role-set[7] rather than others. This brings us to our second conceptual point.

---

cans, rich, poor. Of course as more attributes go into the making of a single subcategory of the non-aligned subsystem, the subcategory becomes narrower and more exclusive. Thus only a few non-aligned actors are both African and rich. (*b*) The second basis for position categorisation that Biddle and Thomas suggested is common behaviour. Thus among members of the non-aligned subsystem, we talked about "militants" and "moderates", and in combining common attribute and common behaviour, the subcategory becomes narrower and more exclusive, *e.g.* militant Asians. (*c*) The third basis for positional (sub)categorisation is the similarity in the behaviour of others toward the actors in question, *e.g.* a neutralised actor. For more details concerning "role theory", see: Shaw, Marvin, and Costanzo, Philip: *Theories of Social Psychology,* New York, McGraw Hill, 1970, pp. 326-347.

[6] Role performance is the behaviour of the individual actor when he is playing the particular role. In contrast to role expectations, which are the "oughts" or the behavioural requirements of a given role, role performance or enactment is the *actual* behaviour exhibited by an actor in a role. Social psychologists affirm that "there may be considerable variation in the manner in which different actors enact the same role, or in the manner in which the same actor enacts the same role on different occasions ... Although any single form of role enactment may be considered to be the most adequate, the enactment of alternative acceptable modes of role behaviour is not precluded." In other words, "role theory does account for the infinite variety of behaviour that an individual [actor] may exhibit. Even though role theory tends to classify people into categories of actors (*e.g.* in our field of International Relations: aligned, non-aligned, bloc leader ...) and though it tends to attribute relatively uniform expectations to a given category, it does not propose that these uniform expectations are met by all relevant actors with the same expressed behaviour." Shaw and Costanzo: *op. cit.,* p. 330.

[7] Merton, Robert: The "Role Set", *British Journal of Sociology,* VIII (1957), pp. 106-120.

2. **Role and Personality**

When Sargent defined in 1951 the actor's role as the "pattern or type of social behaviour which seems *situationally* appropriate to him in terms of the demands and expectations of those in his group", [8] his definition confirms the important function of 'role theory' as a major basis for identifying and placing actors in the social system, *i.e.* the function of 'role theory' for typology-building. But since Sargent's definition seeks to link the functioning of the social system with the behavioural patterns (and hence, types) of actors who make up this system, he brings to mind the (fallacious) dichotomy of societal versus personality variables, sociological versus psychological emphasis, "external" versus "internal effects" in the definition of role. We have already dealt in some detail with this (false) dilemma, and we are not going to dwell on this issue here. Let us just say that as far as our interest in personality and role is concerned, we should emphasise that since role is subject to being played recognizably by *different actors,* it is equally subject to being *performed differently* by different actors. [9] Indeed, if we take the theatre—which has been cited as the originator of the concept of role—we realize that it yields the most revealing empirical examples of how different actors playing the same role may exhibit different role behaviours. No two actors characterising Hamlet, Macbeth or Othello enact the role behaviours in exactly the same way. The dialogue may be the same, but the gestures or vocal intonations are usually different. [10] Consequently, the generality that characterises the five-point official definition of non-alignment of the 1961-Cairo Preparatory Conference, together with the flexibility that characterises its role-demands, allow personality variables to shape behavioural specificities in the non-aligned role-performance [11] even more, especially since the leader is tempted to achieve maximum "self/role congruence" as the means to maximum role-effectiveness (*i.e.* successful foreign policy behaviour).

---

[8] Sargent, S.: "Conceptions of Role and Ego in Contemporary Psychology", in J. Rohrer and M. Sherif (eds.): *Social Psychology at the Crossroads,* New York, Harper, 1950, pp. 355-370, as quoted in Shaw and Costanzo: *op. cit.,* p. 335 (emphasis added).

[9] For a detailed treatment, see Shaw and Costanzo, *op. cit.* (especially pp. 330-332) and the bibliographical sources cited therein.

[10] Giner: *Sociology, op. cit.,* pp. 109-111, and also Shaw and Costanzo: *op. cit.,* pp. 330-332.

[11] Since social psychologists affirm as one of the propositions of "role theory" that the actor is free to vary his expression of a role function within the limits imposed by role expectations or requisites, it follows that since the limits imposed by the expectations of the non-aligned role-set are flexible and elastic, inter-actor variations are given a relatively wider freedom of expression.

For when George Mead [12]—through his concept of self/role congruence—emphasised the belief that "a role is performed better if its requirements are consonant with one's 'natural inclination' (*i.e.* self-concept or self-characteristics as folk psychology expresses it), he was—in fact—saying that the validity or effectiveness of role-enactment is related to the degree of congruence of self and role. Inversely, when self and role characteristics are incongruent or antagonistic, the role-enactment is likely to be invalid and unconvincing. About a hundred years after Mead's birth, William Smelser tested in an experiment the hypothesis of self/role congruence and the result was the empirical confirmation of Mead's proposition. [13]

But if, both conceptually and empirically, personality is correlated with a certain role-enactment, how then to test this hypothesis in our topic on non-alignment ? [14]

3. Nasser's Egypt Versus Nehru's India

We will deal with this personality/political behaviour linkage as a strategy for typology-building through a comparative analysis of Nasser's Egypt versus Nehru's India.

These two actors are very useful samples for comparison, because they manifested a great "concordance of views" which accounts for their close friendship and sustained communication. For instance, Nehru came to have official talks with Nasser for the first time in February 1955, [15] but in the five-month period that followed they visited one another eight times. Moreover,

---

[12] Fletcher : *The Making of Sociology, op. cit.*, pp. 512-542.

[13] Smelser selected two samples of experimental subjects, the members of one group having high scores on the trait "dominance", derived from the California Psychological Inventory, the members of the second having low scores. The subjects, in pairs, were placed in a cooperative work situation and were systematically assigned roles calling for dominant or submissive enactments. The most productive pairs were those where "dominant" subjects had been assigned the "dominant" role and "non-dominant" subjects the "submissive" role. *The least productive pairs were those where the self characteristics and role characteristics had been reversed.* Smelser, William : "Dominance as a Factor in Achievement and Perception in Cooperative Problem-Solving Interactions", *Journal of Abnormal and Social Psychology,* LXII (1961), pp. 535-542, as in Sarbin, Theodore : "Role : Psychological Aspects", *International Encyclopedia of the Social Sciences,* XIII, pp. 446-452 (emphasis added).

[14] The problem becomes more complex since we are moving from the (descriptive) "what" question to the (explanatory) "why" question.

[15] Heikal : *Nasser : The Cairo Documents, op. cit.*, p. 251.

> "whenever Nehru was flying to Europe or America he always stopped in Cairo and even when he had no time to come into the city he would hold his plane for several hours at the airport while Nasser drove out to talk with him". [16]

In addition, both India and Egypt were founder members of the non-aligned subsystem and the most active on its interaction scale (*i.e.* Egypt's top position of 74.6 per cent followed immediately by India's 64 per cent). [17] Both also (with Yugoslavia) represented the subsystem's core sector. [18]

Yet these two actors manifested behavioural differences in their role-enactment. India did not go through a Suez Crisis, become involved in direct military fighting with Europe's two major (military) powers or exchange public recriminations with Krushchev. Moreover, the conciliatory approach of Nehru's India to the Sino-Indian border conflict before 1962 forms a contrast with the "activist" approach of Nasser's Egypt to the Arab-Israeli conflict and the "positivism" of Nasser's "neutralism" generally. [19]

These differences are confirmed by the various quantitative indicators, whether they are measuring behavioural heterogeneity among members of the non-aligned subsystem or militant-moderate patterns in non-aligned actors' role-performance. Thus according to the indicator of behavioural heterogeneity India got — 3 (*i.e.* its non-aligned role-performance can be interpreted as a fairly intermediary position between East and West) whereas Egypt got + 35 (*i.e.* its non-aligned role-performance makes it, comparatively, very near to the Eastern pole). [20] Consequently, full 38 points separated these two non-aligned actors in their role-enactment. This conclusion is even more supported by the measurement of 'militant-versus-moderate' behavioural patterns. Thus Egypt's top score of 260 points is contrasted with India's 66. For Nasser's Egypt emphasised in its role-set the (militant) aspect of anti-colonial revolution (Egypt : 70 points, India : 0) or performing the role of regional leader to the exclusion of major powers (Egypt : 78 points, India : 6). [21]

Heikal, for instance, confirms our hypothesis of personality/political behaviour linkage by implicitly suggesting the personality variable as the

---

[16] *Ibid.*, p. 254.

[17] See above, chapter V, table 11.

[18] *Ibid.*, pp. 174-182.

[19] Even an Indian admirer of Nasser such as Krishna Menon commented on Nasser's (and Nkrumah's) preference for the labellation "positive neutralism' rather than "non-alignment" by saying : "I am afraid I ridiculed it [positive neutralism] with banter." Brecher : *India and World Politics, op. cit.*, p. 7.

[20] See above, chapter V, table 13.

[21] See above, chapter III, table 2.

factor that accounts for both close collaboration as well as 'contrasts' in role-performance. Thus concerning the close collaboration, Heikal describes the Nasser-Nehru first meeting as follows :

> "... they had a deep and instantaneous effect on one another. It was rather like a man looking across a crowded room and falling in love with a woman he had never seen before. The bond between Nasser and Nehru was as immediate as that and as strong as that." [22]

Concerning personality differences which—according to our hypothesis—account for 'contrasts' in role-performance, Heikal has this revealing quotation :

> "What Nasser saw in Nehru above all else was a man who could think, a man who could look at a problem from all its aspects and reason out its origin, its effects and its solution. It was this rational intellect which appealed to Nasser". [23]

And as far as Nehru's side of the personal bond is concerned, he

> "... felt towards Nasser as he would towards a son. And with most fathers there were things about 'his son' which he admired and which at the same time frightened him. He admired Nasser's boldness but he was frightened of it. He was proud of Nasser's capacity for action and he envied it but he was also scared by it—just like an intellectual father whose son goes mountain-climbing." [24]

4.

But though useful, these are still descriptive statements, and Heikal is not concerned with going beyond them to explicit the personality/political behaviour linkage or even to explicit the meaning of personality. [25] For since personality is an "inferred entity", it needs to be traced back to the formative process to make the personality/political behaviour linkage [26] operationally useful. In other words, we have to see how their personalities were formed with the passage of time (*i.e.* their socialisation), and

---

[22] Heikal : *Nasser : The Cairo Documents, op. cit.*, p. 251.

[23] *Ibid.*, p. 252.

[24] *Ibid.*

[25] Heikal does not even use the more specific psychological concept 'personality', but the general term "man", *ibid.*, pp. 251-253.

[26] A pioneer and classical work in the study of personality/political behaviour linkage is : Adorno, T. E. ; Frenkel-Brunswick, Else ; Levinson, Daniel ; and Sanford, R. Nevitt : *The Authoritarian Personality*, New York, Harper, 1950. The authors intended to test the linkage between personality traits and political anti-semitism, as they themselves explicit their objective on page one of the book : "The research to be reported in this volume was guided by the following major hypothesis : that the

—naturally—our emphasis would be on the formative process most linked to their future political behaviour (*i.e.* political socialisation). [27]

The "theory of political socialisation" [28] emphasises the importance of three socialising agents : the family, the school, and job or post-school socialisation. In all three socialising agents, Nasser and Nehru differed. [29]

---

political, economic and social convictions of an individual often form a broad and coherent pattern, as if bound together by a 'mentality' or 'spirit', and that this pattern is an expression of deep-lying trends in his personality. The major concern was with the *potentially fascistic* individual, one whose structure is such as to render him particularly susceptible to anti-democratic propaganda."

[27] "Political socialisation" is a rising subdiscipline of political science. According to the 1968 Biographical Directory Survey conducted under the auspices of the American Political Science Association, political socialisation was the 13th (out of 27) most popular field of primary specialisation. More studies are being done now than three or four years ago, and this trend is increasing. For since in the recent conventions of the American Political Science Association and the joint workshops of the European Consortium for Political Research (*e.g.* Mannheim, 1973, and Strasbourg, 1974), political socialisation is one of the general subject areas for panel meetings, more and more political socialisation studies are likely to be published. This does not prevent the subdiscipline from being in an inchoate state. For instance, students of political socialisation still disagree on the empirical phenomena that constitute the most profitable object of their subdiscipline : is it political attitudes only, or both political attitudes and political behaviour ? Thus in the *Politics of the Developing Areas (op. cit.,* p. 28), Almond defines political socialisation as "the process of induction into the political culture. Its end product it as set of attitudes—cognitions, value standards, and feelings—toward the political system, its various roles and role incumbents. It also includes knowledge of, values affecting, and feelings toward the inputs of demands and claims into the system, and its authoritative outputs." Similarly Lucian Pye (*Politics, Personality and Nation-Building, op. cit.,* p. 45) regards political socialisation as the "process ... through which the individual develops his awareness of his political world and gains his appreciation, judgement, and understanding of political events". Lewis Froman ("Personality and Political Socialisation", *Journal of Politics,* XXIII, May 1961), Richard Dawson and Kenneth Prewitt (*Political Socialization,* Boston, 1969), G. Almond and S. Verba (*The Civic Culture,* Princeton, 1963) adopt the same view. Other social scientists define political socialisation as having both attitudinal and behavioural products. For instance Kenneth Langton ("Assumptions about the Learning of Political Attitudes", *The Annals of the American Academy of Political and Social Science,* CCCLXI, September 1965), D. Easton and Jack Dennis (*Children in the Political System,* New York, 1969), Robert Hess and Judith Torney (*The Development of Political Attitudes in Children,* Chicago, 1967), Robert Le Vine ("Political Socialization and Culture Change", in Geertz : *Old Societies and New States, op. cit.),* Fred Greenstein *(International Encyclopedia of the Social Sciences,* XIV), and William Shonfeld ("The Focus of Political Socialization Research", *World Politics,* XXIII, 1971) adopt this view which we follow here.

[28] Almond and Verba : *The Civic Culture, op. cit.,* pp. 323-374.

[29] Among the most useful sources in this respect are : El-Sadat : *Révolte sur le Nil, op. cit. ;* Nasser : *The Philosophy of the Revolution, op. cit. ;* Nehru, Jawaharlal : *Toward Freedom : The Autobiography of Jawaharlal Nehru,* New York, John Day, 1941 ; Brecher, Michael : *Nehru : A Political Biography,* London, O.U.P., 1959 ;

4.1. *Family*

In addition to the fact that their birth dates were separated by over 28 years (Nehru : 14 November 1889, Nasser : 15 January 1918), their upbringing presented clear contrasts.

4.1.1. Nasser, the son of a postman, had a generally lonely, austere childhood. His family came from the village of Beni Morr (Sons of the Bitter) in Upper Egypt. [30] Nasser's personality was then to be influenced by many of the characteristics of Saïdis or Upper Egyptians (e.g. manliness, warmth, hard work, shrewdness, stubbornness, extreme sensitivity to matters of personal honour which can give rise to vendettas). [31]

Nasser's own early life was as unsettled as that of his country at the time. His father used to be posted to different parts of Egypt and the family had to move. Thus already when he was 6 months old, the family had to change houses in Alexandria, and three years after Nasser's birth the family had to move back to Assiut in Upper Egypt. In 1923, *i.e.* when Nasser was five, his father was sent to Khail El-Arbein (a small village near Suez), [32] then to Khatatba (a small township northeast of Cairo on the edge of the Delta and the desert before Damanhour), then to Alexandria again before being transferred to Cairo.

At the age of six, Nasser was sent to the primary school for railway employees at Khatatba where he could study the *Qur'an* and learn to read and write. But at the age of seven, Nasser "était envoyé au Caire chez son oncle Khalil, par son père lassé de chercher, d'affectation villageoise en poste campagnard, les moyens d'assurer l'éducation du garçon". [33]

Nasser's uncle, Khalil, was a small civil servant in the Ministry of Waqfs (Religious Endowments), with a salary of 5 Egyptian pounds per month. With the help of his uncle, Nasser used to exchange letters with his mother whom he loved intensely, but saw her only on holiday visits

---

Das, M. N. : *The Political Philosophy of Jawaharlal Nehru,* London, Allen & Unwin, 1961 ; Heikal : *Nasser, The Cairo Documents, op. cit.* ; Karanjia, R. K. : *The Philosophy of Mr. Nehru,* London, Allen & Unwin, 1966 ; Karanjia, R. K. : *The Mind of Mr. Nehru,* London, Allen & Unwin, 1961 ; Lacouture, Jean : *Nasser,* Paris, Seuil, 1971 ; Dorothy Norman (ed.) : *Nehru, the First Sixty Years,* 2 volumes, London, The Bodley Head, 1965 ; Stephens : *Nasser, op. cit.* ; St. John, Robert : *The Boss,* London, Arthur Barker, 1961, and Vaucher, Georges : *Gamal Abdul Nasser et son équipe,* 2 volumes, Paris, Juillard, 1959.

[30] For characteristics of people coming from this area—the Sa'idi—see El-Sadat : *Révolte sur le Nil, op. cit.,* p. 33 ; and Lacouture : *Nasser, op. cit.,* pp. 27-28.

[31] Stephens : *Nasser, op. cit.,* p. 24.

[32] Lacouture : *Nasser, op. cit.,* p. 27.

[33] *Ibid.*

when he returned home where three other children were competing for her attention. But from the end of April 1926, she ceased to write to him. "She was ill", or "she went to visit her parents in Alexandria", they said. When he returned during the school holiday, he learnt that she had died a few months before. This "shock of discovery accentuated a natural grief and left a deep and lasting impression on a boy already marked by an appearance of seriousness and reserve". [34] El-Sadat, for instance, felt the effect of this experience when he first met Nasser in 1938, *i.e.* 12 years after the death of the latter's mother. For El-Sadat was struck by the fact that Nasser "... had lost his mother early in life, and he bore the marks of that grief". [35] Nasser himself described this experience as " 'a cruel blow that was imprinted indelibly on my mind' and said that for years afterwards he had kept himself apart from his family". [36]

Thus Nasser's lonely childhood—marked by this sad experience—affected his personality, and indeed many who talked with him and knew him affirm that his mother's early death

> "... gave him a horror of death which led him to avoid bloodshed whenever possible when he came to power. It may also have been a cause of his later persistent fears and suspicions of conspiracies against him ... [At] least his mother's early death must have added another element of insecurity to a disturbed childhood in which he was constantly parted from his family and never had the feeling of a real home. The experience away from his family in early years may have helped to produce that combination of restlessness, suspicion, tension and passion, with patience and ability to conceal his real feelings, which was among his later characteristics as a private conspirator and public figure." [37]

4.1.2. Nehru's early family life presented a clear-cut contrast to Nasser's. Nehru was the son of a distinguished and wealthy barrister, Motilal Nehru, from the aristocratic Kashmiri Brahmin community. Both parents doted on Jawaharlal (the red jewel), and with reason. For Motilal

> "had been married once before, there had been a child, and both mother and child had died. A child had been born to his second wife but it too had died in infancy. Hence Jawaharlal was the object of ... [the parents'] complete devotion and love. And as the only child of a wealthy barrister for eleven years, he was spoiled in a princely fashion." [38]

---

[34] Stephens : *Nasser, op. cit.*, p. 28.

[35] El-Sadat : *Révolte sur le Nil, op. cit.*, p. 36.

[36] Stephens : *Nasser, op. cit.*, p. 28.

[37] *Ibid.*, p. 29.

[38] Brecher : *Nehru* (1961), *op. cit.*, p. 24.

When Nehru was three, the family moved to the "Civil Lines"—an exclusive residential area where only one other Indian family lived at the time. In 1900, when Nehru was eleven, Motilal bought a palatial home, *Anand Bhawan* (Abode of Happiness). Consequently, Nehru could enjoy *Anand Bhawan*'s two swimming pools (one in the palatial garden, another in the house itself). [39] Moreover, young Nehru, a proficient horseman, had a taste for riding which was cared for by one of the most impressive stables in India. Consequently, young Nehru's leisure hours were spent in games: "swimming, cricket, tennis, riding and the like". [40] Amid this atmosphere of lavid luxury and complete security, Nehru was not only brought up as an Englishman in India, but also as an English aristocrat in Britain itself:

> "When I was about eleven", Nehru says, "a new resident tutor, Ferdinand T. Brooks, came and took charge of me . . . He was a keen theosophist who had been recommended to my father by Mrs. Annie Besant. For nearly three years he was with me, and in many ways *he influenced me greatly*." [41]

Not only would this moody, gifted tutor prepare the terrain for Nehru's "Englishness", but he would also prepare him for a career of intellectualism: "Brooks developed in me a taste for reading [and] also initiated me into the mysteries of science . . ." [42]

Some of the influences on Nehru's later personality and future political behaviour that came directly from this mode of early upbringing are aptitude for global vision, complexity of mind and the capacity to notice fine distinctions:

> "Much as I began to resent the presence and behaviour of the alien rulers, I had no feeling whatever, so far as I can remember, against individual Englishmen. I had an English governess, and occasionally I saw English friends of my father's [sic] visiting him. In my heart, I rather admired the English." [43]

4.2. *School*

For young Nasser, however, the English were one bloc who had negative associations. He could not, then, internalise Nehru's fine distinction between the English as positively-associated individuals and the English as (resented) military occupation forces, since he knew only the latter.

---

[39] *Ibid.*, p. 25.

[40] *Ibid.*, p. 28.

[41] Nehru: *Toward Freedom, op. cit.*, pp. 26-27 (emphasis added).

[42] *Ibid.*, p. 28

[43] *Ibid.*, p. 21.

4.2.1. For when young Nasser was sent by his father to study in Cairo and live with his uncle, Khalil had just got out of prison after having been accused of political agitation. Both Khalil and young Nasser continued afterwards to live in the popular and picturesque district of El-Mouski, near the great bazars of Khan El-Khalili, the tomb of Sultan Qalawone, Bab El-Nasr (Door of Victory) and El-Azhar Islamic University. After the village, this busy commercial district was full of Egypt's historical symbols and regrouped mainly the typical strata of Cairo crowds. In the district school—El-Nahhassine (the Coppersmiths)—Nasser spent three years. [44]

Nasser's uncle, Khalil, used to take him to the nearby El-Azhar district, which was then one of the strongholds of nationalist ferment and political demonstrations. The exposure to Islamic and nationalist symbols at this early age accounts for such later characteristic traits as Nasser's Islamic piousness and expressive, manifest anti-colonialism. But in addition to the exposure to these Islamic-nationalist symbols, there were the nationalist talk of his uncle and, of course, the 1927-funeral of Sa'ad Zaghloul, "the father of the nation". Nasser was then only nine, but he must have seen the Egyptian masses pouring into the streets of Cairo and the whole centre of the city closed, so that everyone could attend the funeral of the "national hero" who symbolised Egypt's 1919-nationalist revolution against the British. Nasser himself recalled : ". . . when I was a little child, every time I saw aeroplanes flying overhead I used to shout 'O God Almighty, may a calamity overtake the English'." [45]

Nasser's involvement in the nationalist ferment was—if anything—increased when he learnt of his father's second marriage, so soon after his mother's death. [46] Feeling more and more homeless, he was easily recruited to 'street politics', becoming obsessed with the nationalist cause.

In 1929, at the age of eleven, Nasser's father was posted again to Alexandria. Nasser then went to Ras El-Tin secondary school, near the Summer Royal Palace. It was there that Nasser's active contact with the nationalist ferment would take place through his participation in strikes and political demonstrations that marked Egypt's political system at the time. Students were then called upon to play an active part in politics and they

> ". . . thought of themselves, with encouragement from the rival political parties, as the vanguard of an oppressed and backward nation. It was their duty to protest if their elders were too frightened or too closely controlled to do so. At the same time the students felt an

---

[44] Lacouture : *Nasser, op. cit.*, p. 31.

[45] Nasser : *The Philosophy of the Revolution, op. cit.*, p. 41.

[46] Lacouture : *Nasser, op. cit.*, p. 32, and Stephens : *Nasser, op. cit.*, p. 29.

extra responsibility as the potential educated elite who would not only bring Egypt independence but also modernize her social and cultural life. They were conscious of a wide gulf in this respect between themselves and their parents and elders." [47]

Nasser's participation in his first political demonstration came by accident. He saw the crowd and so followed the lead of slogan-chanting elders. He was hit in the face by a police stick and was taken to spend the night in jail. He then asked his cell-mates about the reasons for the demonstration, and knew it was a clash between the police and *Misr El-Fatah* (Young Egypt) Party. Nasser was the youngest in the cell and he felt proud of it.

In 1933, Nasser's father was posted to Cairo to run a post-office in the old district of *Bab Sharqiyyah* (East Gate) between El-Azbakiyyah—whose gardens Napoleon admired so much—and El-'Abbassiyyah—where Nasser's coup d'état would begin 19 years later. As usual, Nasser's father and his step-mother had a modest flat :

"The three-story building which housed both the post-office and Nasser's family was in a *cul-de-sac* called Khamis el Ads (Lentils Thursday) between a small synagogue of the Karaite Jewish sect and a Jewish chemist's shop. Nasser's family rented a second-floor four-room flat for three or four pounds a month from a Jewish landlord named Samuel who lived next door. Nasser himself had a room at the back of the flat overlooking a courtyard. This was his home for the next four years. With his father's growing family, he can have found little peace at home and he would sometimes go to the quiet courtyard of a nearby old mosque to read." [48]

Nasser would then spend, in this part of Cairo, four decisive years (1933-1937). In Alexandria, he had participated in his first political demonstration by mere accident. In Cairo, on the contrary, he would study, militate, fight, get arrested, enter the faculty of law (centre of political activity), before directing himself resolutely to a military career—an assured means of (successful) political action in a praetorian society.

Nasser pursued his secondary studies at the school of *El-Nahda El-Misriyyah* (Egyptian Renaissance) which precisely had a reputation at the time for performing a leading part in schoolboy and student demonstrations. Nasser occupied the forefront for he became the chairman of the Executive Committe of Cairo Secondary School Students. His involvement in politics was so intense that in his last full year at school (1935-

---

[47] *Ibid.*

[48] *Ibid.,* pp. 31-32. And perhaps it is not a coincidence that he used to go to have some of his meals with the family of the Jewish landlord, Samuel. See also Lacouture : *Nasser, op. cit.,* p. 32.

1936), he spent only 45 days in classes, and was to pass his final secondary school exams only with difficulty. [49]

But active involvement in politics, however, left Nasser some time to read. His reading list comprised mostly history, politics and biographies of famous men by Arab and Moslim nationalist authors. On top of the list comes Mustapha Kamel—an eloquent youth symbolising Egyptian nationalism at the end of the 19th and early 20th centuries—who had inspired the establishment of *El-Hizb El-Watani* (Nationalist Party). But Nasser also read the works of 'Abd El-Rahman El-Kawakibi, "one of the most influential of the early Islamic reformers and anti-imperialists" who had fled from Syria to Egypt to escape Turkish persecution. [50] In his most famous books, *Om El-Qura* (Mother of Villages—the name given to Mecca) and *Tabaï' El-Istibdad* (Characteristics of Tyranny), El-Kawakibi dealt with two issues that occupied Nasser's attention then, and were to become central in his future political attitudes. *Om El-Qura* is "a discussion of how the East can overcome its backwardness and rid itself of foreign domination and it emphasises the central role the Arabs should play in the regeneration of Islamic society". The second book, *Tabaï' El-Istibdad,* argues that "when a Western power occupies an Eastern country it does not bring liberty to the people but combines with local despots and a minority of politicians and religious leaders to exploit them". [51] Nasser also read literature, the nationalist poems of Ahmed Shawqi and especially—as already mentioned—*'Awdat El Roah* (L'Ame retrouvée) by Tawfik El-Hakim. This last work describes

> "the life of a young boy of fifteen, Mohsen, who lives with his uncle in Cairo and goes home to his parent's country estate in the holidays. It gives a sensitive picture of the awakening of a shy but passionate adolescent love, to social conscience and to patriotic self-sacrifice. The background of country and city life is drawn with sensitivity, humour and a feeling for nature ... Nasser could easily have identified with the character and circumstances of Mohsen who lived claustrophopically in an overcrowded Cairo flat, felt the widening gap of culture and generation between himself and his parents, and plunged feverishly into the demonstrations of the 1919 revolution with which the novel ends." [52]

---

[49] *Ibid.*, p. 38, and Stephens : *Nasser, op. cit.*, p. 32.

[50] *Ibid.*

[51] *Ibid.*

[52] Nasser also played the role of Julius Caesar in the school-play marking the yearly celebration of El-Nahda school. For details, see Lacouture : *Nasser, op. cit.*, pp. 33-34 ; Stephens : *Nasser, op. cit.*, p. 33, and Nasser : *The Philosophy of the Revolution, op. cit.*, pp. 43-44.

The reading was, then, attuned to Nasser's emerging political personality and was channelled in the direction of his political action for "the nationalist cause". As he himself explains :

> "At a certain phase of my life, enthusiasm represented 'positive action'. But I later came to realise that I should not be alone in that enthusiasm. To be effective, it should be communicated to others.
>
> I was then a student at the Nahda School, leading many demonstrations in these days, shouting myself hoarse, followed by other fellow-students, in our importunate demand for complete independence. But it was to no avail—our cries died into faint echoes that moved no mountains and blasted no rocks.
>
> Then I came to believe that 'positive action' rested in the solidarity and agreement of all leaders of the nation. So our rebellious roaring ranks went around visiting these leaders, in their own homes, calling on them, in the name of Egypt's youth to agree for concerted action." [53]

Thus with members of the Committee of Secondary School Students —which Nasser chaired—he toured different political organisations ranging from the Fascist 'Misr El-Fatah' to the nationalist Wafd mass party. This direct contact with the pillars of the multi-party system was to prove a very important factor in Nasser's mistrust of the Westminster model of democracy. A close friend of Nasser at the time, Hassan El-Nashshar, described the lesson of this experience :

> "We had decided to contact the leader of a political party, and had fixed an appointment for the 12th of February, 1935. He was an important personality, a minister. When we arrived, he was coming out of his office. Gamal dashed to talk to him and managed to do so in front of the ministry's elevator. He said to him : "We have constituted a group of students and want to have your opinion on the best way to serve the country." The minister advised him to contact the university students, which he did a month later. But what were their main concerns ? Politics ? Struggle ? No. Nothing very serious. Their main concern was how to fill the vacancies in the students' executive committee, who would be the chairman or secretary . . . But as for organising youth against corruption, against imperialism, with this they were not concerned." [54]

The University students' leader whom Nasser went to see, described Nasser of the time in the following way :

> "He had not yet formed clear conceptions or a political programme. He was lost in this disturbed world. He wandered here and there visiting centres of political parties with the hope of finding

[53] *Ibid.*, p. 31.

[54] Lacouture : *Nasser, op. cit.*, p. 35 (my translation).

one that met his nationalist aspirations. But the ideal party, that contained all the necessary elements for the realisation of national aspirations, did not exist."[55]

So he went back to street politics, and it was during one of the political demonstrations of this period that a bullet from a British officer's revolver hit Nasser in the forehead, leaving a permanent scar.[56]

But if this young activist, "égaré dans ce monde bouleversé", was undecided about the choice of his political chief or party, his objective was—however—clear. On September 2, 1935, he wrote to his friend, Hassan El-Nashshar :

> "To-day the situation is critical and Egypt is in an impasse. It seems to me that the country is dying. Despair is great. Who can end it ? . . . Where are the men ready to give their lives for the independence of the country ? Where is the man who can rebuild the country so that the weak and humiliated Egyptian can stand up again and live free and independent ? Where is dignity ? Where is nationalism ? Where is the so-called activity of our youth ? They say the Egyptian is a coward, that he is afraid of the slightest sound. *He needs a leader* to lead him in the struggle for his country. By this means this same Egyptian would become a thunder-clap which would make the walls of tyranny tremble . . ."[57]

At last, and as Nasser had been hoping for so long, the leaders "... did actually agree, but it was on a calamitous decision which destroyed my conviction—they agreed to conclude the 1936 Treaty".[58]

But though disillusioned with this new failure of the ("reactionary") multi-party democracy, Nasser had to think about his final exams at El-Nahda school and about what career to choose. In his last-minute rush to continue his secondary school studies, Nasser was surprised to find the school doors closed in front of him. Unfavorable police reports had signalled him as a political agitator and a scared headmaster refused to permit Nasser to sit for his *baccalaureat*. A wide protest movement was set off among the students, and the headmaster gave in.[59] Nasser did pass his *baccalaureat* in the Summer examinations, and had then to face the big question :

> "What to do then ? He was certainly attracted by political action, but how to materialise it and find the most efficient means for its realisation ? He thought of going to the Cairo faculty of law. After

---

[55] *Ibid.* (my translation).

[56] Stephens : *Nasser, op. cit.*, p. 35.

[57] Nasser : *The Philosophy of the Revolution, op. cit.*, p. 17 (emphasis added) ; Lacouture : *Nasser, op. cit.*, pp. 36-37, and Stephens : *Nasser,* op. cit., pp. 34-35.

[58] Nasser : *The Philosophy of the Revolution, op. cit.*, p. 31.

[59] Lacouture : *Nasser, op. cit.*, p. 38 ; Stephens : *Nasser, op. cit.*, p. 37.

> all, this was the faculty from which the most well-known political leaders had graduated : Zaghloul, Nahas, Ahmed Maher ... He joined the faculty but became disappointed with its atmosphere which did not encourage direct independent action. Dissatisfied and isolated, he abandoned the faculty after seven months.
>
> So why not join the army ? It could provide the effective physical force and the mobilised men that could outdo other political movements and perhaps even take over the political system." [60]

Nasser then chose a military career, and this choice opened a new phase in his life and also in Egypt's.

4.2.2. Not only was Nehru spared the agitational boyhood of Nasser, but also he continued his education like an English aristocrat. In 1904, Nehru was sent to the famous public school, Harrow (where Winston Churchill studied). Thus only at the age of 15 was Nehru to be on his own for the first time—a clear contrast with Nasser's childhood. Here perhaps lies a reason for Nasser's decisiveness and what some termed rashness as opposed to Nehru's well-known hesitation. [61]

Nehru was also very studious, the contrast of Nasser's 'angry young man' type. For contrary to Nasser's neglect of school, Nehru was awarded "the prize for topping the examination list in his form during the third term in 1905 and again in the first term of 1906". [62] Moreover, Dr. Joseph Wood, Headmaster of Harrow, wrote to Motilal :

> "Every master speaks well of your boy, both as to his work and to his conduct. He has distinct ability, is already ahead of his form ... I am fully satisfied with him in every way." [63]

The contrast in school life and studiousness was bound to influence later political attitudes and behaviour. For whereas Nasser could see nothing but British occupation forces and Egypt's perennial demand for "complete independence", Nehru was already building up his interest in internationalism—starting with following the details of British local politics. In his autobiography he tells us :

> "I was greatly interested in the [British] General Election, which took place, as far as I remember, at the end of 1905 and which ended in a great Liberal victory. Early in 1906 our form master asked us

---

[60] Lacouture : *Nasser, op. cit.*, p. 38 (my translation).

[61] Nehru's hesitation is one of his basic characteristics, for he "continually made statements, thought about them, then cancelled them out". Heikal : *Nasser : The Cairo Documents, op. cit.*, p. 253.

[62] Brecher : *Nehru* (1961), *op. cit.*, p. 29.

[63] Nehru : *The First Sixty Years, op. cit.*, Vol. I, p. 10.

about the new Government, and, much to his surprise, I was the only boy in his form who could give him much information on the subject."[64]

Thus whereas English public school pupils of Harrow did not know their country's politics, the Indian—Nehru—did. This interest in "foreign" issues heralded the internationalist emphasis in his non-aligned role-performance. This mode of socialisation was to be accentuated on leaving Harrow for Cambridge.

For in 1907, Nehru went up to Cambridge where he spent three years of mental growth and pleasant, comfortable living. He was enrolled at Trinity College, "famous among other things as the training ground of Prime Ministers".[65] Though his studies were mainly the natural sciences, his "intellectual interests ranged far and wider—into literature, philosophy, economics, politics, history and Greek poetry".[66] It was also during his Cambridge studies that Nehru was introduced to (Fabian) Socialism. In October 1907, he wrote to his father : "I have just come back ... from a lecture on 'Socialism and the University Man' ... The lecturer was George Bernard Shaw, about whom you must have heard a good deal."[67]

And he confirmed in his conversations with Tibor Mende : "I would say that it was really at Cambridge that, broadly speaking, certain socialistic ideas—partly Fabian Socialism, partly some slightly more aggressive socialistic ideas—developed."[68]

Moreover, since "... many of the people I met at Cambridge or during the vacations in London or elsewhere talked learnedly about books and literature and history and politics and economics"[69] and since "... men like Bernard Shaw, Bertrand Russel, Keynes the economist ... were lecturing ..."[70] at the time at Cambridge, Nehru was bound to be influenced by the views of these men and of European thinking at the time. In fact, his classmates—at both Harrow and Cambridge—remember him as a "typical public-school product, polished, urbane and somewhat snobbish".[71] He had internalised English values and cultural norms as he himself—on the eve of his second imprisonment, in 1922—confirmed :

> "Less than ten years ago, I returned from England after a long stay there ... I had imbibed most of the prejudices of Harrow and

[64] Nehru : *Toward Freedom, op. cit.*, p. 31.

[65] Brecher : *Nehru* (1961), *op. cit.*, p. 30.

[66] *Ibid.*

[67] *Nehru : The First Sixty Years, op. cit.*, Vol. I, p. 13.

[68] *Ibid.*

[69] Nehru : *Toward Freedom, op. cit.*, p. 33.

[70] *Nehru : The First Sixty Years, op. cit.*, Vol. I, p. 13.

[71] Brecher : *Nehru* (1961), *op. cit.*, p. 31.

> Cambridge, and in my likes and dislikes I was perhaps more an Englishman than an Indian. I looked upon the world almost from an Englishman's standpoint ... as much prejudiced in favour of England and the English as it was possible for an Indian to be." [72]

Moreover, like a young English intellectual, "... I was much influenced by things like the story of the Italian Republic, by Mazzini, Cavour and Garibaldi ; by the Irish struggle ..." [73]

Once Nehru finished at Cambridge, the question of his career came up, but—opposite to Nasser's case—Nehru was not to take the decision on his own :

> "During my stay at Cambridge the question [arose] as to what career I should take up. For a little the Indian Civil Service was contemplated ; there was a glamour about it still in those days." [74]

Thus, it was a typically conformist and traditional choice: to be recruited to the Indian Civil Service, the "steel frame" of the British Raj [75] as Nehru himself admits candidly in retrospect :

> "It is curious that, inspite of my growing extremism in politics, I did not then view with any strong disfavor the idea of joining the Indian Civil Service and thus becoming a cog in the British Government's administration machine in India. Such an idea in later years would have been repellent to me." [76]

But since "... neither my father nor I was keen on it ...", [77] the possible recruitment to the Indian Civil Service was finally dropped. Working in the Indian Civil Service meant largely that the "red jewel" would be almost constantly absent from his family.

Young Nehru, then, expressed the desire to go to Oxford "to study something besides law". His father had insisted on law but Nehru informed him that

> "Law and Science are all very well in their own way, but no man, however great a lawyer he may be, will or should be excused for his want of knowledge in certain other subjects. I would much rather risk my success at the Bar than go through life as a mere lawyer with no interest in anything save the technicalities and trivialities of law." [78]

---

[72] *Ibid.*

[73] *Nehru : The First Sixty Years, op. cit.,* Vol. I, p. 13.

[74] Nehru : *Toward Freedom, op. cit.,* p. 37.

[75] Brecher : *Nehru* (1961), *op. cit.,* p. 31.

[76] Nehru : *Toward Freedom, op. cit.,* p. 37.

[77] *Ibid.*

[78] *Nehru : The First Sixty Years, op. cit.,* Vol. I, p. 17.

But it was Motilal who insisted on choosing London's Inner Temple. Not even London's School of Economics would be attended for fear that "the study of economics ... might distract" the young Nehru from concentration on law. [79]

As expected, Nehru's two years in London continued to be diametrically opposed to Nasser's El-Nahda School days or his faculty of law days of restlessness, active political agitation and bloody clashes with the police. For Nehru was

> "... debonair in his Bond Street clothes. He frequented the proper clubs and restaurants, whiled away his time at the theatre and at social functions of the young aristocrats. His law studies took up relatively little time, as did serious intellectual pursuits, though he dabbled in Fabian ideas and was interested in the suffragette movement. In the summer [of 1912] he did Europe as was fashionable then and now." [80]

Upon his return to India in 1912 (*i.e.* 23 years old then), Nehru was introduced into active Indian politics. This is again a marked contrast with Nasser who—as a school boy—was hit and imprisoned at the age of sixteen. Moreover, whereas Nasser had been living in the popular districts of Cairo and Egypt's villages, mingling with the *fellahin* and the crowds of Cairo or Alexandria from his earliest days, Nehru—at the age of 23—seemed only to be starting his direct acquaintance with his country. As Nehru himself testifies in his book, significantly entitled *Discovery of India :*

> "India was in my blood and there was much in her that instinctively thrilled me ... Yet I approached her almost as an alien critic, full of dislike for the present as well as for many of the relics of the past that I saw. To some extent I came to her via the West and looked at her as a friendly Westerner might have done. I was eager and anxious to change her outlook and appearance and give her the garb of modernity. And yet doubts rose within me. Did I know India ; I who presumed to scrap much of her past prestige ?" [81]

---

[79] *Ibid.*

[80] Brecher : *Nehru* (1961), *op. cit.*, p. 32.

[81] *Nehru : The First Sixty Years, op. cit.*, Vol. I, p. 18. Consequently Nehru had serious problems of identity. As he himself states it very explicitly and eloquently in his autobiography : "I have become a queer mixture of the East and the West, out of place everywhere, at home nowhere. Perhaps my thoughts and approach to life are more akin to what is called Western than Eastern, but India clings to me, as she does to all her children, in innumerable ways ; and behind me lie, somewhere in the subconscious, racial memories of a hundred, or whatever the number may be, generations of Brahmans. I cannot get rid of either that past inheritance or my recent acquisitions. They are both part of me, and, though they help me in both the East and the West, they also create in me a feeling of spiritual loneliness not only in pub-

Nasser, however, knew his Egypt inside out, and the military profession that he chose symbolised—through the uniform—his manifest "Egyptianness".

4.3.1. Moreover, the military profession also appealed to his emerging personality as a man of action, a personality conditioned by his lonely childhood and austere boyhood. For after his father's second marriage so soon after his mother's death, Nasser became even sadder and could not get along very well with his father. He could not, however, afford to live away from home as a university student. So the Military Academy presented the added advantage of getting away from difficulties at home. [82]

But in the royal and colonised Egypt of the time, admission to the Military Academy was subject to "ascriptive" criteria (*e.g.* family influence, certain social status) and required that one be 'politically clean'. Because of his modest family origin and political 'agitation', Nasser had none of the prescribed requirements. [83] His demand was thus at first rejected, before a second presentation gained acceptance. [84]

In the austere atmosphere of military socialisation, [85] Nasser entertained and satisfied two of the drives which would characterise him as Egypt's charismatic leader : the quest for unquestioned authority and a

lic activities but in life itself. I am stranger and alien in the West. I cannot be of it. But in my own country also, sometimes, I have an exile's feeling." *Toward Freedom, op. cit.,* p. 353.

[82] Stephens : *Nasser, op. cit.,* p. 38.

[83] The first time "Gamal est convoqué devant une commission composée d'officiers supérieurs. Le président : 'Comment vous appelez-vous ?' — 'Gamal Abdel Nasser Hussein.' — 'Que fait votre père ?' — 'Employé à la poste.' — 'D'où venez-vous ?' — 'De Beni-Morr, province d'Assiout.' — 'Vous êtes des paysans ?' — 'Oui.' — 'Personne dans votre famille n'a été officier ?' — 'Non.' — 'Pourquoi voulez-vous devenir officier ?' — 'Pour servir la patrie.' — 'Avez-vous des propriétés ?' — 'Non, je suis un homme du peuple.' — 'Quelqu'un vous a-t-il recommandé ?' — 'Non.' — 'Avez-vous pris part aux manifestations de novembre 1935 ?' — 'Oui.' — Le dialogue s'arrête là." Lacouture : *Nasser, op. cit.,* pp. 41-42.

[84] Nasser, then, went and met General Ibrahim Khairy Pasha, the Under-Secretary of the Ministry of War, who was impressed with him and got him admitted to the Military Academy. *Ibid.* ; Vaucher : *op. cit.,* p. 90.

[85] Though there is a long list of authorship on the role of the military in 'new states', very few studies have tackled the socio-psychological aspect of this new elite. But a relatively useful treatment of the aspects that interest us here is Janowitz, Morris : *The Military in the Political Development of New Nations,* Chicago, University of Chicago Press, 1964. For a critical approach to the "organizational model" in the analysis of the military's intervention in third world political systems, see Price, Robert : "A Theoretical Approach to Military Rule in New States : Reference-Group Theory and the Ghanaian Case", *World Politics,* XXIII (1971), pp. 399-431.

love for reading and instruction. At the Military Academy—unlike at the Secondary School or Faculty of Law—Nasser was a "good subject". His tendency for political 'agitation' and activism was transformed into an applied perseverance. Only six months after his entrance, he was appointed to the 'authoritative' position of a corporal and made the head of a study group.

Nasser's reading list at the time reveals his thirst for education but also certain emphases on what kind of education. The ex-Swiss Consul in Egypt—George Vaucher—in his field research among Nasser's files at the Military Academy, as well as through talks with Nasser's friends and colleagues—gives us the following reading list:

1. *Gordon at Khartoum*	by J. Buchan
2. *Napoleon and Waterloo*	by Becke
3. *My Early Life*	by W. Churchill
4. *Lawrence and the Arabs*	by B. Graves
5. *Bismarck*	by H. Morley
6. *Bonaparte, Governor of Egypt*	by Ch. Roux
7. *Alexander The Great*	by A. Weigall
8. *A Book About Heroic Deeds*	by K. Wynne

In addition he read Arabic literature and works on the glory of Islam and the heroic epoch of Arab conquest (*e.g. Omarieh,* by the Egyptian nationalist poet Hafiz Ibrahim, which is written to the glory of the second Caliph, Omar Ibn El-Khattab—the organiser of the great Islamic conquests).

The full list indicates a marked interest in political and military history, including books about Ataturk, Garibaldi, Foch, as well as five books about Napoleon (who attracted Nasser because he was both the enemy of Great Britain and a poor officer who saw corruption around him and so decided to take over political authority). [86]

Nasser passed his final examination at the Military Academy comfortably on July 1, 1938. Vaucher gives us Nasser's marks:

Military History	13/20
Civic Organisation	14/20
Sciences and Mathematics	17/20
Administration and Organisation	19/20

Clearly he had an aptitude for organisation, for in this branch he obtained his highest mark.

---

[86] Vaucher: *op. cit.,* pp. 66-97.

Nasser was commissioned to Mankabad in Upper Egypt, and as a second-lieutenant's letter [87] to his close friend Hassan El-Nashshar shows, Nasser's adolescent romanticism had not changed and his nationalist fervour was as strong as ever. And if anything, this nationalist fervour would continue to be strong and develop, for in Mankabad

> "there was not much to do . . . in free hours except talk and read or at week-ends to visit Nasser's relatives at Beni Murr. In camp or round the camp-fire out on manoeuvres Nasser and his young officer friends talked mostly professional shop and politics, partly because some of them were politically minded and, as young men in developing countries, felt a special political responsibility, partly because young Muslims especially, lacking feminine society and other entertainment, often have little else but politics to talk about . . . Apart from their careers, there were few other outlets except politics for . . . [their] energy, idealism and romanticism . . . : religion was in doubt, sexual life restricted, good works of a social welfare kind scarcely developed, and literature also highly political in content. Egyptian youth of this generation was uncertain of its identity, surrounded by a bewildering confusion of cultures and even of different languages. Their country seemed to them to be ruled half by foreigners and for the rest by a sham king and a sham parliament : a veneer of constitutionalism concealed a police state and a revolutionary opposition.' [88]

At Mankabad Nasser met the second-lieutenant of infantry Zakaria Moheï ed-Din—whom he was to choose as his successor during the 1967 crisis—and El-Sadat—who was to follow him as Egypt's president. This latter tells us in detail the importance of these Mankabad meetings among social change-conscious youth ; and affirms that ". . . the 23 July Revolution—which was born in Mankabad in 1938 among the young military . . . came from above. It was the work of a small number of a far-sighted, idealistic and determined Egyptians." [89]

The army itself was a microcosm of the shortcomings and failures of the Egyptian political system. For ". . . Egypt was a sick country . . ." and consequently ". . . the social and political unrest in Egypt was the theme of our debates". [90]

It was Nasser, the ". . . true son of the Saïd [Upper Egypt], . . . manly . . . reserved and serious in manner that imposed himself as a leader. If we started a light-hearted conversation", El-Sadat reminisces, "it was invariably Gamal Abdul Nasser who interrupted to bring us back to graver topics". And El-Sadat significantly reminds us : ". . . our orga-

---

[87] Text of letter is in Lacouture : *Nasser, op. cit.*, p. 44.

[88] Stephens : *Nasser, op. cit.*, p. 43.

[89] El-Sadat : *Révolte sur le Nil, op. cit., pp. 32-33* (emphasis added).

[90] El-Sadat, Anwar : *Revolt on the Nile,* London, Allan Wingate, 1957, p. 13.

nisation was *illegal. We worked in darkness,* awaiting the dawn. It was a long-term plan, and *Gamal Abdul Nasser was to be the architect and the strategist* . . .". [91]

For it was as a secret conspirator and plotter that Nasser was to start his preparations to overthrow the regime. Unlike Nehru's direct contact with, and sophistication in grasping, British democracy, Nasser saw this 'democracy' only through colonial occupation and through such instances as the order of Britain's High Commissioner to siege the Royal Palace and to force the king (the legitimate head of the state) either to abdicate or to accept the cabinet chosen by London (February 1942). Moreover, his direct experiences with 'corrupted' political parties helped to internalise his mistrust of the 'multi-party model' and of its "liberal" way of thinking. [92] Consequently, he came to believe that the only way out was the "Revolution", and thus his post-school socialisation continued in an atmosphere of secrecy and plotting, away from the eyes of King Faruq's secret police and the British Intelligence Service. To liberate Egypt from "imperialism, corruption and reactionary elements", Nasser worked with a small group of carefully selected companions on whose loyalty his personal safety and the security of the whole enterprise depended. This mode of socialisation accounts for his future 'personalised' political behaviour and his domination of Egypt's political system where he—either on his own or with the selected few—could decide promptly on the quick counter-moves that characterised his militant pragmatic non-alignment (*e.g.* Suez).

The pattern of Nasser's political socialisation, then, presented a clear contrast to Nehru's attachment and faith in multi-party democracy, his constitutional ascendancy in the ranks of the Congress Party to become its president at the age of forty, and his respect and moral commitment to "principles" and "rules of the game" in the 'democratic' polity (*e.g.* he usually spent long hours in his office in Lok Sabha).

4.3.2. For Nehru was socialised into respecting this type of political system both during his studies at Harrow and Cambridge and upon his return to India at the age of 23. This period (following his return from the metropolis), which witnessed his active participation in local Indian politics and ascendancy in the Congress Party, is characterised by at least three important aspects : (*a*) meeting with Gandhi and *open* political work within the Congress ; (*b*) frequent imprisonment to the point where prison became a second home ; and (*c*) continuation of erudition and internationalist political attitudes.

---

[91] *Ibid.*, pp. 13-15 (emphasis added).

[92] *El-Mithaq* (National Charter) : *op. cit.*, pp. 11-17 ("On the Necessity of Revolution') and pp. 34-49 ("On Sound Democracy).

(*a*) *Gandhi and Political Work Within the Congress*

Nehru described his first meeting with the Mahatma (during Christmas 1916) in the following way: "I was simply bowled over by Gandhi, straight off . . . I worked as a kind of secretary to [him] . . . I was searching for some [satisfying] method of action" [93]; and remarked ". . . [Gandhi] *did not descend from the top; he seemed to emerge from the millions of India,* speaking their language and incessantly drawing attention to them and their appealling condition . . ." [94]

When Nehru states that Gandhi "did not descend from the top" but seemed to "emerge from the millions of India", he was—consciously or unconsciously—emphasising a difference between himself and Gandhi. Though the two studied at the Inner Temple and were imbided with the spirit of English law,

> "Nehru had gone to England as a young boy whose home life was permeated with the modern, secular atmosphere of the West. His real mother-tongue was English. Seven years at Harrow, Cambridge and London deepened his attachment to the British way of life, with the result that he returned to his native land 'more an Englishman than an Indian'. By contrast, Ghandhi's mother-tongue was Gujarati. And by the time he left for England his personality and outlook had been already moulded. Thus two years in London merely provided him with a legal training. He returned to India in 1891 entirely an Indian, in no sense an Englishman." [95]

Consequently, there were bound to be differences in, for instance, political attitudes toward the independence issue. Thus when the Congress—during Gandhi's absence—passed a resolution in 1927 stating that "the goal of the Indian people [was] to have complete national independence", [96] Gandhi criticised Nehru's "extremism" and said:

> "I feel that you love me too well to resent what I am about to write. In any case, I love you too well to restrain my pen when I feel I must write. You are going too fast. You should have taken time to think and become acclimatized . . . By passing such resolutions we make an exhibition of our impotence . . . We have almost sunk to the level of a schoolboys' debating society." [97]

---

[93] *Nehru: The First Sixty Years, op. cit.,* Vol. I, p. 42.

[94] *Ibid.,* p. 43 (emphasis added).

[95] Brecher: *Nehru* (1961), *op. cit.,* p. 35.

[96] For details about divergent political attitudes within the Congress and Nehru's contemplated resignation, see: *Toward Freedom, op. cit.,* pp. 358-359.

[97] Brecher: *Nehru* (1961), *op. cit.,* pp. 57-58.

So not only was Nehru being socialised into attaching a negative value to 'agitational' politics, but also into attaching a positive value to the "purity" of "the means" to any goal. Thus Gandhi again wrote to Nehru :

> "I have concerned myself more with the conservation of the means and their progressive use. I know if we can take care of them the attainment of the goal is assured. I feel too that our progress toward the goal will be in exact proportion to the purity of our means." [98]

Therefore, despite Nehru's English aristocratic upbringing and the fact that he was 20 years younger than Gandhi, the two men ended by being very close to each other. We have seen Gandhi's letter professing love for Nehru, and Nehru's admission of being "bowled over" when he saw the Mahatma in 1916. In 1921, Nehru saw Gandhi in political action at the Nagpur session of the Congress Party (after the arrest of the Ali brothers in mid-September) and he

> "gave up smoking for five years and even flirted with vegetarianism, though only for a brief period. He began reading the *Bhagavad Gita* afresh, with its emphasis on right action, caring less for the consequences. His faith in the importance of means dates from this period, as does his stress on the ethical side of politics . . . Gandhi the man was a model of behaviour for Nehru." [99]

Indeed, it was Gandhi himself who encouraged Nehru's ascendance in the ranks of the Congress. Thus in spite of some protests, Gandhi decided to have Nehru as the Congress President of the 1929 Congress Party's Lahore session (to succeed Motilal). To defend himself against great pressures to assume the leadership himself, Gandhi told the press on July 9, 1929 : ". . . those who know the relations that subsist between Jawaharlal and me know that his being in the chair is as good as my being in it."

Moreover, in 1942 Gandhi publicly designated Nehru as his successor :

> ". . . I have said for some years and say now that not Rajaji [Rajagopalacharia] but Jawaharlal will be my successor. He says he does not understand my language, and that he speaks a language foreign to me . . . *I know this, that when I am gone he will speak my language.*"

And Nehru's classic biographer adds : "It was a prophetic statement which even Nehru must have doubted at the time." [100] And on May 9,

---

[98] *Nehru : The First Sixty Years, op. cit.,* Vol. I, p. 297.

[99] Brecher : *Nehru* (1961), *op. cit.,* p. 43.

[100] *Ibid.,* p. 108 (emphasis added).

1946—at the Congress' first presidential election since 1940—Nehru was elected President for the fourth time, and Gandhi commented: "I told Jawaharlal that he must wear the crown of thorns for the sake of the nation and he has agreed." [101]

But not only did Nehru follow 'democratic' constitutional ascendance, but he was also going up the ladder of political authority through *open* mass party organisation rather than through conspiratorial anti-regime plots. Unlike Nasser, then, Nehru was socialised into mass political action for years before assuming the premiership of the first government of independent India. His description of his 1936-canvassing is both very informative and revealing about his political attitudes and style:

> "... I toured all over India on behalf of Congress candidates, and I imagine that I created some kind of a record in the way of election campaigns. In the course of about four months I traveled [sic] about fifty thousand miles, using every kind of convenience for this purpose, and often going into remote rural areas where there were no proper means of transport. I traveled by airplane, railway, automobile, motor truck, horse carriages of various kinds, bullock cart, bicycle, elephant, camel, horse, steamer, paddle-boat, canoe and on foot.
>
> I carried about with me microphones and loud-speakers and addressed a dozen meetings a day, apart from impromptu gatherings, by the roadside. Some mammoth gatherings approached a hundred thousands; the average audience was usually twenty thousand ... On a rough estimate it can be said that ten million persons actually attended the meetings I addressed, and probably several million more were brought into some kind of touch with me during my journeying by road.
>
> I rushed about from place to place, from the northern frontiers of India to the southern seas, taking little rest, kept up by the excitement of the moment and the enormous enthusiasm that met me ... This election campaign ... stirred up the whole countryside and a new life was visible everywhere ..." [102]

This open political activity through mass party organisation brought Nehru popularity, wide reputation and experience in mass politics. It also brought him repeated [103] imprisonment by the colonial authority.

---

[101] *Nehru: The First Sixty Years, op. cit.,,* Vol. II, p. 195.

[102] *Ibid.,* Vol. I, pp. 477-478.

[103] There is a tale, "perhaps apocryphal, yet nevertheless apposite and poignant, to the effect that, upon being released from prison after a long confinement for speeches he had made, Nehru went directly to a large meeting, stood up and stated quite unaffectedly: "As I was saying ...". *Ibid.,* Vol. II, p. 62.

(*b*) *Frequent Imprisonment*

In 1921 prison was unknown to Jawaharlal, but with the passage of time until he became India's Prime Minister, he was imprisoned 9 times totalling 9 years in all.[104] Looking, for instance, at the 4-year period 1931-1935, he was away from home, family and friends for about 42 months and stayed free only about 6 months.

Thus because of long, repeated seclusion and imprisonment, Nehru has left us—unlike Nasser—his own autobiography : *Toward Freedom :*

> "I wrote my autobiography", Nehru tells us, "entirely in prison, cut off from outside activity. I suffered from various humors in prison, as every prisoner does ; but gradually I developed a mood of introspection and some peace of mind."[105]

He tells us the effect of this solitude and writing experience on his mental growth and tendency for intellectualisation :

> "The primary object in writing these pages was to occupy myself with a definite task, so necessary in the long solitudes of jail life, as well as to review past events in India, with which I had been connected, to enable myself to think clearly about them. I began the task in a mood of self-questioning, and, to a large extent, this persisted throughout . . ."[106]

(*c*) *Consolidation of Erudition and Internationalist Tendencies*

But not only did repeated imprisonment allow Nehru to leave behind him ". . . a record of my own thoughts and moods . . . and . . . what impression . . . external happenings . . . produced on me . . .", but it also accentuated his eruditionist tendency[107] and interest in *global* affairs—heralding the 'internationalist' characteristic in his role-enactment of India's non-alignment. For it was during his fifth term in prison that Nehru began a series of letters to his daughter, Indira, then in her teens. He wrote this "informal survey of world history" to compensate the little girl who was suffering because of her father's preoccupation with politics and his frequent "visits to prison". The series contained "a brief and simple account of the early days of the world". After the communications had been published in book form, and were warmly received, "the idea of continuing them hovered" in Nehru's mind. Although "a busy life full of

---

[104] Brecher : *Nehru* (1961), *op. cit.*, p. 44.

[105] Nehru : *Toward Freedom, op. cit.*, p. 356.

[106] *Ibid.*, p. xiii.

[107] Thus Nehru wrote his important volume, *Discovery of India,* in Ahmadnagar Fort Prison, during five months—April to September 1944. *Nehru : The First Sixty Years, op. cit.*, Vol. II, p. 129.

political activity prevented" the idea "from taking shape . . . prison gave me the chance I needed" at a later date, and "I seized it". [108] The result of these letters to Indira from various Indian prisons between October 1930 and August 1933 is the volume *Glimpses of World History,* which stemmed also from Nehru's "attempt to discover the past in relation to the present". [109]

Nehru's complexity of mind and his 'internationalist' tendency would continue to develop, helped by such activities as a 2-year European tour (1926-1927) when he visited Italy, Switzerland, England, Belgium, France, Germany, Holland, and the U.S.S.R., and where he observed, studied and contemplated on international affairs. A prominent occurrence during this tour was his attendance of the Anti-Imperialist Conference at Brussels [110] (February, 1927). This was followed in the same year by Nehru's visit to Moscow to attend the 10th anniversary of the U.S.S.R., upon which he published *Soviet Russia,* "a series of articles which I sent mostly to the *Hindu Madras* . . . [and which] conveyed some impressions fresh in my mind at the time". [111] The trip developed his interest in the first "Marxist Socialist" experiment and strengthened his already existing tendency to pursue furthet direct contacts at the international level. Consequently, it was inevitable that his political attitude toward, for instance, Marxism and Communism differed from Nasser's, the (young) nationalist officer.

Commenting on his 1926-1927 European sojourn, Nehru confided to Michael Brecher :

> "[It gave] me time to think, to broaden my outlook, to see India from afar, to think on life itself. Until then I was so involved in Indian affairs that I had little time to think about the broad world or about life's problems in general." [112]

And the 'internationalist bias' in his political socialisation would be even more confirmed and allowed to develop when the Congress Party designated Nehru as India's spokesman at the international level. Feeling a

---

[108] *Ibid.,* Vol. I, p. 261.

[109] *Ibid.,* pp. 260-268.

[110] *Ibid.,* p. 119, pp. 121-125, and pp. 126-128 ; also Brecher : *Nehru* (1961), *op. cit.,* pp. 53-54.

[111] Among the chapters in *Soviet Russia* are : The Fascination of Russia ; Impressions of Moscow ; The Soviet System ; The U.S.S.R. Constitution ; Russian Books ; Lenin ; The Peasantry ; Criminal Law ; Minority Problems ; The Peasant and the Land ; Women and Marriage ; Russian Prison ; Russia and India. *Nehru : The First Sixty Years, op. cit.,* Vol. I, p. 129.

[112] Brecher : *Nehru* (1959), *op. cit.,* p. 29.

"sense of duty" beside "personal interest" to follow international affairs closely, Nehru wrote in 1933 :

> "I studied carefully what was happening in Russia, Germany, England, America, Japan, China, France, Spain, Italy, and Central Europe, and tried to understand the tangled web of current affairs. I followed with interest the attempts of each country separately, and of all of them together, to weather the storm ... [the] repeated failures of international conferences to find a solution for political and economic ills and the problem of disarmament ..." [113]

And Nehru makes a revealing statement that could never have been pronounced by Nasser, or even have come to his mind, neither at the time nor twenty years later :

> "In thinking over the troubles and conflicts of the world, *I forgot to some extent my own personal and national troubles.* I would even feel buoyant occasionally at the fact that I was alive at this great revolutionary period of the *world's history.*" [114]

Nehru's 1935-1936 trip to Europe put him again in close contact with the European political context and would—if anything—serve more to strengthen the 'internationalist bias' in his political socialisation. Thus whereas Nasser's 'political socialisation' was marked by its 'nationalist bias' (for he was profoundly influenced by happenings at home such as foreign occupation of his country, royal dictatorship and absolute failure of the "corrupted" multi-party democracy), Nehru's political socialisation had as a concurrent to his involvement in the nationalist movement his following of such developments as the great economic depression, the growth of Socialism, Communism and Fascism, the Spanish Civil War and Munich, the choice between pacifism and rearmament.

Consequently, Nehru's activities during the period contained numerous instances such as his calling for observance of "Abyssinia Day" enunciating an "appeal to the Indian people ... to give country-wide expression to our sympathy and solidarity with the Ethiopian people and our resolve not to submit to the Fascist imperialist menace" [115] (May 5, 1936) ; a resolution of the All-India Congress Committee to "view with grave concern and horror the imperialist aggression of Japan in China attended with wanton cruelty and the bombing of the civil population" [116] (Calcutta, October 1937) ; yet another trip to Europe from June to December 1938 where he made a speech—as the Congress' representative—at a conference organised by International Peace Campaign on the Bombardment of

---

[113] Nehru : *Toward Freedom, op. cit.,* p. 231.

[114] *Ibid.* (emphasis added).

[115] *Nehru : The First Sixty Years, op. cit.,* Vol. I, p. 419.

[116] *Ibid.,* p. 497.

Open Towns and the Restoration of Peace [117] (Paris, July 1938) ; writing a letter to the *Manchester Guardian* about "Betrayal of Czechoslovakia" [118] (September 8, 1938) ; in addition to a visit to Barcelona during the Spanish Civil War at the invitation of the Republican government. [119] Looking at some of Nehru's writings and speeches, one feels that he was akin to the way of thinking of a European liberal imbibed with an internationalist spirit (in addition to being a nationalist). His comments on Chamberlain's "appeasement", [120] and his taking pains to affirm to Congress members that the "Quit India" concept stemmed not from "narrow nationalism, but rather from an international attitude" are clear examples of this. [121] In a very revealing and significant passage, Nehru remarks : "To my misfortune I am affected by international happenings more than I should be . . ." [122]

In a word then, Nehru's political socialisation presents a clear-cut contrast to Nasser's [123] and it follows that their role-performances, as charismatic leaders directing the international behaviour of Egypt and India, were to emphasise different facets of the non-aligned role-set.

5.

Some of the different emphases in the respective enactment of Nehru's India and Nasser's Egypt can, thus, be pointed out :

(i) Because of his education, political experience and involvement in international affairs, Nehru could think out and reflect on India's foreign policy long before his country became independent. Consequently with the declaration of independence, an explicit statement of foreign policy was unambiguously enunciated. This is in contrast to the oscillation of Nasser and his bid for time. We have seen that this made it difficult to locate even the precise starting point of Egypt's non-alignment. [124]

---

[117] *Ibid.*, pp. 571-574.

[118] *Ibid.*, pp. 580-582.

[119] *Ibid.*, p. 561 ; also Brecher : *Nehru* (1961), *op. cit.*, p. 98.

[120] *Nehru : The First Sixty Years, op. cit.*, Vol. I, p. 599.

[121] *Ibid.*, Vol. II, p. 123.

[122] Brecher : *Nehru* (1961), *op. cit.*, p. 101.

[123] We could then continue to trace the pattern of their contrasted socialisation (*e.g.* Nasser's experience in Palestine, Nehru's meeting with Lord Mountbatten . . .) but not very much would be added to our illustrative evidence.

[124] See chapter VII above.

(ii) Nehru's non-alignment has been described as a "doctrine in action" based on declared (universal) norms, and thus his non-aligned role-performance can be evaluated in terms of these norms (hence the accusation levelled against Nehru's India of practising "double standards" as regards the 1956 Suez and Hungarian crises, and the attack on Nehru's "hypocrisy" because of the use of force in Goa). Thus because Nehru was more torn between the moral [125] and the expedient orientation [126] in his role-performance, one can hypothesise that he suffered more than Nasser from role-conflict. [127] For Nasser's non-alignment was essentially a "formula for political action", based primarily on nationalist affectivity, had as its main objective to change an unfavourable national and regional context, and was thus to be judged according to its own criteria of political efficiency. [128]

(iii) Both Nehru's India and Nasser's Egypt have refused membership in East-West bloc alliances, but the bases of this refusal received different emphases and were given different orders of priority. Nehru seemed to be primarily concerned that India should not globalise international antagonism, add to the division of the international system or heighten the probability of conflict. [129] Nehru's analysis of international relations had been thought out for years before he was formally directing India's foreign policy, and consequently his view of the contemporary international system was both complex and sophisticated. His relationship to the East-West conflict tended to be based on his "climate theory" [130] *i.e.* climate of peace versus climate of war. He believed that

---

[125] As Nehru expressed it in talking to Karanjia: "Non-alignment, like *Panch Sheel,* does not necessarily fall simply because this or that country fails to observe the right and proper code of international behaviour, just the same as truth is not sacrificed merely because somebody tells lies! The Five Principles are the obvious and righteous principles of international behaviour, and we do not propose to give them up because some countries do not practice them." Karanjia: *The Mind of Mr. Nehru, op. cit.,* p. 94.

[126] For behavioural reflections of the different role orientations, see Shaw and Costanzo: *op. cit.,* p. 341.

[127] For a conceptual discussion of role conflict, see *ibid.,* pp. 339-340.

[128] Agostini, R.: "Egypte et Inde: Deux conceptions du neutralisme", *Orient,* April 1958, pp. 73-87.

[129] "Non-alignment ...", Nehru used to affirm, "is ... a policy most helpful to the cause of world peace. Once you admit the basic fact that today a major war such as would exterminate humanity is not desirable, then it follows that military alliances, which are the children of the 'cold war' approach, are also not desirable inasmuch as they do not promote that climate of accommodation and peaceful settlement of international problems which is the objective of all the great and small powers of the world to-day." Karanjia: *The Mind of Mr. Nehru, op. cit.,* p. 94

[130] "Peace is not a physical abstention from war, it is an attempt to lessen tensions and create a climate of peace all over the world." *Ibid.,* p. 89, and also p. 92.

"fear, mutual suspicion and misunderstanding, rather than the substantive conflicts of interest and irreconcilable demands that divide nations, are the fundamental roots of war". [131] Consequently, he was manifestly preoccupied with how to create a psychological climate conducive to the relaxation of international tension, the peaceful settlement of systemic conflicts and generally to nurture an environment of negation and mediation (*e.g.* his "zone of peace" approach) and he was thus concerned with the "wider picture".

Nasser used to employ some of these arguments too, but his main emphasis was on Egypt's fear of foreign domination and the curbing of his country's freedom to act : "We do not work either for America or Russia but only for the Egyptians and the Arabs", [132] he stated.

Thus on an issue like Communism, for instance, Nasser and Nehru came to differ. Because of his varied and long reading, his political experience in the inter-war period and his visits to the Soviet Union, Nehru understood Marxism intellectually and had—characteristically—a complex view :

> "... One learns, of course, a great deal from past experience ; and I have always considered the Marxist analysis of the past very scientific and very illuminating. I do not agree with everything Marx says but broadly I have found it useful and rational ..." [133]

Consequently, Communists were given freedom of organisation within India's multi-party system. Nasser, however, regarded communism pragmatically, and considered it dangerous to let this "externally-supported threat" loose in small underdeveloped countries like Egypt or Syria (*e.g.* Nasser's quarrel in 1959 with the Socialist bloc).

(iv) Nasser was thus essentially a radical revisionist whose main concerns were Arab nationalism, Israel as "an imperialist base" and apprehension of big power intervention generally. Whereas Nehru emphasised India's role of "objective mediator" (*e.g.* in the Korean conflict), was tactful with the two blocs, respectful of both views rather than condemning either, Nasser's behaviour toward the superpowers was determined by U.S. and U.S.S.R. policies toward Nasser's concerns closer at home :

> "We are friendly with those who are friends to us and enemies with those who are hostile to us",

---

[131] Lefever : *op. cit.,* p. 107.

[132] Nasser's interview with representatives of 11 American newspapers and 2,500 Broadcasting Stations on March 15th, 1956. *Nasser's Speeches,* Vol. I, pp. 457-458. But this speech is not an isolated example of his approach to non-alignment, for the rest of the volume reflects clearly this approach.

[133] Karanjia : *The Mind of Mr. Nehru, op. cit.,* p. 28.

he asserted as one of the characteristics of Egypt's pragmatic and militant non-aligned role-performance. He preferred to use—rather than be used by—the cold war.

This is why in contrast to Nehru's "pacifism" and his "excessive" concern with the importance and "purity" of means, Nasser emphasised the "positiveness" of his methods. Thus Nasser, the soldier of lower-middle class origin and the man of action, was constantly on the alert to thwart "imperialist threats" in Jordan, in Lebanon or in Yemen, whereas Nehru seemed to believe that his non-alignment could be a practical defence against superpower intervention. Nehru was thus diametrically opposed to any arrangement of regrouping non-aligned actors into a military or even political organisation, while Nasser was actively working to have an Arab or African joint command like the one projected at Casablanca.[134]

There was of course "positivism" in Nehru's role-performance, but it was—as he himself stated—anti-"dramatic» and anti-"agitational".[135] He thus recommended the "persuasive" style of international behaviour and he advised his colleagues at the First Non-Aligned Summit that the superpower cannot be shouted at or ordered around. But Nasser—the lonely, austere child, the young political activist, and the army officer—was ready to make up his mind quickly and answer back promptly. His concentration on "colonial threats" and his learned insensitivity to "unrelated" issues of international relations marked the non-aligned role-performance of a (nationalist) counter-puncher and master of agile footwork in the international system.

---

[134] Cremeans : *op. cit.,* pp. 275-276.

[135] Mallik : *op. cit.,* p. 104. And Nehru said to Karanjia : "Even though we may differ from others, it's no use indulging in all the madness of political slogans and ideological condemnations, angry criticisms and all that." *The Mind of Mr. Nehru, op. cit.,* p. 87. Though this is diametrically opposed to Nasser's style generally, the gap between the two friends tended to narrow. For whereas Nasser became more interested in, and knowledgeable about, the global system, Nehru became more concerned with national problems after the Sino-Indian conflict.

PART FOUR

The Impact of Non-Alignment on the Contemporary International System

CHAPTER IX

Non-Alignment, Stability and Conflict-Management in the Contemporary International System

1.

At the outset of this work, in chapter II, we mentioned the non-aligned actors' claim to constitute an "area of peace" (as Nehru liked to call it), since—according to them—their foreign policy reduces the level of conflict and contributes to systemic maintenance. [1] We also noted that this "peace hypothesis" of non-aligned actors is too broadly formulated to be tested and we decided to deal with it later in the work.

1.1. In picking up this "peace hypothesis" in this last part of the work, we want to emphasise two important postulates underlying the general structure of our research :

(i) Though we have emphasised some limitations of "systems theory" as far as the study of third world foreign policy-making is concerned, we still believe that the analysis of global systemic variables is a must for the general and balanced comprehension of our subject. For, we repeat, it is the systemic macro-context that sets limits on, and offers chances for, the orientation and/or behaviour of actors no matter what their means and ends are. Thus, in emphasising the "national component", we did *not intend it as a substitute* for the global systemic component, but as the key component that has not been duly analysed in the literature in order to provide a balanced comprehension of the policy-making process in non-aligned actors.

(ii) But the emphasis on the "national component" as part of the proposed "situation-role" model raises another conceptual issue : are "systems theory" and the proposed model two juxtaposed frameworks which

[1] See also chapter IV.

could tend to pull our research work in opposite directions ? This is certainly not the view adopted here. We believe that the relationship between international systems analysis and the proposed "situation-role" model is not one of opposition or mutual exclusion but one of complementarity.

As previously mentioned, "systems theory" (as applied by most of its advocates in International Relations theorisation) tended to regard an actor's foreign policy as "a reflection of the characteristics of a social system containing a series of impersonal processes which are external to the actors and constrain them". [2] The proposed "situation-role" model seeks to underline the fact that the actor does not *merely* react to the constraints of the global system, but has its own objectives, its own perception of 'reality', both of which determine its means-end perspective and thus inter-actor variations. In this case, then, one is no longer confined to analysis at the level of the "apparent machine-like character . . . [and] mechanical laws . . . of large social systems", [3] but one equally aims at analysing the actor's voluntaristic perspective.

Thus, taking the limitations of the different levels-of-analysis into account is destined to help prevent us from neglecting one side of the coin and/or being guilty of a "displacement of scope". [4]

1.2. *Non-Alignment and the Level of Conflict in the International System*

As we have seen in chapter II, the so-called "peace function" of non-alignment is not accepted by all International Relations scholars. Both Kripalani and Kissinger have rejected it, basing their refusal on the grounds of the poverty and/or internal instability of non-aligned actors. Though the internal instability of non-aligned actors is based on empirical justifications (as we have seen in previous chapters), neither Kripalani nor Kissinger has offered systematic empirical evidence to support their assumed correlation between internal instability and incapacity to play a regulatory function in the international system. Hence their intuitive

---

[2] Silverman, David : *The Theory of Organisations,* London, Heinemann, 1970, pp. 141-143. This danger of "system's tyranny" is even more easily applicable in the case of small states like the majority of non-aligned actors.

[3] *Ibid.*

[4] Wagner, Helmut : "Displacement of Scope : A Problem of the Relationship between Small-Scale and Large-Scale Sociological Theories", *American Journal of Sociology,* LXIX (1964), pp. 571-584.

generalisations remind us of opposed intuitive generalisations. Thus Sen believed that

> "the most important positive role they [non-aligned actors] can play, and they are expected by both the superpowers to play, is to provide bridges of conciliation when the logic of power struggle pushes the world to the edge of disaster. Here lies the importance of non-alignment or positive neutralism . . .". [5]

These conflicting generalisations reflect the absence of explicit conceptual investigations and systematic empirical evidence as far as the influence of non-aligned actors on the contemporary international system is concerned. They thus point out the difficulties that one might encounter and warn us against accepting the "peace hypothesis" of non-aligned actors except as a working hypothesis. Even its acceptance as a working hypothesis does not eliminate all the problems, for the "peace hypothesis" is too broadly formulated to be falsifiable. Thus this hypothesis needs first to be reformulated and its scope limited in order for it to be usefully treated. We will attempt to do this by investigating the influence of non-aligned actors on two of the crucial variables of the contemporary international system : its structure and its regulatory mechanism.

2. Varieties of Systemic Structure and their Impact on Systemic Stability [6] : Contending "Theories"

Which distribution of capabilities is the most conducive to the prevention of a global war has been the object of conceptualisation in both "classical" and "behavioural" writings. Two opposed "theories" are treated here : the one that contends that the bipolar structure is the most conducive to systemic stability, and the "theory" that claims the contrary and emphasises the 'stability function' of multipolarity.

---

[5] Sen, C. : *Against the Cold War : A Study of Asian-African Policies Since World War II,* Bombay, Asia Publishing House, 1962, p. 49.

[6] Among the authors that will be the centre of analysis in this section, Waltz defined stability as "the peacefulness of adjustment within the international system and ... the durability of the system itself". Waltz, Kenneth : "The Stability of a Bipolar World", *Daedalus,* Summer 1964, pp. 880-310. Deutsch and Singer defined stability as "the probability that the system retains all of its essential characteristics ; that no single nation becomes dominant ; that most of its members continue to survive ; and that large-scale war does not occur". Deutsch, Karl, and Singer, David : "Multipolar Power Systems and International Stability", *World Politics,* XVI (1964), pp. 390-406.

2.1. *Bipolarity and Systemic Stability*

The name of Kenneth Waltz [7] is associated with systematic attempts and the accumulation of arguments to substantiate this contention. Writing in 1964 a full 30-page article devoted exclusively to this subject, Waltz noticed that there is "a widely-accepted ... conventional wisdom" which believes that "a world of many powers is more stable than a bipolar world ...". Consequently, Waltz's main concern is to show that the bipolar structure tends to reduce international violence and, consequently, that this "conventional wisdom" seems to be at variance with empirical evidence. For

> "... the bipolar world of the postwar period has shown a remarkable stability. Measuring time from the termination of the war, 1964 corresponds to 1937. Despite all of the changes in the nineteen years since 1945 that might have shaken the world into another great war, 1964 somehow looks and feels safer than 1937." [8]

Indeed, the bipolar system witnessed serious conflicts and crises, but they are different from those of the multipolar system. In the multipolar system "... the dangers are diffused, responsibilities are unclear and definition of vital interests easily obscured ...".

But in the bipolar system :

> "... attention is focused on crises by both of the major competitors, and especially by the defensive state. To move piecemeal and reap gains serially is difficult, for within a world in confusion there is one great certainty, namely the knowledge of who will oppose whom. One's motto may still be, 'push to the limit', but *limit* must be emphasised as heavily as *push.* Caution, moderation, and the management of crisis come to be of great and obvious importance."

This is why, even though "intensity and breadth of competition and recurrence of crisis limn a picture of constant conflict verging on violence", it is still true that

> "... the relative simplicity of relations within a bipolar world, the great pressures that are generated and the constant possibility of catastrophe produce a conservatism on the part of the two greatest powers. The Soviet Union and the United States may feel more comfortable dealing *à deux* than in contemplating a future world in which they vie for existence and possible advantage with other superpowers. While there is naturally worry about an increase of tensions

---

[7] Waltz : "The Stability of a Bipolar World", *op. cit.*

[8] *Ibid.*

to intolerable levels, there is also a fear that the tensions themselves will lead America and Russia to seek agreements designed to bring a relaxation that will be achieved at the expense of lesser powers."

This is why this bipolar system structure is durable in time, for "... unless some states combine or others dissolve in chaos, the world will remain bipolar until the end of the present century". [9]

But a question might come to one's mind : what about such seemingly "multipolar" phenomena as Gaullist France or the Sino-Soviet split? Did these not change the system's bipolar structure? Waltz does not think so, for he believes that

> "... France and China have demonstrated not their power but their impotence : their inability to change the dominant relation in the world. The solidity of the bipolar balance permits middle states to act with impunity precisely because they know that their divergent actions will not measurably affect the strength of the Soviet Union or the United States, upon which their own security continues to rest ..."

This is why China's and France's "... independence of action ... is at once a product of loosening alliances—the lesser dependence of principals upon their associates—and a protest against it". [10]

Consequently, the direct relationship between the bipolar structure and systemic stability should no longer be—so Waltz reasons—in doubt :

> "The pressures of bipolarity have helped to produce responsibility of action. A relaxation of those pressures will change the situation to one in which it will no longer be clear who will oppose whom. Two considerations then should give one pause : the necessarily unpredictable quality of the third power and the greater instability of a multipower world." [11]

---

[9] *Ibid.*

[10] *Ibid.* In 1967, Waltz reiterated once more this view. "This condition of inequality" (between the superpowers and their allies), he stated, "makes it unlikely that any shifts in the alignment of states would very much help or hurt either of the two leading powers ... Not being dependent upon allies, the United States and the Soviet Union are free to design strategies in accord with their interests. Since the power actually and potentially at the disposal of each of them far exceeds that of their closest competitors, they are able to control in some measure the possibly destabilizing acts of third parties or to absorb their effects ... The extent of the difference in national capabilities makes the bipolar structure resilient. Defection of allies and national shifts of allegiance do not decisively alter the structure. Because they do not, recalcitrant allies may be treated with indifference ; they may even be effectively disciplined" (*e.g.* Suez in 1956). Waltz, Kenneth : "International Structure, National Force and the Balance of World Power", *Journal of International Affairs,* XXI (1967), pp. 215-231.

[11] Waltz : "The Stability of a Bipolar World", *op. cit.*

This bipolar structure, then, should be a source of rejoicing and should even be consolidated, for

> "By making the two strongest states still more powerful and the emergence of third powers more difficult . . . the world . . . [will continue to enjoy] a stability seldom known where three or more powers have sought to cooperate with each other or have competed for existence." [12]

Dealing with this subject three years later, [13] Waltz did not change his view and reiterated :

> "What management there now is in international relations must be provided, singly and occasionally together, by the duopolists at the top. In certain ways . . . the inequality of states in a bipolar world enables the two most powerful states to develop a rich variety of controls and to follow flexible strategies in using them." [14]

2.2. *Bipolarity : A Critique*

Three arguments can be levelled against the 'theory' of bipolarity as the most stable system :

(i) There seems to be confusion in the use of the bipolarity concept itself, for it is supposed to designate two different notions. In one case, bipolarity is applied to international politics as a zero-sum game, where the two superpowers are involved in a global duel for systemic dominance and the "losses" of the one are the "gains" of the other. The other notion is that substantial territorial and/or political changes can take place in the system without affecting directly the status of one superpower and hence overall bipolar systemic stability. Thus the U.S.A., for instance (as Waltz says), can "gain" or lose China, without effect on American previously-held territory.

If this is the case, it is because China is an independent actor in the international system, not merely a factor in Soviet or American capabilities. Consequently

> "there can be important shifts in the international balance which do not upset the basic relation between the U.S. and the U.S.S.R. That relation, however, is no longer bipolar. All changes are either vital in that they directly affect the bipolar balance, or they are not vital in that they fail to do so." [15]

---

[12] *Ibid.*

[13] Waltz : "International Structure, National Force and the Balance of World Power", *op. cit.*

[14] *Ibid.*

[15] Rosecrance, Richard : "Bipolarity, Multipolarity and the Future", *Journal of Conflict Resolution,* X (1966), pp. 314-327.

(ii) Related to the application of two different notions to bipolarity is another confusion between bipolarity and *détente.* Waltz puts as a basis of the bipolar structure the "absence of peripheries" in the system. He also talks about "ingrained habits of the cold war" and "invigorating dangers of a bipolar world". This does not easily lead to the system's stability but rather—and the word is Waltz's—to its "fragility". [16]

Détente, however, is contrary to the basic notion of bipolarity as a zero-sum-game. If the other notion of bipolarity is applied, denoting a looser (non-zero-sum) bipolarity, we are then contradicting a premise of bipolarity in Waltz's thinking : "the absence of peripheries". For loose bipolarity is based—by definition—on the presence of actors outside the two blocs.

Consequently, in dealing with the relationship between the bipolar structure and systemic stability, one has to specify and choose between two systemic structures which can be distinguished :

> "a system in which change can be accommodated without drastic action by the two major camps and in which, as a result, disequilibrium can occur ; or a system in which there is a taut balance maintained by vigilant employment of counterpressure and in which the antagonism between camps is likely to be very great. The first may permit *détente* but is not strictly bipolar ; the second offers stringent bipolarity but rules out accommodation. The two notions are not compatible, and the argument for one undermines the contentions urged on behalf of the other." [17]

(iii) Though bipolarity can help to prevent systemic dominance by one superpower or the other, since a move by the one would call forth countermeasures by the other ; yet this 'counterbalancing' does not reduce the tempo of discord or the possibilities of collision. On the contrary, if Waltz thinks of bipolarity as a zero-sum game, any "advance" of a superpower would be interpreted as a weakening of the other's position and must provoke it to a counter move. In this global spiral of political hostility and "serious and tense" bipolar competition, one of the superpowers is—as Waltz expresses it—"easily led to overreact". This increases the strait-jacket character of the international system, and creates a psychological climate of growing ill-will and misperception. [18] It is likely that in

[16] Waltz : "The Stability of a Bipolar World", *op. cit.*

[17] Rosecrance : "Bipolarity, Multipolarity and the Future", *op. cit.*

[18] This psychological climate of strain and misperception seems to be at the basis of the so-called "climate theory" of non-aligned actors. Lyon expressed the epitome of this "theory" when he stated : "Neutralists tend to place great stress on the role of fear as a tension-breeding factor, and with this often goes the implication that many fears are unwarranted and, hence, removable. They maintain that the mutual fears of the Cold War antagonists create a war-like atmosphere which discourages any possibility of lessening tension and unfreezing the Cold War." Lyon : *Neutral-*

this atmosphere of stress one of the poles may think not only of the risks involved in colliding with its opponent but also of the risks involved in not striking first—thus leaving the initiative to the opponent. With such structural rigidity, "reciprocal fears of surprise attack may grow to such a point that they cannot be endured. Preventive war may seem to be preferable to war at the opponent's initiative". [19]

If this structural rigidity is used as a principal argument against the "theory" of bipolarity as a basis of systemic stability, the structural flexibility characterising a multipolar system is used by this system's advocates to defend their "theory".

2.3. *Multipolarity and Systemic Stability*

Those observers and scholars who emphasise the significance of the multipolar structure are varied and range from Walter Lippmann [20] and Hans Morgenthau [21] to Karl Deutsch and David Singer, [22] passing by Hedley Bull. [23] The Deutsch-Singer contribution provides the systematic arguments for the "stability function" of multipolarity, and it is to them that we should now turn.

---

ism, op. cit., p. 63. Against this *Zeitgeist,* the non-aligned actors aim to create a different psychological climate, a "climate of peace". To achieve this "climate of peace", one should do nothing that contributes to the further enlargement or entrenchment of the "climate of war", but do everything possible toward the shrinkage and 'containment' of the "cold war blocs". See, for instance, Nehru's speech of February 18, 1953 significantly entitled: "The Psychosis of Fear", in *Jawaharlal Nehru's Speeches: 1949-1953,* Delhi, Government of India, Ministry of Information and Broadcasting, The Publications Division, 1954, pp. 243-258.

[19] Rosecrance: "Bipolarity, Multipolarity and the Future", *op. cit.*

[20] Lippmann, in a number of columns written in late 1963 and early 1964 remarked, for instance, that "the paramount theme of this decade, as we know it thus far, is that we are emerging from a two-power world and entering one where there are many powers". "Nato Crisis - and Solution: Don't Blame de Gaulle", *Boston Globe,* December 5, 1963, p. 26.

[21] Morgenthau expressed his belief that in the bipolar structure "the flexibility of the balance of power and, with it, its restraining influence upon the power aspirations of the main protagonists on the international scene have disappeared". *Politics Among Nations, op. cit.,* 3rd edition, p. 350.

[22] Deutsch and Singer: "Multipolar Power Systems and International Stability", *op. cit.*

[23] Bull, in "Atlantic Military Problems: A Preliminary Essay" (prepared for the *Council on Foreign Relations* meeting of November 20, 1963, p. 21) remarked that between 1963 and 1975 "the system of polarization of power will cease to be recognizable: that other states will count for so much in world politics that the two present great powers will find it difficult, even when cooperating, to dominate them". But see also Waltz: "The Stability of a Bipolar World", *op. cit.*

Contrary to the "bipolarity/stability theory", these two authors believe that "as the system moves away from bipolarity toward multipolarity, *the frequency and intensity* of war should be expected to diminish". [24]

They then go on to present

> "two distinct—but related—lines of formal, semi-quantitative, argument as to why the diffusion-stability relationship should turn out as the theoretician has generally assumed and as the historian has often found to be the case". [25]

The main argument is that the greater number of actors which characterises the multipolar structure works for systemic stability through providing greater interaction opportunities among actors and less inter-actor attention than the minimum necessary for involvement in conflict. Each of these points merits more detail :

A. As for the greater number of actors/greater interaction opportunities, it is a characteristic of the multipolar system to witness an increase in the number of (independent) actors. Consequently, there is also an increase in the number of possible dyads or pairs in the international system, *i.e.* increased opportunities of interaction among actors. Since "... one of the greatest threats to the stability of any impersonal social system is the shortage of alternative partners", and since the bipolar structure entails a

> "reduction in the number of possible dyadic relations [which] produces, both for any individual nation and for the totality of those in the system, a corresponding diminution in the number of opportunities for interaction with other actors",

it follows that a

> "logical explanation for the correlation between [increased] number of independent actors and the [reduced] probability of armed conflict lies in the realm of enhanced interaction opportunities, observed in terms of their quantity, diversity and qualities". [26]

---

[24] Deutsch and Singer : "Multipolar Power Systems and International Stability", *op. cit.* (emphasis added).

[25] *Ibid.* Their methodology is essentially a 3-stage conceptualisation. Thus in the first stage, they link up the independent variable (number of independent actors) with the dependent one (stability of the system) by means of an emphasis on "interaction opportunity"—their intervening variable. In the second stage, "the interaction opportunity concept is extended to the point where it impinges on the degree of attention that any nation in the system may allocate to all of the other nations or to possible coalitions of nations". This second stage is followed by a third where "the multipolar and bipolar models are connected with Richardson's model of arms races and similar kinds of escalating conflicts".

[26] *Ibid.*

B. In order to "support the hypothesised correlation between multipolarity and stability", Deutsch and Singer's second argument is based on degree of inter-actor attention/likelihood of inter-actor conflict relationship. Thus after putting their interaction opportunities argument into a statistical formula and a graphic representation, the core of their second argument is verbalised in the following way:

> "It is perhaps not excessive to assume that the minimal attention ratio for an escalating conflict would have to be 1 : 9, since it does not seem likely that any country could be provoked very far into an escalating conflict with less than 10 per cent of the foreign policy attention of its government devoted to the matter.
>
> If we require a minimal attention of 10 per cent for an escalating conflict, the likelihood of such conflicts thus will decline sharply with the decline of the average attention that any one government has available for any one of the remaining actors in the international system."

Moreover, their graphic representation

> "confirms the greater stability of multipolar systems, and it suggests some quantitative findings. It shows that the average share of available attention for any one conflict drops sharply as soon as there are more than three power centers in the system, and more gently after there are more than five such centers; and it further suggests that the stability of the system may depend critically on the *critical attention ratio* ..."

Consequently, they conclude

> "... if some minimum percentage of a nation's external attention is required for that nation to engage in behavior tending toward armed conflict, and the increase in number of independent actors diminishes the share that any nation can allocate to any other single actor, such an increase is likely to have a stabilizing effect upon the system". [27]

2.4. *Multipolarity : A Critique*

There are two main criticisms of the multipolarity/stability correlation:

(i) Though it seems that a multipolar structure might reduce the intensity and consequences of possible conflicts, this reduction does not apply

---

[27] *Ibid.* Deutsch and Singer then proceed with their two basic arguments to "correlate the propositions concerning the greater stability of multipolar systems in international politics ... with Richardson's model of conflict". The confirmation of their multipolarity/stability hypothesis comes out strengthened since they conclude that "the arms race in a *completely rational* world would ... tend to be slower under multipolar conditions than under bipolar ones" (emphasis added).

to the *number* of conflicts in the system. For since the number of independent actors will—by definition—increase, so will the number of national demands and most probably inter-actor frictions. Consequently, in face of this greater gamut of demands and the greater difficulty of their accommodation, the more diverse and complex multipolar structure will tend to result in a greater number of possible conflicts.

(ii) The second problem with the multipolarity/stability correlation is related to the uncertainty and unpredictability of interaction that is inherent in the multipolar system. For though the significance of a change in alignment or capabilities is less than in the bipolar system, it is not as relatively simple to predict its consequences as in this latter. Thus the greater number of (independent) actors makes the number of possible combinations enormous. That is why

> "multipolarity ... raises the difficulty of policy-making. Results may be altogether unforseen ; choice becomes very complex. Since multipolarity raises incalculability, the system finds it more difficult to achieve stable results. War may occur, not through a failure of will, but through a failure of comprehension". [28]

Is it possible to choose between these two contending "theories" ? This does not seem to be the case, for each is valid in some parts of its reasoning. This is why the greatest need here is for a synthesis which takes as its starting point of analysis the international system as it existed from, say, the mid-1950's to the mid-1960's ; that is, the period that witnessed the shaping and consolidation of non-alignment. Moreover, the emphasis in this proposed synthesis is to be on the impact of non-alignment on systemic structure.

3. **Impact of Non-Alignment on Systemic Structure**

The emergence and multiplication of non-aligned actors put an end —by definition—to a structure of tight bipolarity, since there was an increasingly large number of actors outside the two blocs (*i.e.* non-bloc actors). On the other hand, it is an exaggeration to say that the emergence and multiplication of non-aligned actors has replaced bipolarity by multipolarity, for the superpowers continued to feel involved all over the system. In other words there occurred interpenetration between system-wide and subsystemic issues, and the system—becoming more complex—manifested simultaneously features of both bipolarity and multipolarity,

---

[28] Rosecrance : "Bipolarity, Multipolarity and the Future", *op. cit.*

i.e. Rosecrance's "bi-multipolarity",[29] Kaplan's "loose-bipolarity",[30] Holsti's diffuse-bloc[31] system, or Young's "discontinuities model"[32] of the international system.

For at the time the "national liberation movements" were leading to the emergence of "new states", the division of the system into two antagonistic blocs was materialising.[33] These "new states" refusal of bloc-membership reduced the zero-sum element in the bipolar competition by supplying it with abundant objects of competition. In this way the "scarcity of resources" or "positions"—which creates conflict—is reduced. Moreover, the entirety of the system's "resources" was not going to be divided once and for all between the two blocs. The political gains accruing to one bloc were not automatically and necessarily the losses of the other. This means that the opponent's gain could be easily compensated, since (because of the abundant 'no man's land') its 'incremental' or 'marginal utility' could be easily 'swallowed' as it was not strictly 'decremental', but rather one had missed the chance of a potential increment. That is to say, it did not seem to threaten the bloc leader's "chasse gardée" or to diminish the bloc's membership.

Thus the refusal of third world actors to contribute to the rigid division of the contemporary international system between two poles led to the system's structural flexibility.[34] This structural flexibility had as consequences :

(*a*) The blocs moved from conflict in the "centre" of the system (*e.g.* the European scene) where questions of bloc security were paramount, and where accordingly a set-back was not acceptable, towards the "periphery" where a "loss" (*e.g.* in the Congo) could be countenanced. The non-bloc members in this case played the role of a "safety valve" to decrease the pressure of conflict in Europe.

---

[29] *Ibid.*

[30] Kaplan : *System and Process, op. cit.*, pp. 36-43 ; also Kaplan, Morton : "Bipolarity in a Revolutionary Age", in Kaplan (ed.) : *The Revolution in World Politics, op. cit.*, pp. 251-267.

[31] Holsti : *International Politics, op. cit.*, chapter III, but especially pp. 69-94.

[32] Young : "Political Discontinuities in the International System", *op. cit.*, pp. 369-392.

[33] Fliess, Peter : *International Relations in the Bipolar World,* New York, Random House, 1968.

[34] Rosecrance confirmed the analytical arguments adopted here by suggesting : "The relations between two major powers would be strongly conditioned by the presence and activity of other states. This means that international politics would not be a zero-sum competition between two superpowers." This structural flexibility would promote systemic stability since "the resources of the international system would not be entirely divided up between the two major states with future outcomes dependent upon a bilateral competition between them. Rather, resources would

(*b*) The conflict between the blocs shifted to the political arena (*i.e.* competition for the goodwill of non-bloc members) and away from the dangerous military contest involving nuclear weapons.

(*c*) Because non-bloc members were wooed by the superpowers, advantages accrued to their position, the value of alliance membership tended to diminish (*e.g.* Pakistan), and thus the division of the system tended to be less rigid. Thus through a feedback process, a demonstration effect led to more and more structural flexibility in the system.

Other analysts of international systems went even further and implied that this bi-multipolar or loose-bipolar system is the most stable compared with either the rigidity of tight bipolarity or the complexity and unpredictability of absolute multipolarity. [35] This contention is even expressed diagrammatically :

Figure 4. *Non-Alignment and Systemic Regulation*

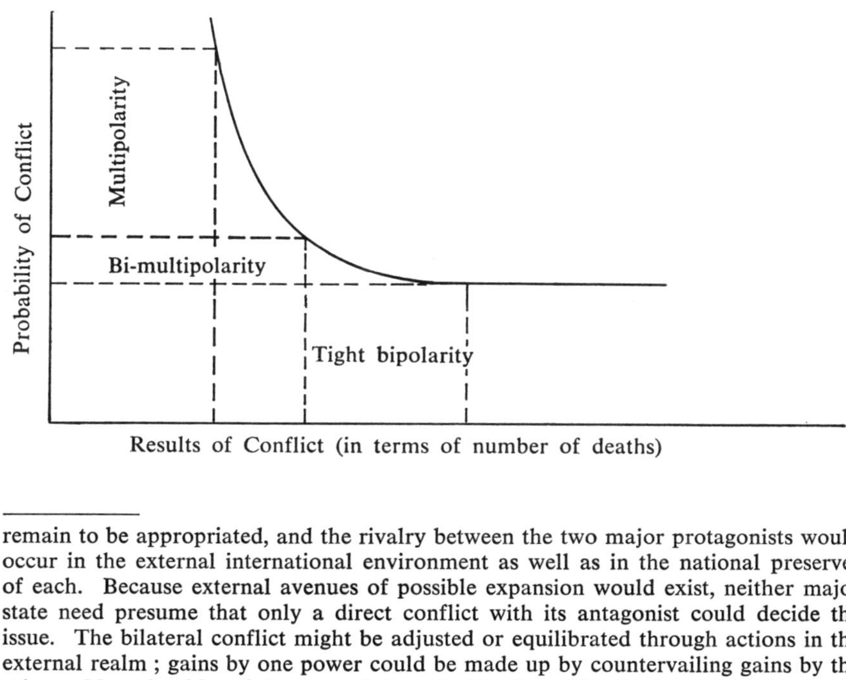

remain to be appropriated, and the rivalry between the two major protagonists would occur in the external international environment as well as in the national preserves of each. Because external avenues of possible expansion would exist, neither major state need presume that only a direct conflict with its antagonist could decide the issue. The bilateral conflict might be adjusted or equilibrated through actions in the external realm ; gains by one power could be made up by countervailing gains by the other. Nor should serial appropriation decide the ultimate fate of the external international world . . . The bipolar powers would continue to seek advantages in the multipolar realm, but they would fail to eliminate multipolar orientations." Rosecrance : "Bipolarity, Multipolarity, and the Future", *op. cit.*

[35] *Ibid.*

Thus—according to this figure—although a multipolar system is by definition complex and the probability of conflict is relatively high, the results are not globally "suicidal" as is indeed the case in a (tight) bipolar system. In the bi-multipolar (or loose-bipolar) system

> "the probability, whether local or general, would be much smaller than [in] a multipolar system. Conflict would be mitigated on two scores : a multipolar buffer might help prevent the two nuclear giants from coming to blows ; and the restraining influence of the bipolar states might in turn prevent extreme conflict among multipolar powers. While simple bipolarity would not exist, the influence of two superpowers would be crucial in limiting the outcomes of the system". [36]

But in addition to the structural flexibility they introduced into the system, have non-aligned actors influenced directly the system's regulatory mechanism and its process of conflict-management ? And if so, in what ways ?

4. Non-Alignment and Regulatory Mechanism in the Contemporary International System

This potential regulatory influence can be materialised when the non-aligned actors succeed, for instance, in consolidating universal norms and/or in suggesting formulas that facilitate the management of conflicts that arise in the system.

4.1. The consolidation of universal norms in the system is brought about essentially through the consolidation of the universal actor, the U.N. On this point, all non-aligned actors are unanimous—as their declarations at Non-Aligned Summit Conferences and outside them clearly show. It is true that the universal actor is destined to perform a regulatory role, but the presence of non-aligned actors is essential to the success of this role. [37] For if the U.N. consisted only of (overcommitted) bloc members, what would be the use of its debates and the resolutions passed in it ? And who would sit there ready, on the whole, to "judge issues on their merits" and vote accordingly ? Whom would the two blocs accept as chairmen of international commissions of enquiry and control ? Whom would the blocs have as a moderating influence on them, and whose views would they care about ?

---

[36] *Ibid.*

[37] Kaplan : *System and Process . . ., op. cit.*, pp. 38-39.

This is why some "systems theorists" explicited that the efficacity and success of the regulatory role played by the universal actor are dependent on non-aligned actors which "coordinate their national objectives with those of the universal actor and subordinate the objectives of bloc actors to those of the universal actor". [38]

And since, in its bipolar competition, each bloc would be trying to gain the favour of non-aligned actors, it would try to appear less intransigent and phrase its demands on the other bloc in ways more consonant with "universalistic" standards, thus consolidating the norms working for the system's regulation and integration. [39] Consequently, the relationship between the choice of non-alignment and systemic stability seems to be positive, since "... the role functions of the non-[bloc] ... actors are essential to the stability of the system". [40]

4.2. It is, however, very probable that "universal norms" do not provide, and/or are not acceptable as, a sufficient basis for conflict-management. Can non-aligned actors still perform a regulatory function in this case ? They can if they manage to "coordinate the expectations" of the conflict protagonists.

We have mentioned in chapter II how nuclear deterrence, for instance, has made a direct war between the superpowers increasingly "unthinkable". The surrender/annihilation zero-sum game avoided, the superpowers are ready to collaborate to find common ground. Yet though some areas of agreement are possible, differences of evaluation, of interpretation and motivation make the concrete principles of the agreement uncertain. Moreover, as the two superpowers are increasingly involved in the global system to protect existing interests and to promote foreign policy objectives, the potentiality for disagreement is heightened (*e.g.* the 1967 Arab-Israeli conflict), and the need is more pressing for establishing acceptable criteria of bargaining. It is in these bargaining situations that the "coordination of expectations" among the opponents plays a decisive role. For the number of concessions and the degree of accommodation given by one opponent to reach agreement depend on what the other opponent expects. For instance, "criteria that have been accepted in the past are known to produce expectations and therefore play a considerable role in the coordination of expectations". [41] Moreover, established criteria—rather than alternative competing ones—are easy to single out and propose as a basis of potential settlement. Thus an established criterion

[38] *Ibid.*, p. 38.

[39] Kaplan : "Bipolarity in a Revolutionary Age", *op. cit.*

[40] Kaplan : *System and Process, op. cit.*, p. 41.

[41] Kaplan : "Bipolarity in a Revolutionary Age", *op. cit.*

increases the bargaining strength of an actor that advocates its application by increasing the probability that the actor will expect a settlement in accordance with it. The probability of coordinating on an alternate criterion is lower and, therefore, the possibility of nuclear war looms larger if the established criterion is not accepted. [42]

Though Kaplan's reasoning is valid, the problem with the contemporary international system is that it is going through a fast process of social change, [43] and consequently established criteria (the basis of the coordination of expectations and potential settlement) are getting less and less. Here lies the contribution of the non-aligned actors, for they compensate for this deficiency. In spite of their military and economic weaknesses, they are functional in determining the criteria of bargaining. This is simply because the interjection of a third-party opinion changes the expectations that parties to a bargain have of the willingness of each to accept a particular criterion of settlement. Provided only that the criterion enunciated by the outside party is not clearly unreasonable, a bargainer 'A', for instance, sees that bargainer 'B' has external support for his arguments. Bargainer 'A' is likely to reason that bargainer 'B' expects him to give in. Bargainer 'B' knows that bargainer 'A' reasons this way, and this increases the incentive of bargainer 'B' to hold out for the arbitrated solution. [44] In this case, by providing "impartial" criteria for potential conflict-management, non-aligned actors as third-party interveners give the needed information as to the possible concessions necessary for the conclusion of a settlement. Of course, the greater the number of non-aligned actors intervening as third parties, and the more "non-partisan" they are perceived, the more true this is. This brings us to the acceptability of non-aligned actors as third parties to manage conflict. [45] This acceptability of non-aligned actors can remain *theoretical acceptability* or be offered the chance to materialise and become *applied acceptability*.

4.2.1. *Theoretical Acceptability:* This depends upon the identity of the parties to a conflict relationship. In other words, the "theoretical acceptability" of non-aligned actors cannot be understood without reference to the structure of conflict in terms of "who are the parties to a con-

[42] *Ibid.*

[43] Davis, Kingsley: "Social Changes Affecting International Relations", in Rosenau (ed.): *International Politics and Foreign Policy, op. cit.*, pp. 130-140.

[44] Kaplan: "Bipolarity in a Revolutionary Age", *op. cit.*

[45] This third party intervention to manage conflict is not to be confined to formal mediation and conciliation, but is used as a general concept to cover the role of non-bloc members. This role may range from "coordination of expectations" between protagonists to acting as mere messengers.

flict relationship". Four possible categories (with illustrative sub-categories) can be conceived :

(i) Inter-bloc conflict :

(*a*) between the two bloc leaders ;

(*b*) between the two blocs *in toto* ;

(*c*) between the bloc leader and a member of the opponent bloc ; and

(*d*) between two members of the antagonistic blocs.

(ii) Intra-bloc conflict :

(*a*) between the bloc leader and one of its members ;

(*b*) between two (or more) members of the same bloc.

(iii) Bloc/non-bloc conflict :

(*a*) between a leader of one of the blocs and a non-bloc actor ;

(*b*) between a member of one of the blocs and a non-bloc actor.

(iv) Intra-non-bloc conflict : conflict between two or more third world actors.

These basic conflict sets determine the "intervening potential" and "theoretical acceptability" of non-aligned actors as third-party interveners :

(i) In the case of inter-bloc conflict and especially bloc polarisation, none of the bloc leaders or bloc members can intervene in a mediatory capacity for they will be involved in the conflict-relationship. This neat confrontation will be dangerous to the international system as a whole. Non-bloc actors will have every interest to intervene in order to arrest the conflict spiral. Moreover, bloc leaders and bloc-members may find non-bloc actors' intervention very useful as offering a new basis for compromise or as a face-saving device. Hence the intervening potential of non-bloc actors will be very high.

(ii) In the second category, intra-bloc conflict, outsiders are generally unacceptable. The other-bloc leader is certainly unacceptable for his mediatory effort will be interpreted either as "interference in family affairs" or as an attempt to drive a wedge in bloc cohesion. Indeed, the other-bloc leader will hesitate to initiate mediation for fear of giving the opponent bloc leader a pretext to interfere in case of future conflict within its own bloc. Moreover, conflict within the bloc may have adverse effects on its cohesion, a possibility that the opponent bloc finds beneficial (*e.g.* Hungary/U.S.S.R., Panama/U.S.A.). As to non-bloc actors, the possibility of their intervention is very limited. Non-bloc actors would consider an intra-bloc conflict as none of their business. Moreover, they would estimate the conflict as not likely to affect their interests (at least not directly) or as not so serious to systemic stability as inter-bloc conflict.

(iii) In the third category, bloc/non-bloc conflict, the most likely interveners would be either the leader of the same bloc or another non-bloc actor. The opposite bloc or its leaders do not have any particular interest in removing the contention, especially if we know that this type of conflict —given the relative military weakness of the non-bloc actors—is not likely to have system-wide disruptive effects. On the contrary, the bloc may benefit from the antagonism between a non-bloc actor and their opposite bloc. But the leader of the bloc involved in conflict will have a special interest in "containing" and "settling" the conflict, for its prolongation may have an adverse effect on the "public image" of its bloc and/ or may help a "rapprochement" of non-bloc actor(s) with the opposite bloc. As to non-bloc actors, their intervention will be motivated by a desire to extend help to their fellow non-bloc actor (through condemnatory statements, *e.g.* Suez) or mediation to "resolve" the conflict.

(iv) In the fourth set, intra-non-bloc conflict, bloc leaders and bloc members may intervene to "score points" in terms of prestige or to "woo" some of the non-bloc actors. But non-bloc actors feel more involved. They regard a conflict within their ranks as dysfunctional to the "cohesion" of the group as a whole and as adverse to their bargaining position "vis-à-vis" the blocs. They may also be motivated by a desire to "preempt" bloc interference in their own affairs, for one of their primary objectives would be to keep out of "the relationship of major tension" in the system.

From this brief description, it appears that non-bloc actors are—in terms of theoretical acceptability—interveners in three out of four basic categories of conflict relationship in a loose bipolar system.

4.2.2. *Applied Acceptability :* The above considerations show that the non-bloc members, precisely because of their "independent" position vis-à-vis the competing blocs can, theoretically, act as interveners in almost all of the possible conflict relationships. However, this theoretical acceptability is not enough in itself to explain either their actual *playing* of the interventionary role or their effectiveness in terms of outcomes. So in order to complete the picture, we argue that there are intervening variables which determine the actual intervention in the conflict process. For instance :

(1) *The communication patterns between protagonists :* the conflict process may be characterised by a dialogue or absence of dialogue between the protagonists. If dialogue is continuous, the need for third-party interveners would diminish ; if the dialogue is discontinuous or blocked, the need for "outsiders" to facilitate the conflict-termination process would increase (*e.g.* the Korean war). Similarly, two actors may be involved in a prolonged process of conflict-interaction, and in this case

learning processes may provide a whole set of techniques to "manage" or to "contain" the conflict within bounds. In this case the possibility of using third-party intervention may be low. (This is the case now between the "superpowers", especially after Cuba). This learning process is important in developing what Boulding calls "long-sightedness" and "the formation of realistic images". [46] The effects of this learning process are conditioned by such factors as the kind of weapons available (*e.g.* the higher their destructiveness, the faster the learning process), the rigidity or flexibility of actors' reciprocal images and the degree of threat-perception (whether actors perceive each other as expansionist or conservationist, for example).

(2) *Interventionary credentials :* it is obvious that some sort of credentials—in terms of social influence—is a perequisite for actual third-party intervention. Though we agree with Young on the absence of physical force in third-party intervention, we believe that the ability of the third-party intervener to offer a reward and/or to inflict punishment constitutes an important credential, though not an indispensable one (*e.g.* the U.N.'s "public disapproval" or "moral condemnation" heighten its credentials as a third-party intervener). Drawing on Young, [47] credentials of third-party interveners include : impartiality (third party is "perceived" as impartial by the conflict protagonists), independence (detachment from the established position of one of the conflict protagonists), salience (third-party's salient position in the international system, "perceived" as such by conflict protagonists), respect, continuity (the intervener acted as such in the past and continues to do so in the present), and possibility of offering reward and inflicting punishment.

(3) *The sequences of the conflict :* analytically speaking, conflict is conceived of as a process, wherein we distinguished four possible cycles ranging from conflict initiation, to response, interaction and termination.

Sequence One	→	initiation : Party 'A' moves from the area of potential conflict to that of actual conflict by manifesting his desire or will, through action, to occupy a position incompatible with the desire or will of party 'B'.
Sequence Two	→	response : 'B' reacts either violently or moderately, slowly or rapidly.

[46] Boulding, Kenneth : "Conflict Management as a Learning Process", in Anthony Renck and Julie Knight (eds.) : *Conflict in Society,* London, J. Y. Churchill, 1966, pp. 243-244.

[47] Young, Oran : *The Intermediaries : Third Parties in International Crises,* Princeton, Princeton U.P., 1967, pp. 80-91.

Sequence Three → conflict interaction : the conflict continues either violently or non-violently, at a high or low speed, for a long or short duration.

Sequence Four → termination (not necessarily synonymous with a final solution) : termination can mean return to the old status quo, acceptance of a new one, or simply a conflict-management (without reaching a definite settlement).

On the basis of this descriptive model of the conflict process, we believe that non-aligned actors can intervene in any of these four sequences. However, the feasibility and "fruitfulness" of their intervention will vary with the sequences. It is possible to distinguish between sequences one, two, and four on the one hand, and sequence three on the other. In the initiation sequence, the third party may intervene either to mollify the harshness of the initial move of 'A' or to induce 'B' not to react violently : this is the pre-commitment sequence and a third party can prevent escalation or offer an alternative position to 'B'. In sequence two, which may mark the beginning of the mutual commitment period, a third party can still intervene quite easily and help preempt the emergence of rigid commitments. In sequence four (termination), it is obvious that the protagonists themselves are willing to terminate their conflict and they will tend to welcome third-party facilitatory efforts. Sequence three witnesses the polarisation of commitments ; once the conflict interaction process is in progress, the possibility of third-party intervention is determined by the dynamics of this process. The possibility of non-aligned actors' intervention is reduced and their success in conflict-management is even lower when at least one of the protagonists perceives the conflict as touching on "vital interests".

5.

Having considered the theoretical and applied acceptability of non-aligned actors as third-party interveners, it is important now to consider some empirical cases of conflict in which non-aligned actors attempted conflict-management and regulatory intervention. Four cases, illustrating three sets of conflict relationships in the contemporary international system, can be treated. These cases are :

1. The Korean conflict.
2. The Cuban missile crisis.
3. The Sino-Indian conflict.
4. The Algerian-Moroccan border conflict. [48].

[48] See chapter V above.

5.1. *The Korean Conflict*

In the early fifties the systemic structure was obviously toward the tight-bipolar end of the continuum, and consequently there was the risk that a local conflict could be easily generalised and threaten the system as a whole.

The Korean conflict corroborates this proposition. As soon as it was declared in June 1950 that North Korean forces had crossed the 38th parallel, not only did the opponent bloc leader—the U.S.A.—feel that the security of its bloc was threatened, but also involved the universal actor—the U.N.—in the bipolar fighting. [49] Thus, rather than playing a regulatory role in the international system, the universal actor (at least at the beginning) took the side of one bloc against the other, and the military conflict was between "the United Nations Command" on the one hand, and the "aggressive Communist forces" on the other.

Even the few existing non-bloc actors could not prevent this rigid bipolarisation of the military conflict. The U.S. resolution adopted by the Security Council on the 25th June, 1950 stated that "the armed attack upon the Republic of Korea by forces from North Korea ... constitutes a breach to peace", and consequently all U.N. members were asked to "render every assistance to the U.N. in the execution of the resolution and to refrain from giving assistance to the North Korean authorities". [50] The resolution was adopted by nine votes in favour, with only one abstention —Yugoslavia. Both India and Egypt voted for the resolution.

But since North Korean forces were advancing rapidly, the U.S. President declared on 27 June 1950 : "I have ordered U.S. air and sea forces to give the Korean government troops cover and support". [51] Though this measure was taken independently of the U.N., the U.S. spokesman affirmed that it was in conformity with the Security Council resolution of 25 June which authorised the giving of assistance to South Korea.

For those who questioned the validity of this "conformity" and the U.S. interpretation of the Security Council resolution, the question soon became an academic one. On 27th of June, the Security Council met to consider a U.S. resolution recommending U.N. members to "furnish assistance to the Republic of Korea as might be necessary to repel the

---

[49] Krishna Menon, Nehru's friend and India's delegate to mediate the Korean conflict, stated that "... the whole of the Korean business was an understanding—I don't use a stronger word—between Trygve Lie on the one hand and the Americans on the other ..." since "the United Nations ... at that time was the United States ...". Brecher : *India and World Politics, op. cit.,* pp. 34-44.

[50] Karunakaran, Kotta P.: *India in World Affairs, February 1950 - December 1953,* London, O.U.P., 1958, especially pp. 95-129.

[52] *Ibid.*

armed attack and restore international peace and security in the area". [52] Seven members voted for the resolution and Yugoslavia voted against. This time neither India nor Egypt participated in the voting due to lack of instructions from their governments. But two days after the voting, Delhi issued a statement accepting the Security Council resolution.

> "The Government of India", the statement said, "have given the most careful consideration to the resolution of the Security Council in the context of events in Korea and also of their general foreign policy . . . The halting of aggression and the quick restoration of peaceful conditions are essential preludes to a satisfactory settlement. The Government of India, therefore, also accept the second resolution of the Security Council." [53]

Indian decision-makers, though, started to have second thoughts, for even if a solution could be reached militarily, the Government of India hoped it would be possible "to put an end to the fighting and settle the dispute by mediation". [54] India's preference for mediation was strengthened when it saw that the conflict was becoming more serious. For on 27th of June, the U.S. Government issued its "Formosa Declaration" which linked the Korean war to the larger China issue. As a result, India's "clear stand against aggression" became subordinated to limiting the conflict and bringing it to an end. Thus on July 7, India abstained from voting when the Security Council passed its third resolution (5/1588) establishing a 16-state U.N. Command under U.S. leadership. In explanation of the Indian position Nehru said : "The best assistance India can render in this grave crisis is to *help limit the area of conflict and in ending it.*" [55]

Consequently the Indian government began to communicate with Britain, China and the two bloc leaders. When Peking, on the 10th of July 1950, expressed "appreciation of the line that India had taken and conveying general agreement with our proposals", [56] Nehru—rather than supporting one bloc militarily—started his policy of bridge-building by sending two identical messages to Stalin and Dean Acheson on July 13, 1950. Nehru stated :

> "India's purpose is *to localize the conflict and to facilitate an early peaceful settlement* by breaking the present deadlock in the Security Council so that representatives of the People's Government

[52] *Ibid.*

[53] *Ibid.*

[54] As quoted in *ibid.*

[55] Steinberg, B. : "The Korean War : A Case Study in Indian Neutralism", *Orbis,* VIII, 1965, pp. 937-955 (emphasis added).

[56] Panikkar, K. M. : *In Two Chinas : Memoirs of a Diplomat,* London, Allen and Unwin, 1955, especially pp. 62-125.

> of China can take their seat in the Council, the U.S.S.R. can return to it and, whether within or through informal contacts outside the Council, the U.S.A., the U.S.S.R. and China, with the help and cooperation of other peace-loving nations, can find a basis for terminating the conflict and for a permanent solution of the problem." [57]

Whereas Stalin replied immediately, accepting the proposal on "the indispensable condition" of the Peking Government being given its seat in the Security Council, [58] the U.S.A. condemned the Indian proposal as "an appeasement to aggression". [59]

In addition to its theoretical acceptability which in turn facilitated its communication with the protagonists, the fact that India abstained from sending any of its armed forces to Korea and sent instead only a symbolic field ambulance, heightened the chances of its applied acceptability as a mediator and increased its *interventionary credentials.* Moreover, Indian dissociation from the actual fighting helped to distinguish between the U.N. as a belligerent in Korea, and the world organization as a universal actor.

India's aloofness and "perceived" impartiality was confirmed in its attitude to resolution 376 (v) of October 7, 1950, establishing the U.N. Commission for the Unification and Rehabilitation of Korea. The resolution, moved by some members who had armed forces in Korea, recommended among other things the establishment of a unified government for the whole of Korea.

India believed that this resolution meant not only the crossing of the 38th parallel, but also the stay of the U.N. forces in the North until Korean unification had been completed.

> "If such is the intention ...", the Indian delegate stated, "my government fears that the result may be to prolong North Korean resistance and even to extend the area of conflict. Our fears may turn out to be wrong, but each government has to judge the situation upon the *best information* at its disposal and act accordingly." [60]

Given the discontinuous, if not non-existent, communication patterns between the protagonists, India had information about Chinese intentions which the Unified Command did not possess. For on the 25th of September, 1950, General Nieh Yen-Jung—the acting Chief of Staff who was

---

[57] Karunakaran : *op. cit.* (emphasis added).

[58] *Ibid.*

[59] Acheson, Dean : *Present at the Creation : My Years in the State Department,* New York, A Signet Book, 1970, especially pp. 524-553, 660-693 and 830-839.

[60] Karunakaran : *op. cit.* (emphasis added). See also : Van Eekelen, W. F. : *Indian Foreign Policy and the Border Dispute with China,* Leiden, Sijthoff, 1964, pp. 66-71.

also the Military Governor of Peking—told India's ambassador in Peking "that the Chinese did not intend to sit back with folded hands and let the Americans come up to their border".[61] This was confirmed to Panikkar by Chou En-Lai himself on the 2nd of October :

> "If the Americans crossed the 38th parallel China would be forced to intervene in Korea. Otherwise he was most anxious for a peaceful settlement, and generally accepted Pandit Nehru's approach to the question ... I asked him whether China intended to intervene, if only the South Koreans crossed the parallel. He was emphatic : The South Koreans did not matter but American intrusion into North Korea would encounter Chinese resistance."[62]

Thus disregarding the advice of the *main channel of communication* that existed among the belligerents at the time, resulted in the extension of the area of conflict rather than in the approaching of a settlement. But the massive entry into the war on November 5, 1950 of the "Chinese people's Volunteers" turned the tide again and the U.N. forces were compelled to withdraw from most of North Korea. Realising that the conflict was getting wider, India was no longer acting by itself, and thus with twelve other states of the newly-formed Arab-Asian group they issued, on the 5th of December, an appeal to China to halt its advance at the 38th parallel,[63] but this appeal was not heeded.

The result was that the conflict began to escalate. When the U.S. —in answer to Chinese intervention—submitted a draft resolution to the U.N. Political Committee, branding China as an aggressor, India opposed the resolution. Delhi was bent on limiting the conflict to facilitate its settlement, and thus branding China as aggressor would not only leave all Far Eastern problems unsolved, but also would make them insoluble, since it would create another barrier to possible negotiations. The Indian delegate failed to understand

> "why it should be so humiliating to confer with a government so as to dispel misunderstanding and to reach a peace settlement without prejudging the issue of aggression, but quite proper first to pronounce that government as aggressor and then to proceed to negotiate with it".[64]

But the branding resolution—with some amendments—was adopted by 44 votes to 7 with 9 abstentions. Burma, India and the Communist-bloc members voted against it.

---

[61] Panikkar : *op. cit.*

[62] *Ibid.*

[63] Steinberg : *op. cit.*

[64] Karunakaran : *op. cit.*

To control the conflict, India was no longer satisfied with acting only as a communication channel and bridge-builder between the belligerents, but—in conjunction with members of the Arab-Asian group—tried to work for a cease-fire. Thus on the 12th of December, 1950, the group submitted a joint draft resolution to the Political Committee requesting the President of the General Assembly to constitute a group of three persons—including himself—to determine the basis on which a satisfactory cease-fire in Korea could be arranged. This time it was the members of the Communist bloc that opposed the draft resolution, but this did not prevent it from being adopted. Peking, however, insisted on the withdrawal of all foreign troops from Korea and Formosa as a precondition for negotiations. In addition, Peking proposed the convening in China of a seven-state conference (the big five, India and Egypt) to discuss Far Eastern problems and to bring about a settlement. Thus non-bloc members were officially invited by one of the protagonists to participate in the conflict-management process. Though this proposal was incorporated in a draft Arab-Asian resolution, the General Assembly rejected it. With the failure of non-bloc members to convince the protagonists to accept their compromise solution, the dimensions of the conflict were getting bigger and there was an increasing demand in the American press and Congress for the use of atomic weapons to halt the Chinese advance. When it was reported early in December 1950 that President Truman was thinking of using the atom bomb in Korea, India's admonitions that the Korean military conflict—if not halted—could easily turn into a world war were substantiated. [65]

When the belligerents realised the impending danger, they shied away from it and opted for contacts and negotiations to find a settlement. General MacArthur was deposed on the grounds that he was "unable to give his whole-hearted support to the policies of the U.S. Government and the U.N. in matters pertaining to his official duties". [66] It seems that the other protagonist, too, was tired of the war, for in a U.N. broadcast on June 23rd, 1951, Jacob Malik—the Soviet representative—declared that the armed conflict in Korea could be settled. He proposed that "as a first step, discussions should be started between the belligerents for a cease-fire

[65] In an informal letter to the Congress, pleading for the use of the atomic bomb in Korea, General MacArthur said "Here, in Asia, is where the Communist supporters have elected to make their play for global conquest ... Here we fight *Europe's war* with arms". The Korean War helped to remind the Asians of the first atomic bomb which was dropped on Asian land, and of the nuclear tests carried out in areas adjacent to Asian lands. Consequently, the Korean War—had it not been halted—could have made Asia once again the battle front to fight Europe's war, and with atomic weapons. Sen : *op. cit.,* pp. 248-249.

[66] Karunakaran : *op. cit.*

and an armistice providing for the mutual withdrawal of forces from the 38th parallel". These discussions officially started in Kaesong on July 8, 1951.

Each party came with its own demands, which were too far apart to permit an easy compromise, and it was difficult to agree *on a basis for bargaining and coordination of expectations.* Moreover, the opponents' lack of faith in each other contributed to the continuous diplomatic stalemate in the negotiations, and to increasing military commitment.

After heated debates and controversies, a provisional draft armistice agreement was reached on November 27, 1951. Though there were still many problems hindering the execution of this agreement, the issue of the repatriation of the prisoners of war constituted the main stumbling-block. [67] Consequently, when the U.N. General Assembly began its ordinary session, the Korean question was naturally debated. The American delegate expressed the Western bloc's view that the U.N. Command was ready to repatriate all prisoners of war, but some of them feared "execution, brutal treatment and imprisonment" if they went back ; even if force were used they would resist their repatriation. The U.S. representative maintained that although the Geneva Convention gave the prisoner the right and the opportunity to go home, there was nothing in it to imply that he must be forced at the end of the bayonet to go back when he did not want to do so. With another twenty U.N. members, he submitted a resolution to this effect. The Soviet representative rejected this 21-state draft resolution and submitted his own.

Thus the deadlock over the repatriation of prisoners of war prevented the conclusion of the cease-fire agreement, and while the fighting continued political bipolarisation between the protagonists was asserting itself again.

It is to be noted that from the time of the resolution branding China as aggressor until the middle of 1952, the Indian Government addressed little attention to the Korean conflict for four main reasons [68] :

1. A major goal of India's foreign policy was achieved when the two belligerents agreed to enter into negotiations in July 1951.

2. Other important problems nearer home occupied India's attention (*e.g.* the 1952 general elections ; the Kashmir problem).

---

[67] Krishna Menon gave the following account : "When I arrived at the U.N. General Assembly in the Autumn of 1952, the Korean position was that an Armistice Treaty with sixty-two clauses had been drafted. There was an agreement between both sides on all but two, and the two were the crucial ones ; those two were connected with repatriation [of prisoners]. The crucial problem was the repatriation business." Brecher : *India and World Politics, op. cit.*, p. 36.

[68] Steinberg : *op. cit.*

3. The conflict was going through the intensive conflict-interaction sequence (*i.e.* sequence 3 mentioned above) when each of the protagonists was committing increasing resources to strengthen its bargaining potential ; consequently the chances of mutual concessions were subordinated to each protagonist's desire to achieve a "position of strength".

4. Since various Indian suggestions and proposals had not been crowned with success, Nehru preferred to wait until he received assurances that India's mediatory efforts would be acceptable to both sides.

Chester Bowles, U.S. ambassador in Delhi, gave this assurance in the Autumn of 1952 when he unofficially suggested to Nehru that India take the "initiative" in breaking the deadlock. On the Chinese side, Panikkar reported to his government that, while opposing voluntary repatriation, Peking agreed with Delhi that no force should be employed in carrying out repatriation. Consequently, Krishna Menon circulated a lengthy resolution on November 17, 1952. What is important about this draft resolution is that it was framed with the knowledge—if not the approval—of Peking, and was drafted after exhaustive consultations with various Arab-Asian delegations. The importance of this resolution justifies a detailed treatment.

The Indian draft resolution, among other things :

1. noted that disagreement between the parties on one remaining issue alone prevented the conclusion of an armistice, and that a considerable measure of agreement already existed on the principles on which this remaining issue could be solved ;
2. expressed the wish to expedite and facilitate the convention of the Political Conference as provided in Article 60 of the draft armistice agreement ;
3. affirmed that the release and repatriation of prisoners of war should be effected in accordance with the Geneva Convention of August 12, 1949 [69] and the practice of international law and the relevant provisions of the draft armistice agreement ;

---

[69] Here is a very clear example of the impact of non-aligned actors on the regulatory mechanism of the international system. They exercise their impact through both the consolidation of "universal norms" and direct intervention to manage conflict. "The basis", Menon stated, "I invented at that time—I think it's correct to use that term—was the Geneva Agreement in regard to Prisoners of War ... I said, if we can bring it down to some formula on a basis which has a wide moral appeal it must be an international agreement in regard to the treatment of POWs. I said in my speech at the U.N., in regard to the prisoners, it should be neither 'push nor pull'. The Geneva Agreement should be the basis." Brecher : *India and World Politics, op. cit.*, p. 37.

4. requested the President of the General Assembly to transmit 17 specific proposals contained in the Indian draft resolution (about the establishment of a Repatriation Commission and its appointment of an Umpire) to the Central Government of the People's Republic of China and to the North Korean authorities, as forming a just and reasonable basis for an agreement ; and to invite their acceptance of these proposals and to make a report to the General Assembly during the seventh session. The resolution also stipulated that

> "at the end of 90 days, the disposition of any prisoners of war whose return to their homelands has not been effected in accordance with the procedure set out above shall be referred by the Repatriation Commission to the Political Conference to be called under article 60 of the draft armistice agreement". [70]

Whereas the British Foreign Secretary—Anthony Eden—found the Indian proposal "timely and constructive", the U.S. delegation believed that the resolution was vague about what would happen to those prisoners who refused repatriation. To get round these differences in the Western bloc, the British delegate proposed the following amendments :

(*a*) in the interests of effective and impartial operation, the "umpire" should be made a full member and president of the Repatriation Commission ;

(*b*) more explicit provision should be made for the welfare of the non-repatriated. [71]

But once these amendments had been incorporated into the Indian draft resolution and the U.S.A. was ready to drop its 21-state draft resolution and support the Indian one, the U.S.S.R. objected strongly to the resolution on the grounds that it was "designed not to put an end to the war but to perpetuate it". [72] Krishna Menon's answer was to dissociate himself from the American position but also to reject Soviet amendments. [73]

The Indian resolution was finally adopted by 53 votes to 5 with one abstention. The Indian resolution is important for at least two main reasons :

1. by the time the resolution was adopted one bloc's dominance over the General Assembly was passing its peak, and an emerging Afro-Asian group—non-aligned in the East-West conflict—was beginning to cohere [74] ;

---

[70] Karunakaran : *op. cit.*

[71] *Ibid.*

[72] *Ibid.*

[73] Eekelen : *op. cit.*

[74] Lyon : *Neutralism, op. cit.*, p. 37.

2. when, at last, an agreement on the repatriation of prisoners of war was concluded on June 8, 1953, its provisions were to a great extent similar to those of the Indian resolution adopted by the General Assembly on December 3, 1952, except that the final disposition of unrepatriated prisoners of war was left to the proposed political conference and not to the U.N. (This was logical, since China was not a U.N. member and the U.N. was the other belligerent in the conflict.)

It was only natural that non-aligned India should be chosen by both blocs to play the important part [75] in the implementation of this agreement and in the Neutral Nations Repatriation Commission (composed of the representatives of Czechoslovakia, Poland, India, Sweden and Switzerland). In fact, the Commission's general terms of reference stipulated that :

> "sufficient armed forces and any other operating personnel required to assist the Neutral Nations Repatriation Commission in carrying out its functions and responsibilities shall be provided exclusively by India, whose representative shall be the umpire . . . chairman and executive agent of the Neutral Nations Repatriation Commission." [76]

Though the Commission was not as successful as non-aligned actors hoped, it scored some achievements :

1. the stumbling-block (the non-forcible repatriation of prisoners of war) that had delayed the conclusion of the armistice and the cessation of mutual killing that had been going on for eight months was removed, to be handled by a "neutral" commission ;
2. though there was bipolarisation within the Commission, the fact that this bipolarisation did not lead to a stalemate and the cessation of dialogue was due to the participation and chairmanship of non-aligned India. The comparison here with another Commission in the same conflict, the Neutral Nations Supervisory Commission, is revealing. This Commission was composed of Czechoslovakia, Poland, Sweden and Switzerland, as representatives of the two belligerents. Consequently,

---

[75] The importance of an "impartial" party beside the two conflicting parties was emphasised. For—as Krishna Menon said—the "Korean experience" showed the necessity of having "one (from the West) and one (from the East) and one (neutral)—there must be a neutral chairman". Brecher : *India and World Politics, op. cit.*, p. 42.

[76] Steinberg, B. : *op. cit.*

> "the classic tradition of the neutral's duties towards all concerned was replaced by a somewhat diffuse concept of the neutral's duties towards the side which had proposed his appointment". [77]

Thus from the very beginning "the Supervisory Commission found itself immobilised from within, as it were, by its own composition and by the fundamentally different concepts which its members had of their mission". [78] The parity basis of representation led to a stalemate division, and since "a majority vote could not be achieved, the Commission was reduced to impotence" [79] ;

3. the fate of non-repatriated prisoners was not allowed to lead to the continuation of the military conflict. For although both protagonists strongly opposed the solution proposed by the Indian representative, both ended by accepting it.

Consequently, *The Times* commented on the work of the Commission by saying [80] :

> "Confused as was the working of this initial venture in neutral arbitration, it is important to remember that it did work", for it "provided a crucible in which several elements were mixed and if they did not all fuse together that was inevitable from their chemical composition."

5.2. *The Cuban Missile Crisis of 1962* [81]

Here is a case of conflict between the two bloc leaders which manifested itself in a most acute form—crisis. Though Cuba was the place of the crisis and was associated with it, the two main protagonists were the U.S.A. and the U.S.S.R. [82] The object of the conflict was the Russian missiles in Cuba, which the other protagonist perceived as threatening its

---

[77] Freymond, Jacques : "Supervising Agreements : The Korean Experience", *Foreign Affairs,* XXXVII (1959), pp. 496-503.

[78] *Ibid.*

[79] *Ibid.*

[80] As quoted in Steinberg, *op. cit.*

[81] The factual background is mainly taken from the following sources : Abel, Alie : *The Missiles of October. The Story of the Cuban Missile Crisis, 1962,* London, MacGibon and Kee (New Edition), 1969 ; Kennedy, Robert : *13 Days. The Cuban Missile Crisis, October 1962,* London, MacMillan, 1969 ; Pachter, Henry : *Collision Course. The Cuban Missile Crisis and Coexistence,* London, Pall Mall Press, 1963 ; *Keesing's Contemporary Archives,* XIII, 1961-1962.

[82] From the various accounts available, it is clear that the Kennedy Administration emphasised the fact that the conflict was with the U.S.S.R. ; Castro, "a new pawn", was to be ignored. (See Patcher, *op. cit.,* pp. 4 and 27.)

core interests.[83] It is because of this perceived threat to core interests that the U.S.A. was not likely to compromise or accept middle-of-the-road measures. It was ready to go to the "last" rung of the escalatory ladder. Secrecy and speed in the preparation of the retaliatory measures were the hallmarks of American strategy. They were meant to take the other party by surprise and thus limit its options (without putting it in a corner). The U.S.S.R., on the other hand (at least on the basis of available accounts which are written by "Western" scolars), did not seem to have core interests at stake in the Cuban crisis.

This does not mean that the U.S.S.R. did not have any intcrests at all. For examplc, the preservation of the revolutionary regime in Cuba and considerations of the Soviet image in the world were at stake. But compared with those of the U.S.A., Soviet interests were, perceptually, less "vital". This element of "non-vitality" of interests, coupled with relative "weakness" in the area of confrontation, explain the bargaining strategy of the Soviet Union, which emphasised the desire to compromise and to accept third-party interveners.[84]

But as the conflict was between the two bloc leaders, and as each bloc leader sought and obtained the support of its allies,[85] a pattern of neat polarization obtained, as we mentioned in dealing with cases of inter-bloc conflict. In this type of conflict, we suggested, only the non-bloc actors could intervene either singly, in combination, or through the U.N. The level of destabilizing forces was very high, and because of this non-aligned actors had a special and direct interest in a prompt termination of the crisis. However, in spite of their theoretical acceptability, the effective intervention of the non-aligned actors was reduced to a minimum, if not

---

[83] These include not only military interests, but also (and mainly) psychological and political interests. Considerations of credibility, posture and image were also important, especially when we realise that, following their meeing in Vienna in 1961, Khrushchev perceived Kennedy as "an inexperienced young leader who could be intimidated and blackmailed". (See Reston, James : "What was killed was not only the President", *The New York Times,* November 15th, 1964).

[84] As an indication of this position, see the positive reply of the U.S.S.R. to the letter of Bertrand Russell and to the letter of the Acting Secretary-General of the U.N. (Patcher, *op. cit.,* pp. 209, 211-212 and 214-215). On the other hand, the Soviet Union seemed to be hoping for an intervention on the part of the uncommitted states, through the U.N., to exert pressure on the U.S.A. (See *Le Monde,* 11-12 November 1962 : "Les Russes semblent avoir cru il y a quelques jours [qu'avec de tels arguments] ils pourraient susciter un mouvement parmi les non-engagés et de cette façon faire pression sur Washington.")

[85] In the case of the U.S.A., the O.A.S. voted a resolution on October 23, declaring support to the American position, and Dean Acheson was sent to Europe to secure support (which he did). As for the Soviet Union a similar bloc solidarity was also visible, at least during the first stages of the crisis, though later on Chinese and Albanian criticism would be audible.

actually neutralized, by the dynamics of the conflict process ; the basic elements being the 'intransigence' of one of the protagonists (which perceived a threat to its core interests) and the speed of the crisis. When the conflict was brought to the attention of the U.N. Security Council by the U.S.A., the non-bloc actors were provided with the opportunity to play a mediatory role. [86] As a result of bloc polarization, the U.N. (the universal actor) was mainly representative of non-aligned actors. In this situation, to requote Kaplan :

> "all non-bloc actors are to coordinate their national objectives with those of the universal actor and to subordinate the objectives of bloc actors to those of the universal actor".

However, the role they played was extremely limited and even moderate. [87] To sum up this role, we can distinguish two phases of non-aligned intervention ; a direct phase and then intervention through the Acting Secretary-General of the universal actor.

A. *The phase of direct intervention :* This intervention took place during the debate on the Cuban crisis in the Security Council. Thus a joint draft resolution was submitted by Ghana and Egypt which requested *inter alia* "... the Acting Secretary-General to confer promptly with the parties directly concerned on the immediate steps to be taken to remove the existing threat to world peace, and to normalize the situation in the Caribbean". From then on they left the matter to U Thant. We might speculate and say that, aware of the gravity of the situation and of their meager resources, they entrusted U Thant to act on their behalf, thus benefiting from the moral authority of the universal actor. It may be noted that this aspect of non-aligned behaviour is in dissonance with rule No. 12 of the loose bipolar system as developed by Kaplan. This rule reads as follows : "universal actors are to mobilize non-bloc ... actors against cases of gross deviancy, for example, resort to force, by a bloc actor". In the Cuban crisis, a different pattern of non-bloc actor behaviour took place, for they took the initiative in asking the universal actor to intervene (instead of being mobilized by it).

B. *Intervention through the Secretary-General :* In his statement to the Security Council on October 24, U Thant revealed that, on the request of a "large number" of member states, he had addressed identically-worded

[86] At that time Ghana and the U.A.R. were members of the Security Council.

[87] In this respect, see *Le Monde* of November 11-12, 1962, which speaks of the fact that "... Les non-engagés sont conscients de leur peu d'influence réelle", that they are still "... sous le coup de la douche froide qu'ils ont reçue au moment où ils s'apprêtaient à aider leurs amis cubains".

messages to President Kennedy and Premier Khrushchev, in which he proposed

> "the voluntary suspension of all armed shipments to Cuba and also the voluntary suspension of the quarantine measures involving the searching of ships bound for Cuba".

In the same statement he also suggested that the protagonists should first discuss the "modalities" of terminating the crisis. Premier Khrushchev accepted U Thant's proposal. But President Kennedy, while stating that "Ambassador Stevenson is ready to discuss promptly [these] arrangements [with you]", was emphatic in saying that

> "the existing threat was created by the secret introduction of offensive weapons into Cuba, and the answer lies in the removal of such weapons".

On the following day (October 25) U Thant wrote again to Khrushchev, hoping that

> "it may be possible to instruct the Soviet ships already on their way to Cuba to stay away from the interception area for a limited time only, in order to permit discussions of the modalities of a possible agreement which could settle the problem peacefully in line with the Charter . . ." ;

and to Kennedy appealing

> "that instructions may be issued to United States vessels in the Caribbean to do everything possible to avoid direct confrontation with Soviet ships . . ."

Both Khrushchev and Kennedy accepted the proposal, but Kennedy still emphasised the importance of withdrawing the missiles from Cuba.

Though the denouement of the crisis was a result of direct American-Soviet agreement, there is another aspect in which the U.N., through U Thant, tried to intervene ; namely on the question of inspection and verification. We know that this was one of the American demands which had to be met before ending the quarantine. U Thant visited Havana on October 29, and raised the matter of land and air inspection with Premier Castro ; but the Cuban leader refused to accept the idea of inspection. On the other hand, there was the problem of inspection of Cuba-bound ships in order to ascertain that they did not transport "offensive" weapons. To get out of the dilemma, the idea of asking the International Committee of the Red Cross to carry out the inspection task was accepted. Accordingly, U Thant contacted the International Committee of the Red Cross on October 30, and it was arranged that a 30-man inspection team would do the job.[88] However, as the U.S. and the U.S.S.R. had reached an agreement on ending the quarantine, U Thant wrote to the International Committee on November 15 :

> "La quarantaine imposée par les Etats-Unis ayant été levée ... il me semble que le recours aux bons offices du CICR à propos de l'affaire cubaine ... n'est plus nécessaire."[89]

These brief considerations show that the non-aligned actors (whether directly or through the U.N.) played a very limited mediatory role, and this was mainly carried out by the Acting Secretary-General. The universal actor, in its limited role as mediator, tried to carry out two main functions :

(*a*) making proposals, and

(*b*) exercising a moderating influence.

As to the reasons for this limited role, we can advance two arguments; first, and by far the most crucial, was that one of the two protagonists, which happened to be a superpower, perceived a threat to core interests and was unwilling to make concessions ; secondly, the non-aligned countries were taken by surprise at the speed of the conflict process, and did not have enough time to work out a coherent interventionary strategy.

5.3. *The Sino-Indian Conflict*

The immediate and direct cause of the 1962 Sino-Indian conflict was about 2,000 miles of border, with maps and treaties often from the last century. But there were larger issues at stake, including the self-assertion of China as a major global actor, the effect of this on the Asian subsystem and the attitude of other major actors in the international system.[90] The fact that at least one of the protagonists (China) regarded the conflict as touching "vital interests" and "basic objectives" made its propensity to

[88] "Le Comité international de la Croix-Rouge et l'affaire de Cuba", *Revue internationale de la Croix-Rouge,* décembre 1962, p. 605.

[89] Comité international de la Croix-Rouge : *Rapport d'activité : 1962,* Genève, 1963, p. 33.

[90] India's Defence Minister at the time of the conflict, Krishna Menon, affirmed: "To China, India strutting across the world stage was virtually the largest and most significant country of a non-aligned group talking on equal terms to great countries in the international field, sometimes trying to bring about compromise solutions to problems between the Soviet Union and the United States in the United Nations. Even at Bandung they found that we were introducing China to the world ; we were making China acceptable. All that must have irked them." Brecher : *India and World Politics, op. cit.,* p. 165.

compromise, and hence the non-aligned actors capacity to elicit concessions, very limited. This also explains why the 242 items of evidence—mainly of a historical nature—which the Chinese produced in 1960-1961, and the no less than 630 items with which the Indians responded, could not prevent the military conflict that ensued. [91]

From the point of view of the structure of the international system, the blocs were not as coherent and clear-cut as in the early fifties, during the Korean conflict for instance. The "looseness" of the bipolar systemic structure was approaching the multipolarity end of the continuum. Moreover, there was ambiguity about how to classify the position of China : whether it was to be considered a full member of the Communist bloc or an aspiring leader of an 'anti-dupolistic' third world. Of course, the Chinese policy-makers themselves did not seem to have this (classification) dilemma, since the two positions were those of an actor playing the same "anti-imperialist revolutionary" role. But the bloc actors were emphasising that it was *Communist* China. This was surely the case with the leaders of the Western bloc.

Britain adopted a firm pro-Indian attitude. The British Prime Minister offered unconditional aid—"what they ask us to do to help them, we will do", Mr. Macmillan said. Thanks to "arms for India" schemes, weapons flowed into the country, and the Secretary for the Commonwealth left for Delhi to have "an informal exchange of views with the Indian and Pakistani Governments on matters arising out of the present situation". An arms agreement "without agreed financial limit" was signed "for the purpose of defending India against Chinese aggression". [92] Implicitly, the purpose was to coordinate efforts between India and Pakistan (a member of both SEATO and CENTO).

The *American* support to India was even more explicit and substantial. On October 31, 1962, the State Department issued a statement explaining the decision to supply "defensive" assistance to India because of "this premeditated *Communist* aggression". Consequently, "in extending assistance to India, we are responding to an urgent need arising from a situation which is of concern not only to this country but *to our allies as well*". [93] J. K. Galbraith, the then American ambassador in Delhi, was even less tactful about the "menace of Communism". [94] Supplies from

[91] D. C. Watt (ed.) : *Survey of International Affairs : 1962,* London, O.U.P., 1970, pp. 404-438.

[92] *Ibid.*

[93] *The Times,* 1 November 1962, as quoted in Watt : *Survey of International Affairs,* 1962, *op. cit.* (emphasis added).

[94] For a detailed account, see Galbraith, John : *Ambassador's Journal : A Personal Account of the Kennedy Years,* New York, New American Library, 1970, pp. 376-454.

U.S. bases in West Germany flowed into India. On November 14, an agreement was signed in Washington between the Indian ambassador and the U.S. Assistant Secretary of State "to furnish assistance to India for the purpose of defence against Chinese aggression directed from Peking" and to provide the necessary facilities for U.S. personnel in Delhi to "observe and review the use of arms supplies". [95]

Even the *Soviet* attitude at the beginning helped to consolidate the impression of China's position as a member of the Communist bloc. A few days after the outbreak of fighting, Moscow urged India to accept China's "constructive" proposals for a "peaceful settlement". [96] East European bloc members reflected the attitude of the bloc leader, and expressed hopes for a peaceful settlement through negotiation, without preconditions. This coincided with the Chinese view. [97]

But whether China was accepted at that time as a full-bloc member or as an aspiring leader of the third world, only non-aligned actors could be *theoretically acceptable* as third-party interveners. This is because each of the two blocs tended to take the position—more or less publicly—of one of the protagonists, which made a mediation attempt by a bloc member suspect to at least one of the protagonists. In addition to their perceived impartiality, non-aligned actors were *practically acceptable* by a fellow-non-aligned India and by a "third world China", keen on securing Afro-Asian non-aligned support. Consequently, the non-aligned actors, encouraged by these *interventionary credentials,* tried to translate their mediatory potential into actuality. The first attempt came from President Tubman of Liberia who sent a telegram on the 19th of October asking for a cease-fire to be followed by third-world mediation. [98] President Nasser cabled to both Chou-En-Lai and Nehru offering to be in touch with them to give a compromise solution, and when both accepted his offer Nasser wrote to the Heads of State of Afghanistan, Indonesia, Algeria, Sudan, Morocco, Ceylon, Ghana, Cambodia, Mali and Guinea. Nasser's first proposals can be summarized as follows :

1. an immediate cease-fire,
2. withdrawal of forces to the positions occupied before the battle began (*i.e.* back to the 8th of September positions),
3. the establishment of a neutral zone between the two armies,
4. negotiation to find an ultimate solution to the basic problems.

---

[95] Watt : *Survey of International Affairs, 1962, op. cit.*

[96] Jansen : *op. cit.,* p. 326.

[97] Moreover, the delay in the delivery of pre-contracted Soviet Mig planes to India strengthened doubts about the Socialist bloc siding with China. Mallik : *op. cit.,* p. 263.

[98] Watt : *Survey of International Affairs, 1962, op. cit.*

Since these proposals coincided generally with India's attitude (especially the withdrawal item), they were approved by Nehru, some leaders were lukewarm and the Chinese rejected them on the 2nd of November. [99]

Nasser's proposals were followed by fairly similar ones from Guinea's Sekou Touré. These suggested a cease-fire, a 20-kilometre withdrawal from either side of the "natural frontiers", an immediate meeting between the two parties, and the "outright condemnation of all foreign intervention". This formulation elicited a letter from Chou-En-Lai to Sekou Touré on November 13 describing the proposals as "equitable, constructive and conducive to a peaceful settlement", and hoping for "a wide, positive response among Asian and African countries" to them.

Then in a meeting at the U.N. headquarters on the 16th of November, another move was initiated by Ghana and Egypt. But since China was not a member of the universal actor, it was doubtful whether China would welcome any proposals elaborated within its framework.

The fact that the non-aligned actors were the main actors that were trying to communicate with, and mediate between, the protagonists encouraged Chou-En-Lai to address messages to them on November 15 to enlist their support. His letter was couched in "third world" language, describing the Sino-Indian border dispute as a "legacy of British imperialist aggression" and condemning U.S. military intervention as detrimental not only to China and India but to the Afro-Asian world as a whole. [100]

China's wooing of the non-aligned actors for support gave them a capacity to 'reward and punish'. It also paved the way for the first institutionalized non-aligned attempt to secure group—rather than individual—action. Consequently Mrs. Bandaranaika—Ceylon's Prime Minister—invited five non-aligned states (Burma, Cambodia, Ghana, Indonesia and the U.A.R.) to attend a meeting at Colombo to discuss mediation between China and India. Her message of November 20 said :

> "The grave international situation arising from the present state of the Sino-Indian border conflict, in my view, requires immediate and concentrated efforts to influence the governments of India and China to avert the outbreak of world war. I *have been in communication* with the Prime Ministers of India and China, and I am aware that several other prime ministers of non-aligned countries have made similar approaches ; but it seems to me that individual approaches have not met with much success. A further deterioration in the situation could lead to the outbreak of war, which *strikes at the very roots of non-alignment.*
>
> It is therefore extremely urgent that Heads of State and Prime Ministers of such non-aligned nations as may be able to assist in influencing India and China should, if possible, meet and consult one

[99] Jansen : *op. cit.*, p. 331.

[100] Watt : *Survey of International Affairs, 1962, op. cit.*

> another and decide upon an *immediate joint approach to India and China.*" [101]

On the 10th of December 1962, the six-non-aligned-state-Conference started in Colombo. The risk arising from conflict-continuation was not only confined to the protagonists, but also affected the non-aligned position as such. Non-aligned actors were worried about big-power intervention in the conflict, the weakening of non-alignment itself, and hence the resurgence of rigid bipolarity. The host to the Conference found that non-alignment was facing its "greatest challenge", for the border conflict had

> "afforded an opportunity for the power politics of the cold war to penetrate as it were into the affairs of the Afro-Asian world. We have seen how India has been obliged to seek arms and assistance from Western powers, and the eagerness with which this has been given. This kind of entanglement with power blocs . . ."

would certainly undermine non-alignment. [102] Though all invitees refused to take sides, the degree of their *impartiality* was not exactly identical. Small states like Burma and Cambodia had to take into account their proximity to the Chinese "super actor" and this might in part explain India's apprehensive attitude toward the Conference. To keep unity within their ranks, the non-aligned actors conceived of their role as that of "friendly third parties" (as Burma's Ne Win expressed it [103]). The Conference should

> "refrain from making any attempt to determine or pass judgement in any way on the rights and wrongs, merits and demerits, of the positions being adhered to by the two parties". [104]

In other words, the Conference's task was certainly not intervening "in the substance of the conflict between India and China" (Indonesia's Dr. Subandrio) but aimed to "lay down the principles which would create the right atmosphere for the resumption of negotiations between the two sides" (U.A.R.'s Ali Sabry [105]).

This position was condoned by all the Conference members, and the official communiqué after the first day of deliberations declared that

> "the Conference decided that its purpose was not to consider the merits and demerits of the dispute but to provide for an exchange of views in order to assist the two countries to resume negotiations with a view to arriving at a peaceful settlement". [106]

---

[101] *Ibid.* (emphasis added).

[102] *Ibid.*, and also Jansen : *op. cit.*, pp. 330-351.

[103] Jansen : *op. cit.*, pp. 330-351.

[104] *Ibid.*

[105] *Ibid.*

[106] *Ibid.*

The principle underlying this peaceful settlement was that "neither side would be in a position to derive benefit from military operations". (This norm of the international system was incorporated in the two-page document entitled "Principles underlying the proposals of the Six", and handed by Mrs. Bandaranaika and Dr. Subandrio to Chou-En-Lai in Peking.)

Since the non-aligned actors believed that *communication* with the protagonists had to be confidential to be successfully maintained, the Conference members

> "decided not to publish the text of their conclusions which are to be communicated to the governments of India and the People's Republic of China, lest a premature disclosure may prejudice their endeavours". [107]

The proposals were officially published on January 19, after Mrs. Bandaranaika had explained their contents personally both in Peking and New Delhi.

In substance the proposals aimed at consolidating the cease-fire until direct negotiations took place. Moreover, they managed to create the "right atmosphere" for the initiation of these negotiations, by providing specific proposals concerning the position of antagonistic troops on the ground. What distinguished these specific proposals is that

> "they did not require the Chinese to do anything which they had not already promised to do ; they also did not require the Indian Army to make any withdrawals and, in the East, permitted it to return to the old frontier". [108]

Consequently the proposals seemed a successful basis for the settlement of conflict since they

> "sought to give China what she wanted in the Western sector—that she considered important—and to satisfy India in the East, which was the vital area for her". [109]

Though the conflict was prevented from worsening, the border dispute was not settled definitively, mainly because India wanted acceptance of the proposals *in toto* whereas China accepted them only "in principle". But one can surmize that whereas the non-aligned actors confined their mediatory effort only to the border dispute, the Sino-Indian conflict involved wider issues. As the *Survey of International Affairs* expressed it :

> "the efforts of the Colombo powers were not misplaced, nor were they wholly without effect, but they had the misfortune to try to

[107] *Ibid.*

[108] *Ibid.*

[109] *Ibid.*

> tackle a problem that came essentially within the scope of the bigger powers". [110]

Yet the members of the Colombo Conference continued to act as a *communication channel and "coordinator of expectations"* between the protagonists. They maintained contacts with the two sides through both diplomatic means and personal visits. Thus during his February 1964 visit to Indonesia, Burma and Cambodia, Chou-En-Lai discussed again the Colombo proposals. The joint Sino-Burmese Communiqué of February 18, 1964 expressed the hope of the two sides

> "that China and India would find it possible to enter into direct negotiations *on the basis* of the Colombo proposals so as to remove progressively the difference between them and finally achieve a friendly settlement" [111]

In other words, the Chinese Premier no longer talked about acceptance "in principle" only. On the other hand, India—as Nehru expressed its attitude to the All-India Congress shortly before his death—still stuck to the Colombo proposals as the basis for negotiation. An eventual settlement of the Sino-Indian dispute on this basis which the two protagonists accept would then justify the Colombo Conference's self-congratulation, as Mrs. Bandaranaika expressed it in her closing speech.

5.4. What do these empirical cases of conflict indicate as regards the impact of non-aligned actors on the conflict-management process in the contemporary international system? Contrary to their relatively direct and easily identifiable impact on the system's structure, the non-aligned actors' influence on the system's conflict-management process is subject to some *intervening variables* (*e.g.* conflict issues, conflict sequence, communication patterns among the protagonists, who the conflict protagonists are . . .).

(i) As far as the *conflict issues* are concerned, sometimes non-bloc members limited themselves to the immediate and direct conflict issue (*e.g.* border demarcation), when the conflict relationship involved broader and more complex issues (as in the Sino-Indian conflict). Though this "narrow definition" of their mediatory function tended to limit their effectiveness as third-party interveners, yet even in this case the protagonists accepted the proposals formulated by non-bloc members as constituting the basis for bargaining and for an eventual settlement of the conflict issue. By performing the function of "coordinator of expectations" between the Indian and Chinese protagonists, non-aligned actors have facilitated a process of mutual concessions ; especially since each prota-

---

[110] Watt : *Survey of International Affairs, 1962, op. cit.*

[111] Eekelen : *op. cit.,* especially p. 126.

gonist does not feel that it is "giving in" to the exigencies of the other. The conclusion is obvious : the intervention of non-aligned actors as third parties has provided a basis conducive to conflict-management—if not definitive solution.

(ii) The *conflict sequence* is another intervening variable that determines the effectiveness and/or limitation of non-aligned actors as third-party interveners in conflict situations. For instance, the massive entry into the Korean conflict of the "Chinese People's Volunteers", and American statesmen's talk of using atomic weapons marked not only the "commitment stage" on the part of the protagonists, but also the lull in India's mediatory efforts. Nevertheless, when the protagonists shied away from conflict escalation and opted for conflict control, the proposals of non-aligned actors constituted the basis of settlement. Moreover, India not only provided the resources for the execution of the agreement terminating the war, but was accorded the chairmanship of the Neutral Nations Repatriation Commission. Thus, the effectiveness of non-bloc members as third-party interveners does not only depend on their "good will", "hard work" and "reasonable proposals", but also on the stage through which the conflict relationship is passing. Thus, in the Cuban missile crisis the swift acceleration of the sequences in the conflict process, to the point of overlapping between conflict "initiation" and conflict "interaction", constituted a further limitation on the intervention of non-aligned actors. This conflict sequence influences the "mood" of the protagonists (amenable to concessions or bent on achieving a "position of strength") and also the communication patterns between these protagonists (*e.g.* whether the dialogue is continuous, discontinuous or lacking altogether).

(iii) Both the Korean conflict and the Cuban missile crisis confirm the importance of this third intervening variable—*communication patterns* between protagonists. When, in the Korean conflict, the belligerents were negotiating in Kaesong, India's role as a channel of communication was not very much needed, and this coincided with a lull in India's influence in the conflict-management process. But it is essentially the Cuban conflict that illustrates the influence of communication between conflict protagonists on third-party intervention. For in this conflict, communication channels were wide open and used extensively, officially and unofficially, [112] directly and indirectly. Moreover, the protagonists themselves

[112] Examples of unofficial and/or indirect communication include : The proposals of Eugene Ivanov (Naval attaché at the Soviet Embassy in London) on October 24, 1962. See Abel : *op. cit.*, pp. 145-147. The conversation between Khrushchev and William Knox (President of Westinghouse International) during the latter's visit to Moscow on October 24. See Abel : *op. cit.*, pp. 151-152. The "lunch proposals" from A. Fomin (counsellor of the Soviet Embassy in Washington) to J. Scali (correspondent of the American Broadcasting Company). See Abel : *op. cit.*, p. 176.

—due to the high stakes involved—wanted to be certain that the messages were clear and undistorted. [113] This is why they did not desire the contribution of non-bloc members in this respect.

(iv) This Cuban missile crisis points out a fourth important intervening variable : *who are the conflict's protagonists ?* Thus the management of the Algerian-Moroccan border conflict, for instance, indicates that the applied acceptability and effectiveness of non-aligned actors are greater in a conflict between members of their own subsystem than in other conflict sets. The superpowers were not willing to get involved in the conflict, and the non-aligned actors themselves were equally keen to keep the conflict out of cold-war entanglements. Not only is applied acceptability stronger in cases of conflict among members of their own subsystem, but also the effectiveness of intervention is greater. Thus whereas they were given the role of arbitrators to "solve" the Algerian-Moroccan conflict, their task in the Sino-Indian conflict was limited to creating the "appropriate atmosphere" and providing a basis for direct bilateral negotiations, and in the Cuban missile crisis the role of non-aligned actors was even more limited and essentially through the universal actor. Their limitations in this last category of conflict (*i.e.* inter-bloc conflict) are even clearer when we notice that in some inter-bloc conflicts (*e.g.* Berlin) the theoretical acceptability of non-aligned actors as third-party interveners was not always translated into applied acceptability or effectiveness. [114]

6.

Does this, in fact, lead us to the conclusion that when the superpowers choose to agree, the efforts of the non-aligned actors are superfluous and when the superpowers refuse to agree, the urgings of the non-aligned are futile ; and—consequently—that the "stability function" claimed by non-aligned actors should be rejected ? Our analysis does not condone this conclusion, for :

1. Not all conflicts in the international system arise only among the superpowers.

---

[113] Due to the influence on him of Barbara Tuchman's book : *The Guns of August,* President Kennedy dreaded war by miscalculation.

[114] Non-aligned actors, however, claim that in such conflicts (*e.g.* Berlin) they have not been completely absent but have played a role similar to that of the chorus in ancient Greek tragedy, whose function it was to predict and warn against the consequences. See, for instance, their views on Berlin during the 1961-crisis as in *Belgrade Conference Report, op. cit.*

2. In actual international interaction, the superpowers and their followers are—most of the time—neither ready to agree fully nor eager to disagree completely. In this intermediate zone, the non-aligned actors have the greatest potency to

> "spur the search for mutually acceptable formulas, assist in such search, devise new formulas or suggest fresh approaches, ... appeal for compromises ... help to cool rising tempers and prolong uneasy truces until the will of accommodation obtains ... keep the channels of indirect communication open ... which could be of supreme value in moments of crisis". [115]

3. Non-alignment has helped to improve the quality of systemic stability nuclear deterrence has initiated. Even when inter-bloc conflicts erupted, the conciliatory and mediatory efforts of non-aligned actors helped to reduce the magnitude of these inter-bloc conflicts (*e.g.* in the Korean conflict). [116]

4. Nor could the alternative to non-alignment (*i.e.* alignment) have proved a panacea or a stronger guarantee of systemic stability. In fact, it could have been more dangerous, for—according to Michigan University's quantitative studies on the Correlates of War Project—in the twentieth century high alliance levels were correlated all too regularly with sharp increases in the frequency, magnitude and severity of war (*e.g.* 1912-1914, 1937-1939). [117]

5. This does not mean, however, that we accept at face value the (politically-exaggerated) "peace function" assertions of non-aligned actors ; nor that we should be satisfied with the non-data-based conceptualisation of some "systems theorists". If this chapter has emphasised the intervening variables that limit the conflict-management capacity of non-aligned actors and thus attempted a more balanced picture of the contribution of non-alignment to systemic stability, it has also pointed out the paucity of literature in this unexplored field, and the need for both conceptual and empirical studies to produce valid generalisations.

---

[115] F. Sayegh : "Anatomy of Neutralism : A Typological Analysis", in Sayegh : *The Dynamics of Neutralism ..., op. cit.,* pp. 90-102.

[116] *Ibid.*

[117] Singer, David, and Small, Melvin : "Formal Alliances, 1816-1965 : An Extension of the Basic Data", *Journal of Peace Research,* VI (1969), pp. 257-283 ; and also Singer, David : "The Correlates of War Project : Interim Report", World Politics, XXIV (1972), pp. 243-270 ; Singer, David, and Small, Melvin : *The Wages of War 1816-1965 : A Statistical Handbook,* New York, Wiley, 1972.

Concluding Remarks

The Findings, the Null Hypothesis and the Fourth Non-Aligned Summit

Recapitulation of the findings of such a research work presents the danger of either taking things out of context or being tempted to repeat the major arguments. But while trying to avoid these real problems, let us concentrate on the immediate payoffs and attempt to answer the question : what do we know now that we did not know before ?

Firstly, on the level of pure information, we do not know of any published study that has treated all third world actors as an international subsystem in the way done here. If chapter V has been the longest in this work, it is precisely to provide the necessary data in this respect. For instance, we know by now the precise level of interaction in the general subsystem as well as the position of individual non-aligned actors. We were no longer confined to investigating Tanzania's position, for instance, in relation to the superpowers, but also (to remedy Crabb's complaint) determined precisely its level of (diplomatic) interaction with a fellow non-aligned actor like Afghanistan. Moreover, through our operationalisation and measurement of behavioural heterogeneity we can now easily situate each subsystem member on the non-alignment continuum, and hence see how distant or close it is to other subsystem fellow members as far as non-aligned role-performance is concerned.

The actor-oriented treatment gave us additional information. As well as its conceptual function as a 'crucial experiment', the analysis of Egypt's non-aligned behaviour made up for the lack of systematic material on this founder-member of the non-aligned subsystem. Thus, rather than being content merely with "comments on current affairs", our scrutiny of historical material and indigenous sources made us realise that the Egyptian desire for 'non-alignment' antedates the post-1945 East-West conflict as such. Moreover, through comparative analysis we know how the charismatic personalities of Nehru and Nasser could bend their countries' foreign policy behaviours in one direction rather than another.

All this information, however, is here given as part of a conceptualisation that aims to disentangle relevant variables, establish their relationships and link the pertinent islands of knowledge. Questions raised are closely related to this objective, and are treated on three levels of analysis :

1. Though the research work is mainly concerned with domestic variables of foreign policy-making, the global level has been treated in two ways : third world actors' position in, and perception of, a stratified international system as a correlate of their non-alignment ; and the impact of this foreign policy orientation on systemic structure and systemic conflict (*i.e.* the hypothetical "peace function" of non-aligned actors).

2. As regards the actor-oriented level, the analysis was centered on the state of the prismatic political system, and the plausibility of the integrative function of non-alignment as a foreign policy was supported.

3. But the third level of analysis—the personality variable—was also dealt with, and it was found that divergent political socialisation processes of charismatic leaders are positively correlated with differences in their countries' non-aligned role-performances, and thus the way is paved for an eventual typology of non-aligned behavioural patterns.

There are at least three other questions that need to be touched upon in these concluding remarks : the relative potencies among foreign policy variables, the null hypothesis, and—thirdly—how do our findings fare in the light of the recently-convened Fourth Summit of Non-Aligned Countries (Algiers, September 1973).

As for the relative potencies of foreign policy variables, we have raised this issue while elaborating the situation-role model in chapter III, but evidence in chapters VI, VII and also VIII indicates that the Rosenau hypothesis (the primacy of the idiosyncratic variable) is confirmed only as far as foreign policy *behaviour* is concerned. As for foreign policy *orientation* (*i.e.* the choice of alignment or non-alignment), we found that when Nasser came to power there was already a "public opinion mood" associating alignment with the continuation—in essence if not in form—of the colonial status. Other national experiences like that of Iraq in the Baghdad Pact point out that this colonialism-cum-alignment "public opinion mood" was not confined to Egypt. Consequently, the so-called "mood theory" seems to be a promising direction, but needs to be further refined and especially applied to non-aligned actors in order for this tentative generalisation to be supported by additional data.

As for the null hypothesis, its explication is of crucial importance in determining the extent to which we can trust the validity and generalisability of the findings presented here. We found that it is such attributes as newly-won independence, Afro-Asian position . . . that are regularly correlated with the adoption of non-alignment as a foreign policy orientation. Though this is confirmed by the Algiers Non-Aligned Summit, which assembled over 90 per cent of the states that gained independence only after the Second World War, we should, nevertheless, not overlook the fact that some actors—both newly-independent and Asian—have participated in East-West alliances, *e.g.* Pakistan. Indeed, data about this country (*e.g.* date of independence, ethnic and linguistic fractionalisation, size of internal security forces, deaths from domestic violence . . .) put Pakistan in the "situational" company of non-aligned actors. Why, then, did Pakistan not adopt non-alignment ?

The basis of this exception to the "general norm" is to be sought in Pakistan's *specific* high threat-perception from India. For when Pakistan achieved independent statehood after massacres and bloodshed, its policy-makers manifested negative identification with both East and West and, in fact, expressed 'non-aligned' overtones. Thus, in a broadcast talk in 1948, Ali Jinnah said that independent Pakistan's foreign policy is ". . . one of friendliness and goodwill towards all the nations of the world". [1] Like non-aligned actors, Pakistan decided to "judge issues on their merits" for, according to Prime Minister Liaquat Ali, its policy was that of sometimes ". . . agreeing with the Western bloc, and sometimes with the communist bloc as the situation and the matter under discussion demanded". [2]

But the increasing threat-perception from India, the conflict with Afghanistan over the Pathan problem, and Pakistan's failure to be incorporated with Arab states in a Moslem association, forced Pakistan either to search for friends and allies even far away, or remain isolated. Thus national security was thought to be guaranteed through participation in Western alliances, and between 1954 and 1965 the total military assistance extended to Pakistan by the U.S. amounted to between 1.2 and 1.5 billion dollars. [3] Pakistan, however, did not make any secret of its prime objective in alliance-participation. A 1959-agreement between Pakistan and the U.S.A. provided for the defence and security of the country without specifying that the "aggressor" had to be communist. Bhutto was even more explicit in revealing Pakistan's prime objective when he stated : ". . . assistance was provided to Pakistan for one set of reasons and received for another". [4]

---

[1] Choudhury, G. W., and Hasan, Parvez : *Pakistan's External Relations,* Karachi, Pakistan Institute of International Affairs, 1958, p. 6.

[2] As quoted in Callard, Keith : *Pakistan's Foreign Policy : An Interpretation,* New York, Institute of Pacific Relations, 1959, p. 14.

[3] Lerski, George : "The Pakistan-American Alliance : A Reevaluation of the Past Decade", *Asian Survey,* VIII (1968), p. 405.

[4] Bhutto, Zulfikar : *The Myth of Independence,* London, O.U.P., 1969, p. 105.

But if it is true that Pakistan's participation in Western alliances was primarily linked to its perception of the threat from India, the dependent variable should vary with the independent one. Indeed, this is what happened. Thus when, for instance, complete Western support for Pakistan against India did not automatically materialise, and when arms shipments (especially after the Sino-Indian conflict) poured into India, Pakistan's policy-makers became increasingly disillusioned with alliance-participation as the panacea for their *specific* problems. Consequently, not only were high official visits and state agreements multiplied with "Communist" China (a target of Western alliance), but also Pakistan seemed to steer more and more toward *de facto* non-alignment. It stopped taking part in the military activities of SEATO and CENTO and reduced its level of representation in their Ministerial Councils. [5] And Pakistan's newspaper *Dawn* added : ". . . even the Soviet Union and China —against whom these pacts were actually designed—. . . appreciated Pakistan's position". [6] Moreover, before the Third Non-Aligned Summit Pakistan conveyed to some non-aligned actors "its keenness" to be an official full-member of the non-aligned subsystem. But, mainly because of India's objections, Pakistan did not receive an invitation to attend the 1970 Dar-es-Salaam Preparatory Conference. *Dawn* commented that though there was "wide Afro-Asian support for its participation because of its independent foreign policy", Pakistan did not insist on participation because "it did not want to disrupt or create difficulties" in the non-aligned subsystem. [7]

If the null hypothesis increases our confidence in the plausibility of this study's tentative conclusions, how do the findings reported here fare following the convening of the Fourth Non-Aligned Summit? To start with, the increasing 'looseness' of the bipolar system has not put an end to non-alignment as the "power paradigm" implied it would, but rather the increase in subsystem membership has continued. Thus 75 full members attended the Fourth Summit, compared to 53 at the 1970-Third Summit (*i.e.* a net increase of 41.50 per cent and triple the number of the non-aligned actors that attended the First Summit 12 years earlier). Moreover, non-aligned actors seem to have increased their interest in their subsystem [8]—if level of representation is used as the indicator to measure this interest. At the First Summit Heads of State or Government constituted 84 per cent of all the representatives ; at the Second Summit this percentage declined to 72 per cent ; and was down to only 41 per cent at

[5] *Dawn,* 10 April 1970.

[6] *Ibid.*

[7] *Ibid.*

[8] Mates, Leo : "New Upsurge of Non-Alignment", *Review of International Affairs* (Belgrade), XXIV (October 20, 1973), pp. 1-3.

the Third Summit. At the Algiers Summit, however, the downward trend was reserved, for the figure went up to 76 per cent. This is why the Fourth Summit's final "Political Declaration" stated, not without self-congratulation, that: "the number and the level of participants and the general tenor of the meeting are an indicator of the vitality and dynamism of non-alignment". [9]

Moreover, non-aligned actors' emphasis (as manifested in their public debate and in the 96-item "Political Declaration") is less on the East-West conflict as such than on their own attributes, which the proposed situation-role model singled out to account for their foreign policy (*e.g.* recent colonial history, their position in a stratified international system bipolarised between North and South . . .). Even when East-West rapprochement was invoked, it was not thought of as the ultimate aim of non-alignment, for item 14 stipulates: "Although substantial progress has been made in the easing of tensions between East and West", peace is "indivisible" and "the fact that nations are faced with colonialism, domination and occupation, neo-colonialism, imperialism and Zionism" limit both the principle and scope of peace. [10] Moreover, out of 13 final resolutions, at least 11 (in addition to a separate "Declaration on the Struggle for National Liberation") are on "colonial, racial" and other issues *specifically* related to the subsystem members, and there was only one resolution on such global systemic issues as "the Matter of Maritime Law". [11]

Moreover, as our treatment of the non-aligned subsystem suggested in chapter V, the 'economic variable' of the 'common situation' continues to be emphasised as the present integrative factor in the subsystem. Not only do economic issues occupy an important place in the final "Political Declaration", but also two additional documents are devoted to it: one entitled "Economic Declaration" [12] and the other: "Action Programme of Economic Cooperation", [13] which no longer formulate only general statements but also provide quantitative data and specific recommendations. [14] This important place devoted to the economic variable reflects the importance it occupied in the public debate, as *Le Monde* expressed it:

> "At the heart of most of the debates was the necessity for the third world to organise itself to assure its independence. Never at

---

[9] *Report on the Fourth Conference of Non-Aligned Countries in Algiers* as published in *Review of International Affairs* (Belgrade), XXIV (September 20, 1973), especially p. 19.

[10] *Ibid.,* p. 20.

[11] *Ibid.,* pp. 23-39.

[12] *Ibid.,* pp. 23-27.

[13] *Ibid.,* pp. 28-31.

[14] *Ibid.,* p. 28.

> any of the preceding Non-Aligned Summit Conferences was this theme dealt with with such vigour and lucidity."[15]

Also, as the situation-role model suggests, the issue of cultural distinctiveness is—for the first time—explicitly emphasised: item 18 of the "Political Declaration" affirms that

> "The peoples of the third world must maintain their identity, revive and enrich their cultural heritage and in all domains promote their authenticity which colonialism seriously alienated."[16]

And in even more detail item XIV of the "Economic Declaration" states:

> "It is an established fact that imperialist action is not restricted to the political or economic sphere, but also includes the cultural and social domains, thus imposing an ideological domination alien to the peoples of the developing world.
> Consequently, the heads of state and government of non-aligned countries underline the need to reaffirm national cultural identity and to eliminate harmful consequences of the colonial era as well as to preserve their cultures and national traditions.
> They feel that the cultural alienation and imported civilization imposed by imperialism and colonialism should be countered by the establishment of a national personality, a continual and resolute return to their own social and cultural values, which define them as a sovereign nation and master of its own resources, so that each nation should exercise effective control over all its wealth and strive for its economic development, giving due respect for its sovereignty, its authenticity, peace and true international cooperation."[17]

Similarly, as our analysis in chapter V stated, the drive toward subsystem institutionalisation continues. Algeria seemed to be going too fast in this direction, for it pushed a proposal to establish a non-aligned secretariat with headquarters in Algiers, but the Summit was unable to agree on it.[18] However, the Conference bureau was transformed into a preparatory committee to guarantee continuity until the Fifth Summit is held in 1976. This holding of "regular sessions" every three years was even more emphasised, for a decision seems to have been already taken to convene the Sixth Summit in 1979 in Latin America.[19]

---

[15] *Le Monde,* 11 September 1973 (my translation).

[16] *Report on the Fourth Conference of Non-Aligned Countries in Algiers, op. cit.,* p. 20.

[17] *Ibid.,* p. 27.

[18] *New York Herald Tribune,* 10 September 1973.

[19] *Le Monde,* 11 September 1973.

This drive toward institutionalisation is not perhaps unrelated to the non-aligned actors' attempt to tackle some of the subsystem's persistent problems that we have emphasised in chapter V : *e.g.* operational criteria of subsystem membership. For when the Palestinian Liberation Organisation endeavoured to obtain full membership in the Fourth Summit, it was asked to constitute a government first—if only a provisional one. Consequently, the presence of a government seems to be the *sine qua non* operational criteria for admitting full members to the subsystem.

As for the subsystem boundary, it is—again as both chapters IV and V suggested—the subjective aspect of the boundary, or the socio-psychological attributes of non-aligned actors that are increasingly emphasised. Whether in the delegates' public speeches or in the official resolutions and Final Communiqué, such labellations as "non-aligned countries", "developing countries" or "third world" states were very often used interchangeably. [20]

[20] See, for instance, item 83 of the Summit's Political Declaration, in *Report on the Fourth Conference of Non-Aligned Countries in Algiers, op. cit.,* p. 23 ; also the opening speech by the Conference President in *ibid.,* pp. 13-16 ; also President Boumedienne's closing speech as reported in *Le Monde,* 11 September 1973. For the complete list of speeches, see *Review of International Affairs* (Belgrade), XXIV (October 5, 1973), pp. 7-40.

Appendices

ON THE APPENDICES

1. Data for these two appendices are collected from *Europa Yearbook,* 1970. When the data sought were either incomplete or non-existent, Europa Yearbook 1971 was substituted.

2. The Complete Data Matrix can yield other information on the non-aligned subsystem. For instance, one can identify diplomatic centres in the subsystem by counting which non-aligned capitals are most used as channels of interaction among subsystem members which do not have direct diplomatic representation. For instance, Cairo comes on top, being used 19 times. This, in fact, confirms data computed in other tables (*e.g.* table 2), and also its top percentage score on the interaction index as in Appendix II.

3. For the methodology used in computing the interaction index of this Appendix II, see p. 209, and table 11.

KEY TO SYMBOLS USED IN THE INTERACTION MATRIX

C.	Chargé d'affaires
E.	Embassy address is not available
H.C.	High Commissioner
SUS.	Diplomatic Relations suspended
T.R.	Trade Relations
*	Recognises the Provisional Government of South Vietnam (the Viet Cong)

Acc.	Accra	Kin.	Kinshasa
Ad. Ab.	Adis Ababa	Lag.	Lagos
Alg.	Algiers	Lond.	London
Ank.	Ankara	Lus.	Lusaka
Ath.	Athens	Mex.	Mexico City
Bagh.	Baghdad	Mosc.	Moscow
Bam.	Bamako	Nair.	Nairobi
Ban.	Bangkok	N.Y.	New York
Bang.	Bangui	Ott.	Ottawa
Beir.	Beirut	Pek.	Peking
Bra.	Brazzaville	P.P.	Pnom Phen
Can.	Canberra	Rab.	Rabat
Con.	Conakry	Ran.	Rangoon
Dak.	Dakar	Rum.	Rumania
Del.	Delhi	Taiw.	Taiwan
D.S.	Dar es-Salaam	Teh.	Teheran
Jak.	Jakarta	Tok.	Tokyo
Jedd.	Jeddah	Wash.	Washington
Kam.	Kampala	Yaou.	Yaoundé
Kar.	Karachi		

COMPLETE DATA MATRIX OF DIPLOMATIC INTERACTION IN THE NONALIGNED SUBSYSTEM AND POSITIONS OF INDIVIDUAL MEMBERS ON THE NONALIGNEMENT CONTINUUM

Nigeria	Ruanda	Senegal	Sierra Leone	Singapore	Somalia	Sudan	Swaziland	Syria	Tanzania	Trin. Tobago	Tunisia	Uganda	U.A.R.	Yemen Arab R.	S. Yemen R.	Yugoslavia	Zambia	China	Taiwan	E. Germany	W. Germany	N. Korea	S. Korea	N. Vietnam	S. Vietnam
						1							5			5		5			5				
		5						5	3C		5	5E	5	3C		5		5						5	*
																	5HC				4HC Lond.				
									5			5E	5			1		SUS			5	1			
5						1					5		5			5					5				
						5										5					5				
						1							5			4 Cairo		5			5				
5						5					1					4 Paris					5	1			
5	5	5				5			5		3C	1	5			5	5				5				
1													5			1		5		1	5	5			*
								5	5				5			5		C3		5					
						1		1					5			4 Ath.					5				
																						1			
5		5			5	5			4 Nair.			4 Nair.	5	5	1	5					5				
		5				1													5		5				4 Taiw.
5		5	5HC			5				4 Mex.	5	5	5			3C					3C				
5		5	5			1			5		4 Alg.	5E	5			5	4 D.S.	5		1	5	5		5	
																5					4HC Lond.				
HC	4 Kam.	5	1	5HC	5	5		5	5HC	5HC	5	5HC	5	4 Cairo	5	5	5HC	3C		1 T.R.	5			1	1
				5	1			5	5		5		5			5		SUS			5				
5					1	5		5			5		5	5	1	5		3C		5		1			
										5HC											4 Lond.				
5					1	5		5			5		5	1		1			5		5				
					5						1	5	5			1		SUS			5				
		1				5		5			5		5	1		1									
																4 Mosc.		3C			4 Paris				5
5		5	5		1	5				1	5		5			5			4 Tok.						
												4 Nair.									4 Lond.				
5		5	5			1			4 Nair			1	5			4 Rome					5				
5					1	5		5			5		5	1		5					5				
1				5HC									5			1					5		5		3C
5		5				1			3C		4 Paris		5			5		5		1 T.R.	4 Bruss.	4 Pek.		5	*
		5						5E			5		5			4 Mosc.		5			5	5			
5		5				1			4 Ad.Ab.		5	4 Ad.Ab.	5	1		5		5			5		4 Tok.		
													5					5			5				
		5	5HC		1	5						5	5			1					5				
									4			1									5				
5			1							4 Wash.	5		5			1					5				
5		1											5			1									
													5			4 Cairo									
						5			5		1		5		5E	1					5	1			
5					5			1	5		4 Cairo	5	5			5V		5		5		1			
1					5	5			3C				5	3C		5		5		5		1		1	
						1						5	5			1		5		5	5				
		4 Ad.Ab.											5												
		5											3C	1		5V		SUS			5				
						1										1					5				
5		5	5	3C	5	5		5	5		5	5		5V	5	5	5	5		5				5	
					5	3		1					5					5		1					
					5E								5					3C		1		1		1	
5		5	1	4 Jak.	4 Tunis	5		5	5		5	5	5	5	1		5	3C		5	5				
		1							5HC			4 D.S.	5			1		5			5	1			
					5	5		5	5			3C	5	5		5V									
	5	5	5																						
					1			5					5			5									
5	5	5	5	5	5				5	5	5	5			5E	5									
					1			5	5				5	4 Cairo	5E										
1		4 Paris	1								1	5													
		1						1	3C				5	4 Cairo		4 Warsaw									
		5																							

From: / To:	Afghanistan	Algeria	Botswana	Burundi	Cameroun	Cent. Af. Rep.	Ceylon	Chad	Congo (Zaïre)	Congo (Braz.)	Cuba	Cyprus	Equat. Guinea	Ethiopia	Gabon	Ghana	Guinea	Guyana	India	Indonesia	Iraq	Jamaica	Jordan	Kenya	Kuwait	Laos	Lebanon	Lesotho	Liberia	Libya	Malaysia	Mali	Mauritania	Morocco	Nepal
Afghanistan							4 Kar.												5	5	5		2 Bagh.				2 Cairo								
Algeria	1				4 Bra.					5	5					5	5		5	5	5		5V	4 D.S.	5		5			5	4 Del.	5	4 Dak.	5	
Botswana																								4 Lus.											
Burundi									5					5										4 D.S.											
Cameroun		5				3C							5	1	4 Bang.		1										1		5	1				5E	
Cent. Af. Rep.					5			5	5	1					1																				
Ceylon	4 Del.										4 CH.					5HC			5HC	5	3C					4 Ran.	4 Cairo				5HC				
Chad					5	5				3				5	1												1			1					
Congo (Zaïre)				5				5				1		5					5															5	
Congo (Braz.)		5			5	1					3C				1												1								
Cuba		5					5V			5		2 Beir.					5		3C	1		1					3C					5		5	
Cyprus									1														1				1								
Equat. Guinea					5																														
Ethiopia				4 Kin.					5	5		1				5	1		5		4 Cairo	1	5	5V			4 Cairo		5	1			4 Dak.	5	
Gabon					5	4 Yaou.				5			4 Yaou.																						
Ghana	4 Del.	5			5	4 Kin.	4HC Del.	4 Kin.	5			1		5					5HC	1	1	1		5HC V			5E		5	1	4HC Can.		4 Dak.	5	
Guinea		5		4 D.S.	4 Lag.			4 Bra.		5	5			5						4 Pek.	4 Cairo			4 D.S.	4 Cairo		4 Cairo		5	1		5	4 Dak.	5E	
Guyana																																			
India	5	5		4 Kam.	4 Lag.		5HC V		3C	5	5	4HC Beir.		5		5HC	5	5HC		5	5	1	4 Beir.	5HC	5	5	5		4 Acc.	4 Cairo	5HC	4 Con.	4 Dak.	5	5
Indonesia	5	5					5V				3C			5		5	5		5		3C					4 P.P.	3C		1		5	5		3C	
Iraq	3C	5					4 Kar.							1		5			5	1			5				5			5	4 Jak.			5	
Jamaica																		5HC																	
Jordan	4 Teh.	5					4 Del.										1		5		5	1					5			4 Tunis				5	
Kenya		4 Cairo							5E					5E					5HC						1										
Kuwait		5												1					5V		5		5	5			5			1	4 Tok.			5	
Laos																			5	4 P.P.											4 Bank.				
Lebanon	4 Teh.	5			4 Dak.	4 Acc.		4 Acc.	1	4 Dak.	5	5		1	1	5	1		5	4 Del.	5	1	5		5E				5	5		4 Dak.		5	
Lesotho			5HC E																					5HC											
Liberia					5				3C E					5		5	5					1		5			3								
Libya		5						5													5		5				5						1	5	
Malaysia							5HC							3C					5HC	1					4 Jedd.										
Mali		4 Paris		4 D.S.	4 Lag.	4 Bra.		4 Bra.	5	5	4 N.Y.			5E	1	5	1							4 D.S.	4 Cairo		1		5				4 Dak.	5E	
Mauritania		5			5									5E			1												1			4 Dak.		5E	
Morocco		5			4 Lag.				5E		3C			5		5	5		5		5		5V	4 Ad.Ab.	5		5			5	4 Kar.	3C	5		
Nepal	4 Del.	4 Cairo					4 Del.												5							4 Pek.	4 Cairo				4 Rang.				
Nigeria		5			5			3C	5			1	5	5		5HC	5		5HC				1	5HC					5			3C		1	
Ruanda									5E	3E				1																					
Senegal		5							5	4 Kin.				5		5	5										5		1			5	5	5	
Sierra Leone																5HC	5										1		5						
Singapore														1					5HC	5											5HC				1
Somalia				4 D.S.					4 D.S.			1		5							4 Cairo			5	4 Jedd.					1					
Sudan	2 Kar.	5			4 Lag.	5	4 Del.	5	5			4 Ath.		5	4 Kin.	5			5		3C		4	5	5		5			4 Cairo				4 Cairo	
Swaziland																																			
Syria	5E	5									3C	3C					5		5V	1	5		5V		5										
Tanzania									5					5					5HC																
Trin. Tobago														5				5HC	5HC			5HC					1								
Tunisia		5			5	4 Kin.		4 Kin.	5					5			1						3C	4 Ad.Ab.	5		5			5		4 Dak	4 Dak.		
Uganda									3CE			1				5HC			5HC																
U.A.R.	5	5	5		5		5		5E	5	5	5		5		5	5		5	1	5	1	5	5	5		5		5	5		5	5	5	
Yemen Arab R.		3C												5							3C						5								
S. Yemen R.																																			
Yugoslavia	5	5			4 Bra.		5	4 Bra.	5	5	5	5		5		5	5		5	5	5		2 Beir.	5	4 Bagh.	4 P.P.	5		4 Acc.	5	5	5	4 Dak.	5	
Zambia			5HC						5					5										5HC											
China		5					5V			5	5						5		3C	Rep. by Rum.	5			5V		3C						5	5	5	5
Taiwan			5		5	5		5	5			5			5							5	5		5		5	5	5	5					
E. Germany											5																								
W. Germany	5			5	5	3C	5	5	5	5		5		5	5	5	5	5	5	1		5	5	5		2 Bank.		1	5	5V	5	5	1	5	5
N. Korea		5								5	5		1				5			5	1											5	4 Bam.		
S. Korea			4 Nair.		4 Lag.			4 Paris	4 Paris					5	4 Paris							1	4 Ank.	5				1	4 Rab.		5			5	
N. Vietnam		5								4 Con.	5						5									5						5	5		
S. Vietnam					4 Rab.				4 Dak.						1								4 Ank.			5	4 Ank.				5			3C	

STRUCTURE OF DIPLOMATIC INTERACTION IN THE NONALIGNED SUBSYSTEM AND POSITIONS OF INDIVIDUAL MEMBERS

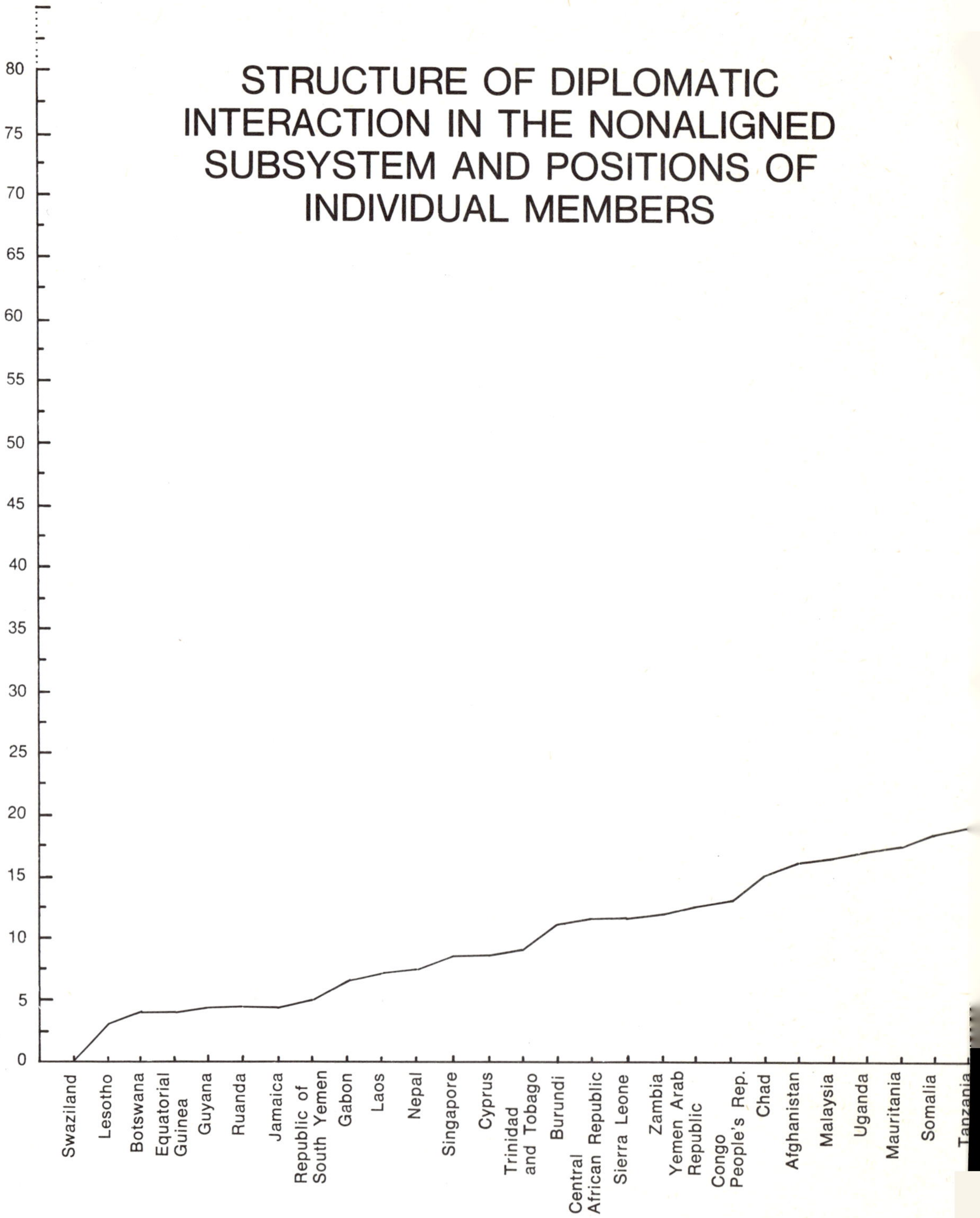

Ceylon
Cuba
Libya
Liberia
Kuwait
Kenya
Syria
Jordan
Cameroon
Indonesia
Mali
Senegal
Iraq
Congo (Zaire)
Tunisia
Guinea
Nigeria
Ghana
Sudan
Morocco
Ethiopia
Lebanon
Algeria
Yugoslavia
India
Egypt

Bibliography

I. Sources and Documents

Consultative Meeting of the Representatives of Non-Aligned Countries. (Belgrade, July 8-12, 1969), Special Documentation Supplement to No. 464-65 of *Review of International Affairs* (Beograd).

EDEN, Anthony. *Full Circle.* The Memoirs of Sir Anthony Eden. London, Cassel, 1960.

EISENHOWER, Dwight. *The White House Years.* Mandate for Change 1953-1956. New York, Signet, 1963.

EISENHOWER, Dwight. *The White House Years.* Waging Peace 1956-1961. New York, Doubleday, 1965.

EL-SADAT, Anwar. *Qissat El-Thawra Kamelah* (The Complete Story of the Revolution). Beirut, Dar El-Qamous, n.d.

EL-SADAT, Anwar. *Révolte sur le Nil.* (Préfacé par le Président Nasser). Paris, Pierre Amiot, 1957.

El-Wathaëq El-'Arabiyya (Arab Political Documents), 1952-1963, Beirut, The American University.

GALBRAITH, John. *Ambassador's Journal.* New York, Signet, 1970.

HASSOUNNA, Abdel Khalek. *Report on the Bandung Conference.* Cairo, the Arab League, 1955.

Ministry of Foreign Affairs, Egypt. *Record of Conversations, Notes and Papers exchanged between the Royal Egyptian Government and the United Kingdom Government, March 1950 - November 1951.* Cairo, 1951.

Ministry of Foreign Affairs, Indonesia. *Asia-Africa Speaks from Bandung.* Jakarta, 1955.

NAGUIB, Mohamed. "Why Egypt Looks to the U.S.". *U.S. News and World Report.* March 27, 1953, p. 28.

NAGUIB, Mohamed. *Egypt's Destiny.* London, Gallancz, 1955.

NASSER, Gamal. *The Philosophy of the Revolution.* Cairo, 1954.

NASSER, Gamal. *Speeches, Declarations and Press Interviews. 1952-1970.* Cairo, Information Department.

NASSER, Gamal. *El-Mithaq* (The National Charter). (Presented by President Nasser to the National Congress of Popular Forces in May 1962). Cairo, Information Department, 1962.

NEHRU, Jawaharlal. *Toward Freedom.* The Autobiography of Jawaharlal Nehru. Ministry of Information and Broadcasting, 1958.

NEHRU, Jawaharlal. *Toward Freedom.* The Autobiography of Jawaharlal Nehru. New York, John Day, 1941.

Nehru. The First Sixty Years. Presenting in his own words the Development of the Political Thought of J.N. Nehru and the Background against which it evolved. 2 vol. Ed. by Dorothy Norman. London, The Bodley Head, 1965.

NKRUMAH, Kwame. *Ghana.* The Autobiography of Kwame NKrumah. New York, Thomas Nelson and Sons, 1957.

NYRERE, Julius. *Uhuru Na Ujamaa / Freedom and Socialism.* A Selection from Writings and Speeches 1955-1967. Dar es-Salaam, O.U.P., 1968.

Official Report of the First Non-Aligned Summit Conference. (Belgrade, September 1-6, 1961). Beograd, Publicisicko-Zddavacki Zavod, 1961.

SÉKOU TOURÉ, Ahmed. *La Lutte du Parti démocratique de Guinée pour l'Emancipation africaine.* Conakry, Imprimerie Nationale, 1959.

SENGHOR, Leopold. *African Socialism.* New York, American Society for African Culture, 1959.

Synopsis of the Second (Summit) Conference of Non-Aligned Countries. (Cairo, October 5-10, 1964). Cairo, Information Department, n.d.

The Belgrade Conference. (Belgrade, September 1-6, 1961). Documents. Cairo, Information Department, n.d.

The Ideologies of the Developing Nations. Ed. by Paul Sigmund, Jr., New York, Praeger, 1963.

The Second (Summit) Conference of Non-Aligned Countries. (Cairo, October 5-10, 1964). *Review of International Affairs* (Beograd), XV, No. 350 (November 5, 1964).

The Third (Summit) Conference of Non-Aligned Countries. (Lusaka, September 8-10, 1970). *Review of International Affairs* (Beograd), XXI, No. 491 (September 20, 1970).

The Fourth (Summit) Conference of Non-Aligned Countries. (Algiers, September 5-9, 1973), *Review of International Affairs* (Beograd), XXIV, Nos. 563-564 (September 20 and October 5, 1973).

The Killearn Diaries 1934-1946. The Diplomatic and Personal Record of Lord Killearn (Sir Miles Lampson), High Commissioner and Ambassador to Egypt. Ed. and introduced by Trefor Evans. London, Sidgwick and Jackson, 1972.

The New Emerging Forces. Documents on the Ideology of Indonesian Foreign Policy. Ed. by George Modelski. Canberra, Australian National University, 1963.

TREVELYAN, Humphrey. *The Middle East in Revolution.* London, Macmillan, 1970.

United Arab Republic. *Arab Socialism.* Cairo, Information Department, 1963.

II. Studies

1. Books and Monographs

ABDEL-MALEK, Anouar. *Dirasat fi El-Thaqafa El-Wataniyya* (Studies on National Culture). Beirut. Dar El-Tali'a, 1967.

— — *Idéologie et Renaissance nationale.* L'Egypte moderne. Paris, Anthropos, 1969.

— — *Egypt : Military Society.* The Army, the Left and Social Change under Nasser. New York, Vintage Book, 1968. (First published in French by Le Seuil in 1962).

ABEL, Elie. *The Missiles of October.* The Story of the Cuban Missile Crisis. London, Macgibbon and Kee, 1969.

ABOU-ZEID, Hekmat. *El-Takayyof El-Igtema'i fi El Rif El-Misri El-Gadid* (Social Adaptation in the New Egyptian Countryside). Cairo. Maktabat El-Anglo, n.d.

ABUL-FATH, Ahmed. *L'Affaire Nasser.* Paris, Plon, 1962.

ACHESON, Dean. *Present at the Creation.* My Years in the State Department. New York, A Signet Book, 1970.

ACIMOVIC, Ljubivoje (ed.) *Nonalignment in the World of Today.* Beograd, Institute of International Politics and Economics, 1969.

ADAMS, Michael (ed.). *The Middle East.* A Handbook. London, Anthony Blond, 1971.

ADORNO, T. E.; FRENKEL-BRUNSWICK, Else; LEVINSON, Daniel and SANFORD, R. Nevitt. *The Authoritarian Personality.* New York, Harper, 1950.

AGWANI, M. S. *Communism in the Arab East.* New York, Asia Publishing House, 1970.

AHMED, Gamal. *The Intellectual Origins of Egyptian Nationalism.* London, O.U.P., 1960.

AHMED, Samir. *The Neutrals and the Test Ban Negotiations.* An analysis of the Non-Aligned States Efforts between 1962-1963. New York, Carnegie Endowment for International Peace, Feb. 1967.

AKE, Claude. *A Theory of Political Integration.* Homewood, The Dorsey Press, 1967.

ALLPORT, Gordon. *Pattern and Growth in Personality.* London, Holt, Rinehart and Winston, 1963.

ALMOND, Gabriel. *Perspectives on Political Development.* Little, Brown and Co., 1970.

ALMOND, Gabriel and COLEMAN, James (ds.). *The Politics of the Developing Areas.* Princeton, Princeton U.P., 1960.

ALMOND, Gabriel and VERBA, Sidney. *The Civic Culture.* Princeton, Princeton U.P., 1963.

AL-SAYYID, Afaf Lutfi. *Egypt and Cromer.* A Study in Anglo-Egyptian Relations. London, Murray, 1968.

AMMAR, Hamed. *Growing up in an Egyptian Village.* London, Routledge and Kegan Paul, 1954.

AMIN, Ahmed. *Qamous El-'Adat wa El-Taqalid El-Misriyya* (A Dictionary of Egyptian Customs and Traditions). Cairo, Matb't Lagnat El-Taaleef wa El-Targaama wa El-Nashr, 1953.

APTER, David. *The Political Kingdom in Uganda.* A Study in Bureaucratic Nationalism. Princeton, Princeton U.P., 1961.

— — *The Politics of Modernization.* Chicago, The University Press of Chicago, 1965.

ARON, Raymond. *Peace and War Among Nations.* A Theory of International Relations. New York, Praeger, 1966. (First published in French by C. Levy in 1962.)

— — *Main Currents in Sociological Thought.* London, Penguin, 1968-1970. 2 vol.

'AWAD, Lewis. *Tarikh El-Fikr El Misri El-Hadith* (History of Modern Egyptian Thinking). Cairo, Kitab El-Hilal, 1969.

'AYROUT, Henri. *El Fallahoon.* Cairo, Moässat El-Halaby, 1968. (Appeared also in French as *Fellahs d'Egypte.* Payot, 1938 and 1952, and in English as *The Egyptian Peasant.* 1962.)

'AZIZ, Sami. *El-Ssahafa El-Misriyyah wa Mawqifoha min El-Ihtilal El-Inglizi* (The Egyptian Press and its Attitude to English Occupation). Cairo, Dar El-Katib El-'Arabi, 1968.

BADEAU, John. *The American Approach to the Arab World.* New York, Harper and Row, 1968.

BAER, Gabriel. *A History of Landownership in Modern Egypt 1800-1950.* London, O.U.P., 1962.

— — *Studies in the Social History of Modern Egypt.* Chicago, University of Chicago Press, 1969.

BAHAA EL-DIN, Hussein. *El-Isloub El-'lmi fi El-'amal El-Siasi* (The Scientific Approach to Political Action). Cairo, El-Nahda, 1968.

BALANDIER, George. *Sociologie actuelle de l'Afrique noire.* Paris, P.U.F., 1963 (2e éd.).

BALES, Robert. *Interaction Process Analysis.* A Method for the Study of Small Groups. Cambridge, Mass., Addison-Wesley Publishing Co., Inc., 1950.

BANTON, Michael. *Roles.* An Introduction to the Study of Social Relations. London, Tavistock Publications, 1965.

BARRACLOUGH, Geoffrey. *An Introduction to Contemporary History.* London, Penguin Books, 1967.

BARRACLOUGH, Geoffrey and WALL, Rachel (eds.). *Survey of International Affairs, 1955-1956.* London, R.I.I.A., O.U.P., 1960.

BARTHOLOMEW, D.J. and BASSET, E. E. *Let's Look at the Figures.* The Quantitative Approach to Human Affairs. London, Penguin, 1971.

BE'ERI, Eliezer. *Army Officers in Arab Politics and Society.* London, Pall Mall Press, 1969.

BELL, Carol, and BENHAM, F. C. (eds.). *Survey of International Affairs, 1954.* London, R.I.I.A., O.U.P., 1957.

BENNABI, Malek. *L'Afro-Asiatisme.* Le Caire, Imprimerie Misr, 1956.

BENOT, Yves. *Idéologies des Indépendances africaines.* Paris, Maspero, 1969.

BERELSON, Bernard and STEINER, Gray. *Human Behavior.* An Inventory of Scientific Findings. New York, Harcourt, Brace and World, 1964.

BERGER, Morroe. *Bureaucracy and Society in Modern Egypt.* Princeton, Princeton U.P., 1957.

— — *Military Elite and Social Change.* Egypt Since Napoleon. Princeton, Princeton University, Center of International Studies, 1960.

— — *Islam in Egypt To-day.* Social and Political Aspects of Popular Religion. New York, Cambridge U.P., 1970.

— — *The Arab World To-day.* New York, Doubleday, 1962.

BERQUES, Jacques. *Dépossession du Monde.* Paris, Le Seuil, 1964.

BHUTTO, Zulfikar. *The Myth of Independence.* London, O.U.P., 1969.

BIERSTADT, Robert (ed.). *A Design for Sociology.* Scope, objectives and methods. Philadelphia, The American Academy of Political and Social Science, 1969.

BINDER, Leonard. *The Ideological Revolution in the Middle East.* New York, Wiley, 1964.

BLACK, Cyril. *The Dynamics of Modernization.* New York, Harper Torchbook Edition, 1967.

BLACK, Cyril ; FALK, Richard ; KNORR, Klaus and YOUNG, Oran. *Neutralization and World Politics,* Princeton, Princeton U.P., 1968.

BLUNT, Wilfrid. *Secret History of the English Occupation of Egypt.* Being a Personal Narrative of Events. London, Martin Secker, 1907.

BOSC, Robert. *Le Tiers Monde dans la Politique internationale.* Paris, Aubier-Montaigne, 1968.

BOUTROS-GHALI, Boutros (avec Simone Dreyfus). *Le Mouvement afro-asiatique.* Paris, Presses Universitaires de France, 1969.

— — *Dirasat fi El-Siassa El-Dawliyya* (Studies in International Politics), Cairo, El-Anglo, 1961.

BRECHER, Michael. *The Foreign Policy System of Israel.* London, O.U.P., 1972.

— — *The New States of Asia.* London, O.U.P., 1963.

— — *Nehru.* A Political Biography, London, O.U.P., 1959 and 1961.

— — *India and World Politics.* Krishna Menon's View of the World. London, O.U.P., 1968.

BRIDEL, René. *Neutralité. Une Voie pour le Tiers Monde ?* Paris, Edition de l'Age d'Homme, 1968.

BRZEZINSKI, Zbigniew (ed.). *Africa and the Communist World,* Stanford, Stanford U.P., 1963.

BUCKLEY, Walter. *Sociology and Modern Systems Theory.* Englewood Cliffs, Prentice-Hall, 1967.

BURTON, John. *International Relations.* A General Theory. London, Cambridge U.P., 1965.

— — *World Society.* London, Cambridge U.P., 1972.

BURTON, John (ed.). *Nonalignment.* London, André Deutsch, 1966.

BUTWELL, Richard (ed.). *Foreign Policy and the Developing Nation.* Lexington, University of Kentucky Press, 1969.

CALLARD, Keith. *Pakistan's Foreign Policy. An Interpretation.* New York, Institute of Pacific Relations, 1959.

CALVEZ, Jean-Yves. *Aspects politiques et sociaux des Pays en Voie de Développement*. Paris, Dalloz, 1971.

CALVOCORESSI, Peter. *World Politics since 1945*. London, Longmans, 1968.

CALVOCORESSI, Peter and ISEPP, Kostanze (eds.). *Survey of International Affairs, 1952*. London, R.I.I.A., O.U.P., 1955.

CAMPBELL, John. *Defence of the Middle East*. New York, Praeger, rev. ed., 1961.

— — *Tito's Separate Road*. New York, Harper and Row Publishers, 1967.

CANTORI, Louis and SPIEGEL, Steven (eds.). *The International Politics of Regions*. A Comparative Approach. Englewood Cliffs, Prentice-Hall, 1970.

CARTER, Gwendolen (ed.). *African One-Party States*. New York, Cornell U.P., 1962.

CHARLESWORTH, James (ed.). *Contemporary Political Analysis*. New York, The Free Press, 1967.

CHILDERS, Erskine. *The Road to Suez*. A Study of Western Arab Relations. London, Macgibbon and Kee, 1960.

CHOPRA, Pran. *Uncertain India*. Bombay, 1968.

CHOUCRI, Nazli. *The Role of Egypt in International Affairs*. Emergence of the Policy of Non-Alignment. Unpublished M. A. thesis, Stanford University, 1964.

CHOUDHURY, Golam. *Pakistan's Relations with India 1947-66*. London, Pall Mall Press, 1968.

CHOUDHURY, Golam and HASAN, Parvez. *Pakistan's External Relations*. Karachi, Pakistan Institute of International Affairs, 1958.

CLUBB, Jerome. *Les Données écologiques dans la Recherche comparée*. Paris, Unesco, 1970.

COHEN, Percy. *Modern Social Theory*. London, Heinemann, 1968.

Colloque sur les politiques de développement et les diverses voies africaines vers le socialisme. (Dakar, 3-8 décembre 1962.) Paris, Présence Africaine, 1963.

COPELAND, Miles. *The Game of Nations*. The Amorality of Power Politics. London, Macmillan, 1969.

COSER, Lewis and ROSENBERG, Bernard (eds.). *Sociological Theory*. New York, The Macmillan Company, 1957.

CRABB, Cecil, Jr. *The Elephants and the Grass*. A Study of Non-Alignment. New York, Praeger, 1965.

CREMEANS, Charles. *The Arabs and the World*. Nasser's Arab Nationalist Policy. New York, Praeger, 1963.

DAHL, Robert. *Modern Political Analysis*. Englewood Cliffs, Prentice-Hall, 1970. (2nd ed.)

DAS, M. N. *The Political Philosophy of Jawaharlal Nehru*. London, Allen and Unwin, 1961.

DEUTSCH, Karl. *Nationalism and its Alternatives*. New York, Knopf, 1969.

— — *The Analysis of International Relations*. Englewood Cliffs, Prentice-Hall, 1968.

DEKMEJIAN, Hrair. *Egypt under Nasser*. A Study in Political Dynamics. Albany, State University of New York Press, 1971.

DUMONT, René et MAZOYER, M. *Développement et Socialisme*. Paris, Seuil, 1969.

DUNN, John. *Modern Revolution*. An Introduction to the Analysis of a Political Phenomenon. London, Cambridge U.P., 1972.

DUROSELLE, Jean-Baptiste ; MEYRIAT, Jean (eds.). *Les nouveaux Etats dans les Relations internationales*. Paris, Armand Colin, 1962.

EASTON, David. *The Political System*. New York, Knopf, 1953.

— — *A Framework for Political Analysis*. Englewood Cliffs, Prentice-Hall, 1965.

— — *A Systems Analysis of Political Life*. New York, John Wiley, 1965.

EL-BARRAWI, Rashed, *Haqiqat El-Inqlab El-Akhir fi Misr* (The Military Coup in Egypt. 1952). Cairo, Maktabat El-Nahda, 1952.

EL-BISHRI, Tareq. *El-Haraka El-Siasiyya fi Misr* (Political Movement in Egypt, 1945-1952). Cairo, El Hayyäa El-Misriyya, 1972.

EL-HADIDI, Ali. *'Abdallah El-Nadim*. Cairo, Maktabat Misr (A'lam El-'Arab, No 9), 1961.

EL-HAKIM, Tawfiq. *'Awdat El Roah* (The Restored Soul). Cairo, Maktabat El-Adab, 1933. (Translated into French as *L'âme retrouvée* but into English as *The Resurrection.)*

— — *'Asfour min El-Sharq* (Sparrow from the East). Cairo, Maktabat El-Adab, 1938.

EL-MUWAILHY, Mohamed. *Hadith 'Eisa bin Hisham* (Tales of Eisa bin Hisham). Cairo, Kitab El-Sha'ab, 1969. 3 vol.

EL-NAGGAR, Hussein. *Lutfi El-Sayed wa El-Shakhssiyya El-Misriyya* (Lutfi El-Sayed and the Egyptian Identity). Cairo, Maktabat El Qahira, 1963.

EL-RAF'I, Abdel Rahman. *Muqaddimat Thawrat 23 Yolyo* (The Preliminaries of the 23 July Revolution). Cairo, El-Nahda, 1959.

EL-SA'ID, Rif'at. *El-Yasar El-Misri* (The Egyptian Left 1925-1940). Beirut, El-Tali'a, 1972.

— — *Tarikh El-Haraka El-Ishtrakiyya fi Misr* (History of the Socialist Movement in Egypt 1900-1925). Beirut, El-Faraby, 1972.

EL-SAYED, Ahmed Lutfi. *Qissat Hayati* (My Life History). Cairo, Dar El-Hilal, 1962.

EL-SAYED, Raouf. *The Baghdad Pact in World Politics*. A Ph. D. Thesis presented to the Graduate Institute of International Studies (Geneva), 1971.

EL-SHARABASSY, El-Said. *Mabadï El-Ishtrakiyya fi El-Islam* (Principles of Socialism in Islam). Cairo, El-Dar El-Qawmiyya, Kutob Thaqafiyya No. 171, n.d.

EMERY, F. E. (ed.). *Systems Thinking*. London, Penguin, 1969.

EULAU, Heinz (ed.). *Behavioralism in Political Science*. New York, Atherton Press, 1969.

'EWAIS, Sayed. *Hadith 'an El-Thaqafa*. Ba'd El-Haqaëq El-Thaqafiyya 'an El-Mogtama' El-Misri El-Mo'asser (A Discussion of Culture. Some Cultural Facts on the Contemporary Egyptian Society). Cairo, Maktabat El-Anglo, 1970.

FANON, Frantz. *Les Damnés de la Terre*. Paris, Maspero, 1966.

FARRELL, Barry (ed.). *Approaches to Comparative and International Politics*. Evanston, Northwestern U.P., 1966.

FARRELL, John and SMITH, Asa (eds.). *Theory and Reality in International Relations*. New York, Columbia U.P., 1967.

FIRST, Ruth. *The Barrel of a Gun*. Political Power in Africa and the Coup d'Etat. London, Penguin African Library, 1972.

FLETCHER, Ronald. *The Making of Sociology*. A Study of Sociological Theory. London, Nelson's University Paperbacks, 1972. Vol. II.

FLIESS, Peter. *International Relations in the Bipolar World*. New York, Random House, 1968.

FOX, Annette, *The Power of Small States*. Chicago, The University of Chicago Press, 1959.

FOX, William (ed.). *Theoretical Aspects of International Relations*. Notre-Dame, Indiana, University of Notre-Dame Press, 1959.

FRANK, André. *Sociology of Development and Underdevelopment of Sociology*. London, Pluto Press, 1971.

FRANKEL, Joseph. *The Making of Foreign Policy*. An Analysis of Decision-Making. London, O.U.P., 1967.

— — *International Politics*. London, Allen Lane, The Penguin Press, 1969.

FREUND, Julien. *The Sociology of Max Weber*. New York, A Vintage Book, 1969.

FRIEDLAND, William and ROSBERG, Carl Jr. (eds.). *African Socialism,* Stanford, Standford U.P., 1964.

FRIEDMAN, Julian ; BLADEN, Christopher ; ROSEN, Stephen (eds.). *Alliances in International Politics,* Boston, Allyn and Bacon, 1970.

GARCEAU, Oliver (ed.). *Political Research and Political Theory*. Cambridge, Mass., Harvard U.P., 1968.

GEERTZ, Clifford (ed.). *Old Societies and New States*. The Quest for Modernity in Asia and Africa. New York, The Free Press, 1963.

GEIGER, Theodore. *The Conflicted Relationship*. The West and the Transformation of Asia, Africa and Latin America. New York, McGraw-Hill, 1967.

GINER, Salvador. *Sociology*. London, Martin Robinson, 1972.

GONDIC, Pierre-François. *L'Etat africain*. Paris, Librairie générale de droit et de jurisprudence, 1970.

GORDON, Morton. *Comparative Political Systems*. Managing Conflict. New York, Macmillan, 1972.

GREENSTEIN, Fred. *Personality and Politics*. Chicago, Markham Publishing Co., 1969.

HAAS, Ernest. *Beyond the Nation State*. Stanford, Stanford U.P., 1964.

HAAS, Michael and KARIEL, Henry (eds.). *Approaches to the Study of Political Science*. Scranton, Chandler Publishing Co., 1970.

HAGEN, Everett. *On the Theory of Social Change*. Homewood, The Dorsey Press, 1962.

HALLE, Louis. *The Cold War as History*. London. Chatto and Windus, 1967.

HALPERN, Manfred. *The Politics of Social Change in the Middle East and North Africa.* Princeton. Princeton U.P., 1963.

HAMON, Léo (éd.). *L'Elaboration de la Politique étrangère.* Paris, P.U.F., 1966.

— — *Le Rôle extra-militaire de l'Armée dans le Tiers Monde.* Paris, P.U.F., 1966.

HANNA, Sami and GARDENER, George. *Arab Socialism.* A Documentary Survey. Leiden, E. J. Brill, 1969.

HAQQY, Yehia. *Quandil Om Hashim* (The Oil Lamp of Hashim's Mother). Cairo, Selselat Eqraä', n.d.

HARRIS, Christina. *Nationalism and Revolution in Egypt.* The Role of the Moslem Brotherhood. The Hague, Mouton and Co., 1965.

HEIKAL, Mohamed. *Nahnu ... wa Amrica* (We ... and the United States). Cairo Dar El 'Assr El-Hadith, 1967.

HEMDAN, Gamal. *Shakhssiyyat Misr* (Egypt's Identity). Cairo, El-Nahda, 1967.

HENSMAN, C. R. (ed.). *From Gandhi to Guevara.* The Polemics of Revolt, London, Allen Lane, The Penguin Press, 1969.

HERZ, John. *International Politics in the Atomic Age.* New York, Columbia U.P., 1959.

HOFFMANN, Stanley. *The State of War.* Essays on the Theory and Practice of International Politics. New York, Praeger, 1965.

HOFFMANN, Stanley (ed.). *Contemporary Theory in International Relations.* Englewood Cliffs, Prentice-Hall, 1960.

HOLSTI, K. J. *International Politics.* A Framework for Analysis. Englewood Cliffs, Prentice-Hall, 1967.

HOLSTI, Ole R.; HOPMANN, P. Terence and SULLIVAN, John. *Unity and Disintegration in International Alliances:* Comparative Studies. New York and London, Wiley-Interscience Publications, 1973.

HOLT, Robert and TURNER, John. *The Political Basis of Economic Development.* An Exploration in Comparative Political Analysis. Princeton, Van Nostrand, 1966.

HOLT, Robert and TURNER, John. *The Methodology of Comparative Research.* New York, The Free Press, 1970.

HOPKINS, Harry. *Egypt, the Crucible.* The Unfinished Revolution of the Arab World. London, Secker and Warburg, 1969.

HOROWITZ, David. *From Yalta to Vietnam.* London, Penguin, 1967.

HOROWITZ, Irving. *Three Worlds of Development.* The Theory and Practice of International Stratification. New York, O.U.P., 1966.

HOSELITZ, Bert (ed.). *Sociological Aspects of Economic Growth.* New York, The Free Press, 1960.

HOURANI, Albert. *Arabic Thought in the Liberal Age.* 1798-1939. London, O.U.P, 1970. (Paperback ed.).

HUDSON, Michael. *The Precarious Republic. Political Modernization in Lebanon.* New York, Random House, 1968.

HUGHES, Anthony. *East Africa. The Search for Unity.* London, Penguin, 1963.

HUNTINGTON, Samuel. *Political Order in Changing Societies.* New Haven, Yale U.P., 1968.

HUNTINGTON, Samuel and MOORE, Clement (eds.). *Authoritarian Politics in Modern Society*. New York, Basic Books, 1970.

HUOPANIEMI, Jukka. *The Roles of Non-Alliance*. Helsinki, Institute of Political Science, University of Helsinki, 1971. (Research Reports No. 23/1971.)

HUREWITZ, J. C. (ed.). *Soviet-American Rivalry in the Middle East*. New York, Praeger, 1969.

JACKSON, Robert and STEIN, Michael (eds.). *Issues in Comparative Politics,* New York, St. Martin's Press, 1971.

JALEE, Pierre. *Le Pillage du Tiers Monde. Paris,* Maspero, 1966.

JANSEN, G. H. *Afro-Asia and Non-Alignment*. London, Faber and Faber, 1966.

JANOWITZ, Morris. *The Military in the Political Development of New Nations*. Chicago, University of Chicago Press, 1964.

JENKINS, Robin. *Exploitation*. The World Power Structure and the Inequality of Nations. London, Paladin, 1971.

JOHNSON, Chalmers. *Revolutionary Change*. Boston, Little, Brown and Co., 1966.

— — *Revolution and the Social System*. Stanford, Hoover Institution Studies, 1964 (No. 3).

JOHNSON, Harry. *Economic Policies Toward Less-Developed Countries*. Washington, Brookings Institution, 1967.

JOHNSTONE, William. *Burma's Foreign Policy*. Cambridge, Mass., Harvard U.P., 1963.

KAHIN, George. *The Asian-African Conference*. Bandung, Indonesia 1955. New York, Cornell U.P., 1956.

KAMEL, 'Adel. *Mellim El-Akbar*. Cairo, Lagnat El-Nashr Lilgami'yyin, 1945.

KAPLAN, Abraham. *The Conduct of Inquiry*. San Francisco, Chandler Publishing Co., 1964.

KAPLAN, Morton. *System and Process in International Politics*. New York, Wiley, 1964 (Science Edition).

KAPLAN, Morton (ed.). *The Revolution in World Politics*. New York, Wiley, 1962.

KAPLAN, Morton (ed.). *New Approaches to International Relations*. New York, Saint-Martin's Press, 1968.

KAPUR, Harish. *The Embattled Triangle. Moscow - Peking - New Delhi*. Delhi, Abhinav Publications, 1973.

KARANJIA, R. K. *The Mind of Mr. Nehru*. London, Allen and Unwin, 1961.

— — *The Philosophy of Mr. Nehru*. London, Allen and Unwin, 1966.

— — *The Arab Dawn*. (With a foreword by President Nasser.) Bombay, Blitz Publications, 1958.

KARPART, K. M. (ed.). *Political and Social Thought in the Contemporary Middle East*. New York, Praeger, 1968.

KARUNAKARAN, Kotta. *India in World Affairs 1950-1953*. London, O.U.P., 1958.

KAUTSKY, John. *Communism and the Politics of Development*. London, Wiley, 1968.

KAUTSKY, J. H. (ed.). *Political Change in Underdeveloped Countries*. New York, Wiley, 1962.

KAY, David (ed.). *The New Nations in the U.N. 1960-67.* New York, Columbia U.P., 1970.

KEBSCHULL, Harvey (ed.). *Politics in Transitional Societies.* The Challenge of Change in Asia, Africa and Latin America. New York, Appleton, Century Crofts, 1968.

KEDOURIE, Elie (ed.). *Nationalism in Asia and Africa.* London, Weidenfeld and Nicholson, 1970.

KENNEDY, Robert. *13 Days.* The Cuban missile crisis, October 1962. London, Macmillan, 1969.

KERR, Malcolm. *The Arab Cold War.* A Study of Ideology in Politics. London, O.U.P., 1965.

KERSTEINS, Thom. *The New Elite in Asia and Africa.* New York, Praeger Special Studies in International Economics and Development, 1966.

KHADDURI, Majid. *Political Trends in the Arab World.* The Role of Ideas and Ideals in Politics. Baltimore, The Johns, Hopkins Press, 1970.

KISSINGER, Henry. *The Necessity for Choice.* New York, Doubleday, 1962.

KNAPP, Wilfred. *A History of War and Peace 1939-1965.* London, O.U.P., 1967.

KNORR, Klaus and ROSENAU, James (eds). *Contending Approaches to International Politics.* Princeton. Princeton U.P., 1970 (paperback ed.).

KUHN, Thomas. *The Structure of Scientific Revolutions.* Chicago, Chicago U.P., (2nd ed.), 1970.

LACOUTURE, Jean. *Quatre Hommes et leurs Peuples. Le Sous-Développement et le Sur-Pouvoir.* Paris, Le Seuil, 1969.

— — *Nasser.* Paris, Le Seuil, 1971.

LACOUTURE, Jean et BAUMIER, Jean. *Le Poids du Tiers Monde.* Paris, Arthaud, 1962.

LACOUTURE, Jean et Simone. *L'Egypte en Mouvement.* Paris. Le Seuil, 1962.

LAGOS, Gustave. *International Stratification and Underdeveloped Countries.* Chapel Hill, University of North Carolina Press, 1963.

LAMBERT, William and LAMBART, Wallace. *Social Psychology.* Englewood Cliffs, Prentice-Hall, 1964.

LANDAU, Jacob. *Parliaments and Parties in Egypt.* Tel Aviv, Israeli Publishing House, 1953.

LAQUEUR, Walter. *Communism and Nationalism in the Middle East.* London, Routledge and Kegan, 1956.

— — *The Struggle for the Middle East. The Soviet Union and the Middle East.* London, Routledge and Kegan Paul, 1969.

LAROUI, Abdallah. *L'Idéologie arabe contemporaine.* Paris, Maspero, 1967.

LEIDEN, Carl and SCHMITT, Karl (eds.). *The Politics of Violence.* Revolution in the Modern World. Englewood Cliffs, Prentice-Hall, 1968.

LERNER, Daniel. *The Passing of Traditional Society.* New York, The Free Press, 1958.

LERCHE, Charles Jr. *The Cold War... and After.* Englewood Cliffs, Prentice-Hall, 1965.

LE VINE, Victor. *Political Leadership in Africa.* Hoover Institution Studies, Stanford University, 1967.

LEVY, Marion Jr. *Modernization and the Structure of Society*. Princeton, Princeton U.P. (2nd ed.), 1969.

LEVY, Reuben. *The Social Structure of Islam*. Cambridge, Cambridge U.P., 1957.

LEWIN, Kurt. *Field Theory in Social Science*. Ed. by D. Cartwright. New York, Harper and Brothers, 1951.

LEYS, Colin (ed.). *Politics and Change in Developing Countries*. Studies in the Theory and Practice of Development. London. Cambridge U.P., 1969.

LIPSET, Seymour Martin. *Politics and the Social Sciences*. New York, O.U.P., 1969.

LISKA, George. *Nations in Alliance*. Baltimore, The Johns Hopkins Press, 1968 (paperback ed.).

— — *Alliances and the Third World*. Baltimore. The Johns Hopkins Press, 1968.

LITTLE, Tom. *Modern Egypt*. London, Ernest Benn, 1968.

LONDON, Kurt (ed.). *New Nations in a Divided World*. New York, Praeger, 1964.

LOUCA, Anouar. *Voyageurs et Ecrivains égyptiens en France au XIXe Siècle*. Paris, Didier, 1970.

LUARD, Evan (ed.). *The International Regulation of Frontier Disputes*. London, Thames and Hudson, 1970.

LYON, Peter. *Neutralism*. Leicester, Leicester U.P., 1963.

LYSTAD, Robert (ed.). *The African World*. A Survey of Social Research. London, Pall Mall, 1965.

MACKENZIE, W. J. M. *Politics and Social Science*. London, Penguin, 1967.

MACRIDIS, Roy (ed.) *Foreign Policy in World Politics*. Englewood Cliffs, Prentice-Hall (2nd ed.), 1962.

MADGE, John. *The Origins of Scientific Sociology*. London, Tavistock, 1963.

MAHFOUZ, 'Afaf. *Socialisme et Pouvoir en Egypte*. Paris, Librairie générale de Droit et de Jurisprudence, 1972.

MAHMUD, Mustafa. *Abdel Nasser*. Qadaya wo Mawaqif (Abdel Naser, Issues and Attitudes). Beirut, Publications of Ssawt El-'Orouba, 1971.

MALLIK, Deva. *The Development of Non-Alignment in India's Foreign Policy*. Allahabad, Chaitanya Publishing House, 1967.

MANSOUR, Sami. *Moätamar Belghrad Li'dam El-Inhiaz* (The Belgrade Non-Aligned Summit Conference). Unpublished Ph. D. Thesis, Cairo University, 1967.

MAQSOUD, Clovis. *Ma'na El-Hyad El-Igabi* (The Meaning of Positive Neutralism). Beirut, Dar El-'Elm, 1969.

MARTIN, Laurence (ed.). *Neutralism and Nonalignment*. New York, Praeger, 1962.

MATES, Leo. *Non-Alignment*. Theory and Current Policy. Belgrade, The Institute of International Politics and Economics, and New York, Oceana Publications Inc., 1972.

MATHISEN, Trygve. *Research in International Relations*. London, Allen and Unwin, 1963.

MAZRUI, Ali. *Violence and Thought*. Essays on Social Tensions in Africa. New York, Humanities Press, 1969.

MAZRUI, Ali (ed.). *The Horizons of African Diplomacy,* Nairobi, East Africa Publishing House, forthcoming.

McCLELLAND, Charles. *Theory and the International System.* New York, Macmillan, 1966.

McCORD, William. *The Springtime of Freedom. Evolution of Developing Societies.* New York, O.U.P., 1965.

McKAY, Vernon (ed.). *African Diplomacy.* Studies in the Determinants of Foreign Policy. New York, Praeger, 1966.

MEAD, Donald. *Growth and Structural Change in the Egyptian Economy.* Homewood, Richard Irwin Inc., 1967.

MEGAHED, Horaya T. *Socialism and Nation-Building in Africa.* The Case of Mali 1960-68. Budapest, Center for Afro-Asian Research of The Hungarian Academy of Sciences, 1970 (Studies in Developing Countries No. 41).

MELIKA,

MERTON, Robert. *Social Theory and Social Structure.* New York, The Free Press (rev. ed.), 1957.

MILLER, J. D. B. *The Politics of the Third World.* London, Chatham House Essays, R.I.I.A., 1966.

MILLER, Linda. *World Order and Local Disorder.* The U.N. and Internal Conflicts. Princeton, Princeton U.P., 1967.

MILLER, Norman and AYA, Roderick (ed.). *National Liberation.* Revolution in the Third World. New York, The Free Press, 1971.

MINTZ Jeanne. *Mohamed, Marx and Marhean.* The Roots of Indonesian Socialism. London, Pall Mall, 1965.

MITCHELL, Richard. *The Society of the Moslem Brothers.* New York, O.U.P. 1969.

MODELSKI, George. *A Theory of Foreign Policy.* London, Pall Mall, 1962.

MODELSKI, George (ed.). *The New Emerging Forces.* Canberra, The Australian National University, 1963.

MONROE, Elizabeth. *Britain's Moment in the Middle East.* London. Methuen and Co., 1965.

MORGENTHAU, Hans. *Politics Among Nations.* New York, Knopf (3rd ed.), 1960.

MOORE, Barrington Jr. *Social Origins of Dictatorship and Democracy.* Lord and Peasant in the Making of the Modern World. London, Penguin, 1969.

MOORE, Clement. *Politics in North Africa.* Berkeley, University of California Press, 1970.

MORQOS, Elias. *Tarikh El-Ahzab El-Shyu'yya fi El-Watan El-'Arabi* (History of Communist Parties in the Arab Homeland.) Beirut, Dar El-Tali'a, 1964.

MORRIS-JONES, W. H. *The Government and Politics of India.* London, Hutchinson (2nd ed.), 1967.

MÜHLMAN, Wilhelm. *Messianisme révolutionnaire du Tiers Monde.* Paris, Gallimard, 1968.

MOUSSA, Pierre. *Les Etats-Unis et les Nations prolétaires.* Paris, Le Seuil, 1965.

MUSTAFA, Ahmed. *Misr wa El-Masäala El-Misriyya* (Egypt and the Egyptian Question). Cairo, Dar El-Ma'aref, n.d.

NEEL, Ann. *Theories of Psychology.* London, University of London Press, 1971.

NETTL, J. and ROBERTSON, Roland. *International Systems and the Modernization of Societies.* London, Faber, 1968.

NIELSEN, Waldewar. *The Great Powers and Africa.* New York, Praeger, 1969.

NORDLINGER, Eric. *Conflict Regulation in Divided Societies.* Harvard University, Center for International Affairs, 1972.

NORTHEDGE, Frederick (ed.). *The Foreign Policies of the Powers.* London, Faber and Faber, 1968.

O'BRIEN, Patrik. *The Revolution in Egypt's Economic System.* From Private Enterprise to Socialism, 1952-1965. London, O.U.P., 1966.

'ODA, Mahmud. *El-Qarya El-Misriyya bina El-Tarikh wa 'elm El-Egtema'* (The Egyptian Village between History and Sociology). Cairo, Maktabat Sa'ïd Raäfat, 1972.

ORGANSKI, A. F. *The Stages of Political Development.* New York, Knopf, 1965.

PACHTER, Henry. *Collision Course. The Cuban Missile Crisis and Coexistence.* London, Pall Mall, 1963.

PAIGE, Glen. *The Korean Decision.* New York, The Free Press, 1968.

PALMER, Monte (ed.). *The Human Factor in Political Development.* Wiltham, Mass., Grinn, 1970.

PALMER, Norman (ed.). *A Design for International Relations Research.* Scope, Theory, Methods and Relevance. Philadelphia, American Academy of Political and Social Science, 1970.

PANIKKAR, K. M. *In Two Chinas. Memoirs of a Diplomat.* London, Allen and Unwin, 1955.

PARSONS, Talcott. *The Social System.* New York, The Free Press, 1964 (paperback ed.).

PENROSE, E. F. *The Revolution in International Relations.* London, Frank Cass and Co., 1965.

PETKOVIC, Ranko. *Non-Alignment in the Contemporary World.* Beograd, Medunardona Politika, 1968.

PHILIPS, Claude Jr. *The Development of Nigerian Foreign Policy.* Evanston, Ill., Northwestern U.P., 1964.

PIAGET, Jean. *Le Structuralisme.* Paris, P.U.F., 1968 (Que Sais-je ?).

POPPER, Karl. *The Logic of Scientific Discovery.* London, Hutchinson, 1968.

POTHOLM, Christian. *Four African Political Systems.* Englewood Cliffs, Prentice-Hall, 1970.

PROCTOR, Harris. *Islam and International Relations.* New York, Praeger, 1965.

PYE, Lucian and VERBA, Sidney (eds.). *Political Culture and Political Development.* Princeton, Princeton U.P., 1965.

QUANDT, William. *Revolution and Political Leadership. Algeria 1954-1968.* Cambridge, Mass., The M.I.T. Press, 1969.

QUEILLE, Pierre. *Histoire de l'Afro-Asiatisme jusqu'à Bandoung.* Paris, Payot, 1965.

QURAISHI, Zaheer. *Liberal Nationalism in Egypt. Rise and Fall of the Wafd Party.* Delhi, Alwaz Publishers, 1967.

RAMADAN, Abdel-'Azim. *Tatawar El-Haraka El-Wataniyya fi Misr* (The Evolution of the Nationalist Movement in Egypt, 1918-1936). Cairo, Dar El-Kitab, 1968.

RANA, Aspy. *A Framework for the Analysis of India's Foreign Policy Strategy in the Nehru Period.* A Ph. D. dissertation submitted to the Graduate Institute of International Studies. Geneva, 1973.

REX, John. *Key Problems in Sociological Theory.* London, Routledge and Kegan Paul, 1970.

RIGGS, Fred. *Administration in Developing Countries.* The Theory of Prismatic Society. Boston, Houghton Mifflin, 1964.

RIVKIN, Arnold. *The African Presence in World Affairs. National Development and its Role in Foreign Policy.* New York, The Free Press, 1963.

— — *Nation-Building in Africa. Problems and Prospects.* Ed. by John Marrow. New Brunswick, N. J., Rutgers U.P., 1969.

ROBERTSON, Roland. *The Sociological Interpretation of Religion.* Oxford, Blackwell, 1970.

ROBERTSON, Roland (ed.). *Sociology of Religion.* London, Penguin, 1969.

ROCHBLAVE-SPENLE, Anne-Marie. *La Notion de Rôle en Psychologie sociale.* Etude historico-critique. Paris, P.U.F., 1962.

ROSECRANCE, Richard. *Action and Reaction in World Politics. International Systems in Perspective.* Boston and Toronto, Little, Brown, 1963.

ROSENAU, James. *Public Opinion and Foreign Policy.* New York, Random House, 1961.

— — *Of Boundaries and Bridges.* A Report on a Conference on the Interdependencies of National and International Political Systems. Princeton University, Center of International Studies, 1967.

ROSENAU, James (ed.). *International Politics and Foreign Policy.* New York, The Free Press, 1961.

— — *International Politics and Foreign Policy.* New York, The Free Press (rev. ed.), 1969.

— — *Domestic Sources of Foreign Policy.* New York, The Free Press, 1967.

— — *Linkage Politics.* Essays on the Convergence of National and International Systems. New York, The Free Press, 1969.

— — *The Scientific Study of Foreign Policy.* New York. The Free Press, 1971.

ROSSI, Mario. *The Third World. The Unaligned Countries and the World Revolution.* New York, Funk and Wagnalls Co., 1963.

ROSTOW, W. W. *The Stages of Economic Growth.* A Non-Communist Manifesto. Cambridge U.P., 1960.

ROTHSTEIN, Robert. *Alliances and Small Powers.* New York, Columbia U.P., 1968.

ROUS, Jean. *Léopold Sédar Senghor.* Un président de l'Afrique nouvelle. Paris, John Didier, 1968.

RUBINSTEIN, Alvin. *Yugoslavia and the Non-Aligned World.* Princeton, Princeton U.P., 1970.

RUDOLPH, Lloyd and Susanne. *The Modernity of Tradition. Political Development in India.* Chicago, University of Chicago Press, 1967.

RUNCIMAN, W. G. *Social Science and Political Theory.* London, Cambridge U.P. (2nd ed.), 1969.

RUSTOW, Dunkwart. *A World of Nations. Problems of Political Modernization.* Washington, D.C., The Brookings Institution, 1967.

RUSSETT, Bruce. *Trends in World Politics.* New York, Macmillan, 1965.

RUSSETT, Bruce. *International Regions and the International System.* Chicago, Rand McNally, 1967.

SAAB, Hassan. *Tahdith El-'Aql El-Arabi* (Modernization of the Arab Mind). Beirut, Dar El-'Elm, 1969.

SABRI, Mousa. *Qissat Malek wa Arba' Wizarat* (The Story of a King and Four Cabinets). Cairo, Dar El-Qalam, n.d.

SAFRAN, Nadav. *Egypt in Search of Political Community.* Cambridge, Mass., Harvard U.P., 1962.

— — *From War to War.* The Arab-Israeli Confrontation 1948-67. New York. Pegasus, 1969.

SAID, Abdul (ed.). *Theory of International Relations.* Englewood Cliffs, Prentice-Hall, 1968.

SAID, Abdul and LERCHE, Charles. *Concepts of International Politics.* Englewood Cliffs, Prentice-Hall, 1963.

SALIH, Tayeb. *Season of Migration.* (Translated from the Arabic by Denys Johnson-Davis.) London, Heineman, 1970 (African Writers Series).

SAYEGH, Anis. *El-Fikra El-'Arabiyya fi Misr* (The Arab Concept in Egypt). Beirut, 1959.

SAYEGH, Fayez (ed.). *The Dynamics of Neutralism in the Arab World.* San Francisco, Chandler Publishing Co., 1964.

SCARROW, Howard. *Comparative Political Analysis.* An Introduction. New York, Harper and Row, 1969.

SCOTT, Andrew. *The Functioning of the International Political System.* London, Macmillan, 1967.

SEALE, Patrick. *The Struggle for Syria.* London, O.U.P., 1965.

SEGAL, Ronald. *The Crisis of India.* London, Penguin, 1965.

SEGESVARY, Victor. *Le Réalisme khrouchtchévien.* Neuchâtel, La Baconnière, 1969.

SEN, C. *Against the Cold War. A Study of Asian-African Policies Since World War II.* Bombay, Asia Publishing House, 1962.

SHAW, Marvin and CONSTANZO, Philip. *Theories of Social Psychology.* New York, McGraw Hill, 1970.

SHA'LAN, Ibrahim. *El-Sha'b El-Misri min Amthalehe El-'Ammiyya* (The Egyptian People through its Popular Proverbs). Cairo, El-Hayäa El-Misriyya Lilkitab, 1972.

SHEPHERD, George Jr. *Non-Aligned Black Africa. An International Subsystem.* Lexington, Heath, 1970.

SHILS, Edward. *Politial Development in the New States.* The Hague, Mouton, 1962.

SHUKRY, Ghali. *Muthakkarat Thaqafa Tahtader* (Memoirs of an Agonizing Culture). Beirut, Dar El-Tali'a, 1970.

SILVERMAN, David. *The Theory of Organizations.* London, Heineman, 1970.

SINGER, David (ed.). *Quantitative International Politics.* New York, The Free Press, 1968.

— — *Human Behavior and International Politics.* Contributions from the Social-Psychological Sciences. Chicago, Rand McNally, 1965.

SINGER, David and SMALL, Melvin. *The Wages of War 1816-1965*. A Statistical Handbook. New York, Wiley, 1972.

SKOLNIKOFF, Eugene. *Science, Technology and American Foreign Policy*. Cambridge, Mass., The M.I.T. Press, 1967.

SMELSER, Neil. *Essays in Sociological Theory*. Englewood Cliffs, Prentice-Hall, 1968.

SMITH, Anthony. *Theories of Nationalism*. London, Duckworth, 1971.

SMITH, Roger. *Cambodia's Foreign Policy*. Ithaca, New York, Cornell U.P., 1969.

SNYDER, Louis. *The New Nationalism*. Ithaca, New York, Cornell U.P., 1968.

SNYDER, Richard ; BRUCK, H. W. and SAPIN, Burton. *Foreign Policy Decision-Making*. An Approach to the Study of International Politics. New York, The Free Press, 1962.

SONDERMAN, Fred ; OLSON, William ; McLELLAN, David (eds.). *The Theory and Practice of International Relations*. Englewood Cliffs, Prentice-Hall (3rd ed.), 1970.

SPANIER, John. *World Politics in an Age of Revolution*. New York, Praeger, 1967.

SPIRO, Herbert. *World Politics. The Global System*. Homewood, The Dorsey Press, 1966.

SPROUT, Harold and Margaret. *Foundations of International Politics*. Princeton, Van Nostrand, 1962.

— — *The Ecological Perspective on Human Affairs*. With Special Reference to International Politics. Princeton, Princeton U.P., 1965.

SRINIVAS, M. N. *Social Change in India*. Berkeley, University of California Press, 1969.

ST. JOHN, Robert. *The Boss*. London, Arthur Barker, 1961.

STEPHENS, Robert. *Nasser. A Political Biography*. London, Allen Lane, 1971.

TAYLOR, Charles ; HUDSON, Michael and al. (eds.). *World Handbook of Political and Social Indicators*. New Haven, Yale U.P. (2nd ed.), 1972.

The Baghdad Pact. Origins and Political Setting. London, R.I.I.A., 1956.

TIGNOR, Robert. *Modernization and British Colonial Rule in Egypt 1882-1914*. Princeton, Princeton U.P., 1966.

THOMAS, L. *Le Socialisme et l'Afrique*. Paris, Le Livre Africain, 1966.

THOMPSON, Scott, *Ghana's Foreign Policy, 1957-1966*. Princeton, Princeton U.P., 1969.

TURNER, Victor (ed.). *Profiles of Change*. African Society and Colonial Rule. London, Cambridge U.P., 1971.

VAN NIEUWENHUIJZE, C. A. O. *Sociology of the Middle East. A Stocktaking and Interpretation*. Leiden, E. J. Brill, 1971.

VATIKIOTIS, P. J. *The Egyptian Army in Politics. Pattern for New Nations?* Bloomington, Indiana U.P., 1961.

— — *The Modern History of Egypt*. New York, Praeger, 1969.

VATIKIOTIS, P. J. (ed.). *Egypt Since the Revolution*. London, Allen and Unwin, 1968. (Studies in Modern Asia and Africa.)

VAUCHER, Georges. *Gamal Abdel Nasser et son Equipe*. Paris, Juillard, 1959 (vol. I) and 1960 (vol. II).

VITAL, David. *The Inequality of States*. Oxford, Clarendon Press, 1967.

VON BERTALANFFY, Ludwig. *General Systems Theory*. New York, Braziller, 1969.

WAHBY, Mohamed. *Azmat El-Tamadon El-'Arabi* (Crisis of Arab Civilization). Beirut, Dar El-'Elm, 1956.

WALLERSTEIN, Immanuel (ed.). *Social Change: The Colonial Situation*. New York, Wiley, 1966.

WATT, D. C. (ed.). *Survey of International Affairs, 1962*. London, R.I.I.A., O.U.P., 1970.

WEBER, Max. *On Charisma and Institution-Building*. Ed. by Shmuel Eisenstadt. Chicago, The University of Chicago Press, 1968.

WEINER, Myron. *The Politics of Scarcity*. Chicago, The University of Chicago Press, 1962.

WEINSTEIN, Michael. *Systematic Political Theory*. Columbus, Ohio, Charles Merrill Publishing Co., 1971.

WELCH, Claude Jr. (ed.). *Political Modernization. A Reader in Comparative Political Change*. Belmont, Calif., Wadsworth Publishing Co., 2nd ed., 1971.

WERTHEIMER, Michael. *Fundamental Issues in Psychology*. New York, Holt, Rinehart and Winston, 1972.

WHEELOCK, Keith. *Nasser's New Egypt*. London, Stevens, 1960.

WILKINSON, David. *Comparative Foreign Relations. Framework and Methods*. Belmont, Calif., Dickenson Publishing Co., 1969.

WILLNER, Ann-Ruth. *Charismatic Political Leadership. A Theory*. Princeton University, Center of International Studies, 1968.

WISEMAN, Victor, *Political Systems*. Some Sociological Approaches. New York, Praeger, 1966.

WOLFENSTEIN, Victor. *Violence or Non-Violence. A Psychoanalytic Exploration of the Choice of Political Means in Social Change*. Princeton University, Center of International Studies, 1965.

— — *The Revolutionary Personality*. Lenin, Trotsky, Gandhi. Princeton, Princeton U.P., 1967.

WORSLEY, Peter. *The Third World*. London, Weidenfeld and Nicholson, 1967.

WRIGGINS, Howard. *The Ruler's Imperative. Strategies for Political Survival in Asia and Africa*. New York, Columbia U.P., 1969.

— — *Ceylon. Dilemmas of a New Nation*. Princeton, Princeton U.P., 1960.

YOUNG, Crawford. *Politics in the Congo*. Princeton, Princeton U.P., 1965.

YOUNG, Oran. *A Systemic Approach to International Politics*. Princeton University, Center of International Studies, June 1968 (No. 33).

— — *Systems of Political Science*. Englewood Cliffs, Prentice-Hall, 1968.

— — *The Intermediaries. Third Parties in International Crises*. Princeton, Princeton U.P., 1967.

ZARTMAN, William. *International Relations in the New Africa*. Englewood Cliffs, Prentice-Hall, 1966.

ZOLBERG, Aristide. *One-Party Rule in the Ivory Coast*. Princeton, Princeton U.P., 1964.

ZURAIQ, Costantine. *Nahnu ... Wa El-Tarikh* (We ... and History). Beirut, Dar El-'Elm (2nd ed.), 1963.

— — *M'ana El-Nakba Mogaddan* (The Renewed Meaning of Disaster). Beirut, Dar El-'Elm, 1967.

2. Articles

A. *Unpublished Articles*

FARAJALLAH, Samaan. "Les perspectives et les limites d'une politique commune des pays non alignés". Paper submitted to the *7th World Congress of the International Political Science Association,* Brussels, September 1967.

GASTEYGER, Curt. "Non-Alignment and Nuclear Weapons". Paper submitted to the *7th World Congress of the International Political Science Association,* Brussels, September 1967.

HOROWITZ, Donald. " Multiracial Politics in the New States. Toward a Theory of Conflict". Paper delivered at the *Annual Meeting of the American Political Science Association,* September 1969.

LEURDIJK, Henk. "From International to Transnational Politics : A Change of Paradigms ?". Paper submitted to the *European Consortium of Political Research (ECPR) Workshop on 'Models of International Relations',* Mannheim, Germany, April 1973.

LIJPHART, Arend. "The Structure of the Theoretical Revolution in International Relations". Paper submitted to the *ECPR Workshop on 'Models of International Relations',* Mannheim, Germany, April 1973.

LYON, Peter, "Neutrality. Neutralism. Non-Alignment". Paper submitted to the *7th Congress of the International Political Science Association,* Brussels, September 1967.

MARK, Max. "The Changing Pattern of Neutralism". Paper presented to the *7th World Congress of the International Political Science Association,* Brussels, September 1967.

MATES, Leo. "Neutrality, Neutralism, Non-Alignment after the Second World War". Paper presented to the *7th World Congress of the International Political Science Association.* Brussels, September 1967.

ORT, Alexander. "La Neutralité dans le Cadre des Relations entre Pays socialistes et Pays occidentaux". Paper presented to the *7th World Congress of the International Political Science Association,* Brussels, September 1967.

RANA, Aspy. "The Identity of India's Non-Alignment : The Nehru Years". Paper presented to the *7th World Congress of the International Political Science Association,* Brussels, September 1967.

SHAW, Timothy. "African States and International Stratification. The Adaptive Foreign Policy of Tanzania". Paper submitted to the *Colston Symposium on 'Foreign Relations of African States',* University of Bristol (England), April 1973.

STAVENHAGEN, Rodolfo. "Decolonising Applied Social Sciences". *Graduate Institute of International Studies,* Geneva, 1971, mimeo.

TON THAT THIEN. "Le Neutralisme en Asie du Sud-Est". Paper presented to the *7th World Congress of the International Political Science Association*, Brussels, September 1967.

WILLETTS, Peter. "Towards a Theory of the Phenomenon of Non-Alignment". Paper submitted to the *ECPR Workshop on 'Models of International Relations*, Mannheim, Germany, April 1973.

B. *Published Articles*

ABDEL-MALEK, Anouar. "La Question agraire en Egypte et la Réforme de 1952". *Tiers Monde*, III (1962) ; pp. 181-216.

— — "Sociologie du Développement national : Problèmes de Conceptualisation" in *Sociologie de la 'Construction nationale' dans les Nouveaux Etats*. Bruxelles, Editions de l'Institut de Sociologie de l'Université libre de Bruxelles, 1968 ; pp. 63-79.

ABI-SAAB, Georges. "Wars of National Liberation and the Laws of War". *Annals of International Studies* (Geneva), III (1972) ; pp. 93-119.

ABUETAN, Barid. "East-West Middle East Policies". *Middle Eastern Affairs*, VII (1956) ; pp. 269-286.

ABU-JABER, Kamel. "Salamah Musa : Precursor of Arab Socialism". *Middle East Journal*, XX (1966) ; pp. 196-207.

ABU-LABAN, Baha. "Social Change and Local Politics". *Journal of Developing Areas*, V (1970) ; pp. 27-43.

ABU-LUGHOD, Ibrahim. "The Transformation of the Egyptian Elite. Prelude to the Urabi Revolt". *Middle East Journal*, XXI (1967) ; pp. 325-45.

AGOSTINI, Régis. "Egypte et Inde : Deux Conceptions du Neutralisme". *Orient*, II (1958) ; pp. 73-89.

AGWANI, M. S. "India, Pakistan and West Asia". *International Studies*, VIII (1966) ; pp. 158-166.

— — "Islam and Modernism in the Arab East". *India Quarterly*, XIX (1963) ; pp. 266-276.

— — "The Reactions of West Asia and the U.A.R. [to the 1962 Sino-Indian Military Conflict]". *International Studies*, V (1963) ; pp. 75-80.

ALGER, Chadwick. "Comparison of Intranational and International Politics". *American Political Science Review*, LVII (1963) ; pp. 406-419.

— — "International Relations" in *International Encyclopedia of the Social Sciences*. New York, The Macmillan Company and The Free Press, 1968, vol. VIII ; pp. 61-69.

— — "Trends in International Relations Research" in *A Design for International Relations Research*, pp. 7-29.

ALGER, Chadwick and BRAMS, Steven. "Patterns of Representation in National Capitals and Intergovernmental Organizations". *World Politics*, XIX (1967) ; pp. 646-663.

ALLISON, Graham. "Conceptual Models and the Cuban Missile Crisis". *American Political Science Review*, LXIII (1969) ; pp. 689-719.

ALLPORT, Gordon. "Prejudice : A Problem in Psychological and Social Causation" in Talcott Parsons and Eward Shils (ed.) : *Toward a General Theory of Action.* New York, Harper and Row, 1965 ; pp. 465-488.

ALMOND, Gabriel. "A Developmental Approach to Political Systems". *World Politics,* XVII (1965) ; pp. 183-215.

AL-SAYYID-MARSOT, Afaf Lutfi. "The Cartoon in Egypt". *Comparative Studies in Society and History,* XIII (1971) ; pp. 2-15.

ANABTAWI, Samir. "Neutralists and Neutralism". *The Journal of Politics,* XXVII (1965) ; pp. 351-361.

ANGLIN, Douglas. "Nigeria : Political Non-Alignment and Economic Alignment". *Journal of Modern African Studies,* II (1964) ; pp. 247-263.

ANIS, Mohamed. "Hadith 4 Fabriar" (The 4th February Incident, 1942). *Al-Ahram,* 6 September 1973.

APTER, David. "Nkrumah, Charisma and the Coup". *Deadalus,* Summer 1968 ; pp. 757-793.

ARDANT, Philippe. "Le Néo-Colonialisme. Thème, Mythe et Réalité". *Revue française de Science politique,* XV (1965) ; pp. 837-855.

ARMSTRONG, H. F. "Neutrality : Varying Tunes". *Foreign Affairs,* XXXV (1956) ; pp. 57-71.

ARON, Raymond. "What is a Theory of International Relations" in Farrell (ed.) : *Theory and Reality in International Relations,* pp. 1-23.

ARORA, V.K. "The Lusaka Conference". *Foreign Policy Reports,* XIX (1970) ; pp. 77-82.

ARRIGHI, Giovanni and SAUL, John. "Socialism and Economic Development in Tropical Africa". *Journal of Modern African Studies,* VI (1968) ; pp. 141-169.

ASHFORD, Douglas. "Contradictions of Nationalism and Nation-Building in the Muslim World". *Middle East Journal,* XVIII (1964) ; pp. 421-431.

AZAR, Edward ; COHEN, Stanley ; JUKAM, Thomas and McCORMICK, James. " The Problem of Source Coverage in the Use of International Events Data". *International Studies Quarterly,* XVI (1972) ; pp. 373-389.

BADEAU, John. "U.S.A. and U.A.R. A Crisis in Confidence". *Foreign Affairs,* XLIII (1965) ; pp. 281-297.

BARNARD, F. M. "Culture and Political Development". *American Political Science Review,* LXIII (1969) ; pp. 379-398.

BAY, Christian. "Politics and Pseudopolitics. A critical Evaluation of some Behavioural Literature". *American Political Science Review,* LIX (1965) ; pp. 39-52.

BELL, Coral. "Non-Alignment and the Power Balance". *Survival,* VI (1963) ; pp. 253-260.

BERG, Elliot. "Socialism and Economic Development in Tropical Africa". *Quarterly Journal of Economics,* LXXVIII (1964) ; pp. 549-573.

BERKI, R. N. "On Marxian Thought and the Problem of International Relations". *World Politics,* XXIV (1971) ; pp. 80-106.

BERNSTEIN, Henry. "Modernization Theory and the Sociological Study of Development". *Journal of Development Studies,* VII (1971), pp. 141-161.

BERNSTEIN, Samuel. "A Schema for the Analysis of Modern Democratic and Totalitarian Regimes". *Orbis,* XIII (1970) ; pp. 1138-1159.

BERQUE, Jacques. "Sciences sociales et Décolonisation. *Tiers Monde,* III (1962) ; pp. 1-15.

BERTIER, F. "L'Egypte et le Pacte de Bagdad". *Politique étrangère,* XXII (1957) ; pp. 535-552.

BILL, James. "The Military and Modernization in the Middle East". *Comparative Politics,* II (1969) ; pp. 41-63.

BINDER, Leonard. "Egypt's Positive Neutrality" in Kaplan (ed.) : *The Revolution in World Politics,* pp. 175-192.

— — "The Middle East Subordinate International System". *World Politics,* X (1958) ; pp. 408-429.

BISCO, Ralph. "Social Science Data Archives. A Review of Developments". *American Political Science Review,* LX (1966) ; pp. 93-110.

BLAU, Peter. "Critical Remarks on Weber's Theory of Authority". *American Political Science Review,* LVII (1963) ; pp. 305-317.

BLECHMAN, Barry. "The Quantitative Evaluation of Foreign Policy Alternatives : Sinai 1956". *Journal of Conflict Resolution,* X (1966) ; pp. 408-427.

BOULDING, Kenneth. "Conflict Management as a Learning Process" in Renck and Julie Knight (ed.) : *Conflict in Society. London,* J. Y. Churchill Ltd., 1966.

— — "National Images and International Systems". *Journal of Conflict Resolution,* III (1959) ; pp. 720-732.

— — "The Content of International Studies in College". *Journal of Conflict Resolution,* VIII (1964) ; pp. 65-71.

BOURDIEU, Pierre. "Structuralism and Theory of Sociological Knowledge". *Social Research,* XXXV (1968) ; pp. 681-707.

BOUTROS-GHALI, Boutros. "Ab'ad El-Ideologia El-Afro Asyawiyya" (Dimensions of Afro-Asian Ideology). *El Siasa El-Dawliyya* (International Politics, Cairo), IV (1968) ; pp. 4-54.

BOUVIER, Paule. " Les Obstacles sociologiques au Développement du Congo". *Tiers Monde,* VIII (1967) ; pp. 435-455.

BOWLES, Donald. "Soviet Russia as a Model for Underdeveloped Areas". *World Politics,* XIV (1962) ; pp. 483-505.

BOYD, Andrew. "Belgrade Notebook". *Encounter,* XVII (November 1961) ; pp. 56-61.

BOYON, Jacques. "Une Idéologie africaine : le Nukrumaïsme". *Revue française de Science politique,* XIII (1963) ; pp. 66-88.

BOZEMAN, Ada. "India's Foreign Policy Today. Reflections upon its Sources". *World Politics,* X (1958) ; pp. 256-274.

BRAMS, Steven. "Transaction Flows in the International System". *American Political Science Review,* XL (1966) ; pp. 880-898.

BRECHER, Michael. "Elite Images and Foreign Policy Choices". *Pacific Affairs,* XL (1967) ; pp. 60-93.

BRECHER, Michael. "The Middle East Subordinate System and its Impact on Israel's Foreign Policy". *International Studies Quarterly,* XIII (1969) ; pp. 117-139.

BRECHER, Michael. "The Subordinate State System of Southern Asia". *World Politics,* XV (1963) ; pp. 213-235.

BRECHER, Michael; STEINBERG, Blema and STEIN, Janice. "A Framework for Research on Foreign Policy Behaviour". *Journal of Conflict Resolution,* XIII (1969), pp. 75-102.

BRONFENBRENNER, Martin. "The 'Structure of Revolutions' in Economic Thought". *History of Political Economy,* III (1971) ; pp. 136-152.

BULL, Hedley. "International Theory. The Case for a Classical Approach". *World Politics,* XVIII (1966) ; pp. 361-378.

BURTON, John. " 'Peace Research' and 'International Relations' ". *Journal of Conflict Resolution,* VIII (1964) ; pp. 281-287.

CANTORI, Louis and SPIEGEL, Steven. "International Regions : A Comparative Approach to Five Subordinate Systems". *International Studies Quarterly,* XIII (1969) ; pp. 361-381.

CARRINGTON, C. E. "Decolonization : The Last Stages". *International Affairs,* 38 (1962) ; pp. 29-41.

CASPARY, William. "The 'Mood Theory'. A Study of Public Opinion and Foreign Policy". *The American Political Science Review,* LXIV (1970) ; pp. 536-547.

CECIL, Charles. "The Determinants of Libyan Foreign Policy". *Middle East Journal,* XIX (1965) ; pp. 20-35.

CHARLES, Bernard. "Le Socialisme africain. Mythes et Réalités". *Revue française de Science politique,* XV (1965) ; pp. 856-884.

CHATTERJI, B. R. "The Welfare State Concept in Indonesia and Cambodia". *India Quarterly,* XVIII (1962) ; pp. 154-167.

CHAUDHURI, J. N. "The Role of Middle Powers". *India Quarterly,* XXV (1969) ; pp. 207-216.

CHOUCRI, Nazli. "The Perceptual Base of Non-Alignment". *Journal of Conflict Resolution,* XIII (1969) ; pp. 57-73.

COHEN, D. L. " The Concept of Charisma and the Analysis of Leadership". *Political Studies,* XX (1972) ; pp. 299-305.

CONE, Winston. "Ghana's African and World Relations". *India Quarterly,* XVIII (1961) ; pp. 258-277.

COTTRELL, Alvin. "The Soviet Union in the Middle East". *Orbis,* XIV (1970) ; pp. 588-599.

COWAN, Gray. "Political Determinants" in *African Diplomacy.* Pp. 119-145.

CRABB, Cecil Jr. "American Diplomatic Tactics and Neutralism". *Political Science Quarterly,* LXXVIII (1963) ; pp. 418-444.

CRECELIUS, Daniel. " Al-Ahzar in the Revolution". *Middle East Journal,* XX (1966) ; pp. 31-50.

CROZIER, Brian. "The Struggle for the Third World". *International Affairs,* XL (1964) ; pp. 440-453.

DAHL, Robert. "The Behavioral Approach in Political Science. Epitaph for a Movement to a Successful Protest". *American Political Science Review,* LV (1961) ; pp. 763-772.

DAS, Parimal. "The Indo-Chinese Crisis and India's Efforts towards Peace-Making, 1959-66". *International Studies* (Delhi), X (1969) ; pp. 303-321.

DASTUR, Aloo. "Twenty-five years of Indian Socialism". *India Quarterly,* XVI (1960) ; pp. 105-120.

DAVIES James. "Political Stability and Instability. Some Manifestations and Causes". *Journal of Conflict Resolution,* XIII (1969) ; pp. 1-18.

— — "Toward a Theory of Revolution". *American Sociological Review,* XXVII (1962), pp. 5-19.

DAVIS, Kingsley. "Social Changes Affecting International Relations" in Rosenau (ed.) : *International Politics and Foreign Policy ;* pp. 130-141.

DAYAL, Rajeshwar. "Crisis in the Lebanon. The Role of the U.N. and the Great Powers". *India Quarterly,* XXVII (1970) ; pp. 123-134.

DECOUFLE, André. "Sociologie politique du Développement. Problèmes et Méthodes". *Tiers Monde,* III (1962) ; pp. 17-26.

DE JOUVENEL, Bertrand. "Political Science and Prevision". *American Political Science Review,* LIX (1965) ; pp. 29-39.

DE LA RUE, Philippe. "Le Neutralisme yougoslave". *Politique étrangère,* XXVI (1961) ; pp. 327-343.

DESOUQI, Kamal. "Dirasa Istetla'yya fi El-Shakhssiyya El-Sudaniyya" (An Exploratory Study of the Sudanese Identity) in Melika : *Qiraat fi 'Elm El-Nafs fi El-Bilad El-'Arabiyya.* Pp. 207-220.

DESOUQI, Mohamed. "Thawrat Rashid 'Ali El-Kilani wa El-Qawmiyya El-'Arabiyya" (The Revolution of Rashid Ali El-Kilani and Arab Nationalism). *El-Siasa El-Dawliyya* (Cairo), VI (1970) ; pp. 586-602.

DEUTSCH, Karl. "Social Mobilization and Political Development". *American Political Science Review,* LV (1961) ; pp. 493-514.

DEUTSCH, Karl and SINGER, David. "Multipolar Power Systems and International Stability". *World Politics,* XVI (1964) ; pp. 390-406.

DEYRUP, Felicia. "Social Mobility as a Major Factor in Economic Development". *Social Research,* XXXIV (1967) ; pp. 333-347.

DINERSTEIN, Herbert. "The Transformation of Alliance Systems". *American Political Science Review,* LIX (1965) ; pp. 589-602.

DOHERTY, Kathryn. "Rhetoric and Reality. A Study of Contemporary Official Egyptian Attitudes toward the International Legal Order". *American Journal of International Law,* LXII (1968) ; pp. 335-364.

DOUTRELOUX, A. "Mythe et Réalité du Colonialisme". *Genève-Afrique,* IV (1965) ; pp. 7-35.

DOWIDAR, Mohamed. "Le Développement économique de l'Egypte depuis 1952". *Tiers Monde,* V (1964) ; pp. 255-273.

DUMONT, René. " Les Problèmes agraires de la R.A.U.". *Politique étrangère,* XXXIII (1968) ; pp. 143-181.

DUTTA, Ratna. "Two Models of the Pattern Variables Paradigm". *Social Research,* XXXVI (1969) ; pp. 433-448.

EASTON, David. "An Approach to the Analysis of Political Systems". *World Politics,* IX (1957); pp. 383-401.

— — "The Current Meaning of Behavioralism" in Charlesworth : *Contemporary Political Analysis.* Pp. 11-32.

— — "The New Revolution in Political Science". *American Political Science Review.* LXIII (1969) ; pp. 1051-1062.

EDWARDS, Michael. " Illusion and Reality in India's Foreign Policy". *International Affairs,* XLI (1965) ; pp. 48-59.

EISENSTADT, Shmuel. "Modernization. Growth and Diversity". *India Quarterly,* XX (1964) ; pp. 17-43.

EL-SHIHAWI, Abdel Khaleq. "Roäya Gadida Lilmasäala El-Zera'iyya" (A New Vision of the Agricultural Problem), *El Kateb* (Cairo). XII (August 1972) ; pp. 23-38.

ETZIONI, Amitar. "Toward a Keynesian Theory of Social Processes". *World Politics,* XXII (1969) ; pp. 139-147.

FARQUHAR, Mac. "The Chinese Model and the Underdeveloped World". *International Affairs,* XXXIX (1963) ; pp. 372-385.

FEIERABEND, Ivo and Rosalind (with SCANLAND III, Franck and CHAMBERS, John). "Level of Development and International Behavior" in Butwell (ed.) : *Foreign Policy and the Developing Nation,* pp. 135-189.

FEIERABEND, Ivo and Rosalind and NESVOLD, Betty. "The Comparative Study of Revolution and Violence". *Comparative Politics,* V (1973) ; pp. 393-425.

FEIT, Edward. "Military Coups and Political Development : Some Lessons from Ghana and Nigeria". *World Politics,* XX (1968) ; pp. 179-194.

FELIX, David. "Economic Development : Take-Offs into Unsustained Growth". *Social Research,* XXXVI (1969) ; pp. 267-294.

FIFIELD, Russel. "The Introductory Course in International Relations". *American Political Science Review,* XLII (1948) ; pp. 1189-1197.

FOSSUM, Egil. "Political Development and Strategies for Change". *Journal of Peace Research,* VII (1970) ; pp. 17-33.

FOÜAD, Ne'mat. "Shakhissiyyat Misr fi El-Adab El-Sha'bi" (Egypt's Identity in Folk Literature) in Melika (ed.) : *Qiräat fi 'Elm El-Nafs El-Igtma'i fi El-Bilad El-'Arabiyya,* vol. II, pp. 537-552.

FREYMOND, Jacques. "How the Small Countries can contribute to Peace" in August Schou and Arne Olav Brundtland (eds.) : *Small States in International Relations.* Stockholm, Almqvist and Wiksell, 1971 (Nobel Symposium) ; pp. 177-186.

— — "Réflexions sur la Structure du Système mondial". *Schweizer Monatshefte,* 52. Jahr, Heft 11 (Februar 1973) ; pp. 785-799.

— — "Supervising Agreements : The Korean Experience". *Foreign Affairs,* XXVII (1959) ; pp. 496-503.

— — "The Crisis of the International System". *International Journal,* XXIV (1969) ; pp. 776-790.

GALINO, Franck. "Patterns of Libyan National Identity". *Middle East Journal,* XXIV (Summer 1970) ; pp. 338-353.

GALLOIS, General Pierre. "Les Conséquences politiques de l'Evolution des Armements" in Hamon (ed.) : *L'Elaboration de la Politique étrangère,* pp. 179-201.

GALTUNG, Ingrid. "The Impact of Study Abroad. A Three-by-Three-Nation Study of Cross-Cultural Contact" (U.A.R., Iran and India). *Journal of Peace Research,* II (1965) ; pp. 258-275.

GILBERT, Stephen. "Soviet-American Military Aid Competition in the Third World". *Orbis,* XIII (1970) ; pp. 1117-1138.

GOLDMAN, Marshall. "A Balance Sheet of Soviet Foreign Aid". *Foreign Affairs,* XLIII (1965) ; pp. 349-361.

GOOD, Robert. "Changing Patterns of African International Relations". *American Political Science Review,* LVIII (1964) ; pp. 632-641.

GOOD, Robert. "State-Building as a Determinant of Foreign Policy in New States" in Martin (ed.): *Neutralism and Non-Alignment,* pp. 3-13.

— — "The Congo Crisis. A Study of Postcolonial Politics" in Martin (ed.): *Neutralism and Non-Alignment,* pp. 34-64.

GORDENKER, Leon and JACOBSON, Harold. "Critical Choices for the U.N. System: The Second Development Decade". *Orbis,* XIV (1970); pp. 43-58.

GORDON, Bernard. "A Political Region of South-East Asia" in *The International Politics of Regions.* Pp. 131-147.

GOYAL, O. P. and Wallace, Paul. "The Congress Party. A Conceptual Study". *India Quarterly,* XX (1964); pp. 180-202.

GREENSTEIN, Fred. "Personality and Political Socialization. The Theories of Authoritarian and Democratic Character". *Annals of the American Academy of Political and Social Science,* CCCLXI (September 1965); pp. 81-96.

— — "Political Socialization". *International Encyclopedia of the Social Sciences,* vol. XIV; pp. 551-555.

GREGOR, James, "Political Science and the Uses of Functional Analysis". *American Political Science Review,* LXII (1968); pp. 425-439.

GRUNDY, Kenneth. "NKrumah's Theory of Underdevelopment. An Analysis of Recurrent Themes". *World Politics,* XV (1963); pp. 438-455.

— — "Political Power and Economic Theory in 'Radical West Africa'". *Orbis,* VIII (1964); pp. 405-424.

— — "Recent Contributions to the Study of African Political Thought". *World Politics,* XVIII (1966); pp. 674-690.

GUPTA, Sisir. "Islam as a Factor in Pakistani Foreign Relations". *India Quarterly,* XVIII (1962); pp. 230-254.

GURR, Ted. "The Revolution-Social Change Nexus: Some Old Theories and New Hypotheses" in *Revolution and Social Change.* Pp. 359-393.

HAAS, Ernest. "The Balance of Power: Prescription, Concept or Propaganda". *World Politics,* V (1953); pp. 442-477.

HAAS, Michael. "International Subsystems: Stability and Polarity". *American Political Science Review,* LXIV (1970); pp. 98-124.

HADSEL, Fred. "Africa and the World. Non-Alignment Reconsidered". *The Annals of the American Academy of Political and Social Science,* CCCLXXII (1967); pp. 93-104.

HAH, Chong-Do and SCHNEIDER, Jeanne. "A Critique of Current Studies on Political Development and Modernization". *Social Research,* XXXV (1968); pp. 130-159.

HALL, A. D. and FAGEN, R. E. "Definition of System". *General Systems,* I (1956); pp. 18-29.

HALPERN, A. M. "The Chinese Communist Line on Neutralism". *China Quarterly* (1961); pp. 90-115.

HALPERN, Manfred. "The Rate and Costs of Political Development". *Annals of the American Academy of Political and Social Science,* CCCLVIII (March 1965); pp. 20-28.

— — "The Revolution of Modernization in National and International Society" in *Issues in Comparative Politics;* pp. 39-60.

HALPERN, Manfred. "Toward Further Modernization of the Study of New Nations". *World Politics,* XVII (1964) ; pp. 157-181.

HAMON, Léo. "Non-Engagement et Neutralisme des nouveaux Etats" in Duroselle and Meyriat : *Les nouveaux Etats dans les Relations internationales,* pp. 353-445.

HANDELMAN, John ; VASQUEZ, John ; O'LEARY, Michael and COPLIN, William. "Color it Morgenthau. A Data-Based Assessment of Quantitative International Relations Research". International Relations Program, Maxwell School, Syracuse University, *Prince Research Studies,* No. 11 (1973).

HANNA, Paul. "The Anglo-Egyptian Negotiation 1950-1952". *Middle Eastern Affairs,* III (1952) ; pp. 213-233.

HANRIEDER, Wolfram. "International and Comparative Politics. Towards a Synthesis ?". *World Politics,* XX (1968) ; pp. 480-494.

— — "The International System. Bipolar or Multibloc ?" *Journal of Conflict Resolution,* IX (1965) ; pp. 299-308.

HARIK, Iliya. "Opinion Leaders and the Mass Media in Rural Egypt. A Reconsideration of the Two-Step Flow of Communications Hypothesis". *American Political Science Review,* LXV (1971) ; pp. 731-740.

HASSNER, Pierre. "La Montée des jeunes Etats et les Relations entre les deux Blocs" in Duroselle et Meyriat : *La Communauté internationale face aux jeunes Etats,* pp. 291-405.

— — "Le 'Système international' et les nouveaux Etats" in Duroselle et Meyriat : *La Communauté internationale face aux jeunes Etats,* pp. 11-61.

HEAPHEY, James. "The Organization of Egypt. Inadequacies of a Nonpolitical Model for Nation-Building". *World Politics,* XVIII (1966) ; pp. 177-194.

HEIKAL, Mohamed. "Igtima' Roäsaä El-Dowal Ghyre El-Monhaza" (The Summit Meeting of Non-Aligned States). *Al-Ahram,* May 26, 1966.

— — "Le Non-Alignement et les nouvelles tendances de la Politique internationale". *Orient,* VII (1963) ; pp. 161-173.

HEINEMAN, Robert. "Primitive Culture and the Individual. The Case of Sub-Saharan Africa". *Journal of Developing Areas,* IV (1969) ; pp. 29-45.

HERMANN, Charles. " The Comparative Study of Foreign Policy". *World Politics,* XX (1968) ; pp. 521-535.

HILAL, Aly. " Thawrat Yolyo wa Qadaya fi El-Manhag" (The July Revolution and some Methodological Issues). *Al-Ahram,* September 29, 1973.

HINSLEY, F. H. "On the Present State and Future Development of the International System". *World Politics,* XX (1968) ; pp. 705-721.

HIRSCHMAN, Albert. "The Search for Paradigms as a Hindrance to Understanding". *World Politics,* XXII (1970) ; pp. 329-344.

HOAGLAND, John. "Arms in the Third World". *Orbis,* XIV (1970) ; pp. 500-510.

HOADLEY, Stephen and HOSEGAWA, Sukehiro. "Sino-Japanese Relations 1950-1970. An Application of the Linkage Model of International Politics". *International Studies Quarterly,* XV (1971) ; pp. 131-159.

HOLSTI, K. J. "National Role Conceptions in the Study of Foreign Policy". *International Studies Quarterly,* XIV (1970) ; pp. 233-310.

— — "Retreat from Utopia. International Relations Theory, 1945-1970". *Canadian Journal of Political Science,* IV (1971) ; pp. 165-178.

HOLT, Robert and TURNER, John. "Insular Polities" in *Linkage Politics.* Pp. 199-236.

HOPKINS, Raymond. "Aggregate Data and the Study of Political Development". *Journal of Politics,* XXXI (1969) ; pp. 71-94.

HOSKYNS, Catherine. "Africa's Foreign Relations. The Case of Tanzania". *International Affairs,* XLIV (1968) ; pp. 446-463.

HOYT, Edwin. "Foreign Policies of India and the United States". *India Quarterly,* XVIII (1961) ; pp. 277-294.

HUDSON, G. F. "The Neutrals and the Afro-Asians". *World Today,* XX (1964) ; pp. 542-548.

HUNTINGTON, Samuel. "Political Development and Political Decay". *World Politics,* XVII (1965) ; pp. 386-430.

— — "The Change to Change : Modernization, Development and Politics". *Comparative Politics,* III (1971) ; pp. 283-322.

HUREWITZ, J. C. "The Beginnings of Military Modernization in the Middle East. A Comparative Analysis". *Middle East Journal,* XXII (1968) ; pp. 144-159.

HVEEM, Helge. "Foreign Policy Opinion as a Function of International Position". *Cooperation and Conflict,* VII (1972) ; pp. 65-87.

HVEEM, Helge and WILLETS, Peter. "The Practice of Non-Alignment" in Mazrui (ed.) : *The Horizons of African Diplomacy,* forthcoming.

ISMAEL, Tareq. "The U.A.R. in Africa". *Canadian Journal of African Studies,* II (1968) ; pp. 175-194.

ISSAWI, Charles. "Social Structure and Ideology in Iraq, Lebanon, Syria and the U.A.R.". *Journal of International Affairs,* XIX (1965) ; pp. 39-46.

IWAN, James. "From Social Welfare to Local Government. The U.A.R. (Egypt)". *Middle East Journal,* XXII (1968) ; pp. 265-278.

JANKOVIC, Branimir. " De la Neutralité classique à la Conception moderne des Pays non alignés". *Revue égyptienne de Droit international,* XXI (1965) ; pp. 89-119.

JARGY, Simon. "Du Neutralisme positif au Non-Alignement". *Orient,* V (2e trim. 1961) ; pp. 15-22.

— — "Quelques Réflexions sur la Conférence de Belgrade". *Orient,* V (3e trim. 1961) ; pp. 19-26.

JHA, C. S. "Le Non-Alignement dans un Monde en Evolution". *Politique étrangère,* XXII (1967) ; pp. 349-369.

— — "The Algiers Conference". *India Quarterly,* XXI (1965) ; pp. 375-387.

JERVIS, Robert. "The Costs of the Quantitative Study of International Relations" in *Contending Approaches to International Politics ;* pp. 177-218.

KAHIN, George ; PANKER, Guy and PYE, Lucian. "Comparative Politics of Non-Western Countries". *American Political Science Review,* XLIX (1955) ; pp. 1022-1042.

KAISER, Karl. "The Interaction of Regional Subsystems. Some Preliminary Notes on Recurrent Patterns and the Role of Superpowers". *World Politics,* XXI (1968) ; pp. 84-108.

KALLEBERG, Arthur. "The Logic of Comparison. A Methodological Note on the Comparative Study of Political Systems". *World Politics,* XIX (1966) ; pp. 69-83.

KAPLAN, Morton. "Bipolarity in a Revolutionary Age" in Kaplan (ed.) : *The Revolution in World Politics,* pp. 251-267.

— — "Systems Theory and Political Science". *Social Research,* XXXV (1968) ; pp. 30-48.

KAPLAN, Morton. "The New Great Debate : Traditionalism vs. Science in International Relations". *World Politics,* XIX (1966) ; pp. 1-21.

KARDELJ, Edward. "Yugoslav Foreign Policy. Some Topical Problems of International Relations". *India Quarterly,* XIV (1958) ; pp. 337-350.

KARUNAKARAN, K. P. "Interrelation between Religion and Politics in Pakistan". *India Quarterly,* XIV (1958) ; pp. 43-62.

KAWALKOWSKI, Al. " Vers la Fin d'une double Hégémonie". *Politique étrangère,* XXIX (1964) ; pp. 260-283.

KAY, David. "The Impact of African States on the United Nations". *International Organization,* XXIII (1969) ; pp. 20-48.

KENDALL, Patricia. " The Ambivalent Character of Nationalism among Egyptian Professionals". *Public Opinion Quarterly,* XX (1956) ; pp. 277-292.

KENNY, Lorne. "Ali Mubarak, Nineteenth Century Egyptian Educator and Administrator". *Middle East Journal,* XXI (1967) ; pp. 35-52.

KEOHANE, Robert. "Lilliputian's Dilemmas : Small States in International Politics". *International Organization,* XXIII (1969) ; pp. 291-311.

KESSELMANN, Mark. "Order or Movement ? The Literature of Political Development as Ideology". *World Politics,* XXVI (1973) ; pp. 139-154.

KHADDURI, Majid. " 'Aziz 'Ali El-Misri and the Arab Nationalist Movement". *Middle Eastern Affairc,* No. 4, ed. by Albert Hourani, St. Anthony's Papers, No. 17 (1965) ; pp. 140-167.

KILSON, Martin. "Authoritarian and Single-Party Tendencies in African Politics". *World Politics,* XV (1963) ; pp. 262-295.

KOROVIN, E. "The Five Principles : A Basis for Peaceful Coexistence". *International Affairs* (Moscow). (May 1956) ; pp. 46-54.

KORTEN, David. "Situational Determinants of Leadership Structure". *Journal of Conflict Resolution,* VI (Sept. 1962) ; pp. 222-236.

KOTHARI, Rajni. "Introduction : La Formation des Nations, ses Constantes et ses Variables". *Revue internationale des Sciences sociales,* XXIII (1971) ; pp. 367-384.

— — "Tradition and Modernity Revisited". *Government and Opposition,* III (1968) ; pp. 273-293.

KRIPALANI, Acharya. "For Principled Neutrality". *Foreign Affairs,* XXXVIII (1959) ; pp. 46-61.

LACHARRIÈRE, Guy. "Aspects actuels du Classement d'un Pays comme 'sous-développé' " *Tiers Monde,* V (avril 1964) ; pp. 157-165.

LACOUTURE, Jean. "A chacun son Neutralisme. Il n'y a pas de Non-Alignement, il y a des Pays non alignés". *Le Monde diplomatique,* No. 90 (October 1961); pp. 4-5.

LANDAU, Martin. "On the Use of Functional Analysis in American Political Science". *Social Research,* XXXV (1968) ; pp. 48-76.

LANGTON, Kenneth. "Assumptions about the Learning of Political Attitudes". *The Annals of the American Academy of Political and Social Science.* CCCLXI (September 1965) ; pp. 1-10.

LASSWELL, Harold. "The Scientific Study of International Relations". *Yearbook of World Affairs* (London), XII (1958) ; pp. 1-29.

"Le Comité international de la Croix-Rouge et l'Affaire de Cuba". *Revue internationale de la Croix-Rouge,* XLIV (1962) ; pp. 605-609.

LEDUC, Gaston. "The Economic Balance Sheet of Colonialism". *Journal of Contemporary History,* IV (1969) ; pp. 37-51.

LEFEVER, Ernest. "Nehru, Nasser and Nkrumah on Neutralism" in Martin : *Neutralism and Non-Alignment ;* pp. 93-121.

— — "State-Building in Tropical Africa". *Orbis,* XII (1969) ; pp. 984-1004.

LERNER, Daniel. "Modernization". *International Encyclopedia of the Social Sciences,* vol. X ; pp. 386-395.

LERSKI, George. " The Pakistan-American Alliance : A Reevaluation of the Past Decade". *Asian Survey,* VIII (1968) ; pp. 400-416.

LEVI, Werner. "Indian Neutralism Reconsidered". *Pacific Affairs,* XXXVII (1964) ; pp. 137-148.

LE VINE, Robert. "Political Socialization and Culture Change" in Geertz (ed.) : *Old Societies and New States,* pp. 280-305.

LIJPHART, Arend. "Comparative Politics and the Comparative Method". *American Political Science Review,* LXV (1971) ; pp. 682-694.

— — "Consociational Democracy". *World Politics,* XXI (1969) ; pp. 207-226.

— — "Cultural Diversity and Theories of Political Integration". *Canadian Journal of Political Science,* IV (1971) ; pp. 1-15.

LINDFORS, Bernth. " The African Politician's changing Image in African Literature in English". *Journal of Developing Areas,* IV (1969) ; pp. 13-29.

LOW-BEER, Francis. "The Concept of Neutralism". *American Political Science Review,* LVIII (1964) ; pp. 383-392.

LYON, Peter. "Neutralism and Polycentrism". *Survey,* No. 58 (January 1966) ; pp. 35-43.

— — "The Foreign Policy of India" in Northedge (ed.) : *The Foreign Policies of the Powers,* pp. 253-288.

MANSINGH, Surjit. "India and the Hungarian Revolution". *India Quarterly,* XXI (1965) ; pp. 138-156.

MARR, Phebe Ann. "Iraq's Leadership Dilemma : A Study in Leadership Trends, 1948-68". *Middle East Journal,* XXIV (1970) ; pp. 283-302.

— — "The Iraqi Revolution. A Case Study of Army Rule". *Orbis,* XIV (1970) ; pp. 714-740.

MASTERS, Roger. "World Politics as a Primitive Political System". *World Politics,* XVI (1964) ; pp. 595-619.

MATES, Leo. "New Upsurge of Non-Alignment". *Review of International Affairs* (Belgrade), XXIV, No. 565 (October 20, 1973) ; pp. 1-3.

— — "Non-Alignment and the Great Powers". *Foreign Affairs,* XLVIII (1970) ; pp. 525-537.

MAZRUI, Ali. "Antimilitarism and Political Militancy in Tanzania". *Journal of Conflict Resolution,* XII (1968) ; pp. 269-285.

— — "From Social Darwinism to Current Theories of Modernization", *World Politics,* XXI (1968) ; pp. 69-83.

— — "Violent Contiguity and the Politics of Retribalisation". *Journal of International Affairs,* XXIII (1969) ; pp. 89-106.

McCLOSKY, Herbert. "Concerning Strategies for a Science of International Politics". *World Politics,* VII (1956) ; pp. 281-295.

MEHTA, G. L. "The Foreign Policy of Dulles". *India Quarterly,* XIX (1963) ; pp. 3-21.

MELIKA, Lewis. "Bina El-Egabiyyah wa El-Lamabalah : Dirasa Li-Itagahat El-Qarawiyyeen Nahwa El-'Aml El-Gam'i fi Khams Sanawat" (Between Active Involvement and Indifference : A Study of Villagers' Attitudes toward Collective Work over a Five-Year Period) in Melika (ed.) : *Qiräat fi 'Elm El-Nafs El-Igtima'i fi El-Bilad El-'Arabiyya,* vol. II ; pp. 611-620.

MELSON, Robert and WOLPE, Howard. "Modernization and the Politics of Communalism. A Theoretical Perspective". *American Political Science Review,* LXIV (1970) ; pp. 1112-1131.

MERTON, Robert. "The Role Set". *British Journal of Sociology,* VIII (1957) ; pp. 106-120.

MITCHELL, William. "Political System" in *The International Encyclopedia of the Social Sciences,* vol. XV ; pp. 473-479.

— — "The New Political Economy". *Social Research,* XXXV (1968) ; pp. 76-111.

MODELSKI, George. "Kautilya : Foreign Policy and International Systems in the Ancient Hindu World". *The American Political Science Review,* LVIII (1964) ; pp. 349-360.

— — "The Communist International System". Princeton University, Center of International Studies, *Research Monograph No. 9,* 1961.

MOORE, Clement. "La Tunisie après Bourguiba ? Libéralisme ou Décadence politique ?" *Revue française de Science politique,* XVII (1967) ; pp. 645-668.

MORGENBESSER, Sidney. "Is it (Economics) a Science ?". *Social Research,* XXXIII (1966) ; pp. 255-272.

MORGENTHAU, Hans. "A Political Theory of Foreign Aid". *American Political Science Review,* LVI (1962); pp. 301-310.

— — "Neutrality and Neutralism". *The Yearbook of World Affairs* (London), XI (1957) ; pp. 47-75.

MORSE, Edward. "The Transformation of Foreign Policies. Modernization, Interdependence and Externalization". *World Politics,* XXII (1970) ; pp. 371-393.

MUKERJEE, Dilip. "India in Transition : Politics of Manoeuvre". *Foreign Affairs,* XLVI (1968) ; pp. 519-531.

MUKHERJEE, Sujit. "Early American Images of India". *India Quarterly,* XX (1964) ; pp. 43-51.

NAIR, N. "Nationalism as a Factor in India's Foreign Policy". *Indian Yearbook of International Affairs,* XI (1962) ; pp. 433-459.

NARAIN, Jaya. "An Essential Requisite of National Integration". *India Quarterly,* XVIII (1961) ; pp. 323-328.

NAYAR, N. "A Study of the Policy of Non-Alignment with Special Reference to African Problems". *Foreign Affairs Reports* (Delhi), X (1961) ; pp. 132-143.

— — "Growth of Non-Alignment in World Affairs". *India Quarterly,* XVIII (1962) ; pp. 28-57.

NEISSER, Hans. "Three Views of Method in Economics". *Social Research,* XXXIV (1967) ; pp. 322-333.

NELSON, Benjamin. "Actors, Directives, Roles, Cues, Meanings, Identities". *The Psychoanalytic Review,* LI (1964) ; pp. 135-160.

NELSON, Joan. "The Urban Poor. Disruption or Political Integration in Third World Cities ?" *World Politics,* XXII (1970) ; pp. 393-415.

NICLAUSSE, M. "La Psychologie des Peuples sous-développés". *L'Afrique et l'Asie,* No. 59 (3e trim. 1962) ; pp. 11-22.

NICOL, Davidson. "Toward a World Order. An African Viewpoint". *Deadalus,* XCV (1966) ; pp. 674-694.

NIMBARK, Ashakant. "Gandhism Re-Examined". *Social Research,* XXXI (1964) ; pp. 94-126.

NORDLINGER, Eric. "Political Development. Time Sequences and Rates of Change". *World Politics,* XX (1968) ; pp. 494-520.

— — "Soldiers in Mufti. The Impact of Military Rule upon Economic and Social Change in the Non-Western States". *American Political Science Review,* LXIV (1970) ; pp. 1131-1149.

'ODA, Abdel Malek. "El-Hizb El-Wahed wa El-Tatbiq El-Ishtraki fi Tanzania" (The One-Party System and Socialist Application in Tanzania). *El-Siasa El-Dawliyya,* III (1967) ; pp. 246-272.

OLSON, Mancur Jr. "Rapid Growth as a Destabilising Force". *Journal of Economic History,* XXIII (1963) ; pp. 529-552.

OLYMPIO, Sylvanus. "African Problems and the Cold War". *Foreign Affairs,* XL (1961) ; pp. 50-58.

PALMER, Norman. "Indian Attitudes toward Colonialism". *Orbis,* II (1957) ; pp. 211-236.

PARKINSON, F. "The Politics of Underdeveloped Countries". *Yearbook of World Affairs* (London), XVII (1963) ; pp. 171-194.

PATEMAN, Carole. "Political Culture, Political Structure and Political Development". *British Journal of Political Science,* I (1971) ; pp. 291-307.

PENNAR, Joan. "The Arabs, Marxism and Moscow. A Historical Survey". *Middle East Journal,* XXII (1968) ; pp. 433-448.

PENNOCK, Roland. "Political Development, Political Systems and Political Goods", *World Politics,* XVIII (1966) ; pp. 415-435.

PFAFF, Richard. "The Function of Arab Nationalism". *Comparative Politics,* II (1970) ; pp. 147-169.

PIERCE, Roy. "Comparative Politics : Liberty and Policy as Variables". *American Political Science Review,* LVII (1963) ; pp. 655-661.

POLK, William. "A Decade of Discovery : America in the Middle East 1947-1958". *Middle Eastern Affairs* (London), No. 2, (St. Anthony's Papers, No. 11), pp. 49-81.

— — "The Nature of Modernization. The Middle East and North Africa". *Foreign Affairs,* XLIV (1965) ; pp. 100-110.

PRICE, Robert. "A Theoretical Approach to Military Rule in New States. Reference-Group Theory and the Ghanaian Case". *World Politics,* XXIII (1971) ; pp. 399-431.

PYE, Lucian. " The Concept of Political Development". *Annals of the American Academy of Political and Social Science,* CCCLVIII (Spring 1965) ; pp. 1-13.

RABI, Hamed. "Hawl El-Ta'hlil El-'Elmi Limafhoum El-Tabe' El-Qawmi El-Misri" (On the Scientific Analysis of Egyptian National Character) in Melika (ed.) : *Qiräat fi 'Elm El-Nafs El Igtima'i fi 'El-Bilad El-'Arabiyya,* vol. II, pp. 519-537.

RAINERO, R. "The Neutralist Idea and its African Characteristics". *Genève-Afrique* (Genève), IV (1965) ; pp. 35-47.

RAJAN, M. "Indian Foreign Policy in Action, 1954-56". *India Quarterly,* XVI (1960) ; pp. 203-237.

RANA, Aspy. "The Intellectual Dimensions of India's Non-Alignment". *The Journal of Asian Studies,* XXVIII (1969) ; pp. 299-312.

RAO, R. "India and Non-Aligned Summitry". *The World Today,* XXVI (1970) ; pp. 393-401.

RAO, T. "Non-Alignment : Trends and Prospects". *Indian Yearbook of International Affairs,* XIV (1965) ; pp. 568-585.

RAPOPORT, Anatol. "General Systems Theory". *The International Encyclopedia of the Social Sciences,* vol. XV ; pp. 452-458.

RATNAM, Prala. "Indian Non-Alignment in the 1970s". *India Quarterly,* XXVI (1970) ; pp. 258-269.

RATTRAM, K. J. " Charisma and Political Leadership". *Political Studies,* XII (1964) ; pp. 341-354.

"Research in Comparative Politics". Report of the Inter-University Summer Seminar on Comparative Politics, Social Science Research Council. *American Political Science Review,* XLVII (1953) ; pp. 641-658.

RIGGS, Fred. "International Relations as a Prismatic System". *World Politics,* XIV (1961) ; pp. 144-182.

— — "Systems Theory : Structural Analysis Reconsidered" in Haas and Kariel : *Approaches to the Study of Political Science.* Pp. 194-235.

— — "The Dialectics of Developmental Conflict". *Comparative Political Studies,* I (1968) ; pp. 197-226.

— — "The Theory of Developing Polities". *World Politics,* XVI (1963) ; pp. 147-171.

— — "The Theory of Political Development" in Charlesworth (ed.) : *Contemporary Political Analysis,* pp. 217-250.

ROBERTS, Geoffrey. "Comparative Politics Today". *Government and Opposition,* VII (1972) ; pp. 38-56.

ROBINSON, James. "Decision-Making. Political Aspects" in *International Encyclopedia of the Social Sciences,* vol. IV ; pp. 55-62.

RONDOT, Pierre. "La République Arabe Unie entre l'Appui soviétique et le Non-Alignement". *Revue de Défense nationale,* XXII (1966) ; pp. 1211-1225.

ROSECRANCE, Richard. "Bipolarity, Multipolarity and the Future". *Journal of Conflict Resolution,* X (1966) ; pp. 314-327.

ROSENAU, James. "Foreign Policy as an Issue-Area" in Rosenau (ed.) : *Domestic Sources of Foreign Policy ;* pp. 11-51.

— — "Pre-Theories and Theories of Foreign Policy" in Farrell (ed.) : *Approaches to Comparative and International Politics ;* pp. 27-93.

— — "The Concept of Intervention". *Journal of International Affairs,* XXII (1968) ; pp. 165-177.

— — "The National Interest". *The International Encyclopedia of the Social Sciences,* vol. XI ; pp. 34-40.

ROSENBLATT, Paul. "Origins and Effects of Group Ethnocentrism and Nationalism". *Journal of Conflict Resolution,* VIII (1964) ; pp. 131-147.

ROTBERG, Robert. "The Rise of African Nationalism. The Case of East and Central Africa". *World Politics,* XV (1962) ; pp. 75-91.

ROTH, Guenther. "Personal Rulership, Patrimonialism, and Empire-Building in New States". *World Politics,* XX (1968) ; pp. 194-207.

ROTHCHILD, Donald. "Ethnicity and Conflict Resolution". *World Politics,* XXII (1970) ; pp. 597-617.

ROTHSTEIN, Robert. "Alignment, Non-Alignment and Small Powers 1945-1965". *International Organization,* XX (1966) ; pp. 397-419.

ROWE, Edward. "The Emerging Anti-Colonial Consensus in the U.N.". *Journal of Conflict Resolution,* VIII (1964) ; pp. 209-231.

RUMMEL, Rudolph. "Dimensions of Conflict Behavior within and between Nations". *General Systems,* VIII (1963) ; pp. 1-50.

RUSSETT, Bruce. "International Behavior Research. Case Studies and Cumulation" in Haas and Kariel : *Approaches to the Study of Political Science ;* pp. 425-444.

— — "Strategies for Comparing Nations." *Journal of Conflict Resolution,* VIII (1964) ; pp. 166-171.

SAAB, Hassan. "The Philosophy of Neutralism in the Arab Mind" in Sayegh (ed.) : *The Dynamics of Neutralism in the Arab World,* pp. 105-111.

SAID, Abdul. "The Impact of the Emergence of the Non-West upon Theories of International Relations" in Said (ed.) : *Theory of International Relations,* pp. 93-107.

SALAMON, Lester. "Comparative History and the Theory of Modernization", *World Politics,* XXIII (1970) ; pp. 83-104.

SARBIN, Theodore. "Role : Psychological Aspects". *International Encyclopedia of the Social Sciences,* vol. XIII ; pp. 446-452.

SARTORI, Giovanni. "Concept misformation in Comparative Politics". *American Political Science Review,* LXIV (1970) ; pp. 1033-1054.

SAYEGH, Fayez. "Anatomy of Neutralism" in Sayegh (ed.) : *The Dynamics of Neutralism in the Arab World ;* pp. 1-102.

— — "Arab Nationalism and Soviet-American Relations". *Annals of the American Academy of Political and Social Science,* CCCXXIV (July 1959) ; pp. 103-111.

— — "Neutralism in the United Arab Republic" in *The Dynamics of Neutralism in the Arab World ;* pp. 163-224.

— — "The Theoretical Structure of Nasser's Arab Socialism", *Middle Eastern Affairs* (London), No. 4, 1965 (St. Anthony's Papers, No. 17) ; pp. 9-56.

SCALAPINO, Robert. "Neutralism in Asia". *American Political Science Review,* XLVIII (1954) ; pp. 49-63.

SCHECHTMAN, Joseph. "Minorities in the Middle East". *India Quarterly,* XVIII (1961) ; pp. 242-258.

SCHWARZENBERGER, Georg. "Beyond Power Politics". *Yearbook of World Affairs* (London), 19 (1965) ; pp. 223-235.

— — "The Scope for Neutralism". *Yearbook of World Affairs* (London), 15 (1961) ; pp. 233-244.

SETHI, J. D. "India as Middle Power". *India Quarterly,* XXV (1969) ; pp. 107-122.

SHARABI, Hisham. "The Transformation of Ideology in the Arab World". *Middle East Journal,* XIX (1965) ; pp. 471-487.

SHAY, Theodore. "Non-Alignment Si, Neutralism No". *The Review of Politics,* XXX (1968) ; pp. 428-445.

SHONFELD, William. "The Focus of Political Socialization Research". *World Politics,* XXIII (1971) ; pp. 544-578.

SGRIDHARANI, Krishnalal. "The Philosophic Bases of India's Foreign Policy". *India Quarterly,* XIV (1958) ; pp. 196-202.

SINGER, David. "The Behavioral Science Approach to International Relations. Payoff and Prospects". *SAIS Review,* X (1966) ; pp. 12-20.

— — "The Correlates of War Project. Interim Report". *World Politics,* XXIV (1972) ; pp. 243-270.

— — "The Global System and its Sub-Systems. A Developmental View" in Rosenau : *Linkage Politics ;* pp. 243-270.

— — "The Level-of-Analysis Problem in International Relations". *World Politics,* XIV (1961) ; pp. 77-92.

SINGER, David and SMALL, Melvin. "Formal Alliances, 1816-1965. An Extension of the Basic Data". *Journal of Peace Research,* VI (1969) ; pp. 257-283.

SINGH, K. R. "The Soviet-U.A.R. Relations". *India Quarterly,* XXI (1969) ; pp. 139-153.

SINGH, L. P. "Political Development or Political Decay in India ?" *Pacific Affairs,* XLIV (1971) ; pp. 65-81.

SIOTIS, Jean. "Social Science and the Study of International Relations". *Yearbook of World Affairs* (London), 24 (1970) ; pp. 1-25.

SKURNIK, Walter. "Léopold Sédar Senghor and African Socialism". *Journal of Modern African Studies,* III (1965) ; pp. 349-369.

SMELSER, Neil. "Personality and the Explanation of Political Phenomena at the Social-System Level. A Methodological Statement". *Journal of Social Issues,* XXIV (1968) ; pp. 111-127.

SMELSER, William. "Dominance as a Factor in Achievement and Perception in Cooperative Problem-Solving Interactions". *Journal of Abnormal and Social Psychology,* LXII (1961) ; pp. 535-542.

SMITH, Brewster. "A Map for the Analysis of Personality and Politics". *Journal of Social Issues,* XXIV (1968) ; pp. 15-29.

SOLHAC, Raymond. "La Neutralité birmane". *Politique étrangère,* XXXII (1967) ; pp. 134-154.

SOLOMON, Robert. "Boundary Concepts and Practices in Southeast Asia". *World Politics,* XXIII (1970) ; pp. 1-24.

SOMIT, Albert and TANENHAUS, Joseph. "Trends in American Political Science". *American Political Science Review,* LVII (1963) ; pp. 933-949.

SONDERMAN, Fred. "The Linkage between Foreign Policy and International Politics" in Rosenau (ed.) : *International Politics and Foreign Policy* (1961) ; pp. 8-18.

SPIRO, Herbert. "Comparative Politics. A Comprehensive Approach". *American Political Science Review,* LVI (1962) ; pp. 577-596.

SPROUT, Harold and Margaret. "The Dilemma of Rising Demands and Insufficient Resources". *World Politics,* XX (1968) ; pp. 660-693.

STANOVNIK, Janez. "The Changing Political Context". *Foreign Affairs,* XLII (1964) ; pp. 242-255.

STEGENGA, James. "Third World Afflictions. An Alarmist's Catalogue". *International Relations,* III (1970) ; pp. 667-679.

STEINBERG, Blema. "The Korean War. A Case Study in Indian Neutralism". *Orbis,* VIII (1965) ; pp. 937-955.

TANTER, Raymond. "Dimensions of Conflict Within and Between Nations, 1958-1960". *Journal of Conflict Resolution,* X (1966) ; pp. 41-73.

TANTER, Raymond and MIDLARSKY, Manus. "A Theory of Revolution", *Journal of Conflict Resolution,* XI (1967) ; pp. 264-281.

TEUNE, Henry and SYNNESTVEDT, Sig. "Measuring International Alignment". *Orbis,* IX (1965) ; pp. 171-190.

THOMPSON, Kenneth. "American Approaches to International Politics". *Yearbook of World Affairs* (London), XIII (1959) ; pp. 205-236.

THOMPSON, William. "The Regional Subsystem". *International Studies Quarterly,* XVII (1973) ; pp. 89-119.

THORNTON, Thomas. "Peking, Moscow and the Underdeveloped Areas". *World Politics,* XIII (1961) ; pp. 491-505.

TILLY, Charles. "Does Modernization Breed Revolution ?" *Comparative Politics,* V (1973) ; pp. 425-449.

TIRYAKIN, Edward. "Typologies". *International Encyclopedia of the Social Sciences,* vol. XVI ; pp. 177-185.

TOUVAL, Saadia. "The Organization of African Unity and African Borders". *International Organization,* XXI (1967) ; pp. 102-127.

TUCKER, Robert. "Theory of Charismatic Leadership". *Deadalus* (Summer 1968) ; pp. 731-756.

VALKENIER, Elizabeth. "Changing Soviet Perspectives on the Liberation Revolution". *Orbis,* IX (1966) ; pp. 953-970.

— — "New Trends in Soviet Economic Relations with the Third World". *World Politics,* XXII (1970) ; pp. 415-433.

— — "Recent Trends in Soviet Research on the Developing Countries". *World Politics,* XX (1968) ; pp. 644-660.

VALLIN, Raymond. "Socialisme musulman en Algérie". *L'Afrique et l'Asie,* No. 69 (1er trim. 1965) ; pp. 14-32.

VAN DER KROEF, Justus. "Interpretations of the 1965 Indonesian Coup". *Pacific Affairs,* XLIII (1970) ; pp. 557-577.

VANDEWEGHE, Luc. "Le Neutralisme afro-asiatique". *Chronique de Politique étrangère,* XIII (1960) ; pp. 179-225.

VATIKIOTIS, P. "Foreign Policy of Egypt" in Macridis (ed.) : *Foreign Policy in World Politics,* pp. 335-359.

VERBA, Sideney ; BRODY, Richard ; PARKER, Edwin ; NIE, Norman ; POLSBY, Nelson ; EKMAN, Paul and BLACK, Gordon. "Public Opinion and the War in Vietnam". *The American Political Science Review,* LXI (1967) ; pp. 317-333.

VERNANT, Jacques. "Le Développement du 'Non-Alignement' au Moyen-Orient". *Politique étrangère,* XXX (1965) ; pp. 350-369.

— — "Politique et Diplomatie. Le Neutralisme hier et aujourd'hui". *Revue de Défense nationale,* XXI (1965) ; pp. 1609-1617.

VIET, Jean. "La Notion de Rôle en Politique". *Revue française de Science politique,* X (1960) ; pp. 309-335.

VON BERTALANFFY, Ludwig. "General Systems Theory". *General Systems,* I (1956) ; pp. 1-11.

VON DER MEHDEN, Fred. "Southeast Asian Relations with Africa". *Asian Survey,* V (1965) ; pp. 341-349.

WAGNER, Helmut. "Displacement of Scope. A Problem of the Relationship between Small-Scale and Large-Scale Sociological Theories". *American Journal of Sociology,* LXIX (1964) ; pp. 571-584.

WAKIN, Edward. "The Copts in Egypt". *Middle Eastern Affairs,* XII (1961); pp. 198-208.

WALTZ, Kenneth. "International Structure, National Force and the Balance of World Power". *Journal of International Affairs,* XXI (1967); pp. 215-231.

— — "The Stability of a Bipolar World". *Deadalus,* XCIII (1964); pp. 881-910.

WEINER, Myron. "Neutralism and Non-Alignment". *International Encyclopedia of the Social Sciences,* vol. XI; pp. 166-172.

— — "Struggle against Power. Notes on Indian Political Behavior". *World Politics,* VIII (1956); pp. 392-404.

WEINSTEIN, Franklin. "The Uses of Foreign Policy in Indonesia. An Approach to the Analysis of Foreign Policy in Less Developed Countries". *World Politics,* XXIV (1972); pp. 356-382.

WILD, Patricia. "The Organization of African Unity and the Algerian-Moroccan Border Conflict". *International Organization,* XX (1966); pp. 18-36.

WILKENFELD, Jonathan. "Domestic and Foreign Conflict Behaviour of Nations". *Journal of Peace Research,* V (1968); pp. 56-70.

— — "Some Further Findings Regarding the Domestic and Foreign Conflict Behaviour of Nations". *Journal of Peace Research,* VI (1969); pp. 147-157.

WILLNER, Ann. "The Underdeveloped Study of Political Development". *World Politics,* XVI (1964); p. 468-482.

WILLNER, Ann and Dorothy. "The Rise and Role of Charismatic Leaders". *Annals of the American Academy of Political and Social Science,* CCCLVIII (March 1965); pp. 77-89.

WINHAM, Gilbert. "Political Development and Lerner's Theory. Further Test of a Causal Model". *American Political Science Review,* LXIV (1970); pp. 810-819.

WOLF, Charles Jr. "Some Aspects of the Value of Less-Developed Countries to the U.S.A.". *World Politics,* XV (1963); pp. 623-635.

WOLFERS, Arnold. "The Actors in International Politics" in Fox (ed.): *Theoretical Aspects of International Relations,* pp. 83-103.

WRIGGINS, Howard. "Impediments to Unity in New Nations. The Case of Ceylon". *American Political Science Review,* LV (1961); pp. 313-320.

YALEM, Ronald. "Toward the Reconciliation of Traditional and Behavioral Approaches to International Theory". *Orbis,* XIII (1969); pp. 578-600.

YOUNG, Kenneth Jr. "New Politics in New States". *Foreign Affairs,* XXXIX (1961); pp. 494-504.

YOUNG, Oran. "Intervention and International Systems". *Journal of International Affairs,* XXII (1968); pp. 177-188.

— — "Political Discontinuities in the International System". *World Politics,* XX (1968); pp. 369-392.

ZANINOVICH, George. "Pattern Analysis of Variables within the International System". *Journal of Conflict Resolution,* VI (1962); pp. 253-268.

ZARTMAN, William. "Africa as a Subordinate State System in International Relations". *International Organization,* XXI (1967); pp. 545-564.

— — "Intervention among Developing States". *Journal of International Affairs,* XXII (1968); pp. 188-198.

ZHUKOV, E. "The Bandung Conference of African and Asian Countries and its Historic Significance". *Journal of International Affairs* (Moscow), (May 1955); pp. 18-32.

ZINKIN, Taya. "Indian Foreign Policy. An Interpretation of Attitudes". *World Politics,* VII (1955) ; pp. 179-209.

ZOLBERG, Aristide. "The Structure of Political Conflict in the New States of Tropical Africa". *American Political Science Review,* LXII (1968) ; pp. 70-88.

ZOPPO, Ciro. "Soviet Ships in the Mediterranean and the U.S.-Soviet Confrontation in the Middle East". *Orbis,* XIV (1970) ; pp. 109-129.

III. Newspapers, Periodicals and Data Sources

Africa-Asia (Paris).

Al-Ahram (Cairo).

Al-Akhbar (Cairo).

BANKS, Arthur and TEXTOR, Robert. *A Cross-Polity Survey*. Cambridge, Mass., The M.I.T. Press, 1968.

Cahiers de l'Orient contemporain (Paris).

Christian Science Monitor (Corvallis, Oregon).

Chronology of Arab Politics (Beirut).

Dawn (Karachi).

DE BLIJ, Harm. *A Geography of Sub-Saharan Africa.* Chicago, Rand McNally and Co., 1964.

Documentation française (Paris).

Egyptian Economic and Political Review (Cairo).

Egyptian Gazette (Cairo).

Egyptian Mail (Cairo).

El-Gomhouriyya (Cairo).

El-Siassa El-Dawliyya (Cairo).

El-Tali'a (Cairo).

Europa Yearbook (London).

Foreign Affairs Reports (Delhi).

Hindu (Madras).

Hsinhua (Peking).

Information Please Alamanac (New York).

International Affairs (Moscow).

Jeune Afrique (Paris).

Keesings Contemporary Archives (London).

L'Afrique et l'Asie (Paris).

La Bourse égyptienne (Cairo).

Le Commerce du Levant (Beirut).

Le Mois en Afrique (Paris).

Le Monde (Paris).

L'Orient (a Lebanese daily, Beirut).

Middle East Journal (Washington, D.C.).

Middle Eastern Affairs (New York).

Misr El Mo'assera (L'Egypte contemporaine, Cairo).

Orient (Paris).

O.F.N.S. (Overseas Foreign News Service, London).

Review of International Affairs (Beograd).

Statesman's Yearbook (London).

Straits Times (Kuala Lumpur).

The Daily Telegraph (London).

The Economist (London).

The Guardian (London).

The International Herald Tribune (Paris).

The Military Balance (Institute of Strategic Studies, London).

The New York Times (New York).

The Sunday Times (London).

The Times (London).

The Times of India (Bombay).

U.A.R. Statistical Yearbook (Cairo).

United Nations Statistical Yearbook (New York).

Who's Who in the Arab World. Beirut, 3rd ed., 1971-1972.

Worldmark Encyclopedia of Nations : Africa. New York, Harper and Row, 1967.

Worldmark Encyclopedia of Nations : Asia and Australia. New York, Harper and Row, 1967.

World Handbook of Political and Social Indicators. Ed. by Charles Taylor, Michael Hudson et al. New Haven, Yale U.P., 2nd ed., 1972.

Index

Name Index

Subject Index

Achevé d'imprimer
sur les presses de l'Imprimerie Vaudoise,
à Lausanne,
en décembre mil neuf cent soixante-quinze.

Imprimé en Suisse